CASTLES AND GALLEYS

A Reassessment of the Historic Galley-Castles of the Norse-Gaelic Seaways

edited by

Paula Martin

Islands Book Trust

![IBT logo]

Published in 2017 by the Islands Book Trust

www.theislandsbooktrust.com

© Islands Book Trust 2017

ISBN: 978-1-907443-76-3

Text © individual authors

The Islands Book Trust would like to thank Dr Paula Martin
for her assistance in the publication of this volume.

Islands Book Trust
Laxay Hall
Laxay
Isle of Lewis
HS2 9PJ
Tel: 01851 830316

Typeset by Erica Schwarz (www.schwarz-editorial.co.uk)
Cover design by Raspberry Creative Type, Edinburgh
Printed and bound by Short Run Press, Exeter

Contents

Contents

LIST OF CONTRIBUTORS

Dr Colin Breen
Reader, Environmental Sciences Research Institute, Ulster University,
cp.breen@ulster.ac.uk

Dr David Caldwell
Retired Keeper of Archaeology, National Museums Scotland,
current President, Society of Antiquaries of Scotland,
dh.caldwell@btinternet.com

Dr Barbara Crawford
Honorary Professor, University of the Highlands and Islands,
Honorary Reader in History, University of St Andrews,
bec@strathmartine.demon.co.uk

Dr Peter Davey
Honorary Senior Research Fellow, Centre for Manx Studies,
Department of Archaeology, School of Histories, Languages and Cultures,
University of Liverpool, pjd1@liv.ac.uk

Dr Sarah Jane Gibbon
Lecturer, University of the Highlands and Islands Archaeology Institute,
sarahjane.gibbon@uhi.ac.uk

Professor R Andrew McDonald
Department of History, Brock University, Canada, amcdonald@brocku.ca

Brigadier John Macfarlane
Independent scholar, john.m.macfarlane@btinternet.com

Rory Macneil
Chief of Clan MacNeil, CEO of ResearchSpace

Dr Tom McNeill
Retired Senior Lecturer, Queens University Belfast,
temcneill44@yahoo.co.uk

Dr Alan Macniven
Senior Lecturer in Scandinavian Studies, University of Edinburgh,
alan.macniven@ed.ac.uk

Jamie MacPherson

District Architect – Central West, Conservation Directorate,
Historic Environment Scotland, james.macpherson@hes.scot

Dr Donald McWhannell

Retired Chartered Mechanical Engineer, 8 Seaforth Road, Dundee,
DD5 1QH, d_mcwhannell@onetel.com

Dr Colin Martin

Honorary Reader, School of History, University of St Andrews,
cjmm@btinternet.com

Professor Richard Oram

Dean of Arts and Humanities, Professor of Medieval and
Environmental History, University of Stirling, r.d.oram@stir.ac.uk

Dr John Raven

Deputy Head of Casework (Ancient Monuments) – West,
Historic Environment Scotland, john.raven@hes.scot

David Sellar LL.D

Historian and lawyer, former Lord Lyon King of Arms

Dr Geoffrey Stell

Scottish Centre for Conservation Studies, University of Edinburgh,
former Head of Architecture, RCAHMS, geoffrey.stell@ed.ac.uk

Dr Domhnall Uilleam Stiùbhart

Senior Lecturer, Sabhal Mòr Ostaig, University of the
Highlands and Islands, ds.smo@uhi.ac.uk

Dr Mark Thacker

Postdoctoral Research Fellow, University of Stirling,
mark.thacker@stir.ac.uk

About the Editor

Dr Paula Martin is an archaeologist and editor, based in Fife and Morvern. She has worked on wrecks of the Spanish Armada in Donegal and Fair Isle, and on two small 17th-century warships in the Sound of Mull. Paula and her husband Colin are engaged in a long-term study of the maritime landscapes of Scotland's western seaboard. For ten years she edited the *International Journal of Nautical Archaeology*, and is now an editor for *Scottish Archaeological Internet Reports*.

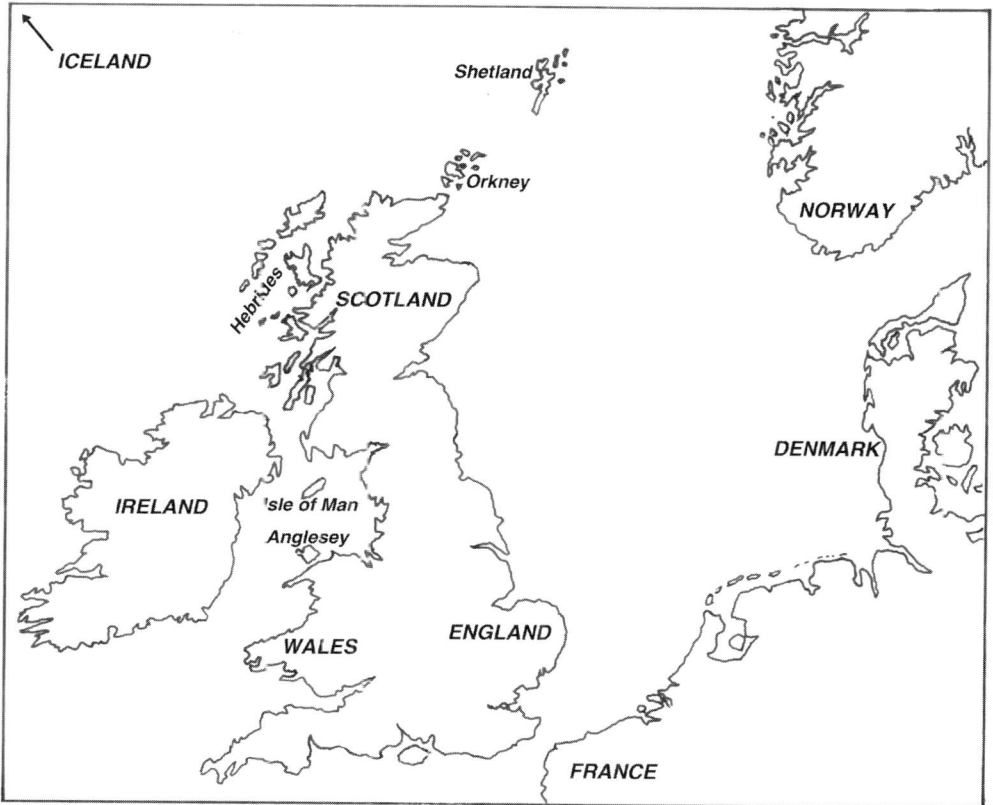

Figure 1. The Norse-Gaelic (or Norse-Celtic) seaways. (Colin Martin)

Figure 2. Barra, with inset detail of the area around Castle Bay. B = Bàgh Thalaman; P = portage; LT = Loch Tangasdail; DM = Dun Mhic Leoid; C = Crubisdale; BB = Bàgh Beag; M = market-place. (Colin Martin)

I

Ian Macneil's Challenge to Hebridean Castle Historiography

Rory Macneil

In his article 'Kisimul Castle and the Origins of Hebridean Galley-Castles: Preliminary Thoughts', originally delivered at the Society for Northern Studies conference in Barra in 2002, Ian Macneil set out a series of fundamental challenges to Hebridean castle historiography.[1] These challenges, and his subsequent, as yet unpublished, work in this area, were the inspiration for this conference. So, to start the conference, it makes sense to ask: why was Ian dissatisfied with the prevailing historiography?

A definition: Hebridean galley-castles

Ian began his critique by coining a term. He defined Hebridean galley-castles as follows:

- 'Hebrides' and 'Hebridean' include not only the Norse Sudreys, but also the adjacent mainland.

- A 'galley' is any galley-type boat, but is typically Norse, Hebridean, or Irish.

- A 'castle' is any lime-mortared or drystone structure combining residence and defence, of the period 800–1600, far longer than in conventional definitions.

- A 'galley-castle' is any castle close enough to the sea directly or by portage to have been significantly influenced by the existence of galleys when they were a dominant military factor. Most castles in both the Hebridean islands and the Hebridean mainland shores are galley-castles.

Debatable assumptions

The first step in Ian's critique was to focus on four often unstated, usually unsupported, and, he argued, incorrect assumptions which underlay prevailing scholarship about Hebridean galley-castles. The first is what he termed 'Scottish diffusionism' – a diffusion of cultural influences moving northwards from the Battle of Hastings in 1066 to eastern-central Scotland and thence, gradually and belatedly, outward, finally reaching 'remote' areas like the Hebrides. The second is lack of indigenous evolution in the development of Hebridean castles. The third, which follows from the first two, is that castles are late unless proved to be early. The fourth, again stemming from the first two, is that Hebrideans were too primitive to build castles at early periods. A fundamental effect of these four assumptions was the assigning of late dates to castles.

Inadequate attention to context

With that foundation, Ian moved on to the next stage of his critique, which is that prevailing scholarship pays inadequate attention to the context, or contexts, in which the castles were built and operated. One manifestation of this was ignoring what came before; that is, 'what was already there when it was built'. A second was what he viewed as misuse of charters and other early written accounts in Hebridean castle scholarship. He went into considerable detail on this topic, which includes a full discussion of Fordun, arguing that the only list Fordun made was of islands, with unorganised references to structures, including castles, notwithstanding which, castles not referred to by Fordun have been mistakenly said to have not existed prior to *c.*1370.

Failure to adopt a comprehensive approach

At this point Ian begins a transition from identifying weaknesses in existing approaches to setting forth a vision for new and more productive ways of approaching Hebridean galley-castle historiography. Central to this vision is a move to what he termed 'comprehensive studies'. The failure to adopt a comprehensive approach in existing scholarship is evidenced by:

- Failure to start with a set that includes at a minimum all Hebridean castles.
- Limiting study to castles only, for example not covering the use or non-use of lime mortar in all stone structures of the period.
- Failure to enlarge the geographical scope of reference to adjacent areas such as the Northern Isles, the Isle of Man, the Clyde, Galloway, Norway and Ireland.
- Too many individual castle analyses.

Suggested remedies: the elements of a comprehensive approach

With this as background, Ian elaborated in some detail what a comprehensive approach to the study of galley-castles would look like. This is arguably the heart of his essay, and the most complex, for in addition to identifying the elements of a comprehensive approach, he goes further and comments on the substance of what some, but not all, of those elements, might be.

Ian identifies the following remedies:

- Recognition of the lack of comprehensiveness in existing studies and the limitations and distortions it introduces into our understanding of galley-castles.
- Examining the broadest set of possible galley-castles, for example by giving 'shadow-castles', which are lost in obscurity, just as much attention as 'calendar-castles',

and by including in the range of structures studied those 'failing to fit conventional definitions, such as drystone duns either built or occupied after 800'.

He goes on to enumerate a set of subjects needing comprehensive study:

- Physical: construction and archaeological finds, of which the most fundamental is the use of lime-mortar construction.

- Historical, such as the use of charters and place-name evidence.

- Functions, for example the locations of the castles relative to seaborne commerce, communications and warfare.

- Relations, in particular location relative to other galley-castles, and for example a possible relationship between the building of many of the galley-castles and Somerled's mid-12th-century empire-building.

Revisions of prevailing frames of reference

In the final section Ian moves from suggestions for more 'scientific rigour' in studies of the origins of Hebridean castles to a self-consciously more substantive suggestion, namely the revision of prevailing frames of reference relating to these castles. The three specific suggestions Ian made follow logically from the critique of existing scholarship, and build on them. The first was that although galley-castles shared a range of basic functions with other medieval castles, they differed in a crucial respect, namely that their symbiotic relationship with galleys means that the galley should be the central focus of thinking about these castles. The centrality of the galley in galley-castle studies leads to a second revision to the appropriate frame of reference, namely the need to take the period 800–1600 as the best relevant time-frame, since that is the period when galleys dominated both trade and military activities. The third revision relates to location, in the micro sense that each area in which a castle existed must be understood first and foremost on its own terms rather than as an adjunct to somewhere else, that galley-castles are sea-oriented rather than land-oriented, and, finally, that to achieve these goals the best term for the central area of study is 'Hebrides and Hebridean mainland', and the best term for the more global area of which this forms a part is the 'Norse-Celtic Seaways' (Figure 1).

Ian's subsequent work

In conjunction with the preparation of his talk at the Northern Studies conference for publication, and right up until his death in February 2010, Ian engaged in a series of galley-castle projects, starting to explore some of the new avenues he had identified. He completed one of these, a comprehensive investigation of possible galley-castles throughout the Norse-Celtic seaways. This involved several years of painstaking research, looking at a wide range of sources including maps, charters, articles and books, in which Ian followed the principles he had suggested by adopting a comprehensive approach, over a longer time-frame, and including of a broad range of structures in the initial sample reviewed for possible inclusion. The results were compiled in a database of possible galley-castles and a series of maps, which can be found at http://www.ed.ac.uk/literatures-languages-cultures/delc/nordic-research/resources.

At the time of his death two articles, one on the misuse of information about castles in Fordun in medieval-castle scholarship, and the other on medieval Scottish castle historiography, were partially complete, and in addition Ian left hundreds of handwritten notes in the books and articles he was using as reference material, setting out comments, ideas and questions.

The world has moved on

In the 13 years since the Northern Studies conference medieval Scottish castle historiography has not stood still; on the contrary, this period has seen a steady flow of work, some of it bringing to bear fresh perspectives and new techniques. This includes new work on castles, including galley-castles, new perspectives on the Hebrides and other areas of the Norse-Celtic seaways, the application of new techniques such as laser-scanning of buildings and DNA analysis, and fresh perspectives such as considering the impact of climate on historical developments.

Our Conference – designed to stimulate comprehensive approaches

These new perspectives, techniques and developments doubtless will be reflected in the talks we will have an opportunity to listen to over the next two days. In addition, it is worth noting that the structure of the conference and the particular topics included are designed to stimulate adoption of the approaches Ian suggested. The focus on castles in particular areas – Ulster, Orkney, the Isle of Man and the Sound of Mull and Loch Awe – will hopefully result in an examination of groups of castles and shared characteristics, and, taken together, similarities and differences between galley-castles generally. Several speakers will be looking at physical aspects of castles, including using lime mortar for dating, and materials used in constructing castles. Other speakers will focus on the specific locale of the castles, including their relation to harbours, and sourcing of materials for construction. Galleys and sailing-patterns will also be subjects of exploration.

Some Barra examples worthy of investigation

Finally, as food for thought as the conference begins, to illustrate the point that you do not have to look too far to find promising subjects for exploring the avenues Ian pointed us towards, here are several right here on Barra, possibly related to a prime example of a galley-castle, Kisimul Castle (Figure 2; Plates 1–4). All are worthy of future detailed exploration.

Note

1. Ian R Macneil, 2006, 'Kisimul Castle and the Origins of Hebridean Galley-Castles: Preliminary Thoughts', in A Kruse and A Ross (eds), *Barra and Skye: Two Hebridean Perspectives* (Edinburgh), pp.21–46.

The Galley-Castles and the Norse-Gaelic Seaways: Movement, Mobility and Maritime Connectivity in Medieval Atlantic Scotland c.1000–1500

R Andrew McDonald[1]

Sveinn Ásleifarson, Alan of Galloway, and the primacy of the maritime world

> This was how Svein used to live. Winter he would spend at home on Gairsay, where he entertained some eighty men at his own expense … In the spring he had more than enough to occupy him, with a great deal of seed to sow which he saw to carefully himself. Then when that job was done, he would go off plundering in the Hebrides and in Ireland on what he called his 'spring-trip', then back home just after midsummer, where he stayed till the cornfields had been reaped and the grain was safely in. After that he would go off raiding again, and never came back till the first month of winter was ended. This he used to call his 'autumn-trip'.[2]

The notorious Orkney chieftain and pirate Sveinn Ásleifarson (d. *c.*1171), the subject of this famous paragraph, is one of the most colourful and significant characters in *Orkneyinga Saga*, the early-13th-century saga-history of the rulers of Orkney and Caithness. Sveinn's career is of interest for many reasons, but although he is most often considered principally within the context of the Northern Isles, it is noteworthy that Sveinn frequently raided in the Hebrides and the Irish Sea, and is also said to have resided for extended periods in the Isle of Man (where he married a Manx widow) as well as in Tiree and Lewis.[3] In fact the saga informs us that Sveinn's reach extended all the way to the Isles of Scilly, the small island group lying *c.*45km off Land's End in Cornwall, where he plundered on one occasion.[4] Sveinn's exploits therefore spanned the British Seas, but what is really striking, however, is the manner in which Sveinn moves seamlessly and with apparent ease through the maritime environment of the Atlantic shores of Scotland; the seaways facilitate rather than impede mobility, and there appear to be few social or cultural boundaries within this watery world. Highlighting the point, when Sveinn returned to Orkney following his sojourn in the Isle of Man, his Manx wife, Ingiríðr Þorkelsdóttir, and stepson, Sigmundr Andrésson

'Fishhook', accompanied him; his stepson soon found a place in the retinue of Earl Rǫgnvaldr Kali of Orkney (d.1158) where he acquired some fame as a skaldic poet.[5]

Many similar examples of such maritime mobility and connectivity could, of course, be cited from a wide range of sources including Norse sagas, Latin chronicles and annals, and Gaelic praise-poems. But these themes are perhaps best encapsulated in a brief anecdote found in *Hákonar saga*, the saga-biography of King Hákon IV Hákonarson of Norway (r.1217–63) composed by the Icelander Sturla Þórðarson soon after the king's death. The saga relates how, in the summer of the year 1230, the Manx king Óláfr the Black (d.1237) arrived in Norway with disturbing news:

> He told of great strife from the west out of the Isles. He said he had fled out of the Isles and Man, because the earl Alan had gathered together a great host, and meant to fall on the men of Man. He repeated many of the earl's big words as to the men of Norway. He said the earl called the sea no more difficult to cross to Norway than from Norway to Scotland, and that it was no worse off for havens there to him who wished to harry.[6]

Alan (d.1234) was Lord of Galloway in south-west Scotland, a great sea-captain and a major player in Irish Sea politics as well as Constable of Scotland. Described by the saga-man as 'the greatest warrior in that time' he is said to have commanded 'a great host and crowd of ships', and to have 'harried round the southern Isles and Ireland'.[7] Alan had, throughout the late 1220s, been heavily involved in the Manx civil war raging between the brothers Óláfr and Rǫgnvaldr, as an ally of the latter, and, despite Rǫgnvaldr's death in 1229, the threat of further intervention from Alan was potent enough to spur the panicked flight of Óláfr to Norway the following year.[8] In fact, Óláfr's concerns may have been justified: a few years earlier, in 1224, Alan had written to the English king Henry III (r.1216–72) stating that he had been in the Western Isles, going from island to island with his army in his galleys, ready to cross to Ireland in order to act against Hugh de Lacy, when a messenger arrived with news of an agreement between the king's justiciar of Ireland and de Lacy.[9]

Alan's 'big words' about island-hopping, whether between the Hebrides and Ireland or the Hebrides and Norway, and whether actually spoken or not, articulate what has been called in another context (the pre-modern Mediterranean) the 'conceptual primacy of the maritime world': a perspective in which the sea is no barrier to communication, but rather represents what has been called 'the principal agent of connectivity'.[10] This paper uses Sveinn Ásleifarson's journey and Alan of Galloway's big words as a point of departure for some reflections on themes of maritime mobility and interconnectivity and the notion of the 'conceptual primacy of the maritime world' as it manifests itself in Atlantic Scotland between roughly 1000 and 1500 – that is to say, from the zenith of the earldom of Orkney and Caithness to the demise of the later medieval MacDonald Lordship of the Isles.

Of course, Scotland famously 'is, and always has been, a maritime nation'[11] (Plates 5–6), and the concept is well entrenched in Scottish scholarship. But the point is still worth making. Around the Mediterranean, for example (and also the Irish Sea and North Sea), maritime links are taken for granted;[12] and, as I hope to show, recent approaches to archipelagic history and the study of islands and islandscapes may offer new avenues of thinking about Atlantic Scotland in the middle ages, perhaps not least by the application of concepts borrowed from the maritime history of other regions. In any event, as Ian Macneil urged in his appeal for a re-examination of the galley-castles, any investigation of these castles as a group must be situated within the broader context of the maritime societies of medieval Atlantic Scotland which produced them,[13] and this is ultimately the overarching goal of this paper.

The essay is divided into two parts. The first examines islands, islandscapes, connectivity and marginality in medieval Atlantic Scotland – broadly speaking, it is about environment. The second part then examines these themes as they apply to the four principal units of lordship which dominated Atlantic Scotland through the central and later middle ages, *c*.1000 to 1500. In the interests of space, I concentrate on the secular, although much could certainly be said on the ecclesiastical front with regard to these themes as well. Throughout, I use the term 'Atlantic Scotland' as shorthand for what archaeologists have come to call the 'Atlantic province of Scotland', that is, the west coast, western islands, northern mainland and northern isles.[14] I include in this definition the Clyde islands even though they are not usually considered part of the Hebrides, and I also include the Isle of Man, the main power-centre of the Manx sea-kings who also controlled some of the Hebrides between the late 11th and mid 13th centuries. Although Man is not now considered to be one of the Hebrides, its history throughout the middle ages was closely connected with these islands,[15] and such a broad sweep seems appropriate given the wide-ranging geographical scope of the conference and inclusion of castles from Orkney, Caithness, and Man as well as the Hebrides and Argyll.

Returning briefly to *Orkneyinga saga* and *Hákonar saga*, it is worth noting that these texts are of great significance for the study of the galley-castles since they provide the earliest written evidence for stone-built castles in Atlantic Scotland (and indeed for Scotland as a whole). *Hákonar saga* contains an account of the three-day-long siege of a castle on Bute (undoubtedly Rothesay) undertaken by the Norse led by the Hebridean chieftain Uspak (Óspakr) in an expedition to the Isles in 1230:

> The Northmen ran in to the castle, and made a hard assault on it. But the Scots defended themselves well, and poured down on them boiling pitch and lead. Then fell many of the Northmen and many were wounded. They bound over them 'flakes' of wood [wickerwork shields], and after that they hewed at the wall, for the stone was soft; and the wall crumbled before them … Three days they fought with the defenders before they got the castle won.[16]

This passage is also significant in that it represents the earliest account of a siege in all of Scotland.[17] *Orkneyinga saga* also contains an important early description of the stone castle built by Kolbein *hrúga* on Wyre: 'At that time there was a very able man called Kolbein Heap farming on Wyre in Orkney. He had a fine stone fort there, a really solid stronghold'.[18] This has been identified as Cubbie Roo's castle, substantial remains of which still survive; it is mentioned in *Hákonar saga* as well and is generally agreed to represent one of the earliest stone-built castles in Scotland, dating from the 12th century.[19]

Another stone fortress, at Lambaborg in Caithness, also features in the narrative and provides the setting for some of Sveinn Ásleifarson's characteristically dramatic exploits. The saga says that it, 'stood on a sea-cliff with a stoutly built stone wall to landward. The cliff stretched quite a distance along the coast'.[20] (Besieged in the fortress, Sveinn escaped by lowering himself from the walls of the stronghold into the sea.) This fortress has not been identified with certainty, but Bucholly Castle in Caithness is one potential candidate.[21] Taken together these references constitute some of the earliest written evidence for stone-built castles in Atlantic Scotland and, indeed, for Scotland in general.

Extended archipelagos: islands, islandscapes, connectivity and marginality in Atlantic Scotland

Sveinn resided on the island of Gairsay in the Orkney Islands, and his world was a maritime one. The islands in which he lived, and through which he journeyed, form an important, if neglected, part of the Atlantic Archipelago that is the British Isles – what one scholar has called, perhaps a little unfortunately, the 'Other British Isles'.[22] The British Isles, broadly defined, embraces not only the two main islands of Great Britain and Ireland but also thousands of offshore islands forming an 'Atlantic Archipelago' which stretches from the Shetland Islands, half-way to Norway, to the Scilly Isles off the south-western tip of Land's End in Cornwall (Figure 1). The British Isles also include the UK crown dependencies of the Isle of Man, and by tradition, the Channel Islands (the Bailiwicks of Guernsey and Jersey), although the latter are strictly speaking an archipelago off the coast of Normandy rather than part of the Atlantic Archipelago of the British Isles. Although precise numbers are difficult to establish, estimates for the total number of islands range between *c.*5000 and *c.*6000 with a measurable coastline, though only a small proportion are inhabited.[23]

This Atlantic archipelago is in fact subdivided into a variety of constituent but distinct archipelagos.[24] In the north, the Shetland and Orkney Islands – collectively, the Northern Isles – stretch like stepping-stones in the North Atlantic between Scotland and Norway. The Orkney Islands lie only 10km off the northern tip of Scotland, at latitude 58–59° north, and comprise about 70 islands spread out over *c.*50km east to west and 85km north to south. Some 80km to the north-east of Orkney are the Shetland Islands, *c.*100 islands spread out over a distance of some 160km, straddling latitude 60° north (the same latitude as southern Greenland). Shetland has, with good reason, been called the crossroads of the North Sea: Norway is just over 320km to the east and the Faroe Islands lie about the same distance to the north-west. (London, on the other hand, lies nearly 1000km to the south.) From this nodal location one could sail southward, round the stormy seas off Cape Wrath (the name of which has nothing to do with anger but is derived from Old Norse *hvarf*, 'turning point'[25]), to the Hebrides or Sudreys (Southern Isles), the double chain, divided into Inner and Outer Hebrides, of more than 500 islands of widely varying topography, arcing through some 400km off the west coast of Scotland. At the southern end of this archipelago lies the Isle of Man, a small (570km²) but fertile island in the middle of the Irish Sea, roughly equidistant from the surrounding lands of England, Ireland and Scotland, with Wales lying a little further to the south.

In maritime terms, our frame of reference is the so-called British Seas: the North Sea (also known as the German Sea or German Ocean), Sea of the Hebrides, Sea of the Minches, Malin Sea, Irish Sea, and the Celtic Sea (the English Channel is also one of the British Seas but it will have little place in this discussion).[26] It is truly remarkable to consider that Sveinn had traversed this Atlantic Archipelago (and most of the British Seas) from one end to the other in the course of his life – and he was by no means unique: among those whose travels within the Atlantic Archipelago can be traced are figures like King Magnús *berfœttr* of Norway (d.1103); Óláfr the Black of Man (d.1237); the Hebridean chieftains Uspak (Óspakr) (d.1230) and Eógan son of Donnchad, lord of Lorn and king in the southern Hebrides (d. c.1275); and King Hákon IV of Norway (d.1263) – and these represent only some of the great and good whose itineraries have been preserved in written sources. There must have been many anonymous soldiers, pirates, pilgrims, merchants and others who had also voyaged through these islands but whose journeys have left little or no imprint on the written record.

This is not the place to rehearse knowledge of these 'Other British Isles' in the works of medieval writers, but authors who mentioned these islands frequently characterized them as situated on the edge of the habitable world, beyond which there lay nothing but frozen northern ocean. In the Jerusalem-centric world-view that characterized medieval geographical knowledge, the British Isles lay at the edge of the known world; the northern oceans and the islands lying in them were consequently poorly known and were often depicted as lands of darkness. To take a few examples, Giraldus Cambrensis (Gerald of Wales) writing in the late 1180s described Ireland as situated in 'the farthest western lands' and observed that 'beyond those limits there is no land, nor is there any habitation either of men or beasts – but beyond the whole horizon only the ocean flows and is borne on in boundless space'.[27] Adam of Bremen, writing c.1075, included a detailed discussion of the islands of the North in his *History of the Archbishops of Hamburg-Bremen*; while it is true that Adam does briefly mention Orkney and the Hebrides as well as Thule, Iceland, Greenland, and Vinland, his description of an expedition of King Haraldr Hardrada of Norway (d.1066) into the Northern Ocean is perhaps more telling:

> The very well informed prince of the Norwegians, Harold, lately attempted this sea. After he had explored the expanse of the Northern Ocean in his ships, there lay before their eyes at length the darksome bounds of a failing world, and by retracing his steps he barely escaped in safety the vast pit of the abyss.[28]

A particularly telling comment on European knowledge of the islands and their inhabitants is to be found in Pope Urban II's speech at the Council of Clermont in 1095, famous for launching the First Crusade, as recounted in the English chronicler William of Malmesbury, writing *c*.1125. Describing the three continents of the world, Asia, Africa, and Europe, the pope observed that Christians inhabited only a small part, adding: 'For all those barbarous peoples who in far-distant islands frequent the ice-bound ocean, living as they do like beasts – who could call them Christians?'[29] As one modern commentator on this rhetoric has observed, 'Northern Europeans, some of whom in Norway and Sweden had indeed not been converted to Christianity at the time of Urban's speech, are therefore equated by the Mediterranean pope with the sea-monsters who live at the world's end'.[30] These remarks call to mind inaccuracies in cartographic representations of the region in famous maps of the British Isles such as those by the 13th-century monk Matthew Paris (d.1259) or the anonymous 14th-century Gough map.[31]

Yet, as the examples of Sveinn Ásleifarson and Alan of Galloway cited above suggest, the 'Other British Isles' were hardly as isolated or as remote as medieval commentators perceived: interconnected with one another and with surrounding lands, these islands formed a unique archipelagic medieval water-world (or several water-worlds) which arced hundreds of kilometres from the Shetland Islands south to the Isle of Man and which embraced both islands and adjacent mainland territory (Figure 1). Their history, to apply an expression originally coined by the historian J G A Pocock, one of the pioneers of conceptualizing British history as archipelagic in nature, must be conceived in 'pelagic, maritime, and oceanic' terms,[32] in order to challenge terrestrial bias and land-bound perspectives. Thanks to relatively recent developments in island studies and Atlantic studies, with particularly useful contributions from archaeology (island archaeology seems a flourishing field at the moment),[33] islands and oceans figure more prominently in our understanding of the past than they did even a decade or two ago. Islands, in particular, we are told, are special places, at once surrounded and delineated by the 'protecting perimeter' of the sea,[34] yet also interconnected with one another and with mainlands by the thoroughfares of the seaways.[35]

Islands and islandscapes can, therefore, be defined both by isolation and by interconnectivity, while nevertheless guarding against generalizations and always allowing for regional variations.[36] As Sir Barry Cunliffe put it, the inhabitants of the Atlantic façade were 'in many ways remote from neighbours by land, yet easily linked to others by the sea'.[37] Similar sentiments have been expressed by other scholars as well: 'The sea … unites conceptually as well as topographically', remark Horden and Purcell of the pre-modern Mediterranean:

> It is no barrier to communications, but the medium of all human intercourse from one region to another. Moreover, to the sea in the literal sense we must add the very important cases in which water-borne contacts extend the sea into the land.[38]

Far from being isolated at the edge of the known world, then, it is possible to conceptualize the islandscapes of Atlantic Scotland as forming their own 'core' or 'centre'. Viewed from this perspective, the further one moves away from the water, the more one moves towards the margins, in a sort of inside-out geography, where, the world of the sea is 'normal' (the interior), and the land is the fringe, its marginality increasing with its distance from the water. Distance is, in effect, inverted: places linked by sea are always 'close', while neighbours on land may … be quite 'distant'.[39]

Ian Armit, in his important study of the archaeology of Skye and the Western Isles, used the term 'island-centred geography' to denote a perspective in which 'travel by sea was of prime importance and where modern political perceptions were simply irrelevant'[40] – and the point has been made in other contexts as well.[41] Indeed, Armit asserts that it is the Scottish and British mainland authorities which have made the islands peripheral, 'due in part to their cultural and economic distance from the relatively recent centres of power'.[42] Marginality – or centrality for that matter – thereby becomes entirely a matter of perspective.

The premise is an important one if we are properly to understand the galley-castles of the western seaboard. While it is true that they are remote and difficult of access from a modern land-based (or air-travel based) perspective which treats Glasgow and Edinburgh as centres and the western seaboard and islands as peripheral, the careful siting of the castles, almost without exception in commanding situations astride the western seaways and sailing-corridors of Atlantic Scotland, speaks to a different perception on the part of their builders (see conclusion, below).[43] Indeed, as Martin MacGregor has observed, 'Meshing the matter of sovereignty with the role of galleys and castles permits identification of the nodal points on the strategic and military map of the late-medieval Highlands' – and the map that emerges is predominantly a maritime one.[44] A similar point emerges from the choice of Lismore in Loch Linnhe as the seat for the bishop of Argyll in the 1180s: relatively remote and difficult of access today, at the time of its establishment it was apparently regarded as an attractive nodal location from which to administer a far-flung diocese (although within less than a century there were complaints about its remote location).[45]

As a final point here, the resemblance of these islandscapes of Atlantic Scotland to the west coast of Norway with its archipelagos and fjords is often noted. As it has been aptly put, 'One could sail down through the Inner Hebrides to the Irish Sea as though it were one of the Norwegian archipelagos, and beyond beckoned the Isle of Man'.[46] In fact, the sailing-routes of Atlantic Scotland comprise a northern section of a larger whole that has been described as the western seaways (sometimes the Celtic seaways), a series of long-distance maritime routes linking the Atlantic façade of Europe from Scandinavia to the Iberian Peninsula. First identified and articulated by archaeologists over a century ago, the concept received further definition in the 1930s by scholars like O G S Crawford and Sir Cyril Fox, the former concentrating on post-Roman journeys and especially the maritime activities of the Celtic saints.[47] In the 1960s and '70s the western seaways were further elucidated by E G Bowen, whose main focus was also the travels of the Celtic saints.[48] Reflecting on this phenomenon, A R Lewis described what he called a 'Celtic Christian thalassocracy' and a 'Celtic maritime empire' which extended from Dalriada to Brittany and perhaps Spain: 'It was to endure for centuries', he concluded, 'until it forged the Celtic peoples into a cultural area with a common and peculiar set of Christian practices, art, literature and language – as well as a common naval tradition'.[49] The phenomenon of the *papar* (seafaring Celtic priests, monks, and/or hermits) and their voyages, settlement, and distribution throughout the North Atlantic has received considerable scholarly attention of late.[50]

The arrival of the Norse and their settlement in the region from the 9th century created a Scandinavian thalassocracy. Norse expansion linked the islands around Britain with the North Atlantic islands of the Faroes, Iceland, and Greenland, creating a tightly connected network which spanned the North Atlantic: summing up the Scandinavian achievement, Benjamin Hudson observed that 'The Scandinavians made the Atlantic Ocean their highway, their larder, and their private lake'.[51] The integration of Norse and Celtic sea-routes has led to their designation as the 'Celtic sea-route of the Vikings',[52] although the term Gaelic-Norse seaways is equally appropriate. The concept of the western seaways has not gone without critics, but the existence of extensive and well-defined maritime contacts linking the Atlantic façade of Europe is now well established.[53]

Having said all this, and Alan of Galloway's boasts notwithstanding, the ease of travelling the sea-road must never be exaggerated. Hazards were abundant. A great deal more could be said on the topic, but, briefly, medieval writers commented on the dangers of whirlpools (several of which were well known along the sea-routes) and tidal surges, not to mention storms and even more drastic events such as the mysterious phenomenon known as 'sea-hedges' described in the 13th-century Norwegian text *Konungs skuggsjá* (*King's mirror*).[54] The precarious nature of travel along the sea-road is vividly depicted in the 13th-century *Hrafns saga Sveinbjarnarsonar*, where a shipload of Icelanders, storm-driven into the Hebrides, feared that 'no man could pilot them through; and most men expected that the ship would be wrecked, and the men drowned'.[55]

They were saved, but others were less fortunate: the Manx king Haraldr Óláfsson, for example, perished with his new bride and entire retinue in a shipwreck off Sumburgh Head in the Shetland Islands while returning from Norway in the autumn of 1248, and another Manx dynast was lost when his ship foundered and sank in a storm off the Welsh coast ten years earlier.[56] *King Hakon's saga* relates how one of King Hákon's vessels, returning home following the 1263 expedition to the isles, was swallowed up in the Pentland Firth by the tidal race known as the Swelkie,[57] and, indeed, the late-season equinoctial gales of that year played a crucial role in disrupting the Norwegian expedition.[58] Giraldus Cambrensis, better known as Gerald of Wales (d.1220x23), observed that, 'The Irish Sea, surging with currents that rush together, is nearly always tempestuous, so that even in the summer it scarcely shows itself calm for a few days to them that sail'. Gerald had first-hand experience, having lived on its shores and crossed it several times himself; in another work he devoted an entire chapter to the subject of storms.[59]

Although the 13th to 15th centuries are famous as the age of the first portolan charts and of the sailing-directions known as 'rutters' (from French *routier*), the earliest surviving Scottish text of this nature dates only from the mid 16th century.[60] By the later Medieval or Early-Modern period, however, writers like

Donald Monro (d. *c*.1575) commented on local conditions and mentioned tides, currents, and other local hazards as well as frequently noting the location of good havens for galleys. Monro observes, for instance, that between the islands of Jura and Scarba, 'thair runs ane stream above the power of all sailing and rowing with infinite dangeris callit Arey brekan [Corybrekan]'.[61] The famous 14th-century Gough map, sometimes described as the first road-map of the British Isles, although notoriously inaccurate in its rendering of much of the Scottish coast, includes a drawing of a ship with a broken mast possibly caught on rocks in the sea between Orkney and Norway; the precise meaning of the vignette is unclear but it illustrates the ever-present danger of shipwreck in this watery world.[62] What Mollat calls, 'The ambiguity of the sea, both a source of life and a realm of death', is a prominent and well-known theme in maritime history and literature.[63]

An important aspect of the environment of Atlantic Scotland is the close interlocking of mainland and island, resulting in an environment which facilitates inter-island and island-mainland communication, and in which it is often impossible to make a firm distinction between shore and offshore, or between the extent of different islands.[64] It is well known that the western seaboard of Scotland is characterized by its 'fjord-like littoral',[65] with long narrow sea-lochs jutting far inland, and peninsulas embracing offshore islands. In fact, the coastline of the modern county of Argyll (smaller than its medieval namesake), stretches for some 3000 miles (*c*.4800km);[66] for comparison, that is more than the coastline of France (4668km) or Iceland (4675km); one ramification of this serrated coastline is the fact that no place in Argyll is more than *c*.30km from the sea.[67] Thanks to the branch of modern mathematics known as fractal modelling, it is actually possible to quantify the 'wiggliness' of a coastline using what is called a fractal dimension. Where a value of 1 represents a very smooth/straight coast (and 2 is the highest possible), the value for the west coast of Great Britain overall is given as about 1.25; only Norway has a wigglier coast, which has been assigned a value of 1.52. The value for at least part of the west of Scotland has been calculated at 1.3.[68]

Fractal modelling aside, this aspect of the environment of the west coast was certainly known to medieval writers.[69] The *Saga of Magnús berfœttr* in Snorri Sturluson's (d.1241) massive collection of Norwegian kings' sagas, *Heimskringla* (*c*.1230), for instance, describing King Magnús's (d.1103) famous expedition to the Isles in 1098, explains that as part of that ruler's expedition, 'his men went west about all the firths of Scotland behind the islands, both inhabited and uninhabited, and took possession of all of them for the king'.[70] *King Hakon's saga* describes a well-known episode that formed part of the 1263 expedition which highlights some of the implications of this environment for movement and mobility. The saga relates how, following unsuccessful negotiations with the Scots king, Hákon dispatched 60 ships up Loch Long:

> And when they got up into the firth they took their boats, and drew them up there over the land to a great lake which is called Loch Lomond. … There were also very many islands on that lake which were well tilled. Those isles the Northmen wasted with fire and sword. They burned too the whole district round the lake, and wrought there the greatest mischief.[71]

Edward J Cowan has elucidated the meaning of the episode within the broader context of the campaign,[72] but of significance here is the manner in which naval technology and environment permitted the movement of vessels overland across what is known as a 'peninsular road'.

The portaging described in the saga is represented on the ground in the form of place-names, both Norse and Gaelic in origin. Perhaps the best known of these are the Gaelic *tairbeart* place-names, which are common in the west of Scotland and mean literally an 'over-bringing' or 'portage'.[73] Examples are Tarbet on the narrow isthmus separating Loch Long and Loch Lomond – undoubtedly the location of the feat described in *King Hakon's saga* just noted – as well as Tarbert at the northern end of the Kintyre peninsula, the site of two legendary and spectacular feats that stand as representative of the principles of mobility and interconnectivity under consideration here. I refer of course to Magnús *berfœttr* and Robert I allegedly having themselves hauled over the narrow isthmus at Tarbert in ships with sails set in 1098 and *c*.1315 respectively.

King Magnús's feat is detailed in both *Heimskringla* and *Orkneyinga saga*, where we are informed that Magnús came to an agreement with King Malcolm of Scotland [*recte* King Edgar] to the effect that 'King Malcolm would let him have all the islands off the west coast which were separated by water navigable by a ship with the rudder set'. The saga then continues:

> When King Magnús reached Kintyre he had a skiff hauled across the narrow neck of land at Tarbert, with himself sitting at the helm, and this is how he won the peninsula. It juts out from the west of Scotland, and the isthmus connecting it to the mainland is so narrow that ships are regularly hauled across.[74]

King Magnús then had his men sail both northward and southward close to the shore, and that is how he claimed all the islands west of Scotland', we are told.

Some two centuries later, Robert I (r.1306–29) is said to have accomplished the same feat. John Barbour describes, in his epic poem *The Bruce* (*c*.1375), how King Robert accomplished a similar feat in the context of his Irish campaigns *c*.1315:

> To Tarbart thai held thar way
> In galayis ordanyt for thar far,
> Bot thaim worthyt draw thar schippis thar,
> And a myle wes betwixt the seys
> Bot that wes lownyt all with treis.
> The king his schippis thar gert draw,
> And for the wynd couth stoutly blaw
> Apon thar bak as thai wald ga
> He gert men rapys and mastis ta
> And set thaim in the schippis hey
> And sayllis to the toppis tey
> And gert men gang tharby drawand,
> The wyind thaim helpyt that wes blawand
> Sua that in a litill space
> Thar flote all our-drawin was.

> They held their way to the Tarbert in galleys ordered for their journey. But there they had to draw their ships, and it was a mile between the seas, [which] was all sheltered by trees. The king had his ships dragged there, and because the wind was blowing strongly upon their backs, [in the direction] they wanted to go, he had men take stays and masts, raise them up in the ships, tie sails to the yards and go beside [the ships] pulling [them]. The wind that was blowing helped them, so that in a little time their fleet had been completely drawn over. When those who were in the Isles heard how the good king had had his ships go there with sails, over between the two Tarberts, they were all utterly dejected. For they knew by an old prophecy that whoever should have ships go between those seas with sails should so win the Isles for himself that no-one could withstand him by force.[75]

In their study of the pre-modern Mediterranean, Horden and Purcell argue that, in an environment characterized by the close interconnection of mainland and island, it is the maritime milieu which 'dominates pockets of the land-world with which it comes into contact'.[76] The examples of Magnús *berfœttr* in 1098 and Robert I in *c*.1315 illustrate an identical phenomenon in the western seaways. By having themselves hauled over land in a ship with sails set, we see the way in which Kintyre – physically a part of the mainland, although often described as an island in medieval texts[77] – is defined in terms of its relationship to an offshore island rather than vice versa. All three episodes illustrate the manner in which 'water-borne contacts extend the sea into the land'[78] in such a littoral environment.

The age of the sea-kings and sea-lords

In these often turbulent waters off the Atlantic facade of Scotland, ambitious chieftains and warlords carved out far-flung archipelagic lordships, kingdoms, and empires between *c*.900 and 1500. Although there remains a dearth of scholarship on Atlantic Scotland as a whole in the central and later middle ages, and these lordships are seldom discussed outside specialized scholarship on the region (e.g. studies of the Isle of Man, Hebrides, Northern Isles, or of individual islands), they nevertheless deserve attention as a remarkable assemblage of medieval thalassocracies.

There had been rulers styled kings or lords of the Isles from the late 9th and 10th centuries, but we know little about them.[79] Between the 10th and 15th centuries, however, four major units of lordship developed and flourished in the maritime environment of Atlantic Scotland: the joint Earldom of Orkney and Caithness, ruled by the Scandinavian jarls of Orkney until the demise of the Norse line of earls in 1231; the Hiberno-Norse kingdom of Man and the Isles, lorded over by a dynasty based in Man but also controlling some of the Hebrides from 1079 to 1265; a second kingdom of the Isles, an offshoot of the kingdom of Man and the Isles established in the 1150s; and the later-medieval MacDonald Lordship of the Isles (1336–1493) which can be regarded as a successor state to the kingdom of Man and the Isles, a sort of state-within-a-state or sub-kingdom of later-medieval Scotland. These polities and their rulers dominated the history of Atlantic Scotland in the middle ages, but they were by no means unique. Other notable sea-lords included the Lords of Galloway, a major power in the Irish Sea (Alan of Galloway has been mentioned above), as well as the Stewarts in the Firth of Clyde; the MacSweens in Knapdale; the MacLeans of Duart; the MacLeods in the North Minch; or the MacNeils of Barra.

In considering what characterized these lordships, it is their archipelagic and oceanic nature that stands out: all embraced both insular and mainland territory (though the realm of the Manx sea-kings was the most insular). The territory of the Lordship of the Isles, for example, has been aptly described as 'scattered but homogeneous', while the kingdom of Man and the Isles has been called a 'discontiguous water-world' (although I am less comfortable now than I was in 2007 about the utility of the term 'discontiguous' here).[80] A 13th-century Gaelic praise-poem on Aongus mac Domnaill, lord of Islay (d. *c*.1295), summed it up in more poetic fashion when it observed that his lordship extended 'from Mull to the Mull' – that is, from the Isle of Mull to the Mull of Kintyre.[81] The close integration of island and mainland into homogenous maritime lordships finds concrete expression in the remarkable group of galley-castles which form the subject of this volume: distributed across mainland, islands, islets or tidal islets, the castles all demonstrate a maritime orientation in which any distinction between island and mainland is largely irrelevant. For example, the key strongholds of the MacDougall lords of Lorn, the most powerful of Somerled's descendants through most of the 13th century, included fortresses on the mainland at Dunstaffnage in Lorn, north of Oban (Plate 7), as well as on a variety of islands including Aros and Duart on Mull, and Cairn na Burgh in the Treshnish Isles (Plate 8) (and may have included others at Dun Chonaill in the Garvellachs and Dunollie near Oban) – quite a remarkable assemblage (information on which, it might be noted, is scattered through no fewer than three of the RCAHMS inventories of Argyll).[82]

The jarls (earls) of Orkney and Caithness lorded it over a dominion which stretched nearly 400km from Unst, the most northerly of the Shetland Islands, to Caithness on the northern Scottish mainland, and in which the Pentland Firth was no political barrier at all.[83] It was claimed of Earl Þorfinnr Sigurðarson (d. *c*.1065) that, 'he won for himself nine Scottish earldoms, along with the whole of the Hebrides and a considerable part of Ireland', and the saga records a verse attributed to Arnórr Þórðarson jarlaskáld (*fl. c*.1045–75):

> The raven-feaster ruled
> right from Dublin –
> what I say is certain –
> To the Giants' Skerries.[84]

Doubt has been expressed about Þorfinnr's rule over nine Scottish earldoms and a portion of Ireland, but there is no question about the wide extent of the hegemony of the Orkney earls in the early 11th century which may well have extended to Dublin and Man.[85] The power of the Orkney earls steadily declined from the mid 12th century, however: Shetland was forfeited to the king of Norway in 1195 and the line of Norse earls died out soon after in 1231.

The weakening of Orkney influence and a power vacuum in Norway probably opened the way for new polities to develop in the Sudreys or southern Isles. Guðrøðr Crovan (d.1095), a survivor of the battle of Stamford Bridge in 1066, conquered the Isle of Man in 1079;[86] he and his descendants also ruled a far-flung sea-girt lordship based in Man, but, in addition, they also controlled all, later only some, of the Hebrides. Guðrøðr died on Islay in 1095, and most of his successors visited the Hebridean portion of their kingdom, some of them spending considerable time in residence there, where Skye and Lewis appear to have been power-centres.[87] In the late 1150s this kingdom was shattered with the rise to power of Somerled (Sumarliði), styled *rí Innse Gall & Cind tire* (d.1164).[88] He defeated Guðrøðr Crovan's grandson, Guðrøðr Óláfsson (d.1187), in two naval battles in the late 1150s; the mid-13th-century *Chronicles of the kings of Man and the Isles* explains that, 'the kingdom has existed in two parts from that day up until the present time, and this was the cause of the break-up of the kingdom from the time the sons of Somerled got possession of it'.[89] (The statement incidentally also betrays something of the text's status as an in-house chronicle for the Manx rulers).[90] The precise boundaries between the two dominions are uncertain and in any case were frequently contested, but in broad terms Somerled wrested the Islay and Mull groups of islands from the grasp of the Manx kings, and he and his descendants also controlled adjacent mainland territories from Kintyre to Knoydart. The Manx kings, however, retained control of Skye and most (perhaps all) of the Outer Hebrides, including Lewis; we may also note in passing that they possessed land and resources in Ireland, where King Rǫgnvaldr (d.1229) was granted lands in Carlingford by King John (r.1199–1216) in 1212, and on the Scottish mainland at Glenelg, by charter of the Scottish kings (an inventory of documents in 1282 included a 'charter of Glenhelk [Glenelg] which belonged to the king of Man').[91]

Rivalry between the Manx kings and the descendants of Somerled and within the Clann Somhairle itself form dominant and defining themes in the history of the western seaboard between the 1150s and the 1260s. Somerled's death in 1164 was followed by what has been aptly described as an 'extended civil war' among his descendants as his dominion fragmented.[92] Although the exact details are often murky, it appears that, by the middle of the 13th century, the MacDougalls held Lorn, Benderloch, and Lismore, the Garvellachs, north Jura, Mull, Tiree, Coll and the Treshnish Isles; the MacDonalds held Islay, south Jura, Colonsay, Oronsay, part of Kintyre, and probably Ardnamurchan and Morvern; and the MacRuaídrís held Garmoran (Moidart, Arisaig, Morar and Knoydart) as well as Eigg, Rum, Barra and the Uists.[93] The cession of the Hebrides to Scotland by the treaty of Perth in 1266 caused little disruption of existing holdings; rather, it was the period of the wars of Scotland in the late 13th and early 14th centuries that upset the equilibrium of these holdings when the pro-Balliol MacDougalls, who had been dominant through much of the 13th century, lost out to the pro-Bruce MacDonalds and MacRuaídrís.[94] The MacDonald Lordship of the Isles (1336–1493), with its 'capital' at Finlaggan on Islay, effectively re-created the vast insular and mainland territory of Somerled.[95]

Guðrøðr Crovan's galleys: ships and sea-power in the western seaways

The exercise of power within this stormy maritime arena required above all else large fleets of ships. Giraldus Cambrensis, writing about the Northern and Western Isles and their Norse masters *c*.1200, observed that: 'the Norwegians, who keep their eyes ever on the ocean, lead, above any other people, a piratical life. Consequently, all their expeditions and wars are decided by naval engagements'.[96] A sea-king without ships was by definition next to helpless. King Sverri of Norway (r.1184–1202) recognized as much when he opined in the early 1180s that, 'From this have come all our distresses, that we lost all our ships'.[97] Both statements incidentally also represent fine examples of the conceptual primacy of the maritime that has been referred to above.

Kings and chieftains in the Isles across many centuries would have understood that sentiment perfectly. *Orkneyinga saga*, in the brief pen-portrait of King Rǫgnvaldr of Man near its conclusion, describes him as 'the greatest fighting man in all the western lands', and goes on to remark that 'For three whole years he had lived aboard longships and not spent a single night under a sooty roof'.[98] Gaelic praise-poems on figures like King Rǫgnvaldr and Aongus of Islay present them as sea-kings, riding the waves in their magnificent vessels: 'You are the man of the brindled barques, the shore you will reach is cursed'.[99] Shores were places to be pillaged. Ships and their warriors were celebrated. We even learn the name of King Rǫgnvaldr's flagship, the *Swan* (or perhaps the *Black Swan*).[100]

Power was won and lost in this maritime arena first and foremost through sea-battles. One of the key events in the history of the medieval Isles was the division of the kingdom of Man and the Isles between Guðrøðr Óláfsson and Somerled, determined by two sea-battles in 1156 and 1158.[101] In another defining moment, Somerled himself perished in an amphibious invasion of the Scottish mainland near Renfrew in 1164.[102] *Orkneyinga saga* records several naval battles such as those between Earl Þorfinnr (d. *c*.1065) and the enigmatic Scottish ruler called Karl Hundason at Deerness; Earl Rǫgnvaldr Brúsason (d.1046) and Þorfinnr, fought off Roberry; or that at Tankerness between Earls Páll Hákonarson (d. *c*.1137) and Rǫgnvaldr (d.1158).[103] The well-known Gaelic verses in the early-16th-century *Book of the Dean of Lismore* describing Eòin Mac Suibhne's voyage to Castle Sween of (possibly) *c*.1310 celebrate the ships and men of this episode which may belong to the period of the Wars of Scotland.[104] The Battle of Bloody Bay, fought between John of Islay, Lord of the Isles and Earl of Ross (d.1503), and his son, Angus Óg (d. *c*.1490), in the early 1480s off the coast of Mull, represents not only a significant event in the history of the Lordship of the Isles but also one of the famous sea-battles of the era.[105] By the early 17th century, the age of the galley was over: Martin MacGregor notes that the Islay rising of 1615, which took the form of a land-based campaign fought in a maritime environment with ships reduced to a supporting role, highlights the passing of the dominance of the naval power of the Isles.[106]

The fleets commanded by these rulers were considerable, although they varied widely across time and space, and there seems to have been a general reduction in the size of fleets in the later middle ages.[107] Fleets of 30, 60, 90 and even 100 vessels are attributed to the Manx sea-kings in various sources at various times, and Somerled is said to have undertaken his invasion of the Scottish mainland in 1164 with 160 vessels.[108] Alan of Galloway is said to have amassed a fleet of 150 or 200 vessels in 1230; this made him a major player in the politics of the Irish Sea and he was perceived as a threat by Manx and Norwegian rulers.[109]

Orkneyinga saga shows the earls travelling and fighting with relatively small numbers of vessels, with anywhere from two to about a dozen very common. Larger fleets are, however, sometimes mentioned, as in the early 1150s when Earl Rǫgnvaldr set off on Crusade.[110] One of the larger naval confrontations in the saga is that between earls Rǫgnvaldr, with 30 ships, and Þorfinnr, with 60 (the saga incidentally provides a very detailed description of a sea-battle in this account).[111] John, the first Lord of the Isles (d. *c*.1387), is said to have had a fleet of 60 ships, and in Donald Dubh's uprising of 1545 he is said to have been followed by 17 chiefs with 180 galleys.[112] All these numbers clearly need to be treated with circumspection, as medieval sources are prone to inaccuracies and exaggeration, but taken altogether, and given the maritime nature of the territories they controlled, there can be little doubt about the relative strength of these rulers where naval power was concerned.

Manx fleets in particular seem to have been especially valued by rulers around the shores of the Irish Sea, who often sought to hire them out on a mercenary basis, as occurred possibly in the 1090s, when Manx ships were put at the disposal of Gruffudd ap Cynan, prince of Gwynedd (d.1137), or a century later when King Rǫgnvaldr provided naval power for King William in his struggle with Earl Haraldr Maddaðarson (d.1206) over Caithness. King Guðrøðr Óláfsson (d.1187) sent 30 vessels to support the Hiberno-Norse counter-attack against English-held Dublin in 1171, while an entry from the *Annals of the Four Masters* under the year 1154 describe how Muircheartach Mac Lochlainn, over-king of the Northern Uí Néill, as part of his ongoing bid for the kingship of all Ireland, 'sent persons over sea to hire (and who did hire) the fleets of the Gall-Gaeidhil [Galloway], of Ara [Arran], of Ceann-tire [Kintyre], of Manainn [Man], and the borders of Alba [Scotland] in general, over which Mac Scelling was in command'.[113] Access to Manx naval power may well have been a consideration in the marriage-match between John de Courcy, conqueror of Ulster (d. *c*.1219), and Affrica, the sister of King Rǫgnvaldr: certainly when de Courcy found himself out of favour with King John in the early 13th century (1204–05) his brother-in-law Rǫgnvaldr provided Manx vessels in a bid for reinstatement.[114]

Perhaps the best barometer for the sea-power commanded by the insular rulers, however, is its harnessing by 13th-century English kings to guard the English and Irish coasts and patrol the waters of the northern Irish Sea basin. Thus in 1235, for example, King Óláfr Guðrøðarson (d.1237) was tasked by Henry III with,

> guarding, at his own cost, the coast of the sea of England towards Ireland, and towards the Isle of Man, and likewise the coast of the sea of Ireland toward England, and towards the aforesaid Isle of Man, lest injury might happen to the aforesaid our lands of England and Ireland, by sea, upon these coasts.[115]

A great fleet also denoted a substantial force of warriors with which to man it, and the armies commanded by the lords in the isles also reflect the maritime interconnectivities of the region. Indeed, the way in which leaders from one region were able to recruit forces from throughout the broader arena of the western seaways is a notable feature of the military history of the region. Somerled's invasion of the Scottish mainland in 1164, for example, was undertaken with forces from Argyll, Kintyre, the Hebrides and Dublin.[116] Forty years later, when King Rǫgnvaldr led an army to Caithness *c*.1200, it also comprised forces from the Hebrides, Kintyre, and Ireland; this probably reflects his close connections with Ireland, including Ulster, and, indeed, as late as 1251 the Manx king Magnús was recruiting troops in Ireland.[117] The English chronicler Roger of Howden relates how, in 1196, Earl Haraldr Maddaðarson (d. *c*.1206) journeyed to the Isle of Man in order to recruit ships and men against his Norwegian-appointed rival for the earldom, Haraldr the Younger; we are told that Haraldr the Younger also journeyed to Man, although not whether he too was seeking ships and men.[118]

No discussion of the warriors of Atlantic Scotland could fail to make mention of the famous galloglass, a class of professional mercenary soldier first appearing in the mid 13th century in the Hebrides and playing a prominent role in Hebridean, Irish Sea, and Irish affairs through the later middle ages and into the Early-Modern era. As the Galloglass project puts it: 'The location of the galloglass at the intersection of Scottish and Irish politics, warfare and culture in the late middle ages is frequently alluded to and has long been recognized'.[119] In the space available it is not possible to examine in detail the place of the galloglass in our maritime world, but it is worth noting that the role of galloglass in the lands bordering the Irish Sea provides another prominent example of maritime connectivity and mobility between regions.[120]

As some of the foregoing (particularly Sveinn Ásleifarson's career) suggests, sea-borne raiding and plundering was a prominent activity of the kings and chieftains of the Isles and is encountered regularly in the sources. Among the best-known examples is that of Ruaídrí the son of Ragnall son of Somerled who, as late as 1212 and 1214, was pillaging in Derry along with Thomas of Galloway (d.1231), younger son of Roland of Galloway (d.1200).[121] Other illustrations are provided by the praise-poems composed in honour of Rǫgnvaldr king of Man and Aongus mac Domnaill of Islay. Rǫgnvaldr is said to have conducted cattle-raids on Ireland, and the lord of Islay is depicted in similar light: 'You've circled Ireland, scarce the shore where you've not taken cattle', says the poet.[122]

The role of plundering and especially of cattle-raiding is of course well known in early Irish society, but it is perhaps open to question whether these 13th-century praise-poems accurately portray the situation or whether they are idealizations representing a conservative literary tradition. But, though we must use their evidence with caution, there can be no doubt that both Rǫgnvaldr and Aongus did undertake expeditions to Ireland: in 1218, for example, there is a reference to the excesses committed in Ireland by the Manx king, and as late as 1256 the English king ordered his Irish bailiffs to curb the activities of Aongus and other Scottish malefactors there.[123] Seán Duffy suggests that Aongus might well have been providing military service to his

Irish associates as part of what has been called 'the prehistory of the galloglass'.[124] Also to be noted is an episode which occurred in 1258 when what looks like another MacSorley-led piratical raid took place along the coast of Connacht. The *Annals of Loch Cé* record that,

> A great fleet came from Innsi-Gall with Mac Somhairle; and they passed round Erinn westwards to Conmaicne-Mara, where they robbed a merchant-vessel of all its goods, both wine and clothing, and copper and iron.

The raiders were intercepted by Jordan de Exeter, the sheriff of Connaught, who was killed along with many of his men in the ensuing battle on an offshore island. The entry concludes with the comment that 'Mac Somhairle went afterwards exultingly, enriched with spoils, with the triumph of victory, to his own country'.[125] The name of Mac Somhairle is not supplied, but suspicion has been cast on Dubgall mac Ruaídrí of Garmoran (d.1268), the first cousin of Aongus mac Domnaill; political as well as economic and opportunistic motives have also been suggested for these and other episodes of MacSorley plundering in Ireland.[126]

W Stanford Reid highlighted the importance of sea-power in the Anglo-Scottish wars of the 13th and 14th centuries,[127] and no discussion of piracy in the arena of the western seaways would be complete without mention of the (in)famous sea-captain Thomas Dun whose activities formed a significant chapter in the Irish Sea theatre of war in the 1310s. Barbour relates how Dun's ships ferried Edward Bruce's men across the Bann in 1315, and in autumn of that year Dun and his fleet were harassing English shipping around Holyhead. By 1317 Dun's activities were so troublesome that two new English vessels were constructed solely for the purpose of intercepting him – a task at which they were eventually successful following a huge sea-battle in July 1317.[128] The English directive to construct those vessels specified their purpose: 'to destroy Thomas D[un] mariner, who is infesting the sea towards the west with a crew of Scots, doing great damage to traders coming to England'.[129] On the other side of the conflict, John MacDougall of Argyll (d.1316) served Edward II as 'Admiral and Captain of our Fleet of Ships' (*admirallum et capitaneum flotae nostrae navium*) from 1311 and was tasked with hunting down the king's enemies on the west coast. John expelled the Scots from the Isle of Man in 1315 and later that year he captured 23 Scottish rebels on 'the sea coast of Scotland'.[130] Although his career in this capacity has ultimately been judged as unsuccessful, John must have brought important local knowledge and personal experience of the marine environment of the western seaboard to his task.[131] The failure of the English to control the seas has been regarded as a contributing factor to their lack of success in Scotland.[132]

Ships carried more than just kings, warriors, and pirates, of course. The west highland galley was a notably versatile vessel, and trade and commerce also flowed along the western seaways, although the sources are not nearly as forthcoming as the historian would like, and references are scattered and often frustratingly vague. As far as west highland trade is concerned, the burghs of Tarbert, Dumbarton and Glasgow dominate the picture.[133] In 1275, for instance, there is a reference to the bishop of Glasgow's merchants going to and returning from Argyll with merchandise, the nature of which is unfortunately not related.[134] Also in 1275, some of Alexander of Argyll's (d.1310) men were arrested with their vessel and goods in Bristol on suspicion of piracy; the value of the goods was given at 160 marks but the nature of the merchandise was not mentioned.[135]

The fact that the crew of the ship could be suspected of piracy is perhaps a reflection of the interchangeability of commerce and piracy, but perhaps more informative is the fact that we find men and vessels from the Isles at Bristol, a major English port. In 1292 Edward I granted letters of safe conduct to Alexander of Argyll, Aongus the son of Domnaill, and his son Alexander, in which it was stated that these men frequently sent merchants with goods to Ireland to both buy and sell.[136] A letter of King Óláfr of Man of *c.*1228 refers specifically to his merchants (presumably Manx), and in 1342 the Manx arranged a year's truce with the Scots to allow merchants from England, Ireland and Wales to come safely to the island.[137] *Orkneyinga saga* relates how Kali Kolsson, the future Earl Rǫgnvaldr, accompanied a trading expedition to Grimsby in his youth; the saga says that 'There was a large gathering of people there from Orkney, Scotland and the Hebrides'.[138]

The saga of Hrafn Sveinbjarnarsonar, the biography of the famous Icelandic *goði* (chieftain) and physician (d.1213), relates how, en route from Iceland to Norway in 1202, Hrafn and the bishop-elect of Hólar, Guðmundr Arason, were storm-driven into the Hebrides, where they feared for their lives in rough seas; they were saved, and eventually found shelter on Sandey, where they encountered a king of the Isles named Óláfr (probably Óláfr Guðrøðarson). Given the status of its passengers, it is easy to lose sight of the fact that Hrafn and Guðmundr sailed on a trading vessel and that most of the Icelanders on board were in fact merchants; *vaðmál* (homespun) constituted at least part of their cargo, and the episode sheds some illumination on further potential commercial connections.[139] We would like to know more about all these episodes, of course, but taken together they reveal that long-distance trade over the seaways was important throughout the Medieval and Early-Modern periods. Resources and manpower used in the construction of the galley-castles must have travelled this way, too, though there is virtually nothing in the written record on this topic.

The traffic flowing along the sea-road is exemplified by the spectacular find of 78 chess-pieces (with 14 plain disks and one belt-buckle) at Uig Bay on the west coast of the island of Lewis in 1831: the so-called 'Lewis chessmen'. Made of walrus-ivory and crafted, in all likelihood, in Norway (though an Icelandic origin has also been suggested), the chess-pieces were prestigious items and were probably buried by a merchant traveling the well-established route from Scandinavia to Ireland via the Hebrides. They can be fairly closely dated to the second half of the 12th century, and Ian Armit has observed that the chessmen indicate 'the relative wealth and close contacts with the mainstream Norse world of at least some inhabitants of the Hebrides well into the Medieval period'.[140] Similar patterns of trade have been revealed by recent archaeological work on the other Outer Hebridean islands of North and South Uist, at The Udal, Bornais, and Cille Pheadair, which have excavated late Norse settlements with extensive North Atlantic connections.[141] Painstaking archaeological work by James Barrett on Quoygrew in Orkney has also done much to illuminate changing patterns of production, trade and interaction across the Medieval period in the Northern Isles.[142]

As a final point here, it is worth noting that, although the economy of the region is often regarded as being backward and depressed, this may require reassessment. The question of how such a supposed economic backwater could sustain what has been described as 'the most remarkable collection of thirteenth-century lords' strongholds to be found in any single region of Britain'[143] has yet to be examined in detail, much less satisfactorily answered.

Conclusion: the galley-castles, the Norse-Gaelic seaways, and the supremacy of the maritime

'Eòin has reached a happy haven/In the breast of Knapdale, a voyage at sea ...'. So says the poet in *A Meeting of a Fleet Against the Castle of Suibhne*, one of the great late-medieval Gaelic poems from the *Book of the Dean of Lismore* (compiled 1512–42) and one of the few surviving literary references to a galley-castle (Castle Sween) on the western seaboard.[144] The poem is of interest for many reasons, both historical and literary, but here we may note the maritime context of the castle and its close association with the sea: Eòin is bringing a fleet to lay siege to the castle, the spectacular remains of which still stand on a rocky ridge on the east shore of Loch Sween with commanding prospects of the sea-loch (Plate 9). Among other things, then, the poem is a reminder that the castles of the western seaboard (as with most monuments of the region) existed within a context that was, to use Pocock's phrase, 'pelagic, maritime, and oceanic'.[145] This maritime and oceanic orientation is reflected in the physical remains of medieval Atlantic Scotland, a significant proportion of which are situated in coastal locations, often placed on rocky outcrops, offshore islands, or in sheltered bays.[146] If they represent 'tangible illustrations of the physical horizons of [the] maritime lordships'[147] which created them, then those horizons were, unsurprisingly, dominated by the sea – literally as well as figuratively, since the landward vistas of many of the galley-castles are often restricted (as at Kisimul in Barra and Mingary in Ardnamurchan, for example) and fortification was sometimes required to secure approaches from the landward side (as at Mingary, or Duart in Mull, for example).[148]

A well-known and defining characteristic of the galley-castles is their location at strategic situations with respect to the western seaways: they are usually (but not always) sited to provide commanding prospects of the sea-lanes, and often (though again, not always) have good landing-places and havens for galleys nearby. Thus, to take but a few examples, Dunstaffnage in Lorn commands the seaward approach to Loch Etive and the Pass of Brander, and also overlooks the Firth of Lorn and the eastern entrance to the Sound of Mull.[149] Similarly, Duart castle in Mull has been described as occupying

> one of the most commanding [sites] in the whole area of the western seaboard, lying as it does at the intersection of three major waterways, namely the Sound of Mull,

Loch Linnhe and the Firth of Lorn. Observation can also be kept from the castle upon vessels passing through Loch Etive, while the neighbouring castles of Dunstaffnage, Dunollie, Achadun and Ardtornish are all clearly visible (Plate 10).[150]

So closely tied to the seaways are the galley-castles that producing a map of the castles also serves effectively to delineate the main sailing-routes and thoroughfares of the region. Castles and galleys therefore existed in what has been described as a state of 'perfect symbiosis' in the west; 'a network of stone and ships' as Steve Boardman has put it.[151] Indeed, bearing in mind the intervisibility of a number of important castles lining the Sound of Mull (mentioned above), there may have been a sense in which castles were intended to function as part of a system or network: inter-visibility (as well as inter-audibility) forms an important aspect of the definition of 'microregions' in Horden and Purcell's study of the pre-modern Mediterranean, and the concept might be worth further investigation in the context of the galley-castles of Atlantic Scotland.[152] To take but one possible example, *Orkneyinga saga* describes a system of signal-beacons in the Northern Isles which apparently acted as a sort of Late Norse Distant Early Warning system, and the early-modern institution of Watch and Ward in the Isle of Man may have had Late Norse and/or medieval antecedents; given this, one may legitimately speculate as to whether a similar system existed in the Hebrides and Argyll, particularly if the burning beacon or fiery mountain on the MacLeod of The Lewes coat-of-arms represents such an institution, perhaps originally related to the MacNicol coast-watchers.[153]

Not every castle, however, is ideally located for dominating seaborne communication, convenient landing, or easy seaward approaches; the limitations and situational peculiarities of some of the monuments suggest the importance of other roles as well, particularly the symbolic.[154] Geoffrey Stell has drawn attention to some of the limitations of the siting of Mingary castle in Ardnamurchan, for example: in addition to lacking good anchorage close to hand, the castle 'almost recklessly faces west in the teeth of virtually every gale that blows' and the seaward approach to the castle is not an easy one. 'To conclude', says Stell, 'that Mingary is a site of "considerable strategic importance in respect of sea-borne communication" is thus to gloss over some unanswered peculiarities of its local position'.[155] The island fortress of Cairn na Burgh in the Treshnish Isles, despite its impressive situation, similarly lacked nearby convenient anchorage, and landing was dependent on weather and tidal conditions which are often difficult.[156] It has also been suggested that the relative lack of stone castles in Skye and the Outer Hebrides points to their value as status-symbols (although of course a strong strategic situation and a role as a status-symbol are not mutually exclusive).[157]

Whether constructed to command and control strategic sea-lanes, or as prestige architecture to impress, advertise, or overawe, the galley-castles reflect the power and status of the sea-lords of Atlantic Scotland in the middle ages. Recent scholarship has drawn attention to the importance of places where sea and shore interact, particularly islands and islets, as being possessed of special qualities: 'That islands were liminal places, neither entirely of the land nor of the sea, would have endowed them with unusual power in the minds of those who lived at the interface between land and ocean'.[158] The point was not made with the galley-castles of Atlantic Scotland in mind, but it may prove useful nevertheless in helping to assess the significance of these structures. Some, at least, of the galley-castle sites appear to have been occupied in Prehistoric and Early-Historic times before being reoccupied and rebuilt in the Medieval period, and in some instances it is difficult to draw distinctions between castles and earlier structures such as duns and roundhouses. Ian Armit has observed of Kisimul castle, for example, that, 'the choice of an island for the construction of this major symbol of authority in Barra appears to echo again the long tradition of islet occupation in the Hebrides'.[159]

There are many reasons why earlier sites may have been re-used by medieval castle-builders, of course, but it may be pertinent to reflect on the degree to which the situation of the castles in liminal spaces between land and sea relates to their role as symbols of power and prestige, or perhaps, following recent work undertaken on Iron Age settlements in the Outer Hebrides, there is even something to be learned about identity here.[160] Of particular relevance might be those castles situated on tiny islets, tidal or otherwise, like Kisimul or Eilean Tioram (Plate 11).[161] Whatever the case may be, in the final analysis these castles, situated at the dynamic interface between sea and shore, provide a potent reminder of the primacy of the maritime in medieval Atlantic Scotland as well as important insight into the lost worlds that created them.

Notes

1. I am very grateful to the organizers for the opportunity to participate in the conference. I would also like to thank Benjamin T Hudson, Barbara Crawford, John Sainsbury and Angus A Somerville for discussing the paper with me at various stages of its development and for providing helpful advice and criticism, although they are by no means responsible for any errors that may remain, which are, of course, my own.
2. *Orkneyinga saga: the history of the earls of Orkney*, transl. H Pálsson & P Edwards, 1981 (London), ch. 110, p.215. Hereafter *OS*. This edition is used except where otherwise indicated.
3. *OS* chs 66, 78, 79.
4. *OS* ch. 100, p.207. There is no comprehensive study of Sveinn but see J Barrett, 2005, 'Svein Asleifarson and 12th-century Orcadian society', in O Owen (ed.), *The world of Orkneyinga Saga: 'the broad-cloth Viking trip'* (Kirkwall), pp.213–23.
5. *OS* chs 78, 87, 88, pp.144–6, 169–74, 174–81.
6. *Icelandic Sagas and other historical documents relating to the settlements and descents of the Northmen on the British Isles*, vol. 4, 1894, *The saga of Hacon, and a fragment of the saga of Magnus, with appendices*, transl. Sir G Dasent (London), ch. 166, p.152. Hereafter *HS*; all subsequent references are to this translation. A new edition of the text is: *Hákonar saga Hákonarsonar*, Þ Hauksson & S Jakobsson (eds), 2013, 2 vols (Reykjavík).
7. *HS*, ch. 163, p.150. On Alan see K J Stringer, 1993, 'Periphery and core in 13th-century Scotland: Alan son of Roland, Lord of Galloway and Constable of Scotland', in A Grant & K J Stringer (eds), *Medieval Scotland: crown, lordship and community* (Edinburgh), pp.82–113.

8. R A McDonald, 2007a, *Manx Kingship in its Irish Sea Setting, 1187–1229: King Rǫgnvaldr and the Crovan dynasty* (Dublin).

9. *Calendar of documents relating to Scotland preserved in Her Majesty's Public Record Office, London*, J Bain (ed.), vols 1–4, 1881–8 (Edinburgh); vol. 5, J D Galbraith & G G Simpson (eds), 1896 (Edinburgh), vol.1, no. 890 pp.158–9. Hereafter *CDS*.

10. P Horden & N Purcell, 2000, *The Corrupting Sea: A Study of Mediterranean History* (Malden MA & Oxford), p.133.

11. S Murdoch, 2010, *The Terror of the Seas? Scottish Maritime Warfare 1513–1713* (Leiden & Boston), p.i.

12. M Pye, 2015, *The Edge of the World: How the North Sea made us who we are* (London); M McCaughan & J Appleby (eds), 1989, *The Irish Sea: Aspects of Maritime History* (Belfast).

13. I R Macneil, 2006, 'Kisimul Castle and the Origins of Hebridean Galley-Castles: Preliminary Thoughts', in A Kruse with A Ross (eds), *Barra and Skye: Two Hebridean Perspectives* (Edinburgh), 21–46, see esp. 42–44.

14. See E MacKie, 2000, 'The Scottish Atlantic Iron Age: Indigenous and Isolated or Part of a Wider European World?', in J C Henderson (ed.), *The Prehistory and Early History of Atlantic Europe. Papers from a session held at the European Association of Archaeologists 4th Annual Meeting in Göteborg 1998*, BAR S-861 (Oxford), pp.99–100.

15. Late-medieval writers like John of Fordun and Walter Bower included the Isle of Man in their listings of the islands between Scotland and Ireland: see for example *Scotichronicon by Walter Bower in Latin and English*, D E R Watt *et al.* (eds), 1987–97, 9 vols (Aberdeen), vol. I, bk II, ch. 10, pp.186–7.

16. *HS*, ch. 167 p.152–4. I have revised the translation slightly, and I am grateful to Angus Somerville for advice on the passage.

17. C Tabraham, 1997, *Scotland's Castles* (London), p.31. The saga contains another reference to a castle at the Mull of Kintyre in its account of events of 1263: ch. 320, pp.149–50.

18. *OS*, ch. 84 p.155.

19. A Ritchie, 1996, *Orkney* (Edinburgh), pp.93–4. *HS*, ch. 170 p.156, where the castle is described as 'a very unhandy place to attack'.

20. *OS* chs 82–3 p.151.

21. *OS* p.249, but *cf Orkneyinga saga: A new translation with introduction and notes*, A B Taylor, 1938 (Edinburgh), p.390 where a case is made for Broch of Ness on the south of the Bay of Freswick.

22. D W Moore, 2005, *The other British Isles: a history of Shetland, Orkney, the Hebrides, Isle of Man, Anglesey, Scilly, Isle of Wight and the Channel Islands* (Jefferson NC & London).

23. A Lew, C Hall & T Dallen, 2008, *World Geography of Travel and Tourism: A Regional Approach* (Oxford), p.94; see also http://www.sovereignty.org.uk/features/articles/uk6. html. Another estimate, considering only those islands which are 0.2 hectares (half an acre) or more in area and are islands at all states of the tide, places the total about 4400. http://www.theguardian.com/notesandqueries/query/0,5753,-1934,00.html.

24. There is a good discussion of the maritime environment of Atlantic Scotland in B Crawford, 1987, *Scandinavian Scotland* (Leicester), pp.11–27; a good overview of the Hebridean environment is W H Murray, 1973, *The Islands of Western Scotland* (London). F H Groome, new edn 1895, *Ordnance Gazetteer of Scotland: A Survey of Scottish Topography*, 6 vols (London), remains useful and is now accessible online: http://www. gazetteerofscotland. org.uk.

25. Crawford, *Scandinavian Scotland*, p.21.

26. J Hardisty, 1990, *The British Seas: An introduction to the oceanography and resources of the north-west European continental shelf* (London & New York).

27. *History and Topography of Ireland*, Gerald of Wales, trans. J J O'Meara, 1982, revised edn (London), p.31.

28. Adam of Bremen, 2002, *History of the Archbishops of Hamburg-Bremen*, transl. with intro. & notes by Francis J Tschan, with a new intro. & selected bibliography by Timothy Reuter (New York), pp.219–20.

29. William of Malmesbury, *De gestis regum Anglorum. History of the English Kings*, ed. and transl. R A B Mynors, R Thomson & M Winterbottom, 1998–99 (Oxford), I, pp.600–01.

30. M T Clancy, 1983, *England and its Rulers 1066–1272* (London), pp.22–3.

31. N Millea, 2007, *The Gough map: the earliest road map of Great Britain?* (Oxford), pp.45–7.

32. J G A Pocock, 2005, 'The Atlantic Archipelago and the War of the Three Kingdoms', in *The Discovery of Islands: Essays in British History* (Cambridge), p.78 (essay originally published 1996).

33. See for example G Noble, T Poller, J Raven & L Verrill (eds), 2008, *Scottish Odysseys: The Archaeology of Islands* (Stroud).

34. B Cunliffe, 2001, *Facing the Ocean: The Atlantic and its peoples 8000 BC–AD 1500* (Oxford), p.31.

35. See especially the influential work of C Broodbank, 2000, *An Island Archaeology of the Early Cyclades* (Cambridge).

36. The study of 'Islandscapes' encompasses both landscapes and seascapes, and recognizes individual islands as well as archipelagos and adjacent mainland. See Broodbank, cited above, and also R Van De Noort, 2011, *North Sea Archaeologies: A Maritime Biography, 10,000 BC to AD 1500* (Oxford), pp.26, 126–36.

37. Cunliffe, *Facing the Ocean*, p.viii. Cf M Mollat, 1993, *Europe and the Sea*, transl. T L Fagan (Oxford), p.ix.

38. Horden & Purcell, *Corrupting Sea*, p.133.

39. Horden & Purcell, *Corrupting Sea*, p.133.

40. I Armit, 1996, *The Archaeology of Skye and the Western Isles* (Edinburgh), pp.5–6.

41. J R Coull, 1996, 'Shetland: the land, sea and human environments', in D Waugh (ed.), *Shetland's northern links: language and history* (Edinburgh), pp.66–77.

42. Armit, *Archaeology*, p.5.

43. A fact regularly commented on in the RCAHMS inventories: see notes 82 and 148–50 below.

44. M MacGregor, 2014, 'Warfare in Gaelic Scotland in the Later Middle ages', in E M Spiers, J A Crang & M Strickland (eds) *A Military History of Scotland* (Edinburgh), p.214.

45. MacKie, 'Scottish Atlantic Iron Age', p.100; see also I B Cowan, 1978, 'The Medieval Church in Argyll and the Isles', *Scottish Church History Society Records* 20.I, pp.5–29 at 20–23; *Fasti Ecclesiae Scoticanae Medii Aevi Ad Annum 1638*, D E R Watt & A L Murray (eds), 2003 (Edinburgh), pp.34–5.

46. J Leirfall, 1979, *West Over Sea: Reminders of Norse Ascendency from Shetland to Dublin*, transl. K Young (Belfast), p.23.

47. O G S Crawford, 1936, 'The Western Seaways', in D Buxton (ed.), *Custom is King* (London); C Fox, 1932, *The Personality of Britain* (Cardiff:). There is a succinct overview of the development of the topic in Cunliffe, *Facing the Ocean*, pp.16–18.

48. E G Bowen, 1970, 'Britain and the British Seas', in D Moore (ed.), *The Irish Sea Province in Archaeology and History* (Cardiff), pp.13–29; E G Bowen, 1977, *Saints seaways and settlements in the Celtic lands* (Cardiff).

49. A R Lewis, 1958, *The Northern Seas: shipping and commerce in northern Europe AD 300–1100* (Princeton), p.64.

50. See for example B E Crawford (ed.), 2002, *The Papar in the North Atlantic: Environment and History* (St Andrews), http://www.paparproject.org.uk; and now K Ahronson, 2015, *Into the Ocean: Vikings, Irish and Environmental Change in Iceland and the North* (Toronto).

51. B T Hudson, 2012, 'Prologue: The Medieval Atlantic Ocean', in B T Hudson (ed.), *Studies in the Medieval Atlantic* (New York & London), p.9.

52. E Ridel, 2007, 'From Scotland to Normandy: the Celtic Sea Route of the Vikings', in B Ballin Smith, S Taylor & G Williams (eds), *West Over Sea: Studies in Scandinavian Sea-Borne Expansion and Settlement before 1300* (Leiden & Boston), pp.81–94.

53. See discussion in J M Wooding, 1996, *Communication and Commerce along the Western Sealanes AD 400–800,* BAR S654 (Oxford), esp. ch. 1.

54. *The King's Mirror (Speculum Regale-Konungs Skuggsjá)*, transl. L M Larson, 1917 (New York), pp.137–8.

55. *Hrafns saga Sveinbjarnarsonar*, G Helgadóttir (ed.), 1987 (Oxford), pp.20–22. Transl. in *Early Sources of Scottish History AD 500 to 1286*, ed. and transl. A O Anderson, 1922, 2 vols (Edinburgh); reprint 1990 (Stamford), ii, p.358.

56. *Cronica regum Mannie & Insularum: chronicles of the kings of Man and the Isles BL Cotton Julius Avii*, ed. and transl. G Broderick, 1996, 2nd edn (Douglas), ff.46v–47r (wrongly dated 1249 in the text), ff.45r–45v. Hereafter *CRMI*.

57. *HS*, ch. 327, p.364. The name is from Old Norse *svelgr* = whirlpool: Crawford, *Scandinavian Scotland*, p.21. It is mentioned in the 12th-century *Historia Norwegie*, ed. I. Ekrem & L.B. Mortensen, transl. P Fisher, 2003 (Copenhagen), ch. VI, pp.64–5, where it is described as 'the most gigantic of all whirlpools'.

58. E J Cowan, 1990, 'Norwegian Sunset – Scottish Dawn: Hakon IV and Alexander III', in N Reid (ed.), 1990, *Scotland in the Reign of Alexander III 1249–86* (Edinburgh), p.122.

59. Gerald of Wales, *History and Topography of Ireland*, p.58; *Expugnatio Hibernica. The conquest of Ireland*, ed. and transl. A B Scott & F X Martin, 1978 (Dublin), ch. 36, *De Tempestatibus.*

60. Alexander Lindsay, *A Rutter of the Scottish Seas (c.1540)*, ed. I H Adams & G Fortune, 1980 (Greenwich). A good overview of the development of portolan charts is T Campbell, 1987, 'Portolan charts from the late thirteenth century to 1500', in J B Harley & D Woodward (eds), *The History of Cartography, Vol. 1 – Cartography in Prehistoric, Ancient, and Medieval Europe and the Mediterranean* (Chicago), pp.371–463.

61. Donald Monro, *Description of the Occidental i.e. Western Islands of Scotland* in *A Description of the Western Islands of Scotland circa 1695; A voyage to St. Kilda by Martin Martin with A Description of the Occidental i.e. Western Islands of Scotland by Donald Monro*, introduction by Charles J Withers & R W Munro, 1999 (Edinburgh), p.303.

62. Millea, *Gough Map*, pp.11, 43–44.

63. Mollat*, Europe and the Sea*, p.192.

64. G W S Barrow, 2003, *Kingship and Unity: Scotland AD 1000–1300*, 2nd edn (Edinburgh), pp.130–31; G Noble & F Stevens, 2008, 'An island of fluctuating perceptions: the landscape and archaeology of Bute', in *Scottish Odysseys*, p.40; J Wright, 2008, 'Islandscapes and Standing Stones: Changing perceptions', in *Scottish Odysseys*, p.63.

65. I A Fraser, 'The Place-names of Argyll', in D Omand (ed.), 2004, *The Argyll Book* (Edinburgh), pp.243–54 at 245.

66. Argyll and the Isles Tourism: http: www.exploreargyll.co.uk, accessed 1 September 2015.

67. D G Sutherland, 1997, 'The Environment of Argyll', in G Ritchie (ed.), *The Archæology of Argyll* (Edinburgh), p.10. Note that Scotland comprises less than 1% of Europe's total area but about 8–10% of its total coastline! www.snh.gov.uk, accessed 1 September 2015.

68. B B Mandelbrot, 1967, 'How long is the coast of Britain? Statistical self-similarity and fractional dimension', *Science* 156, pp.636–8 (http://users.math.yale.edu/~bbm3/web_pdfs/howLongIsTheCoastOfBritain.pdf); see also G Boffetta, A Celani, D Dezzani & A Seminara, 2008, 'How winding is the coast of Britain? Conformal invariance of rocky shorelines', *Geophys. Res. Lett.* 35.3 (http://www.fisica.unige.it/~seminara/publications/rocky.pdf).

69. The 15th-century chronicler Walter Bower took considerable interest in the lochs of western Scotland: *Scotichronicon*, vol I, bk II, ch. 10, pp.190–91.

70. Snorri Sturluson, *Heimskringla: History of the Kings of Norway*, transl. L Hollander, 1991 (Austin TX), pp.677–8.

71. *HS*, ch 323, pp.354–5.

72. Cowan, 'Norwegian Sunset – Scottish Dawn', pp.121–23.

73. W J Watson, 2004, *The History of the Celtic Place-names of Scotland*, with an introduction by Simon Taylor (Edinburgh), pp.505–06; see now Alan Macniven, 2014, 'Navigating the nomenclature: the validity of Gaelic *Tairbeart* as evidence for pre-Norse survival in Lewis and the west of Scotland', in D H Caldwell & Mark A Hall (eds), *The Lewis Chessmen: New Perspectives* (Edinburgh), pp.121–50. See also E Nyman, 2006, 'Words for "portage" in the Scandinavian languages, and place-names indicating old portages', and C Phillips, 2006, 'Portages in Early Medieval Scotland: The Great Glen Route and the Forth-Clyde Isthmus', both in C Westerdahl (ed.), *The Significance of Portages: Proceedings of the First International Conference on the Significance of Portages, 29 Sept. – 2 Oct 2004, Lydal, Vest-Agder, Norway*, BAR Int. Ser. 1499 (Oxford), pp.169–72 and 191–8.

74. *OS*, ch 41 p.86.

75. John Barbour, *The Bruce*, ed. and transl. A A M Duncan, 2007 (Edinburgh), bk 15, lines 276–90, pp.564–5.

76. Horden & Purcell, *Corrupting Sea*, p.133.

77. Interestingly, the authors of *Heimskringla* and *Orkneyinga saga* knew better: Kintyre is accurately described in both texts as a peninsula attached to the mainland by a narrow isthmus.

78. Horden & Purcell, *Corrupting Sea*, p.133.

79. See R A McDonald, 1997, *The Kingdom of the Isles: Scotland's Western Seaboard c.1100–c.1336* (East Linton), pp.30–33; A Woolf, 2004, 'The Age of Sea-Kings: 900–1300', in D Omand (ed.), *The Argyll Book* (Edinburgh), pp.94–109.

80. *The Acts of the Lords of the Isles 1336–1493*, J Munro & R W Munro (eds), 1986 (Edinburgh), p.xxiii; McDonald, *Manx kingship*, p.17.

81. *The Triumph Tree: Scotland's Earliest Poetry, 550–1350*, ed. T O Clancy, 1998 (Edinburgh), p.288.

82. I Fisher, 2005, 'The Heirs of Somerled', in R Oram & G Stell (eds), *Lordship and Architecture in Medieval and Renaissance Scotland* (Edinburgh), pp.85–96; RCAHMS, 1974, *Argyll: An Inventory of the Ancient Monuments Vol. 2: Lorn* (Edinburgh), nos 286–7, pp.194–8, 198–211; RCAHMS, 1980, *Argyll: An Inventory of the Monuments Vol. 3: Mull, Tiree, Coll and Northern Argyll* (Edinburgh), nos 333, 335, 339, 345, pp.173–7, 184–90, 191–200, 209–17; RCAHMS, 1984, *Argyll: An Inventory of the Ancient Monuments Vol. 5: Islay, Jura, Colonsay and Oronsay* (Edinburgh), no. 402 pp.265–8.

83. B E Crawford, 2013, *The Northern Earldoms: Orkney and Caithness from AD 870 to 1470* (Edinburgh), pp.15–16.

84. *OS*, ch. 32 p.75.

85. Crawford, *Northern Earldoms*, p.162.

86. An important study is S Duffy, 2002, 'Emerging from the mist: Ireland and Man in the eleventh century', in P J Davey & D Finlayson (eds), *Mannin revisited: twelve essays on Manx culture and environment* (Edinburgh), pp.53–62.

87. Discussed at length in McDonald, *Manx kingship*, pp.92–5; the accomplishment of these kings in ruling such a far-flung kingdom, divided into two halves with a central wedge controlled by a rival dynasty, merits some consideration. See now S Duffy & H Mytum (eds), 2015, *New History of the Isle of Man Vol. 3: The Medieval Period 1000–1406* (Liverpool).

88. 'The Annals of Tigernach', ed. and transl. W Stokes, 1897, *Revue Celtique* 18, pp.9–59, 150–303 at 195, (CELT: Corpus of Electronic Texts: a project of University College Cork, College Road, Cork, Ireland (2010) at http://www.ucc.ie/celt/published/T100002A/index.html).

89. *CRMI*, f.37v.

90. McDonald, *Manx kingship*, pp.98–100.

91. Carlingford grant: *Rotuli chartarum in turri Londinensi asservati vol I pars I ab anno MCXCIX ad annum MCCXVI*, T D Hardy (ed.), 1837 (London), p.186; Glenelg charter: *The Acts of the Parliaments of Scotland*, T Thomson & C Innes (eds), 1814–75, 11 vols (Edinburgh), vol. i, p.110; further discussion in McDonald, *Manx kingship*, chs 3–4.

92. Woolf, 'Age of Sea-Kings', p.107.

93. See *Acts of the Lords of the Isles*, pp.xx–xxi; K A Steer & J W M Bannerman, 1977, *Late Medieval Monumental Sculpture in the West Highlands* (Edinburgh), p.202.

94. McDonald, *Kingdom of the Isles*, chs 5–6. See also R Oram, 2004b, 'The Lordship of the Isles: 1336–1493', in D Omand (ed.), *The Argyll Book* (Edinburgh), pp.123–39.

95. *Acts of the Lords of the Isles*, pp.xxiii–xxxviii. On the Lordship see important contributions by J Bannerman, 1977, 'The lordship of the Isles', in J Brown (ed.), *Scottish society in the 15th century* (London: Arnold), pp.209–40; and A Grant, 1988, 'Scotland's "Celtic fringe" in the late middle ages: the MacDonald lordship of the Isles and the kingdom of Scotland', in R R Davies (ed.), *The British Isles, 1100–1400: Comparisons, contrasts, and connection* (Edinburgh), pp.118–42. On Islay: D H Caldwell, 2008a, *Islay: The Land of the Lordship* (Edinburgh), and D H Caldwell & N A Ruckley, 2005, 'Domestic Architecture in the Lordship of the Isles', in R Oram & G Stell (eds), *Lordship and Architecture* (Edinburgh), pp.97–122.

96. *History and Topography*, transl. O'Meara, pp.65–6.

97. *Sverris saga*, G Indrebø (ed.), 1920 (Kristiana: Riksarkivet), ch. 73 p.79; *Sverrissaga: The saga of king Sverri of Norway*, transl. J Sephton, 1899 (London), repr. 1922 (Felinfach), p.92.

98. *OS*, ch. 110, p.221.

99. *Triumph Tree*, pp.236–41, 288–91; quote at 239.

100. *Triumph Tree*, pp.239, 241.

101. *CRMI*, ff.37v–38r.

102. *CRMI*, f.39r.

103. *OS*, chs 20, 26, 65.

104. D E Meek, 1997, '"Norsemen and Noble Stewards": The MacSween Poem in the Book of the Dean of Lismore', *Cambrian Medieval Celtic Studies* 34, pp.1–49. There is considerable doubt as to whether or not the expedition actually took place: K Simms, 2007, 'Images of the galloglass in poems to the MacSweeneys', in Duffy (ed.), *World of the Galloglass* (Dublin), regards it as 'a visionary one': pp.106–23 at 110–11.

105. D Rixson, 1998, *The West Highland Galley* (Edinburgh), pp.87–8.

106. MacGregor, 'Warfare in Gaelic Scotland', pp.212–13.

107. A good study is Rixson, *West Highland Galley*; see also J MacInnes, 1974, 'West Highland Sea Power in the Middle ages', *Transactions of the Gaelic Society of Inverness* xlviii, pp.518–56.

108. See R A McDonald, 2007b, 'Dealing death from Man: Manx sea power in and around the Irish Sea, 1079–1265', in Duffy (ed.), *World of the Galloglass*, pp.45–76 (with further discussion and references); Somerled's invasion force in *CRMI*, f.39r.

109. *HS*, ch. 167, p.153; see Anderson, *Early Sources*, ii, p.476 n.12 for variation of the number of vessels involved in different manuscripts of the text.

110. *OS*, ch. 86, p.165 gives 15 ships.

111. *OS*, ch. 26 p.65.

112. See Rixson, *West Highland Galley*, ch. 5 generally on numbers and sizes of boats and ch. 6 on naval battles.

113. *Annala Rioghachta Eireann: Annals of the kingdom of Ireland by the four masters from the earliest period to the year 1616*, J O'Donovan (ed. and transl.), 1851, 7 vols (Dublin), vol. ii, pp.1112–13 s.a. 1154; discussed in Duffy, "The prehistory of the galloglass," in Duffy (ed.), *World of the Galloglass*, pp.1–2. The identity of MacScelling is uncertain but Duffy points out that Somerled is said to have had an illegitimate son of that name.

114. *CRMI*, f.41r.

115. *Foedera, conventiones, literae et cujuscunque generis acta publica, inter reges Angliae et alios quosvis imperatores*, T Rymer (ed.), 1739–45, 10 vols (Hagae Comitis), I.I, p.118; printed with translation in *Monumenta de Insula Manniae, or a collection of national documents relating to the Isle of Man*, J R Oliver (ed. and transl.), 1860–62, 3 vols (Douglas), ii, pp.72–3.

116. Sources for the invasion and Somerled's demise are conveniently collected in Anderson, *Early Sources*, ii, pp.253–8.

117. *OS* ch. 110, p.221; Magnús recruiting in Ireland: *Calendar of Documents relating to Ireland, 1171–1307*, H S Sweetman (ed.), 5 vols (London), vol. I, no. 3206. Hereafter *CDI*.

118. *Chronica magistri Rogeri de Houedene*, T Arnold (ed.), 1868–71, 4 vols (London), iv, pp.10–12; discussion in A A M. Duncan, 1999b, 'Roger of Howden and Scotland, 1187–1201', in B Crawford (ed.), *Church, chronicle and learning in medieval and early Renaissance Scotland* (Edinburgh), pp.143 and 155 notes 51, 55.

119. Galloglass project website: http://galloglass.ucc.ie/index.php.

120. For which see now Duffy (ed.), *World of the Galloglass*.

121. *Annala Uladh: Annals of Ulster: otherwise, Annala Senait, annals of Senat: a chronicle of Irish affairs*, W H Hennessy & B MacCarthy (eds and transl.), 1887–1901, 4 vols (Dublin), vol. ii, pp.252 (s.a. 1212), 256 (s.a. 1214); http://www.ucc.ie/celt/published/T100001B/index.html.

122. *Triumph Tree*, pp.236–41, 288–91, quote at 290.

123. *Foedera,* T Rymer (ed.), I.I, p.75; *CDI* ii, 490.

124. Duffy, 'The prehistory of the galloglass', p.16.

125. *The Annals of Loch Cé: a chronicle of Irish affairs from AD 1014 to AD 1590*, W M Hennessy (ed. and transl.), 1871, 2 vols (London), vol. ii, pp.427–9.

126. Duffy, 'The prehistory of the galloglass', pp.15–19.

127. W S Reid, 1960, 'Sea-power in the Anglo-Scottish War, 1296–1328', *Mariner's Mirror* 46, pp.7–23.

128. There remains no detailed study of Dun's activities, but see C MacNamee, 1997, *The Wars of the Bruces: Scotland, England and Ireland, 1306–1328* (East Linton), pp.173–6, 180–84.

129. *CDS*, iii, no. 549 p.106.

130. *CDS* iii, nos. 420–21, p.80.

131. Like Dun, John's career would repay further study. See brief discussion in McDonald, *Kingdom of the Isles*, pp.180–82. R M Haines, 2003, *King Edward II: His life, his reign, and its aftermath, 1284–1330* (Montreal & Kingston), p.294, describes John as 'senile'.

132. T O'Neill, 1987, *Merchants and Mariners in Medieval Ireland* (Dublin), p.120.

133. See generally McDonald, *Kingdom of the Isles*, pp.149–57; B T Hudson, 1999, 'The changing economy of the Irish Sea province', in B Smith (ed.), *Britain and Ireland 900–1300: Insular responses to medieval European change* (Cambridge), pp.39–66, and J Barrett, 2007b, 'The Pirate Fishermen: The Political Economy of a Medieval Earldom', in B Ballin Smith, S Taylor & G Williams (eds), *West Over Sea: Studies in Scandinavian Sea-Borne Expansion and Settlement before 1300* (Leiden), pp.299–340, are both important contributions. There is also much of value in O'Neill, *Merchants and Mariners in Medieval Ireland.*

134. *The Acts of Alexander III King of Scots 1249–1286*, C J Neville & G G Simpson (eds), 2012, *Regesta Regum Scottorum* IV.I, (Edinburgh), no. 272 p.220.

135. *Acts of Alexander III*, Neville & Simpson (eds), nos. 92, 278, pp.127, 221–2.

136. *Documents illustrative of the history of Scotland from the death of king Alexander the Third to the accession of Robert Bruce*, J Stevenson (ed.), 1870, 2 vols (Edinburgh), vol. i, no. 276, pp.336–7.

137. *CDS* v no. 9 p.136; truce of 1342 discussed in O'Neill, *Merchants and Mariners*, p.121.

138. *OS* ch. 59 p.109.

139. On *vaðmál* and its importance, see J Byock, 2001, *Viking Age Iceland* (London), pp.263–8; see also Hudson, 'The changing economy of the Irish Sea Province', pp.39–66 in general.

140. Armit, *Archaeology*, pp.203–04. On the Lewis chessmen see now D H Caldwell & M A Hall, 2014, *The Lewis Chessmen: New Perspectives* (Edinburgh).

141. M Parker-Pearson, N Sharples & J Symonds, 2004, *South Uist: archaeology and history of a Hebridean Island* (Stroud), p.144.

142. J H Barrett (ed.), 2012a, *Being an Islander: Production and identity at Quoygrew, Orkney, AD 900–1600* (Cambridge).

143. Barrow, *Kingship and Unity*, p.137.

144. 'Dál Chabhlaigh ar Chaisteál Suibhne' (A Meeting of a Fleet Against the Castle of Suibhne), in *Duanaire na Sracaire: Songbook of the Pillagers. Anthology of Scotland's Gaelic Verse to 1600*, W McLeod (ed.) & M Bateman (ed. and transl.), 2007 (Edinburgh), p.227; see also Meek, 'Norsemen and Noble Stewards', pp.1–49.

145. See n.32 above.
146. G Stell, 1988, 'By Land and Sea in Medieval and Early Modern Scotland', *Review of Scottish Culture* 4, p.26.
147. Stell, 'By Land and Sea', p.26.
148. RCAHMS *Argyll* 3, no. 339 pp.191–200, no. 345, pp.209–17.
149. RCAHMS *Argyll* 2 no. 287, pp.198–211.
150. RCAHMS *Argyll* 3, p.191.
151. MacGregor, 'Warfare in Gaelic Scotland', p.213; S Boardman, 2007, *The Campbells 1250–1513* (Edinburgh), p.56.
152. Horden & Purcell, pp.124–32. The issue is addressed in a Hebridean context, but for an earlier period, in R Rennell, 2010, 'Islands, islets, experience and identity in the Outer Hebridean Iron Age', *Shima: The International Journal of Research into Island Cultures* 4.1, pp.47–64, http://www.shimajournal.org/issues/v4n1/g.%20Rennell%20 Shima%20v4n1%2047-64.pdf.
153. See *OS*, chs 67, 69–71; on Watch and Ward see B R S Megaw, 1941, 'A thousand years of watch and ward: from Viking beacon to home guard', *Journal of the Manx Museum* 5.64, pp.8–13, and A Johnson, 2002, 'Watch and ward on the Isle of Man: the medieval re-occupation of Iron Age promontory forts', in P J Davey & D Finlayson (eds), *Mannin revisited*, pp.63–80. On the MacLeod coat of arms see W D H Sellar, A Maclean & C B H Nicholson, 1999, *The Highland clan MacNeacail (MacNicol): a history of the Nicolsons of Scorrybreac* (Waternish, Skye), pp.10–11.
154. I Fisher, 2005, 'The Heirs of Somerled', in Oram & Stell (eds), *Lordship and Architecture*, pp.90–91; Stell, 1988, 'By Land and Sea', pp.27–8.
155. Stell, 'By Land and Sea', p.27; cf. RCAHMS *Argyll* 3, no. 345, pp.209–217.
156. RCAHMS *Argyll* 3, no. 335 pp.184–90 at 186; Fisher, 'Heirs of Somerled', p.92
157. Armit, *Archaeology*, pp.218–21; R Miket & D L Roberts, 1990, *The Mediaeval Castles of Skye and Lochalsh* (Portree), p.5.
158. Cunliffe, *Facing the Ocean*, p.31.
159. Armit, *Archaeology*, p.220. Evidence of earlier occupation at Kisimul in S Foster, 2006, 'Kisimul Castle: Recent work by Historic Scotland', in Kruse & Ross, *Barra and Skye*, pp.63–64.
160. Rennell, 'Islands, islets, experience and identity in the Outer Hebridean Iron Age', pp.47–64, http://www.shimajournal.org/issues/v4n1/g.%20Rennell%20Shima%20v4n1%20 47-64.pdf.
161. The name Kisimul may derive from Old Norse *kjóss* = 'small bay' and *múli* = 'headland', and it was famously described by Monro as 'ane castell in ane Ile upon ane strenthie craig': Monro, *Description*, p.325. On the derivation of the name see A B Stahl, 2006, 'On the Verge of Loss: Lesser Known Place-names of Barra and Vatersay', in Kruse & Ross, *Barra and Skye*, pp.94–114, at 108.

3

Clans, Castles and DNA: Macneils, MacNeills and the Families of Cowal, Knapdale and Glassary

David Sellar

I am in complete agreement with Ian Macneil's demolition of much 20th-century historical writing about the Hebrides and its castles and its centrist approach; and I am more than happy with the notion of Norse-Celtic seaways.[1] My approach in this paper will be partly genealogical, looking at what has been claimed or demonstrated about the origins of some leading West Highland families: the Macneils of Barra and the MacNeills of Taynish and Gigha, who spell their name differently, and may or may not be related; looking also at the origins of the leading families of Cowal, Knapdale and Glassary, particularly the MacSweens, the Lamonts and the MacLachlans, revising and expanding on an article I wrote some years ago.[2] I shall also say something about West Highland castles and the seaways associated with them, and the exciting and often surprising advances made by recent DNA research.

Looking first to the Macneils of Barra, it has often been claimed, for example by Robert Lister Macneil, the present chief's grandfather, that the chiefs of Barra descend in the direct male line from the semi-historical Niall of the Nine Hostages, High King of Ireland in the early 5th century at the dawn of recorded history.[3] Many Irish families claim descent from Niall, including the O'Neills and the O'Donnells, who continued to rule in the north of Ireland until c.1600 (that is, more than 1000 years after the time of Niall of the Nine Hostages). Confusingly, the eponym of the O'Neills was another Niall: Niall Glundubh, King of Ailech in northern Ireland, killed in battle with the Vikings in AD 919.

That great genealogist and historian of the Highland Clans, Sir Iain Moncrieffe, also supported the claim to descent from Niall of the Nine Hostages, a claim which is reflected in the current Arms of Macneil of Barra, one quartering of which shows nine fetterlocks in allusion to the Nine Hostages. The fetterlocks also appear in earlier versions of the Barra Arms, matriculated in 1806 and 1822 respectively, and the vaunted descent is referred to in Gaelic poetry.[4] Others, however, including the late Ian Macneil of Barra in private conversation, and John Lorne Campbell, have been more sceptical about this alleged descent. Another notable doubter 100 years ago or so was Duke Niall of Argyll, a great expert on West Highland families.

Another matter on which opinions have differed is whether the Macneils of Barra on the one hand, and the MacNeills of Taynish and Gigha on the other, are one family or two unrelated families. Robert Lister Macneil and Iain Moncreiffe both thought that the northern Macneils and the southern MacNeills were branches of one and the same family. Again, others have differed; and some have even suggested that the southern MacNeills hived off from the Macleans in the 14th century, the ancestral Neil in this case being a Maclean![5]

The common ancestor of the major families of Cowal, Knapdale and Glassary was named Dunsleve (Gaelic Donn Sleibhe) – which gives the modern Irish surname Donleavy – and I have named the genealogical chart 'The Dunsleve kindred' accordingly (Figure 3.1). This shows the immediate descendants of Dunsleve. Although Dunsleve himself does not appear on record many of his descendants do. I take him to be a historical figure who must have flourished in the second half of the 12th century. MacSweeney family tradition, as set out in the early-16th-century Irish *Leabhar Chlainne Suibhne* (Book of Clan Sween), gives Dunsleve 12 sons, four of whom are named on the chart.[6] The first of these, Suibhne Ruadh (Sweeney the Red) is generally credited with building Castle Sween on Loch Sween in Knapdale *c.*1200, one of the oldest surviving stone castles in Scotland (Plate 9). Suibhne is the eponym of the Scottish MacSweens and the many Irish families of MacSweeney galloglass who operated as mercenary soldiers there for upwards of three centuries *c.*1300 – 1600.[7] The name 'Suibhne', incidentally, is Gaelic Suibhne, a common name in early Ireland, and not, as is sometimes said, Scandinavian Sveinn or Sweyn. That would give Suain in Gaelic and MacSwan in English.

From Ferchar, the second son on the chart, descend the Lamonts through Ferchar's grandson Lagmann or Laumon, the Lamont eponym, and also the lesser-known MacSorleys of Monydrain (a few miles north of Lochgilphead). From Gilchrist, the third son, descend the Argyll MacGilchrists, later shortened to Gilchrist, and the MacLachlans who take their name from Lachlan Mor, son of Gilpatrick, son of

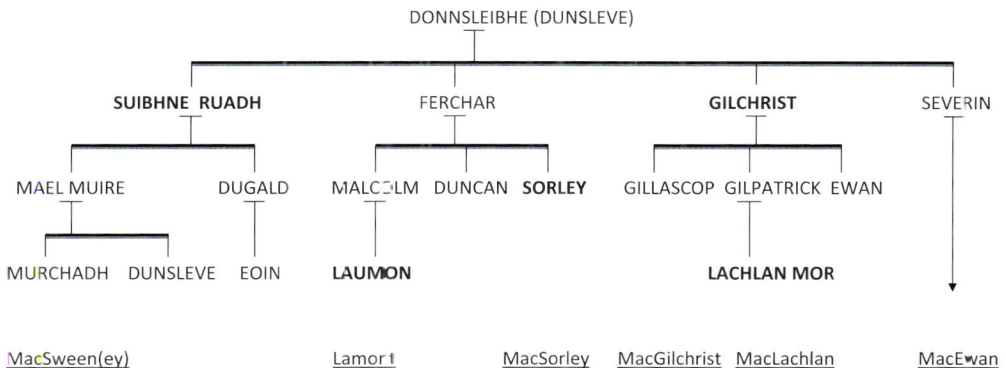

Figure 3.1. The Dunsleve kindred. (David Sellar)

Gilchrist.[8] The MacEwans of Otter Ferry which links, or linked, the two sides of Loch Fyne, descend from a further son of Dunsleve whose name appears to have been Severin.[9]

Three major clans, then, descend from Dunsleve: the MacSweens, the Lamonts and the MacLachlans; and three minor: the MacSorleys of Monydrain, the MacGilchrists and the MacEwans of Otter. The evidence for these relationships is pretty much conclusive, the sources being a combination of medieval Gaelic genealogies from both Scotland and Ireland, including the celebrated Scottish 'MS1467', and contemporary record evidence from the 1230s onwards, mainly from the Register of the Monastery of Paisley (*Paisley Registrum*).[10] There are a number of further points worth noting about these families. One is the predominance of Gaelic forenames among the two or three generations after Dunsleve – although there are exceptions, the most notable being Laumon or Lagman.[11] Another is the emergence among the descendants of Dunsleve of separate lineages about this time (separate 'clans' if you like, *c*.1200–1250, see at the foot of the chart). This can be compared to the emergence of separate clans among the descendants of Somerled/*Somhairle* around the same time: originally named as *Clann Somhairle* after Somerled, in the course of the 13th century they split up into the separate clans of MacDougall, MacDonald, MacRuairi and MacAllister. A further comparison, again about the same time, is the emergence from among the descendants of Cormac, son of Airbertach, of the separate clans of MacKinnon, MacQuarrie and MacMillan.[12]

At the height of their power, about the mid 13th century, the Dunsleve kindred owned a great swathe of contiguous territory (Figure 3.2). The MacSweens owned nearly all of Knapdale. As already noted, Suibhne is given the credit for building the famous stone castle which bears his name. The important castle of Skipness on the east side of Kintyre, which looks across to the north of Arran, was owned by his son Dugald/Dufgallus, if not by Suibhne himself. In April 1247 Pope Innocent IV granted protection to Dugald, 'lord of the land of Macherummel in Kintyre', and confirmed his gift of the church of St Colmanelo in Kintyre to Paisley Abbey. I have not been able to discover where Macherummel is unless it is the two Rummels by Machrimore. In 1261 Dugald ('*Dufgallum filium Syfin*') confirmed his gift of the patronage of St Colmanelo to Paisley.[13]

In the following year, at Paisley, Dugald '*filius Suvyn*' granted Skipness, Killislate, the two Unguys MacCrummel (presumably the same as 'Macherummel') and Belelach in Trolstyn to Walter, earl of Menteith. Dugald appended his own seal to the charter, the witnesses to his charter including his nephew Murchadh the son of Mael Muire, Roland (Lachlan) the son of Dugald's cousin Gilpatrick, and Dunsleve brother of Murchadh.[14] Geoffrey Barrow has pointed to this charter as an early example of the adoption of feudal ways by a Gaelic magnate. He notes, in particular, that Dugald granted these lands in Knapdale and Kintyre, with an outlying estate in Cowal (Belelach), to be held as Dugald himself had held them of the king 'as a free barony' (*in libera baronia*) for two-thirds of a knight's service in the king's army.[15] The following day, at Erskine, Walter, earl of Menteith, confirmed Dugald's gift of the church of St Colmanelo the previous year, the witnesses including Dugald himself (*Dufgallo filio Sewen*), Murchadh the son of Mael Muire, his nephew, and Dunsleve brother of Murchadh. Murchadh died in the earl of Ulster's prison in 1267.[16] His son Murchadh Mear is the ancestor of all the later MacSweeney Irish galloglass families. Kenneth Nicholls has recently suggested amendments to the generally accepted MacSween genealogy in the 13th and 14th centuries.[17]

The Lamonts, named for Laumon son of Ferchar son of Dunsleve, owned most of Cowal, including Inveryne on Loch Fyne and originally including also Kilmun in the east of Cowal, later the burial-place of the Campbell chiefs. At some date between 1232 and 1241 Duncan son of Ferchar, and Laumon the son of Malcolm and nephew of Duncan, gave Paisley the pennyland of Kilmore by Loch Gilp which lies by the chapel of St Mary, and the three half-pennylands which they and their ancestors had at Kilmun. This was witnessed by Walter the Steward, Malcolm son of the earl of Lennox and others. About the same time Laumon son of Malcolm gave Paisley the church at Kilfinan on Loch Fyne, and appended his seal; the witnesses including Walter fitz Alan, Steward and Justiciar, *Dufgallo filio Moysi*, *Dufgallo filio Syvin* and Gilpatrick son of Gilchrist.[18] I do not know who Dugald son of Moysi was, but Dugald son of Suibhne and Gilpatrick son of Gilchrist were both first cousins of Laumon's father Malcolm. In 1260 Angus son of Duncan son of Ferchar confirmed the gifts of his father Duncan and of Laumon, a witness

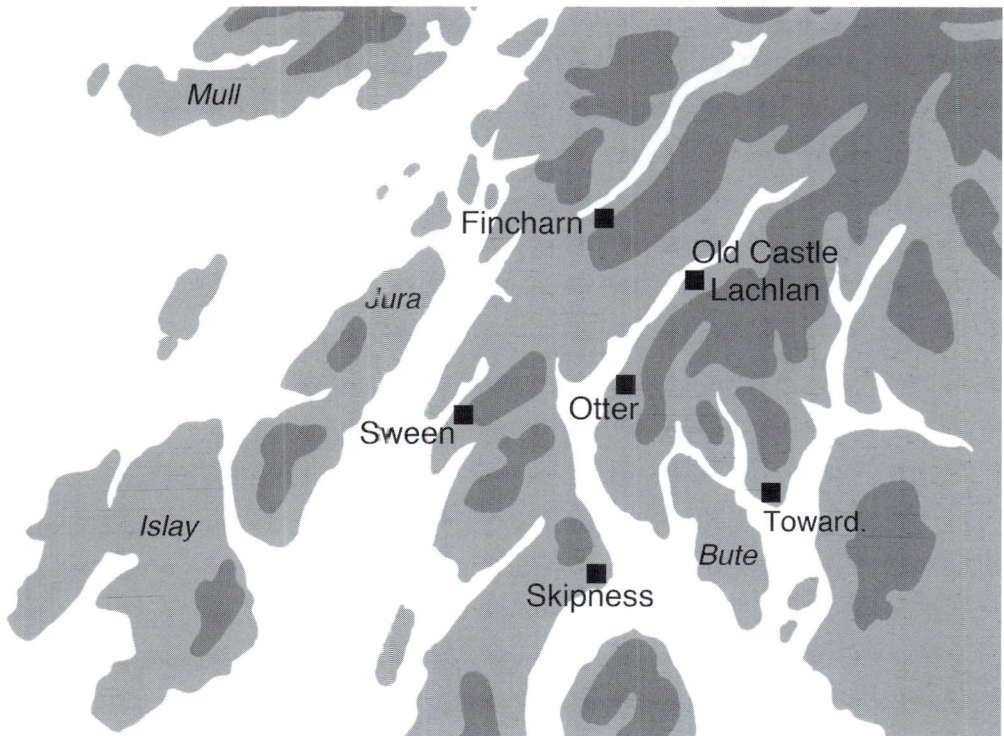

Figure 3.2. Castles mentioned in the text. (Edward Martin)

being Laumon's son Mael Muire.[19] In 1269 Bishop Laurence of Argyll inspected the charters of 'Dufgallus son of Sifyn', Duncan son of Ferchar, Laumon son of Malcolm nephew of Duncan, and also of Angus son of Donald.[20] In 1295 Malcolm, son and heir of the late Laumon, granted a charter of land pertaining to the church of Kilfinan; 'signed with his own seal, and with that of James the Steward which is better known'.[21]

Glassary went to the descendants of Gilchrist son of Dunsleve; lands soon to be divided between the 'Glassarie' family, with its *caput* initially at the Castle of Fincharn, at the south-east side of Loch Awe, descending to the Scrymgeours via an heiress; and the MacLachlans with their *caput* at Old Castle Lachlan in Strathlachlan on the east side of Loch Fyne.[22] Gilchrist had at least three sons: Gillascop, Gilpatrick and Ewan. Gillascop was granted a charter of much of Glassary by Alexander II in 1240.[23] Gilpatrick's son Lachlan Mor, the MacLachlan eponym, appears at least once as a charter witness under the guise of 'Roland'.[24] John son of Ewan was forfeited in the Wars of Independence.[25] A further possible son of Gilchrist is the Donald MacGilchrist, lord of Tarbert, Loch Fyne, who appears *c*.1250.[26]

The Glassary lands covered a considerable area extending from Fincharn on Loch Awe to Strathlachlan on the east side of Loch Fyne and south to Ederline and Kilmichael Glen, Dunadd and Monydrain (the home of the MacSorleys for 500 years) and Lochgilphead. The Lamont chiefs remained in Cowal until the end of the 19th century; while the MacLachlans are still in Strathlachlan today within sight of the ruins of Old Castle Lachlan. It is apparent that the lands were shared between the various branches of the Dunsleve kindred: Knapdale and parts of Kintyre falling to Suibhne and his descendants, the major part of Cowal to Ferchar and his descendants, with 'an outlying estate in Cowal' as Barrow describes it, granted by Dugald son of Suibhne in his charter to the earl of Menteith; and the major part of Glassary to Gilchrist and his descendants, with Strathlachlan in Cowal falling to Lachlan, a grandson of Gilchrist. When all this is taken into account it is apparent that the distribution of the lands in Glassary, Cowal and Knapdale owned by the Dunsleve kindred must have been the result of carefully considered family planning and agreement a generation or two before. It is also apparent that unitary succession corresponding to the later Scots law of heritage was not followed, at least not in the earlier generations succeeding Dunsleve.

It is also clear that the building of the castles on the lands of the Dunsleve kindred was carefully planned to dominate the seaways as much as the land. Castle Sween guarded the approaches to mid-Argyll from the west and offered a safe harbour. Skipness Castle guarded the passage between Kintyre and Arran. MacEwan's Castle guarded Otter Ferry further up Loch Fyne, while further still up the Loch, short of Strachur, stood Old Castle Lachlan. The Lamont castle of Toward stood at the south end of the easternmost point of Cowal, while the MacGilchrist castle of Fincharn was at the south-east end of Loch Awe not far from the parish church of Kilneuair. Altogether six castles strategically situated, all of which belonged to one or other of the Dunsleve kindred. To which should probably be added the precursor of Robert

Bruce's castle of Tarbert, on Loch Fyne overlooking the harbour and the famous portage from east to west Loch Tarbert.

It is entirely fitting that MacSween control of the sea should be commemorated in the famous Gaelic poem, which begins 'Tryst of a fleet against Castle Sween', and has been translated and annotated by two distinguished Celtic scholars, William J Watson and Donald Meek. It purports to describe a naval expedition directed against Castle Sween under the command of Eoin/John MacSween with a view to retaking the castle and returning it to the MacSweens, its original owners. How far the poem describes an actual expedition, and how far it is poetic fancy is not clear; as Meek points out it certainly draws on earlier elaborate literary accounts of war-fleets of King Cnut and of his father King Sven.[27]

Returning to the origins of the MacNeills, north or south, they do not appear on the contemporary record until the 15th century (that is, assuming that they are not Macleans). Nor, so far as I am aware, does their pedigree appear in medieval Gaelic genealogies, Scottish or Irish. It has been suggested, although on rather slim grounds, that the Macneils of Barra should be counted among the descendants of Dunsleve. I was guilty of giving some credence to this myself in my earlier paper. The first clear mention of the Macneils of Barra is in 1427 when 'Gilleonan son of Ruairi son of Murchadh son of Neil' was granted a charter of Boisdale in South Uist, and of Barra, by Alexander, Lord of the Isles.[28] A Roderic Macneil, presumably the father of this Gilleonan, appears as a charter witness in 1409.[29] Is Neil, the great grandfather of Gilleonan, the eponym of the Barra Macneils? I suspect that he may be, and I think it likely, as has been suggested by Sir Iain Moncreiffe among others, that the Macneils inherited Boisdale and Barra, as well as the distinctive name of 'Ruairi', from the MacRuairi descendants of Somerled. Where the rare name 'Gilleonan' (formerly 'Gil-Adamnan' after St Adamnan) came from is more of a puzzle. It is now sometimes rendered in English as 'Jonathan'.

The earliest MacNeill of Taynish and Gigha on record is Torcuil/Torquil MacNeill who was granted a charter of lands in Knapdale and also the office of Constable of Castle Sween by the same Alexander, Lord of the Isles, in 1440.[30] The grant of the Constableship of Castle Sween suggests to me that Torquil may have been related in some way to the MacSweens, perhaps a junior cadet.

The traditional story of the origins of Dunsleve and the clans of Cowal, Knapdale and Glassary is set out in *Leabhar Chlainne Suibhne* (The Book of Clan Sweeney), written in Gaelic in Ireland in the early 16th century. The MacSweeneys claimed that they descended from an O'Neill king named *Flaithbhertach an Trostain*, that is 'Flaherty of the Pilgrim Staff', who went on pilgrimage to Rome and died there in 1036. I argued for the accuracy of this tradition some years ago, and would still support it, but many have been more sceptical, including Gerard A Hayes-McCoy, and more recently Katharine Simms and Sean Duffy.[31] They argued that the MacSweeneys were of Norse descent rather than Gaelic, as more recently has D C McWhannell.[32]

I would certainly agree that society in the West Highlands and Islands had been mixed Gaelic and Norse for many generations before the eponymous Suibhne, but would still argue that the MacSweens and the other families discussed, whose relationship to each other is, I believe, incontrovertible, were of Gaelic descent in the male line. According to the medieval Irish genealogical collections and the Scottish MS1467, Dunsleve/Donn Sleibhe was the son of Aodh Alainn (the Handsome). Aodh Alainn is regularly given the further name, or alias, of Buirrche or An Buirrche in the pedigrees, although it is not clear why. He is given as the son of Anrothan in the pedigrees and Anrothan as the son of Aodh Athlamhan O'Neill, king of Ailech who died in 1033, three years before his father Flaherty of the Pilgrim Staff, previously king of Ailech.[33] Aodh Athlamhan was the last king of Ailech of the O'Neill line for several generations: the O'Neills did not regain the throne of Ailech until Aodh Toinleasg in 1176. The names of the three intervening generations between Aodh Athlamhan and Aodh Toinleasg – Conchobar, Flaithbhertach and Domhnall – are given in the genealogies, but little if anything is known about them. According to *Leabhar Chlainne Suibhne* it was Anrothan (Dunsleve's grandfather) who migrated to Scotland where he married the king's daughter and was given a generous grant of land.

There are some further considerations which tend to support the authenticity of the genealogies at least as far back as the father of Dunsleve. I would put more emphasis now than before on the fact that the Lamonts are sometimes referred to in Irish sources as 'Meg' or 'Mag' 'Buirrche', that is 'MacBuirrche'. I mentioned before that the O'Clery Collection of Genealogies heads the Lamont Genealogy '*Genelach Meg Buirrce*' and starts 'Duncan son of John son of Malcolm son of Laumon' after Laumon and the three succeeding chiefs, his son, grandson, and great grandson. However, there are further references to the same effect in contemporary Irish annals. For example, in 1305 the *Annals of Connacht* record that 'Mag Buirrche', chief of the galloglass, was killed along with the heir of Clan Suibhne, and in 1346 the *Connacht Annals* record the killing of 'Mag Buirce', the galloglass of O'Rourke.[34] It is very rare for the eponym of a Gaelic family not to be a real person. The fact that Buirrche is being used as an eponym suggests that the pedigree is reliable at least as far back as the father of Dunsleve. The fine-tuning that has clearly gone into the division of the territory of the Dunsleve kindred also suggests existence as a kindred before his time.

Is the story about the arrival of Anrothan in Scotland, his marriage, and his acquisition of land credible? It sounds like a familiar fairy story. On the other hand, how else can one explain the accumulation of so much land in the hands of the Dunsleve kindred. If the claimed ancestor of the kindred was an incomer to Scotland he must have been a man of considerable status. Also, to repeat what I have written in my earlier article, 'The meagre details that have survived of the marriages of the members of the Cowal and Knapdale families fully bear out the impression of status which can be inferred from the extent of their lands'.[35] For example, Mael Muire, son of Suibhne, was married to a granddaughter of Ruairi O'Connor, High King of Ireland; and the mother of Aodh O'Donnell, king of Tyrconnell intermittently from 1281 to 1333, was a MacSween. Add to this the fact that Suibhne built the earliest surviving stone castle in Scotland (*c.*1200), and that his son Dugald's charter of Skipness and other lands has been described by Geoffrey Barrow as an early instance of the adoption of feudal ways by a Gaelic magnate (see above), and it is clear that the Dunsleve kindred belonged to the first rank of the Gaelic aristocracy. It is also worth noting that Dugald mac Suibhne used a seal in 1262, as did Laumon, as early as 1232 x1241, as noted above, and as did Laumon's son Malcolm in 1295. Unfortunately none of these seals has survived.

Finally I should like to consider briefly how the impact of DNA research, and in particular Y-chromosome research, has affected speculations about family origins, and doubtless will continue to do so. The work of Brian Sykes is now well known in the world of DNA [36] He was the first to identify tentatively the Y-chromosome of Somerled by researching and comparing the Y-chromosomes of a random sample of MacDonald, MacDougall and MacAllister descendants. He then persuaded four MacDonald chiefs and one MacAllister to give him a sample of their DNA. This revealed that they all shared the Y-chromosome in question, thus verifying his hypothesis about Somerled. The MacDonalds, of course, have always gloried in their Gaelic ancestry. Their traditions and Gaelic praise-poetry – some of it apparently recited before the battle of Harlaw in 1411 – trace them back to the legendary Conn of the Hundred Battles, High King of Ireland, by way of his equally legendary grandson Colla Uais. The MacLeods, by contrast, have boasted of their High Norse ancestry, which has been celebrated again and again in their poetry.

At a conference of the Scottish Medievalists held some 15 years ago Brian Sykes set the cat among the pigeons by declaring that his researches showed that it appeared that the Y-chromosome of the MacDonalds was distinctively Scandinavian while the Y-chromosome of the MacLeods was distinctively Celtic. A few years later a group of historians and scientists based at Trinity College, Dublin, were able to show that tens of thousands of men living in the north of Ireland today were descended from a single individual who must have lived *c*.AD 400. More than that, many of these belonged to families who, according to Irish history and traditional genealogies, descended from Niall of the Nine Hostages, in some cases demonstrably so. The conclusion was inescapable. Many hundreds of Scots have been found to carry the same Y-chromosome. My first thought on learning of this survey was that, if there are so many descendants of Niall of the Nine Hostages around in the world today, does that not make the traditional account of the descent of the Macneils of Barra from Niall more credible? However, as many will now know, at the beginning of this year it was reported in the Press that a survey of Macneil of Barra descendants world-wide had shown that their Y-chromosome was not Celtic but was distinctively Norse.

What about the Dunsleve kindred: the MacSweens, Lamonts, MacLachlans and others, some of whom, as we have seen, especially the MacSweens, claim to descend from the O'Neills, and therefore from Niall of the Nine Hostages, as well as from Niall Glundubh and Flaithbhertach an Trostain? I am no expert on the most up-to-date Y-chromosome research, but, so far as I can ascertain, it suggests that the Y-chromosome of the Dunsleve kindred is Celtic rather than Norse, and that they may indeed be descended from Niall of the Nine Hostages. If the MacSweens have inherited this Y-chromosome, so too must the Lamonts and the MacLachlans.

Equally, if it turns out that the MacSweens are of Norse descent so too must be the Lamonts and the MacLachlans. I do not know whether any DNA research has been carried out yet on the MacNeills of Taynish and Gigha, but the results would certainly be interesting: Will such research show that they too belong to the families of Cowal, Knapdale and Glassary; or will it show that they come from the same stock as the Macneils of Barra, or even the Macleans; or, indeed, none of these? There may still be many surprises in store.

Acknowledgements

I would like to thank Alastair Campbell of Airds for his generous hospitality and encouragement over the years. I am also indebted to the website 'People of Medieval Scotland' (PoMS, www.poms.ac.uk) for providing a ready and speedy check on many of the people mentioned in the article.

Notes

1. I R Macneil, 2006, 'Kisimul Castle and the origins of Hebridean Galley-Castles: preliminary thoughts', in A Kruse & A Ross (eds), *Barra and Skye: Two Hebridean Perspectives* (Edinburgh).
2. W D H Sellar, 1971, 'Family Origins in Cowal and Knapdale', *Scottish Studi*es 15, pp.21–37.
3. R L Macneil, 1923, *Clan Macneil* (New York); 1964, *Castle in the Sea* (London & Glasgow).
4. The Arms matriculated in 1805 and 1822 are recorded in the *Lyon Register*, as are the more recent recordings.
5. N Maclean-Bristol, 1995, *Warriors and Priests: The History of Clan Maclean, 1300–1570* (East Linton).
6. *Leabhar Chlainne Suibhne*, P Walsh (ed.), 1920 (Dublin), hereafter *LCS*.
7. S Duffy (ed.), 2007b, *The World of the Galloglass: Kings, warlords and warriors in Ireland and Scotland* (Dublin), contains many articles of Scottish interest, particularly on the *Clann Suibhne*. See also J Marsden, 2003, *Galloglas: Hebridean and West Highland Mercenary Warrior Kindreds in Medieval Ireland* (East Linton).
8. One manuscript variant makes Gilchrist the brother of Dunsleve, rather than his son, but chronology suggests that son is correct. As will be seen, Lachlan witnesses a charter as 'Roland', a known 'polite' equivalent of Lachlan.
9. This name in MS 1467 has proved difficult to read and a number of variants have been proposed. I read it as Saibaran which I take to be Severin.
10. The Gaelic Pedigrees in MS 1467 (NLS Adv. MS 72.1.1) have been transcribed and commented on in recent years both on the web, and in a series of ground-breaking articles published by Ronald & Mairi Black in *West Highland Notes and Queries*, 2007–14, which replicate the names as they actually appear in the manuscript; *Registrum Monasterii de Passelet*, J Stuart (ed.), 1832 (Maitland Club) (hereafter *Paisley Registrum*).
11. The name 'Lagman' is Norse for a lawman. It later became a personal name as 'Lagman', and in Scotland as Laumon (variant spellings) the eponym of the surname Lamont. The standard work on the Lamonts is H McKechnie, 1938, *The Lamont Clan 1235–1935* (Edinburgh).

12. W D H Sellar, 1981, 'Highland Family Origins – Pedigree Making and Pedigree Faking', in Loraine Maclean (ed.), *The Middle Ages in the Highlands* (Inverness), pp.105–08.
13. *Paisley Registrum*, p.120.
14. NLS MS Adv 29.4.2 (Hutton Collection) ii, 27.
15. G W S Barrow, 1980, *The Anglo Norman Era in Scottish History* (Oxford), p.138.
16. *Annals of Connacht* s.a.1267.
17. Duffy (ed.), *The World of the Galloglass*, pp.86–105.
18. *Paisley Registrum*, p.132–3.
19. *Paisley Registrum*, p.133.
20. This is Angus Mor mac Donald; *Paisley Registrum*, p.136.
21. *Paisley Registrum*, pp.138–9.
22. 'Glassarie Writs', in J R N MacPhail (ed.), 1916, *Highland Papers* ii (Edinburgh), pp.121–4.
23. 'Glassarie Writs', pp.121–4.
24. Witnessing Dugald MacSween's charter of Skipness above.
25. 'Glassarie Writs', pp.136–7.
26. Another possibility is that this Donald son of Gilchrist, lord of Tarbert, was a MacFarlane, and that the Tarbert in question is at Loch Lomond: names, father's names, dates and place-names fit both possible candidates.
27. D E Meek, 1997, '"Norsemen and Noble Stewards", the MacSween poem in the Book of the Dean of Lismore', *Cambrian Medieval Celtic Studies* 34, pp.1–49. Meek's edition of this poem is commented on by Katharine Simms in her 'Images of the galloglass in poems to the MacSweeneys' in Duffy (ed.), *The World of the Galloglass*, pp.110–11.
28. *Acts of the Lords of the Isles, 1336–1493*, J & R W Munro (eds), 1986 (Edinburgh), p.34.
29. *Acts of the Lords of the Isles*, p.28.
30. *Acts of the Lords of the Isles*, p.50.
31. G A Hayes-McCoy, 1937, *Scots Mercenary Forces in Ireland, 1565–1603* (Dublin & London); K Simms, 2007, 'Images of the galloglass in poems to the MacSweeneys', and S Duffy, 2007a, 'The prehistory of the galloglass', in S Duffy (ed.), *The World of the Galloglass* (Dublin).
32. D C McWhannell, 2014a, 'Difficulties with the Ua Neill pedigrees, Anrothan and the ancestry of Donnsleibhe, father of Suibhne, *West Highland Notes and Queries* (January); 2014b, 'The family of Donnsleibhe the father of Suibhne, *West Highland Notes and Queries* (May). (This article considers nomenclature).
33. *Annals of Ulster*, s.a.1033.
34. K Nicholls, 2007, 'Scottish mercenary kindreds in Ireland, 1250–1600', in S Duffy (ed.), *The World of the Galloglass*, p.30 (*Annals of Connacht* 1305; *Annals of Connacht* 1346). Nicholls suggests that both men killed in 1305 might have been MacSweens.
35. Sellar, 'Family Origins', p.30 n.2.
36. B Sykes, 2004a, *The Seven Daughters of Eve* (London); 2007, *The Blood of the Isles* (London).

4

—

Sailing-Times in the Norse-Gaelic Seaways

Donald McWhannell

West Highland galleys were central to the exercise of power and the maintenance of a society dominated by the needs of a warrior aristocracy. Galleys were used for personal transport and display, as troop-transports, as assault-craft and for trading. The rowing and sailing galleys, birlinns (Gaelic *bírlinn* (s.), *bírlinnean* (pl.)) and smaller craft were well suited to the seas and lochs in which they operated, since these vessels remained in use for some 900 years. West Highland galleys and *bírlinnean* were linked to the lordships of Argyll and the Isles and to west-coast lordship in general. From the time of Robert I, King of Scots, such vessels are specifically associated with holding lands through Crown ship-service charters. Later similar ship-service charters were issued to subordinates by local magnates such as the Campbells of Argyll.[1] West Highland and Island galley-owning magnates in general also possessed castles.

West Highland galleys were significant cultural icons. There is a large corpus of vibrant poetry associated with the sea and the galleys of the Gael. The image of the galley is widely employed on West Highland and Island grave-slabs and crosses (Plates 3–4). As lymphads they appear as charges on the majority of West Highland arms.[2] The total lack of any galley or *bírlinn* wreck-sites has hampered the study of the realities of sailing and rowing such vessels, as it is not possible to reconstruct an authentic historical vessel.

In 1635 Campbell of Glenorchy had a new *bírlinn* constructed which matched the feudal requirement for ship-service for his lands in Lorn. In 1642 this vessel is likely to have been used to transport Inverliever's Company to Ireland, since the Marquess of Argyll required such a *bírlinn* to be made available by Glenorchy for this purpose. The original boatbuilder's bill of materials used and labour employed for this vessel survives, as does a later 1695 account for a 12-oared 'great boat'. The detail provided in these accounts allows an intelligent estimate to be made as to the form of these two vessels.[3]

The Gaelic poets' views of galleys

Galleys (Gaelic *long* (s.), *loingeas* (pl.)) and *bírlinnean* appear in a range of Gaelic poems from the incitement to Eòin MacSuibhne, *Dál Chabhlaigh ar Chaistéal Suibhne*, by Artúr Dall MacGurcaigh, to the lament for Eòin MacDhomhnaill,

An Iorram Dharraich. In the mid-13th-century Irish poem *Ceannaigh duain t'athar a Aonghas*, an address to Aonghus Mór mac Dhomhnaill of Islay, the poet expresses his regret at the lack of a land-bridge from Ulster to Islay, his hatred of sailing in galleys, and his perhaps-justifiable fear of two maelstroms, Coire dhá Ruadh and Coire Bhreacán, near the sailing-route.

Possibly the most famous galley-related poem is the visceral 18th-century *Bírlinn Chlann Raghnaill* by Alasdair mac Mhaighstir Alasdair, a poetic masterpiece which imaginatively and yet realistically evokes a voyage by Clan Ranald's *bírlinn* from South Uist via the Sound of Islay to Carrickfergus. The poet gives a vivid description of the qualities of the skipper and crewmen, describes their assigned duties and provides a lively depiction of the vessel being rowed to the sailing-point, of sailing the seaways as it travels to Ireland, and of surviving a violent storm.[4]

Below is a stanza taken from a 16th-century praise-poem to Gill'Easbaig, 4th Earl of Argyll, which encapsulates an anonymous Gaelic poet's view of the Campbell galleys (*An Duanag Ullamh*, version b, *c*.1550).[5]

Loingeas leathann làidir luchdmhor	Broad robust laden galleys
Dealbhach dìonach	Sound and shapely
Sleamhain sliosrèidh ro-luath ràmhach	Sleek-sided, swift oars bristling
Dairchruaidh dìreach	Oak-hard, deadly

The Norse-Gaelic seaways

'Atlantic Europe', from Gibraltar to Shetland, has existed for *c*.6000 years. There is archaeological evidence of coastal traffic for 4000 years and the trading of goods from 2300 BC.[6] From the time of the Massaliote Periplus (early 6th century BC) and the voyage of Pytheas (330–300 BC) these seas have provided challenges and opportunities to mariners. The Picts, *Gàidheal*, *Gaill* and *Gall-Ghàidheil* all ventured out on these seas under oar and sail in hope of success and profit, while Irish monks sailed north as far as Iceland in search of solitude.

Gildas (d. *c*.569) writes of the Scotti and Picti possessing fleets of boats having both oars and sails. The large sailing and rowing currachs (Gaelic *curach* (s.), *curaichean* (pl.)) of the Gaels were seagoing vessels. *Curaichean* engaged in trade, raiding, voyages of exploration and missionary voyages. A mid-5th-century trading-fleet of 50 *curaichean* led by Brecán mac Maine maic Néill Naoigiallach, when attempting the voyage from Ireland to Scotland, was, it seems, overwhelmed in the tide-race between Rathlin and the Antrim coast.[7] The Picts, who were able to settle Orkney, Shetland and the Western Isles of Scotland, had significant naval assets, as is indicated by the loss of a Pictish fleet of 150 ships in 729.[8] This loss occurred some time between Easter and August. The ships were possibly overwhelmed off Troup Head.

It appears that the Picts may have used both hide-covered and plank-built vessels. The only known illustration of a Pictish vessel is the depiction of what appears to be a clinker-built vessel with a steering-oar on the late-9th-century St Orland's stone at Cossans in Angus. The *curach* remained in use for transporting warrior-bands until at least the first half of the 7th century. The 8th-century Irish law-tract the *Uraicecht Becc* notes a *lerlong*, a seagoing ship, a '*barc*' which is not suitable for sea-voyages, and the hide-covered *curach*.[9] In 1963 a successful re-enactment of the voyage of Colm Cille from Derry to Iona took place in a *curach* crewed by 13 enthusiasts. Since then further re-enactment voyages between Northern Ireland and Iona have taken place in the 40-foot, 12-oared *curach Colmcille*. These voyages have taken between 5 and 8 days. The *Colmcille* has also made trips to north-west England, Brittany and northern Spain and has circumnavigated Ireland.

Ship-service in Argyll is first documented in the levy of the naval forces of Dál Riata given in the *Senchus fer n-Alban* compiled in the mid 7th century. The three Dalriadic kindreds, together with their Airgíalla vassals, had the capability of deploying a sea-borne host of *c*.2000 men.[10] The 7-benched ship-service vessels may possibly have been constructed using clinker planking. Although the exact form of vessels used by the Dalriadic peoples is not known, it is significant that Adhamhnán in his *Life of St Columba* refers to both planked and skin-covered vessels.[11]

The arrival of the Scandinavians

The Northern Isles plus areas of the coastal mainland of Caithness and Sutherland and the western islands and coastlands from Lewis to Argyll were raided and ultimately conquered in the period from 795 to *c*.825 by Scandinavian forces originating mainly from western Norway. Scandinavian settlers brought with them their language and new social, economic, political and power structures. Norse domestic architecture, fishing techniques and diet were introduced. Scandinavian forms of weapons, ship-service and maritime technologies modified or replaced the indigenous systems during the period of Norse and *Gall-Ghàidheil* lordship in western Scotland.

Evidence for the cultural impact of the Scandinavians can be seen in:

(a) the historical dominance over both skin-covered and carvel-built vessels of clinker-built ships and boats constructed in a similar way to Scandinavian vessels;
(b) Norse place-names which occur in areas settled by the Scandinavians;
(c) the introduction, adoption and adaptation of some Norse personal names into Irish and Gaelic;
(d) the historic use of Norn as the language of Orkney and Shetland;
(e) the vocabularies of Old and Middle Irish and Gaelic which acquired significant numbers of Norse loan-words, which were particularly applied extensively to ships and maritime activities.

A unit used by the Scandinavians was the *vika*, which may be considered to be a distance of 6 nautical miles (NM). In coastal waters a 'day's rowing' (12 hours) was reckoned as six *vikur* or 36NM, giving an average speed of 3 knots (NM/hr). In later times the men of Lewis were stated to be capable of 'pulling an oar all day long', thus matching the performance of their Scandinavian forebears. At sea a 'day's sailing' (24 hours) was reckoned to be 24 *vikur* or 144NM, giving an average speed of 6 knots.[12]

Lordship, castles and ships

Fortified promontory sites, brochs, duns and medieval castles were centres of power. Medieval castles facilitated the social, cultural, administrative and political interactions of the lord and his household as well as providing some level of security for their persons, personal goods and treasure. Ships allowed the projection of power, the short- and long-distance exchange of goods and the movement of troops, merchants, civilians, ideas and wealth. Castles with adjacent protected anchorages, harbours, slips or beaching-areas were clearly important within the context of the Norse-Gaelic thalassocracy. Some examples of such castles are Dunstaffnage (Plate 7), Dùn Mhuirich and Castle Sween (Argyll) (Plate 9), Rubh' an Dùnain (Skye) (Plate 12), Dùn Ara (Mull), Breacadhadh Castle (Coll), Castle Rushen and Peel Castle (Isle of Man), The Brough of Birsay and Cubbie Roo's Castle (Orkney) and Carrickfergus Castle (Antrim).

Although *Leabhar na gCeart* (*Book of Rights*, an 11th- or early-12th-century document) may describe an idealised set of relationships between the high king of Ireland, regional kings and lesser client kings, there is a clear indication of extensive and organised gifting of ships throughout Ireland. The east, south and west coasts, and in particular Ulster, were to be given significant numbers of ships through a system which had similarities to the *leiðangr* arrangements of Scandinavia. Ships were a significant element of the *tuarastal* system of gifts, obligations and the sharing of the spoils of war. *Leabhar na gCeart* is geared to Ua Briain interests and, due to a state of war that existed between the Ua Briain and the kings of Aileach, there are no mentions of ships being gifted to the kings of north-west Ireland.[13]

The Uí Mháille and Uí Fhlaithbheartaigh were two west-Connacht kindreds who deployed fleets of galleys. The Uí Mháille also possessed merchant ships which traded as far as Spain and Portugal. In 1396 Conchobhar Ua Flaithbheartaigh raided west Connacht, but all his crew except one were drowned between Aran and Ireland. In December 1599, 'There are three very good galleys belonging to Tibbot ne Longe, sone of Grany O'Malley, his brother and O'Malley that will carry 300 men apiece'.[14]

Types of vessel

'Lymphad' derives from Gaelic *long-fhata* (*long* (f.) = ship, *fata* (adj.) = long). *Long-fhata* describes a long, slender rowing-and-sailing vessel similar to the Scandinavian *langskip*, is related to the Latin *navis longa,* and refers to a warship. The *hafskip,* or *knarr*, was the primary ocean-going Scandinavian sailing vessel and carried people, goods and animals on long voyages in the North Atlantic. A galley, as defined by the Scottish Crown in 1615, was a vessel of 18–24 oars, while a *bírlinn* was a vessel of 12–18 oars.[15] *Bírlinn* is a Gaelic word deriving either from Norse *byrðingr*, a small cargo ship, or from Middle English *berling*, a pole, spar or tent-sill. *Bírlinn* in the form *birrling* first occurs in a maritime context in the Middle Irish tale *Cath Finntrágha*.[16] Any vessel of 12 oars or fewer may be considered to be a boat. Boats were four-, six-, eight- and ten-oared, while 12-oared 'great boats' also existed.[17] A *curach* was a skin-covered wickerwork vessel. In Ireland large sea-going *curaichean* existed from early times until the 17th century. Small *curaichean* may have continued in use in Scotland as late as the 18th century.

It is known that a *bírlinn* was built for MacLeod of Macleod in 1706. A brief list of the materials used and the costs for this work have been published. The number of clench-nails and roves, the quantity of oak and the yardage of sailcloth used would seem to indicate that this *bírlinn* was small, perhaps of only 12 oars. This is likely to have been one of the very last of these vessels to have been built.[18]

The extempore poem recited by Domhnall Gorm Mór (d.1616) of the Sleat family, when in a somewhat poor humour, to MacNéill of Barra's boatwright is of much interest. Domhnall Gorm was regarded as an expert in boatbuilding and a bard of considerable standing. He was also a warrior chieftain. It is understood that when questioned by his host MacNéill about the design of a *bírlinn* he declined to discuss the matter due to his dissatisfaction with the hospitality he was receiving at Caisteal Chiosmuil. Finally, as he was about to embark to leave the sea-girt castle he offered his advice in poetic Gaelic in such a way as to make his meaning difficult for MacNéill and his boatwright to interpret. The text of the poem is as follows:

Leagail bheag is togail bhog	A narrow garboard and soft rising above
Snìomh fada 'ga ghoid 's i gun tuim	a long twist and without room for bilge water
Sliasaid agus gualainn chruinn	quarters and shoulders well rounded
'S ma bhios trì troighean 'na druim	and if there be three feet of keel
Biodh troigh 'na tobhta chrainn dorn	there could be a foot of mast thwart, a fist's width
A leth uibhir sin 'na cliabh	the equivalent of half that at the breast
'S a dha thrian a liad 'na tòin	and two thirds breadth at stern.[19]

Early navigation in the European Atlantic Zone

The Iron Age seagoing peoples of the Atlantic coast appear to have had an intimate knowledge of winds, tides, currents, time-measurement and astronomical data. The celestial bodies of importance were and are the fixed stars, the sun and the moon. Seasonal changes in sea-conditions and the regular trans-oceanic migrations of birds will most probably have been noted. Seamen will also have had great understanding of the performance of their vessels, including leeway in various wind-strengths and sea-states, and are likely to have practised the art of 'steering by the run of the sea' for short periods when out of sight of land. The use of the sounding-lead and bottom-sampling to establish the possibilities of safe passage in murky inshore tidal waters, and also to check for a good bottom for anchoring, are likely to have been developed in early times.

Cave-art shows that large seagoing ships with sails and oars existed on the Iberian coast by the late Bronze Age. Before the 6th century BC large skin-boats, given a fair wind, were able to sail from Brittany to Ireland in two days. By the 1st century BC the Veneti in Brittany had robust plank-built ships which were capable of sailing to Britain.[20] Much later an informative guide to Norwegian seafaring practice is found in the first part of the *Konungs Skuggsja* (King's Mirror), written *c.*1250.[21]

In the West Highlands and Islands there are many portage locations referred to as 'tarberts' (from the Gaelic *tairbeart*, derived from Old Irish 'to carry across'). It is probable that many such tarberts were used to transfer goods between ships rather than to move ships across them. However it is known that for military reasons in AD 1263 some 60 ships were dragged from Arrochar on Loch Long to Tarbet on Loch Lomond.[22] On one famous occasion *c*.1098 King Magnús Berfœttr of Norway, while sitting in a ship holding the tiller, had himself dragged across the isthmus between East and West Loch Tarbert, Kintyre.[23] Near West Loch Tarbert there may be archaeological evidence for the remains of a timber 'roadway' to aid the movement of vessels. Vessels were likely to have been dragged between East Loch Tarbert and West Loch Tarbert to avoid the long passage round the Mull of Kintyre. Tarberts played a significant part in trading-routes and were used in warfare.[24]

Early navigators were greatly dependent on orally-transmitted traditional lore. In northern waters written sailing-directions seem only to have come into use from the 13th century. The Scottish rutter produced by Alexander Lindsay is associated with the voyage of James V to the Western Isles in 1540.[25] Lindsay's rutter covers the whole Scottish coast plus the north-east coast of England to the Humber, and mentions Ardglass in Ireland, and the Isle of Man. Late-medieval rutters make reference to 'kennings' (14 Scots miles or 20 English miles or 17.4 NM) and 'courses'. It is thought that Lindsay used two pre-existing rutters in compiling his sailing-directions for the west coast. It is not, however, known whether either of these was a Gaelic source. In Paris in 1583 Nicholas de Nicolay published the first known chart of Scottish waters.

Without access to charts and rutters an essential addition to any ship's crew will have been an experienced local pilot. Assuming that West Highland galley crews did not possess rutters, compasses or charts, then orally-transmitted knowledge and the memory of past experiences would have been central to safe navigation. As late as 1746, persons seeking either to capture or to assist in the escape of Charles Edward Stuart needed the assistance of local pilots.[26] Giraldus Cambrensis, in his *Topography of Ireland* (*c*.1188), comments on the strong currents in the Irish Sea and the ebb and flow of the tide therein. He states that 'the Irish Sea being agitated by opposing currents is almost always troubled, so that navigators scarcely ever find it tranquil even for a few days in summer'.[27] Chaucer, in his *Canterbury Tales* (late 14th century), writes:

> A shipman was ther, wonynge fer by weste …
> But of his craft to rekene wel his tydes,
> His stremes and his daungers hym bisides,
> His herberwe, and his moone, his lodermenage,
> Ther nas non swich from Hulle to Cartage.[28]

In making predictions about the often-treacherous tides and currents of northern European waters, medieval navigators needed to correlate lunar and solar time and to remember the lunar tidal regimes for each port. The schema that was adopted used the points of the compass as an aid. Quoting from Lindsay's rutter,

> At the Mull of Cantyre the moone southwest, full sea. On the costes of Arran and Buit the moone south, full sea. At Wrwyn and Air and along the cost of Carrik, the moone south to est, full sea. At the Mulle of Galloway the moon south, full sea. From the Mull of Galloway alongis the cost unto Solway the mone south to est, full sea.[29]

Such stratagems enabled the navigator to construct in his mind the information which the modern navigator obtains, after checking the date and time of day, from tide-tables and tidal atlases.

Prior to the introduction of the magnetic compass in the 14th century, Northern European oceanic navigators were dependent on the pole star and the sun to estimate latitude and heading. They had only the possibility of somewhat inaccurate dead-reckoning to give an indication of longitude in terms of the distance west or east of the starting-point of the voyage. It was helpful to use adventitious aids to navigation such as the smell of the land, changes in the sea's temperature, colour and salinity, the presence or absence of insects, seabirds, fish and whales, the occurrence of fresh driftwood, the types of sea-bird to be seen and their flight paths, clouds forming over islands, ice-blink and wave-pattern changes near coasts and islands.

Admiration for the achievements of the Norse in long-distance, often latitude sailing in the stormy north Atlantic is fully justified. Latitude sailing at 61° north takes a vessel starting off from opposite Hernar in Norway, north of Shetland and south of both Færoe and Iceland, to arrive safely in eastern Greenland. Equally it takes great skill to navigate narrow seas with strong currents, hazardous headlands, uncharted rock-strewn coasts and drying harbours. These difficulties are particularly challenging during adverse weather and poor visibility.

Tidal atlases indicating tidal flows for spring and neap tides around the British coast are available, as are atlases for the four seasons of the year showing the power of the wind and the height of the waves. It is very clear from the tidal atlases that headlands and narrow passages are areas of strong tidal flows, particularly at spring tides. The power of the wind varies with the seasons. Winter winds are significantly more powerful, as can be clearly seen from the seasonal atlases. Wave-height varies with the seasons. It varies in relation to both wind-power and the available fetch (the distance travelled by the wind over open water). Compared to the Atlantic, reduced average wave-heights, as shown on wave-energy resources charts, indicate why the Minch is also known as An Cuan Sgìth (The Tired Sea).[30]

Availability of vessels

The climate of the British Isles has not altered greatly in the last 300 years. However the warm climax of the 13th century was followed by a period of increasing cold which reached its lowest point in the 17th century. Since then there have been fluctuations between cooler and warmer periods, which may now be increasing in both amplitude and frequency. For the days of sail and oar it has been estimated that men could work at sea off the west coast of Scotland for the following number of days per month (Table 4.1). Hence it is possible to infer that galleys would have been able to be used

Table 4.1. Average number of days per month that boats in the days of sail and oar could be at sea (data based on E McKee, 1983, *Working Boats of Britain*, pp.19–22).

	Rowing (days)	Sailing & Rowing (days)	Stormbound (days)
January	1	23	7
April	1	28	1
July	2	29	0
October	1	27	3

Table 4.2. Daylight hours available in Islay.

Mid January	Mid April	Mid July	Mid October
7hr 41min	14hr 10min	16hr 57min	10hr 30min

for about 87% of the year. Although galleys did sail at night it is interesting to note the daylight hours available in Islay, a fairly central geographical location within the Norse-Gaelic seaways (Table 4.2).

Overcast skies and sea-fogs caused Norse mariners to have real navigational difficulties, described as *hafvilla* – a state of total lack of sense of direction and position. Coastal fog was and is of great concern to all mariners (without good radar and GPS systems), particularly in relation to hitting nearby rocks, sandbanks or other ships and in missing landfalls. The frequency of fog in the southern Hebrides is greater than in the northern Hebrides. The Minch has fog for less than 100 hours per year. Much of the western side of the Long Island is fog-free except along the coast of the Uists where fog may occur for up to 200 hours per year.[31]

Pre-scientific weather-lore was based on observations of the clouds, the moon, the sky at sunrise and sunset and the behaviour of birds, animals, fish, leeches, and insects, together with a memory of seasonal variations in temperature, precipitation and wind-strength and direction. There was likely to have been a good understanding of what we now call a depression, and of the arrival of fronts. The general behaviour of both warm and cold fronts, and in particular the wind-shifts and squalls linked to cold fronts, will have been noted. A rule for such forecasting is still remembered in the sayings about 'red sky at night' and 'red sky in the morning'. What is not generally known is the need to also note wind-direction, which in these instances affects the possibility of a correct forecast being made.

The performance of modern interpretations of medieval Scandinavian vessels and of an experimental *birlinn*

Campbell feudal ship-service 40-oared galleys, being longer, may have had slightly higher, but comparable, performance capabilities to the Gokstad ship. The large

Table 4.3. The performance under oars of modern interpretations of medieval Scandinavian vessels and of an experimental *birlinn* *Aileach* plus the Trans-Atlantic passage-time under sail and oar for the Gokstad ship interpretation *Viking*.

Vessel	Length (m)	Width (m)	Oars	Calm-water cruising (knots)	Calm-water sprint (knots)	From	via	To	Time (days)
Gokstad ship	23.3	5.2	32						
Gokstad (scale-model, tank-tested)[32]				5.7	6.8				
Gokstad ship *Viking*						Norway	Scotland	Newfoundland	28
Helge Ask (snekkja)	17.5	2.5	26	2	4				
Havhingsten (langskip)	29.26	3.8	60	2.5	4+				
Aileach (birlinn)	12.2	3.05	16	3	4				

Table 4.4. The performance under sail of modern interpretations of medieval Scandinavian vessels and of an experimental *birlinn* *Aileach* plus two passage times under sail and oar for the *langskip* interpretation *Havhingsten*.

Vessel	Length (m)	Width (m)	Oars	Fair wind (knots)	Strong wind (knots)	From	via	To	Time (days)
Roar Ege (byrðingr)	14	3.4	5	<6.3	8–10				
Helge Ask (snekkja)	17.5	2.5	26	6–8	12–15				
Havhingsten (langskip)	29.26	3.8	60	5–7	15+	Roskilde	Shetland	Dublin	45 (inc. stops)
Havhingsten (langskip)	29.26	3.8	60	5–7	15+	Dublin	English Channel	Roskilde	42 (inc. stops)
Ottar (knarr)	16.5	4.5	4	<10	12				
Aileach (birlinn)[33]	12.2	3.05	16						

slender 60-oared Scandinavian warships powered by warrior rowers are believed to have averaged 5 knots over long distances under oars (Table 4.3).

Roar Ege (Table 4.4) has only five oar-ports and is primarily a sailing vessel, and has been tested using both linen and woollen sails and has been found to achieve the following performance figures:

> Running double-reefed in 32 knots true wind, boat-speed 8.6 knots.
>
> Beating in 12 knots true wind, boat-speed 4 knots, velocity-made-good 1.7 knots.
>
> Beating in 19 knots true wind, boat-speed 4.8 knots, velocity-made-good 2 knots.

An improvement in performance was anticipated with the second woollen sail which has an improved weave and treatments.[34]

As vessels such as *Helge Ask* have no effective keel, the velocity-made-good to windward is generally poor at *c*.1 knot. Clearly such a vessel must always be rowed to windward, and is only effective under sail on reaches and runs. The *curach Colmcille*, rowing and sailing between Northern Ireland and Iona, achieved a shortest passage-time of 5 days and a longest of 8 days (including stopovers). *Colmcille* sustains 3–4 knots under oars and 6–8 knots broad reaching or running under sail.

Aileach appears to have been designed with more emphasis on rowing performance than on performance under sail, and is of much lighter displacement than *Roar Ege*. *Aileach* appears to be less efficient to windward than *Roar Ege* with a best windward performance of around 5 knots at 75° to the true wind for a velocity made good of 1.3 knots in strong winds, and *Aileach* has safely reached 12 knots when running in strong winds. On passage to and from the Faeroes, during which time adverse weather was encountered, *Aileach's* average speed was 2.8 knots. In 1991, crewed by amateurs, *Aileach* completed an inshore voyage from western Ireland to Stornoway, during which she suffered a broken mast and broken oars. In 1992, having gained experience, *Aileach* was sailed from Scotland to Færoe and back despite suffering a broken rudder due to stress of weather on the outward leg. The outward voyage did, however, involve requiring outside assistance on two occasions.[35]

The *Brendan*, a reconstruction of a large sea-going *curach*, was sailed some 4500 miles from Ireland to Newfoundland via the Hebrides and Iceland between May 1976 and June 1977. A repair to a tear in the skin of the *curach* was able to be carried out while at sea.[36]

> By strange channellis, fronteris and forlandis
> Onkouth costis and many wilsum strandis
> Now goith our barge, for nowder hawk [hulk] nor craike [carrack]
> May heir brake sail, for schald bankis and sandis.[37]

The shallow draft of galleys and *birlinnean*, combined with their performance under oars during calms and in light airs, may have been useful in avoiding heavier-displacement English naval sailing vessels which were of much deeper draft, were armed with cannon and patrolled off the Irish coast.

The following extracts from Norse literature reflect the very real situation of shipping water in an open boat in a rough sea and the urgent need to keep bailing.

Menn sé 'k ausa	I see six men
í meginveðri	bail on Elliði
sex á Elliða	in stormy weather
en sjau róa.	and seven are rowing.
Þat er gunnhvǫtun	The one in the stem
glíkt í stafni	who strains at the oars
Friðþjófi, er fram	resembles battle-doughty
fellr við árar.	Friðþjófr.
Jusu vér, meðan	We, cheerful fellows
yfir gekk svǫlór	bailed for eighteen days
bragnar teitir,	while cold spray
á bæði borð	(from waves)
tíu dœgr ok átta.	came over both gunwales.[38]
Hví samir hitt at dúsa	Why is it fitting for an unbending
hirðmanni geðstirðum	retainer to lie there and rest?
vest nú (þott kjǫl kosti)	Be active now, old knight
knár riddari enn hári:	although the keel [ship] is sorely tried:
þats satt at bÿðk byttu	It's true that I tell Giffarðr
(breiðhúfuðum) reiða	to swing the bucket
(austrs til hár í hesti	the bilge water is too high
hvaljarðar) Giffarði.	in the broad-bellied horse [ship] of the whale land [sea].[39]

Voyaging

Assuming that a close-winded galley was able to sail a course 68° off the true wind, then the galley would have a sector of 136° to windward incapable of being reached other than by tacking or by dropping sail and rowing. In navigating his vessel the galley skipper would need to be particularly prudent in relation to his position off lee and exposed shores, taking account of not only the condition of his hull, rudder, mast, sails, and rigging but also of his oars and the strength and endurance of his oarsmen. A 15th-century Dublin merchant, Bartholomew Rossynell, indicated that a heavily-laden merchant ship took 24 hours to sail from Man to Dublin, that it took 30 hours to sail from the Irish Sea to Orkney with a 'good wind', while a voyage from the north of Ireland to Iceland took 5 days in 'good sailing weather'.[40] In the British Isles a south-westerly wind prevails during the winter, summer and autumn but in spring and during April and May in particular, the frequency of north-easterlies is about equal to that of south-westerlies. In some decades the prevailing wind during these months has been north-easterly. Seasonal variations in wind-direction will have been observed and then exploited by early mariners.

These mariners, Picti, Scotti, *Gàidheil, Gaill* or *Gall-Ghàidheil,* all had an expectation of success when they set out to sea for war, profit or social reasons. Doubtless first paganism and later Christianity provided comfort in the face of danger. Successful voyaging was underpinned by great skill and experience in ship-design, shipbuilding and seamanship. However, knowledge and experience could not prevent accidents occurring; for example Iain Garbh Mac Gille Chaluim, when attempting to sail back from Lewis to Raasay on the evening of Easter Monday 1671 after attending the christening of a child of the Earl of Seaforth, was capsized by a stormy gust and he and his crew of 16 were all drowned. This tragic event was recorded in poetry, song and a *piobaireachd, Cumha Mhic Ghille Chaluim,* by Pádruig Óg MacRuimein.[41] A sound, well-maintained vessel and gear, a fit and experienced crew, good food and water, a good navigator and a wise skipper are all necessary elements for successful voyaging.

A good example of a voyage under sail and oar is the record of a voyage of 12 days by an oared sailing boat from Inveresragan to Poolewe in 1732.

> Starting at 11.00 on 07/06 from Inveresragan, Loch Etive, rowed constantly for 35 hrs, passing Duart Castle at 22.00 08/06.
>
> At 01.00 on 09/06, a fair sailing wind took the boat up the Sound of Mull to round Ardnamurchan by 10.00. Anchored somewhere beyond Ardnamurchan as the wind fell away in the evening.
>
> At 10.00 on 10/06, a fair wind set in taking the boat to Eigg. A headwind then arose at 16.00 and stayed fresh until 01.00 on 11/06 when a calm set in. With much laborious rowing the boat made Sleat by nightfall.
>
> At 10.00 on 12/06 left Sleat, rowing to Glenelg Barracks.
>
> Left Glenelg at 12.00 on 13/06 (without the boat's skipper) for the entrance to the narrows at Kyleakin. After lying to anchor at the entrance the tide became very strong and endangered the boat. A local pilot took the boat back to Sgeir na Caillich, 'a safe harbour', and later when the tide eased the boat was rowed along the shore back to Kyleakin (the skipper then rejoined the boat and another pilot was found to take them to the Gairloch).
>
> At 10.00 on 14/06 sailed with fair wind for the Crowlin Islands but before getting there the wind rose against them and the boat returned to Kyleakin where it lay for two days.
>
> At 01.00 on 17/06 sailed with a fair wind which held for about 14 hrs.
>
> Arrived at Poolewe at 03.00 on 18/06.[42]

Conclusions

The distances between castles, anchorages and beaching-places suitable for galleys in the sea areas of the Minch, Firth of Clyde, Solway and Irish Sea are relatively short, and therefore voyaging between these locations may have been readily accomplished within suitable weather and tidal windows. Opportunities for voyaging were available throughout the year but the risks increased during the early spring, late autumn and winter months. Longer passages and sailing at night are required when travelling between the Outer Hebrides and the Northern Isles or Ireland. Late spring, summer and early autumn are the best times for these longer voyages. Galley-castles, as is true for many other castles throughout Europe, were situated on or near significant trade and expeditionary routes. These locations gave their owners the opportunity to levy dues from passing cargo ships and to monitor and perhaps control the passage of warships.

The vigorous tidal flows in the North Channel are by turns benign (a fair wind and the tidal stream in similar directions), or potentially hazardous (a strong wind and the tidal stream in opposing directions). Unique tidally-induced hazards such as those near Rathlin or the whirlpools of Coire Bhreacain between Scarba and Jura and the Swilkie off Stroma are to be avoided; likewise significant overfalls such as occur off the Mull of Oa, off Sumburgh Head and in the Pentland Firth are likely to have presented a threat of swamping for a galley or *bírlinn*. Passage-making between Man and eastern-central Ireland, north Wales and Anglesey, north-western England and Galloway is relatively easily accomplished, while passage-making through the North Channel, going north or south, requires suitable winds, tides and timing. Waiting at anchor for the turn of the tide or for a fair wind is likely to have been a common experience for galley crews.

Despite benefitting from the use of modern navigational aids, the *Colmcille*, *Brendan*, *Roar Ege*, *Aileach*, *Helge Ask* and *Havhingsten* (Plate 13) voyages do give some indication of the capabilities of *curaichean*, *bírlinnean* and *loingeas*. The original *bírlinnean* and galleys, skippered by experienced mariners and manned by hardy crewmen were, as history shows, very capable of voyaging in the Norse-Gaelic Seaways. Accidents with loss of life and of vessels did happen, and at all times the sea must be respected. The weather-lore, forecasting abilities, retained tidal knowledge and the geographic memory of early and medieval sailors seem to have generally been excellent.

Successful oared sailing vessels must achieve the appropriate balance between rowing-performance and sailing-performance for the duties they are required to carry out and for the sea areas they operate in. Good performance under oars is important when navigating inshore waters. Rowing songs (*iorraim*) were used from early times. In the 12th-century *Prophecy of Berchán* Scotland is described as *Alba eathair-bhinn* (Scotland of melodious boats). Oared sailing vessels must have good sea-keeping ability, be fast under both oar and sail, be capable of being beached and must needs be constructed within the available materials and skills base. That galleys and *bírlinnean* remained in use for some 900 years is a tribute to the appropriateness of these vessels for voyaging in the Norse-Gaelic seaways and indeed to the skills of their builders and their crews. That *curaichean* are still in use in Ireland is a fine testament to these very ancient vessels' fitness for purpose in Atlantic waters.

Notes

1. D C McWhannell, 2002, 'The Galleys of Argyll', *Mariner's Mirror* 88.1, pp.14–32.
2. A Campbell, *West Highland Heraldry*, www.heraldry-scotland.co.uk/westhigh.html.
3. D C McWhannell, 2003, 'Campbell of Breadalbane and Campbell of Argyll Boatbuilding Accounts 1600 to 1700', *Mariner's Mirror* 89.4, pp.405–24.
4. A Riach, 2015, *The Birlinn of Clanranald* (Newtyle, Angus).
5. *Duanaire na Sracaire*. W McLeod & M Bateman (eds), 2007 (Edinburgh), pp.381–7.
6. J C Henderson, 2007, *The Atlantic Iron Age* (Abingdon), pp.1–2.
7. J Hornell, 1946, *Water Transport: origins and early evolution* (Cambridge), p.142; see also www.asnc.cam.ac.uk/irishglossaries/search.php?sText=Breccan.
8. *Tri l. long Picardach do brisidh i r-Ross Cuissine sa bliadain cetna* (see *The Annals of Tigernach* www.ucc.ie/online/ G10002A/text013html): T729.2.
9. P O'Neill, 2014, 'Control of the Means of Production in Early Irish Law', *Studia Celtic Finnica* 10, p.87 (available online); see also *Corpus Iuris Hibernici*, D A Binchy (ed.), 1978 (Dublin).
10. J MacInnes, 1974, 'West Highland Sea Power in the Middle Ages', *Transactions of the Gaelic Society of Inverness* 48, pp.519–520.
11. Adamnan, Abbot of Hy, *Life of St Columba founder of Hy*, W Reeves (ed.), 1874 (Edinburgh), introduction.
12. R Morken, 1968, 'Norse Nautical Units and Distance Measurement', *Mariner's Mirror* 54.4, pp.393–401.
13. C Swift, 2004, 'Royal Fleets in Viking Ireland, the Evidence of Lebor na Cert, AD 1050–1150', in J Hines, A Lane & M Redknap, *Land Sea and Home, Proceedings of a Conference on Viking-Period Settlement, at Cardiff, July 2001* (Society for Medieval Archaeology Monograph), pp.189–208.
14. *CSP Ireland of the Reign of Elizabeth*, ccvi, p.355.
15. *Register of the Privy Council of Scotland*, vol. 10, 1891 (Edinburgh), 25 June 1615.
16. W Sayers, 2006, 'What's in a Nonce?', *Scandinavian Studies* 78, pp.111–28.
17. D C McWhannell, 2000, 'Ship Service and Indigenous Sea Power in the West of Scotland', *West Highland Notes & Queries* ser. 3.1, p.5.
18. A MacLeod, 1933, *Sàr Orain* (Glasgow), p.126.
19. I Grant, 1959, *The Macleods: the history of a clan, 1200–1956* (London), pp.359–60.
20. S McGrail, 2014, *Early Ships and Seafaring: Water Transport within Europe* (Barnsley), p.134.
21. *The King's Mirror (Speculum Regale-Konungs Skuggsjá)*, transl. L M Larsen, 1917 (New York), pp.86–99.
22. A Findlay, 2004, *Fagrskinna: A Catalogue of the Kings of Norway* (Leiden), p.247.
23. *Icelandic Sagas and Other Historical Documents Relating to the Settlements and Descents of Northmen on the British Isles*, 2012, Gudbrand Vigfusson (ed.), vol. 4 (Cambridge), p.xxxiii.
24. D A McCullough, 2000, *Investigating Portages in the Norse maritime landscape of Scotland and the Isles*, unpublished PhD thesis, University of Glasgow (available from ethos.bl.uk).
25. Alexander Lindsay, 1980, *A Rutter of the Scottish Seas (c.1540)*, eds I H Adams and G Fortune (Greenwich).
26. J S Gibson, 1967, *Ships of the '45* (London), pp.77, 86, 128, 140ff.

27. *Giraldus Cambrensis, The Topography of Ireland*, T Forester (transl.) & T Wright (ed.), 1894 (London), p.33.

28. C D Frake, 1985, 'Cognitive Maps of Time and Tide Among Medieval Seafarers', *Man* new ser. 20, pp.254–70.

29. Lindsay, *Rutter of the Scottish Seas*, p.52.

30. *Atlas of UK Marine Renewable Energy Resources*, 2008, www.renewables.atlas.info/@ Crown Copyright.

31. B E Crawford, 1987, *Scandinavian Scotland* (Leicester), fig. 15, (see also www.paparproject. org.uk/hebrides_introduction.pdf).

32. These speeds are based on towing-tank testing of a scale model, a propulsive efficiency of 70% for the oars and a developed power of 0.25hp per oar, cruising and 0.4hp per oar, sprinting. It has also been estimated that in a true head-wind of 8 m/s the cruising speed would drop to 4.9 knots.

33. In a headwind and sea *Aileach's* speed dropped to 2 knots or lower. It was, it seems, only possible to row effectively in wave-heights of less than 4 feet or winds below Force 4 (Beaufort Scale). Two men pulling on one oar was effective. It was found however that the thwarts, placed 35 inches apart, were too close for large modern oarsmen to achieve a long stroke. Complete extension of the arms resulted in hitting the back of the oarsman in front.

34. J Bennett (ed.), 2009, *Sailing into the Past* (Barnsley: Seaforth), p.65 (see also www. vikingeskipsmuseet.dk web pages ref. "Roar Ege").

35. W Clark, 1993, *The Lord of the Isles Voyage* (Bowmore, Islay), pp.141–50.

36. T Severin, 1978, *The Brendan Voyage* (New York), p.242.

37. Gawin Douglas, *The Æneid of Virgil, The Proloug of the Thyrd Buke*, Bannatyne Club 64.1 (Edinburgh), p.124.

38. R Perkins, 2011, *Verses in Eric the Red's Saga* (London), p.15, (extract from *Friðþjófs Saga ins frækna*, 1901, pp.29, 32).

39. Perkins, *Verses in Eric the Red's Saga*, p.xx (text and translation as in *Morkinskinna*, pp.200, 304).

40. J V Sigurðson & T Bolton, 2014, *Celtic-Norse Relationships in the Irish Sea in the Middle Ages* (Leiden), p.viii.

41. www.ceolsean.net, www.sorleymaclean.org

42. Data extracted from NRS RH4/93/3–4, 'Report of Voyage' by Edward Nixon and James Watson 20/06/1732. Nixon, an Irishman, was master of the ship *Hereward* trading to Oban in 1729. He became a partner with four other Irishmen in The Glenorchy Firewood Co. and The Glenkinglass Furnace Co. Watson is described as a 'shopkeeper' in the Loch Etive Trading Co. Records. Photographs of the original 'Report of Voyage' document were kindly made available by R Black.

5

The Ruins of Danish Forts?
Exploring the Scandinavian Heritage of
Hebridean Galley-Castles

Alan Macniven[1]

IN HIS 2006 CONSIDERATION of the origins of Kisimul Castle in Barra, the late Ian Macneil highlighted a number of more general issues in the historiography of the Hebridean galley-castles. His main point of contention was the assumption that all such structures were a result of mainland Scottish influence in the later Middle Ages, with minimal indigenous input in their design or evolution. Macneil's response was Post-Colonial in nature – a call to rewrite the narrative from a local perspective. By defining the subject broadly to include all stone-built structures combining residence and defence which appeared in the Norse 'Sudreys' and adjacent mainland between AD 800 and 1600, he hoped to inspire a comprehensive reappraisal of Hebridean fortifications.

He was optimistic, moreover, that a contextualised and comparative analysis of individual structures would point to origins for at least some of the corpus in the earlier part of that period. This might, as Macneil suggested, mean the empire-building activities of Somerled MacGillebrigte in the mid 12th century. But with the 'Isles to the West of Scotland' at least nominally subject to the crown of Norway until 1266, there is also ample scope for a Scandinavian influence. In the absence of systematic contemporary accounts of the construction or early use of these structures, or, indeed, of the modern evaluation of their remains, it is difficult to establish the extent of that influence, let alone how direct or early it might have been. However, if the focus is shifted away from the castles themselves and onto the sites where they were built, cues can be taken from the Central Place theory originally devised by Walter Christaller, and developed more recently by Stefan Brink, Søren Sindbæk and others, to identify structures of power in prehistoric landscapes.[2]

By examining the proximity of galley-castle sites to nearby settlements, antiquities and topographical features, it is possible to gauge more clearly how they fit into long-standing patterns of political and economic exploitation. In a Hebridean context, where the sea is omnipresent, and boats have always played a vital role in communication and commerce, this is bound to reveal a certain degree of continuity. It would be surprising, for example, if there were not at least a few points of commonality with the widely distributed duns, forts and brochs of the Iron Age, or the probable military concerns of the Pictish and Dál Riatan elite who dominated the area during its Early Historic era. It is clear from the originally 7th-century origin-myth and naval census known as the *Míniugud Senchasa Fher nAlban* (Old Irish 'History of the [Gaelic-speaking] men of Scotland'),[3] and the numerous early accounts of Pictish maritime activity, that both groups set great store by naval prowess.[4] But given the late-8th-century arrival of the Vikings, and the subsequent rebranding of the Western Isles as *Innse Gall* (Gaelic 'The Islands of the [Scandinavian] foreigners'),[5] it would be unwise to imagine that the long-term transmission of these traditions was entirely seamless.

One way forward is to analyse seascapes in oblique and aerial photos from a seafaring perspective. As is discussed elsewhere in this volume, this technique has proved fruitful in the identification of undocumented early harbours. It should be noted, however, that although a number of these sites, including Rubh' an Dùnan in Skye,[6] have been mooted as possible Viking shipyards, the connection has yet to be verified. Indeed, it is worth stressing that there have, as yet, been no confirmed discoveries of Viking Age military infrastructure in the Isles. With no clear type-sites to go by, identifying the most promising targets for future excavation is no easy task. But in narrowing down the possibilities, it might be worth considering whether the most successful harbours, with the best chance of yielding diagnostic material, have evolved as a direct result of their utility to the land-based population. In this respect, the incoming Scandinavians have graced us with a large body of other cultural markers in the landscape with potential to develop the narrative even where material evidence is in short supply, the originally Old Norse elements in the names of local places. In theory at least, the careful cultivation of this material could also help to establish the Vikings' place in the overarching chain of continuity, whether this was a result of accident or design, and possibly also whether it was achieved by fair means or foul.

Some context

In April 2015, the initial conclusions of MacNeil and Buchanan's *MacNeil Surname Y-DNA Project* were released to a mixed response in the clan diaspora. For the Macneils of Barra, there had been expectations of scientific corroboration for traditional genealogies linking them back to the 5th-century Irish warlord, Niall *Noígiallach* (Irish 'Niall of the Nine Hostages'). Disappointingly for some, what the DNA evidence seemed to suggest was that the clan's genetic inheritance was not from Ireland, nor even from the wider Celtic world, but from the Scandinavian colonists who made their home in the Hebrides during the Viking Age.[7] Playing to standard clichés on Viking activity, the news was jokingly spun as a mitigating circumstance for the MacNeils' more recent 'pirating' activity. When it comes to Barra in particular, however, it should be noted that the few surviving accounts of the Old-Norse-speaking population portray them in a rather more civilised light. The runic dedication on the Christian cross-slab at Cille Bharra to a certain

Þorgerðr Steinarsdóttir, for example, shows that they were literate.[8] The celebration of the poet Ormr *Barreyjarskáld* (Old Norse 'The Bard of Barra') as part of the wedding entertainment at Reykhólar in Iceland in 1119 demonstrates that they were cultured.[9] And finally, the ancestry of Álfdís *Barreysku* (Old Norse 'The Barra Lass') presented in *Laxdæla saga*, *Grettis saga Ásmundarson* and *Landnámabók* (Old Norse 'The Book of Settlements') implies that they had an innate capacity for kindness. According to *Landnámabók*, Álfdís' paternal great-grandfather was none other than Ölvir *barnakarl* Einarsson (Old Norse 'The Children's Man'), a Viking warrior who gained his nickname for steadfastly refusing to spear the children of his Celtic victims![10]

Despite the consternation they have caused, the results of MacNeil and Buchanan's survey are not without precedent. A number of earlier studies focusing on the modern male descendants of Somerled have also pointed to a shared genetic marker, in this case a subgroup of haplogroup M17, known to be extremely rare in Celtic-speaking areas of Scotland, but very common in Norway.[11]

For students of Hebridean place-names, none of these genealogical revelations is entirely unexpected. From an onomastic perspective, the arrival of the Vikings in Barra, as elsewhere in the Isles, is synonymous with change. Surveys of the traditional farm-names of the Outer Hebrides have for more than 140 years now stressed the prospect of complete cultural disjuncture,[12] with a recent review of the Islay material by the present author suggesting much the same thing for the Inner Isles.[13] Previous generations of scholars may have laboured under romantic misapprehensions of a hybrid 'Gall-Gaidheal' or Norse-Celtic society in the West,[14] observing that the recorded Old Norse names for the larger islands, such as *Ljóðhús* for Lewis, *Skíð* for Skye and *Íl* for Islay, have been adapted from pre-existing native material.[15] But with advances in our understanding of how the creation and transmission of place-name material actually works, the idea that these names demonstrate early assimilation has also been called into question. Rather than pointing to mutual acceptance and cultural blending, the development is more realistically explained as the cold pragmatism of minimally-informed Scandinavian colonists in a hurry to apportion an as-yet-vaguely-defined new territory.[16] Attention can also be drawn to the many names in the Ordnance Survey Gazetteers for the area whose recent forms comprise both Old Norse and Gaelic elements. Contrary to popular belief, there are vanishingly few which warrant the description of 'hybrid' in a strict linguistic sense,[17] and cannot be readily explained in terms of routine developments in local naming-practices in the centuries after the Viking Age, but before their crystallised, written forms took shape.

Further changes in the form and interpretation of the Hebrides' Old Norse nomenclature can be traced to the agenda-driven *dinn senchus* (Gaelic 'folk-etymology') of the later Middle Ages. By this point, the collective memory of Scandinavian culture in the Scottish *Gàidhealtachd* had been reframed as a meme for un-Christian 'otherness'.[18] Where Old Norse names had ceased to function in an appellative sense, they might be re-imagined with a more desirable Gaelic etymology.[19] The Islay hill-name Beinn Tart a'Mhill, for example, was traditionally seen as a rather contrived Gaelic rendering of 'Hill of the Thirsty Hill', when the context points more clearly to Old Norse *Hjartafjall* 'Stag Mountain'.[20] A similar, albeit less extreme, example is provided by the island-name Barra. Although the popular understanding of this name is as a commemoration of the 6th-century Irish saint, Finbarr of Cork,[21] in combination with the Old Norse generic *ey* (f), meaning 'island', more convincing and topographically appropriate etymologies are provided by the completely Norse *Barrey*, 'Rough Island' and *Berrey*, 'Bare Island'.[22]

That is not to dismiss the medieval provenance of the chapel known as *Cille Bharra* (Gaelic 'The Cell or Chapel of St Finbarr') at Eoligarry (Old Norse 'Oli's Farm') in the north of the island.[23] But with the results of an as-yet-unpublished geophysical survey by Historic Scotland revealing the outline of two rectilinear structures directly underneath the chapel,[24] it seems unlikely to be especially early, or the source of inspiration for the island name. In fact, given the similarity of the outlines to the diagnostically Scandinavian settlement-structures now being uncovered elsewhere in the Hebrides, especially in South Uist,[25] this particular chapel should probably be interpreted as the later adornment of a prosperous Viking settlement with a place of Christian worship. On balance, it is likely that any eventual cultural blending in the Isles began from a baseline of large-scale Scandinavian settlement through an intermediate period of ethnic apartheid or worse. Suspicions that Gaelicisation occurred only much later, as an unavoidable consequence of changing political circumstances, are gaining increasing traction among linguists researching the formative impact of Old Norse on Scottish Gaelic.[26]

Although there is little contemporary detail on the early stages of the Viking Age in the Hebrides, these seem certain to have been characterised by violence. Two generations or more of raiding, pillaging and slaving would have destabilised the area to the extent that large-scale immigration became viable by the mid 9th century.[27] While it would be surprising if temporary fortifications had not been erected during this period, it is pertinent to ask why a culturally uniformly Scandinavian community would have needed more permanent defensive structures.

Under constant threat from the dispossessed and disgruntled Hebridean nobility, the territorial aspirations of their Celtic rivals in Ireland or mainland Scotland, and even their Scandinavian neighbours elsewhere in the Isles, the Norse settlers would have had to invest heavily in military infrastructure to embed successfully enough for their place-name legacy to have survived. The historical evidence for this investment may be disparate and indirect, but if the timescale is extended to include the later Middle Ages, and allowances are made for a certain amount of retrospective extrapolation, there are enough clues to begin framing the narrative.

Given what is known of the land-tenures of later-medieval Norway, the Kingdom of Man and the Isles, and the MacDonald Lordship of the Isles, for example, it seems likely that the process of political entrenchment involved the development of systems of *leiðangr* (m) (Old Norse 'naval levy'),[28] a presumption supported by the later evolution of the Viking longship into the Gaelic *bìrlinn* (f) or West Highland galley.[29] While these warships represented a considerable asset to the Lordship, not least for their capacity to transport thousands of fighting men around the west coast and Irish Sea,[30] where they were actually kept when not in use is far from certain. As in later periods, it can be assumed that many individual vessels were stored or maintained on or near the farms supplying them. The Scandinavian experience suggests that there would also have been a number of minor and major gathering-points, including custom-built harbours.[31] However, references to this kind of facility in the Hebrides tend to be very late or anecdotal. One of the most interesting was gathered by the Welsh traveller Thomas Pennant while visiting the Isle of Islay in the late 18th century. In his *Tour of Scotland and Voyage to the Hebrides* of 1772, Pennant recounts a local tradition of the 'Great MacDonald' having had his harbour at Tràigh an Luig at the head of Loch Indaal, adding that it was once served by piers with doors to secure shipping, as evinced by 'a great iron hook, one of the hinges, having lately being found there'.[32] For the Viking Age itself, such accounts are non-existent. But with galley-castles often controlling the most sheltered or strategically-important bays in their localities, it would be reasonable to imagine a certain amount of continuity of resort.

Where to start?

In attempting to trace the chain of continuity back to the Viking Age, it makes sense to begin with the earliest castles. Identifying these structures is not exactly straightforward. The area encompassed by Macneil's proposed survey boasts many hundreds of stone-built fortifications. Whereas those of the dry-stone variety can probably be classified as pre-Norse, and therefore too early, this still leaves scores of lime-mortared structures which meet his definition. As a starting-point, however, the list is still too long. Macneil had begun to address this problem by compiling a spreadsheet of early castles off the west coast. With a distinct lack of documents covering the Isles or their built environment prior to the 15th century, he turned to the list of 'The Islands of Scotia, apart from the Orkneys' comprising chapter 10 of John of Fordun's *Chronica Gentis Scottorum*, thought to have been written in the 1370s. As Macneil takes pains to point out, Fordun's list is far from exhaustive, covering only 34 Hebridean islands (or 35 if Tioram off the coast of Moidart is included), eight in the Firth of Clyde, and a further four locations including the islands of Man, Rathlin, Stroma, and the promontory of Durness in Sutherland. The criteria for selection are, moreover, unclear. While Fordun also refers to a number of domestic, fortified, and ecclesiastical structures, coverage of the islands listed is neither systematic nor complete. Excluding Man, Rathlin, Stroma and Durness, Fordun lists only 11 fortifications. By way of comparison, Martin Coventry, in the latest edition of his *Castles of Scotland*, lists 70 or more castles on the same islands occupied by Fordun's 11.[33] Needless to say, not all of the castles known today are early. But by cross-referencing them with the typological assessments listed in Historic Environment Scotland's monuments record, Macneil was able to identify 30 sites in the Hebrides and Clyde estuary likely to have supported a castellated structure before the end of the 14th century (Figure 5.1).

Establishing the significance of the associated sites to the Norse communities of the Viking Age poses a number of challenges. While entertaining, the somewhat frivolous association of at least three of them with 'Vikings' in local folklore must be dismissed as colourful embellishment. Analysing the language background of the names of the castles, along with those of the islands, parishes and districts where they can be found seems to point to a strong Scandinavian heritage, as does a variety of other discrete names in their immediate locality (see Table 5.1 [end of chapter] and Appendix 1). But this is precisely what we would expect of a region whose medieval history has been defined by blanket settlement and cultural apartheid at the hands of the Vikings, even if they had no particular military interest in the sites under investigation. It is entirely possible that some of them only gained military importance with later advances in naval technology, such as the need for nearby and sheltered mooring for much larger, ocean-going ships. Conversely, even where the proportion of Old Norse place-names in a given locality seems low, as in the immediate vicinity of the Lordship Centre on Eilean Mòr in Loch Finlaggan on the Isle of Islay, this can often be explained in terms of post-Norse developments in landownership, land-tenure, and

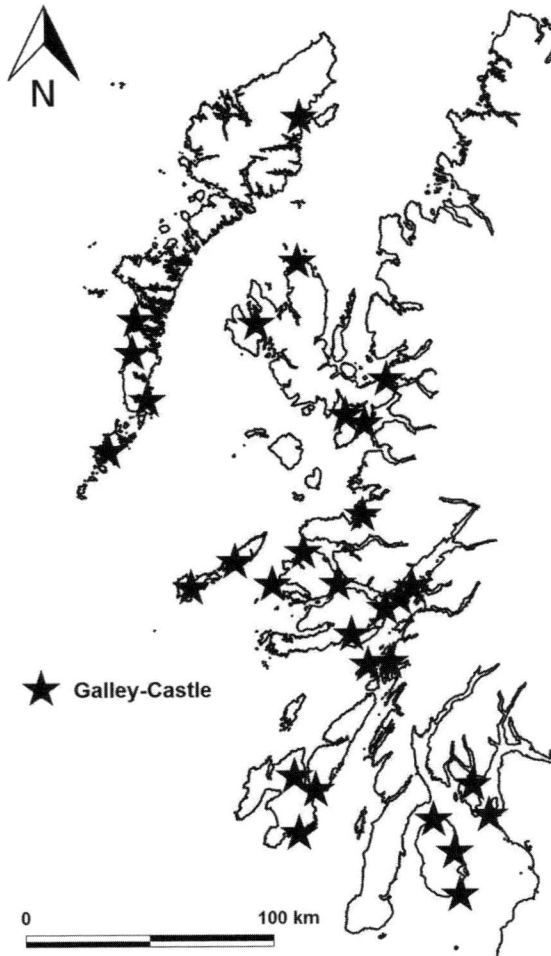

Figure 5.1. Galley-castles in the Hebrides and Clyde Estuary c.1370. (Alan Macniven)

agricultural emphases, not to mention periods of settlement expansion and retraction which would have greatly accelerated the statistical re-Gaelicisation of the local nomenclature.[34]

Late prehistoric fort-building in Scandinavia?

By and large, the most successful Scandinavian settlements in the Sudreys as elsewhere are likely to have been continually used to the present day, or developed in scale to the extent of obscuring traces of ancient infrastructure. To have any realistic chance of identifying other sites likely to have been favoured for their naval amenity during the Viking Age, it is crucial to establish the perspective of the incoming Scandinavians themselves. The Viking colonists who settled in the Hebrides came from a venerable tradition of fort-building, whose Iron Age floruit rivalled that of Atlantic Scotland. The many hundreds of drystone, turf and vitrified *bygdeborger* and *fornborgar*, or hillforts, of Norway, Denmark and Sweden cover a wide range of types, sizes and locations, pointing to a variety of different uses, including ritual, agricultural and domestic.[35] However, their common juxtaposition to topographical features such as bogs, waterways, ridges and hilltops implies that an important feature of most was defensibility. The inter-visibility of forts around several major waterways, including Mjøsa in Norway and Store Bælt in Denmark, suggests that some were also used to control communications or resources from a relatively early date.

While the so-called Roman Iron Age (*c.*AD 0–400) witnessed a general decline in the hillfort phenomenon, the military use of enclosures seems to have become increasingly important from precisely that point. In Norway, the appearance of *ring-tun* or *tunanlegg* (Norwegian 'court(yard) sites') comprising an array of barrack-like longhouses with the short ends facing a central courtyard, may have been inspired by Roman practice. Their discovery at the mouths of major river-valleys in the north of the country points to a role in the colonisation or control of Sámi lands,[36] whereas examples in the south and south-west have been interpreted as bases for forays into what was to become Denmark.[37] Although confined to the Iron Age in Norway, the advent of the Viking Age saw the concept resurface in Denmark on a substantially grander scale. Ringforts dating to the reign of Haraldr *blátönn* (Old Norse 'Bluetooth') Gormsson, or his son Sveinn *tvéskegg* Haraldsson (Old Norse 'Forkbeard') have been found in a number of strategic locations across Denmark and Skåne. Circular on plan, these *trelleborger* (from Old Norse *præll* (m) 'thrall, serf, slave' and *borg* (f) 'fort') comprise a turf rampart and ditch, with inner diameters ranging from 120 to 240m, housing a symmetrical pattern of as many as 48 longhouse barracks. There is some debate as to what the traditional name for these structures might mean, whether it indicates that they were originally built by slaves, or played a role in slaving activity, or whether their outer walls were protected by wooden staves known in Danish as *trælle*. With origins in the late 10th century, however, it is generally agreed that their primary function was to control Denmark in a time of political unrest.[38]

Compared to Denmark, the Viking Age and following period in Norway are characterised by a conspicuous dearth of fortifications. This may be because the trend was to build in timber alone, as for example the late-12th-century reference to Archbishop Eysteinn Erlendsson's *Treborg* or 'timber fortifications' outside Trondheim,[39] with the structures leaving little or no trace. It could also be because the nature of Norwegian society was changing, perhaps as a result of increasing political centralisation.[40] But the need for military installations may also have been minimised by the fractured, fjordic character of the landscape, framed as it is by dramatic mountains and waterways.[41] Beyond the occasional beacon or timber palisade, the topography in much of Norway would have been sufficient to hinder the progress of enemies long enough to help the locals prepare for fight or flight. It can nevertheless be assumed that their *höfðingjar* (m pl) (Old Norse 'chieftains') were familiar with a wide variety of fortifications through their economic and political connections and military activities abroad. Later-medieval saga references to the walled cities of *Rómaborg* (Rome) and *Jórsalaborg* (Jerusalem), for example, are likely to have a long antecedence.

Although typologically very different, a selection of native duns and brochs in *Scotia Scandinavica* are recognised in the surviving Old Norse nomenclature for the area as 'borgs'.[42] Similar in range to Gaelic *dùn* (m), the Old Norse noun, *borg* (f) was the standard Scandinavian word for 'fortification' before the terms *kastali* (m) and *slott* (n) were borrowed from continental Europe along with advances in castle design in the later Middle Ages. It is also the origin of the archaeological term *broch* via the Norn dialects of Orkney and Shetland.[43] Perhaps the most well-known of these in Scotland is the *Móseyarborg* (Old Norse 'Broch of Mousa') mentioned in *Egils saga Skalla-Grímssonar*, where Björn Brynjólfsson, a chieftain's son from Norway, is said to have spent the winter after abducting Þóra *hlaðhönd* ('Lace Cuff') Hróaldsdóttir.[44] Reflexes of the element can be found throughout the Scandinavian settlement-zone in Scotland. In the West Highlands and Islands, however, the subsequent influence of the Gaelic language has transformed it, in some cases almost out of recognition. On further investigation it appears that the Ordnance Survey 1:50,000 Inventory preserves more than 130 examples, covering a range of written forms including *borg, borgh, brogue, borve, bhuirg, bor, borre, borro, bhorra, bhora, barra* and *broc* (Figure 5.2). While closer scrutiny of older and smaller-scale maps would no doubt reveal others, it is important to note that this corresponds to only a small fraction of the drystone fortifications in the region. This is due in part to the later-medieval language shift from Old Norse to Gaelic, and the likely replacement or (part-) translation of local names containing Old Norse *borg* with others based on Gaelic *dùn*. It is tempting to imagine, however, that the word *borg* as used in the Hebrides had acquired a narrower meaning than 'fortification' in general, and may never have been a particularly common feature of Hebridean naming patterns.

It has been suggested by the present author that prehistoric fortifications with names building on the element *borg* may once have functioned as central places in the administrative districts of early historic Islay, the boundaries of which were later repurposed by incoming Norse communities (Figure 5.3).[45] That is not to assume, as was popularly believed until the later 19th century, that the structures themselves had actually been built by Scandinavians,[46] or even that they had been re-used by them. The available archaeological evidence for Atlantic Scotand on the whole, as typified

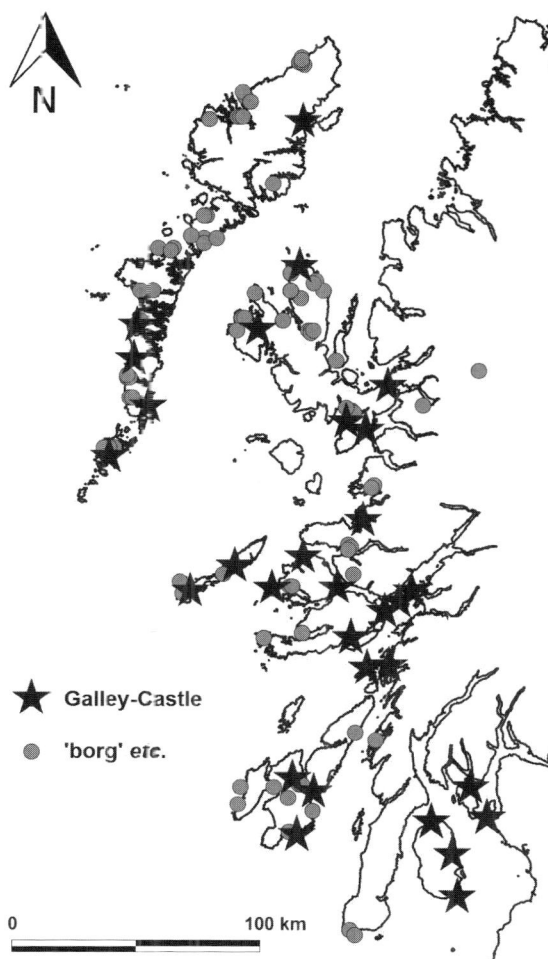

Figure 5.2. *Galley-castles and 'borg' sites in the Hebrides and Clyde Estuary. (Alan Macniven)*

by the broch of Dun Vulan near Bornais in South Uist,[47] points to wide-ranging abandonment not long after the beginning of the Viking Age, dispelling any notion that they might be considered the ruins of 'Danish' forts. Establishing similarly complex patterns for the rest of the Hebrides would require an extensive settlement-historical survey, which is likely to be hampered by the relative lack of early fiscal records for the other islands compared to Islay. In the first instance, however, there is plenty of scope to investigate the association of Old Norse *borg* names with medieval central places.

The importance of ships and harbours

The Vikings were certainly capable of employing temporary fortifications to good effect in their military campaigns abroad.[48] In the British Isles, this can be seen from contemporary annalistic references to Norse naval camps known as 'Longphorts' in Ireland in the 840s,[49] or the fortification of the church at Repton in the English Midlands

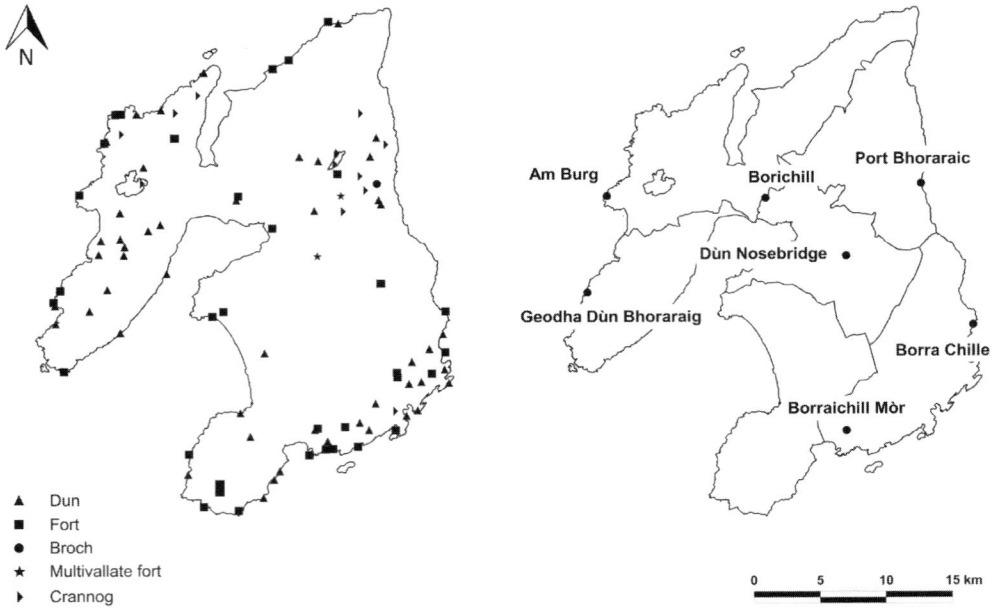

Figure 5.3. ON borg names and reconstructed early parishes in Islay. (after Macniven 2015: 3, 101)

by the Danes in 874.[50] They were also capable of appropriating and administering large walled towns, such as York,[51] in addition to 'destroying and plundering' native forts, such as Dumbarton Rock.[52] When it came to protecting their more permanent settlements in the Hebrides, however, it seems that, as in Norway, the emphasis was placed, not on fortified structures, but on the landscape and on ships. Although the first written suggestions of ship-service in Norway are encountered in Snorri Sturluson's 13th-century biography of Hákon *góði* (Old Norse 'The Good') Haraldsson, who died in AD 961, there are hints that similar systems were developing elsewhere in the diaspora at around the same time. Annalistic references to the *Lagmannaibh nan-Innsedh* (from Old Norse *lögmenn* or 'lawmen' of the Isles), who accompanied Scandinavian kings of Man and Dublin on military expeditions to Ireland,[53] strengthens the possibility of a functioning levy-system in the Hebrides by the late 950s.

As in Norway itself, it would be surprising if this had not involved the construction and maintenance of specialist harbours, jetties, slipways and portages. In Scandinavia generally there is a growing body of research on the cognitive landscape of naval warfare and defence dedicated to identifying sites of this type for the purposes of settlement-historical study or excavation[54] In recent years considerable progress has been made in the use of maritime naming-elements as indicators of coastal power in south-west Norway, the likely homeland of many of Scotland's Viking colonists.

In their 2003 article, 'Place-names as evidence for ancient maritime culture in Norway', Frans-Arne Stylegar and Oliver Grimm present an overview of the place-name record for three parishes in Vest-Agder, carefully gathered from modern inventories, the monumental *Norske Gaardnavne*, and the lesser-known Norwegian archives covering agricultural improvements in the 19th century. They focus on three major categories of naming element.

1. Those alluding to major vessels, ranging from the generic *skip* (n) 'ship', through the long and broad warships known as *dreki* (m) and *snekkja* (f), the long and narrow *skeið* (f) and slightly later *skúta* (f), to the trading vessels known as *byrðingr* (m) 'ship of burden' (the source of Gaelic *bìrlinn*), *buza* (f) and *knörr* (m) (gen. *knarrar*) (both types of merchant ships adapted from earlier warships).

2. Those alluding to the sheltering of major vessels, including *höfn* (f) (gen. *hafnar*) 'harbour', *naust* (n) 'boathouse', *stöð* (f) 'landing-place', *topt* (f) 'site (of boathouse ruins)' and *uppdráttr* (m) 'slipway'.

3. Those alluding to the *leiðangr* (m) or 'naval levy' system, such as *herr* (m) 'host/force/army', *konungr* (m) 'king', and *skipreiða* (f) 'ship-service (district)'.

Rather than highlighting the significance of any individual naming elements in the *identification of late prehistoric harbour sites*, Stylegar and Grimm stress the importance of a co-ordinated approach. Their preferred starting-point is known central places or otherwise significant settlements around the coast, as evident from early accounts. Where none are recorded, consideration of the place-name material is used in conjunction with a number of material factors to deduce their one-time presence. This might include the close proximity of later medieval ecclesiastical structures, pointing to the continued wealth and influence of local landowners into the later Middle Ages. They also stress the importance of contemporary antiquities, such as boathouses, of which 17 'huge' examples are known from south-west Norway, with the largest, at Vikum in Høyanger municipality, Sogn og Fjordane, measuring 40 x 15m.[55]

Adapting this approach for the Hebridean material requires a number of adjustments, not least a toning-down of expectations. Compared to south-west Norway, the sources available for local place-names predating the 19th century are limited in both number and detail. Moreover, given the significant changes to the local namescape which can be assumed for the centuries separating the earliest records from the end of the Norse period, it is likely that many diagnostic examples have been lost or obscured. The chances of missing relevant names can be minimised by an awareness of the major linguistic changes typifying the adaptation of Old Norse name material into Gaelic, including lenition, back-formation, projection and prosthesis.[56] If attention is also paid to the potential impact of (part-)translation, phonetic adaptation and lexical substitution, the range of potential examples can be widened. It is possible, for example, that some Viking Age place-names building on Old Norse *skip* (n) 'ship' have been translated with Gaelic *long* (f) 'ship', or preserved through replacement with the loanword *sgiob* (f). Allowances should also be made for the re-imagining of Old Norse word material as Gaelic through lexical substitution and folk etymology. Old Norse *drag*, for example, might be transformed into Gaelic *tràigh* (f) 'strand'; *skeið* rendered as *sgiath* (m) 'wing, tip, fin' or *sgaoth* (f) 'shoal, flock, swarm'; or *snekkja* as *sneachd* (m) 'snow'. Consideration of topographical and cultural contexts are crucial here.

Unlike in south-west Norway, it would perhaps also be unrealistic to expect to find evidence for early boathouses, whether 'huge' or otherwise, particularly in the Outer Hebrides, where access to the longer timbers needed for roofing may have been limited or prohibitively expensive. It can be speculated that this is also one of the reasons behind the apparent development of the later medieval *bìrlinn* not from the *skeið* but the *byrðingr*. In any case, more recent maritime practices in the Long Island have seen the portage of smaller ships from the sea to smaller bodies of fresh or brackish water for longer-term berthing, where close enough to the coast. This had the multiple benefits of protecting the boats from winter storms, ridding them of molluscs and other marine parasites which can only survive in salt water, and preventing the hulls from drying out, meaning they could be recommissioned relatively quickly without the need for re-swelling.[57] If this recent culture of dragging and carrying boats across land is a legacy of the Norse period, it would make sense to add an additional category of naming element to the search: those alluding to portage, including *bor* (from *bera* (v)) 'bear, carry', *eið* (n) 'isthmus/portage', and *hlunnr* (m) 'roller (for moving a ship on land)'.[58]

Discussion

On the basis of location and cultural significance alone, there are good grounds to assume that the majority of galley-castle sites in the Norse Sudreys have ancient pedigrees, with most being close to both successful settlements and ancient ecclesiastical sites (see Table 5.2 [end of chapter] and Appendix 1). While allowances must be made for the conflation of island- and parish-names, and the names of castles with settlements, it is also fair to say that most can be found in conspicuously Norse onomastic contexts. Closer analysis of the discrete elements in the surrounding place-names is less conclusive. Of the 30 sites listed in Table 5.1, 11 can be linked to an Old Norse *borg* name, including 5 of the 11 fortifications mentioned by Fordun, 2 in the names of castles themselves, and 4 in names describing nearby locations. Fewer sites have associations with other elements indicating naval infrastructure. Of those which have, only Dunscaith in Skye, a possible derivation from Old Norse *skeið*, which probably alludes to the berthing or racing of ships,[59] is also relatively close to a cluster of *borg* names, pointing perhaps to its suitability for further scrutiny.

While the coincidence of galley-castles with borg names seems relatively weak, this may be a reflection of the limitations of the available evidence, with so much of the original Old Norse material now lost. Even so, it would be wrong to assume that all known galley-castles were built on long-standing Norse skipreiða sites. Advances in naval technology and armaments in the undocumented part of the Hebridean Middle Ages would no doubt have seen new sites of Norse heritage developed for their suitability to watch out for or repel larger ships of deeper draft sailing further from the coast, even where the opportunities for the landing or storage of such vessels nearby was limited. With the Hebrides being so much smaller than Norway, it might also be imagined that their levies operated on a smaller scale, without the need for as many dedicated facilities, and possibly also with a greater degree of overlap between military and mercantile utility. But if the galley-castle sites provide only a partial correlation to the earlier Norse infrastructure, that still leaves the question of where the rest of it might be sought.

The most promising solution as things stand is to return to the element *borg*. Of the clusters observed in the Ordnance Survey 1:50,000 Inventory (Figure 5.4) a number display convincing combinations of the features described above. In Skye, the settlement district known as Borve in Snizort, with its commanding dun, faces onto the sheltered inner part of Loch Snizort. The nearby Skeabost Island, where the River Snizort enters the loch, once housed the late-medieval cathedral of Sodor and the Isles,[60] pointing to the previous 'centrality' of the location. The name Skeabost itself is almost certainly an Old Norse *bólstaðr* (m) or 'farm' compound. While the specific element is unclear,[61] it would be reasonable to imagine a reconstructed *Skeiðabólstaðr*

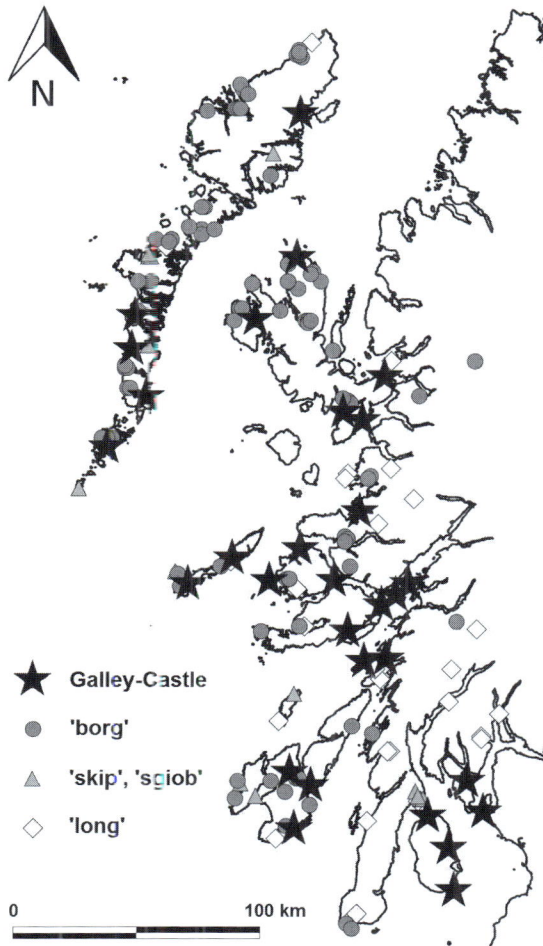

Figure 5.4. *'Skip', 'sgiob' and 'long' names in the West of Scotland in the Ordnance Survey's 1:50,000 Inventory. (after Macniven 2015: 3, 101)*

'Ship Farm'. In Trotternish, the promontory fort of Dùn Skudiburgh dominates the approach to both Scuddaborg Farm and the sheltered bay and settlement of Uig, from Old Norse *Vík, meaning 'Bay'. While Forbes suggests derivation of the element *Scud etc.* from Gaelic *scut* or *sgut* meaning 'cluster',[62] a ready alternative for the whole name is provided by Old Norse *Skútaborg* 'Ship Fort'.

In South Uist, excavations at the Viking settlement site at Bornais, from Old Norse *Borgnes* 'Fort Headland', have produced an assemblage of diagnostically Scandinavian material as rich as that from anywhere else in Scotland, and without clear signs of cultural continuity from the preceding Pictish period.[63] With the settlement district of Kildonan adjacent to the south, complete with burial-ground and chapel-site, and the later Ormaclett Castle nearby to the north, the location has clearly retained its importance over the centuries. At the same time, the surrounding area abounds in Old Norse place-names, with Bornais likely to have been the Viking Age name for the adjacent headland, known in Gaelic as Rudha Ardvule. This would make Dùn Vulan the eponymous *borg*, and its apparent abandonment *c.*AD 800 highly significant. There are also a number of inland lochs nearby, including Loch Ardvule at the very end of the peninsula, immediately adjacent to both the broch and the sea.

Further south, in Islay, the ancient promontory fort of Am Burg faces out onto the Atlantic from the coast of Kilchoman parish, not far from the freshwater Loch Gorm, the site of the early chapel at Kilchoman, where the Cawdor Campbell lairds of Islay are said to have had a mansion in the 17th century,[64] and the farm at Ballinaby, whose soils and sand-dunes have preserved an array of high-status Viking burials.[65]

Elsewhere in the Hebrides there are a number of other important locations whose close proximity to the sea, freshwater lochs, and Iron Age fortifications combines with local place-names derived from Old Norse *borg*. These include Borerary in North Uist, Borve in Barra, and Borve Lodge in Harris, *c.*450m inland from a sheltered *slochd* known as Sta, with possible derivation from Old Norse *stöð* or *stöðvar*. If the search were expanded to take in other place-name inventories, however, it is almost certain that more would be uncovered. A case in point here is Rothesay Castle in Bute. Although the Ordnance Survey 1:50,000 Inventory does not seem to record any local 'borgs', the 1st edition six-inch-to-the-mile sheet shows a Dun Burgidale, from Old Norse *Borgadalr*, 'Fort Valley', *c.*2.8km to the WNW. While Dun Burgidale is clearly not a physical precursor to Rothesay castle, the small distance that separates the two does not preclude it from being a conceptual forebear within the same district. Both are close to Cnoc an Rath,[66] whose earthworks have been compared with known Norse *þing* (n) or 'assembly' sites,[67] and appear to have been in use as such throughout the consolidation phase of Norse settlement in the latter part of the 9th century.[68]

Closer scrutiny of more general terms for ships, such as Old Norse *skip* or Gaelic *long*, may also help here (Figure 5.4), as might the identification of more specific terms for mercantile activity such as *(lað)hella* (f) 'rock from which one can load a ship'; *torg* (n) 'square, market-place', *markaðr* (m) 'market' and their Gaelic equivalents.[69] Given the close association of both mercantile and military activity with the Norse 'establishment', there are also grounds for seeking connections with other administrative and cult practices, through place-names containing elements such as *þing*,[70] *hörgr* (m), '(stone) altar, roofless place of worship, sacrificial cairn', or *hóf* (n) 'hall, temple'. If, in time, this leads to the discovery and excavation of a Viking Age type-site, it should be possible to further refine the narrative. But until that happens, the broad conclusions that can be drawn are likely to remain as follows. The Viking warlords arriving in the Hebrides in the 9th century would have been well aware of native patterns of landscape exploitation, including the location of their defensive structures, landing-places and harbours – even without formal or friendly exchange. Where there were clear advantages in so doing, they would have appropriated and adapted these systems, with the subsequent settled communities continuing to enjoy the practical or strategic advantages of individual sites, albeit from a Scandinavian perspective. In this respect, the incoming Norse might be regarded as 'accidental' custodians of long-standing tradition. It seems unlikely, however, that they were responsible for building the surviving galley-castles or even their immediate precursors. Whether the proportions, block-work, or mortaring techniques employed in the later-medieval structures show signs of local innovation, or have been imported in their entirety from the Scottish mainland, is a matter for close architectural-historical study. For students of the Hebridean Viking Age the real value of the galley-castles is as markers of localities within which we might hope to find other clues as to the nature and distribution of Norse maritime activity.

Notes

1. The author would like to express his gratitude to the Islands Book Trust for their kind invitation to participate in the Galley-Castles Conference in Barra, to the other delegates for their willingness to discuss the ideas presented in this paper, and to Dr Arne Kruse at the University of Edinburgh for doing the same. He is especially grateful to Dr Rory Macneil for providing access to his late father's unpublished datasets, which provided the core structure for the information presented in the Appendix.

2. W Christaller, 1933, *Die zentralen Orte in Süddeutschland* (Jena); S Brink, 1996, 'Political and Social Structures in Early Scandinavia: A Settlement-historical Pre-study of the Central Place', *TOR Tidskrift för arkeologi* 28, pp.235–8; Brink, 1997, 'Political and Social Structures in Early Scandinavia II: Aspects of Space and Territoriality – The Settlement District', *TOR Tidskrift för arkeologi* 29, pp.389–437; Brink, 1999, 'Social Order in the Early Scandinavian Landscape', in C Fabech & J Ringtved (eds), *Settlement and Landscape*, pp.423–39 (Århus); S M Sindbæk, 2009, 'Open Access, Nodal Points and Central Places: Maritime Communication and Locational Principles for Coastal Sites in South Scandinavia, c.AD 400–1200', *Estonian Journal of Archaeology* 13.2, pp.96–109.

3. J W M Bannerman, 1974, *Studies in the History of Dalriada* (Edinburgh); D Ó Corráin, 1980, 'Book Review: Studies in the History of Dál Riada, John Bannerman', *Celtica* 13, pp.168–82; D N Dumville, 2002, 'Ireland and North Britain in the Earlier Middle Ages: Contexts for Miniugud Senchasa Fher nAlban', in C Ó'Baoil & N R McGuire (eds), *Rannsachadh na Gàidhlig 2000* (Obar Dheathain), pp.185–211; A Woolf, 2007, *From Pictland to Alba 789–1070* (Edinburgh); J E Fraser, 2009, *From Caledonia to Pictland: Scotland to 795*, New Edinburgh History of Scotland, Vol. I. (Edinburgh).

4. See, for example, the *Annals of Tigernach* 792.2, which reports that, 'A hundred and fifty Pictish vessels were wrecked at Ross Cuissine'.

5. W D H Sellar, 1966, 'The Origins and Ancestry of Somerled', *Scottish Historical Review* 45, p.135; Woolf *From Pictland to Alba*, pp.64, 100.

6. C J M Martin, 2014a, 'The Sea World of the Chessmen', in D H Caldwell & M A Hall (eds), *The Lewis Chessmen: New Perspectives*: 185–99 (Edinburgh).

7. http://www.heraldscotland.com/news/13197315.Macneil_clan_shocked_as_DNA_checks_force_rewrite_of_history/ (accessed 24 May 2016).

8. CANMORE Site Number: NF70NW3.4 (NGR: NF 7051 0738).

9. P Meulengracht-Sørensen, 2000, 'The Prosimetrum Form 1: Verses as the Voice of the Past', in R E Poole (ed.), *Skaldsagas: Text, Vocation, and Desire in the Icelandic Sagas of Poets* (Berlin), pp.183–4.

10. *Íslendingabók, Landnámabók. Íslenzk Fornrit I. Bindi*, J Benediktsson (ed.), 1986 (Rejkjavík), pp.145, 379.

11. B Sykes, 2004b, *Adam's Curse: A Future Without Men* (London), pp.220–25; A Moffat & J Wilson, 2011, *The Scots: A Genetic Journey* (Edinburgh), pp.192, 239.

12. F W L Thomas, 1876, 'Did the Norsemen Extirpate the Inhabitants of the Hebrides in the Ninth Century?', *PSAS* 11, pp.472–507; M Oftedal, 1954, 'The Village Names of Lewis in the Outer Hebrides', *Norsk tidsskrift for sprogvidenskap* 17, pp.363–409; A Jennings & A Kruse, 2005, 'An ethnic enigma – Norse, Pict and Gael', in A Mortensen & S V Arge (eds), *Viking and Norse North Atlantic, Selected Papers from the Proceedings of the Fourteenth Viking Congress, 19–30 July 2001, Tórshavn, Faroe Islands* (Tórshavn), pp.251–63; A Jennings & A Kruse, 2009, 'From Dál Riata to the Gall-Ghàidheil', *Viking and Medieval Scandinavia* 5, pp.123–49.

13. A Macniven, 2015, *The Vikings in Islay: The Place of Names in Hebridean Settlement History* (Edinburgh).

14. For a discussion see T O Clancy, 2008, 'The Gall-Ghàidheil and Galloway', *Journal of Scottish Name Studies* 2, pp.19–50; Jennings & Kruse, 'From Dál Riata to the Gall-Ghàidheil'.

15. P Gammeltoft, 2006, 'Scandinavian Influence on Hebridean Island Names', in P Gammeltoft & B Jørgensen (eds), *Names through the Looking-Glass. Festschrift in Honour of Gillian Fellows-Jensen. 5 July 2006* (Copenhagen); G Broderick, 2013, 'Some Island Names in the Former "Kingdom of the Isles": A Reappraisal', *Journal of Scottish Name Studies* 7, pp.1–28.

16. P Gammeltoft, C Hough & D Waugh (eds), 2005, *Cultural Contacts in the North Atlantic Region: The Evidence of the Names* (Lerwick), pp.141–56.

17. See for example R A V Cox, 1989, 'Questioning the value and validity of the term 'hybrid', in Hebridean place-name study', *Nomina* 12, pp.1–9.

18. J Shaw, 2008, '"Gaelic/Norse Folklore Contacts" and Oral Traditions from the West of Scotland', in T A Gunnell (ed.), *Legends and Landscape: Articles based on Plenary Lectures Presented at the 5th Celtic-Nordic-Baltic Folklore Symposium, Reykjavík, 2005* (Reykjavík).

19. P Gammeltoft, 2004, 'Scandinavian-Gaelic contacts. Can place-names and place-name elements be used as a source for contact-linguistic research?', *Nowele* 44, pp.51–90; Gammeltoft, 2007, 'Scandinavian naming-systems in the Hebrides – A way of understanding how Scandinavians were in contact with Gaels and Picts?', in B Ballin-

Smith *et al.* (eds), *West Over the Sea: Studies in Scandinavian Sea-Borne Expansion and Settlement Before 1300*, pp.479–95 (Leiden).

20. Macniven *Vikings in Islay*, pp 11–19, 34–41.

21. CANMORE Site Number: NF70NW3 (NGR: NF 7051 0738).

22. A B Stahl, 1999, Place-Names of Barra in the Outer Hebrides, unpublished PhD thesis, University of Edinburgh, p.139. Further alternatives are suggested by etymological work on similar sounding names and naming elements elsewhere in the Hebrides. See, for example, the discussion of Camus Barravaig under CAMUS and Barrapol under LOCH AN EILEAN in the Appendix.

23. Stahl, Place-Names of Barra, p.198.

24. Pers. comm. Dr John Raven, Historic Environment Scotland.

25. See for example N Sharples & R Smith, 2009, 'Norse settlement in the Western Isles', in A Woolf (ed.), *Scandinavian Scotland – Twenty Years After. The Proceedings of a Day Conference held on 19 February 2007* (St Andrews).

26. Gammeltoft, 'Scandinavian-Gaelic contacts'; T W Stewart, 2004, 'Lexical Imposition: Old Norse vocabulary in Scottish Gaelic', *Diachronica* 21.2, pp.393–420.

27. Jennings & Kruse 'From Dál Riata to the Gall-Ghàidheil'.

28. D G E Williams, 1997, 'The Dating of the Norwegian leiðangr system: A Philological Approach', *Nowele* 30, pp.21–5.

29. D Rixson, 1998, *The West Highland Galley* (Edinburgh).

30. D H Caldwell, 2008b, 'The Lossit Cymba', *West Highland Notes and Queries*, ser. 3.12, pp.3–11; Caldwell, 2015, 'The Sea Power of the Western Isles of Scotland in the late Medieval Period', in J H Barrett & S J Gibbon (eds), *Maritime Societies of the Viking And Medieval World*, pp.350–68 (Leeds).

31. C Westerdahl, 1989, *Norrlandsleden I* (Örnsköldsvik).

32. A Simmons (ed.), 1998, *A Tour in Scotland and Voyage to the Hebrides 1772 by Thomas Pennant* (Edinburgh), p.209.

33. M Coventry, 2006, *The Castles of Scotland*, 4th edn (Edinburgh), pp.22–38.

34. See for example, Macniven, *Vikings in Islay*, pp.55–60.

35. G Fisher, 1956, 'Borg', in J Brøndstedt, J Danstrup & L Jacobsen (eds), *Kulturhistorisk leksikon for nordisk middelalder fra vikingetid til reformationstid Bd. II* (København), pp.135–8; B Solberg, 2003, *Jernalderen i Norge: c.500 f.Kr–1030 e.Kr* (Oslo); E Roesdahl, S M Sindbaek, A Pedersen & D M Wilson (eds), 2014, *Aggersborg. The Viking Age settlement and fortress* (Højbjerg); for Sweden see also Riksantikvarieämbetet's online search engine *Fornsök* (http://www.fmis.raa.se/cocoon/fornsok/search.html).

36. B Myhre, 1998, 'The Archaeology of the Early Viking Age in Norway', in H B Clarke, M Ní Mhaonaigh *et al.* (eds), *Ireland and Scandinavia in the Early Viking Age* (Dublin), pp.3–35.

37. F-A Stylegar & O Grimm, 2004, 'Court sites in SW Norway – reflections of a Roman period political organisation?', *Norwegian Archaeological Review* 37.2, pp.111–33; A E Herteig, 1989, 'The Coastal Courtyard-Sites in Norway from the 1st Millenium AD', in H Galinié (ed.) *Les Mondes Normands (VIIIe-XIIe s.)* (Caen), pp.11–12.

38. E Roesdahl, 2001, 'Trelleborg Fortresses', in P Crabtree (ed.), *Medieval Archaeology An Encyclopedia* (New York), pp.344–7.

39. Fisher 'Borg', p.135.

40. For an interesting discussion of political centralisation in early medieval Norway, see A Kruse, 2015, 'Laithlinn', *Namn og Nemne* 32.3, pp.49–86.

41. Fisher 'Borg', p.135.

42. This term was coined by W F H Nicolaisen, 1969, 'Norse settlement in the Northern and Western Isles', *Scottish Historical Review* 48, pp.6–17, to describe the Viking Age Scandinavian settlement zone in what is now Scotland.

43. *Dictionary of the Scots Language*, 'broch': http://www.dsl.ac.uk/entry/snd/broch_n1_v.

44. *Egils saga Skalla-Grímssonar. Íslenzk Fornrit II. Bindi: 363–409*, A Nordal (ed.), 1933 (Reykjavík), pp.85–6.

45. Macniven, *Vikings in Islay*, pp.93–104.

46. This topic is discussed at length in J Graham-Campbell, 2004, '"Danes … in this Country": discovering the Vikings in Scotland', *PSAS* 13, pp.201–39.

47. CANMORE Site Number: NF72NW1; N Sharples & M Parker-Pearson, 1999b, *Between Land and Sea: Excavations at Dun Vulan, South Uist* (Sheffield); but see also A Jennings & A Kruse, 2005, 'An ethnic enigma – Norse, Pict and Gael', in A Mortensen & S V Arge (eds), *Viking and Norse North Atlantic, Selected Papers from the Proceedings of the Fourteenth Viking Congress, 19–30 July 2001, Tórshavn, Faroe Islands* (Tórshavn), pp.251–63.

48. C D Stanton, 2015, *Medieval Maritime Warfare* (Barnsley), p.195; J C Besteman, 1999, 'Viking Silver on Wieringen', in H Sarfatij (ed.), *In Discussion with the Past* (Zwolle), p.253.

49. See for example *Annals of Ulster* 841.4; F McDonald & E Keogh, 2010, 'Fortress uncovered: Co Louth Viking site of international importance', *The Irish Times. 17th September 2010*: http://www.irishtimes.com/news/fortress-uncovered-co-louth-viking-site-of-international-importance-1.651715; See also the website for the Linn Duachaill project: http://www.linnduachaill.ie/2010/12/03/report-from-local-historian-micheal-mckeown/ (accessed 24 May 2016).

50. M Biddle & B Kjølbye-Biddle, 1992, 'Repton and the Vikings', *Antiquity* 66, pp.36–51.

51. Richard Hall, 2010, *Viking Age Archaeology* (Princes Risborough).

52. *Annals of Ulster* 870.6.

53. *Annals of the Four Masters* 960.14, 970.13.

54. C Westerdahl, 2002, 'The cognitive landscape of naval warfare and defence. Toponymic and archaeological aspects', in A N Jørgensen, J Pind, L Jørgensen & B Clausen (eds), *Maritime Warfare in Northern Europe. Technology, organisation logistics and administration 500 BC–1500 AD*: 169–90 (Copenhagen).

55. F-A Stylegar & O Grimm, 2003, 'Place-Names as Evidence for Ancient Maritime Culture in Norway', *Norsk Sjøfartsmuseum Årbok* 2002, pp.93–5.

56. Macniven *Vikings in Islay*, pp.34–41.

57. Pers comm Jamie MacPherson.

58. A Macniven, 2014, 'Navigating the nomenclature: the validity of Gaelic *Tairbeart as evidence for pre-Norse survival in Lewis and the west of Scotland', in D H Caldwell & M A Hall (eds), *The Lewis Chessmen: New Perspectives* (Edinburgh), pp.121–50; D Waugh, 2005, 'What is an aith? Place-Name evidence for portages in Shetland', *The New Shetlander* 232, pp.33–8; Waugh, 2006, 'Place-Name Evidence for Portages in Orkney and Shetland', in C Westerdahl (ed.), *The Significance of Portages: Proceedings of the First International Conference on the Significance of Portages, 29 Sept – 2 Oct 2004, in Lyngdal, Vest-Agder, Norway* (BAR S-1499, Oxford), pp.239–49; Waugh, 2010, 'On *eið*-names in Orkney and other North Atlantic islands', in J Sheehan & D Ó Corráin (eds), *The Viking Age in Ireland and the West* (Dublin), pp.545–54.

59. See notes on DUNSCAITH in the Appendix.

60. S E Thomas, 2014, 'From cathedral of the Isles to obscurity – the archaeology and history of Skeabost Island, Snizort', *PSAS* 144, pp.245–64.

61. P Gammeltoft, 2001, *The place-name element bólstaðr in the North Atlantic area* (Copenhagen), p.149.

62. A R Forbes, 1923, *Place-Names of Skye and Adjacent Islands with Lore: Mythical, Traditional and Historical* (Paisley), p.318.

63. CANMORE Site Number: NF73SW8. N Sharples & M Parker-Pearson, 1999a, 'Norse Settlement in the Outer Hebrides', *Norwegian Archaeological Review* 32, pp.41–62; see also Jennings & Kruse, 'An Ethnic Enigma'.

64. Macniven *Vikings in Islay*, p.330.

65. Macniven *Vikings in Islay*, pp.293–4.

66. CANMORE Site Number: NS06NE 5.

67. G Márkus, 2012, *The Place-Names of Bute* (Donnington), pp.324, n.7.

68. The findings from the site at Cnoc an Rath on the Isle of Bute were presented by Dr Paul Duffy of Brandanii Archaeology and Heritage in his paper 'Powerful place-names: Collaborative Archaeology in Practice on Bute' at the Scottish Place-Name Society conference in Rothesay on 7 May 2015. A brief report was published by the Herald newspaper the following day: http://www.heraldscotland.com/news/14478238. Viking__parliament__site_uncovered_on_Scottish_island/ (accessed 24 May 2016).

69. A Christophersen, 1991, 'Ports and Trade in Norway during the transition to historical time', in O Crumlin-Pedersen (ed.), *Aspects of maritime Scandinavia AD 200–1200. Proceedings of the Nordic Seminar on Maritime Aspects of Archaeology 1989* (Roskilde), pp.159–70.

70. See for example A Sanmark & S J Semple, 2010, 'The topography of outdoor assembly sites in Europe with reference to recent field results from Sweden', in H Lewis & S J Semple (eds), *Perspectives in Landscape Archaeology* (Oxford: BAR S-2103), pp.107–19. For further material on Norse *þing* sites, see the international Thing Project: http://www.thingproject.eu/content/general (accessed 24 May 2016).

Table 5.1. Galley-castles in the Hebrides and Clyde Estuary: location and place-name context (Appendix 1).

Castle name	NGR	Island	Fordun		Viking folklore	Old Norse origins for name of					
			Castle	Island		Castle	Farm	Island	Parish	District	Environs
Achadun	NM 8043 3927	Lismore		✓			✓				✓
Aros	NM 5629 4498	Mull	✓	✓		✓	✓	✓			✓
Bheagram	NF 7611 3711	South Uist		✓		✓	✓	✓	✓		✓
Borve	NF 7733 5050	Benbecula	✓	✓		✓	✓		✓		✓
Breacachadh	NM 1599 5390	Coll		✓			✓	✓	✓		✓
Brodick	NS 0155 3786	Arran	✓	✓		✓	✓	✓			✓
Cairnaburgh Mor	NM 3058 4485	Treshnish	✓	✓		✓		✓		✓	✓
Calvay	NF 8175 1811	South Uist		✓		✓	✓	✓	✓		✓
Camus (Dun Horavaig)	NG 6714 0871	Skye		✓		✓	✓	✓	✓		✓
Claig	NR 4714 6270	Jura		✓					✓		✓
Coeffin	NM 8536 4377	Lismore	✓	✓	✓	?	?				
Con	NM 7658 1360	Torsa	✓	✓		✓	✓	✓	✓		✓
Duart	NM 7489 3532	Mull	✓	✓		✓					
Dun Ara	NM 4271 5771	Mull	✓	✓				✓			✓
Dun Chonnail	NM 6805 1266	Garvellachs		✓	✓	✓			✓		
Dunakin	NG 7580 2634	Skye		✓				✓			
Dunscaith	NG 5952 1207	Skye		✓		✓	✓	✓	✓		✓
Duntulm	NG 4099 7435	Skye		✓		✓	✓	✓		✓	✓
Dunvegan	NG 2474 4910	Skye		✓	✓	?	?	✓	✓	✓	✓
Dunyvaig	NR 4059 4549	Islay	✓	✓				✓			✓
Finlaggan	NR 3882 6810	Islay		✓				✓			✓
Kildonan	NS 0363 2091	Arran	✓	✓				✓			✓
Kisimul	NL 6651 9794	Barra		✓		✓		✓	✓		✓
Little Cumbrae	NS 1524 5234	Little Cumbrae		✓		✓		✓	✓		
Loch an Eilean	NL 9859 4353	Tiree	✓	✓			✓	✓	✓		✓
Lochranza	NR 9331 5067	Arran		✓		✓		✓			
Moy	NM 6167 2475	Mull		✓			✓	✓	✓		✓
Rothesay	NS 8078 6458	Bute	✓	✓		✓	✓	✓	✓		✓
Stornoway	NB 4213 3267	Lewis		✓		✓	✓	✓	✓		✓
Tioram	NM 6621 7243	Eilean Tioram		✓		✓		✓		✓	✓

Table 5.2. Contextualising data for galley-castles in the Hebrides and Clyde Estuary (Appendix 1).

Castle name	Island	Proximity to: (metres)					*borg* name	*skeið* etc.
		Sea	Inland water	Settlement	Eccles. Antiquity	Early fort		
Achadun	Lismore	300	150/50	730	1200	n/a		
Aros	Mull	<50	<50/<50	150	1800	n/a	✓	
Bheagram	South Uist	1150	<50/750	480	750	n/a	✓	
Borve	Benbecula	730	400/200	180	450	880	✓	
Breacachadh	Coll	<50	n/a	1100	1900	940	✓	
Brodick	Arran	220	1250/<50	1600	2700	n/a		
Cairnaburgh Mor	Treshnish	<50	n/a	n/a	n/a	120	✓	
Calvay	South Uist	<50	n/a	3000	n/a	n/a		✓
Camus (Dun Horavaig)	Skye	<50	n/a	300	420?	n/a	✓	
Claig	Jura	<50	n/a	730	3270	n/a		
Coeffin	Lismore	<50	n/a	720	770	n/a		
Con	Torsa	<50	n/a	1200	170	n/a		
Duart	Mull	110	n/a	<50	n/a	n/a		
Dun Ara	Mull	80	n/a	2000	950	1500		
Dun Chonnail	Garvellachs	<50	n/a	n/a	1500	n/a		
Dunakin	Skye	<50	n/a	250	n/a	n/a		
Dunscaith	Skye	<50	450/100	300	1400	n/a	✓	✓
Duntulm	Skye	100	550/310	60	n/a	100		✓
Dunvegan	Skye	<50	n/a	700	1400	n/a		✓
Dunyvaig	Islay	<50	n/a	250	560	3750	✓	
Finlaggan	Islay	4500	<50/4000	700	<50	70	✓	
Kildonan	Arran	90	n/a	360	360?	n/a	✓	
Kisimul	Barra	<50	880	70	600?	n/a		
Little Cumbrae	Little Cumbrae	<50	280/200	80	50	n/a		
Loch an Eilean	Tiree	1000	<50/1000	260	1500?	n/a		
Lochranza	Arran	<50	n/a	150	1350	650		
Moy	Mull	<50	<50/<50	<50	350	n/a		✓
Rothesay	Bute	120	990/890	<50	300?	2800	✓	
Stornoway	Lewis	150	n/a	350	n/a	n/a		
Tioram	Eilean Tioram	<50	<50/<50	2000	650	n/a		

Appendix 1

Contextualising data for Macneil's list of 30 pre-1370 Hebridean and Firth of Clyde galley-castle sites is presented below. **HEADWORDS** are followed by an 8-digit Ordnance Survey National Grid Reference for the location, Historic Environment Scotland's CANMORE Site Number, the name of the parish in which the site can be found, the name of the island or district if this differs, and the name of the locality (in brackets) if this is significant.

Where an Old Norse form of any of these names is given in the later medieval Icelandic Sagas, it is shown after the relevant name in ***bold print***. Reconstructed Old Norse forms are preceded by an asterisk (*). This information is followed by a brief etymology of the **HEADWORD** giving the source language(s), a reconstructed original form if this differs substantially, and an interpretation of the original appellative meaning. Next comes a survey of the topographical context including distance to the sea, and proximity to inland-water bodies close to both the castle-site and the sea. The final selection of observations covers cultural markers including the name and proximity of the nearest settlement, with a brief etymology as above unless this has already been presented or is readily apparent, the proximity of ecclesiastical antiquities and other early fortifications, and a survey of the wider place-name context. This last section focuses on traces of Old Norse name material.

NB: Unless otherwise stated, the forms of the place-names given below the **HEADWORD** are taken from the 1st edition Ordnance Survey six-inch-to-the-mile sheets for that area. Distances have been gauged on the basis of (http://maps.nls.uk/geo/explore/). CANMORE Site Numbers and other archaeological data are taken from (https://canmore.org.uk/).

Abbreviations

G = Gaelic, ON = Old Norse, SEn = Scots (English)

* = reconstructed form, pn = personal name, m = masculine, f = feminine, n = neuter

ACHADUN (NM 8043 3927; NM83NW3) Lismore
Etymology: G *Achadh Dùn* 'Fort Field'.
Sea: The ruins of Achadun lie *c.*300m S of the sheltered Achadun Bay, and 190m E of a relatively sheltered *slochd* in Bernera Bay (ON *Bjarnarey* 'Björn's Island' (MacBain 1922: 91–2)).
Inland water: An un-named lochan lies 150m to the WNW, 50m ESE of the sea.
Settlement: Achadun lies 730m to the E.
Eccles. Antiq: The site of a chapel and burial-ground can be found on the adjacent Bernera Island, 1.2km to the W via An Dòirlinn.
Early forts: No others nearby.
Place-names: The headland of Rubh' Ard Eirnish lies 500m to the N, joined to Bernera Island to the W by An Dòirlinn. Given that G *doirling* (f) means 'pebbly part

of a shore, narrow sound separating an islet from the mainland, and liable to ebb dry' (Dwelly 2011: 39), it seems likely that the headland derives its name from ON *Eyrnes* 'Pebble Point'. The settlement known as Frackersaig (an ON *vík* (f) or 'bay' name) is 2.3km to the ENE, adjacent to the 'fort' known as Dùn Cuilein.

AROS (NM 5629 4498; NM54SE1) Kilninian & Kilmore, Mull (*Mýl*)

Etymology:	ON *Áróss* 'Rivermouth', which accurately describes the location (MacBain 1922: 38, 154, 170; Maclean 1997: 190).
Sea:	The relatively sheltered bay of Port an Toibre (G 'Bay of the Well') is immediately adjacent to the N.
Inland water:	The estuary of the River Aros is immediately adjacent to the S.
Settlement:	Aros Mains lies 150m to the NW. There are several others within a 1km radius, all with G names.
Eccles. Antiq:	Cill an Ailein lies 1.8km to the WNW.
Early forts:	No others nearby.
Place-names:	The names of the topographical features surrounding the castle are G. The name of the adjacent river, however, the valley through which its flows and the castle itself are all derived from an ON original. On the opposite site of the Sound of Mull, *c.*5.3km to the ENE, the river Amhainn Salachainn enters the sea, having followed a course through a valley draining from Coire Bhorradail, around 3.9km further to the NNW. The element *Bhorradail (<ON *Borga(r) dalr* 'Valley of the Fort') seems likely to preserve the ON name for the valley, and point in turn to an important or conspicuous fort in the area.

BHEAGRAM (NF 7611 3711; NF73NE 4) South Uist (*Ívist*)

Etymology:	ON *Bekraholmr* 'Ram Island' (see MacBain 1922: 170).
Sea:	1.15km to the W over land, adjacent to Sgeir Dremisdale.
Inland water:	The castle lies on Eilean Bheagram in the middle of the inland Loch an Eilein, once connected to the adjacent mainland by a now-submerged causeway. Loch an Eilein is *c.*750m to the E of the sea over land, but connected to the estuary of Bun na Feathlach via Loch Eilean a' Ghille-ruaidh and Loch Rigarry through a series of canalised watercourses *c.*2.2km long. Whether this route was complete or navigable in antiquity is difficult to say.
Settlement:	Dremisdale (an ON *dalr* (m) or 'valley' compound) lies 480m to the NW.
Eccles. Antiq:	There is a complex of ecclesiastical ruins around Howmore, 750m SSW, including Caibeal nan Sagairt, Caibeal Dhiarmaid and Teampall Mòr.
Early forts:	No others nearby.
Place-names:	Howmore (<ON *Haugr* '(Burial) Mound' + G Mòr 'Big') 750m SSW on W bank of Loch Rigarry (possibly *ON *Rygjargerði* 'Farm of the Lady/Housewife', or *Hryggjargerði* 'Farm on the Ridge'). Several Old Norse topographical names within the vicinity of the castle, including: Loch Grunavat (<ON *Grunnavatn* 'Shallow Lake') 1.3km to the S; the hilltop of Haarsal (<ON *Hársalr* 'High Saddle'), 1.8km to the SE; Glac Huravat (preserving an ON *vatn* (n) or 'lake compound') 1.8km to the ESE; Loch Stilligarry (another ON *gerði* (n) or 'farm' compound) 600m to the N; and Sgeir Dremisdale, 1.5km to the W of Castle Bheagram, and 1.1km to the W of Dremisdale. Of even

greater interest, however, are the remains of Dùn Altaburg (possibly <G *Dùn Allt (n)a* 'Fort of the Stream of' *Burg* (<ON *Borg* 'Fort'); or G *Dùn* 'Fort' *Altaburg* (<ON *Alftaborg* 'Swan Fort')) on a small island in the NE corner of Loch Altaburg, *c*.2.9km to the SSW of Caisteal Bheagram. Loch Altaburg itself is only 220m to the E of the sea over low-lying flat terrain. It shares the same, rich ON nomenclature, and ecclesiastical sites as Bheagram. The settlement complex of Ceann a'Mòil 1.2km to the WSW boasts a smithy and a school, with the ancient Crois Chnoca Breaca a further 400m to the WSW and two graveyards 900m further still.

BORVE   (NF 7733 5050; NF75SE12) South Uist (*Ívist*), Benbecula

Etymology:	ON *Borg* 'Fort'.
Sea:	730m to the NE of an un-named, but relatively sheltered bay at the NW extremity of Bagh Nam Faoileann, the important sea-loch separating Benbecula from South Uist. But also 880m E of an un-named, open stretch of coast running N-S.
Inland water:	Borve Castle is 400m SE from the inland loch, Loch a Chinn Uacraich, which in turn is only 240m from the W coast.
Settlement:	Borve Castle is surrounded by the low-lying and fertile settlement district known as Borve. The nearest farm-buildings are *c*.170m to the WNW.
Eccles. Antiq:	The ruins of Teampull Bhuirgh lie 450m to the SW.
Early forts:	Dùn Shunish is 800m to the NE. It is possible that the site of the 'Erd House' identified on the promontory known as Sìthean Bhuirgh (G 'Fairy Mound of *Bhuirgh* (<ON *Borg* 'Fort'), 1km to the SW, marks the location of another early fort.
Place-names:	The settlement known as Griminish (ON *Grímunes* 'Headland of the Halter/ Hood', or *Grím(s)nes* 'Headland of Grímr), 1.4km to the NNE, appears to be derived from Old Norse, possibly named for the headland of Culla (<ON *kúla* (f) or *kollr* (m) '(round) hill') 2.6km to its W.

BREACACHADH (NM 1599 5390; NM15SE1) Coll (*Kollr*)

Etymology:	G *Breacachaidh* 'Speckled Field'.
Sea:	The castle overlooks the inner end of the S-facing Loch Breachacha, with its many convenient *slocan*.
Inland water:	N/a
Settlement:	The small settlement of Uig (<ON *Vík* 'Bay'), lies 1.1km to the ENE. Arileod, containing the Old Norse loan-name *Ljótr* (pn m) is nearby.
Eccles. Antiq:	The ancient burial-place of the Maclean family lies 1.9km to the SW.
Early forts:	The remains of a 'fort' overlook the sea at Port Garbh, 940m to the SSW. Dùn an Achaidh lies 2.4km to the ENE, adjacent to the settlements of Acha and Kilbride.
Place-names:	The majority of topographical names in the vicinity are G. The old pier at Port na Luinge (<G 'Bay of the Boats') lies to the SSE. From the name of another port, Port Aoir Ard-innis, some 550mm back towards the castle, it seems that the headland occupied by both was once known by the ON generic *nes* (n) 'headland, point'. Whether there was a specific element or what it might have been is impossible to tell. 4.8km to the SW is the strait known as Caolas

Eilean Bhoramuil separating the Isle of Coll from the offlying islet known as Eilean Bhoramuil (<ON **Borga(r)múli* 'Ridge or Headland of the Fort', possibly named for its place on the inbound route to the site of Breacacha).

BRODICK	(NS 0155 3786; NS03NW2) Kilbride, Arran (***Hers ey/Herey***)
Etymology:	ON **Breiðavík* 'Broad Bay' (see Fraser 1999: 72).
Sea:	Brodick Castle lies 220m inland to the N of the N end of Brodick Bay.
Inland water:	N/a. However, 1.25km to the SSE, the mouth of the Glenrosa River (<ON **Hrossá* 'Horse River' (Fraser 1999: 129)), may have been wide enough to berth ships.
Settlement:	The settlement district of Brodick is *c.*1.6km to the SSW.
Eccles. Antiq:	The site of a chapel is shown 2.7km to the SSW, with Kilmichael a further 500m to the SW.
Early forts:	No others nearby.
Place-names:	Ormisdale (<ON **Ormsdalr* 'Orm's Valley'), is 2.1km to the S. The bay is overlooked by the mountain known as Goatfell (<ON **Geitafjall* 'Goat Fell' (Fraser 1999: 130)), 4.4km to the NW.

CAIRNABURGH MOR	(NM 3058 4485; NM34SW1) Kilninian & Kilmore, Treshnish (**-nes*)
Etymology:	G *Cairn na *Bhurgh Mòr* (< ON **Borg* 'Fort') 'Big Cairn of the Fort' **OR** ON **Kvernaborg* 'Mill Fort' + G *Mòr* 'Big'.
Sea:	The ruins of the castle lie in the centre of the islet of the same name at the W entrance to Loch Tuath. A relatively sheltered harbour is provided by Slochd Bran *c.*50m to the NW.
Inland water:	N/a
Settlement:	N/a
Eccles. Antiq:	N/a
Early forts:	The adjacent islet of Cairn na Burgh Beg, 120m to the NE, is also the site of an ancient fort.
Place-names:	While relatively few place-names have been recorded for the Treshnish islands, it is significant that the archipelago itself takes its name from an obscure ON *nes* (n) 'headland, promontory' compound. Two of its more southerly islands also have ON names, Fladda (<ON **Flatey* 'Flat Island') and Lunga (possibly from ON **Lungey*, with *lung* (n) being an obscure poetical synonym for ship, possibly borrowed from Welsh (IED: 399), or Gaelic). The latter terminates in the SW at An Calbh (<ON **Kálfr*, 'The Calf'), where the name seems to describe a small islet, just off the SW tip of the island. The term '*kalven*' is still used in Norway to refer to something smaller that lies beside something bigger. It is particularly common in island and inland-lake names (Sandnes & Stemshaug 1990: 179).

CALVAY	(NF 8175 1811; HES NM34SW1) South Uist (***Ívist***)
Etymology:	ON **Kálfey* 'Calf Island'. As with An Calbh (under CAIRNABURGH MOR, above), it is surely significant that the ruins of Castle Calvay lie on a tiny island just off the N coast of Calvay island.
Sea:	The island of Calvay lies just off the S coast at the entrance to Loch Boisdale (from an ON *dalr* (m) or 'valley' compound, but see Forbes 1923: 88), with its many sheltered bays, and easy access to inland watercourses.
Inland water:	N/a

Settlement:	Loch Boisdale lies 3km to the WNW and South Loch Boisdale 3km to the WSW.
Eccles. Antiq:	N/a
Early forts:	No others nearby.
Place-names:	Large number of topographical features in the vicinity still retain Old Norse names: *eg.* Durnish (<ON *Dýrnes* 'Deer Point'), Gasay (possibly <ON *Gásey* 'Goose Island'), Maulaig Bay (<ON *Melvík* 'Gravel or Pebble or possibly Dune Bay'). Glen Noustapal (<ON *Naustapollr* 'Pool of the Boatshed') meets the coast 2.8km to the NNW.

CAMUS (aka **KNOCK,** built on the site of **DÙN HORAVAIG**) (NG 6714 0871; NG60NE4) Sleat (**Slétta*), Skye (*Skíð*)

Etymology:	Dùn Horavaig < G Dùn (Fort) **Horavaig* (<ON **Torf(u)vík* 'Turf Bay' or **Þórrvík* 'Þór's Bay' *etc.* (see Macniven 2015: 148–9 on Rhubha Thòrrnish; see also Forbes 1923: 215).
Sea:	The ruins of Camus overlook the relatively sheltered Knock Bay.
Inland water:	N/a
Settlement:	The farm-buildings at Knock are *c.*300m to the NW, and adjacent on the E to the settlement district known as Teangue (<ON **Tunga* 'Tongue (of Land)' (Forbes 1923: 401)).
Eccles. Antiq:	None, although there was a Free Church and manse in Teangue on the 1st edition OS 6" map.
Early forts:	No others nearby.
Place-names:	2.2km to the ENE is Camas Baravaig (<ON **Barravík).* While Forbes (1923: 450) saw this as 'Head or Point Bay', it may also represent ON **Borga(r)vík* or 'Fort Bay'), and the settlement district known as Baravaig. Loch Baravaig is 550m to the WNW of the bay. Although the origins of the district name Sleat are debated (see Forbes 1923: 333), it could reasonably be seen to derive from ON **Slétta* 'Level Field/Plain', which accurately describes a significant part of the locality.

CLAIG (NR 4714 6270; HES NR46SE3) Jura (**Dýrey*)

Etymology:	G *Claig* (m) 'trench' in reference to the steep-sided ravine in front of the entrance.
Sea:	Claig Castle sits *c.*50m from the sea at the SE end of the islet known as Am Fraoch Eilean off the S tip of Jura (ON **Dýrey* 'Deer Island') at the S entrance to the Sound of Islay.
Inland water:	N/a
Settlement:	The island on which the castle sits is offshore from the old settlement district of Ardfin. The farm-buildings at Achadun lie 730m to the E.
Eccles. Antiq:	Cladh Cill Ian is *c.*3.27km to the ENE.
Early forts:	No others nearby.
Place-names:	This area is surrounded, albeit at a distance, by a number of place-names building on ON *dalr* (m) 'valley', including: Brosdale, 1.66km to the NE; Allt Leac Earnadail, which enters the sea at Leac Earnadail 4.8km northwards along the W coast; and Gleann Ghàireasdail and Gleann Choireadail 3km across the Sound of Islay (see Macniven 2015: 175, 284).

COEFFIN (NM 8536 4377; NM84SE2) Lismore

Etymology:	Uncertain. Traditionally thought to be named for a Viking prince called Caifen, although this seems unlikely.
Sea:	An un-named *slocbd* in an un-named bay *c*.30m to the SSW, sheltered from Poll nan Cnaimh by the rocky point of Sgeir nan Uan.
Inland water:	N/a
Settlement:	Clachan lies 720m SE. There are several others within 1km radius, all with G names.
Eccles. Antiq:	There is an ecclesiastical complex adjacent to Clachan, which includes the remains of the Cathedral of St Maluag, 770m to the ESE, the site of a chapel, nunnery and sanctuary.
Early forts:	No others nearby.
Place-names:	The names of the topographical features adjacent to the castle ruins are G, but of the phrasal type with a medial article considered by Watson (1904: xl–xli) to be very late. Whether the earlier names were also G or ON is impossible to say.

CON, CAISTEAL NAN (NM 7658 1360; NM71SE3) Kilbrandon & Kilchattan, Torsa (**Þórsey*)

Etymology:	G 'Castle of the Hound'.
Sea:	The ruins of Caisteal nan Con overlook the sea on the NW coast of the island of Torsay (<ON **Þórsey* 'Þór's/Þórir's Island), guarding the S approach to the inner part of Seil Sound.
Inland water:	N/a
Settlement:	The farm-buildings of Torsay are *c*.1.2km to the SSE.
Eccles. Antiq:	None, although the adjoining Eilean na h-Eaglaise, 170m to the N, was probably at one time connected to the Church.
Early forts:	No others nearby.
Place-names:	With very few place-names recorded for this island, it is significant that the name of the island itself, and the only settlement now left on it are derived from ON.

DUART (NM 7489 3532; HES NM73NW1) Torosay (**Þórsetr*), Mull (*Mýl*)

Etymology:	G **Dubh Àird* 'Black Promontory' (Maclean 1997: 5).
Sea:	The ruins of Duart Castle occupy the promontory known as Duart Point, *c*.110m to the S of the Sound of Mull. The E end of Duart Bay lies *c*.300m to the SW
Inland water:	N/a
Settlement:	The farm-buildings at Duart lie *c*.20m to the SW.
Eccles. Antiq:	There is a burial ground *c*.200m to the E of the settlement of Kilpatrick, *c*.1.4km to the SW.
Early forts:	No others nearby.
Place-names:	The closest obviously ON place-name belongs to the farm of Scallastle (<ON **Skáladalr* 'Shieling Dale' (Maclean 1997: 33)) on Scallastle Bay, *c*.5.68km to the WNW. It should also be noted that the parish name, Torosay, is ON. While Johnston (1903: 313) suggests derivation from **Þórsey*, Maclean (1997: 36) points out that there is no island, nor a river, which would give **Þórsá* and develop in a similar way. There are nevertheless a number of viable alternatives including **Þórsetr* 'Þór's Farm' * *Þórrissetr* 'Þórrir's Farm' etc.

DUN ARA (NM 4271 5771; NM45NW1) Kilninian & Kilmore, Mull (*Mýl*)

Etymology:	G *Dùn Aire* 'Lookout Fortress' *cf* the nearby Sròn na h-Aire (G 'Lookout Headland') (Maclean 1997: 58, 88).
Sea:	Dùn Ara lies at the NW extremity of Sorne Point *c.*80m to the E of the sea.
Inland water:	N/a
Settlement:	Sorne lies 2km to the ESE.
Eccles. Antiq:	An 'Old Burial Ground' is shown *c.*950m to the S.
Early forts:	The ruins of An Sean Dùn (G 'The Old Fort') lie 1.5km to the SSE overlooking the inner reaches of Loch Mingarry. With the /ng/ in this name not being pronounced, it seems likely that derivation is from ON *Miklagerði* or *Miklagarðr* 'Large Farm' (see MacBain 1922: 167, 172; Forbes 1923: 265; Maclean 1997: 31). The more recent Glengorm Castle lies *c.*1.3km to the ESE.
Place-names:	The names in the vicinity appear to be G.

DUN CHONNAIL & DUNKERD (NM 6805 1266; NM61SE 6) Jura (*Dýrey*), Garvellachs

Etymology:	G 'Connal's Fort'; G *Dùn na Ceard* 'Fort of the Smith'.
Sea:	The remnants of the old fortifications straddle the central plateaux on the small islet known as Dùn Chonnuill, guarding the Firth of Lorne at the NW extremity of the archipelago. No part of it is more than 130m from the sea.
Inland water:	N/a
Settlement:	N/a
Eccles. Antiq:	There is an ancient burial-ground *c.*1.5km to the SW on the adjacent Garbh Eileach.
Early forts:	No others nearby.
Place-names:	While all the local place-names on the 1st edition OS 6in map appear to be G, their inclusion of ON loanwords such as *sgeir* (skerry) proves that some of them are at least post-Norse.

DUNAKIN (aka **CAISTEAL MAOL**) (NG 7580 2634; NG72NE1) Strath, Skye (*Skíð*)

Etymology:	G 'The Fort of *Acunn (<ON *Hákon* (pn m)', possibly the Hákon Hákonarson who led a Norwegian expeditionary force to Largs in 1263 (see Forbes 1923: 230)); Maol <G *maol* (m) '(brow of a) rock/promontory/cape/(bare) rounded hill'.
Sea:	Dunakin overlooks the sea and an un-named but sheltered bay at the entrance to An t-Òb (although probably G, meaning 'The Bay or Tidal Inlet', it should be noted that the generic is a borrowing from ON *hóp* (n) meaning much the same thing, and allowing for origins in ON *Hóp*).
Inland water:	N/a
Settlement:	Kyleakin (G 'The Strait of *Acunn (<ON *Hákon* (Forbes 1923: 230))) lies 250m to the W.
Eccles. Antiq:	N/a
Early forts:	No others nearby.
Place-names:	The headland of *An Cnap* lies 350m to the WNW. Although this could derive from G *cnap* (m) 'knob, little hill, lump' (see Forbes 1923: 117), it could also derive from ON *knappr* (m) 'knob, button' from which the word is in any case loaned.

DUNSCAITH (NG 5952 1207; NG51SE1) Sleat (**Slétta*), Skye (*Skíð*)

Etymology: This fort has long been associated with the warrior-queen Sgathach, said to have trained the mythical Irish hero Cuchullan. As Forbes (1923: 371) points out, however, the queen's apparent name is actually a title derived from the name of the fort, which in turn appears to derive from the local topography. While Forbes suggests what would have to be seen as the extremely rare linguistic Gaelic-Norse hybrid **Sgàth vik*, 'Narrow Bay', a more realistic alternative is provided by ON **Skeiðavík* 'Bay of the Ships/Bay where the ships are raced' (see Hallan 1982: 91–6).

Sea: Dùn Scaith sits atop a sea stack at the NE seaward extremity of Òb Gauskavaig (<ON **Austvík* 'East Bay' (see Forbes 1923: 386)).

Inland water: While there doesn't appear to any nearby on the 1st edition OS map, aerial photography suggests that a patch of land 450m to the E, which itself is around 100m NE from the high-water mark, has been drained.

Settlement: The settlement of Tokavaig (<ON **Tókavík* 'Tóki's Bay' (see Forbes 1923: 401)) begins *c.*300m to the E and continues for another 1km or so.

Eccles. Antiq: Teampuill Chaon lies 1.4km to the NE.

Early forts: No others nearby.

Place-names: There is a large number of ON names in the vicinity: Dùn Sgaith guards the S bank of the SW approach to Loch Eishort (<ON **Eiðsfjörðr* 'Portage Channel'); the very sheltered bay of Inver Aulavaig (<ON **Óláfsvík/Ólavík* 'Óláf's or Óli's Bay'), lies 1.1km to the NE; the settlement of Tarskavaig (<ON **Þorskavík* 'Cod Bay' (see Forbes 1923: 401)) begins *c.*1.9km to the SSE; and Sgiath-bheinn Chrossavaig (<ON **Krossavík* 'Cross Bay', or **Hrossavík* 'Horse Bay' (see Forbes 1923: 365)) lies 2.5km to the ESE. Although the origins of the district name Sleat are debated (see Forbes 1923: 333), it could reasonably be seen to derive from ON **Slétta* 'Level Field/Plain', which accurately describes a significant part of the locality.

4.4km to the NNE on the far side of Loch Eishort, is the ancient fort of Dùn Boreraig (<ON **Borga(r)vík* 'Fort Bay' (see Forbes 1923: 84–5)) in the SW of the settlement-district known as Boreraig.

DUNTULM (NG 4099 7435; NG7SW1) Kilmuir, Skye (*Skíð*), Trotternish (**Þróndarnes*)

Etymology: G **Dùn an t-*Ulm* (<ON **Hólmr* 'Islet' (see also Forbes 1923: 168–71)).

Sea: Duntulm Castle overlooks the bay of Port Duntulm *c.*100m from the NW extremity of Ru Meanish (<ON **Mjónes* 'Narrow Promontory' (Forbes 1923: 265)).

Inland water: Loch Cleat lies *c.*550m to the E of the castle, but only *c.*310m from the NE end of Port Duntulm, to which it is connected by a stream.

Settlement: Duntulm lies 360m to the ESE.

Eccles. Antiq: N/a

Early forts: Duntulm Castle overlooks the bay of Port Duntulm *c.*100m from the NW extremity of Ru Meanish.

Place-names: There are too many ON topographical and settlement names in this area to list. Of the more directly significant to this survey, the long and narrow islet known as Tulm Island (<ON **Hólmr* 'Islet') lies *c.*250m offshore, sheltering Port Duntulm. Around 2km to the SE is Connista (possibly <ON

Konungsstaðir 'King's Farm' (but see also Forbes 1923: 135–6)). 4km to the SW across Lùb Score is Bornaskitaig (*Bornsciataik* in 1689. This appears to be an ON loanword *borg* (f) 'fort', and an ON place-name *Skitaig* in a G matrix, joined by the article *na*. Forbes (1923: 82) suggests origins for the latter in *Skagavík* which he interprets as 'Low Cape', but which the Norwegian experience would suggest meant something like 'Pointy Bay' (see Sandnes & Stemshaug 1999: 278). However, it is also possible that the name derives from *Skútuvík* 'Ship Bay' or 'Bay where the ships are raced' (see Hallan 1982: 91–6). 2km to the E of Bornaskitaig is Herbister (<ON *Herrabólstaðr* 'Lord's Farm', *Hærrabólstaðr* 'Higher Farm' (Forbes 1923: 214; Gammeltoft 2001: 122), or possibly *Herbólstaðr* 'Host/Levy/Army Farm'). The district-name, Trotternish is also ON (< *Þrándnes* 'Þránd's Headland' or the 'Boar-Shaped Headland', or *Þrondarnes* 'Headland of the People of Trøndelag' (see Forbes 1923: 434–5; Macniven 2015: 187–8)).

DUNVEGAN (NG 2474 4910; NG24NW7) Duirinish (*Dýranes*), Skye (*Skíð*), Waternish (*Vatnnes*)

Etymology:	Uncertain. Vegan is popularly believed to derive from an Old Icelandic male personal name, 'Bekan' (Forbes 1923: 171–7). Given the lack of suitable comparators, however, this seems unlikely.
Sea:	Dunvegan Castle sits just above the high-water mark on the north shore of the sheltered inner part of Loch Dunvegan.
Inland water:	N/a
Settlement:	The settlement of Dunvegan is c.700m to the S.
Eccles. Antiq:	None, although the ruins of the church at Kilmuir are c.1.4km to the SE.
Early forts:	No others nearby.
Place-names:	There are a large number of ON names in the vicinity: This includes both the parish name, Duirinish (<ON *Dýranes* 'Deer Point' (see also Forbes 1923: 160)), and the district-name, Waternish (<ON *Vatnnes* 'Lake (or Water) Point' (see Forbes 1923: 446)). 900m to the SSE on the opposite side of Loch Dunvegan is Uiginish (<ON *Víknes* 'Bay Point' (Forbes 1923: 442)); 4.3km to the SE is Heribost (<ON *Herrabólstaðr* 'Lord's Farm', *Hærrabólstaðr* 'Higher Farm' (Forbes 1923: 214; Gammeltoft 2001: 122)). As the land around the present farm-centre doesn't appear conspicuously higher than that on the neighbouring farms, it is also tempting to imagine an original *Herbólstaðr* 'Host/Levy/Army Farm'). Of even greater interest is the complex of names further towards Dunvegan Head on the S bank of the loch c.6.6km to the NW. These include the ancient fort of Dun Boreraig (<ON *Borga(r) vík* 'Fort Bay' (Forbes 1923: 84–5)), which overlooks the sea c.1km from the settlement-district of Boreraig to the NE and Ùig (<ON *Vík* 'Bay') to the SW. The OS 1st edition 6in map shows several contemporary boatslips along this stretch of coast.

DUNYVAIG (NR 4059 4549; NR44NW24) Kildalton, Islay (*Íl*)

Etymology:	G Dùn *Yvaig (< ON *Útvík* 'Outer Bay' (Macniven 2015:168–9)).
Sea:	The remains of Dunyvaig Castle overlook Port an Dùin, the likely referent of the ON name, on the SE extremity of Lagavulin Bay.

Inland water: N/a

Settlement: Lagavulin (G 'Hollow of the Mill' (Macniven 2015:167–9))) is *c.*250m to the NW across Lagavulin Bay (nearly 400m round the coast).

Eccles. Antiq: Cill Màire is *c.*560m to the NW. The old chapel-site of Callumkill is 1.1km to the N.

Early forts: N/a, but there are numerous duns and forts in the surrounding area, including that of Borraichill Mòr (<ON *Borga(r)hóll* 'Hill of the Fort (Macniven 2015: 182–3)), 3.75km to the WNW.

Place-names: The old farm-district of Surnaig (possibly <ON *Surn(ár)vík* 'Bay of the River Surn' (Macniven 2015: 179–80)) is *c.*400m to the WSW across Lagavulin Bay. It is likely that this name preserves the Old Norse designation for the Bay.

FINLAGGAN (NR 3882 6810; NR36NE6) Kilarrow & Kilmeny, Islay (*Íl*)

Etymology: From Port an Eilean Fhindlagan, with 'Finlaggan' being a diminutive of Findlug, the subject of the dedication of the chapel on Eilean Mòr (G 'Big Island' (Macniven 2015: 263–5)).

Sea: The ruins of the MacDonald castle-complex on Eilean Mòr are *c.*4.5km to the WSW of Port Askaig (< ON *Askvík* 'Ash-Tree Bay' (Macniven 2015: 277–8)) on the Sound of Islay (ON *Ílarsund*). The Sound itself, however, is known to have been used as a staging-point for the fleets of the Lords of the Isles during the later Middle Ages (Caldwell 2015).

Inland water: Although surrounded by Loch Finlaggan, *c.*4km at its closest point from the sea, it seems unlikely that this watercourse would have been used for the harbouring of ships. The beach at Tràigh an Luig (G 'Strand of the Hollow') is 11.2km to the WSW. Although distant, this is where the 'Great MacDonald' is said to have had his harbour (see above), presumably at the same time that the fortifications on Eilean Mòr were in use. Given the level of control held by the MacDonalds over the area, an infrastructure connecting Finlaggan and Loch Indaal is entirely possible.

Settlement: The farm-buildings at Finlaggan lie 700m to the NE.

Eccles. Antiq: The ruins on Eilean Mòr also boast a chapel. However, the old parish centre of Kilmeny is *c.*2.75km to the S (Macniven 2015: 269–70).

Early forts: The remains of an early dun have been identified on top of an even earlier crannog that forms the basis of the adjacent Eilean na Comhairle (G 'Council Isle' (Macniven 2015: 265)) *c.*70m to the SSW.

Place-names: The broch of Dùn Bhoraraic (< ON *Borga(r)vík* 'Fort Bay'), *c.*3.6km to the SE, commands a cultural landscape which may have been a Norse prestige-centre during the Viking Age (Macniven 2015: 273–4).

KILDONAN (NS 0363 2091; NS02SW10) Kilbride, Arran (*Hersey/Herey*)

Etymology: G *Cill Donain* 'Church of St. Donan' (see Fraser 1999: 83).

Sea: The ruins of Kildonan Castle lie 90m to the NNE of the coast.

Inland water: N/a

Settlement: The farm-buildings at Kildonan are a further 360m inland to the N.

Eccles. Antiq: None, although the name Kildonan suggests that there was at one time a chapel and/or burial-ground nearby.

Early forts: No others nearby.

Place-names: The small island of Pladda is 1.6km to the SW across the Sound of Pladda (from ON *Flatey* 'Flat Island' (see Fraser 1999: 138–9). Otherwise, all of the local place-names appear to be SEn or G.

KISIMUL (NL 6651 9794; NL69NE3) Barra (*Barrey*)

Etymology: ON *Kjósamúli* 'Rock of the Small Bay' (see Stahl 1999: 214).
Sea: The Castle lies on a small island in the NE part of Castle Bay.
Inland water: The very sheltered and enclosed bay of Bàgh Beag lies 880m to the W beyond the headland of Horogh.
Settlement: The modern development of Castlebay surrounds the harbour, 70m to the N.
Eccles. Antiq: None, although there are 3 more recent churches within a radius of 600m to the N.
Early forts: No others nearby.
Place-names: 600m to the W is the settlement of Horogh (ON *Hörgr* 'Pile of Stones/ Place of Heathen Worship' (Stahl 1999: 212)). 3.5km to the NNW is the settlement district of Borve (<ON *Borg* 'Fort'), which lies to the E of the site of Dùn Borve, itself 300m to the ENE of the sea at Stoung Beg (<ON *Stöng* 'Mast' + G *Beg* 'Little' (see Whaley 2005: 244–69 for an interesting discussion of 'The Semantics of Stöng/Stang')). Around 1.57km to the SW of Borve and less than 50m from the sea is the small Loch na Doirlinn. About 770m to the WNW of Borve are the ruins of the chapel of St Brendan.

LITTLE CUMBRAE (NS 1524 5234; NS15SE14) Cumbraes (*Kumrey*)

Etymology: ON *Kumrey* 'Island of the Britons'.
Sea: The ruins of the castle overlook the sea at the N end of the elongated tidal islet known as Castle Island, just off the E coast of Little Cumbrae. The islet provides several sheltered harbours.
Inland water: The now-drained Tom's Loch is 280m to the W, 200m inland.
Settlement: The buildings at South Quay face Castle Island 80m across the sands to the W.
Eccles. Antiq: The site of St Vey's Chapel is 650m to the NW.
Early forts: No others nearby.
Place-names: While the island itself appears to have an ON name, all of the names around the castle are SEn or G.

LOCH AN EILEAN (NL 9859 4353; NL94SE10) Tiree (*Tyrvist*)

Etymology: G 'Loch of the Island' (Holliday 2014: 96).
Sea: 1km to the SSE.
Inland water: The ruins of the castle sit on a spur of land projecting out into the small freshwater loch of Loch an Eilean. The loch itself is connected by the Crossapoll Burn (<ON *Krossaból* 'Cross Farm' (Gammeltoft 2001: 304–5; Holliday 2014: 80–1)) to the sea 1km to the SE at Crossapoll Point.
Settlement: The loch and the castle are located in the settlement-district known as Heylipoll (possibly an ON *ból* (n) 'farm', or *pollr* (m) 'pool' compound, albeit obscure (see Gammeltoft 2001: 307; Holliday 2014: 94–6)). The closest farm-buildings are 260m to the SE.
Eccles. Antiq: None nearby, although there is a more recent church 1.5km to the S.
Early forts: The ruins of Dùn Ceann a'Bhàig lie 1.95km to the NNE.

Place-names: Many Old Norse. The farm-buildings at Crossapoll are 1.1km to the E. The adjacent settlement district to the W is known as Barrapoll (<ON *Barraból* 'Barley Farm', or *Barrapollr* 'Barley Bay' (see Gammeltoft 2001: 301; Holliday 2014: 62–3)). Loch Stanail (from an ON *hóll* (m) 'rounded hill' name (Holliday 2014: 123)) is 1.95km to the NW, and Cnoc Bhirceapol (<ON *Birkiból* 'Birch-Tree Farm' or *Birkipollr* 'Birch-Tree Pool' Gammeltoft 2001: 302; Holliday 2014: 68)) 2.2km to the WNW.

LOCHRANZA (NR 9331 5067; NR95SW1) Kilmory, Arran (*Hers ey/ Herey*)

Etymology: G *Loch *Ranza* (<ON *Reynisá* 'Rowan-Tree River' (see Fraser 1999: 87–8, 135)).

Sea: The ruins of Lochranza Castle lie on a narrow spit of land which juts nearly all the way across the inner end of Lochranza, providing a sheltered natural harbour.

Inland water: N/a

Settlement: The ruins of the castle are 150m to the NE of the conjoined settlements of Urinbeg (G possibly *Aorainn Beg* 'Lesser Headland' (Fraser 1999: 96)) and Clachurin (G *Clach an Aorainn* 'Stoney Foreland' (Fraser 1999: 73)).

Eccles. Antiq: The site of an old chapel lies 1.35km to the SE. The presence of Margnaheglish, 875m to the SE (G *Marg na h-Eaglaise* 'Merkland of the Church' (Fraser 1999: 89)) suggest an early ecclesiastical connection.

Early forts: The ruins of the ancient fort at Torr an t-Sean Chaisteil (G 'Hill of the Old Castle') lie 650m inland to the SW.

Place-names: Apart from the name Lochranza itself, which derives from ON, the other place-names in the surrounding area appear to be SEn or G.

MOY (NM 7658 1360; NM71SE3) Torosay (**Þórsetr*), Mull (*Mýl*)

Etymology: G **a' Mhoigh*, the locative of *magh* (m) 'field' (Maclean 1997: 31; MacBain 1922: 158)).

Sea: Moy Castle sits *c.*40m to the NE of the point where the Lochuisg River enters the sea.

Inland water: The Lochuisg River follows a course to the NE where it joins Loch Uisg after *c.*1km at a point *c.*650m to the NNE of the sea. The easternmost point of Loch Uisg is separated by around 650m of level land from Loch Spelve, allowing sheltered access to the Firth of Lorne.

Settlement: The farm complex of Lochbuie lies 50m to the N.

Eccles. Antiq: The area around Moy Castle abounds in sites of ecclesiastical and spiritual importance, both ancient and modern. Within a 1km radius there are is a church, a chapel, several burial-grounds, standing stones and a 'druidical circle'. An Caibeal, for example, is 350m to the NW.

Early forts: No others nearby.

Place-names: The tidal island of Eilean Mòr lies *c.*600m to the SE, providing a series of harbouring possibilities. On the E side of the island, within line-of-sight of Castle Moy, is the sheltered natural bay of Port na Sgitheig (possible from ON *skeiðavík* 'Ship Bay'). It should also be noted that the parish name, Torosay, is ON. While Johnston (1903: 313) suggests derivation from **Þórsey*, Maclean (1997: 36) points out that there is no island, nor a river, which would give **Þórsá* and develop in a similar way. There are nevertheless a number of viable alternatives including **Þórsetr* 'Þór's Farm' * *Þórrissetr* 'Þórrir's Farm' etc.

ROTHESAY (NS 0878 6458; NS06SE3) Rothesay (**Ruðrisey*), Bute (*Bót*)
Etymology:	ON **Ruðrisey* '*Ruðri's Island' (Márkus 2012: 508).
Sea:	The ruins of Rothesay Castle lie 120m to the SSE of Rothesay Bay.
Inland water:	There are 3 lochs within 2km: Greenan Loch, 1.9km to the WSW and 1.7km to the sea; Loch Fada/The Kirk Dam, 990m to the SSW and 1.1km to the sea; and Loch Ascog (<ON **Askvík* 'Ash-Tree Bay' or **Askskógr* 'Ash-Tree Bay' (Márkus 2012: 146–51)), 1.5m to the SE, but only 890m to the sea at Ascog Bay. The latter two are both linked to the Rothesay side of the Firth of Clyde by a burn. Whether it was possible to transport ships along them is difficult to say.
Settlement:	The castle sits in the middle of Rothesay.
Eccles. Antiq:	Rothesay and the surrounding area are home to numerous modern and ancient churches and chapel-sites.
Early forts:	Dunburgidale (from ON **Borgadale* 'Fort Valley') lies 2.8km to the WNW.
Place-names:	Apart from Rothesay, and the names building on Ascog c.2.14km to the ESE, the place-names in the surrounding area are all G or SEn.

STORNOWAY (NB 4213 3267; NB43SW 6) Stornoway (**Stjörnuvágr*), Lewis (*Ljóðhús*)
Etymology:	ON **Stjörnuvágr* 'Steerage Bay' (Oftedal 1954: §84).
Sea:	The castle is c.150m to the N of the sheltered inner part of Stornoway Harbour.
Inland water:	N/a
Settlement:	Stornoway lies c.350m to the E.
Eccles. Antiq:	N/a
Early forts:	No others nearby.
Place-names:	There are too many place-names of ON origin in the surrounding area to list (see Oftedal 1954).

TIORAM (NM 6621 7243; NM67SE1) Glenelg, Moidart (**Móðafjörðr*)
Etymology:	G 'Dry Castle'.
Sea:	The remains of Castle Tioram overlook the NW edge of a small tidal island on the seaward side of Cùl Doirlinn, guarding the entrance to Loch Moidart via the South Channel, and the mouth of the River Shiel.
Inland water:	See above.
Settlement:	Shielfoot is c.2km to the S on the S bank of the River Shiel.
Eccles. Antiq:	The site of St Vey's Chapel is 650m to the NW.
Early forts:	The remains of a large vitrified fort can be found c.2.2km to S, overlooking the River Shiel at Shielfoot.
Place-names:	The district name Moidart (<ON *Móðafjörðr* 'Large (or loamy) River/Firth' (MacBain 1922: 93)) is one of a large number of ON *fjörðr* (m) 'firth/sea-loch' names in the region. The larger island of Riska (<ON **Eiríksey* 'Eirík's Island' (MacBain 1922: 169)) lies across a narrow channel to the N, on the way to the skerry known as Sgeir Srath Luinga 300m to the WNW and Port Thaibeirt Dheas c.1km to the N. Although (late) Gaelic, both of these names point to maritime activity involving ships (G *long* (f)) and portage (G *tairbeart* (f)).

6

—

WAR OR COMMERCE IN THE GALLEY-CASTLE?
AN EXAMINATION OF TWO CASTLES

Tom McNeill

WHEN ACADEMICS divide up monuments into types, they usually do so either to construct a chronology or to define a purpose for the buildings. Thus, in the case of castles, we used to talk of 'motte-castles', which were assumed to be 'early' because the use of earth and timber was seen in modern times as primitive and better replaced by stone. There were 'keep-castles', defined by having a great tower which could be used as an ultimate strong-point to retreat into in the case of attack. The types assume a line of development for castles, along which we may place each individual example; depending on its position compared to others in the group, it then becomes either advanced or old-fashioned. The line of development depended on the assumption that the main purpose of a castle was defence in war, and so all designs could be judged by the yardstick of how efficient we perceived them to be for this.

However, we now reject such types precisely for the reasons which caused them to be used. As we have studied castles over the last 40 years it has simply been impossible to maintain the idea of a single line of development, especially one based on siege. Revision of dating, the study of the internal buildings, their design and layout, and a sceptical view of their use in war, have all combined to cause the old ideas to be abandoned, at least in academic circles if not by those who present castles to the public. Instead, we now see them as the seats of lordship, places from where lords governed their estates, centres of administration and finance on the one hand, buildings to project the social and political prestige and power of the lord on the other. This debate is very relevant to the idea of the 'galley-castle' and to any consideration of its use. We are faced with a question: are galley-castles a real group, built for a common purpose and a particular form of lordship, or do they simply share one feature, their siting beside the sea?

Against this background, this paper seeks to analyse the purpose behind the construction of two castles, both of which could be called galley-castles. They were built in the lordship of Clan Ian Mor, or Clan Donald South,[1] whose lands straddled the North Channel, at the junction of the Hebrides, Ireland and the northern Irish Sea, encompassing south-west Scotland and the Isle of Man. One is well-known, the castle of Dunivaig on Islay, sited beside a good anchorage near the good land along the south coast of Islay; it served as the *caput* of the lordship. The other is

Claig, sited on an islet off the south-west corner of Jura, at the southern end of the Sound of Islay. Both have been described by the Royal Commission on Ancient and Historical Monuments of Scotland to their excellent standards,[2] so there is no value in reviewing their description of the remains on these sites. This paper, however, seeks to add information to the Commission's description. In part this reflects the general change in the analysis of castles and their functions which has taken place since the publication of the account: in part it is based on the evidence of the physical and social environment of the castles. Its aim is to re-assess the functions of the two sites, as examples of galley-castles.

Dunivaig is a classic sea-castle of the Western Isles. The site is made up of four elements: a harbour with an anchorage;[3] an area of flat land north and east of the castle, and the castle, itself in two parts, the higher inner core and a lower enclosure (Figure 6.1; Plate 14). Its core is a steep rock overlooking the entrance to a sheltered bay; apart from the narrow entrance, the bay and anchorage are almost completely surrounded by land. The Royal Commission concentrated their description on the remains of the castle on the rock, surmounted by a rectangular, two-storey block, and the lower enclosure, defined by a stone wall with two entrances and containing the foundations of four or five buildings. One of the gates opens north-east towards the land approach, while the other is wider and opens westwards towards the anchorage.

The Commission's description is framed in terms of a 'normal' castle: the 'hall-like' building on the top of the rock, connected to the main, outer, courtyard below,

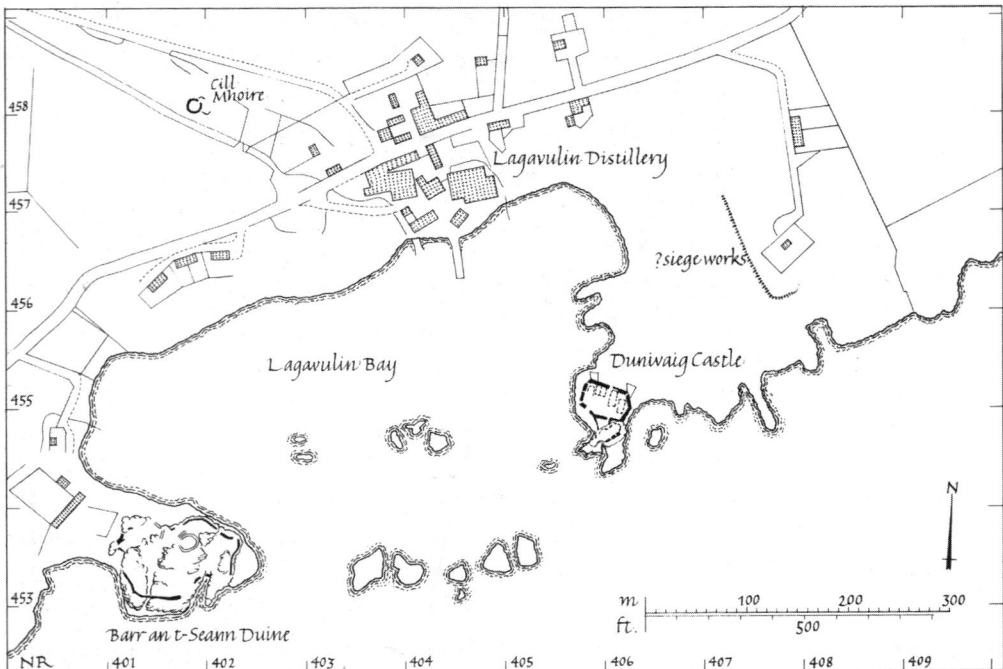

Figure 6.1. Dunivaig Castle and Lagavulin Bay, Islay.
(SC 423754 © Historic Environment Scotland)

through a small, intermediate space. Between them, these elements comprise the castle. Although the castle is mentioned in the 14th century, most of the written history is from the 17th, mainly references concerned with the sieges of the castle in 1615 and 1647. The documents draw the reader's attention in two ways. The first, which combined with the Commission's general caution on dating castle-remains earlier than necessary, has been to focus the dating on the 16th and 17th centuries. The second is to allow a military role, perhaps unconsciously but very much a product of the time of its publication (1984), to dominate any reference to the function of the castle: a good example of this is the way that the wide gate towards the landing-place is linked to the besieged garrison launching a boat in 1615. As with other references, where the account of a siege may help to identify a structure, the actual document is valuable, but the impression left is unhelpful.

In truth, the site does not read well as a 'normal' castle, such as Castle Sween or Kisimul, where the curtain-wall and gate enclose the classic buildings of medieval lordship; the great hall where the public events of the castle were staged, requiring a kitchen and service rooms, and the lord's more private chamber or chambers. The structure on top of the rock, although it is large and rectangular, does not look like a hall. It is reached up a steep, winding path broken by a drawbridge, denying the open public access usually found in a hall. Neither storey is high, unlike a first-floor hall over an undercroft. It has a privy attached to the upper, and possibly the lower story, but otherwise has no indication of any service buildings or lodgings connected to it. It looks much more like a private lodging. If so, on the analogy of Threave in Scotland, Warkworth in England or Askeaton and others in Ireland, where the lord's lodgings are in towers isolated from the rest of the castle, especially the great hall, this could be for the MacDonald. However, these examples of isolated lords' towers have a considerable number of chambers. At Dunivaig, the much simpler block is more likely to have been built to provide accommodation for a principal officer of his household.

The buildings in the enclosure below the rock are long and narrow and unconnected to each other; they are not like lodgings or other domestic accommodation. Instead, they appear to be storehouses, with relatively narrow openings. The wide gate towards the harbour is probably approached from a landing-place, which might be identified as a slip to draw boats up, possibly to take them through the gate; this would be in line with the idea of the galley-castle.[4] Two features cast doubt on this interpretation. The slip is steep and boulder-strewn, and the Royal Commission identified a central pillar in the opening. The pillar-base is now difficult to see or identify as such, but it would make it impossible to draw a boat through the gate, and the space inside is very restricted for one. Instead, it is much easier to see this as a landing-place for goods, which were then carried in through the gate to be stored in the houses of the courtyard. This leaves the castle bereft of hall and lodgings, the key social and political equipment for a 'normal' castle to function effectively as the centre of a lordship as Dunivaig was.

The answer probably lies in the two other elements of the site, noted above. The anchorage is not only that, as described by Martin (this volume), but on the east side lies a bay, north of the rocks around the outer enclosure of the castle. The flat soft, sandy mud of the bottom of the bay is exposed at low tide and is clear of rocks – whether naturally or by human activity is unclear. This would form a classic medieval landing-place, a better place than the slip beside the castle for a larger vessel to come in from anchoring in the wider bay, settle at high tide and be emptied at low tide. It faces towards the second element, the flat land north and east of the castle. Here we might expect to find two things. The first is the great hall, so essential to lordship, and chambers of the lord, both presumably of timber, if the block on the castle-rock did not serve as the lord's chamber. The second is a further settlement, a township set around the lord's accommodation. The land concerned is very marshy and cut up by drains but, as the Commission records,[5] there are the remains of houses there, even a partial stone vault. Again, in line with their cautious dating, the Commission has dated the structures to the 18th century; there is no reason given why they should not be 15th- or 16th-century, when the site was at the height of its importance.

Claig castle is a complete contrast to Dunivaig. It consists of a single tower on the small island of Am Fraoch Eilean, just off the south-western corner of Jura (Plate 15). There are the remains of a small enclosure backing onto a natural cleft across the island, which contains a rectangular stone building, *c*.5m by a little less than 9m within its thick walls of roughly-coursed rubble. The ground floor is divided into two poorly-lit rooms without any domestic features, such as a fireplace or privy. The Royal Commission suggests reasonably that the first floor may have had a single room, with an attic or upper storey above that.[6] This is not a castle for a major lord, such as the head of the Clan Ian Mor. Either it was built to accommodate the household of a lesser lord, which is unlikely given its position on a small island away from any resources, or for a more restricted purpose.

For its interpretation, its siting is all. The island lies just off the Jura shore at the southern end of the Sound of Islay, which is here about a nautical mile and a half wide. North-west of the island, between it and the Jura shore, lies a small anchorage, which is reached from the Sound by a channel between Fraoch Eilean and the Black Rocks to the west. The Sound of Islay is a vital line of communication, but the tides, at flood and ebb, run through it at up to five knots; the anchorage is important because it offers a place for a vessel to wait until the tide turns. To the Royal Commission, the purpose of Claig was as a military post, housing a garrison not a lord: 'Commanding as it does the two main sea-lanes … the Sounds of Jura and Islay, the site is one of considerable strategic importance'.[7] In rejecting a domestic purpose, they are surely correct, but we may doubt its military effectiveness. In order to command the Sounds, there would have to have been a force stationed at Claig, equipped and constantly ready to take to a galley and attack an intruding, hostile vessel. Whether the lordship could afford such a force may be questioned, but we must have other doubts.

The Sound of Jura, between Jura and Kintyre, is some 12 miles wide at this point; seeing a boat against the Kintyre shore would be difficult; identifying and challenging it before it passed by, well-nigh impossible. The same applies to the Sound of Islay. If we imagine a group of three galleys coming southwards down the Sound, with the flood-tide, they would be travelling at up to ten knots and keeping to the Islay shore. They would come into view from Claig when they were about three nautical miles away; travelling at ten knots, they would pass Claig some 20 minutes later. Within this time, the force in Claig would have to see the galleys, identify them as hostile, get out to their own galley lying in the anchorage, make it ready, and take it out one-and-a-half miles across the tidal stream in order to attack a larger force. With a castle at the south end of the Sound only, there was nothing to inhibit a force attacking the east coast of Islay from the north. Claig, therefore, cannot have been built to function as a military post, but its position still demands that we consider a maritime role for it. The answer, which also would involve a body of men stationed there for a significant part of the year, should be some sort of civil control. The likeliest would be the collection of tolls from passing commercial shipping. Tolls depend, not on immediate force, but on the merchants' tacit consent to pay, so that they more or less voluntarily stop at the customs-post, either for fear of later punishment or to purchase protection. Claig's position and probable power would be much better suited for this than for war or piracy.

Such a statement, contrasting trade with piracy and war, contains much ambivalence. To the merchant who pays, there may be little difference between tolls levied by a lord and piracy; the distinction is one of distinguishing between a legal authority and an unlicensed one; but who defines the legality? The safe and capacious anchorages which served to collect war-fleets could also harbour the sites where traders came, and vice versa; after all, not only are the topographical needs the same, but socially it makes good sense to use traditional collecting-points for trade. The vessels themselves were not to be distinguished in their purpose; the ships at the battle of Sluys were not specialised warships, but trading vessels used in war. Merchants were not always peaceful. If we are to disentangle these overlapping things, then we need to make a distinction between what we may term trade and commerce.

For this, trade is essentially the simple fact of the exchange of goods. The evidence for its occurrence is usually anecdotal: either an individual mention of an event in a document, or the finding of an exotic artefact or material which has been traded. While the fact of such contact is important in our study of prehistoric or protohistoric periods, in the medieval period it is of little interest. We know that men and women of the Islands made contact with the rest of Scotland, England and Ireland on a regular basis in political manoeuvres, while the Church provided even wider contacts. What we are interested in is not anecdotal trade but systematic commerce. In this there are regular voyages along repeated routes to well-known sites where trade takes place.

In most histories of the medieval economy, this commerce is defined by the presence of towns and coinage. The towns demonstrate the existence of a class of professional merchants, while we are so used to the convenience of coinage that we find it difficult to imagine organised trade and profit without it. In fact, this is a model derived from the economies of Continental Europe, where they were, indeed, essential to commerce. If the trade is simpler and more one-sided, however, involving professional merchants who traded in a small range of goods, extracting them from primary producers in a region, neither towns nor coins are necessary. The activity may be seasonal and the trading-places only occupied for parts of the year, so that permanent towns are not essential; this does not affect the possibility of systematic commerce. There can be fixed exchanges, especially if there are relatively few goods traded, while sometimes items such as bolts of cloth in Iceland may substitute for coin. We see this in the fish-trade of the North Atlantic. There are professionals, fishermen, seamen and merchants from Germany, Spain and England on the one side. On the other are the locals, Icelanders, Irishmen or the men of the Orkney, Shetland and Faroe islands, who caught and processed the fish on a small-scale, individual basis. They did not need the towns and coin; seasonal landing-sites and exchange of goods served well. On the other hand, a crucial threshold is crossed when the lords of these lands begin to take an active part in the commerce, focusing it on their centres, or moving their centres to the trading-places. This means a new source of income and prestige for them; levies on the merchants; access to prestige goods for themselves, above all, in the Middle Ages, access to wine for banquets.

This is what our two castles seem to offer evidence for. The stone remains of Dunivaig lead us to the idea that this was a depot for the gathering of goods, which came by sea to be stored and either traded or used in lordly entertainment. The rock-top building, well insulated from the rest, would serve for the lord's bailiff or official who controlled the stores kept in the buildings in the ward. The castle, as we see it now, is ill-suited for the rest of the lord's political and social activities, which require a hall and chambers, presumably elsewhere. Claig extends the story of control further. The building of Claig provides evidence for a large volume of shipping for at least part of the year through the Sound of Islay. Instead of being content with attracting commerce to their *caput*, the MacDonalds set out to exact tolls from trading vessels going through the Sound. This shows two things: that there was a steady stream of vessels, and that this was big enough to justify the costs of building the tower and the effort of maintaining a ward within it.

The ships presumably came from the ports of Ayrshire and Galloway, but may easily have arrived from further south, from ports along the west coast of England. Many of them may have been headed for the lands of Clan Donald South, but many must also have been headed further north, to Mull and beyond. In the building of the two castles, the MacDonalds of Clan Ian Mor showed themselves keenly interested in commerce, in both controlling and profiting from it. The Gaelic lordships of Ulster have been shown to have taken part in such systematic commerce; crucially, we can see how their castles were in some cases sited so as to take part in, and control, the trading-places.[8]

The MacDonalds of Dunivaig had since *c*.1400 controlled the northern part of east Antrim, the Glens. During the middle of the 16th century, or some time before, they expanded their lands to take over the north coast of the county. In 1565 the MacDonalds had a castle called the New castle or Ballycastle, the present name of the place. The same site is also recorded under two other names, English and Irish, but both naming it as a market. In 1568, and on other occasions afterwards, English soldiers are recorded as camping there, at 'Market Town Bay'. The friary there and the river are called after the Irish *margaidh* (anglicised 'Margy'), meaning a market.[9] Like their fellow lords westwards along the Ulster coast, the MacDonalds were closely involved in commerce, in this case probably the sale of salmon for wine and, later, guns. The remains of Dunivaig, however, are likely to be older, probably of the 15th century, and fit well with this interpretation of a commercial use under direct lordly control.

This reasoning may well have a bearing on galley-castles in general. As a term, it is perhaps one of those which, as noted above, are applied to a variety of castles. Indeed, the two examined here have little in common beyond their coastal location. More importantly, it has also attracted a connotation or association with a picture of lords who used the sea for wars and piracy. As so often, it is the episodes of violence which attract the attention of the writers of contemporary chronicles, get repeated and embroidered through folk-tales, and get picked up by historians because they are the only references that they have to their contemporary use. This is the case with the account of Dunivaig, but the references are late and to only two episodes in its history. The image of sea-borne conflict carries over into the picture of Claig as controlling the seas around it militarily. By contrast, a study of the remaining structures takes us in an opposite direction, from war to commerce.

Two important questions remain. One is whether other sites can also be re-interpreted in the same way or whether this is something which only affected the southern Inner Hebrides. It seems very unlikely that the economic pattern implied in Clan Ian Mor's lands did not spread to other lordships, if only because they, too, needed to import wine and arms. The second is: what were the goods being traded out of the Islands? In Ulster the traders came above all for salmon. In South-West Ireland it was herring which provided the staple trade.[10] The fish-trade grew enormously in late-medieval Europe, from Ireland to Norway, the Northern Isles and Iceland, while both herring and salmon are found in the Hebrides. Again it seems most unlikely that the commerce would not have spread to the rest of the Western Isles. If so, we might look at some of the galley-castle sites with different eyes, less as the bases of romantic warriors and more as the centres of lords with a real interest in promoting and controlling trade.

Notes

1. S Kingston, 2004, *Ulster and the Isles in the Fifteenth Century* (Dublin), gives an account of this lordship, but very much from a political-military viewpoint.
2. RCAHMS, 1984, *Argyll 5, Islay, Jura, Colonsay and Jura* (Edinburgh), no. 400, pp.263–4; no. 403, pp.268–75.
3. C Martin, 2014b, 'A Maritime Dominion – sea power and the Lordship', in R D Oram (ed.), *The Lordship of the Isles*, pp.176–99 (Leiden), illus 7.1 shows it at high tide.
4. Martin, 'Maritime Dominion', p.180.
5. RCAHMS, *Argyll 5*, p.274.
6. RCAHMS, *Argyll 5*, p.273.

7. RCAHMS, *Argyll 5*, p.263.

8. M Gardiner & T E McNeill, 2016, 'Sea-borne trade and the commercialization of fifteenth and sixteenth century Ulster', *Proceedings of the Royal Irish Academy* 116.C, pp.1–34.

9. T E McNeill, 2004, 'Excavations at Dunineny castle, Co. Antrim', *Medieval Archaeology* 48, p.191.

10. C Breen, 2001, 'The maritime cultural landscape in Gaelic Ireland', in P J Duffy, D Edwards & E Fitzpatrick (eds), *Gaelic Ireland c.1250–c.1650; land, lordship and settlement* (Dublin), pp.418–35; C Kelleher, 2007, 'The Gaelic O'Driscoll lords of Baltimore, Co. Cork', in L Doran & J Littleton (eds), *Lordship in medieval Ireland* (Dublin), pp.130–59.

7

Construction of Galley-Castles – Materials and Sources

Jamie MacPherson

This is a piece of stone from Kisimul Castle, which we had analysed by the British Geological Survey (BGS). I have got a wet cloth which I will hand round with it in order to keep the clean surface damp. What I want you to look at is the strata in the stone, because there was a conundrum with that 'green' stone. From 2009 until the end of last year I was working closely with the Macneil family on Kisimul Castle. Rory Macneil's father, Ian Roderick, had identified South Uist as a potential source of that stone. However, every time we mentioned that particular stone, and its potential source, to geologists, they would say 'Oh no. It doesn't come from there', and I would say 'Where does it come from?', and they would say 'Well we don't know'. So today I have a big exclusive to reveal.

I am going to read to you some of the information from the BGS report. Then we will discuss where the bulk of the stone for Kisimul came from, and how the lime mortar was made. I am also going to discuss an outreach project relating to traditional materials and techniques for building such galley-castles. That slide shows the light from the experimental lime-kiln which you can still see just on the shore here in Castlebay, which was great fun.

Within the area I now cover on behalf of HES I look after 56 separate monuments. Of these I chose four galley-castles to have their masonry scientifically analysed – Sween, Skipness, Dunstaffnage and Kilchurn. This is useful information for when we are stone-matching for repairs in conserving these monuments. The BGS were commissioned by Historic Scotland to assess the character and provenance of 'decorative stones' in these four 'galley-castles' in Argyll.[1] A single sample of 'decorative stone' from Kisimul Castle was included in the assessment – the one I have passed around. Why were these particular castles selected?

Decorative stones

The term 'decorative stone' is used here to refer to any stone which would have been selected to stand out visually or to perform a particular function in the castle masonry. In this context it includes easily-worked, or visually-distinctive stone that was used to form, for example, window and door surrounds, copes, quoins and corbels, lintels and sills.

The main bedrock in Argyll is a thick sequence of sedimentary strata with intrusions and extrusions of igneous rock (the Dalradian Supergroup). The entire sequence was folded and metamorphosed during a major geological event (the Caledonian Orogeny) 470 million years ago. The evidence from the BGS study suggests that metamorphic, sedimentary and igneous rocks from the Dalradian Supergroup were selected for their functional properties during the construction of the Argyll galley-castles; they are not from a common source, and were probably collected from the nearest available source of the strongest foliated stone that was known to the castle builders. All the metamorphosed rock in the Dalradian Supergroup has a weak-to-strong *foliation* (a planar, parallel arrangement of the constituent minerals along which the rock splits preferentially, producing tabular blocks).

Outcrops of sandstone are relatively rare in Argyll, but small exposures occur in several localities close to the mainland coast and on some of the outlying islands. Beds of Devonian sandstone crop out close to the coast between Dunstaffnage and Knapdale. In places, sandstone strata of Carboniferous, Permian, Triassic, Jurassic and Cretaceous age crop out in coastal exposures where they are preserved beneath beds of Palaeogene lava that erupted due to a period of rapid crustal thinning as the Atlantic Ocean opened 60 million years ago. In all the Argyll castles, the main walling-stones are derived from the local Dalradian Supergroup bedrock and/or from loose (superficial) deposits lying on top of the Dalradian bedrock. In each case, the walling-stones very probably would have been sourced close to the castle.

Castle Sween

In Castle Sween tabular blocks of metamafite, used mainly to form lintels and sills, were almost certainly sourced from outcrops close to the shore of Loch Sween, possibly including the nearby quarries at Doide. The main decorative stone is light brownish-grey, poorly consolidated aeolian (desert) sandstone. An outcrop of stone with similar characteristics is described in BGS records at Muasdale on the west coast of Kintyre, and is considered to be the likeliest source of the sandstone dressings in Castle Sween, though further evaluation is required to test this.

Skipness Castle

In Skipness Castle tabular blocks of the local bedrock have been used to form lintels and sills. The original (and main) decorative stone is pink sandstone which is typical of Permian sandstones and almost certainly came from Arran. Blocks of white sandstone were used in the 16th century to form structural corbels on the tower, and as scattered replacements for pink sandstone dressings. This sandstone shares several characteristics with the pink sandstone and may be a 'bleached' Permian sandstone from Arran.

Dunstaffnage Castle

The oldest sandstones in Dunstaffnage Castle (Plate 7), a white-to-buff and a light-buff sandstone, are likely to be Carboniferous sandstones, and probably come from the Inninmore Bay/Ardtornish area of Morvern. Tabular blocks of purplish Devonian sandstone, probably from nearby outcrops of the Kerrera Sandstone Formation, were introduced in the 16th century and used to form arched openings, lintels and sills and some walling-stone blocks. Blocks of white sandstone have been used to form two fireplaces in the 16th-century dwelling-house, and a large column (possibly a recycled lintel?) now supporting a more recent stairway. This sandstone may have been sourced from the Lochaline White Sandstone Formation, at Lochaline in Morvern. A single tabular block of pyrite-bearing metamorphosed mudstone has been used to form a lintel in the 16th-century dwelling-house. This is likely to have come from the Easdale Slate Formation, probably from the Easdale and 'slate islands' area.

Kilchurn Castle

In Kilchurn Castle, virtually all the decorative stones consist of metamorphosed igneous rock. There may be two types: metamorphosed intrusive mafic igneous rock, and metamorphosed pyroclastic rock. Both were probably sourced from outcrops around the north end of Loch Awe. In the three other Argyll castles most of the decorative stone is sandstone, but a small proportion is flaggy metamorphosed rock. The sandstones have come from many sources, probably all of which were in the Argyll coast and Arran area. The castle-builders were clearly prepared to transport these 'decorative stones' over considerable distances by sea.

From the scientific evidence produced by the BGS, it was possible to map out the sourcing of the 'decorative stone' for the four Argyll castles. Figure 7.1 (p.104) shows this very well. With the science to back it up, the map perhaps starts to pose more intriguing questions about trade and co-operation between those who controlled the wider landscapes and contexts of these galley-castles at the time of their construction and/or alteration. I doubt very much that the MacFarlanes? who built Dunstaffnage originally also controlled the south of Mull, or the Morvern peninsula. The quantity of stone, and the time it would take to win it from source and transport it, perhaps suggest a degree of planned, seasonal co-operation and shared knowledge of resources? Perhaps this also explains some of the common construction details we see in the castles, if the castle-builder were also sharing construction techniques, or as trends and fashions in construction came and went? The rarity of sandstone in Argyll, as the BGS report noted, makes it a valuable resource even today, and the natural exposure of it on the coastline lent itself usefully to sea transportation in history as it does today (for example the Lochaline silica mine reopened in 2012, and ships sand to Merseyside for processing).

The themes below are described from first-hand experience.

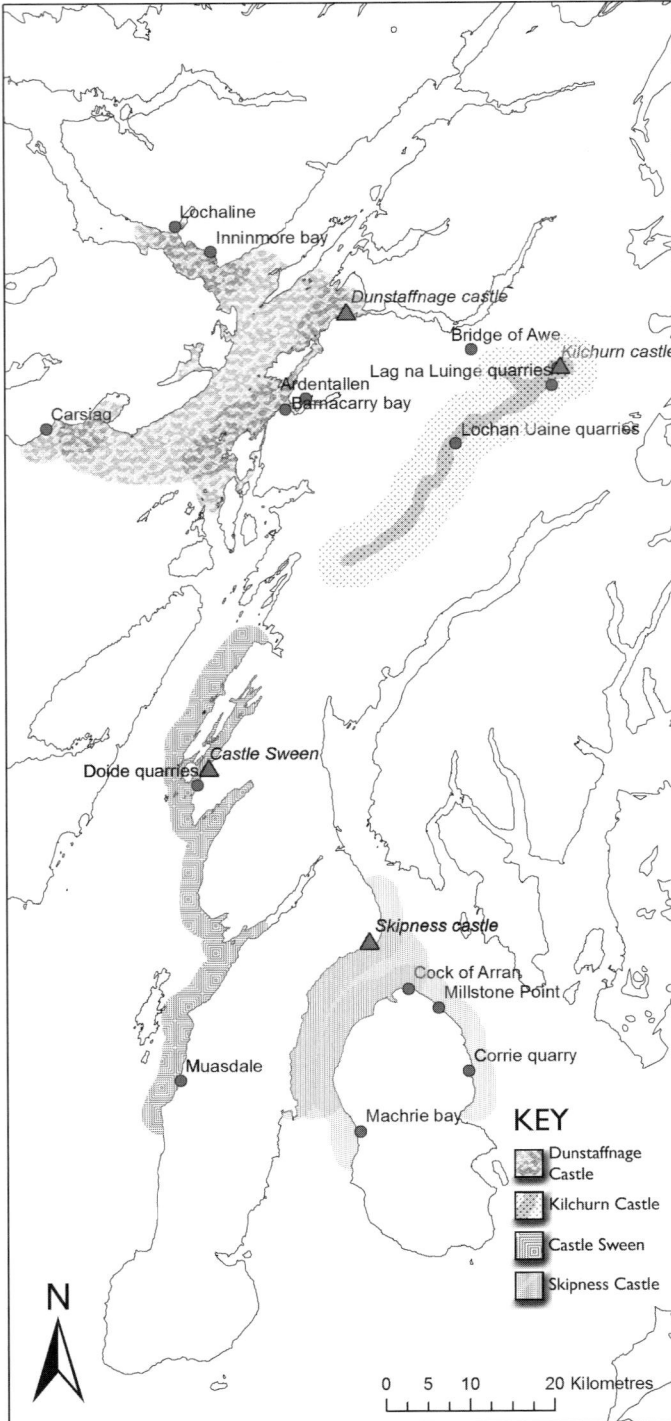

Figure 7.1. Map showing sources of building stone.
(Janette MacPherson, and Stacie Allan (HES))

Kisimul mass-masonry

The term 'mass-masonry' is used here to describe all stone used in the construction of the castle which falls outwith the 'decorative stone' description. Mass-masonry therefore represents the bulk masonry forming the mass of the castle. Kisimul is slightly different from the other four castles analysed here, in that there is no immediate source of even a proportion of mass-masonry to hand at site, or even within its Castlebay context. The local geology simply does not permit this. Built on an island as it was, all material would have been brought in by sea, and the importance of sea transportation here is tangible. Sourcing the quantity of stone required to construct Kisimul was only made possible through a knowledge of the seas and the geology elsewhere around Barra and surrounding islands.

I was keen to investigate and attain knowledge of where the Kisimul masonry may have come from. Three potential sources for the bulk of the masonry used in the construction of Kisimul were suggested to me by Calum MacNeil, Nasg. These were Ard a Caolas on Vatersay, Rubha Mor, and one potential site on Sandray. All of these are coastal. Calum had advised of the traditional technique of heating the rock with fires, and allowing the tide to quench it in order to crack it and separate transportable portions of stone out of the bedrock. On visiting the first two locations on foot (I was unable to visit Sandray) I was struck by how inaccessible these locations are by land. I took the time to explore these areas and assess how rock could have been won.

Ard a Caolas

Ard a Caolas covers a large area of coastline, and the geology changes as you round the headland, as I did, from south to north. A promising start was made in terms of the type of rock evident, but the distance to the shore/beach and the exposure to the Atlantic may have made this a difficult quarry-source. Continuing round the headland, the viability of the coast as a quarry dropped off to virtually nil as the shoreline became steep and dangerous. Further on, and now facing back to Barra itself, the shore becomes less steep and there is a change in the geology, and distinct slabs of rock are evident. Heading east along the north shore of Vatersay, still overlooking Barra, there are some viable sources of slab rock, and potential boat-landings.

There is historical evidence for the movement of heavy rock in this part of Vatersay. A clearly-defined line of rock has been set out, perhaps to define a boundary, but whatever the reason this feature has made it onto historic OS maps, and is formed of stones far heavier than those used at Kisimul. It is noteworthy that this area of Vatersay and Barra has been quarried at different times using ever more modern techniques. The blast-quarry for the causeway is the most obvious, but an early small drilled-and-blasted outcrop of rock near the end of the road at Aird a Caolas was also noted while traversing the headland. The rock is far more easily won by blast technology, but it is interesting to consider the old technique of heating and quenching and the effort and resources this requires in terms of fuel and manpower.

At the end of the road sat a recently-demolished 20th-century house. In its demolished state it serves as a useful reminder of the extensive volume of stone required to build even a small dwelling. Quarry-marks remain on individual stones, and the lime-mortar is shell-based. I shall touch on lime-mortar later in relation to Kisimul, but it is worth noting that the 1st edition OS maps of Vatersay denote the only lime-kiln I have found formally recognised on Barra or Vatersay. This lime-kiln is marked as being only *c.*500 yards from the demolished house. On visiting this location I could find very little evidence of a kiln. Elsewhere, I do wonder if some lime-kilns have been erroneously considered as kelp-kilns on Barra, as the absence of formally-recognised lime-kilns is unusual.

Rubha Mor

The Rubha Mor is part of Barra itself and is just as inaccessible by foot as Ard a Caolas. As I reconnoitred this location it was again noted that the coastline heading east and then south from Brevig was not suitable either for quarrying or for landing boats for transportation. However to the south of Rubha Mor there is a rocky bay with numerous *slochd*s or hollows which serve as quarries for naturally-exposed rock and as sheltered landing-points for boats. So useful are these *slochd*s for this dual purpose, that I would feel confident in using them for these purposes today. Kisimul is relatively close to this location, and in fact is roughly half-way between Ard a Coalas and Rubha Mor. A good amount of rock could have been won from either location while waiting for the right tides and seas to transport it. It should have been possible to travel either way depending on the prevailing weather. At both locations, it is primarily the dark basalt extrusions that have eroded to form the *slochd*s, and its tendency to split into relatively small, angular blocks made it the obvious 'quarriable' resource. Certainly the amount of basalt at Kisimul (now silvered through exposure) would back this up.

Lime-mortar at Kisimul

The shell of the cockle makes the whitest, if not the strongest lime; they lie in great banks on the sea side, where a small vessel may be loaded in a tide.[2]

The quote above comes from *The Book of Barra*, kindly gifted to me by Rory Macneil of Barra. It is a very useful reference to the origin of the calcium carbonate used historically on Barra as the basis for lime-mortar. I used this source myself in 2014 when Historic Scotland built a lime-kiln and burnt cockle-shell in it, using peat as fuel. The lime-kiln itself was based on the remains of a kiln at Iochar on South Uist. Local stone was sourced (from blast quarries) and a drystane kiln erected on the foreshore in Castlebay in sight of Kisimul Castle (Plate 16). As an aside, when I was asked through work to visit Mingary Castle, Ardnamurchan, some years ago I first did some checking of the mapping evidence for the site. Immediately adjacent to the castle are the remains of a lime-kiln. I suspect this is fairly common.

The purpose of the kiln in Castlebay was to recreate the lime used in the construction of the castle. As an experiment it proved very successful, and, working closely with the primary and secondary schools, we proved that lime made from cockle-shell does indeed make a very white lime product. Where I would question the quotation from the *Book of Barra* is in regard to the strength of the lime. It is not immediately obvious how hard a lime product will become as it carbonates (drawing CO_2 back from the atmosphere). Certainly the evidence from the existing lime remains at Kisimul would suggest that the cockle makes for a very durable lime-mortar. The extent of the surviving lime-mortar and harl is remarkable given the level of exposure it is subjected to. These lime remains have weathered to a grey appearance through time, giving the false impression that they date to the 1960s refurbishment of the castle, which introduced a lot of cement-based mortars and concretes. Consider, however, that the castle would originally have appeared very white from the cockle-based lime. The harl would have completely obscured the masonry build, which had the net effect of presenting a homogenous mass of defence and an imposing presence in the bay.

Elsewhere, at Castle Sween, I have noted evidence of the charcoal fuel used in burning the calcium-carbonate source (limestone?) to create the castle-building mortars. A portion of the castle was blasted off in the 1960s and lies on the foreshore below. A good-sized piece of charcoal can be seen within the exposed core of the wall-remains. This charcoal still exhibits the bark remains of what appears to be hazel-wood, a common timber used for charcoal.

Decorative stone at Kisimul: the 'green stone'

Back to the sample of green stone I handed around earlier, which I found on the foreshore outside the great hall of the castle. This sample represents a small piece of the 'decorative stone' used on the wallheads at Kisimul as the 'saddle and trough' detail to shed water off the tower masonry. This appears to be the only application of what is termed here as 'decorative stone'. Essentially all other window and door details and fire-surrounds appear to have been formed from selected pieces of the locally-sourced mass-masonry described earlier. The saddle-and-trough detail is common in castles of this type, and it is fair to say that the local mass-masonry available to the castle-builders did not offer easily-foliated tabular blocks in the quantity required to finish the top of the tower and maintain a water-shedding detail. Archaeology undertaken at Kisimul within the courtyard unearthed a large, apparently unused, portion of this stone-type. Enough flint has also been found in the various excavations to suggest prehistoric occupation of the island on which Kisimul stands.

The sample of decorative stone from Kisimul Castle is very strongly foliated (mylonitic) metamafic rock. The sizes and arrangement of the crystals in the rock are different from the samples from Argyll. The Kisimul sample shows evidence of major compressive stress and ductile deformation (as in liquid plasticine). Here is the exciting new evidence I promised at the beginning of this talk. The intensity of deformation is typical of rocks from the Outer Hebrides Fault Zone, and the rock was probably sourced from an outcrop near to Kisimul Castle. With this knowledge I was keen to try and track down the source, especially if this was located on Barra or immediately adjacent islands such as Vatersay.

Immediately prior to the conference I scoured the areas in Barra and Vatersay where the geology maps identified the line of the fault zone. This zone occurs where an eastern geological plate rode up and over a western plate, creating the ductile deformation mention earlier, and the hills on the eastern sides of Barra and the Uists. Unfortunately, and frustratingly, I was unable to locate any rock of the same appearance as the green sample. I did, however, notice some quarries (of unknown date) along the line of the fault where decent building-stone could have been won. I also noticed further viable locations for quarrying for Kisimul stone at the east end of Vatersay, with good sandy beaches for landing boats. They can be seen from Kisimul itself, and are within easy transportation distance of the castle.

Postscript

After delivering my paper I was approached by Alasdair MacEachen who suggested a potential source of stone with a green appearance on South Uist, perhaps similar to that of the Kisimul sample. This is where Iain Roderick Macneil had suggested a potential source. A friend of Alasdair's had a fireplace built of it. This was immediately of interest to me, and as it turned out Alasdair was able to procure a sample of this stone which he very kindly delivered to my office in Edinburgh on 18 December 2015. The sample appeared to be a very close match visually. Thin-section analysis of Alasdair's sample has now been carried out.[3] The island of Stulaigh may well be the source.

Notes

1. P A Everett, M R Gillespie & A E Tracey, 2015, Provenance of building stones in four 'galley castles' in Argyll (British Geological Survey, Nottingham), http://nora.nerc.ac.uk/511801/.
2. E MacQueen, 1998, 'Barra in 1794', in J Lorne Campbell, *The Book of Barra* (Stornoway), p.63.
3. Paul Everett, 2016, Building stone assessment: comparison of stone samples from Kisimul Castle (Barra) and the island of Stulaigh (by South Uist) (British Geological Survey), http://nora.nerc.ac.uk/514351/.

8

—

Early Harbours and Landing-Places on Scotland's Western Seaboard

Colin Martin

> Nowhere does the sea hold wider sway; it carries to and fro in its motion a mass of currents, and, in its ebb and flow, is not held by the coast, but passes deep inland and winds about, pushing in among highlands and mountains as if in its own domain.

IN THESE MEMORABLE WORDS Tacitus, writing in the late 1st century AD, characterises the maritime landscapes of north-west Britain. This is a region of great geographical complexity, in which land and sea mingle inextricably. Although much of it is exposed to the prevailing south-westerly winds from the open Atlantic, the lee sides of islands and the many deeply-indented bays and sea-lochs mean that shelter is usually close at hand, and there are few places where land is not in view, at least when visibility allows. Most locations can be accessed by boat, and the potential for seaborne communication across the region is virtually unrestricted. Long arms of the sea reach to settlements deep inland, while other centres of population and activity project far into the ocean on peninsulas and islands.

A tidal range of up to 4m induces complex currents as water ebbs and flows into and out of partially-enclosed basins and through narrow constrictions. Winds, according to their direction and velocity, can hasten, retard, or modify currents and sea-conditions in ways modern hydrographers still find difficult to predict. These variables can be exploited by those who understand them, and who know from experience how the shifting phases of the tidal cycle and vagaries of the wind create hazards to be avoided or advantages to be gained. Such knowledge is power, for locals who possess it enjoy an overwhelming superiority over strangers who do not.

Within the orbit of the North-Western Seaways (a loose geo-political zone which includes the Northern Isles, the Scottish west coast and islands, Ireland, the Irish Sea, and the Isle of Man), complex networks of voyaging and contact can be envisaged, shifting through time and responding to historical and climatic imperatives, in which most individual voyages were seasonal and relatively short. Influences and ideas might spread directly or by overlapping stages, at times forging mutually-beneficial relationships or negotiating compromises, and at others violently clashing. In these processes the sea was a facilitator of movement and not, as often perceived today, a barrier. As a consequence centres of various kinds emerged as focal points of activity or influence, each with peripheral areas merging with neighbouring ones to create zones of mutual opportunity, competition, or conflict.[2]

The labyrinthine seaways of western Scotland encouraged 'short-hop' voyaging in which passages were normally undertaken in daylight, during the summer months, whenever possible in good weather (although Atlantic weather is often unpredictable), in sight of land, and never far from a safe haven. Such a philosophy lent uncertainty as to when a voyage might be conducted but relative certainty that, once begun, it would be completed swiftly and safely. Time-based schedules were less important than seasonal imperatives and optimum conditions, a mind-set still evident in the timing of weather-dependent activities in the area today. The philosophy is nicely expressed in a passage from the Norwegian manuscript *The King's Mirror* of *c.*1250, in which a merchant advises his son:

> Have [your ship] thoroughly coated with tar in the autumn and, if possible, keep it tarred all winter … keep your ship attractive, for then capable men will join you and it will be well manned. Be sure to have your ship ready when summer begins and do your travelling when the season is best. Keep reliable tackle on shipboard at all times, and never remain out at sea in late autumn, if you can avoid it.[3]

Sensible seafarers always seek to minimise risk. A cautious 'safety first' attitude is evident in Alasdair Macdonald's 18th-century epic poem, *The Birlinn of Clanranald*, which contrasts the heroic physical virtues of warriors – the poem is a metaphor for Gaeldom's lost maritime culture – with the considered, restrained, and collaborative qualities expected of the same individuals when functioning as members of a ship's crew. Men were expendable, ships were not.[4]

Early seaborne transport

Early evidence for human voyaging in the Hebrides comes from the island of Rum, where a mesolithic site at Kinloch at the head of Loch Scresort has yielded flint and bloodstone tools together with pollen and other environmental material dating back nearly 9000 years.[5] Discoveries from a site at Rubha Port an t-Seilich, on Islay (NR 431 674), have recently pushed the earliest date for human activity in this area back a further 3000 years.[6] These hunter-gatherers could only have come by sea. We have no evidence for the kinds of vessels they used, but boats made of hides stretched over a light framework seem the most likely. Such craft are much more seaworthy than the only practical alternative, the logboat, of which examples of late-mesolithic date are known from the sheltered waters on the Danish Baltic coast.[7] Ethnological studies of skin-boats in Ireland and Greenland demonstrate their excellent open-water capabilities,[8] and they are recorded in western Scotland during the early-historic period.[9] Skin-boats can be made from resources readily available in such an environment – hides, hair, sinew, bone, fats and oils, vegetable-fibre, and light timber. Their construction would use skills hunter-gatherers naturally possessed for survival in a periglacial landscape – cutting, scraping, drilling, bending, sewing, binding, and waterproofing with resins and fat.

Bloodstone is an inferior alternative to flint as a raw material for stone tools. The only source in the Inner Hebrides is Rum, which explains its predominance in the Kinloch assemblage. Its distribution is a useful indicator of prehistoric maritime connections. Bloodstone artefacts have been identified on mesolithic sites extending from Morvern, Sunart, and Ardnamurchan in the south to Loch Torridon in the north, all within 70km of Rum. This suggests a localised waterborne network of contact centred on Rum and defined by the distance a boat might travel in good weather during summer daylight hours. A similar pattern has been noted for the distribution of Arran pitchstone.[10]

Adomnan's *Life of Columba*, written in the late 7th century AD of events 100 years earlier, contains much information about seafaring and water-craft.[11] Both skin-boats and plank-built vessels are mentioned, the latter being constructed of dressed oak and pine. Oars and sails were used for propulsion. Cargoes including wattles for building were carried on board, while larger and more awkward items such as structural timbers for the monastery on Iona were towed. Without archaeological evidence for boats of this period it remains uncertain whether the planked wooden craft of Columba's time were built of overlapping rivet-joined planks in the clinker tradition, but there is no inherent reason why they should not have been. A pre-Viking clinker-built ship of imposing dimensions dating to the early 7th century is known from a burial at Sutton Hoo in Suffolk.[12] Metalwork from the early-historic fortified site at Dunadd, including moulds for making distinctive bird-headed brooches, shows strong affinities with Anglo-Saxon England,[13] so knowledge of vessels like the Sutton Hoo ship might well have been transmitted, directly or indirectly, to boatbuilders on the west of Scotland. Influences could also come from further afield, such as those which might have been brought (along with distinctive E-ware pottery) by the Gaulish merchant-ships known to have visited the area in the 6th century AD.[14] Ships are highly mobile entities, and both the technologies embedded in their construction and ideas in the minds of their occupants can be disseminated over considerable distances and across wide networks.

In AD 794 the *Annals of Ulster* record the 'devastation of all the islands of Britain by the gentiles'.[15] This is the earliest written evidence for seaborne incursions from Scandinavia, though they may have begun earlier, following the North Sea rim and probing the estuaries and rivers of eastern England as their Saxon predecessors had done centuries before. Others mainly from Norway's long Atlantic seaboard, made the open-water passage to Orkney and Shetland before running south-westwards towards the Sea of the Hebrides with its easily-navigated waters and tempting shorelines. There were fertile regions to be settled, centres of secular and ecclesiastical wealth and power to be looted, and human resources to be raided, subdued, taxed, married, or enslaved.

The artefact behind this explosion of aggressive energy and maritime power-projection was the ocean-going clinker-built oared sailing ship. Its origins lie in Scandinavia during the Late Prehistoric period with vessels such as the overlapping-plank boats from Hjortspring (*c* 350 BC) and Nydam (*c*.AD 320), both of which appear to have been designed for armed warriors and were paddled or rowed.[16]

Some time during the Early Historic period the full clinker form was developed and a sailing rig added to create a formidable instrument of war, the Viking longship. Its predatory zenith is represented by the Gokstad ship of *c.*850.[17] Rather later vessels from Skuldelev in Denmark include a broad-beamed cargo-carrying *knarr* of a kind which might have sustained long-distance voyaging such as Leif Eiriksson's expedition to Vinland *c.*AD 1000.[18]

West Highland galleys

From these roots the West Highland galley evolved. No archaeological remains of such a vessel have yet been identified, and our understanding of their form and construction depends almost entirely on iconographic representations, mainly late-medieval grave-slabs (Plates 3–4).[19] The classic example is on the tomb of Alasdair Crotach at Rodel in Harris (1528), which shows all the essential features – a single mast with square sail, clinker-built hull, high end-posts, a stern-hung rudder, and oarports along the sides.[20] MacAulay has attempted a classification of types and sizes on the basis of Gaelic and Norse terminology, suggesting that West Highland galleys were probably beamier and of deeper draught than Viking longships.[21] It is quite likely that the average *bírlinn* (if such a thing existed) was more akin to the Skuldelev *knarr* than to the Gokstad warship, and was a multi-role vessel which in its military capacity was mainly employed for transporting armed men. It is likely that *bírlinnean* had much in common with medieval ship-finds in Scandinavia.[22] The hung rudder was not, as sometimes suggested, a *bírlinn*-specific innovation, but a Europe-wide development of the Later Medieval period.[23]

It is not the purpose of this paper to chronicle specific episodes of naval warfare during the heyday of the galley, or to speculate why such warfare was conducted. The limited historical sources available are well covered in the literature (and see McDonald, this volume).[24] Overall they suggest that three basic principles of warfare were applied.[25] The first two were mobility and surprise. An ability to determine when, where, and in what strength to strike an enemy without his prior knowledge enabled a chosen objective to be overwhelmed before its defenders had time to organise an effective response or muster reinforcements. In an age before radar and aerial reconnaissance, seaborne transport was uniquely suited to this approach. The third principle depended on the first two. Long-distance mobility combined with surprise allowed force to be concentrated precisely where it could be applied with best effect, so that when it reached its objective it was locally superior, however strong an enemy's overall resources might be elsewhere. Unless a countering force was in the right place at the right time it was impotent against an unexpected and carefully targeted attack. In modern military parlance a galley's primary strength was its ability to act as a 'force multiplier', exemplified by the strategic use of air-transport today. A galley's usual role was not to fight, but to deliver efficiently, without warning, and in the right place, the forces necessary to prevail.

Seen from this perspective, galley-power in the Hebrides and adjacent mainland appears to have been applied in two ways. The first was low-intensity raiding by small groups or even single vessels which could attack isolated settlements such as farms or monasteries virtually with impunity. The second, much rarer, form was large-scale incursions when fleets of ships, sometimes numbering hundreds, transported whole armies to engage in formal military campaigns on shore. This was logistically complex and required lengthy planning, which often compromised surprise.[26] On rare occasions fleets might clash in the seaborne equivalent of a land battle, each side sometimes tying their ships together to maintain linear cohesion and protect the flanks. Spears, swords, axes and bows were the main weapons, supplemented by heavy stones at close range.[27] Such battles usually inflicted heavy casualties on both sides, often without achieving a positive outcome for either.

Elite galleys also provided personal transport for the chiefly class and their retinues on formal progressions around their dominions, visiting subordinate kinsfolk and vassals to reinforce loyalty, hold feasts, dispense justice, display prowess, arrange marriages, and grant favours as they went. The process was known as 'sorning', and depended on the elite's right to demand food and hospitality as they progressed. Such journeys were equivalent to the peripatetic system of kingship which was a driving element in state-formation processes in medieval north Britain.[28] The practice was explicitly banned under the Statutes of Iona in 1609, though by then sorning had largely degenerated into opportunistic protection rackets and piracy, usually conducted by landless and clanless 'broken' men.[29]

Seaworthy boats and skilful seamanship can be assumed for all periods, since natural selection in a demanding maritime environment such as this quickly weeds out poorly-designed or badly-built vessels and inadequate crews. Good navigation was also vital. Much of the western seaboard's juxtaposition of land and sea is visually distinctive, and easily-recognised features abound. We can be confident that early Hebridean seafarers usually knew exactly where they were, in cognitive if not in spatial terms.[30] The use of landmarks to establish intersecting lines-of-sight, and so define precise positions or avoid hazards, is second nature to inshore mariners, and the varied seascapes of the area, with their mountainous backdrops and distinctive foreground islands and rocks, lend themselves to visual navigation. Such knowledge was filed away in a seafarer's mental store of experience and passed to succeeding generations. A rare recorded example defining fishing-grounds to the east and north-east of the Flannan Isles was drawn from memory in later life by George Macleod of Lewis, whose family had fished there for generations.[31] Knowledge of changing current-patterns at different phases of the tidal cycle in the vicinity of islands and coastal features also aided navigation, especially at night or in poor visibility. As late as the 1970s this technique was still used by Jerry Stout, skipper of Fair Isle's mail-boat *Good Shepherd*.[32] Depth is another guide to position. Sounding-leads were known to the Romans and attested in medieval Europe, though it is not known when they were introduced in northern waters.[33] These devices not only record depth but also, by means of a smear of grease in a hollow at the head, retrieve a sample of the sea-bed which, to practised eyes, fingers, and noses, can impart useful navigational information.

Seafaring networks require an infrastructure of landing-places, harbours, and supporting land-based facilities. Until quite recently almost all such places in the Hebrides and adjacent mainland were provided by nature. The complex geomorphology of the region has created numerous bays and beaches on which vessels can ground on a falling tide for loading or unloading, and float off as the water rises, an adaptable and efficient technique which sailing smacks and puffers have used into recent times. The safest way to secure a boat when not in use is to haul it ashore, a procedure which can be used for quite substantial craft if enough helpers are available. This perhaps explains the oddly-expressed arithmetic of the *Senchus Fer nAlban* (History of the Men of Scotland), a 10th-century compilation incorporating mid-7th-century sources, which notes that Dalriada contained 1410 households, every 20-strong group of which was obliged to provide two seven-benched boats for the king's service.[34] Why did it not simply specify 10 households per boat? The answer may be that the combined population of 20 households – say 100 able-bodied people – was needed to haul each boat ashore. With this level of available man-power (incorporating, no doubt, women, children, and co-operative animals) vessels of full *bírlinn*-size might be drawn to safety. Paired townships totalling 20 houses have been recognised in later land assessments.[35] For a modern example of the boat/community equation, the viability of continued habitation on Fair Isle was called into question in the early 1950s when the number of men available to operate the hand-winch by which the mail-boat *Good Shepherd* was hauled ashore fell below the required 14. In this instance the difficulty was solved by the acquisition of a powered winch, and the island has since prospered.[36]

Other advantages might flow from the administrative and operational pairing of galleys as prescribed by the *Senchus*. It would foster social cohesion among the crews and their extended families, and stimulate healthy competition, while in action the vessels could provide one another with mutual support, either as a pair or as part of larger formations in the manner of modern fighter aircraft.[37]

Landing-places and harbours

The Gaelic prefix '*port*' is widespread throughout the area, though its meaning is not as obvious as it sounds. It appears to denote any coastal feature, almost always a natural one, which may be useful to seafarers in particular circumstances. Some may offer good shelter from one direction, but be a death-trap from others. Others might be suitable for grounding to load or offload cargoes at defined states of the tide. Yet others may be locations where boats could be hauled ashore and secured. Like taxi-drivers imbibing the 'knowledge' of streets and shortcuts in towns, experienced seafarers would possess an intimate familiarity with these places throughout their region, and know how to exploit or avoid them as circumstances dictated.

Port names rarely possess suffixes which explain their particular associations or uses, though Port na Curaich (NM 262 216) commemorates Columba's traditional landing-place on Iona while Port na Birlinn (NM 746 352), a sandy inlet beside Duart Castle, is clearly where the Maclean chief's galley was kept. It was used until recent times by the annual coal puffer, which could ground on the sand (a concrete enclosure for the offloaded coal survives), and the family still launch their glass-fibre dinghy there. A location on the west coast of Barra is known in local tradition as Sloc a' Churaich (Hollow of the Currach) (NF 656 024).[38] Other words which denote harbour associations include *acarsaid, cala, laimhrig, ob/oban*, and *longphort. Bagh* is less specific. It may be applied to a harbour-related feature, but equally well be used in a purely geographical sense. Similes also find their way into harbour names with words such as *dorus* (door), *geata* (gate), or *cuil* (corner or nook).[39]

Although most harbours and landing-places until the modern era were entirely natural, a few appear to have undergone limited modification by the clearance of stones or the provision of nousts or boat-shelters (this Norse-derived word seems to be in more general use than the Gaelic *bara*). It is often possible to postulate likely landing-places in the vicinities of known settlement-sites, especially structures which appear to be of a defensive or high-status nature. A recent programme of coastal aerial survey undertaken by the writer in partnership with RCAHMS has examined the topographical settings of pre-modern defensive structures in the area to identify potential landing-places in their vicinities. Examples include the complex roundhouse at Eilean na h-Ordaig (NM 497 230) near the head of Loch Scridain on Mull.[40] The mound on which it stands is surrounded by water at high tide, giving access to a complex of muddy creeks at its rear, where boats could be laid up safely. A similar arrangement is evident at the complex roundhouse at Dun nan Gall north of Ulva (NM 433 431),[41] also on Mull. Another island fortification at Eilean nan Gabhar near Croig in north Mull (NM 402 542) is adjacent to a good anchorage and landing-place, as confirmed by its present-day use by yachts and the bay's name of Laimhrig.

The complex roundhouse at Dun Mor Vaul on Tiree (NM 042 492) (Plate 17)[42] is close to a narrow creek with a sandy beach at its head, protected by a semi-circular earthwork (NM 041 492) which incorporates the foundations of a rectangular structure. The proposition that this might be a defended landing-place associated with the roundhouse is worth testing. Another typical location for early fortified sites is on a strip of land running parallel with the shore, to which it is linked by a narrow neck in the manner of a letter 'H' on its side. An example is the fort at Eilean Uillne at the north end of Morvern (NM 544 566).[43] The H-shaped morphology gives boats a choice of shelter from the north or south, and back doors by which to escape from threats in either direction.

A more elaborate manifestation of this configuration is evident around the complex roundhouse at Dun Fiadhairt north of Dunvegan on Skye (NG 231 504), on a peninsula with no fewer than five sheltering creeks facing in different directions. One, some 50m south-west of the building, is known as Ob an Dúin, a name with strong harbour connotations.[44] This site has produced a pottery votive model of a wool-bale of probable Roman date, indicative perhaps of the broch's wide maritime connections in the Later Prehistoric period.[45]

Two recurring features observed at postulated harbour-sites related to Atlantic roundhouses may be relevant. Many are not readily visible from seaward, and this invisibility appears to be deliberate. Dun Ghallain in Loch Sunart (NM 647 600) is typical.[46] It stands on a tall tidal islet with an enclosed bay behind it. The bay is shielded by the main stack and an adjacent one, leaving a narrow deep-water channel overlooked by the dun. There are entrances in both directions. Boats drawn up on shore would be hidden from seaborne strangers, but could put to sea themselves at a moment's notice. In times of danger they could therefore choose whether to lie low, launch a surprise attack, or escape from the threat by whichever entrance happened to be the 'back door'. This characteristic was noted at Fionnsbhagh in Harris in the late 17th century by Martin Martin, who observed that the bay is 'an excellent, though unknown harbour; the land lies low, and hides it from the sight of seafaring men'.[47] A second feature to note is that the natural harbours associated with defensive or high-status structures are almost always quite small, and with rare exceptions would not accommodate more than a couple of vessels. The implication is that ships within a defined administrative or power-focused area such as a lordship were generally dispersed among scattered habitations rather than concentrated in some form of central fleet-base.

The otherwise-natural harbour at Dun Ghallain reveals some limited human modification – a strip cleared through the stony foreshore below the dun for launching and drawing up boats. This enhancement may be seen as a first stage in developing a harbour artificially, a process which might be said to begin when human intervention first clears a pathway up a beach to make it easier to drag a boat. A second (and perhaps contemporary) stage might be to use the cleared stones to create a rudimentary quay on one side of the strip. Such a structure could then be said to constitute a built harbour of the simplest kind (since Dun Ghallain was apparently occupied in relatively recent times this may of course be a late feature).

Such features are difficult or impossible to date, and the evidence may sometimes be misleading. Adjacent to a prehistoric fort at Haunn on the north-west coast of Mull (NM 333 470) is a classic H-shaped natural harbour enhanced by a cleared strip and roughly-built quay.[48] There is no identifiable settlement of any other date in the vicinity, so it might reasonably be supposed that fort and harbour may be contemporary. However a 19th-century Admiralty chart labels the same harbour as an embarkation point for the nearby Treshnish Isles, which at that time would have been uninhabited but used for grazing. In medieval times the twin Treshnish islands of Cairn na Burgh More and Cairn na Burgh Beg were complementary parts of a single castle of refuge,[49] latterly belonging to the Macleans. So is the harbour at Haun prehistoric, medieval, or modern? Or was it used in all these periods, modified through time from its natural state until it reached its present form?

Dating is further complicated by the evident later re-use of many prehistoric structures, and presumably their associated landing-places, into Historic times. A small fortification at Dun Ban, on a rock in the narrow sound between Ulva and Gometra (NM 384 415),[50] probably has earlier antecedents though in its present form it appears to be of late-medieval or early-modern construction, as evidenced by the foundations of a small rectangular building on its summit. A stone-built causeway leads to the rock, and nousts for at least two medium-sized vessels are cut into the adjacent foreshore.

The western and northern coasts of North Uist, with their low-lying machair and loch-strewn margins, have several island duns in lochs, separated from the sea by narrow spits of land over which boat-portage would be easy. Many have causeways, and some were clearly re-used in Historic times. A fine example is Dun an Sticer (Fort of the Sulker) (NF 897 776),[51] which stands on an island in a loch adjacent to a sea inlet called Port an Long (Ship Harbour). The earlier structure is an Iron Age complex Atlantic roundhouse or broch, within which has been inserted a rectangular tower or hall once occupied by a late-16th-century sea-raider, Hugh Macdonald.[52] Two smaller rectangular buildings lie outside the walls. The island is linked to the loch margins and to a larger island, Eilean na Mi-Chomhairle (Council Island) by three stone causeways, and it is difficult to avoid the conclusion that the place was used for the secure harbourage of boats, probably during several periods.

A similar roundhouse-related boat-harbour has been identified nearby at Dun Aonais (NF 856 738), which appears to have accommodation for a vessel of up to 20ft long and 7 or 8ft wide.[53] Two rectangular buildings have been inserted inside the earlier roundhouse. Similar sites with what appear to be attached boat-landing structures have been excavated at the aisled house at Garry Iochdrach (NF 772 742), and at Dun Thomaidh (NF 758 758).[54] Iron rivets have been found at both sites. These are not illustrated in the reports but the likelihood that they are fastenings for clinker-built boats is strong.

The functions of this concentrated group of harbours in North Uist, situated in small lochs or estuaries with associated fortified islands along an indented shallow-water northern coast, and apparently dating from the Prehistoric to Early-Modern periods, cannot be determined with certainty, although water-depth would have restricted them to small craft. No doubt they engaged in subsistence fishing and local communication for much of the time, but their number, proximity, and defensive character might indicate a different function. When incorporated into a coherent administrative structure such as a lordship they may have served boats belonging to vassals on the Dalriadan *Senchus* model, but in more chaotic times they perhaps operated on a more independent, predatory basis. That the north shore of North Uist was a nest of piracy in the first half of the 16th century is confirmed by Dean Monro, who wrote *c.*1546 that 'thair is sundrie coves and holes under the earth coverit with hedder above, quhilk fosteris money rebellis in the cuntry of the north heid of Vyist'.[55]

Small-boat piracy is often endemic in remote coastal regions in times of political collapse or economic stress, as evidenced on Somalia's seaboard today. Particularly dangerous places were those bounded by shallow water from which small vessels could dash out and return but which bigger deep-draught vessels could not reach.[56] Once ashore, the North Uist landscape with its maze of lochs and waterways would make it easy for locals on foot to escape pursuers unfamiliar with the confusing and hazardous terrain. High ground in the vicinity was another factor which locally-based piracy could exploit. Cruising in the open sea in the hope of encountering a random victim was both inefficient and dangerous, for it rendered the predator vulnerable to counter-attack by larger and better-armed ships beyond the safety of his inshore bolt-holes. Elevated vantage-points on shore would enable potential victims to be monitored and the best moment to strike identified. This tactic was used effectively during the Napoleonic Wars in the central Mediterranean, where French privateers operated along the coasts 'from Cape Falcon to Malta, which are scarcely ever seen until they are close to their prey, for they keep under the land in little creeks, and often have men looking out on the hills, so they do not go out until a vessel is seen'.[57] An incident is recorded in Ireland as late as the famine of the 1840s when 34 starving men in 11 curraghs emerged from Blacksod Bay to plunder a ship 10 miles off the Mayo coast.[58]

Another notorious focus of piracy on Scotland's western seaboard was the approach to Kyleakin and Loch Alsh, centred on the islands of Scalpay, Pabay, Longay, and the Crowlins. This was a favoured rendezvous for Dutch and eastern Scottish fishing-fleets in the 16th and 17th centuries. Pabay in particular was noted as 'a maine shelter for theevies and cutthrots'. A little to the north, Rona with its excellent natural harbour of Acairseid Mhor was 'a heavin for hieland Galeis … quiet for the fostering of thieves, ruggaris and reevaris till await upon the pailing and spuilzeing of poor mens geir'.[59] And during many periods in its long history Clan Macneil engaged in raiding and piratical activity from its commodious and secure bases on Barra, particularly against the western coastlands of Ireland.[60] More locally-based opportunistic piracy is evidenced on the Stack Islands off Eriskay, where a small tower, perhaps originally a watch-post, was used by an outlaw, probably in the 16th century, from which he preyed on vessels anchored in Barra Sound.[61] In Ireland, Broad Haven on the Mayo coast was a notorious pirate lair, described by Sir William Monson who extirpated it in 1614 as the 'well-head of all pirates'.[62] Aspects of 'domestic' piracy on Scotland's western seaboard during this period are discussed by Murdoch.[63]

That ships were generally dispersed throughout an area rather than concentrated in central locations is implied in the *Senchus Fer nAlban*, cited above, which specified that each 20-household community should provide two seven-benched boats for the king's service. Like the earlier fortified structures in the area, most castles also appear to have possessed only limited harbour facilities in their immediate vicinities. Duart's Port na Birlinn, a natural sandy cove 300m from the castle, has space for beaching a couple of galley-sized ships. Similar levels of accommodation might be postulated for the natural landing-places adjacent to Castles Sween in Knapdale (NR 712 788) (Plate 9), Coeffin on Lismore (NM 853 437) (Plate 18), or Tioram in Moidart (NM 662 724) (Plate 11). Even castles without apparent landing facilities may be deceptive. Below Duntulm Castle on Skye (NG 409 743) is a groove in the rocky foreshore known as Barr nam Biorlainn, said to be a slipway for the castle's galleys.[64] While the rocky foreshore fronting Mingary Castle in Ardnamurchan (NM 502 631) could only have served small boats in good weather, it is within a mile of the sheltered landing inside Rubha Aird an Iasgaich (NM 492 626) where the modern ferry-pier is situated. Close to Ardtornish Castle in Morvern (NM 691 426), at one time a seat of the Lords of the Isles, a later boathouse and cleared landing at Inninbeg may have had medieval predecessors. The castle is less than two miles by land or sea from the commodious and sheltered Loch Aline, where good anchorage and shore facilities would have been available. However, the main seat of the Lords of the Isles at Finlaggan (NR 388 681) on Islay and the Maclean stronghold in Tiree (NL 985 435) were in lochs with no direct access to the sea.

The built harbours associated with the castles of Aros (NM 563 449) (Plate 19) and Dun Ara on Mull (NM 427 577), and Kisimul on Barra (NL 665 979), would likewise accommodate no more than a couple of medium-sized vessels. Dunyvaig (NR 405 454) on Islay, another castle associated with the Lords of the Isles, is served only by a narrow cleared strip leading to a sea-gate, while its approach through Lagavoulin Bay is strewn with dangerous reefs. The choice of this apparently hazardous location may have been for defensive reasons, since local mariners would know where the safe passages lay while strangers would not. The availability close by of substantial permanent harbourage or laying-up facilities does not therefore appear to have been an essential factor in the siting of maritime castles, though most appear to have had the capacity to support one or two vessels, presumably for everyday use.

A few maritime castles, however, appear to possess no adjacent landings or laying-up facilities for galley-sized vessels. The adjacent fortified islets of Cairn na Burgh More (NM 306 448) and Cairn na Burgh Beg (NM 308 449) in the Treshnish Isles (Plate 8), which together constitute a place of strength off the west coast of Mull, are without secure landing-places or anchorages for any but the smallest craft. A similar lack is apparent at Dun Chonnuill (NM 680 126) in the Garvellach Islands, though both Cairn na Burgh and Dun Chonnuill have narrow landings suitable for small boats in calm conditions.[65] Such harbourless island-castles are best regarded as places of refuge. Both have natural water supplies, and given adequate provisions, stored in advance, might hold out almost indefinitely. An attacking force, on the other hand, would be vulnerable to the vagaries of weather, especially if it intended to mount an extended blockade, while if it attempted an opposed landing against a difficult shore the advantages would lie with the defenders.[66] A well-documented example of such a strategy is the prior provisioning in 1615 of Bhacsaigh (NB 115 370), a fortified island in Loch Roag on the west coast of Lewis, by the outlaw Neil Odhar MacLeod as 'a fort invincible … in the tyme of his strictest necessity'.[67]

The above considerations suggest that, as postulated for earlier eras, galleys were not normally concentrated around single terrestrial places of strength but dispersed throughout kin-based and politically-coherent territories of maritime lordships or other groupings. Galleys were at their most vulnerable when beached or concentrated: dispersal in small groups at scattered locations from which they could easily put to sea would thus increase security on both counts.[68] It is unlikely that many vessels were specialised warships in any conventional sense, but multi-purpose craft which would normally be employed on the workaday activities of communities within the group to which they owed allegiance. Since the primary requirement of war-galleys was to transport armed men, the roles were easily interchangeable. Providing, maintaining, and manning these vessels within small communities would represent a strong focus of social cohesion, pride, and hierarchical loyalty. Fleets were not therefore centrally-based permanent entities but created when required, like medieval armies, by calling out the fighting men of the clan(s) with their weapons and galleys. All that was needed was for someone with the appropriate authority and loyal following to choose and promulgate a time and place.

Once assembled, a galley fleet had no need of a castle to protect it. It was, of itself, a concentration of offensive and defensive power wherever it went. The castles, particularly when grouped under an over-arching authority such as the Lordship of the Isles, provided a network of surveillance and communication within which such fleets could be mobilised, assembled, and directed. Elements of what were probably systems of watch- and warning-posts survive in place-names such as Torr na Fhaire (NM 677 454) and Fire Hill adjacent to the Sound of Mull, and in small structures which may be observation-posts at Caisteal Dubh nan Cliar, Kilchoan (NM 473 631), and Torr Mór near Shielfoot (NM 662 708).[69] A tradition on Eigg asserts that a watch-post on a high point at the island's north end, Dùnan Thalasgair (NM 481 905), was linked to a corresponding post at Rubh' an Dúnain (NG 395 159) on Skye, 25km distant, where 'there was always a watchman … day and night and if he fell asleep he had to die'.[70] Similar systems in Scandinavia are described by Crumlin-Pedersen,[71] while the *Orkneyinga Saga* speaks of beacons 'built on Fair Isle and North Ronaldsay and on most of the other islands, so that each of them could be seen from the others'.[72] The tallest peak on Fair Isle, at the north end of the island, is still called Ward Hill. A report written in the late 1590s notes that fire- or smoke-signals were sometimes sent from the cliffs at Dunluce Castle in Antrim to summon mercenary aid from the Southern Hebrides, the number of beacons indicating how many thousand men were required.[73]

Numerous wide and sheltered locations are available on the western seaboard for assembling fleets, as they were for merchant convoys during the Second World War. Some, for example Dunstaffnage (Plate 7), Castle Bay, Stornoway and Tarbert (Loch Fyne), were overlooked by castles, but many others were not. A list of anchorages on the west coast capable of sheltering fleets is provided by Alexander Lindsay's *A Rutter for the Scottish Seas*, evidently in preparation for James V's proposed 'daunting' of the west in 1540.[74] Though probably not intended to be comprehensive it includes, running from the north: Handa Island in Sutherland; Loch Ewe and Gairloch in Ross and Cromarty; the Inner Sound of Raasay; Loch Alsh; the Shiant Islands south-east of Lewis; Loch Tuath, Tobermory, Aros Castle and Loch Spelve on Mull; Seil Sound and Loch Melfort; the Tarbat of Jura; the Sound of Islay; Loch Ranza and Lamlash Bay on Arran; and the Sound of Bute. Other galley muster-places are recorded by Dean Monro in the 16th century. They include: Luing, Oronsay, Eilean Chalmain (Ross of Mull), Staffa, Fladda (Treshnish), Tiree, Muck, Eigg, Rona and Barra (North Bay). Monro classifies other harbours and anchorages as 'good roads' for shipping: Sanda (south of Kintyre), Rothesay (Bute), Jura, Isla, Gometra, Tobermory, Crowlin Island and Gairloch.[75]

Duart Castle is 12km from the entrance to Loch Spelve on Mull, which was a traditional mustering-place for Maclean galleys. A fortification on the small islet of Eilean Amalaig (NM 707 299) has been associated with their protection.[76] There is a small cleared landing-strip on its east side. Aros Castle (NM 563 449), another seat of the Lordship, is within easy reach of Tobermory Bay, perhaps the best anchorage in the area. A large, well-sheltered harbour at Loch Aineort in South Uist (NF 798

274) is attested by Martin Martin, who noted that a Cromwellian frigate was wrecked in its narrow entrance, Sruth Beag.[77] Local sources report currents there of up to 7 knots. Perhaps this is another instance of exploiting local knowledge of dangerous passages as a defensive strategy. Other natural havens along the eastern seaboard of the Long Island include Loch Boisdale, Loch Skipport, Loch Maddy, Loch Tarbert and Stornoway.

A final category of galley-related installation has recently been recognised. Although most vessels, as argued above, were probably normally kept dispersed, a number of secure centres for building, repairing, and over-wintering galleys would also have been required. One such location has been provisionally identified on the peninsula of Rubh' an Dúnain, on the south-west coast of Skye (Plate 20).[78] Close to its seaward tip there is a shallow loch linked to the sea by an artificial canal. Halfway along the canal are two stone-lined boat nousts (or possibly covered boathouses on the Scandinavian model),[79] set below a promontory on which stands a headland fort of probable Iron Age origin which appears to have been modified in later periods. A stone-built quay, now submerged, runs on either side of the canal's entrance to the loch. Within the loch a boat-timber identifiable as a *bite* from a Norse-type *faering* has been recovered and C14-dated to *c*.AD 1100.

This evidence allows a three-phase chronology to be postulated. Phase I is the building of the fort, probably in the Late Iron Age, its siting dictated by the availability of a suitable rocky headland with a good anchorage close by and an adjacent natural inlet with a safe boat-landing. Phase II is the enhancing of the access channel by stone-clearance and the provision of nousts. This probably occurred during the Early Historic period and is likely to have involved Norse occupation. Phase III, which again probably had Norse associations, saw a continuation of the canal into the loch and the provision of quays on either side of the entrance. This phase probably pre-dates the arrival of the 12th-century *faering* into the loch.

In later years Rubh' an Dúnain was the traditional wintering-place for Macleod galleys under the supervision of their coast-watchers, the Macaskills, a clan with Norse antecedents.[80] The drained loch at Laig on Eigg (NM 471 878), where two end-pieces of a Norse-type boat were found in the 19th century, may have been a similar facility. Tradition asserts that the Norsemen 'used the loch as a winter harbour for their galleys'.[81] Another loch site with possible galley-wintering connotations is Loch Gorm on Islay with its island castle of Eilean Mór (NR 234 655) and potential short portage (1.2km) from the sea along the Saligo River. Caldwell (2008: 333) has suggested that the name of a nearby hillock, Sunderland (NR 246 638), may be derived from the Old Norse *Sjóvarping*, the assembly-place by the lake.[82]

A preliminary investigation of features and topography in the vicinity of Kisimul Castle during the Galley-Castles conference in September 2015 revealed a probable conjunction of all the galley-related features discussed above. The castle stands on a rocky islet and possesses a rare example of a galley-dock on its western side, capable of accommodating two medium-sized vessels (Plate 4). Adjacent to it are the remains of an extra-mural stone building identified as a crew-house.[83] On the shore opposite, where the island's main shopping centre and ferry terminal are now located, is a small protected bay named Port na-h-Airde – 'port of the promontory'. Its landward slope used to be called Cnoc na Féille – 'hill of the Market' – so it may well have been the location of a beach-market of the kind associated with maritime trade on the Norse model.[84]

Castle Bay and the adjacent Vatersay Bay, which within the past century have accommodated vast fleets of herring drifters, would have provided superb anchorages for galley musters. Locally-based boats might have found more permanent moorings, or been drawn up on shore, in Bagh Beag to the west of the castle, where, despite its awkward entrance (perhaps left unimproved for defensive purposes), modern vessels still lie secure in their nousts. Evidence of relatively-recent boatbuilding activity has been noted on the slope at Crubisdale, 700m from Bagh Beag (NL 648 988).[85] For another potential secure boatbuilding and repair yard with an enclosed winter harbour akin to Rubh' an Dúnain we need look no further than 2.5km from Kisimul as the crow flies, or 10km by sea, to Bàgh Thalaman, where there is a tradition of boat-portage of less than 1km across almost-level dunes to Loch Tangasdail (pers. comm. Calum MacNeil, Barra). There, on the site of an earlier roundhouse, is a small unvaulted building (NL 647 996) described c.1620 as 'a little toure of stone and lyme builded on ane litle Illand in the midst of this Logh'.[86] It is not a high-status dwelling but the rather cramped quarters of a few ordinary folk, perhaps security guards or watchmen, closely paralleled by the postulated crew-house at Kisimul. On the east side of the loch is a small peninsula called Am Marbh (The Slain), where human bones and fragments of weapons have been found.[87] This suggestion of a battle hereabouts underlines the importance of the location. The waters of this loch, and around Kisimul's island, merit a programme of well-directed underwater investigation in a quest to understand better the dynamics of maritime castles and their associated infrastructures on Scotland's western seaboard.

Kisimul itself is admirably located to exercise surveillance over the southern part of the Outer Hebrides and its approaches. Though itself low-lying and with restricted views, within a 4km radius of the castle are the peaks of Heiseabhal Mòr (190m, NL 626 963) on Vatersay to the WSW, Beinn Tangabhal (332m, NL 638 990) to the WNW, with Heabhal (383m, NL 678 995) and Hartabhal (356m, NF 682 001) to the north-east. Between them these high-points command unimpeded views over all Barra's coastline and approaches for as far as visibility permits, and from each location simple visual signals might be transmitted directly to the castle. The receiver of such information will no doubt have been Kismul's documented 'Gockman', or lookout, stationed on the tower, who (in accordance with his responsibilities) denied Martin Martin entry to the castle during an unannounced visit in the late 17th century.[88] More complex messages could be conveyed by downhill runners from any of these points in half an hour or less. Beinn Eireabhal (201m, NF 690 043) overlooks the galley-anchorage recorded by Dean Monro in the vicinity of North Bay,[89] and a watch-post sited there could have communicated with Kisimul via an intermediate station on Heabhal, while at the northern tip of the island Beinn Sgurabhal (79m, NF 696 089) commands the seaward approaches to the Sound of Barra. It is perhaps significant that the names of all six peaks end in the Norse root *bhal* (hill), and are the only such hill names recorded on the 1:25,000 OS Map of Barra and the Small Isles.[90] Norse names in the Hebrides are often associated with navigation and related matters, and as well as being prominent landmarks from seaward this group of distinctive and distinctively-named peaks are admirably placed to have served as lookout points in a postulated Kisimul-centred network of maritime surveillance and communication.

These observations underline the timeliness of Ian Macneil's call in 2002 for the special character of castles on Scotland's western seaboard to be recognised.[91] Most were indeed galley-castles, since their coastal locations, frequent topographical intervisibility, and the maritime mobility that connected them, imply systems of deploying and controlling oared sailing warships in ways their land-bound cousins could not emulate. But in other respects they functioned conventionally as places of strength and surveillance, statements of power and prestige, accommodation for elites and their retinues, focuses of hospitality and allegiance, prisons, storehouses, administrative and judicial centres, just as castles did elsewhere. It is the maritime element which distinguishes these particular strongholds, and while they will often have maintained a close military association with galleys and galley-related warfare, their sea-dominated environments would have involved them in much else besides – the exploitation of maritime resources, markets, trade, taxation, and the projection of seaborne power and influence in various guises. So why not broaden the definition and call them simply 'maritime castles'?

Notes

1. H Mattingly (transl.), 1948, *Tacitus on Britain and Germany* (Harmondsworth), p.61.
2. B Cunliffe, 2001, *Facing the Ocean* (Oxford), pp.9–63; J C Henderson, 2007, *The Atlantic Iron Age* (Abingdon), pp.27–56.
3. *The King's Mirror (Speculum Regale – Konungs Skuggsjá)*, transl. L M Larsen, 1917 (New York), pp.83–4.
4. J MacAulay, 1996, *Birlinn: Longships of the Hebrides* (Cambridge), pp.73–109; C J M Martin, 2014b, 'A Maritime Dominion – Sea Power and the Lordship', in R D Oram (ed.), *The Lordship of the Isles* (Leiden), pp.178–9.
5. C R Wickham-Jones, 1990, *Rhum: Mesolithic and Later Sites at Kinloch, Excavations 1984–86* (Edinburgh).
6. *Current Archaeology* 319, 2016, p.6.
7. O Crumlin-Pedersen, 2010, *Archaeology and the Sea in Scandinavia and Britain* (Roskilde), p.53.
8. C MacCárthaigh (ed.), 2008, *Traditional Boats of Ireland* (Cork), pp.417–578; H C Petersen, 1986, *Skinboats of Greenland* (Roskilde).
9. C J M Martin, 2009, 'Maritime Transport on the Western Seaboard from Prehistory to the Nineteenth Century', in K Veitch (ed.), *Transport and Communications* (Edinburgh), pp.141–2.
10. Wickham-Jones, *Rhum*, pp.84–90; C R Wickham-Jones, 1986, 'The Procurement and Use of Stone for Flaked Tools in Prehistoric Scotland', *PSAS* 116, pp.1–10.

11. *Adomnán's Life of Columba*, ed. and transl. A O Anderson & M O Anderson, 1961 (Edinburgh).

12. R Bruce-Mitford, 1975, *The Sutton Hoo Ship Burial, vol. 1: excavations, background, the ship, dating, and inventory* (London).

13. M R Nieke, 2004, 'Secular Society from the Iron Age to Dálriata and the Kingdoms of the Scots', in D Omand (ed.), *The Argyll Book* (Edinburgh), pp.66–70, pl.18.

14. Cunliffe, *Facing the Ocean* pp.480–81.

15. B E Crawford, 1987, *Scandinavian Scotland* (Leicester), p.40.

16. Crumlin-Pederson, *Archaeology and the Sea*, pp.63–8.

17. A W Brøgger & H Shetelig, 1971, *The Viking Ships: Their Ancestry and Evolution* (London), pp.72–103.

18. J Graham-Campbell, 2001, *The Viking World,* 3rd edn (London), pp.82–5.

19. K A Steer & J W M Bannerman, 1977, *Late Medieval Monuments in the West Highlands* (Edinburgh); D Rixson, 1998, *The West Highland Galley* (Edinburgh); D C McWhannell, 2002, 'The Galleys of Argyll', *Mariner's Mirror* 88.1, pp.14–32.

20. Steer & Bannerman, *Late Medieval Monuments*, p.181.

21. MacAulay, *Bìrlínn*, pp.21–38.

22. Crumlin-Pedersen, *Archaeology and the Sea*, pp.107–24.

23. G Hutchinson, 1994, *Medieval Ships and Shipping* (London), pp.50–55.

24. See for example Crawford, *Scandinavian Scotland*; R A McDonald, 1997, *The Kingdom of the Isles: Scotland's Western Seaboard, c.1100–c.1336* (Edinburgh); R D Oram, 2014d, *The Lordship of the Isles* (Leiden); and McDonald this volume.

25. D K Palit, 1953, *The Essentials of Military Knowledge* (Aldershot).

26. M Ravn, 2016, *Viking-Age War Fleets: shipbuilding, resource management and maritime warfare in 11th-century Denmark* (Roskilde).

27. J MacInnes 1974, 'West Highland Sea Power in the Middle Ages', *Transactions of the Gaelic Society of Inverness* 48, pp.540–41.

28. S T Driscoll, 1998, 'Formalising the Mechanisms of State Power: Early Scottish Lordship from the Ninth to the Thirteenth Centuries', in S Foster, A Macinnes & R MacInnes (eds), *Scottish Power Centres from the Early Middle Ages to the Twentieth Century* (Glasgow), pp.32–58.

29. R A Dodgshon, 1998, *From Chiefs to Landlords: social and economic change in the Western Highlands and Islands, c.1493–1820* (Edinburgh), pp.103–07.

30. Hutchinson, *Medieval Ships*, pp.164–82; A J Parker, 2001, 'Maritime Landscapes', *Landscapes* 2.1, pp.34–41.

31. G Macleod (Seòras Chaluím Sheòrais), 2005, *Muir is Tir* (Sea and Shore) (Stornoway), pp.105–13.

32. A Whitfield, 1995, *Island Pilot* (Lerwick), pp.34–5.

33. Hutchinson, *Medieval Ships*, p.175.

34. J W M Bannerman, 1974, *Studies in the History of Dalriada* (Edinburgh), p.110.

35. Dodgshon, *From Chiefs to Landlords*, pp.145–9.

36. G Stout, nd, *Eight Acres and a Boat* (Dundee).

37. R L Shaw, 1985, *Fighter Combat: Tactics and Maneuvering* (Wellingborough), p.269.

38. A A MacGregor, 1929, *Summer Days Among the Western Isles* (Edinburgh & London), p.292.

39. E Dwelly, 2011, *The Illustrated Gaelic-English Dictionary,* facsimile edn (Edinburgh).

40. RCAHMS, 1980, *Argyll Volume 3: Mull, Tiree, Coll & Northern Argyll* (Edinburgh), p.113.

41. RCAHMS, *Argyll 3*, pp.94–5.
42. RCAHMS, *Argyll 3*, pp.93–4.
43. RCAHMS, *Argyll 3*, p.84.
44. RCAHMS, 1928, *Ninth report with inventory of monuments and constructions in the Outer Hebrides, Skye and the small isles* (Edinburgh), pp.157–8.
45. J Curle, 1932, 'An Inventory of Objects of Roman and Provincial Origin found in Sites in Scotland not Definitely Associated with Roman Constructions', *PSAS* 66, p.290.
46. RCAHMS *Argyll 3*, p.108.
47. Martin Martin, *A Description of the Western Islands of Scotland c.1695*, intro. by C J Withers & R W Munro, 1999 (Edinburgh), p.32.
48. RCAHMS *Argyll 3*, p.109.
49. RCAHMS *Argyll 3*, pp.187–90.
50. RCAHMS *Argyll 3*, p.202.
51. RCAHMS, *Outer Hebrides*.
52. H Haswell-Smith, 1996, *The Scottish Islands* (Edinburgh), p.245.
53. RCAHMS *Outer Hebrides*, p.68.
54. E Beveridge & J G Callander 1931, 'Excavation of an Earth-house at Foshigarry, and a fort, Dun Thomaidh, in North Uist', *PSAS* 65, pp. 319, 321; E Beveridge & J G Callander, 1932, 'Earth-houses at Garry Iochdrach and Bac Mhic Connain, in North Uist', *PSAS* 66, pp.34, 41.
55. Martin Martin, *Description of the Western Islands,* p.328.
56. G E Manwaring & W G Perrin, 1922, *The Life and Works of Sir Henry Mainwaring*, 2 vols (Navy Records Society 54), vol. 2, pp.14–15.
57. J Davey, 2015, *In Nelson's Wake: the navy and the Napoleonic Wars* (New Haven & London), p.232, citing NMM, PRV/58/1, Observations on the State of Affairs in the Mediterranean, 1810, pp.11–12.
58. C Woodham-Smith, 1962, *The Great Hunger: Ireland 1845–9* (London), p.136.
59. Martin Martin, *Description of the Western Islands*, pp.321–2.
60. K Branigan, 2012, *Barra: Episodes from an Island's History* (Stroud), pp.64–6.
61. J MacPherson, 1992, *Tales from Barra Told by the Coddy,* J L Campbell (ed.) (Edinburgh), pp.59–60.
62. M Oppenheim (ed.), 1902, *The Naval Tracts of Sir William Monson,* vol. 3 (Navy Records Society 43), p.59.
63. S Murdoch, 2010, *The Terror of the Seas: Scottish Maritime Warfare 1513–1713* (Leiden), pp.134–40.
64. A A MacGregor, 1930, *Over the Sea to Skye* (London), p.234; 1966, *The Enchanted Isles* (London), pl. opp. p.104.
65. RCAHMS, 1992, *Argyll, An Inventory of the Ancient Monuments Vol. 7, Mid Argyll & Cowal, Medieval & Later Monuments* (Edinburgh), pp.184–90); RCAHMS, 1984, *Argyll Vol. 5: Islay, Jura, Colonsay and Oronsay* (Edinburgh), facing p.266.
66. Martin Martin, *Description of the Western Islands*, p.317.
67. I F Grant, 1959, *The Macleods: the History of a Clan 1200–1956* (London), p.215.
68. N Maclean-Bristol, 1999, *Murder Under Trust: the crimes and death of Sir Lachlan Mor Maclean of Duart, 1558–1598* (East Linton), p.187.
69. RCAHMS, *Argyll 3*, pp.88–9, 190.
70. C Dressler, 1998, *Eigg: The Story of an Island* (Edinburgh), p.4.
71. Crumlin-Pedersen, *Archaeology and the Sea*, pp.131–2.

72. *Orkneyinga Saga, The History of the Earls of Orkney*, H Pálsson & P Edwards (eds), 1981 (Harmondsworth), p.129.

73. Maclean-Bristol, *Murder Under Trust* p.80.

74. Alexander Lindsay, *A Rutter of the Scottish Seas Circa 1540*, I H Adams & G Fortune (eds), 1980 (Greenwich), pp.51–3.

75. Martin Martin, *Description of the Western Islands*, passim.

76. RCAHMS, *Argyll 3*, p.120.

77. Martin Martin, *Description of the Western Islands*, p.61; Angus MacLellan, 1962, *The Furrow Behind Me*, transl. J Lorne Campbell (London), pp.177–8.

78. C J M Martin, 2014a, 'The Sea World of the Chessmen', in D H Caldwell & M A Hall (eds), *The Lewis Chessmen: New Perspectives* (Edinburgh), pp.185–99.

79. See Crumlin-Pedersen, *Archaeology and the Sea*, pp.140–41.

80. A Nicolson, 1994 (3rd edn, ed. Cailean Maclean), *History of Skye* (South Lochs), p.20.

81. N MacPherson, 1879, 'Notes on Antiquities from the Island of Eigg', *PSAS* 12, pp.577–97.

82. RCAHMS, *Argyll 5*, pp.282–3; D H Caldwell, 2008a, *Islay: The Land of the Lordship* (Edinburgh), p.333.

83. S Foster, 2006, 'Kisimul Castle: Recent Work by Historic Scotland', in A Kruse & A Ross (eds), *Barra and Skye: Two Hebridean Perspectives* (Edinburgh), pp.47–65.

84. A B Stahl, 2006, 'On the Verge of Loss: Lesser-Known Place-Names of Barra and Vatersay', in A Kruse & A Ross (eds), *Barra and Skye: Two Hebridean Perspectives* (Edinburgh), p.109; O Owen, 1999, *The Sea Road: A Viking Voyage Through Scotland* (Edinburgh), p.23; B E Crawford, 2013, *The Northern Earldoms: Orkney and Caithness from AD 870 to 1470* (Edinburgh), pp.87–8.

85. K Branigan & P Foster, 2002, *Barra and the Bishop's Isles* (Stroud), pp.134–5.

86. J Lorne Campbell (ed.), 1936, *The Book of Barra* (Edinburgh & London), p.38.

87. MacGregor, *Summer Days*, p.288.

88. Martin Martin, *Description of the Western Islands*, pp.64–5, 326.

89. Martin Martin, *Description of the Western Islands*, p.326.

90. OS Explorer 452 (2015).

91. I R Macneil, 2006, 'Kisimul Castle and the Origins of Hebridean Galley-Castles: Preliminary Thoughts', in A Kruse & A Ross (eds), *Barra and Skye: Two Hebridean Perspectives* (Edinburgh), p.45.

9

Norse Period Hebridean Dun Re-occupation and Castle-Building

John Raven

CASTLES ARE PERHAPS the most readily recognised symbols of medieval lordship. This is especially so along Scotland's western seaboard, where they continue to make such a significant contribution to the picturesque qualities of the landscape, and provide a huge attraction for those investigating their genealogical heritage in the homelands of the clans. Their study allows us to reconstruct narratives about the world of their builders and occupants; their perceptions and identities, the cultural influences they responded to and the social and cultural messages they hoped to transmit to the people with whom they came into contact. Castles also represent a mediation of their patrons' enculturated models of society, lordship and hierarchy. These messages were presented through their position in the landscape, form, architectural details and decoration, how they were used, and how internal space was organised. Added to what a castle's builders were trying to communicate, we, today, can add understanding through deciphering their date of construction, subsequent additions and the wider historical and cultural context of their initial building and later changes.

It is generally accepted that the western seaboard exhibits evidence for some of the earliest non-royal masonry castles in Scotland.[1] Indeed, as will be discussed briefly below, this has proved a conundrum for many scholars. It has also proved a source of some contention, as earliness has become equated with significance, and there has been a scrabble to prove which is the earliest.[2] Nevertheless, some are undoubtedly 13th-century and possibly 12th-century in origin. They therefore belong to a period when many Hebrideans were shifting allegiances between Norway and Scotland and were torn between competing cultural, economic and social models: feudal and Gaelic. Castle-building was both a product of and a medium for expressing these conflicting concepts, and their remains present an opportunity for the study and understanding of medieval lordly Hebridean society. However, castles were not the only form of Hebridean fortification in this period, nor were they the only forms of lordly expression. Miket and Roberts[3] were among the first to realise the potential relevance of Hebridean medieval castles being sited on top of prehistoric predecessors, and it is to this subject that we must turn to understand the foundations of castle-building throughout the western seaboard.

Before progressing, it might be helpful to put the period of castle-building into its historical context. After the Vikings arrived, *c.*800, it took some time for a structured, functional settlement-pattern to emerge. This was, initially at least, predominantly Norse in character. However, the signing of the Treaty of Perth in 1266, when the Norwegian king handed what was probably only nominal control of the Hebrides to the King of Scotland, only marked a way-point in what was an ongoing, and by that point largely inevitable, transition from Norwegian rule. As much as it was to bring the Hebridean kingdoms more directly back under the Norwegian heel, the Largs campaign that led to the Treaty was an attempt to redress Scottish incursions westward, which had been under way, albeit intermittently, for at least a century or two. The Hebrides had not been under any unified control, and had had strong political and cultural connections with Ireland and the Irish-Sea zone throughout the Norse period. The Hebrides were also strongly linked to Gaelic areas of the Scottish mainland, including the Scottish kingdom.

It might also be helpful to provide a very broad-brush archaeological background to the monuments which existed in the Norse-period landscape and are relevant to this study. Throughout the Hebridean Iron Age the most prevalent monuments were brochs and duns (for ease of reference in the rest of this paper, the term 'dun' will often be used as a catch-all for brochs and duns), perhaps best described as monumental dry-stone houses, often sitting on artificial islands or crannogs, or in prominent locations, occasionally within hillforts. Few new duns appear to have been built during the late Iron Age or Pictish period. Houses were, instead, being built within structures that were by this point often centuries old. There seems to have been a gradual shift away from duns, with those remaining in occupation finally being abandoned *c.*800. The reasons are unclear, but it may not be a coincidence that this is roughly when the Vikings arrived.[4] It is also a period, however, when in Ireland there was a shift away from many small secular fortifications towards larger royal and/or ecclesiastical sites.[5] Further east, on the Scottish mainland, there is not the same pattern of disruption, and some fortifications appear to have continued in use.

Only a small handful of Hebridean fortifications could potentially date to within the three centuries that followed. One is the small sub-rectangular enclosure with timber walls but no internal structures which was identified at the Udal, North Uist, and which its excavator dated to the Viking *landnám* in the 9th century.[6] Two more are Dun Nosebridge and Dun Guaidhre in Islay. These have a passing resemblance to the Viking ringworks or *longphort*s associated with mobile armies or marauding bands in England and Ireland, which possibly, but unsurprisingly, seem to follow Scandinavian traditions. However, there is no hard evidence for their dating or use. They could equally be seen as a Hebridean interpretation of mottes or 'Anglo-Norman' ringworks. All three sites are exceptional; they do not reflect wider settlement norms. More generally, once established, Norse settlement in the Hebrides largely reflected the pattern visible elsewhere in the Norse Atlantic diaspora, characterised by longhouses, with influence and wealth expressed through the erection of large, decorated halls. Although the halls of the most influential perhaps sat at the centre of small clusters of buildings occupied by adherents, they were effectively unfortified farmsteads, sitting within farmland and distributed throughout the landscape.[7]

Although abandoned, duns were not forgotten; they remained part of the landscape and often appear to have been imbued with some significance. In Caithness and the Northern Isles they were often associated with ancestral burial mounds, occasionally becoming the focus for new inhumations. A 9th-century burial at Dun Mor Vaul, Tiree,[8] suggests this may have been a widespread initial response to dun mounds in the early Viking era. But in the east many do not seem to have been adopted by the Norse, and broch-mounds retained their association with pre-Norse inhabitants, as perhaps evidenced by place-names like 'Pictish Howe'.

There are a few possible exceptions, however. Mousa, in Shetland, twice attracted the attention of the compilers of the sagas. In the 10th century, we are told, the broch was used for shelter over the winter by an eloping couple after they became shipwrecked nearby,[9] and in 1153 Erlend the Young is credited with taking his betrothed there 'where everything had been made ready',[10] presumably for occupation and defence. However, even if we accept that the sagas, written about three centuries after the first event and a century after the second, can be treated as unproblematic source material, the fact that these events were considered sufficiently noteworthy to mention the location may suggest that the scribes identified the occupation of a broch as atypical. The association with a significant landmark and the resemblance of both episodes potentially suggests a romantic motif and further raises suspicions about the accuracy of these two episodes.

The Norse settlements at Bornish, South Uist and Loch na Berie, Lewis,[11] were both sited relatively close to, but not alongside, dun sites. Excavations at Bornish have identified a high-status settlement, dating from the end of the 10th century onwards. The prefix from the place-name appears to derive from the Norse word *borg* for fort,[12] and therefore directly references Dun Vulan located on the headland 1.5km away. Although modern occupation may have truncated any evidence, excavations at Dun Vulan produced no evidence for re-use of the interior, or immediately outside, contemporaneous with the first few centuries at Bornish.[13] This suggests that the broch was seen as more than simply a landscape feature and was initially treated as something to respect but set apart from everyday settlement, similar to the pattern seen in Caithness, Orkney and Shetland.

However, whereas the Norse and medieval inhabitants of the Northern Isles continued to treat duns as 'other', those throughout the western seaboard followed a different trajectory. A wide range of excavated duns, brochs and crannogs show evidence for re-occupation and modification through the erection of buildings across and inside them, a process which began in the 12th to 14th centuries. The earliest dun excavations usually consisted of simply emptying out the interiors. In this way any later structures and finds which might have been used to date them were lost. In some cases linear walls were noted and care was taken to recover finds in the fill, although their find-spots and stratigraphy were often ignored. Nevertheless, a background noise indicating activity beginning in the late Norse Period can be identified. Erskine Beveridge found a dirk and clinker nails, usually associated with clinker-built boats, belonging to a later structure built within Dun a'Ghallain, North Uist.[14] Likewise, by the time Callander recorded the excavations at Dun Beag, Skye, the five internal structures recorded by 18th-century travellers had already been gutted, but a number of currently un-dated metal objects, which Callander suggested could be Scandinavian in character, were recovered, along with a number of coins, the earliest of which were of Henry II and Edward I.[15]

Slightly more concrete evidence has been uncovered in the later 20th century, mostly by prehistorians primarily interested in seeking the Iron Age deposits underneath. As a result, although they recorded the evidence, its importance was often put to one side. At Kildonan, Kintyre, Fairhurst identified that after a long period of abandonment the interior was levelled and roughly cobbled or paved, the galleries were in-filled and blocked, and the entrance remodelled. Within the interior were constructed six relatively small and ephemeral huts. These structures were, based on comparisons with pottery then known elsewhere, dated to the 13th or early 14th century.[16] At Dun Lagaidh, Wester Ross,[17] similar modifications were made to a prehistoric dun. The existing entrance was blocked, but this time with lime-mortared masonry, and the internal floor was cleared out and levelled. Radial walls were also constructed, linking the dun to an earlier hillfort and possibly forming a bailey-like enclosure. A hoard of English coins from under the collapse of one of the radial walls strongly suggests their deposition, post-dating the dun re-modification, around or shortly after 1230. Although later medieval occupation obscures evidence for earlier use, recent excavations at Dun Mhuirich, Knapdale, indicate that substantial re-modifications took place some time between the 12th and 14th centuries.[18] Early work at Dun Fhinn, Kintyre, produced a 16th-century coin within a much-disturbed upper soil matrix. However, later excavations, not yet fully published, recorded a post-built structure with wattle-and-daub partitions, presumably below the disturbed horizons.[19] The use of structural posts would be consistent with a 12th- to 13th-century date.

At Tirefour Castle, Lismore, at least one building was constructed immediately outside the broch, dated through the recovery of a 12th-century pin.[20] Tirefour's interior has been cleared in the past, presumably to enhance the visual aspect of the tower. Recent excavations remain unpublished but little has been made of any potential Norse finds from inner floor-levels in the available literature. The absence of visible internal structures is not therefore necessarily definitive. At Dun Vulan, South Uist, after at least four centuries of abandonment and possibly as early as 1300, the entrance was blocked with rubble and at least one, rather ephemeral, building was constructed against the dun walls. Occupation in the 1940s may have removed internal evidence, and the interior was not fully excavated, but hard evidence for medieval activity was confined to the broch's exterior.[21] While the evidence is not strong, together these cases could hint that in some instances re-use of duns was restricted to external buildings, either through reluctance or because the interiors served a separate function which did not involve habitation. The separation of settlement from fortifications is something we will return to below in relation to castles.

The number of duns and crannogs with later settlement in, at, around and over them is considerable. However, dun re-occupation was a phenomenon that lasted into the 17th century, and it is not possible to be certain of the origins of medieval occupation and re-use without excavation. The number of duns with Norse period re-use is nevertheless likely to be much higher than these few excavated examples can attest. Re-evaluation of many previous excavations may also produce further evidence for occupation in this period, especially those relying on dates from pottery assemblages. Hall's research at Baliscate, Mull, has revealed that a number of handmade Hebridean pottery forms there, which were previously believed to be later medieval, were actually in use as early as the 12th century.[22] The lime-bonded tower inserted into Dun Cuier, Barra, is believed to have been late- or post-medieval, on the basis of post-medieval finds which appear to corroborate the belief that accompanying small bag-shaped jars with everted rims and stab decoration are 15th to 17th century in date.[23] The revised pottery dating at Baliscate could have implications for our understanding of the longevity and complexity of re-use at this site and many others.

It is worth noting that when those sites that show evidence of Norse-period occupation are compared with those duns where there is no sign of re-occupation, there seems to be a general, but not universal, association with the sea; being coastal, often located near to small harbours (perhaps accommodating no more than one boat) and with wide views out over the sea and maritime routeways. There is also, often, a correlation between these sites and units of tax-assessment (such as ouncelands, quarterlands, pennylands) and, along with other high-status farmsteads, with chapel-sites; presumably private chapels directly serving their occupants.[24]

The re-occupation of duns created central places of a fortified, or rather monumentalised, nature. This marks a significant departure from earlier Norse patterns of dispersed farmsteads and architectural styles, and reveals major changes in cultural identity and societal structures. There does not appear to have been any major political or military change which would provide a functional explanation of a sudden need for defence. Instead, the re-occupation and appropriation of sites which were old before the Viking Age, and which Norse-period Hebrideans would have recognised as such, clearly belongs to the cultural and political realignment away from Norway, when a newly emerging, or at least increasingly Gaelic, identity was being deliberately recreated. Hebridean lords no longer wished to perceive themselves simply as foreign interlopers, but wanted to emphasise their indigenous roots and (re-)claim a Gaelic, and thereby implicitly a non- and pre-Norse, heritage.

We can perhaps see parallels here in the modification of many clans' genealogical histories to expunge any links to the Norse and insert Irish origins.[25] One example is the claim of the Macneils of Barra to descend from the 7th-century Irish king, Niall of the Nine Hostages, and an oral tradition which recorded the clan being forced into exile by the Norse and then triumphantly returning to drive the Norse out of its previously owned castles.[26]

These attempts to link duns to genealogical progenitors are also evident in naming-patterns. Numerous duns are suffixed by the name of a significant figure in the founding of a local lineage. Two of the Glenelg brochs are named after founders of the local MacLennan families, and Dun Torcuill in North Uist is named after one of the major MacLeod lineages. Sadly, antiquarians bottomed out the Glenelg brochs, leaving only the slightest hint of re-use in one of the three, and, while Dun Torcuill shows hints of re-use, it remains unexcavated.[27] Duns associated with named historical individuals, especially where those place-names were only recorded in more recent times, cannot always be relied on. However, it is curious how often these associations can be backed up by archaeological evidence.

As noted above, Dun Mhuirich, in Knapdale, has evidence for medieval occupation. Its name probably derives from one of two historically-attested Knapdale lords. One is Aodh Álainn an Burriche, the father of Donnsléibhe the founder of a number of dynasties throughout Knapdale and Cowal, but himself considered noteworthy enough for at least one lineage to refer to themselves as the 'MacBurriches', and who may have lived in the 12th century. The other is Murchadh, son of the Sween who provided the MacSweens with their eponym, and great-grandson of Aodh Álainn an Burriche, who was sufficiently powerful to appear in the saga record of the Largs campaigns, and whose death in Ireland was thought worth recording in Irish annals.[28]

The survival of the name of Dun Mhuirchaidh, on Benbecula, reveals the veracity of some of these names. In its entirety the site consists of an artificial or heavily-modified island, sitting next to an adjacent larger natural island and with a submerged crannog also nearby. At the heart of the main island is a prehistoric dun, surrounded by a cluster of building-footings, some of which are much more recent, all enclosed within a massive dry-stone wall. This is unlike any other dun, but in its general layout and relationship with other islands has parallels with Finlaggan and other lordly Gaelic sites, which often have 12th-century beginnings. The Siol Mhuirchaidh may have had ascendency over some of the Uists before being displaced the MacRuaris. Oral tradition suggests that they were ejected from the dun by their new overlords who then maintained it as their own seat until they built Borve Castle on the other side of the island. It seems unlikely that there would have been any benefit in preserving the tradition that the dun was founded by a competing lineage unless there was at least some grain of truth in the story.[29]

Dun Raouill, on South Uist, is another, peculiar, structure with a place-name which appears to tie it to the MacRuaris, albeit in an oddly-corrupted form; this association is supported in oral histories. It remained in use until the 17th century but it is not clear how much it has been modified between its original construction and its present form, nor is it clear whether the buildings on a nearby island were associated with the dun throughout its use or only belong to later periods. Unlike the other examples above, however, it does not appear to have been built on an earlier site, and is unique in being a monumental rectangular structure, and, while of dry-stone construction, is more akin to what might be recognisable as a castle.[30] Could it be some form of 'missing link'?[31]

While dun-occupation facilitated Hebridean lords' attempts to realign their cultural identities, it may have also been a relatively easy way to express 'castellation' and demonstrate their adoption of feudal symbolism. Indeed, the concepts are not mutually exclusive. The process demonstrating that they were inheritors of indigenous governance over the islands, linked to the land, but also showing that they were elevating themselves above their social inferiors – whom they had previous lived alongside in similar, if not more ornate, farmsteads – and entering into the up-to-date European social model by becoming the builders, inheritors, owners and/or occupiers of something that in most appearances was very similar to a castle.

This is further supported by the number of re-occupied prehistoric duns which went on to be developed into what might more readily be appreciated as castles. Most western seaboard castles are built on earlier fortifications or sites. This is not unusual; setting aside where there may have been more-or-less continuous occupation, many English castles were famously built on Roman and Iron Age sites, and in Scotland, Dundonald and Crookston castles,[32] for example, which were curiously within the Gaelic sphere, were built on top of Iron Age or Dark Age hill-forts. However, the Hebridean and Argyll examples perhaps depart from this pattern in that there often appears to be an intermediary stage of dun re-occupation as outlined above. Where new western seaboard castles were not built on re-occupied sites there was often a direct correlation with or visual reference to an earlier site, or one with genealogical connotations: for instance, Castle Sween and Dun Mhuirich are inter-visible.

Dating castles has proved notoriously difficult. Even where there is documentary evidence, which is rare in a Hebridean context, it is often not easy directly to relate the dating or signing of a charter to specific phases of what survives today. Castles may pre-date their mention in charters by some centuries, or not be specifically mentioned. Even when they are excavated, relating what survives to primary or later building phases can prove problematic. Often, as is the case at Mingary, in Ardnamurchan, later construction work cleared out all evidence for earlier activity.[33] Instead, castellologists are usually reliant on comparisons between the character of the masonry or architectural features at the few dated examples and those which are less well dated. In some cases the evidence can be even flimsier. There is no hard dating for the earliest phase of Castle Sween, yet it is widely claimed to be among the earliest masonry castles in Scotland, largely on the basis of the link to the eponymous 12th-century Sween, provided by the place-name and later medieval oral tradition, and some vague architectural comparisons (it does, however, appear on record in the following century).[34] The mortar-dating technique being pioneered in Scotland by Mark Thacker has the potential to redress this situation and to allow for a much more informed debate in the future.

Despite this note of caution, however, a number of masonry castles along the western seaboard can quite confidently be dated to the 13th century, with some writers making less-credible claims that a few could belong to the 12th. This is particularly remarkable as at this time most nobles in Scotland, Ireland and Scandinavia were only building earth-and-timber castles. Masonry castles, in all three areas, were predominantly the prerogative of royal or courtly households. This divergence is often interpreted as being a self-professed expression of the independence and importance of western Gaelic lords, either filling the vacuum left by declining Norwegian influence, or under encouragement, or even direct patronage, from the Scottish court to form a bulwark against the west.[35]

The MacDougalls and MacSweens were both powerful dynasties. In the 1200s the MacDougalls were in the ascendency over the other MacSorley lineages. Although their holdings included some of the Hebrides, such as Mull, they were most firmly established in the old Dalriadic kingdom of Lorn, on whose *caput* they decided to erect their main castle. By the time Castle Sween was built, the MacSweens appear to have inherited or extended into Cowal and Knapdale, possibly also an older Dalriadic kingdom,[36] sandwiched between the expansive ambitions of the Stewarts to the east and the MacDonalds to the west. All three kindreds had a vested interest in asserting their own position, reflecting a rejection of or assertion of independence from western and Norwegian influence, but perhaps also in demonstrating their Scottish loyalty and exploiting that in order to resist or displace Norse and western influences in favour of themselves. It is curious that the main castles of both lineages (Dunstaffanage, Lorn, and Duart, Mull, are often attributed to the MacDougalls, while Castle Sween is linked to the MacSweens) could all be grouped together in terms of vague plan, overall form and architectural detail, as many scholars have, into a single typological group: 'castles of enclosure', or 'curtain-wall castles'.[37] However, it is difficult to see how helpful this classification is; each is as different from the others as it is similar. Other potential examples, the dates and patrons of which are less clear, also appear to reflect either builders who were more mainland-orientated or the eastern, mainland extent of wider Hebridean lordships: for example, Mingary, Ardnamurchan, whose origin has recently been much debated, and Eilean Tioram, which may be later but unquestionably was originally the seat of the MacRuaris, whose lordship was predominantly island-based.[38] Eilean Donan, built by the mainland-centric MacKenzies before 1300,[39] may also be a candidate for this group.

Another group of castles can also be easily dated to the Norse Period, or at least to the 13th century, broadly classifiable as 'hall-houses' or 'chamber-castles'. Like enclosure-castles, while they share some characteristics, they also vary considerably in size, decoration and form, and it is questionable how useful the term might be. There are a few examples, such as Skipness and Ardtornish, scattered along the mainland coastline, alongside the enclosure-castles, and others in the Argyll heartland, such as Fincharn. In the Isles, though, they are the commonest castle form. The most decorative examples are perhaps Skipness, in Kintyre, and Aros, on Mull, which are large, have ornate windows and appear to have been built on virgin sites.

A simpler representative can be found at Borve, on Benbecula. Borve, or *Buirgh*, is the Gaelic derivative of the Norse term *borg*, noted above, which perhaps indicates an earlier date, when Norse was the predominant Hebridean tongue. It could also suggest that the castle sat on or replaced an earlier dun. The association between the castle and the place-name is slightly problematic, as early charters refer to the castle as *Bheinn A Mhaoil*, an earlier name for Benbecula, rather than Borve. However, it is related to a nearby chapel and along with re-occupied duns nearby, correlates to the layout of ouncelands and quarterlands, suggesting it developed out of the pre-existing Norse farming system and was not imposed on it.[40] While there are medieval chapels near to Aros, the clearest relationship between castles and chapels is at Fincharn, Skipness and Dunstaffnage. All appear to be early (the incorporation of chapels inside castles seems in general to be a much later phenomenon); it is possible, therefore, that these also developed with reference to and out of pre-existing landholding networks. More work needs to be done to identify whether there is any wider correlation between castles and administrative units, but it is interesting to note that Fincharn was associated in its earliest grant with five pennylands,[41] which would be equivalent to a quarterland in the Western Isles, a unit potentially equated with noble status.

Borve's surroundings have changed considerably due to sand-accumulation since the 17th century; it was originally located by an enclosed bay by the sea. Unlike many Hebridean castles of similar date, or, indeed, most later Hebridean castles, it was also directly sited alongside and overlooking large stretches of arable ground.[42] The reasons for this are not clear. It is possible that this was simply the result of a castle being built on top of an early high status site, most of which were set within farmland. However, it may equally show that Borve's builders were attempting to follow the model set by the majority of Lowland and European castles, and to demonstrate dominance over arable resources. Most other Hebridean castles were predominantly or only focussed on a coastal setting and the most enduring were often beside good harbours.

These coastal settings reflect a maritime outlook in terms of views out over routeways and/or harbours, but also about both being seen and presenting an impressive face when approached by sea. It is unlikely to be a coincidence that castle-building coincided with the sudden increase in fishing throughout the North Atlantic in the 12th century, for both domestic use and export, and the increasing exploitation of Hebridean waters by English and European fishing-fleets allowed many lords to grow rich on the back of taxes for access to their fisheries and harbours, and provided trading opportunities. Indeed, it seems probable that these revenues provided lords with the surplus resources necessary to invest in castle-building, and that there is a strong link between castles, harbours and fisheries.[43] It was also by sea that dignitaries and visitors would come, from elsewhere in their own lordships, from other lordships, from Ireland, and on occasion from the courts of England or Scotland. The lime-washed masonry castle, sitting on a cliff above an anchorage, was as much intended to impress the visitor with the sophistication of the builder and owner, as it may have been to awe the captains of fishing vessels, or provide a level of defence.

Work at Castle Sween and Dunstaffnage has revealed ranges of internal timber buildings contemporary with their earliest phases and the Norse period. Unfortunately, however, much of it has been truncated by later development and it is not clear what activities were taking place within these ranges.[44] Neither of these castles appears to have been surrounded by a cluster of outbuildings, and 'castletowns' are almost completely absent throughout the western seaboard. It must be presumed, therefore, that the ranges accommodated chambers, halls and functional buildings, but their arrangement and spatial grammar remain obscure.

Around some of the hall-houses, such as Ardtornish and Aros, there are small clusters of structures, some of which are relatively spacious. The date of these buildings has not been verified but 16th-century sources suggest that most of the activity around Irish castles took place in outbuildings and external halls, with the castle being relegated to the function of a defensive sleeping-chamber.[45] It is possible that this was a late development, or even one peculiar to Ireland, but it is equally possible that this arrangement was reflected at Norse-period Hebridean hall-houses. Certainly, separate sleeping-chambers seem to have been a secondary consideration at many early masonry castles, and remained so even at very high-status ones into the 14th century, as at Dundonald.[46] This may indicate that there was no perceived need to have secluded chambers, that rooms were multi-functional, or that most activity was conducted outwith the castle, so that initially there was no conflict between chamber and other functions.

It is only in later periods that we witness additional construction-phases to provide additional masonry chambers, halls and other buildings at most enclosure-castles. This was possibly in recognition that masonry was perceived as a much more appropriate medium for hall-based activity than timber, but could potentially suggest that the functions which took place within halls were not intended within the earlier ranges. Whatever the answer, this seems to indicate that enclosure-castles were initially seen to serve a different function to hall-houses. In this context it is interesting to note that in several instances where pairs of castles belonged to one lordship, one was an enclosure-castle, the other a hall-house: for instance, Castle Sween and Skipness were both held in the 1260s by the MacSweens, albeit by separate individuals,[47] and Borve and Eilean Tioram by the MacRuaris, although it is unclear whether the two were constructed around the same time.

It is difficult to perceive of grand masonry halls with decorative windows, like Aros or Skipness, if not any of the others, as anything other than forums for gathering, feasting, judicial display, and events such as document signings, and that the difference in form reflects the need to display the hall rather than keep it hidden behind a high enclosing wall. The enclosure around Aros appears to have been low and probably late. The later transformation of Skipness into an enclosure-castle, alongside the building of halls at enclosure-castles, may reflect that any distinction between the functions of differing types of castle was becoming obsolete, or that there was increasing recognition of the multiplicity of roles castles could perform.

Most Hebridean castles, and especially the hall-houses, bear more similarity to examples from Ireland and the Scottish mainland than to Scandinavian ones. While some hall-houses share some characteristic features with castles which are generally thought to be Norse in Caithness, in that they are relatively simple architecturally, plain, un-vaulted and with first-floor entrances,[48] they differ in that the Hebridean examples are rectangular rather than the predominantly squarer Caithness examples. The precise influences and architectural models adopted by Hebridean castle-builders therefore remain obscure, and it may be that the search for architectural inspiration is a red herring, and Hebridean castle-building should, instead, be perceived as simply part of pan-European tradition.

Nevertheless, the re-occupation of prehistoric sites, the early adoption of castellated masonry building and the increasing maritime focus, which developed throughout the Norse Period, reflects the development of a new, distinct and seignorial Hebridean identity, influenced by, but distinct from, Norse, Scottish and/or Irish. It also reflects a tension between this new Gaelicised identity and feudalised social and cultural models, channelled through Scandinavia, Scotland and Europe. These tensions, and the particular Hebridean reaction to them, were to develop further, in modified forms, as the Middle Ages progressed; but that is the subject of another paper.

Acknowledgements

I would like to thank William Wyeth, joint Historic Environment Scotland and Stirling University PhD student, for discussing his thoughts on aspects of this paper as it was being written. Any errors, however, are my own.

Notes

1. E.g. S Cruden, 1960, *The Scottish Castle* (Edinburgh); J Dunbar, 1981, 'The Medieval Architecture of the Scottish Highlands', in L MacLean (ed.), *The Middle Ages in the Highlands* (Inverness), pp.38–70; A A M Duncan & A L Brown, 1957, 'Argyll and the Isles in the Earlier Middle Ages', *PSAS* 90, pp.192–220; RCAHMS, 1997, *Argyll Castles in the Care of Historic Scotland* (Edinburgh), pp.1–7; C J Tabraham, 1986, *Scottish Castles and Fortifications* (Edinburgh); C J Tabraham, 1997, *Scotland's Castles* (London).

2. See G Stell, 2006, 'Castle Tioram: A Statement of Cultural Significance', http://www.historic-scotland.gov.uk/tioram-stell-fullversion-part1and2.pdf. This is perhaps a reflection of modern castle-studies' origins in the Inspectorate of Ancient Monuments and the resulting need to classify national importance ahead of designation.

3. R Miket & D L Roberts, 1990, *The Mediaeval Castles of Skye and Lochalsh* (Portree).

4. Mary MacLeod-Rivett and Val Turner, in a paper given at the EAA Glasgow Conference in 2015, entitled 'Incoming & Accommodating: Localising Models of Scandinavian Settlement in the Northern and Western Isles', suggested that archaeologists are not finding Pictish and Viking settlement from 800–1000 because it remained transient during and immediately after the raiding period, there was a blurring of the cultural markers used to recognise them, or people have been looking in the wrong places.

5. For a good summary see A O'Sullivan, F McCormick, T Kerr & L Harney, 2013, *Early Medieval Ireland, AD 400 – 1100: The Evidence from Archaeological Excavations* (Dublin), pp.325–32.

6. I A Crawford, 1981, 'War or Peace – Viking Colonisation in the Northern and Western Isles of Scotland Reviewed', in H Bekker-Nielsen, P Foote & O Olsen (eds), *Proceedings of the Eighth Viking Congress* (Odense), pp.266–7; I A Crawford, 1996, 'The Udal', *Current Archaeology* 147, pp.86–9; I A Crawford & R Switsur, 1977, 'Sandscaping and C14: the Udal, N. Uist', *Antiquity* 51: 124–36. All three descriptions are brief and slightly conflicting on the nature of the build; the recently commenced post-excavation programme may be able to shed some light on this.

7. M Parker-Pearson, N Sharples & J Symonds, 2004, *South Uist: Archaeology and History of a Hebridean Island* (Stroud), pp.125–44; J Raven, 2005, Medieval Landscapes and Lordship in South Uist, unpublished PhD thesis, University of Glasgow, pp.147–60; N Sharples, 2005c, *A Norse Farmstead in the Outer Hebrides: Excavations at Mound 3, Bornais, South Uist* (Oxford), pp.55–7; N Sharples & M Parker-Pearson, 1999a, 'Norse Settlement in the Outer Hebrides', *Norwegian Archaeological Review* 32, pp.41–62.

8. E MacKie, 1974, *Dun Mor Vaul: An Iron Age Broch on Tiree* (Glasgow:), pp.90–91, 214.

9. *Egil's Saga*, H Palsson & P Edwards (eds), 1976 (Harmondsworth), p.82.

10. *Orkneyinga Saga*, H Palsson & P Edwards (eds), 1978 (Harmondsworth), p.190.

11. I am grateful to Mary MacLeod-Rivett for making me aware of the existence of the crop-marks reminiscent of a series of Norse longhouses at Loch na Berie, Lewis; J Raven & M MacLeod-Rivett, forthcoming, '*Morentur in Domino libere et in Pace*: Cultural Identity and the Remembered Past in the Mediaeval Outer Hebrides', in S Stoddart (ed.), *Gardening Time: Reflections on Memory, Monuments and History in Sardinia and Scotland* (Cambridge).

12. Raven & MacLeod-Rivett, 'Cultural Identity'.

13. M Parker-Pearson & N Sharples, 1999, *Between Land and Sea: Excavations at Dun Vulan, South Uist* (Sheffield).

14. E Beveridge, 1911, *North Uist; Its Archaeology and Topography* (Wiltshire), p.197.

15. G Callander, 1921, 'Report on the Excavation of Dun Beag. A Broch Near Struan, Skye', *PSAS* 55, pp.110–31.

16. H Fairhurst, 1939, 'The Galleried Dun at Kildonan Bay, Kintyre', *PSAS* 73, pp.185–228.

17. E MacKie,1969, 'Dun Lagaidh', *Current Archaeology* 12, pp.8–13; E MacKie, 2007, '*The Roundhouses, Brochs and Wheelhouses of Atlantic Scotland, c.700 BC – AD 500: Architecture and Material Culture* (BAR 444: Oxford), p.765.

18. R Regan, 2012, *Dun Mhuirich, North Knapdale*, http://www.kilmartin.org/docs/dunMhurichExcavation2012DSR.pdf; R Regan, 2013, *Dun Mhuirich, North Knapdale*, http://www.kilmartin.org/docs/dunMhurichExcavation2013DSR.pdf.

19. H Fairhurst, 1956, 'The Stack Fort on Ugadale Point, Kintyre', *PSAS* 88, pp.15–21; RCAHMS, 1971, *Argyll, an Inventory of the Ancient Monuments Vol. 1: Kintyre* (Edinburgh), pp.83–4.

20. Pers. comm. Simon Stoddart and Ewen Campbell.

21. Parker-Pearson & Sharples, *Between Land and Sea*, pp.35, 196–7, 348.

22. D Hall, forthcoming, 'The Pottery', in C Ellis (ed.), 'Excavations at Baliscate, Mull', *Scottish Archaeological Internet Reports*.

23. A Young, 1956, 'Excavations at Dun Cuier, Isle of Barra, Outer Hebrides', *PSAS* 89, pp.290–328; see E Campbell, 2003, 'The Western Isles Pottery Sequence', in B Ballin Smith & I Banks (eds), *In the Shadow of the Brochs: The Iron Age in Scotland* (Stroud), pp.139–44; Raven, Medieval Landscapes, pp.375–9 for a discussion on pottery sequences.

24. This at least holds true for the southern Outer Hebrides, see Raven, Medieval Landscapes.

25. W Gillies, 1987, 'Heroes and Ancestors', in B Almqvist, P Ó Héalaí & S Ó Catháin (eds), *The Heroic Process: Form, Function and Fantasy in Folk Epic* (Dublin), pp.57–74; W Gillies, 1994, 'The Invention of Tradition, Highland-Style', in A MacDonald, M Lynch & I Cowan (eds), *The Renaissance in Scotland* (Leiden), pp.144–56; W D H Sellar, 1966, 'The Origins and Ancestry of Somerled', *Scottish Historical Review* 45, pp.124–42; W D H Sellar, 1971, 'Family Origins in Cowal and Knapdale', *Scottish Studies* 15, pp.21–31.

26. A A MacGregor, 1929, *Summer Days Among the Western Isles* (Edinburgh), pp.198–9.

27. W Matheson, 1950, 'Traditions of the MacKenzies', *Transactions of the Gaelic Society of Inverness* 40, p.203; Beveridge, *North Uist*, pp.149–52. For a fuller discussion of names and re-use of the Glenelg brochs see Raven, Medieval Landscapes, pp.149–52.

28. Sellar, 'Family Origins in Cowal and Knapdale'.

29. For a fuller discussion on Dun Mhuirichaidh see Raven, Medieval Landscapes, pp.202–04.

30. See Raven, Medieval Landscapes, pp.222–3.

31. Macewens Castle, Cowal, a small sub-ovoid timber-and-turf palisaded enclosure surrounding a number of huts, with occupation dating from the 12th century onwards (D Marshall, 1983, 'Excavations at Macewen's Castle, Argyll, in 1968–69', *Glasgow Archaeological Journal* 10, pp.131–42), reveals that some new, small, non-castellated fortifications were still being built throughout this period. Ditches and earthen banks surrounding Dunollie (L Alcock & E Alcock, 1987, 'Reconnaissance Excavations on Early Historic Fortifications and other Royal Sites in Scotland, 1974–84: 2, Excavations at Dunollie Castle, Oban, Argyll. 1978', *PSAS* 117, pp.119–48) and Dunstaffnage (C Breen, W Forsythe, J Raven & D Rhodes, 2010, 'Survey and Excavation at Dunstaffnage Castle, Argyll *PSAS* 140, pp.165–78) may indicate another building tradition predating the castles, but may belong to the Wars of Independence based on material in their infill.

32. G Ewart & D Pringle, 2004, 'Dundonald Castle Excavations 1896–93', *Scottish Archaeological Journal* 26, pp.4–13, 24–48, 123–27; W D Simpson, 1953, 'Crookston Castle', *Transactions of the Glasgow Archaeological Society* 12, pp.1–14.

33. Pers. comm. Tom Addyman.

34. E.g. Cruden, *Scottish Castle*, pp.22–6; Dunbar, 'Medieval Architecture', p.44; RCAHMS, Argyll Castles, pp.78, 89; W D Simpson, 1967a, 'Castle Sween', *Transactions of the Glasgow Archaeological Society* 15, pp.3–14.

35. E.g. Cruden, *The Scottish Castle*, p.38; A Grant, 1988, 'Scotland's 'Celtic Fringe' in the Late Middle Ages: The Macdonald Lords of the Isles and the Kingdom of Scotland', in R R Davies (ed.) *The British Isles, 1100 – 1500: Comparisons, Contrasts and Connections* (Edinburgh), pp.118–41; G Stell, 1985, 'The Scottish Medieval Castle: Form, Function and "Evolution"', in K Stringer (ed.), *Essays on the Nobility of Medieval Scotland* (Edinburgh), p.201.

36. Sellar, 'Family Origins in Cowal and Knapdale'.

37. Following Cruden, *Scottish Castle*, and Dunbar, 'Medieval Architecture'.

38. See R D Oram, nd, *Mingary Castle, the MacIans and the Lordship of Ardnamurchan.* http://www.mingarycastletrust.co.uk/mingarycastletrust/history/analytical-and-historical-assessment/, and J S Petre, 1992, 'Mingary in Ardnamurchan: A Review of Who Could Have Built the Castle', *PSAS* 144, pp.256–76, for debates on Mingary, and Stell, 'Castle Tioram', for Eilean Tioram.

39. N Toop, 2009, Eilean Donan Castle, Ross-shire, unpublished Archaeological Evaluation Report, Field Archaeology Specialists.

40. It is also tempting to suggest that the development of castles with large halls and central, open hearths (as perhaps suggested by the lack of evidence for fireplaces or vents, in albeit ruined structures) were a continuum of the internal layout of Norse farmstead halls, but, unfortunately, this cannot be verified by excavation. Miket & Roberts, *Mediaeval Castles of Skye and Lochalsh*, p.9, also suggested that some of the architectural grammar and layout of internal mural passageways and stairs might directly reference broch architecture.

41. RCAHMS, 1992, *Argyll. 7: Mid Argyll and Cowal: Medieval & Later Monuments* (Edinburgh), p.285.

42. For a fuller discussion on Borve Castle and it setting see Raven, Medieval Landscapes, pp.233–4, 314, 351–5, 366.

43. For discussions on the 12th-century fishing explosion see J Barrett, R Nicholson & R Cerón-Carrasco, 1999, 'Archaeo-Ichthyological Evidence for Long-Term Socio-Economic Trends in Northern Scotland: 3500 BC to AD 1500', *Journal of Archaeological Science* 26, pp.353–88; J Barrett, 2007a, 'Sea Fishing and Long-Term Socio-Economic Trends in North-Western Europe', in J Graham-Campbell & M Valor (eds), *The Archaeology of Medieval Europe Vol. 1: Eighth to Twelfth Centuries AD* (Aarhus), pp.201–03; for evidence on Hebridean exploitation and the resulting socio-economic impacts see Raven, Medieval Landscapes, pp.154, 167, 367.

44. G Ewart & J Triscott, 1996, 'Archaeological Excavations at Castle Sween, Knapdale, Argyll and Bute, 1989–90', *PSAS* 126, pp.517–77; J Lewis, 1996, 'Dunstaffnage Castle, Argyll & Bute: Excavations in the North Tower and East Range, 1987–94', *PSAS* 126, pp.559–603.

45. C Lennon, 1981, *Richard Stanihurst the Dubliner, 1547–1618* (Dublin); R Loeber, 2001, 'An Architectural History of Gaelic Castles and Settlements, 1370–1600', in P Duffy, D Edwards & E Fitzpatrick (eds), *Gaelic Ireland: Land Lordship & Settlement, c.1250 – c.1650* (Dublin), pp.271–314; see Raven, Medieval Landscapes, for a fuller discussion of Scottish examples.

46. Ewart & Pringle, 'Dundonald Castle Excavations', pp.64–79, 143–53.

47. See Sellar, 'Family Origins in Cowal and Knapdale', for the relationship between Murchaidh and Dugald. RCAHMS, *Argyll Castles*, p.26 also notes that Dugald may have held Skipness from the MacDonald Lords of the Isles, rather than independently.

48. Dunbar, 'Medieval Architecture', pp.56–7, under recent scrutiny by W Wyeth, pers. comm.

10

Galley-Castles by Land and Sea

David H Caldwell

THE WEST HIGHLANDS AND ISLANDS were heavily militarised in the medieval period, so there should be little surprise that clan chiefs and lords built themselves castles. Geographical factors meant that most of these castles were by the sea, whether on the mainland or on islands, or else on significant inland waters like Loch Awe. Hence the usual means of access was directly by boat, and facilities for sheltering and unloading boats are evident at many sites. All this may seem self-evident, but our understanding of these so-called galley-castles would be greatly enhanced if we were able to place these considerations in a wider context of what the castle-builders wanted from their investments in mortar and stone. This paper is a modest attempt to explore what else we ought to know or want to discover about the purposes or functions of these castles.

We are not at a stage in our understanding where we can confidently date many of the castles in question, and even the owners and occupants are often obscure to us. For the most part, however, we can reasonably assume that they are works built for local lords.[1] Politically and culturally, from the 12th to the 16th century, we are dealing with a world dominated by the Kingdom of the Isles and then by its successor, the MacDonald Lordship of the Isles along with the lordship of the Campbells. Throughout these centuries it was a region largely distinct from the rest of Scotland. Thus, although the castles display a great variety of traits and designs, most of which can be paralleled elsewhere, including provisions for access by sea, there is some merit in selecting them as a group for study. Within our study area there are castles which are not adjacent to significant stretches of navigable water, as well as lordly residences which do not count as castles. The major such site, Finlaggan in Islay, inland and lacking defences for much of its history, is included in our discussions below for the practical reasons that it was part of the world which produced the galley-castles, and extensive excavations there have uncovered much relevant evidence.

Status symbols

Architectural historians have classified castles, coining names like 'tower-house', 'enclosure-castle' and 'hall-house', since no convenient medieval terminology has come down to us. These types may reflect changing fashions, different functions or different levels of wealth, and such variations might well explain a situation like that encountered on the island of Lismore with its two castles, Achanduin (Plate 21) and Coeffin (Plate 18), visible from each other and both with obvious provision for access from the adjacent Loch Linnhe.[2] They must surely have created different effects when viewed from the sea, Achanduin as a rectangular, walled enclosure and Coeffin as tower-like with its hall-house dominating a pinnacle of rock. Coeffin would appear to offer less in terms of facilities and space for its occupants than Achanduin, consisting merely of the hall-house – a large irregularly-shaped first-floor chamber, presumably all or mostly occupied by a hall, 16m by up to 6.5m, over an unvaulted ground floor with three external entrances. The ruins of up to three smaller buildings form an adjacent bailey or enclosure which RCAHMS, perhaps wrongly, assumed were of late-medieval date rather than 13th century like the hall-house.

In attempting to understand Achanduin we can benefit from the archaeological data recovered by the late Dennis Turner in extensive excavations undertaken in the 1970s.[3] These indicate a likely date of construction for the enclosure walls and the south-east range at the very end of the 13th or at the beginning of the 14th century. The range is interpreted as having a first-floor hall, up to *c*.8m by 21.5m in size. Surviving details in the upstanding walls indicate the intention of the builders to construct another internal range, but this did not happen. The excavations produced evidence for a sequence of less-substantial buildings in the north corner of the courtyard, probably representing private quarters for the castellan.

Perhaps, however, our impression that Coeffin offered less space and fewer facilities than Achanduin is misleading, especially if we factor in the possibility that the turf-covered traces of buildings immediately to the north-east actually relate to the castle's medieval occupation. We might expect that the requirements of the castellans' rank and status might have influenced their design choices for their castles. Dennis Turner supposed that Achanduin was built by the MacDougalls but given by them some time afterwards to the bishops of Argyll, with whom it remained.[4] The extensive excavations failed to turn up anything which was obviously ecclesiastical or related to administering a bishopric. Proprietorship of Coeffin is a mystery. The likely choices appear to be the MacDougalls or else the MacDonalds. After all, it was a dispute over lands on Lismore that was one of the causes of enmity between the two kindreds from the late 13th century.[5]

To our modern eye, if not our medieval ancestors', the prominence of the feasting-hall at Coeffin is more suggestive of status than the blank walls of Achanduin, and the ability to entertain lavishly was one of the attributes of great lords in this medieval world. Especially when seen from the sea, their castles with feasting-halls dominating their settings, like Ardtornish and Aros on either side of the Sound of Mull and Dunyvaig in Islay, must have impressed their followers, potential rivals and guests.[6]

The apparent lack of any fortifications at two major residences of the Lords of the Isles raises an interesting question. There are no traces of a defensive wall enclosing the hall-house and its ancillary buildings at Ardtornish, and at Finlaggan the walls, towers and gateway of the 13th-century castle were destroyed and not replaced, creating an open settlement surrounded only by the shallow waters of the loch. Might it be the case that the lack of castle walls helped demonstrate the status of the MacDonald Lords, their dependence on men rather than fortifications?

No doubt the tower-houses built from the 14th to the 16th century were intended to be eye-catching and suggest the status of their builders. At Kisimul on Barra, at Breacachadh on Coll (Plate 22) and at Dunollie beside Oban it is such a tower, rather than a feasting-hall, which dominates relatively small walled enclosures.[7] Perhaps this marks them out as of lesser status than the castles just mentioned with obviously lordly feasting-halls. At other enclosure-castles similar to Achanduin, including Skipness in Kintyre, Sween in Knapdale and Duart in Mull, their appearance and amenities were greatly enhanced by the addition of towers.[8]

Fortifications

As fortresses it might be anticipated that defence will have been a major consideration in the design of galley-castles. Certainly strong walls and battlements are characteristic, but any expectation that a detailed study of them will be rewarded with much evidence for sophisticated military design will rapidly be disappointed. There are a few architectural flourishes like the 15th-century box machicolations over the entrances at Breacachadh and Kisimul,[9] and the 13th-century arrow-slits at Skipness in Kintyre and Dunstaffnage in Lorn.[10] It is worth recalling that local warriors fought as archers, but it is not necessary to have specially-designed slits and embrasures to mount an effective defence with bows.[11] A report on the Isles written in 1596 by John Cunningham (see below) comments that by that time many of the local bowmen were armed with firearms,[12] which helps explain the provisions for the use of guns evident in some castles where battlements survive. They include the remodelled parapets at Mingary Castle in Ardnamurchan and Breacachadh on Coll. Both may date to the late 16th century.[13] Archaeological evidence for the importance of guns at this time comes from the assemblages of gunflints and lead shot excavated at Dùn Èistean, a stronghold of the Morrisons on a stack at the north end of Lewis. Though difficult of direct access by sea, and not identified as a castle in recent research reports, it can be included as a galley-castle.[14]

There are also a few galley-castles which were adapted in the late 16th century for defence by or against artillery. Here we will concentrate our attention on Breacachadh Castle on the island of Coll, now sensitively restored to its 16th-century form.[15] The castle stands at the head of a sheltered sea-loch, Loch Breacachadh, adjacent to a beach where boats could be drawn up. Immediately to its south there is a rocky outcrop with an alignment of boulders jutting into the sea, probably representing the remains of a medieval jetty or breakwater (Plate 22). To landward of the castle is relatively fertile land, cultivated in earlier times.

Breacachadh was the main seat of the MacLeans of Coll, represented in the late 16th century by Lachlan of Coll, but his lands and the castle were possessed by his uncle, Lachlan Mor MacLean of Duart, who had purchased the youngster's ward, relief and marriage in 1583. Young Lachlan had to go to law in December 1596 to have his uncle removed.[16] Earlier that year the uncle had been visited in Coll by an

Edinburgh merchant, John Cunningham, then acting for the English Government, which was concerned to keep the MacLeans from supporting the uprising in Ulster led by the Earl of Tyrone, if not buy their active support.[17] The report apparently written by Cunningham for his political masters survives, including a description of Breacachadh Castle. It says

> ane castell callit Brekauche, quhilk is an great strenth be reason of the situation thairof verie neir to the sea, quhilk defendis the half thairof, and hes three walls about the rest of the castell and thairof biggit with lyme and stane, with sundrie gude devises for defending of the tower. Ane uther wall about that, within the quhilk schippis and boittis are drawin and salvit. And the third and the uttermost wall of tymber and earth, within the quhilk the haill gudes of the cuntrie are keipit in tyme of troublis or weiris.[18]

This clearly does not square well with the castle as we see it today and begs some explanation. The castle now consists, essentially, of a tower-house to which is attached a barmkin with a round tower projecting at the corner opposite the tower-house. The tower-house is the 'great strenth' of Cunningham's description and the barmkin the 'three walls about the rest'. Cunningham may have had the round tower in mind when he mentioned 'sundrie gude devises for defending of the tower', and certainly the box-machicolations over both castle gates and the parapets with loops for firing guns, both on the tower-house and around the barmkin wall.[19]

What of Cunningham's outer wall within which ships and boats could be drawn for protection? Partly cladding the west and north external faces of the tower-house are the remains of a structure identified by the Royal Commission as the unfinished remains of a massive, stone-faced, early-17th-century artillery-battery, apparently built over earlier structures, including a kitchen. Could it be that this was in fact a late-16th-century bastion, pointed to the north and with flanks to east and west, typical of those which formed the major elements in contemporary *trace italienne* schemes of fortification?[20] Since Cunningham's account describes a completed work we have to imagine the medieval tower-house and barmkin enclosed in a fort with at least two other large bastions, one adjacent to the shore to the south of the castle and another to the south-west, each providing covering fire to each other and the bastion adjacent to the tower-house. The walls of the medieval castle would have offered little lasting protection from siege-guns, and their upper portions would have remained exposed to bombardment. Interestingly, the interior of the barmkin was filled up with stonework, apparently in the late 16th century. Perhaps the intention, unrealised, was to reduce the towers in height and turn the castle into a solid defensive platform protected by the bastioned trace beyond. Finally, there is Cunningham's outermost wall of timber and earth which could shelter the 'haill gudes of the cuntrie' in time of war. We can postulate that this would have been a strong timberwork fence set in an earthen bank, surrounding the outer wall and castle itself.

The author is the first to admit that his interpretation of Cunningham's description is highly speculative, but not necessarily fanciful. Concentric lines of fortification including *trace italienne* schemes are a feature of some of the English forts in contemporary Ulster, including Mount Norris, the third Blackwater Fort and Charlemont Fort, as shown in plans by English map-makers. Inisloughan Fort in County Antrim, captured by the English from Brian MacArt O'Neill in August 1602, is a particularly interesting example from the point of view of interpreting Breacachadh, since it is shown to have consisted of a stone-walled structure with two bastions (circular, however, rather than pointed) surrounded by two concentric timberwork defences separated by water-filled moats.[21]

To Lachlan Mor must go the credit for adapting the medieval castle at Breacachadh into a sophisticated fort. One possible avenue for his acquisition of the knowledge and will to do so is provided by events of 1588–89. In those years he had, notoriously, pressed into his service for fighting against the MacDonalds Spaniards and guns from the Armada ship which ended up at Tobermory in Mull.[22] These Spaniards would undoubtedly have included men with a knowledge of the latest trends and thinking in fort-design.

There is a tantalising clue in contemporary documentation about Lachlan Mor's interest in erecting and using gun-forts elsewhere. In March 1597/8 his secretary, John Auchinross, wrote to George Nicolson, the English agent in Edinburgh, about how the MacLeans could co-operate with the English in subduing the rebellion of the earl of Tyrone in Ireland. Auchinross rehearses a plan, perhaps already discussed, for a 'strength' in Lough Foyle that would be built in a month using a combination of Lachlan Mor's men and English pioneers. The English would also supply a ship and a little pinnace with ordnance. This fort would act as a base for raids by 200–300 of Lachlan's men into Tyrone's territory while the English used their regular troops to go after Tyrone himself. Auchinross's letter was passed on to Lord Burghley in London. It is clear that the idea was taken seriously by some in English government circles, especially in Dublin, where there was a fear of Tyrone receiving support at this time from King James VI.[23]

A strong fort in Coll would have made strategic sense to Lachlan Mor in his struggle for local dominance with the MacDonalds and in pursuing his military and political aims in Ireland. Loch Breacachadh offered better shelter for his ships than the treacherous waters of the Sound of Mull off Duart Castle. From Coll, and his nearby island fortress, Cairn na Burgh Castle in the Treshnish Islands (Plate 8), which had no shelter for ships, he was well placed to police or disrupt ship-movements of friends and foes. It is probable that it was at Breacachadh that Lachlan had his force of 600 men garrisoned in 1595 when he was attempting to discourage contingents of MacDonalds, MacLeods and others from Skye, Lewis, Harris and other areas to the north of his territories in Mull from joining with Clann Iain Mhoir (Clan Donald South) in an expedition to Ireland to support Tyrone.[24] Whatever the extent of Lachlan Mor's work and ambitions at Breacachadh they came to an end with his untimely death in battle in 1598 at the hands of his nephew Sir James MacDonald of Knockrinsay. In reclaiming their heritage Lachlan Maclean of Coll and his descendants may have been determined to undo the militarisation of their castle – a unique experiment in a Scottish context – and turn it back into a home.

At the MacDonald castle of Duntulm in Skye the lines of the courtyard walls were reconfigured, perhaps in the late 16th century, to create an angled bastion with an earlier round tower at its apex, reduced in height. The intention was probably to create a platform for guns and provide enfilading fire along the adjacent walls.[25] At Eilean Donan in Wester Ross a 'hornwork' or bastion was created, probably in the late 16th century, for the defence of the landward side of the castle. It has a small hexagonal bastion at its tip.[26]

Other contemporary artillery forts have already been identified in the Western Isles, specifically a series in Islay and Colonsay associated with Sir James MacDonald of Knockrinsay. They date to the uprising he led in 1615 and are represented today by physical remains. Two of them, at Loch an Sgoltaire in Colonsay and Loch Gorm in Islay, both island sites, are characterised by massive stone-faced earthworks with circular flanking bastions.[27] Sir James could readily have got his inspiration for them from the gun-fort on Calton Hill, Edinburgh, apparently erected *c*.1571 by the Regent Lennox as part of a plan to wrest control of Edinburgh, town and castle, from the supporters of Mary Queen of Scots. The fort is depicted on Gordon of Rothiemay's 1647 plan of Edinburgh as square with a circular bastion at each corner, and Sir James would no doubt have had plenty of opportunity to view it during his long enforced stay at court.[28] Sir James may also have been responsible for the two pointed bastions added to the landward wall of his ancestral castle of Dunyvaig in Islay, but they clearly do not demonstrate an understanding of the principles of *trace italienne* fortification.[29]

Access by water and for ships

In so far as galleys and other smaller ships were of considerable importance to our castle-owners, future research might usefully consider what provisions were made to protect these assets, not just from tide and weather but from human interference. Landing facilities were often protected by proximity to castle walls, for example at Moy in Mull, Kisimul in Barra (Plates 1–2) and Castle Sween in Knapdale (Plate 9), but the situation at Dunyvaig in Islay, where sizeable boats could be drawn within the castle walls, seems unusual.

Dunyvaig was the main residence of the MacDonald chiefs of Clann Iain Mhoir, and the outer courtyard has remains of a substantial sea-gate, almost 6m wide, fronted by a boat-landing (Plate 23). A 16th-century date for it has been suggested by RCAHMS but, as previously pointed out by the author, the style of masonry is comparable to 12th- and 13th-century work in churches elsewhere in Argyll and the Isles, for example Iona Nunnery and Saddell Abbey in Kintyre, suggesting that it could be of comparable date.[30] It was presumably through this gate at Dunyvaig that a group of renegades under Ranald Og MacDonald escaped by boat while under siege in 1614, and Coll Ciotach, one of the leaders of Clann Iain Mhoir, launched a boat with a few other supporters on the evening of 2 February 1615, rather than surrender to the Laird of Cawdor with the rest of the garrison after the castle had been subjected to two days of artillery bombardment.[31]

It is not our intention in this paper to consider any further the provisions made by castellans for their own boats. There are, however, some castles where we can surmise that the relationship with ships was more complex than providing access for the castellan. The large area enclosed by King Robert Bruce in his building operations at Tarbert Castle in Kintyre, guarding the strategically important boat-crossing point across a narrow isthmus, may be explicable as protected parking-space for boats, just as the outer stone enclosure at Breacachadh described in 1595/6. If so, Tarbert and Breacachadh would be capable of providing shelter for the ships of a sizeable force, perhaps 600 men in the case of the latter (see above). Alongside it in functional terms might be placed the headland fort at Rubh' an Dùnain in Skye, assuming its occupancy extended into the Medieval period. It was ideally placed to protect and control the adjacent winter-harbour with its docks and quay, perhaps used by the MacLeods of Harris (Dunvegan) (Plates 12 and 20).[32]

When Alexander (Alasdair Crotach) the chief of that family was given a royal charter in 1498 of those lands in Harris and Skye he had previously held of the Lord of the Isles it was stipulated that he was to provide the service of one galley of 26 oars and two galleys of 16 oars.[33] We know from the previously-mentioned report of 1595/6 by John Cunningham that the lands in question were assessed as supporting 1200 warriors, 500 of them from the Skye lands.[34] If we assume three men to an oar, the MacLeods would have needed more than three galleys to ship all of these, more like six galleys for the Skye contingents alone.[35]

Finally, on the subject of castles and ships, attention should be drawn to Claig Castle on a small island (Am Fraoch Eilean) near the shore of Jura in the Sound of Islay (Plate 15). It is likely to have served as the estate-centre for the lands in Jura retained by the Lords of the Isles. Its ruins have been interpreted as a tower-house, possibly with one or two adjacent subsidiary structures, clearly none of which could have provided appropriate facilities for long-term residence by the Lords, their household and retinue. A further use is suggested by its proximity to a sheltered beach on Jura and a report by a Bristol merchant in August 1569 who reported seeing in the Sound, when sailing through it from Mull, a naval force of 32 galleys along with other boats getting ready to sail for Lough Foyle. He was informed that there were 4000 men and one of the main leaders was Sorley Boy MacDonald. If this was a usual place for Clann Iain Mhoir to muster its forces, Claig Castle would make sense as an administrative and supply centre for naval expeditions.[36]

Access by land and for horses

Claig Castle along with Kisimul, and with Innis Chonnell and Fraoch Eilean, both in Loch Awe, could only be accessed by boat, but the majority of the castles in our study area had entrances to landward which in practical, day-to-day terms, may have been their main entrances, their front doors. There are few signs that any architectural effort was invested in making direct access from ship to castle memorable. Some of our galley-castles, however, have imposing landward entrances, ones that could be ridden through. The prominence of ships as a means of transport in our study area has meant that the importance of horses as a means of locomotion by the great and for mounting warriors has been given little consideration. The chess knights of *c*.1300 from the hoard discovered in Lewis very probably mirror a class present in the kingdom of the Isles,[37] while images of mounted warriors are to be found in later medieval West Highland sculpture.[38]

A grand entrance for riding through may have been a very significant factor for some castellans in keeping up appearances, not just in our study area but more generally in medieval Europe. How high and how wide did such an entrance have to be? Those are questions which it is hard to give precise answers to, especially if, as might reasonably be supposed, it was normal to ride ponies and horses smaller in size than modern breeds. Few gates survive in complete enough condition for measurements of height as well as width to be made, but the entrance to Skipness, almost 3m wide and *c*.2.5m high was surely large enough for horsemen (Plate 24). It is considered to date to the late 13th or early 14th century.[39] The landward (north-east) entrance to Achanduin, originally *c*.1m wide, appears too small, and yet this is the castle from which Bishop George Lauder of Argyll rode in 1452 to his cathedral some two and a half miles away, where he was assaulted and pulled off his horse.[40]

Horses could have been led in through the Achanduin entrance, as through those of many other castles. The only evidence for horses from the extensive excavations at Achanduin is a fragment of a horse-shoe, probably of medieval date, from the castle courtyard (no. 21).[41] There are also two horse-shoes from medieval rubble and midden deposits within the north tower of Dunstaffnage Castle, and a snaffle-bit and probable part of a horse's mouth-piece from debris of 17th century date in Castle Sween.[42] Neither of these castles appears to have had large or easy gateways for riders to enter by. What is totally lacking is any evidence in these castles or others in our area for stabling. Perhaps it will be found in ancillary, adjacent structures.

Some extramural considerations

Stabling for horses, storage of their fodder, a source of water for them to drink, all may appear mundane facilities compared to the symbolic and military functions of castles, but nevertheless these were vital considerations for castellans in making their residences viable. They were just a part of a wider infrastructure providing storage facilities for produce from the land, whether farmed by the owner himself or rendered as payments in kind for rent and other customary services; and for supplies, for example of wine, which had to be bought in. A traditional and not unreasonable view among castellologists is that foodstuffs and drink for the owner's table would have been kept in the undercroft of his hall or the cellar of his tower-house, but a large estate and a powerful lord would have had storage needs which expanded well beyond victuals alone, not to mention other items like fuel and equipment.

Water was not the drink of choice for humans, but a good supply of it was clearly essential for cooking and washing, generally for a reasonable quality of life. A study of the access to, and security of, water-supplies in different galley-castles would clearly be useful. Fortunate were the residents of castles like Innis Chonnell who could draw water from the adjacent loch (but how did they deal with sewage?), or Dunstaffnage and Skipness where wells were dug within the castle walls. The evidence is presently lacking for several other castles, and in some cases indicates supply difficulties. At Breacachadh the kitchen and its spring-fed water-supply was outside the stone walls of the medieval castle, and at Achanduin it has been suggested that the early (14th century?) addition of the 'forework' was largely to do with creating a cistern, possibly spring-fed. The prominent hexagonal bastion, perhaps of later-16th-century date, at Eilean Donan Castle in Wester Ross, contains a cistern, and there is a small rock-cut one on the rocky islet occupied by Castle Stalker in Loch Laich, Appin.[43]

Then there might be a need to retain officials, specialists and craftsmen and provide space, both public and private, for different types of meetings in which the castellan may have exercised a lordship or judicial role. This listing is clearly sketchy and not exhaustive, and is intended merely to raise the question of to what extent many of our castles were stand-alone entities or could only function in relation with other buildings and facilities outside their walls. There is an obvious need to analyse castles and what they contained on a place-by-place basis. No doubt there was much variation in what was deemed necessary to be encompassed in a castle's walls and what could remain outside, or be entirely dispensed with. Other factors like the wealth and status of the owner and the regularity and length of occupation in any one year would come into play.

This is not the time and place to develop this theme any further, but we might note some clues for further study. Firstly, there are the documentary sources for great lords retaining large bodies of warriors. The Lords of the Isles, who had a bodyguard of 360 men, are said to have kept them when resident at Finlaggan, in guard-houses on the shore of the loch.[44] Now admittedly Finlaggan, a site on two islands in a freshwater loch, was not a galley-castle, nor even, for much of its history, what we would understand as a castle, but although it had an area of *c.*7500m[2] it was apparently still not large enough to be self-contained. The outer lines of fortifications described in 1596 at Breacachadh may well have been intended for sheltering the 600 warriors Lachlan MacLean of Duart informed Robert Bowes, the English agent in Edinburgh, in the previous year that he had maintained in garrison for three months.[45]

Secondly, there is the archaeological evidence at several castles, like Coeffin as already mentioned, of nearby buildings, the date and relevance of which have to be explored. A striking case is Ardtornish in Morvern where adjacent to the hall-house are the foundations of over 15 buildings, apparently unenclosed. Ardtornish appears to have been a favourite residence of the Lords of the Isles and the hall-house alone could surely not have provided the facilities and accommodation for their household and retinue.[46]

Thirdly, there are the physical relationships to be explored between galley-castles and churches. In fact, the norm seems to have been that they were well apart from each other.[47] It is two 13th century exceptions which are intriguing. They are Skipness, which had a chapel adjacent to a hall-house, and Dunstaffnage with a chapel within easy walking distance of the enclosure-castle. Neither was a parish church, but it is possible that their presence can best be explained not by the piety of the castellans but by their status as great lords, if not kings, with a consequent need for clerics to provide their services as administrators. Again, Finlaggan might be compared, with its 14th-century chapel actually within the residential complex of the Lords of the Isles. Here such a facility was of more pressing need given the attendance of bishops and abbots at council meetings and inauguration ceremonies.[48]

Residences

At the core of every one of our galley-castles was a residence, in some cases a permanent home, in others an occasional or seasonal dwelling-place. More detailed analysis of the elements contained in these residences ought to tell us more about the function of galley-castles. Central to our understanding is the knowledge of the importance in medieval homes right across Europe of halls, which can readily be identified as prominent structures in our galley-castles. Some, like the so-called hall-houses, were free-standing structures with first floor halls, others like Finlaggan, and apparently Dun Ara in Mull, were stand-alone ground-floor halls. In other cases the halls were tied into castle walls and were integrated with other rooms. A complex example is Dunstaffnage, where it appears the original 13th-century plan was for a first-floor hall on the east curtain wall sandwiched between the north tower, probably containing private accommodation for the castellan, and the gatehouse tower.

The full range of factors affecting these design variations has still to be adequately explored. More a teaser than an explanation is the comment on Finlaggan by Donald Monro, Dean of the Isles, in 1549. He describes the main island (Eilean Mor) as being 'well biggit in palace-work according to their auld fassoun'.[49] The description applies to buildings dismantled 50 years previously but of which there was no doubt considerable memory in Monro's time. Was it the fact that they were a complex of several structures around a stand-alone hall rather than a suite of rooms, as at Dunstaffnage, which attracted Monro's attention? We can compare the early-16th-century account by Alexander Myln of the bishop's palace at Dunkeld at the beginning of the previous century – in Highland fashion with large houses built on the ground. Interestingly, Myln goes on to say that Bishop Robert Cardeny then erected a tower to improve security, and a hall with a larder and granaries underneath it.[50]

The halls tended to be long rectangular rooms, many potentially with floor areas of $c.130m^2$ to $170m^2$ or more. This may have been rather smaller in practice, with a service area screened off at one end, as is clearly the case in the hall at Finlaggan. There, in the end wall opposite the service area, there was a large fireplace, presumably adjacent to where the lord would have sat. The ground-floor hall at Breacachadh had its fireplace in one of its long walls where it might have helped distribute heat more evenly throughout the building.[51] Key questions might be whether this reflects different seating arrangements and whether this is to do with the different status of the owners of the two halls, or results from fashions which changed with time.

What we should be aware of is the importance placed on seating arrangements in the hall, as exemplified in a story in a 17th-century MacDonald history concerning a feast held at Aros by Alexander Lord of the Isles some time about the 1430s or 1440s.

His steward, MacLean, presumably realising the difficulty of keeping all the guests happy by ordering them according to their perceived rank and status, gave up the job to John MacDonald, Tutor of Moidart. MacDonald, however, wilfully insulted MacLean, MacNeil of Barra, MacLeod of Harris and MacLeod of Lewis by calling them to be seated last of all, where they pleased. Three of them left in a rage.[52]

Since the obvious function of these halls was to provide space for eating or feasting, this begs the question of what arrangements there were for food-preparation and cooking. Even where, as at Breacachadh, Kisimul and Sween, kitchens can be identified, we are none the wiser about what food and drink was processed and how. The lack of significant evidence for kitchen facilities at major castles like Aros and Ardtornish is striking. While excavations at Achanduin did uncover an oven or kiln used for some domestic process, and perhaps the suggestion of other kitchen activity in the undercroft of the hall,[53] it is only at Finlaggan, admittedly not in any way a typical site, that there is a reasonable amount of evidence for the scale and complexity of kitchen facilities. This has only become apparent thanks to extensive excavations. They show that the kitchens, with excavated evidence for three kilns or ovens, were in a range estimated as having an area of *c.*8m by 20m, adjacent to the hall.[54] We might expect that other important residences of the Lords of the Isles at Aros and Ardtornish, also with great halls, would have had equally large kitchens.

Apart from a hall and kitchen facilities a castellan had need of private space where he could live with his family and conduct private business. That is potentially what tower-houses of 14th century and later date offered. Some appear to have contained kitchens and halls for more private use by the owner, his family and close associates. It is not apparent that any of our galley-castles, with possible exception of one or two, consisted solely of a tower-house unsupported by other buildings.[55] An obvious example of the latter, only because it is on a small island with no space for other structures, is Castle Stalker, dating to the mid 16th century. Its two entrances, one on the ground floor and the other on the first, are probably a clue to the requirement of separating access and space between family and retainers. The large fireplace on the first floor could have been used for preparing food while the second floor served as a hall or more private chamber for the owner and his family, with sleeping accommodation in the garret.[56]

Accommodation for guests and retainers is harder to identify. It is probable that for most of these categories for much of the time the facilities on offer were very basic, the opportunity to sleep in the hall or some other building not exclusively devoted to the purpose. An account of the meeting at Mulindry in Islay (not a castle) between Angus MacDonald, chief of Clann Iain Mhoir and Lachlan MacLean of Duart in July 1586, a meeting which ended in bloodshed, has the MacLean contingent, 88 strong including Lachlan himself and Angus's young son James (retained as a hostage), provided with accommodation in a long-house somewhat separate from the other houses.[57]

It is possible that many guests would have welcomed the offer of accommodation in a kiln (barn) as it could be guaranteed to be dry and possibly warm from the firing of the kiln. According to later clan traditions, however, the chief of the MacKenzies

(Coinneach a' Bhlàir), invited to spend Yule (Christmas) with Angus Og, son and heir of John II Lord of the Isles, at Balconie Castle in Easter Ross some time about the 1480s, saw the proposed arrangement as an affront to his dignity.[58] There is a curious tale in another 17th-century history of how John II Lord of the Isles was insulted by his son, the same Angus Og, by being forced to spend a night sleeping under an up-turned boat at his (unnamed) residence in Islay.[59] Perhaps such shelter was not untypical for retainers.

Within the framework of castle walls there is much analysis that should be done on the relationships and accessibility of rooms. The arrangement of such facilities as fireplaces and toilets are potential indicators for how galley-castles functioned, though even with the evidence of upstanding walls and archaeological excavations both might be difficult to detect since for the one movable braziers could be used, and for the other there was no need for plumbing.

The original arrangements of the Breacachadh tower-house were for five stories including a ground-floor unvaulted cellar and a garret, each floor essentially consisting of a single chamber. There were latrines in mural chambers on the first and third floors, each provided with chutes discharging outside the castle. It would be possible to interpret the arrangements in this tower-house as two suites of two stories each, over storage at ground-floor level. The better-appointed suite at first and second floor level possibly had provisions for brazier-hearths.[60] It would have been for the owner of the castle while the suite above, accessible from the original stair system without entering the first and second floor chambers, might have been for retainers or other family members. There are no obvious facilities in this tower-house for food-preparation, suggesting that it was occupied only by private chambers and was not a stand-alone residence for the castle owner.

A comparable type of analysis can be made of the tower-house at the superficially similar castle of Kisimul. There, however, the most imposing chamber, for the use of the castellan, was positioned at second-floor level above one provided with a loft, perhaps to provide extra sleeping accommodation for retainers.[61] The tower that was created in the early 16th century out of the earlier east range at Skipness has three stories of single chambers provided with latrines and fireplaces, over a ground-floor cellar.[62] More research and analysis of galley-castles might well reveal a preference by castellans for retaining halls for communal dinning throughout the medieval period while providing themselves and their families with more private accommodation, especially in tower-houses from the 15th century onwards.

There is much else that we do not understand about galley-castles. Perhaps our greatest challenge is identifying how women and children of all ranks were provided for, were integrated into male society, and lived and worked within our castle walls. In the present state of our knowledge it is difficult to identify any artefacts from excavations in galley-castles which are exclusively or unambiguously female in character. That gender appears so far to be represented in the castle archaeological record solely by a late-16th-century carving of a lady from the MacDougall castle of Gylen in Kerrera.[63]

An embarrassment of riches

Contemporary documentary sources for galley-castles are sparse and there is little expectation that more will be discovered. That means that archaeological research is the most obvious avenue for increasing our database of knowledge. While excavations at castles like Achanduin, Sween and Dunstaffnage, as well as Finlaggan, have amply demonstrated that there is a wealth of material to be uncovered and processed, if only we can design and fund appropriate research projects, this is no reason to ignore the sources already available. As I hope has been demonstrated in this paper there is already a good corpus of information, not least the walls of the castles themselves. Perhaps to call them an embarrassment of riches is an exaggeration, but we should certainly reconsider why we have not subjected them to more rigorous examination, and sought an understanding of them beyond their purely military role.

Notes

1. The obvious exceptions are Tarbert Castle, with building phases assigned, putatively, to King Alexander II and more certainly to Robert I and James IV, and also Kilkerran near Campbeltown, erected for James IV *c*.1498. See RCAHMS, 1971, *Argyll, An Inventory of the Ancient Monuments vol. 1, Kintyre* (Edinburgh), pp.160, 179–84.
2. RCAHMS, 1974, *Argyll, An Inventory of the Ancient Monuments vol. 2, Lorn* (Edinburgh), pp.168–71, 184–7. Note that Achanduin is given as Achadun by RCAHMS.
3. D H Caldwell, G P Stell & D J Turner, 2015, 'Excavations at Achanduin Castle, Lismore, Argyll, 1970–75: findings and commentary', *PSAS* 145, pp.349–69; D H Caldwell & G P Stell, forthcoming, *Achanduin Castle, Lismore, Argyll: an account of the excavations by Dennis Turner, 1970–75* (Edinburgh: SAIR).
4. D Turner, 1998, 'The bishops of Argyll and the Castle of Achanduin, Lismore, AD 1180–1343', *PSAS* 128, pp.645–52.
5. N Murray, 2002, 'A House Divided Against Itself: a brief synopsis of the history of Clann Alexandair and the early career of "Good John of Islay" *c*.1290–1370', in C Ó Baoill & N R McGuire (eds), *Rannsachadh Na Gàidhlig 2000* (Obar Dheathain), p.222.
6. For Aros see RCAHMS 1980, *Argyll, An Inventory of the Ancient Monuments vol. 3, Mull, Tiree, Coll & Northern Argyll* (Edinburgh), pp.173–7; Ardtornish, *ibid*, pp.170–73; Dunyvaig (Dunivaig), RCAHMS, 1984, *Argyll, An Inventory of the Ancient Monuments vol. 5, Islay, Jura & Colonsay* (Edinburgh), pp.268–75.
7. For Kisimul see Dunbar, 1978, 'Kisimul Castle, Isle of Barra', *Glasgow Archaeological Journal* 5, pp.25–43; Breacachadh (Breachacha) RCAHMS, *Argyll 3*, pp.177–84; Dunollie, RCAHMS, *Argyll 2*, pp.194–8.
8. For Skipness see RCAHMS, *Argyll 1*, pp.165–78: Castle Sween, RCAHMS, *Argyll, An Inventory of the Ancient Monuments vol. 7, Mid Argyll & Cowal, Medieval & Later Monuments* (Edinburgh), pp.245–59; Duart, RCAHMS, *Argyll 3*, pp.191–200.
9. RCAHMS, *Argyll 3*, pl. 42.A, E; Dunbar, 'Kisimul Castle', pl. 5.
10. RCAHMS, *Argyll 1*, fig. 169; RCAHMS, *Argyll 2*, fig. 186.
11. Although medieval warriors from the West Highlands and the Isles depicted themselves on their monuments as being armed with swords, spears and axes (K A Steer & J W M Bannerman, 1977, *Late Medieval Monumental Sculpture in the West Highlands* (Edinburgh))

they are described in contemporary documentation as archers, for example as the 'Irish archers' led by the Earl of Argyll at the battle of Pinkie in 1547 (D H Caldwell, 1991, 'The Battle of Pinkie', in N Macdougall (ed.), *Scotland and War AD 79–1918* (Edinburgh), p.75, using information derived from William Patten). See also D H Caldwell, 2007, 'Having the right kit: West Highlanders fighting in Ireland', in S Duffy (ed.), *The World of the Galloglass* (Dublin), pp.162–4.

12. D H Caldwell, 2013, 'An Intelligence Report on the Hebrides, 1595/6', *West Highland Notes & Queries* ser. 3.23, p.6.

13. RCAHMS, *Argyll 3*, p.214; D J Turner & J G Dunbar, 1970, 'Breachacha Castle, Coll: Excavations and Field Survey, 1965–8', *PSAS* 102, p.166.

14. R C Barrowman, 2015, 'A local response to a wider situation: the archaeology of the clan stronghold of Dùn Èistean, Isle of Lewis', *Post–Medieval Archaeology* 49.1, pp.17–56; D H Caldwell, 2014a, 'Breacachadh Castle 1595', *West Highland Notes & Queries* ser 3.24, pp.24–8.

15. The following account of Breacachadh originally appeared in Caldwell, 'Breacachadh Castle 1595'.

16. N Maclean-Bristol, 1999, *Murder Under Trust: The Crimes and Death of Sir Lachlan Mor Maclean of Duart 1558–1598* (East Linton), pp.211–12.

17. For a fuller analysis of this see Caldwell, 'Intelligence Report on the Hebrides', and Caldwell, 2015, 'The Sea Power of the Western Isles of Scotland in the late Medieval Period', in J H Barrett & S Gibbon (eds), *Maritime Societies of the Viking And Medieval World* (Leeds), pp.350–68. Cunningham possibly arrived in Coll prior to 25 March and hence, as far as contemporaries were concerned, in 1595 rather than 1596.

18. W F Skene, 1880, *Celtic Scotland: a history of Ancient Alban* (Edinburgh), vol 3, pp.436–7.

19. RCAHMS, *Argyll 3*, p.182, dates the wall-head defences on the tower-house to the early 17th century.

20. For early *trace italienne* fortifications in a Scottish context see D H Caldwell & G Ewart, 1998, 'Excavations at Eyemouth, Berwickshire, in a mid-16th-century *trace italienne* Fort', *Post-Medieval Archaeology* 31, pp.61–119.

21. G A Hayes-McCoy, 1964, *Ulster and other Irish Maps* (Dublin), Mount Norris, no. II; the third Blackwater Fort, no. III; Charlemont Fort, no. IV; Inisloughan Fort, no. VI.

22. Maclean-Bristol, *Murder under Trust*, pp.95–7.

23. *CSP Scotland*, XIII, 1597–1603, pt.1, pp.175–6, no. 129. See also Maclean-Bristol, *Murder under Trust*, p.230; *CSP Ireland*, 1598–99, pp.128, 140.

24. Lachlan Mor wrote in July 1595 to Robert Bowes, the English agent in Edinburgh, that he had just disbanded a force of 600 men whom he had had in garrison for three months, *CSP Scotland 1593–95*, no 581.

25. R Miket & D L Roberts, 1990, *The Mediaeval Castles of Skye & Lochalsh* (Portree), pp.67–8.

26. Miket & Roberts, *Mediaeval Castles of Skye & Lochalsh*, pp.108–09.

27. RCAHMS, *Argyll 5*, pp.281–3; D H Caldwell, 2009, 'The Campbell takeover of Islay – the archaeological evidence', in A Horning & N Brannon (eds), *Ireland and Britain in the Atlantic World* (Dublin), pp.89–110; D H Caldwell, 2011, *Islay, Jura and Colonsay: a historical guide* (Edinburgh), pp.184–6.

28. A detail of Gordon's plan showing the fort on Calton Hill is reproduced in RCAMS, *Edinburgh*, p.37, fig. 150.

29. RCAHMS, *Argyll 5*, illus 269B; Caldwell, 'The Campbell takeover of Islay', p.97; Caldwell, *Islay, Jura and Colonsay*, pp.166–7.

30. RCAHMS, *Argyll 5*, p.268; D H Caldwell & N A Ruckley, 2005, 'Domestic Architecture in the Lordship of the Isles', in R Oram & G Stell (eds), *Lordship and Architecture in Medieval and Renaissance Scotland* (Edinburgh), pp.101–02; Caldwell, *Islay, Jura and Colonsay*, pp.164–7.

31. D H Caldwell, 2008a, *Islay: The Land of the Lordship* (Edinburgh), pp.97, 99.

32. C J M Martin, 2014a, 'The Sea World of the Chessmen', in D H Caldwell & M A Hall (eds), *The Lewis Chessmen: New Perspectives* (Edinburgh), pp.191–7.

33. *Register of the Great Seal of Scotland 1424–1513*, J B Paul (ed.), 1882 (Edinburgh), no. 2420.

34. Caldwell, 'Intelligence Report on the Hebrides', pp.5–6. We have excluded from the numbers of warriors from Skye the contingent of 500 due from Trotternish. It is not clear if and when the MacLeods of Harris might have had effective control of that land. See *Acts of the Lords of the Isles, 1336–1493*, J Munro & R W Munro (eds), 1986 (Edinburgh), pp.xxix, l, li, 187, 227–8.

35. The figure of three men to an oar is derived from a report on West Highland ships presented to the Scottish Privy Council in 1615. See Caldwell, 'Having the right kit', pp.144–51.

36. The calendared version of Sumpter's report in *CSP Ireland, vol. 1*, H C Hamilton (ed.), 1860 (London & Dublin), p.416 does not give all this detail. The author has relied on the fuller version transcribed by G G Smith, 1895, *The Book of Islay: documents illustrating the history of the island* (Edinburgh), p.73. The original document is in TNA (SP63/29/38). Sumpter got some of his data from one of 'McAlane's men'. By McAlane he would have meant the Earl of Argyll (MacCailean Mhoir) rather than 'Macklane' (MacLean of Duart) whom he notes was Lord of Mull. The expedition was to accompany Lady Agnes Campbell, the widow of Sir James MacDonald of Dunyvaig and the Glynns, for her marriage to Turlough Luineach O Neil. See G A Hayes-McCoy, 1937, *Scots Mercenary Forces in Ireland, 1565–1603* (Tunbridge Wells), pp.94–109.

37. Caldwell, 'Breacachadh Castle 1595'.

38. The examples known to the author are on crosses at Kilchoman and Kilarrow in Islay (RCAHMS, *Argyll 5*, nos 366/12, 359/18; Saddell and Kilkeran (two) in Kintyre (RCAHMS, *Argyll 1*, nos 296/2, 285/2–3; Kilmory in Knapdale, Inverary (RCAHMS, *Argyll 7*, nos 76/37, 36; Kirkapoll in Tiree, RCAHMS, *Argyll 3*, no 310/3; and on two grave-slabs in Iona, RCAHMS, 1982, *Argyll, An Inventory of the Ancient Monuments vol. 4, Iona* (Edinburgh), nos 6/149 and 159. In general terms all can be dated to the 14th or 15th century.

39. RCAHMS, *Argyll 1*, pp.165–78.

40. *The Asloan Manuscript: a Miscellany in Prose and Verse written by John Asloan in the Reign of James the Fifth*, W A Craigie (ed.), 1923, vol. 1 (Edinburgh), pp.222–4.

41. Caldwell & Stell, *Achanduin Castle*.

42. These finds were reported on by the author in the excavation reports by G Ewart & J Triscott, 1996, 'Archaeological excavations at Castle Sween, Knapdale, Argyll & Bute, 1989–90', *PSAS* 126, nos 28–9, p.539, and J Lewis, 1996, 'Dunstaffnage Castle, Argyll & Bute: excavations in the north tower and east range, 1987–94', *PSAS* 126, no. 42, p.587.

43. Miket & Roberts, 2009, *Mediaeval Castles of Skye & Lochalsh*, pp.108–09; RCAHMS, *Argyll 2*: p.189.

44. This figure of 360 is derived from a statement in the previously-mentioned 1596 report on the Isles to the effect that Islay, in addition to its quota of 800 men, supplied a gentleman from each markland (hence 360) to be household-men to their master (Skene, *Celtic Scotland*, p.438). Martin Martin, *A Description of the Western Islands*

of Scotland circa 1695 (1999 (Edinburgh), p.273), observed at the end of the 17th century the ruins of their houses, and they were pointed out to Pennant in 1772 (1998, *A Tour in Scotland and Voyage to the Hebrides 1772* (Edinburgh), p.214). See also Caldwell, *Islay, Jura and Colonsay*, p.179.

45. *CSP Scotland, Vol. 11 (1593–95)*, no. 581.

46. RCAHMS, *Argyll 3*, fig. 201. For clues to the importance of Ardtornish see *Acts of the Lords of the Isles*, pp.14–18, 27–8, 108–16, 287.

47. The author is dismissing as unlikely the tradition that a building in the courtyard at Kisimul was a chapel. See Dunbar, 'Kisimul Castle', p.39. There does, however, seem to have been a chapel in the island castle of Eilean Dearg at the head of the Kyles of Bute (RCAHMS, *Argyll 7*, pp.282–3).

48. D H Caldwell, 2003, 'Finlaggan, Islay – stones and inauguration ceremonies', in R Welander, D J Breeze & T O Clancy (eds), *The Stone of Destiny: artefact & icon* (Edinburgh), pp.62–5, 69–72; D H Caldwell, 2014b, 'The Kingdom of the Isles', in D H Caldwell & M A Hall (eds), *The Lewis Chessmen: New Perspectives* (Edinburgh), p.80.

49. R W Munro (ed.), 1961, *Monro's Western Isles of Scotland and Genealogies of the Clans 1549* (Edinburgh), p.57.

50. *Vitae Dunkeldensis Ecclesiae Episcoporum A Prima Sedes Fundatione Ad Annum MDXV*, A Myln (ed.), 1823 (Edinburgh), p.16.

51. The excavators of this feature, however, expressed doubt about it being a fireplace because 'occupation-layers' extended into it from the hall. This writer does not share their concern. See Turner & Dunbar, 'Breachacha Castle'.

52. J R N MacPhail (ed.), 1914, *Highland Papers*, vol. 1 (Edinburgh), pp.45–6.

53. Caldwell & Stell, *Achanduin Castle*.

54. This estimate is based on the writer's excavations at Finlaggan, trenches 2 and 12.

55. Chris Tabraham (1988, 'The Scottish medieval towerhouse as lordly residence in the light of recent excavation', *PSAS* 118, pp.267–76) challenged the prevailing notion among scholars that many tower-houses were self-contained residences in a study of Douglas castles in the south of Scotland.

56. RCAHMS, *Argyll 2*, pp.188–94.

57. R Gordon, 1813, *A Genealogical History of the Earldom of Sutherland* (Edinburgh), p.189. Gordon's account is preferred by this writer to the one in *The Historie and Life of king James the Sext*, T Thomson (ed.), 1825 (Edinburgh), pp.217–22. In the latter the meeting took place at an unnamed place in Kintyre.

58. The story is retailed by Mr Hector Mackenzie in his manuscript history of the Mackenzies (1710), now in Glasgow City Archives (Mitchell Library): MS 591702. The author is most grateful to Aonghas MacCoinnich of Glasgow University for providing him with a transcript of the relevant passage (ff.24v–26v).

59. MacPhail, *Highland Papers,* vol. 1, p.47.

60. RCAHMS, *Argyll 3*, p.180, identified socket-holes in the walls as for beams to support brazier-hearths on the first and second floors.

61. W MacKay MacKenzie, 1927, *The Mediaeval Castle in Scotland* (London), p.126, compared the arrangements in the tower at Kisimul to the earlier towers at Threave in Kirkcudbrightshire, Halforest in Aberdeenshire and Lochleven in Kinross-shire in that the main chamber or hall was at second-floor level.

62. RCAHMS, *Argyll 1*, pp.174, 176–8.

63. RCAHMS, *Argyll 2*, pl. 65G.

Plate 1. Kisimul Castle showing the galley-dock partly exposed to the left. (Paula Martin)

Plate 2. Kisimul Castle showing the small upstanding wall of the extramural 'crewhouse' on the right. (Paula Martin)

Plate 3. *Dun Mhic Leoid, a small stone tower in Loch Tangasdail, Barra, with an adjacent artificial platform. The loch may have been used for over-wintering galleys. (Colin Martin)*

Plate 4. *The stone-built galley-harbour beside Kisimul Castle, seen from the top of the tower. The basin can be entered at high tide. (Colin Martin)*

Plate 5. *Armed warriors in a galley. Detail from a West Highland graveslab at Kiel, Lochaline, Morvern (Iona school, early 16th century). (Colin Martin)*

Plate 6. *A galley drawn up in front of a castle. Detail from a West Highland graveslab at Kiel, Lochaline, Morvern (Iona school, late 15th century). (Colin Martin)*

Plate 7. Dunstaffnage Castle with its sheltered anchorage. (Colin Martin)

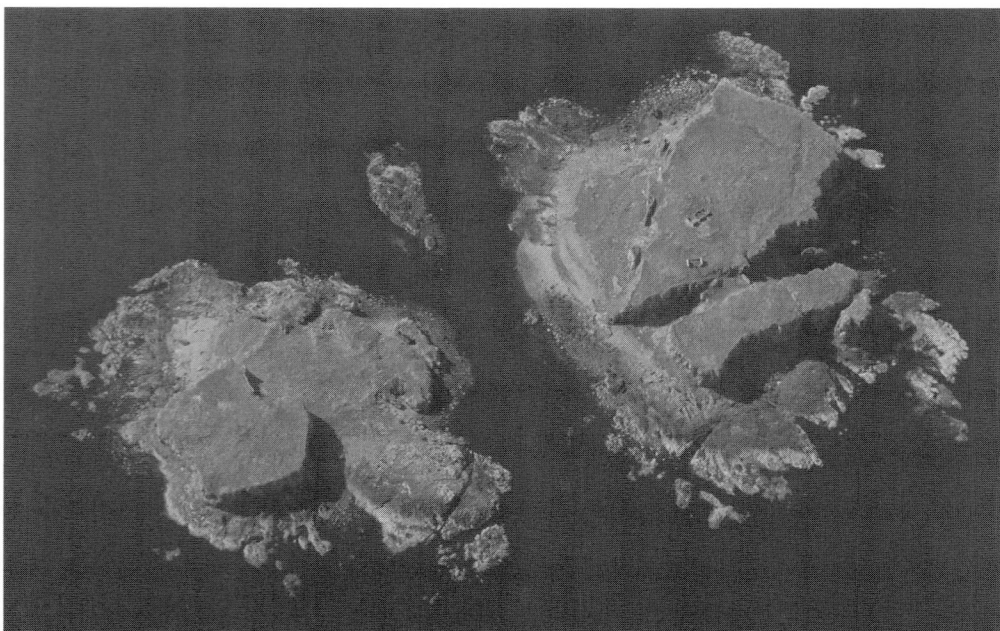

Plate 8. Cairn na Burgh Beg (left) and Cairn na Burgh Mor (right), in the Treshnish Isles. Traces of buildings can be seen on both islands. (Colin Martin)

Plate 9. *Castle Sween, Knapdale, with its boat-landing to the left. (Colin Martin)*

Plate 10. *The castles of Ardtornish (left foreground) and Duart (right background) overlooking the east end of the Sound of Mull. (Colin Martin)*

Plate 11. *Castle Tioram on its tidal islet. (Colin Martin)*

Plate 12. *The headland fort at Rubh' an Dùnain, Skye. (Paula Martin)*

Plate 13. Havhingsten *off Caisteal Dhubhairt. (© The Viking Ship Museum, Roskilde, Denmark; Photograph: Werner Karrasch)*

Plate 14. *The castle of Dunivaig, Islay, seen across the anchorage. (Tom MacNeill)*

Plate 15. The Sound of Islay, looking north-west. Am Fraoch Eilean (centre) is the smaller island off the south-western corner of Jura. The anchorage lies between it and Jura; rising ground on Jura hides most of the Sound from Claig. (Colin Martin)

Plate 16. *A drystone lime-kiln erected on the shore at Castlebay, a community project to produce lime from cockle-shells. (Jamie MacPherson)*

Plate 17. *The complex Atlantic roundhouse at Dun Mor Vaul, Tiree (lower right). At top left is a narrow gully with a sandy beach. Beyond the beach is a curved earth-work (far left) which may be associated with the boat-landing. (Colin Martin)*

Plate 18. *Castle Coeffin, Lismore, with a cleared boat-landing, which is respected by a fish-trap. Below the castle, at right-angles to the landing-strip, are the remains of a stone-built quay. (Colin Martin)*

Plate 19. *Aros Castle, Mull, with the remains of a small harbour on the foreshore (upper left). (Edward Martin)*

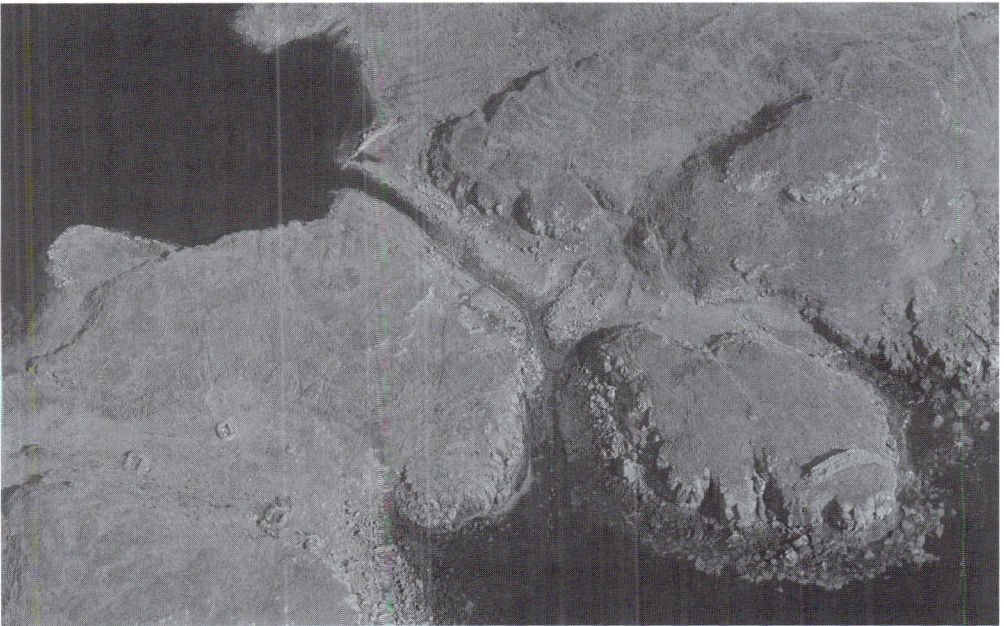

Plate 20. *Rubh' an Dùnain, Skye, with the headland fort (lower right), and the canal leading into the loch (upper left). (Colin Martin)*

Plate 21. *Achanduin Castle, Lismore, on its mound. (Colin Martin)*

Plate 22. *Breachacha Castle, Coll. (Colin Martin)*

Plate 23. The sea-gate at Dunivaig Castle, Islay. (David Caldwell)

Plate 24. The main gate at Skipness Castle, Kintyre. (David Caldwell)

Plate 25. *Castle Fincharn, Loch Awe, mid-Argyll, from the farmland to the east. (Mark Thacker)*

Plate 26. *Overlooking the farm at Fincharn from the south; limestone outcrops above enclosed fields and woodland with Loch Awe in the distance. (Mark Thacker)*

Plate 27. Ash (Fraxinus) standards with hazel (Corylus) underwood. Relict woodland on Loch Aweside. (Mark Thacker)

Plate 28. Castle Fincharn from the south; a lime-coated living agent of lordship. (Mark Thacker)

Plate 29. Cronk yn Howe Mooar from the south-east. Bradda Hill is in the background. (Peter Davey)

Plate 30. Peel Castle from the north, showing St German's cathedral, St Patrick's round tower and chapel as well as a suite of military structures. (Peter Davey)

Plate 31. *Castle Rushen from the air; the island's capital and main naval and military base until the 19th century. (Peter Davey)*

Plate 32. *The unexcavated promontory fort of Purt ny Ceabagh seen from the west. It has clear views to Hango Broogh, 3km to the south, and Castle Rushen, 5km to the south-west. (Peter Davey)*

Plate 33. *The MacSweeney castle at Doe, County Donegal. (Colin Breen)*

Plate 34. Dunluce Castle, County Antrim, first built by the MacQuillans c.1500 but later restructured by the MacDonnells. (Colin Breen)

Plate 35. Rockfleet Castle, County Mayo, one of the primary O'Malley castles. (Colin Breen)

Plate 36. *Moy Castle, Lochbuie, Mull. (Paula Martin)*

Plate 37. *Dundonald Castle: although located inland, the Stewarts' stronghold in Kyle and its Early Historic predecessor controlled a maritime hinterland in the outer Firth of Clyde from the nearby beaching-places on Barassie strand. (Richard Oram)*

Plate 38. Rothesay Castle, Bute: from the later 1220s this castle and its adjacent sheltered anchorage formed the springboard for Stewart domination of the southern Argyll peninsulas. (Richard Oram)

Plate 39. Dunstaffnage Castle: the plan and details of the 13th-century castle of the MacDougall lords of Lorn underscore its owners' engagement with contemporary innovations in elite architectural expression. (Richard Oram)

Plate 40. *Tarbert Castle: on its ridge-top site overlooking East Loch Tarbert and controlling the portage route across the isthmus between Knapdale and Kintyre, King Alexander II's castle projected Scottish royal power into the southern Hebrides. (Colin Martin)*

Plate 41. *Dunvegan Castle, Skye: the late-14th-century addition of a great tower to the MacLeods' 13th-century enclosure-castle is a bold statement of the family's claims to membership of the aristocratic top flight. (Richard Oram)*

Plate 42. *Moy Castle, Lochbuie, Mull: the boat-landing. (Paula Martin)*

Plate 43. Lochbuie, Mull, from the south: Lochbuie House stands top centre, Moy Castle with its boat-landing to its right and closer to the shore. The entrance to the large harbour is to the right of it, and beyond that a later small quay and boat-landing. (Colin Martin)

McGillechrist's Castle: An Environmental Study in Medieval Buildings Archaeology from Argyll

Mark Thacker

THE MEDIEVAL RUINS of Castle Fincharn lie atop a small but steep rock escarpment with extensive views up Loch Awe and inland over the woods and fields of the surrounding farm (Plate 25). The monument was first visited by the author in early 2013 as part of a project investigating the masonry techniques of North Atlantic Europe, and subsequently became a more comprehensively recorded regional case-study.[1] Although the 'North Atlantic' is often characterised as an inherently challenging environment, the province actually encompasses a huge range of contrasting regional environments which have variously enabled how different communities materially constructed their lives. To an archaeologist used to the wind-battered coasts of the Western Isles, looking out from the ruins of this once-fine medieval building, it was the heavy richness of this mid-Argyll landscape that was most salient.

This paper will explore that mid-Argyll landscape as a very simple example of the archaeological potential of standing-building survey and materials analysis. As a result of this work, Castle Fincharn became the first medieval building in Scotland to be directly radiocarbon dated, and that has allowed me to draw together other forms of evidence to present a more holistic narrative of environmental exploitation and change. The primary form of evidence throughout, however, will be the surviving masonry of the ruin itself.

The castle

Castle Fincharn is a rectangular masonry building which occupies the whole level summit of the rectangular rock-outcrop on which it stands, with an additional small enclosed 'bailey' area at the northern end.[2] Although there are large sections of masonry missing, particularly from the south and south-west walls which are reduced to footings only, much of the longer east and west walls are still standing to almost two full storeys, *c.*6m high. These side-walls display evidence of first-floor joist-sockets, narrow ground-floor slit opes and larger arch-headed first-floor window openings, whilst a surviving lintel in the north wall suggests the main entrance of this building was on the ground floor.

Although this degree of ruination undoubtedly means that many architectural details have been lost, the mix of substantially upstanding and completely collapsed masonry here is ideal for examining the general masonry fabric in three dimensions. Most importantly, the collapse has enabled very good visual and physical access to primary wall-cores in full cross-section, allowing the relationship between core, bedding- and facing-mortars to be evaluated, while the concomitant survival of reasonably large sections of wall-face also allows the stone emplacement technique and bonding strategies to be examined and recorded.

The internal and external faces of the walls of Castle Fincharn are of similar character, described by Miller and Kirkhope as of 'Early West Highland type'.[3] The rubble stone surviving in the general wall-faces displays no clearly visible evidence of knapping or dressing, but the regularity of the natural planes of cleavage in the stone and the good organizational technique of the medieval mason has allowed the face-work to be laid in a very consistent formally-coursed masonry style. This comprises often edge-laid blocks of hard, crystalline, dark-coloured and coarsely textured schistose and mafic rocks, which present a large surface area at the wall-face and define the height of each masonry course as between 400 and 450mm.

These blocks were pinned and the wall-courses levelled with smaller fissile flat-laid stones of some different lithologies, including a blue meta-limestone, a red coarsely-porphyrtic possible felsite, and a more-sandy-textured schist or psammite. The building has been raised in reasonably sharply defined and level courses which are evident in cross-section right through the core-rubble and both faces of each wall. Externally the corners of the building are softly rounded on the ground floor and, where they survive, angular on the first floor, with fine sandstone external window-dressings evident at one ground-floor slit-window, while internal quoins and arch-heads generally employ the same small flat-laid fissile rubble schistose stone.

Where visible in full cross-section, the mortar profile across the depth of the masonry is bound with a completely contiguous single-phase lime-based mortar, which had been only very lightly tempered with rounded sands and gravels. That this mortar is a wood-fired limestone-lime was betrayed by a remarkably high concentration of coarse kiln-relict inclusions, including both charcoal and angular-to-subangular calcareous clasts ranging in size up to 60mm. These clasts presented a spectrum of textural evidence for heat-alteration, and some displayed concentric zoning with well-heated/part-calcined rims surrounding poorly-heated relatively-unaltered cores. Examination of these cores *in situ* and in loose hand-sample suggested that the lime provenance was a very dark-blue/black, coarsely-crystalline meta-sedimentary limestone.

The church

The upstanding remains of the parish church of Kilneuair lie *c*.1000m WSW of the castle, and survive as a ruined structure of two main phases with remarkably contrasting masonry styles. The east end is certainly the earlier and, like the castle, displays formally coursed masonry which approaches course-and-snecked, although the larger boulders are generally touching. Although in different proportions, these building-stones are of similar eroded local stone-types to the castle, and have been placed to present a large edge-laid face, levelled and packed by much sharper flat-laid fissile rubble. Although large areas of collapse enable masonry cross-sections and wall-cores to be inspected in many contexts, vigorous moss-growth made characterisation more challenging, and no external coatings appear to have survived. This is, however, a single-phase, contiguous core, bed and internal-coating mortar which, as at Castle Fincharn, is a wood-fired limestone-lime displaying high kiln-relict concentrations including charcoal and heated limestone. This mortar appears more heavily tempered than at the castle, however, with a very well-sorted bimodal sub-millimetric lithic material including large sub-rounded to sub-angular unheated temper clasts to 30mm.

The single upstanding window-jamb of primary masonry to the south of the east wall strongly suggests that the east wall originally contained twin lights, and their internal obtuse-angled quoins, like the trefoil-headed piscina within the south wall, are chisel-dressed and surface-finished. The west end of the church is clearly secondary and the masonry is much less formal, with wall-faces dominated by flat stretchers laid in an uncoursed masonry style, in a limestone-lime more consistently tempered with a fine, generally sub-millimetric aggregate, and a medium-to-high concentration of kiln-relicts.

There is an *ex situ* dressed-stone font within the site, which is probably medieval, and the surrounding burial-ground contains a large range of monuments including some late-medieval graveslabs. These all suggest that this was a medieval parish church.

The environment

The wider environment around the castle, church and farm is largely defined by its underlying metamorphic geology, and the undulating topography of this south-east slope of the Loch Awe syncline rises from the loch-shore to hills up to 400–450m. Today this landscape presents a patchwork of different grazing and woodland types and, in response to the building surveys this was explored through a series of walkovers.

Two possible sources of meta-limestone were identified within a wider geology dominated by metamorphosed formations of the south-west Highland Dalradian, and both are black.[4] Sandy 'Shira' limestone is reported within the region's Ardrishaig phylites, and can be seen outcropping in quarries above the western shore of Loch Phearsain and south to the east of Kilmelfort,[5] whilst 'Tayvallich' limestone is much more widely distributed and reported much closer to our site. Indeed, walkover confirmed the location of one outcrop of this material between the farm of Fincharn and Kilneuair church, within which a classic 19th-century square lime-kiln (also containing kiln-relicts) and quarry were encountered and recorded. In this locality, bluffs of eroded limestone inter-bedded with a coarse young conglomerate and swarms of basalt dykes rise quite suddenly above the cleared and enclosed pasture below, and protrude through the shallow clay-rich soil/overburden in a number of places (Plate 26). The limestone of this outcrop is oriented in beds between vertical and a western dip of *c*.45°, and is generally coarse-grained and very dark blue, with regular veining in two planes (of *c*.70°) and a high concentration of large quartz grains (to 5–7mm). These quartz clasts are often remarkably protruding as they emerge from the eroding meta-sedimentary matrix in which they are held.

Large detrital rubble stones around the shore of Loch Awe adjacent to the castle displayed very similar geomorphologies to those noted within the castle walls and are a likely source for building-stone. Identifying possible sources of mortar-temper, however, was less straightforward as, although the rounded-to-subangular lithic clasts noted within the *in situ* mortars could represent either a terrigenous or aquatic source, local sources appeared restricted to the loch-shore and nearby Fincharn River. These may seem obvious aggregate sources but both contexts displayed insignificant gravel volumes at the time of survey, perhaps explaining the apparently lightly-tempered texture of the mortar within the castle walls.

During walkover, a mature woodland was noted adjacent to Loch Awe on the steeper topography north-east of Castle Fincharn and, despite significant changes in the character of the woodland in the wider region since the Medieval period, this area is conspicuously depicted as wooded on all historical maps of the lower Loch Awe area; including recent, 19th century (1st edn OS), 18th century (Roy Map) and even 16th century documents (Pont 14). For the current project, a 2.8km stretch of this woodland (from NM 9333 06193 to NM 91038 04746) was surveyed in 400m sections over a 4-hour period, during which tree taxa and habits were generally described. A woodland morphology of particular character emerged, generally dominated by tall, very straight ash (*Fraxinus* sp.) standards with a hazel-included underwood of striking 'self-coppice' habit, in which multiple narrow shoots of varying ages grew from a stool below ground (Plate 27). Other tree taxa included low concentrations of oak and some localised populations of birch in seasonally-flooded low-lying areas.

Microscopic analyses

Ultimately 15 mortar samples from Castle Fincharn, two limestone samples from regional outcrops and a sample of detrital gravel from the loch-side were recorded and removed or collected for microscopic analysis and comparison. Three of these mortar samples and both limestones were thick- and thin-sectioned to thicknesses of 1mm and 30microns respectively, and the gravel sample was cast and thin-sectioned also. That the mortar samples removed from the walls of the castle appeared to contain limestone inclusions with remarkably clear concentrically zoned textural and colour variation has already been briefly described during the on-site survey work, but this spectrum of textural alteration was especially clear at microscopic levels of analysis and has significant archaeometric interest.[6] In summary, this heat-alteration was more developed at clast rims, where source-texture had been almost completely lost, while the less-altered cores displayed a coarse heterogeneous metacarbonate with sparry veining and coarse quartz inclusions. Comparison with the loose but representative limestone samples collected from outcrops within the district very clearly confirmed that these kiln-relicts were characteristic of the local Tayvallich lithology, while the quartz-rich schistose gravels sampled from the nearby loch-side also matched those of the mortar-temper source.

Twelve charcoal samples were examined by the author to establish sample porosity and morphology (in order to ensure that at least some of the assemblage had radiocarbon-dating potential) before further characterization to genus or species level was undertaken by Dr Mike Cressey. It is worthwhile stressing that, despite their exposed Highland depositional environment, the charcoal samples were generally very coherent, although many had spring vessels which were completely full of very fine lime. Most importantly ten of the 12 samples were initially characterised as diffuse-porous taxa with roundwood morphologies, suggesting good radiocarbon-dating potential in the assemblage, and of these nine were ultimately interpreted as hazel (*Corylus* sp.), two were oak (*Quercus* sp.), and one was birch (*Betula* sp.).

Documentary evidence

The volume of medieval documentary evidence which might relate to the wider barony of Glassary is unusually rich, and begins with a 1240 royal charter granting lands at Fincharn and elsewhere to Gillescop MacGillechrist.[7] There is, however, no direct reference to any type of castle at Fincharn in this or any subsequent medieval texts, and interpretations of documents which might refer to this building, to the site or to the barony have been widespread and varied. For instance, while both Macphail and RCAHMS doubt Bain's assertion that the 1297 memorandum by Alexander of the Isles which refers to a 'certain castle and barony by the name of Glasrog' is describing Glassary,[8] this association is accepted by Ewart and Baker in their discussion of nearby Carrick.[9] Moreover, although a second royal charter of 1374 to 'Gilbert de Glascestre' describing the '*terras de Glascestre et castrum*' is widely accepted as referring to a castle within the barony of Glassary,[10] many commentators have highlighted that the location of this building has not been identified, perhaps tacitly implying that MacPhail's allusion to Fincharn here does not convince.[11]

Importantly, a more explicit reference identifying Fincharn as the *caput* of this lordship does finally emerge in a 1563 retour confirming to the Scrymgeour family 'the lands of the lordship and barony of Glasre … with the messuage or manor place of the said lordship named Nether Fincharn',[12] although whether this reflects the physical reality on the ground by this period may be doubted (see below). Furthermore, and most significantly for our understanding of the cultural context for the construction of the castle, whether this supposed late-16th-century relationship between a building at Fincharn and the rest of the lordship existed in the preceding three centuries has not been demonstrated.

Architectural evidence

In Glassary, as elsewhere, a more informed perspective on this relationship between castle and lordship has been undermined by the variety of interpretations of the ruined building itself. While some commentators have simply accepted the 1240 royal land-charter as evidence of its construction-date,[13] some have suggested the building is *c*.1300,[14] while others have insisted on architectural grounds that this 'must be a later castle' – and that the ruins at nearby Caol Chaorunn can more convincingly be attributed to this early period.[15] Coventry's description of Castle Fincharn as 'a strong but ruined 16th-century tower-house and courtyard'[16] supports this interpretation, but Millar and Kirkhope's characterisation that the ruined building is 'of uncertain date' is probably a fair summary given that no consensus appears to have been reached.[17]

Coventry's characterisation of Castle Fincharn as a 'tower house',[18] however, highlights a typological ambiguity to add to the chronological one surrounding this particular structure. Elsewhere Castle Fincharn has been described as a 'hall-house', although the typological basis on which similar rectangular two-storied structures in England and Ireland have been interpreted as independent public halls (rather than private-chamber blocks within more complex castle structures) has been convincingly overturned.[19] The structural similarities on which this structural typology was based, however, remain, and within this Fincharn had previously been regarded as the smallest example of a further geographically-defined 'West Highland' group.[20]

Usefully, many of the Irish comparanda have construction and abandonment dates well constrained by documentary evidence, even to particular years,[21] but a more refined international Insular architectural typological approach is undermined by the generally much broader Scottish chronologies which regularly ascribe foundation-dates in terms of centuries or even longer periods only. It is argued here that the constructional form and chronologies of these Scottish buildings need to be refined through archaeological analysis and independent dating at individual sites first, before the social, cultural and political negotiations which the architecture might express, or wider comparative building typologies, are considered further (see postscript below).

Radiocarbon data

On the basis of their short-lived taxonomies, young roundwood morphologies and range of deep-core masonry contexts, five of the charcoal kiln relicts removed and characterised from Fincharn Castle were submitted to SUERC for AMS radiocarbon analysis. Importantly for this study, these samples returned radiocarbon dates which span such a narrow chronological range that (applying Chauvenet criteria) we can suggest the wood-fuel used to fire the lime-kiln was probably cut in a single event. This is significant in supporting previous interpretations that the surviving castle masonry is predominantly single phase, but also allows the data to be combined to produce a more refined date with reduced error. Indeed, calibrated against Int. Cal. 13 the data from Fincharn indicates that a date-range of 1219–1269 cal. AD (at 95.4% probability) should be accepted for the cutting of the lime-kiln fuel.

Although requiring more work, we might push the interpretation of this narrow range of radiocarbon dates to suggest that much of the wood was cut live for the specific purpose of firing the lime-kiln for the castle's construction. The spectrum of Type 3–4 limestone kiln-relicts within the mortar does evidence a wide range of kiln temperatures,[22] but the fuel must have had a reasonably calorific value given that much of this geogenic carbonate was heated to dissociation at significantly over 700°. As hazel does not burn green, this suggests some degree of seasoning of the wood-fuel, and that this process was managed in some way is not unsupported by the lack of evidence for post-mortem taphonomy in the (admittedly small) relict mortar-fuel assemblage. During the woodland walkover a fraction of standing deadwood within the hazel population was often noted, but I would speculate that this is unlikely to remain standing for very long or retain coherence once on the wet woodland floor. A very small seasoning ('old-wood') offset might therefore be appropriate, but within the data this is unlikely to be statistically significant. The high overall concentration of fuel and carbonate kiln-relicts within the mortar also suggest the lime was not refined after slaking to produce a putty or powder, but is a 'hot-lime', which has been slaked, tempered with gravel and mixed in one operation. During construction this hot-lime mortar is likely to have been deposited within the building very soon after burning, making any 'old mortar' effect also insignificant. It is probable that construction was completed over more than one season, so broadening the chronological range very slightly, but the combined calibrated range of 1219–1269 remains a reasonable lower terminus for the construction of Castle Fincharn, and this accords very well with the 1240 royal charter for the surrounding land.

Map evidence

Some of the ambiguity around the identity of Fincharn Castle as the 'castle of Glassary' may relate to the evidence from later periods, although a brief analysis of this material further informs our understanding of the social, geographical and chronological context of the building. In the late 16th century Pont identified the 'castell in Glassrie [as] called Duntreoir', and this name is translated within the margin as 'Duntruyne' (1583–96: 83) apparently confirming the RCAHMS statement that Fincharn castle does not appear on Pont's maps of the region.[23] However, the southern tip of Loch Awe and Glassary are covered in two overlapping sections of his manuscripts (Pont 1583–1614, Map 14: mid-Argyll from Dunoon to Inverary and Loch Awe; Map 15: Argyll north of the Crinan Canal), and within Pont 14 a significant building is clearly drawn on the south shores of Loch Awe, west of the settlements of Fincharn Mor and Beag. This does not appear to be one of Johnson's later additions, and clearly depicts a two-storey building with an arched opening. Although slightly inaccurately positioned, no other archaeological or historical context for this structure is known to this author, and it is possible that this building should be identified as Fincharn Castle.[24]

If this identification can be accepted, we should then also question why no roof-structure has been drawn – a missing feature which clearly contrasts with Pont's depictions of the other Loch Awe castles of Innes Chonnel and Kilchurn on the same manuscript (Pont 14), both of which, unlike single-phase Fincharn, have 16th-century phases, and that Fincharn Castle is not redrawn on the overlapping section of Map 15 may also suggest further ambiguity about the status of this apparently roofless building. Although again cartographically apparently misplaced, in the text of the same document Pont describes Kilmichael (not Kilneuair) as the parish church of Glassary and, although the reasons for the translation have until now remained obscure, in this case it is well known that at some time around the Reformation the parish church had been moved to this more central location.[25] It is therefore possible that these texts and depictions describe the late-16th-century political reality in the region as centred on Duntrune and Kilmichael, and this may allow further chronological refinement for the biography of Castle Fincharn.

By the mid 18th century Fincharn Castle is labelled on the Roy Map (1747–55) but is shown as a simple open square which (like the building in Pont 14) has no roof, and by the mid 19th century the ruin of the castle at some distant unspecified date had already passed into local folklore.[26] Oral tradition recounts that the castle was ruined by an act of arson, perpetrated by angry vassals, and this finds some support from a 1501 petition to the Pope written by James and John Scrymgeour (respectively rector and patron of the parish church of Kilneuair) requesting the excommunication of certain,

> 'wild men' who at that time lived 'even within the limits of this parish … [and] who cannot be coerced or punished by secular judge or power and within the said limits and surrounding vicinity, especially at the … castle of Fynchaers … [who] … habitually carry out many homicides, thefts, robberies, burnings, oppressions, vulgarly called lesornyng'.[27]

Ironically, therefore, the first documentary reference to Castle Fincharn as the lordly *caput* of the barony of Glassary, which was written in 1563 and included the patronage of the rectory and vicarage of the Church of Kilneuair, may (on the eve of the castle's ruin) evidence another truth entirely.[28] If we can accept that this retour at least suggests that the castle was in some way habitable, then this allows a lower terminus for the building's ruin, while Pont's maps, depictions and descriptions appear to allow an upper terminus for both the ruin of the castle and the translation of the parish church. The evidence therefore suggests the movement of the secular and ecclesiastical centre of the lordship at some time between 1563 and 1593.

The woodland

The short-lived taxa and roundwood morphologies of the relict-fuel within the lime-mortar of the castle conforms to the self-coppicing habit of the hazel population of the woodland growing near Fincharn today, and allows us to speculate that a similar hazel-included underwood habitat may have pertained in the Medieval period. In terms of context this may be supported by the longevity of this woodland context in map evidence dating back to the 16th century, and a mid-19th-century description specifically identifying 'a considerable portion of natural wood [as opposed to the previously described 'plantations'] as oak, hazel and birch etc, along Lochaweside'.[29]

Given its high concentration in walkover survey, however, the lack of ash (*Fraxinus*) within both this 19th century account and the mortar-fuel assemblage from the castle is salient. Moreover this is the reverse of the situation to that presented by the excavated material from nearby Castle Carrick, where ash was a significant fraction of the excavated structural-timber assemblage but was not represented in putative fragments of relict native woodland local to this Loch Goil site.[30] Crone speculates that the lack of ash evidence within current populations near Carrick might suggest local over-exploitation at an early date, but this region does also present a largely non-calcareous underlying geology and in this respect Fincharn is always likely to be more conducive to ash growth and regeneration. Accepting that environmental diversity is therefore likely to be a significant factor in building evidence, the more remarkable contrast between these broadly-contemporary buildings is that the structural timber evidence at Castle Carrick is dominated by ash, oak and pine, while the lime-kiln-relict assemblage at Castle Fincharn is dominated by hazel. Indeed, this structural evidence at Carrick appears to foreshadow the later medieval baron-court records forbidding quite precisely the cutting of oak, ash and pine,[31] and, although we have no upstanding evidence at Fincharn, these taxa are perhaps likely to have formed the structural assemblage here also.

Comparing the two sites archaeologically, ecologically and geologically may indicate more extensive intra-regional trade of structural timber, converted or otherwise, than has been previously acknowledged. The ubiquitous 'self-coppicing' morphology of the hazel shrubs recorded during the walkover survey of Fincharn, however, is a 'natural' habit and, although this does not preclude more anthropogenic coppice morphologies at various times in the past,[32] this would be difficult to assess without root-stock examination.

With some minor variation, the map evidence appears to suggest that before the emergence of large softwood plantations in the 20th century, a fairly static general picture of woodland-distribution pertained around Loch Awe between the late 16th and 19th centuries. This is important in suggesting that significant deforestation had probably already taken place around Fincharn before 18th-century improvement and enclosure, and this may be supported by the *Statistical Accounts* which describe how peat was the general fuel of a parish which 'cannot by any means be said to be wooded'.[33] Unusually at Fincharn, we can tentatively push this post-medieval documentary evidence back into the late-medieval period, as the 1501 Scrymgeour petition to the pope, noted above, describes Kilneuair as being in 'quite a wooded place near the sea shore'.[34] That a slightly dubious geographical description and estimation of the local tree-density should be offered in a petition seeking the excommunication of the current 'wild' residents of Castle Fincharn is curious, and suggests that we should treat this apparently incidental reference carefully, but if the locality could at that time reasonably be described as a 'wooded place', then by late-medieval standards this probably indicates quite extensive tree coverage, and is in direct contrast with the later evidence discussed above.

To investigate the woodland history around Fincharn before this late-medieval map and documentary evidence, however, we must return to the physical evidence which survives in the Argyll landscape today. In an important study describing the complex development of woodland in Upper Loch Awe, through historical, ecological and especially palynological research, Philip Sansum divided the medieval changes in woodland pollen here into two main phases or 'zones'. The first, of AD 800–1240, describes a generally 'open woodland … of oak, alder and hazel … [with an] … influx of birch … [peaking in the 12th century and] … mediated by grazing', while in the second period, 1240–1590, 'pollen accumulation rates are appreciably lower … signify[ing] a long period when the woodland on the site became more open than that represented in the previous zone … and wetter'.[35]

That this evidence is also presented on the less calcareous geologies of Upper Loch Awe might, once more, account for the lack of *Fraxinus* in these results, and allows us to speculate that this excellent timber may have been a valuable trade-commodity. In this regard, whether or not lime-kiln fuel-types are more reflective of local rather than regional or inter-regional resources remains to be demonstrated and, as the preliminary evidence appears to suggest some geographical and chronological variation in woodland resources even in mid-Argyll, this will be an important issue for the archaeological potential of the materials used throughout Scotland going forward. On a smaller scale, however, it is important to recognise that the major human impact on the woodland of Upper Loch Awe in the late 16th century highlighted by Sansum's research is also apparent in the documentary evidence associated with Castle Fincharn, while significant vegetational change was initiated in the district from the same *c.*1240 date.

McGillechrist's Castle

As the first directly radiocarbon-dated medieval building in Scotland, my investigation of Castle Fincharn demonstrated how a more chronologically refined understanding of the upstanding archaeology can allow many other types of evidence to be correlated to present a more holistic narrative of lordship construction in this period.

In situ archaeological analysis of the mortar and masonry of the church of Kilneuair suggests that the earliest phase of this building was erected within the same 'early Highland' masonry traditions as Castle Fincharn, while architectural typology suggests that this church was also built in the mid 13th century. By the late 13th century the parish and lordship of Glassary had become co-extensive[36] and, although sited on its northern edge, the political link between castle and church in the Medieval period was so strong that it was only when Castle Fincharn was finally ruined in the late 16th century that the parish church eventually translated to the more conveniently sited Kilmichael-Glassary. It is this shared medieval biography of castle and church which suggests most strongly that Castle Fincharn is indeed the 'castle of Glassary' throughout the period, and this is supported by the somewhat remote location of both church and castle within these polities.

If this can be accepted, then the documentary evidence also allows a 1297 upper terminus for the construction of the castle building to complement the 1219 lower terminus provided by the radiocarbon data. That the 1240 charter does not mention this building, however, also suggests this is a likely documentary lower terminus, and the archaeology of the mortar fuel indicates the castle was probably constructed shortly after this date. This refined chronology also then allows the building to be more confidently ascribed to a significant historical figure – this is Gillescop MacGillechrist's castle.

Discussion

That the material evidence from Castle Fincharn has much wider significance for our understanding of the chronology and regionality of high-medieval lordship and parish-formation within Glassary, Argyll and the wider North Atlantic is discussed in much greater detail elsewhere,[37] but it is worth noting here that the origins of the northern *locus* of this particular lordship are probably geo-historical and of long standing. For thousands of years lower Loch Awe would have been a crossroads where land- and water-routes down the loch met the north-south routeway between Kintyre and Lorn, and this location provides a context for us to speculate further about the position of Fincharn and MacGillechrist within a medieval landscape of lordship in mid-Argyll.

As convincingly argued by Sellar, Gillescop, Ewen, GilPatrick and (possibly) Dovenaldus MacGillechrist were all nephews of Sween the Red, and the clan has promoted an ancestral narrative rooted within the much earlier medieval histories of Ireland and Argyll.[38] Within this scheme the 13th-century MacSween, MacFerchar, and especially MacGilchrist cousins appear to control land within an earlier consolidated polity of 'Knapdaill and Glassrie', of which a 17th-century account describes Sween as 'thane'.[39] That this Campbell history was written in English, however, suggests that it is very likely to be a late translation of an orally-transmitted reference to Sween as '*toísech*' of Knapdaill and Glassrie with concomitant implications in terms of Gaelic kinship and lordship. The title of *toísech*, and its relationship to 'thane' and 'mormaer', has been much discussed by scholars with reference to the emergence of feudal high-medieval lordship from Pictish eastern Scotland,[40] but the term might be much more simply translated in Argyll, where the Scottish crown was less powerful and where Sween's lordship was much closer in extent to an Irish *tuath*.

Although the southern boundary of this putative *tuath* has been delimited in the hills south of Skipness, this is an otherwise nicely topographically constrained unit of land which others, extrapolating from evidence contained within the *Senchus fer n'Alban*, have speculated may correspond somewhat with the southernmost sept of the *cenél Loairn*.[41] If this can be accepted, the unusually large prehistoric burial-cairn on the farm at Fincharn, after which the castle and farm are named, may very well have served as a prominent 'ancestral' marker for the northern boundary of the kingdom, as has been reported in 8th-century Ireland,[42] and the symbolism appropriated by later elites and communities. Given recent scholarship surrounding the apparent disappearance of Dál Riata, bridging the documentary gap between this putative 8th-century political geography and the 10th-century emergence of MacGillechrist's ancestors in Argyll is a challenge for historians, but it does appear likely that this region continued to be organized around a system of local kingdoms within which we may glimpse smaller polities.[43]

It is likely that the geology, topography and geography of Fincharn had always made the place a fertile focus for settlement, but that deeply-rooted ancestral lordship provided a symbolic context for the location of MacGillechrist's castle, as well as his status within his kin, is resonant given the accelerating rate of cultural, environmental and political change suggested by the archaeological evidence within the 13th-century building and landscape. I am not seeking to underplay the significant changes in mid-Argyll society around the turn of the millennium, but medieval buildings and their environments are contingent and reflexive mediators of power, and the emergence of mortared masonry within the archaeological record of any region is always a moment of huge social and cultural import. Whether associated with castles, churches or burial-monuments, lime-mortars and coatings animate buildings to serve as powerful living agents of authority which physically, symbolically and legally co-represent 'the body of the chief' and the body of the saints (Plate 28).[44] In mid-13th-century Glassary, Castle Fincharn represented Gillespic MacGillechrist, a man capable of commissioning some of the earliest masonry buildings in the region to symbolise and mediate his power and ancestry.

Comparison of the materials used to construct this building with those available in the wider environment demonstrates their overwhelmingly local provenance as MacGillechrist exploited the Fincharn environment, as the 1240 charter allowed, '*in bosco et plano*'.[45] Comparing the taxa-specific fuel-evidence in Castle Fincharn with structural evidence from elsewhere in mid-Argyll suggests MacGillechrist and other castle-builders were exploiting their woodland resources in particular ways, but that in Loch Awe, from this same mid-13th-century period, tree cover would begin to 'decline … under stress [involving] elements of climate, grazing and depletion of the wood resource by an expanding human population'.[46]

Gillespic MacGillechrist's *floruit*, however, coincided with a period of complex cultural tides and by 1300 his lordship and the whole Sween *tuath* would have been largely lost to kindreds from further south and east. From this perspective, as the crown sought greater control in the west, MacGillechrist's castle may also represent an attempt to negotiate his position and accommodate his lordship within the larger kingdom of Scotland. But that Sansum cited climate-change and population-growth as factors in the post-1240 change in the woodland history of Loch Awe is also very pertinent to our discussion of this building's wider context. Quite clearly during this period there were much larger environmental as well as political forces in motion, in mid-Argyll as elsewhere, which were essentially outwith MacGillechrist's control (Oram, this volume), and from this perspective the castles of Sween, Fincharn, Skipness and Tarbert are an important last brief masonry glimpse of this powerful family before they were overwhelmed.

Postscript – The Scottish Medieval Castles and Chapels C-14 Project

A more detailed description of the work undertaken at Fincharn and a number of other medieval sites is presented within the author's PhD thesis,[47] and the palaeo-environmental methodologies developed therein have now been incorporated within a national medieval-buildings survey and analysis project, called the 'Scottish Medieval Castles and Chapels C-14 Project' (or 'SMCCCP'). From that perspective, although it is clear that the results from this preliminary analysis of Castle Fincharn have implications for our understanding of a number of other buildings in Argyll and elsewhere (perhaps particularly at the nearby castles of Sween, Skipness, Tarbert, Coeffin, Ardtornish and Fraoch Eilean), as investigations at these buildings are at a much earlier stage there has been no attempt to speculate further on these relationships here. More archaeologically and chronologically refined individual case-studies, like Fincharn, are required to inform interdisciplinary comparative debate while the SMCCCP is also seeking to develop the archaeological, palaeo-environmental and dating potential of Scottish medieval building-materials more widely.

Given that the author's materials research in this field began with a study of the medieval and later shell-limes of the Western Isles, however,[48] it is entirely appropriate that the first results of these methodologies should be publicly presented here, and this paper is dedicated to Lachie Morrison of Gearradubh, Grimsay.

Acknowledgements

The author would like to gratefully acknowledge the support and advice of John Raven, Allan Rutherford and Rod McCullagh (all HES); Angus Wilson (the owner of Castle Fincharn) for his enthusiastic support and permission to work on the site; Geoff Bromiley (School of Geosciences, University of Edinburgh) for supervising the thesis research from which details of this case-study have been taken; Mike Cressey (CFA Archaeology, Edinburgh) for archaeobotanical analysis, verification and discussion; and the staff at SUERC (in particular Gordon Cook and Tony Krus) for radiocarbon analysis and discussion. HES funded the archaeobotanical and radiocarbon analyses.

Notes

1. M Thacker, 2016, Constructing Lordship in North Atlantic Europe: the archaeology of masonry mortars in the medieval and later buildings of the Scottish North Atlantic, unpublished PhD thesis, University of Edinburgh.
2. RCAHMS, *Argyll, An Inventory of the Ancient Monuments* vol. 7, *Mid Argyll & Coual, Medieval & Later Monuments* (Edinburgh).
3. H Millar & J Kirkhope, 1964, 'Fincharn Castle', *Discovery & Excavation in Scotland*, p.9.
4. See G Borradaile, 1970, 'The west limb of the Loch Awe syncline and the associated cleavage fan', *Geological Magazine* 107.5, pp.459–67; P Gower, 1977, 'The Dalradian rocks of the west coast of the Tayvallich peninsula', *Scottish Journal of Geology* 13, pp.125–33, although the BGS now favour the term 'neoproterozoic'.
5. G Borradaile, 1977, 'The Dalradian rocks of northern Loch Awe', *Scottish Journal of Geology* 13, pp.155–64.
6. Thacker, Constructing Lordship in North Atlantic Europe.
7. J R N MacPhail (ed.), 1916, *Highland Papers*, vol. 2 (Edinburgh), pp.114–5.
8. Macphail, *Highland Papers*, vol. 2, p.149; RCAHMS, *Argyll 7*, p.286; *Documents illustrative of the history of Scotland from the death of king Alexander the Third to the accession of Robert Bruce*, J Stevenson (ed.) 2 vols, 1870 (Edinburgh), p.191.

9.   G Ewart & F Baker, 1998, 'Carrick Castle: symbol and source of Campbell power in south Argyll from the 14th to the 17th century', *PSAS* 129, p.998.
10. MacPhail, *Highland Papers*, vol.2, pp.148–9.
11. E.g. G W S Barrow, 1980, *The Anglo Norman Era in Scottish History* (Oxford), p.69.
12. MacPhail, *Highland Papers*, vol.2, p.206.
13. M Campbell, 1984, *Mid-Argyll: an archaeological guide*, p.33; RCAHMS, *Argyll 7*, p.285; H James, 2009, Medieval Rural Settlement: a study of Mid-Argyll, Scotland, unpublished PhD thesis, University of Glasgow, p.250.
14. https://canmore.org.uk/site/22777/fincharn-castle
15. M Campbell & M Sandeman, 1962, 'Mid-Argyll: a field survey of the historic and prehistoric monuments', *PSAS* 95, pp.86–7.
16. M Coventry, 1997, *The Castles of Scotland* (Edinburgh), p.179.
17. Millar & Kirkhope, 'Fincharn Castle', p.9.
18. Coventry, *Castles of Scotland*, p.179
19. J Blair, 1993, Hall and chamber: English domestic planning 1000 – 1250, in G Meirion-Jones & M Jones, *Manorial Domestic Buildings in England and Northern France* (London), pp. 1–21; T O'Keeffe, 2014, 'Halls, "hall-houses" and tower-houses in medieval Ireland: disentangling the needlessly entangled', *Castle Studies Group Journal* 27, pp.252–62.
20. P Sweetman, 1998, 'The hall-house in Ireland', *Archaeology Ireland* 12.3, p.15; RCAHMS, *Argyll 7*.
21. P Holland, 1996, 'The Anglo-Normans and their castles in County Galway', in G Moran & R Gillespie, *Galway: History and Society* (Dublin), p.11.
22. Thacker, Constructing Lordship in North Atlantic Europe.
23. RCAHMS, *Argyll 7*, p.285.
24. As has also been suggested by James, Medieval Rural Settlement, p.136, although without further discussion.
25. Cosmo Innes (ed.), 1851, 1854, 1855, *Origines Parochiales Scotiae: The Antiquities Ecclesiastical and Territorial of the Parishes of Scotland* (Edinburgh), vol. 2, p.43.
26. D Campbell, 1844, 'The Parish of Glassary', in *New Statistical Account of Scotland*, vol. 7, pp.675–700.
27. *Calendar of Papal Letters xvii, part 1, 1492–1503*, A Fuller (ed.), 1994, no. 493; also referenced in S Boardman, 2006, *The Campbells 1250–1513* (Edinburgh).
28. MacPhail, *Highland Papers*, vol.2, p.206.
29. Campbell, 'Parish of Glassary', p.681.
30. A Crone, 1998, 'Wooden objects', , in G Ewart & F Baker, 'Carrick Castle: symbol and source of Campbell power in south Argyll from the 14th to the 17th century', *PSAS* 129, p.981.
31. F Watson, 1997, 'Rights and responsibilities: woodland management as seen through baron court records', in T Smout (ed.), *Scottish Woodland History* (Dalkeith), pp.100–114.
32. Contra P Sansum, 2004, Historical resource-use and ecological change in semi-natural woodland: western oakwoods in Argyll, Scotland, unpublished PhD thesis, University of Stirling, p.129.
33. *Old Statistical Account*, 1791–9, J Sinclair (ed.), vol. 13, p.664.
34. *Calendar of Papal Letters xvii, part 1, 1492–1503*, no. 493.
35. Sansum, Historical resource-use and ecological change; P Sansum, 2005, 'Argyll Oakwoods: Use and ecological change 1000 to 2000 AD – a Palynological-Historical investigation', *Botanical Journal of Scotland* 57.1–2, pp.214, 219.

36. Boardman, *The Campbells*, p.12.
37. Thacker, Constructing Lordship in North Atlantic Europe.
38. W D H Sellar, 1971, 'Family Origins in Cowal and Knapdale', *Scottish Studies* 15, pp.21–37.
39. Sellar, 'Family Origins in Cowal and Knapdale'; Macphail , *Highland Papers*, vol.2, p.82.
40. J Bannerman, 1993, 'MacDuff of Fife', in A Grant & K Stringer (eds), *Medieval Scotland*: 20–38 (Edinburgh); A Grant, 1993, 'Thanes and thanages', in Grant & Stringer, *Medieval Scotland*, pp.39–81; see S T Driscoll, 1998, 'Formalising the Mechanisms of State Power: Early Scottish Lordship from the Ninth to the Thirteenth Centuries', in S Foster, A Macinnes & R MacInnes (eds), *Scottish Power Centres from the Early Middle Ages to the Twentieth Century* (Glasgow), pp.32–58.
41. M Lobay, 2009, *Contextual landscape study of the early Christian churches of Argyll. The persistence of memory* (BAR 488: Oxford), p.53.
42. E O'Brien & E Breathnach, 2011, 'Irish boundary Ferta their physical manifestation and historical context', in F Edmonds & P Russell, *Tome: Studies in Medieval Celtic History and Law* (Woodbridge), pp.53–64.
43. See D Dumville, 2011, 'Political Organisiation in Dál Riata', in F Edmonds & P Russell, *Tome: Studies in Medieval Celtic History and Law* (Woodbridge), pp.41–52.
44. Raven, 2005, Medieval Landscapes and Lordship in South Uist, unpublished PhD thesis, University of Glasgow, p. 273; Thacker, 2011, An archaeology of the lime and shell-lime mortars of the Western Isles, unpublished MA dissertation, University of York.
45. Macphail, *Highland Papers*, vol. 2, p.122.
46. Sansum, Historical resource-use and ecological change in semi-natural woodland, p.233.
47. Thacker, Constructing Lordship in North Atlantic Europe.
48. Thacker, An archaeology of the lime and shell-lime mortars of the Western Isles.

THREE ARCHIPELAGOS: PERSPECTIVES ON EARLY MODERN BARRA

Domhnall Uilleam Stiùbhart

IN THIS PAPER I shall try to resolve two straightforward but challenging questions. Given the paucity of relevant sources, and their diverse provenance, to what extent can we construct a coherent, convincing, and suitably contextualised interpretation of the history of a small, under-researched Hebridean kindred during a crucial moment in its past? And how might such a history contribute to the ongoing reassessment of the early modern history of the western Gàidhealtachd over the past generation – a reassessment to which this article is strongly indebted?

The dearth of conventional archival documents relating to the island of Barra and its MacNeil chiefs makes for a demanding task. There are no surviving family muniments, and the smattering of relevant sources are unclear concerning the legal chiefly succession, and even on occasion the identity of the chiefs themselves. The period under discussion is comparatively brief: the lifetime of one, albeit long-lived, chief of the MacNeils, the charismatic Ruairidh an Tartair (Roderick the Tartar), who was active in the final quarter of the 16th and the first quarter of the 17th centuries. Ruairidh's biography is complicated by his having had two families of sons by two different women. Contemporary evidence is contradictory, but the most persuasive modern interpretation, that of the Gaelic scholar John Lorne Campbell, proposes that the chief's legitimate wife was Mòr or Marion MacDonald, sister to Dòmhnall mac Ailein, Captain of Clan Ranald, and Raghnall mac Ailein of Benbecula, while his other partner – island tradition alluded to a 'love-match' – was Màiri MacLeod, daughter of Uilleam, chief of the MacLeods of Harris, wife of Donnchadh Campbell of Castle Sween and mother to Sir Dùghall Campbell of Auchinbreck[1] (Figures 12.1 and 12.2). Perhaps to a greater extent than most of his contemporaries, the political strategies adopted by Ruairidh an Tartair were shaped by the need to unify his fractured kindred in order to prevent a lethal feud breaking out between these two groups of sons, their relatives, and their respective supporters.

The convoluted history of the MacNeils of Barra during this period unfolds within three different geographical scales, in three nested archipelagos. Firstly, there is the local micro-archipelago: Barra and its surrounding islands, stretching from the tail of the Bishop's Isles to the south, to the constellation of islets off Barra's north-east shore,

The sons of Ruairidh an Tartair

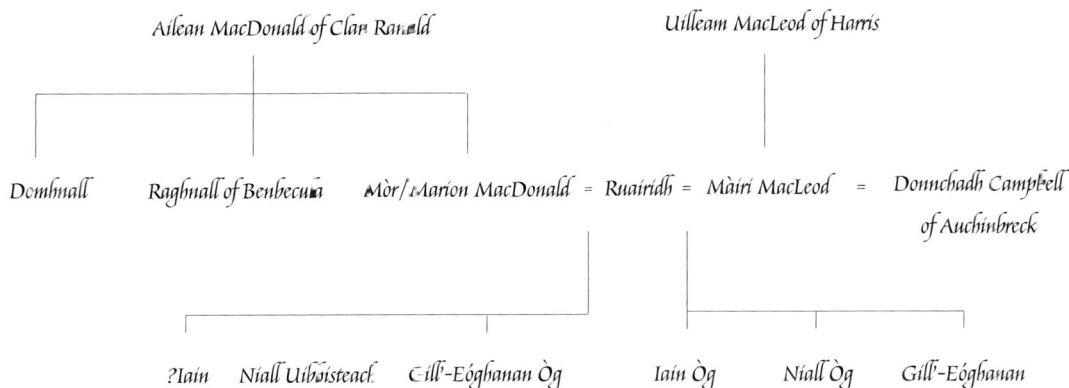

Ailean MacDonald of Clan Ranald   Uilleam MacLeod of Harris

Domhnall   Raghnall of Benbecula   Mòr/Marion MacDonald = Ruairidh = Màiri MacLeod   = Donnchadh Campbell of Auchinbreck

?Iain   Niall Uibhisteach   Gill'-Eóghanan Òg   Iain Òg   Niall Òg   Gill'-Eóghanan

Figure 12.1.

The marriages of Lachlann Barrach

son of Lachlann Mór Maclean of Duart and probable foster-son of Ruairidh an Tartair

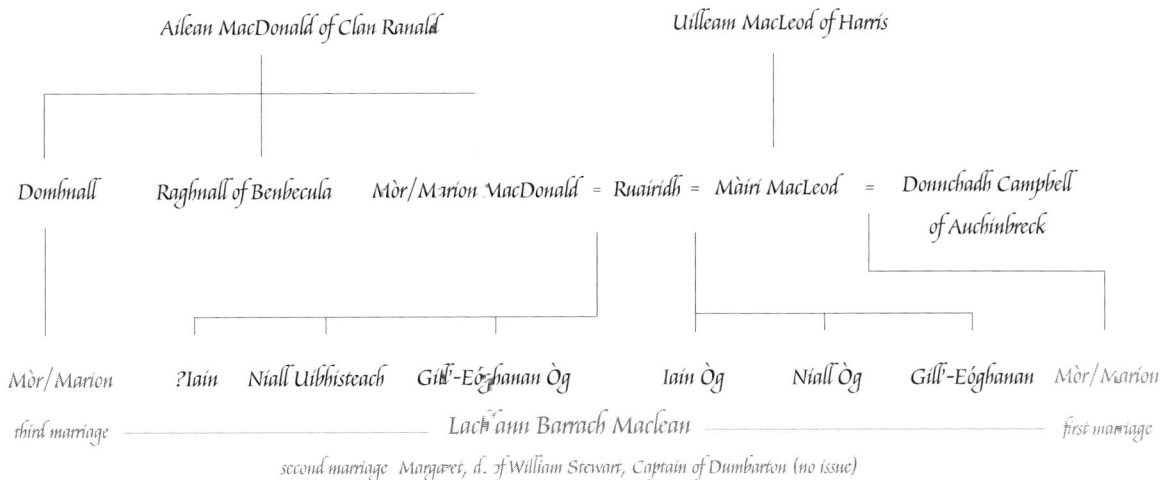

Ailean MacDonald of Clan Ranald   Uilleam MacLeod of Harris

Domhnall   Raghnall of Benbecula   Mòr/Marion MacDonald = Ruairidh = Màiri MacLeod   = Donnchadh Campbell of Auchinbreck

Mòr/Marion   ?Iain   Niall Uibhisteach   Gill'-Eóghanan Òg   Iain Òg   Niall Òg   Gill'-Eóghanan   Mòr/Marion

third marriage ————————————— Lachlann Barrach Maclean ————————————— *first marriage*

second marriage Margaret, d. of William Stewart, Captain of Dumbarton (no issue)

Figure 12.2.

then, still further north-east, to the 'lost patrimony' of the island of Eirisgeigh/Eriskay and the district of Baghasdail/Boisdale in South Uist, ceded to the MacDonalds of Clan Ranald at the end of the 16th century. At least nine of these islands were inhabited up to the 19th century, and evidence suggests that during the clan era the Barra micro-archipelago served a variety of economic and social functions within the wider estate: as pasturage for cattle and sheep, for fishing, for fowling, and as hunting reserves for deer and grouse. I cannot investigate this context in detail in this paper, but I shall allude to it in the addendum when analysing the account of Barra by Martin Martin.

Secondly, there is the regional meso-archipelago: not only the chain of the Outer Hebrides of which the Barra micro-archipelago occupies the southern extremity, but the entire western seaboard of the Scottish Gàidhealtachd. As we shall see, throughout much of the 16th century and beyond the Clan MacNeil was closely associated with, and nominally subordinate to, a major kindred of the southern Inner Hebrides: the Macleans of Duart on the island of Mull.

Finally, there is the international macro-archipelago, or more specifically, the western approaches to the North-East Atlantic Island Group incorporating Scotland, Ireland and England. Intriguing evidence suggests that, to a greater extent than most contemporary Hebridean kindreds, the MacNeils of Barra operated within this wider maritime framework. Unable to carry out cattle-raids by land, and trusting to their relative inaccessibility and insignificance in regional and national politics, the clan undertook extensive voyages, established affiliations with other maritime communities, and – like many of their coastal contemporaries throughout these islands – took advantage of the burgeoning opportunities for small-scale plunder and exchange offered by increasing commercial trade on the one hand, and regional conflict and disorder on the other.

We can tentatively, and roughly, divide this period in Barra's history into four phases, typified by a narrowing of focus, loss of power, and restriction of movement. Firstly, in the last quarter of the 16th century, years of long sea-voyages to Ireland, and possibly to the Northern Isles, the MacNeils operated as independent actors involved in piracy and raiding.[2] During this phase, the MacNeils were followers of the Macleans of Duart and allies of the MacLeods of Harris, fighting beside them in both Ireland and Scotland. Secondly, after the disastrous defeat of their principal patrons at the Battle of Gruinard in 1598, and the dwindling of the Macleans' potential military value to the English Crown after the conclusion of the Nine Years' War in Ulster, the focus of MacNeil operations shifted to the Outer Hebrides. There they played a significant role in aiding, abetting, and possibly directing the MacLeods of Lewis in their struggle against the colonial plantation enterprise of the Fife Adventurers. A third phase ensued following the defeat of two successive attempts at plantation by the Adventurers, and increased pressure from the Edinburgh authorities as a result of the kidnapping of most Hebridean chiefs in 1608. As the ageing Ruairidh an Tartair lost his authority, a short interval of bloody internecine struggle erupted in Barra itself as two different factions within the family jockeyed for position, using neighbouring clans and state power against their rivals. Finally, the conflict was resolved through an uneasy reconciliation brought about by the re-imposition of Maclean suzerainty under the lordship of a new regional powerbroker, Ruairidh MacKenzie of Coigach.

⌘ ⌘ ⌘

The MacNeils of Barra were unique among clans in the Outer Hebrides in not holding a mainland or 'quasi-mainland' territorial wing opposite their island possessions. Their northern rivals, the MacDonalds of Clan Ranald, held the mainland districts of Moidart, Arisaig, south Morar, and, until the early 17th century, Knoydart in the Rough Bounds. As well as North Uist, the MacDonalds of Sleat possessed Trotternish and the fertile peninsula of Sleat itself on the island of Skye, as well as enjoying access to other MacDonald territories on the mainland opposite until the end of the 16th century. The MacLeods of Harris were proprietors of Dunvegan and Minginish in Skye, and the district of Glenelg on the mainland. Finally, until their dispossession by the MacKenzies in the early 17th century, Sìol Thormoid, the MacLeods of Lewis, occupied extensive territories ringing the entire north Minch basin (Figure 12.3).

The doubling of island and mainland territories outlined above may be a local modification of the medieval multiple estate, where a more fertile, lower-lying core was complemented by an altogether rougher and more mountainous margin. For an estate to function successfully, especially in such a risk-laden and occasionally disorderly environment as the Scottish Gàidhealtachd, it was advantageous to possess both types of territory, benefitting from their different produce and the different people inhabiting them. More immediately pertinent, however, is the fact that kindreds possessing extensive island territories required secure timber reserves with which to build, equip, and maintain the galleys vital to safeguard control of the seas around these territories – their maritories, to use the term currently in vogue – as well as to ensure regular communication with and transport to and from their islands. Such

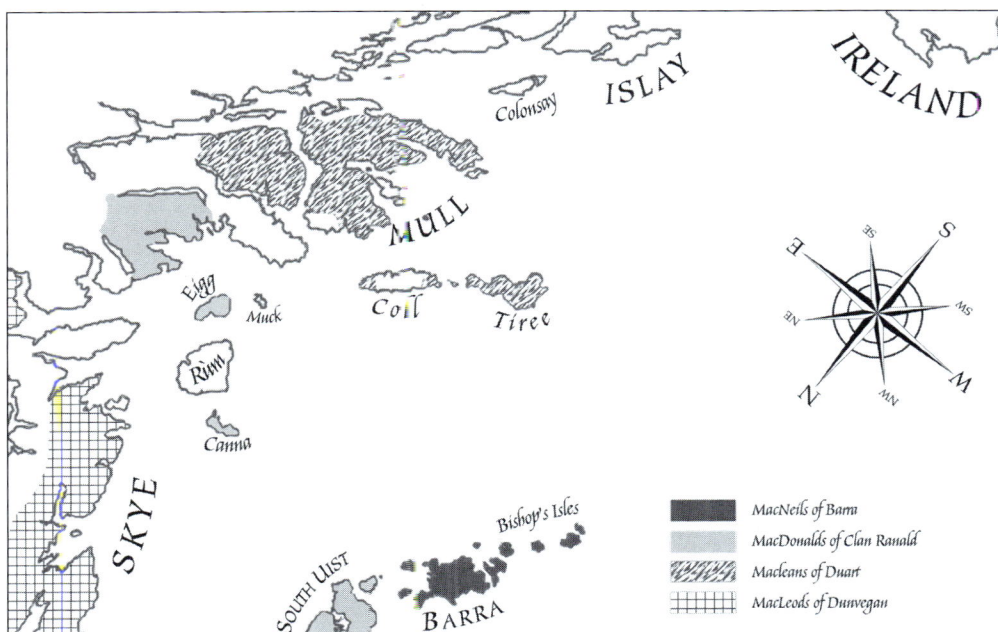

Figure 12.3. *A vernacular vantage-point: the view from Barra c.1610. (Domhnall Uilleam Stiùbhart)*

supplies were not to be met with in the windswept, treeless Outer Hebrides. Island clans therefore required access to districts with substantial reserves of woodland.[3] But what of the Clan MacNeil of Barra, with no such mainland possessions?

Since the collapse of the MacDonald Lordship of the Isles in the latter half of the 15th century, the Macleans of Duart, the MacLeods of Harris, the Mackinnons of Strath, and the MacNeils of Barra regularly co-operated in a loose strategic coalition in order to counter the still-formidable strength of Clan Donald. Documentary evidence makes it clear that the MacNeils lay within the sphere of influence of the Macleans of Duart, whose territories embraced much of the Isle of Mull, the Isle of Tiree, and the two ends of the Isle of Coll. It is probable that they depended on the more powerful kindred for ships' timber, as well as construction expertise.[4] In return, the MacNeils of Barra operated as a subservient clan to the Macleans. Thus we find, for example, in an obligation to the Bishop of the Isles in 1585, Ruairidh MacNeil of Barra describing the chief Lachlann Mór Maclean of Duart as his 'chief and master'.[5] 'Johne and Murdo, sones to Rory Mckneill of Barray' were among the hostages given to Aonghas MacDonald of Dùn Naomhaig in order to release the aforesaid chief, Lachlann Mór Maclean of Duart, in 1587, while MacNeil's brother is said to have fallen fighting with the Maclean forces in the Battle of Glenlivet, 1594.[6] Politically, then, Barra was as much part of what contemporaries referred to as the 'Southern Isles' – that is, the islands south of Ardnamurchan Point – as it belonged to the northern Hebrides.

Nevertheless, despite the small size and relative poverty of the MacNeil estate, the chiefs of Barra were significant players in the politics of the western Gàidhealtachd at the time. Although the figures may well be inflated, contemporary reports estimated that Barra and its adjacent islands could raise the respectable figure of 200 or even 300 fighting men.[7] The kindred's real strength, however, lay in sea-power, seamanship, and the boldness and charisma of its chief.[8] During the early 1580s, the summer plundering-season took the men of Barra as far afield as Munster, an archipelagic reach that entangled them in politics and conflict far beyond the Hebrides:

> MacNeil Barra (McNeale Barroh) who was reputed the best seafaring warrior in the Islands and is most remote to the north and by west, as I take it, is a follower to MacLean and has been accustomed to invade Ulla in Connaught (Conoght) in Ireland, being O'Mallye's country and to prey in the sea coast of Connaught aforesaid, Thomond, Kyerye and Desmond in Ireland. Whereupon Grany ny Mallye and he invaded one another's possessions through far distant. I have heard some of MacNeil's sept have come with the Mallyes to prey Valensia, an island in McCarty More's country, with borders adjoining.[9]

The MacNeils' ambition comes through in a somewhat untrustworthy contemporary anecdote recorded by the anonymous compiler of a description of Barra *c*.1620. It was probably narrated by the aged Ruairidh an Tartair himself:

> the Superior or Laird of Barray is called Rorie [blank] Mcneill he is sex or sevin score of yeares as himself did say, This ancient man in tyme of his yewth being a valiant and Stout man of warr and heareing from Skippers that oftymes wer wont to travell to ane

Illand which the Inhabitants of the Illand alledged this Mcneill and his predicessors should be there Superiors which Illand is sein oftymes ffrom the tope of the Mountanes of Barray. This Rorie heareing oftymes the same Newes reported to him & to his predecessors he ffraughted a shipe but nowayes could ffind the Illand At last was driven to Ireland on the west syd theroff And took wp a Spreath [*spréidh* or plunder] And returned home yrefter.[10]

Two intriguing references suggest that the MacNeils' piratical expeditions ventured even beyond the south-west coast of Ireland, into the Bristol Channel. In 1580 the MacNeils plundered cargo worth £1200 out of the *White Hart* of Bridgewater in Devon.[11] Around the same time, a young boy, John MacNeil, of MacNeil gentry background, was fostered out to William Nycoll, a merchant from the parish of Northam in Devon.[12] Whether or not this act represents a pragmatic blending of Gaelic adoptive kinship and English apprenticeship customs, it certainly suggests an attempt by the MacNeil kindred to forge or formalise an allegiance with a regional go-between. Piracy was not only a matter of procuring plunder, but also of the subsequent disposal of spoils through clandestine local networks of commerce, gift-giving, companionship, and hospitality, where land-based suppliers enjoyed economic advantage over pirates themselves.[13]

Rather than limiting themselves to the sporadic, opportunistic coastal raiding supposedly characteristic of Scottish and Irish Gaeldom, these references suggest that the MacNeils were no strangers to the piratical activities endemic to the south-western approaches to Britain in the second half of the 16th century, an illicit commerce involving participants from Devon, Somerset, south Wales, Munster, and Connemara.[14] Far from being the denizens of a remote Hebridean backwater, the MacNeil kindred were enthusiastic, skilful, and apparently successful participants in an oceanic black market taking advantage of rapidly expanding international trade-flows, a network of plunderers, fences, and hangers-on stretching throughout the North Atlantic from Munster to Morocco to Newfoundland. Ruairidh an Tartair might best be understood as one of the group of 'career pirates' who emerge around this time.[15]

A later incident at Ciosmul Castle suggests that even after the kindred's range of operations was curtailed, the MacNeils of Barra continued to use their business acumen and access to extensive networks of underhand commerce. In November 1603 the *Anthony* of London, driven by bad weather to Barra during a voyage to supply the English garrison at Lough Foyle, was lured into the harbour at Bàgh a' Chaisteil on the pretext that there it would be safe from the predatory MacDonalds of Clan Ranald. As soon as the ship weighed anchor, the locals ransacked its cargo. As Aonghas MacCoinnich remarks, the presence of Lowland Scottish middlemen in Barra suggests 'a well-practised operation'.[16]

The reputation for archipelagic maritime reach, and their long-standing association with the powerful Macleans of Duart, allowed the MacNeils a small but noteworthy and clearly lucrative role as combatants and, not to put too fine a point on it, pirates on the western seaboard of Scotland, Ireland, and beyond during the confused and violent latter half of the 16th century.[17] A pride in the kindred pervades contemporary waulking songs, for example in the lines in *An Spaidearachd Bharrach* ['The Barra Flyting']:

Mo cheòl-ghàire Ruairi an Tartair!	My joy of laughter Ruairidh the Tartar!
Bheireadh am fion d'a chuid eachaibh,	Who'd give wine to his horses,
Chuireadh crùidhean òir fo'n casan,	Who'd put golden horseshoes on their feet,
'S iomadh claidheamh glégheal lasrach,	Many a sword flaming white,
'S iomadh targaid fuilteach stracach,	Many a targe bloody and rent,
Chunnaig mo shùil anns a' chaisteal –	My eye saw in the castle –
'S a chuid dhaoine mar na farspaich	And his men like the black-backed gulls
'S gach ian eile thà 's an ealtainn …[18]	And every other bird that is in the sky …

or in a version of the well-known *Latha dhomh 's mi 'm Beinn a' Cheathaich*:

'S ann agam fhin a bha t athar (joy)	I felt joy
Faicinn do bhataidh ga gabhail	Seeing your boat under sail
Toirt a cinn o'n t seana chuain dhomhainn	Turning in from the old deep ocean,
Bhiorlain dhubh 's i seoladh leatha	A black galley sailing with her
Mach o dhuthaich Mhic Ille sheathain	Out from Maclean's Country
Steach gu Ciosmal an athan	Into Ciosmul of the granary
Far a faighte cuirm ri gabhail	Where a banquet would be held
S ol fion o dh oi[dh]che gu latha.[19]	Wine being drunk from night to daytime.
	(my translation)

A further illustration of the importance of the MacNeils of Barra might be the remarkable, and apparently successful, efforts made by Lachlann Mór Maclean of Duart – up to and including lobbying Queen Elizabeth of England herself – to ensure the safety and repatriation from prison in England of John MacNeil, the 'special kinsman of McNeill of Barray' fostered out in Devon, now renamed 'Johne Neale', and languishing in prison on a charge of manslaughter after a shipboard brawl.[20] Another mark of the significance of the MacNeils to the Macleans of Duart is that we can be virtually certain that Lachlann Mór's second son Lachlann Òg was fostered in Barra in the chief's household: the nickname given to him in a near-contemporary source, the Wardlaw MS compiled by the Reverend James Fraser of Kirkhill (1634–1709), is Lachlann Barrach: that is, Lachlan the Barraman.[21] We shall return to him later.

Nevertheless, the power of the MacNeils should not be exaggerated. Far-flung plundering expeditions were a remarkable demonstration of Barra seamanship; it is notable, however, that these lengthy voyages prudently sidestepped closer, more turbulent and dangerous areas of Ulster and the western Highlands. Lachlann Mór Maclean's endeavours to gain pardon for John MacNeil, the young boy who had been fostered with the Devon merchant and ended up being accused of murder, might not have been purely an act of goodwill towards his dependents, the MacNeils, but could also be read as part of a wider initiative by Lachlann to open up channels of communication with Elizabeth's court, and to enhance his own personal standing and authority therein. Finally, it is possible to interpret the ambitious voyages of the

MacNeils not so much as an exercise of power, but rather as a symptom of internal weaknesses. Expeditions could function as a safety-valve, undertaken not only for the straightforward economic reasons of acquiring specie and exotic portable wealth, but also because of pragmatic social contingency, in order to foster mutual loyalty, collective prestige, and a common sense of purpose and honour among a clan élite riven by dissension and rivalry.[22]

As we have seen, Ruairidh MacNeil had two sets of sons by two women: Mòr or Marion, of the MacDonalds of Clan Ranald; and Màiri, of the MacLeods of Harris. A rough transcription of a somewhat cryptic, and now apparently lost, bond of obligation dated 1585, made in 1838 by the Victorian peerage lawyer John Riddell (1785–1862), illustrates the wider entanglements that resulted from the MacNeils' internecine vendetta.[23] The document states that Ruairidh an Tartair would not allow his son and heir John to succeed him unless certain unspecified payments were made to 'marrian mykloid Uilleyeam makloide off harray umquhylle is dochter' – that is, his other wife, Màiri MacLeod daughter of the chief William MacLeod of Harris. The cautioner to ensure the chief's orders were to be carried out was named as 'Donald makneill person of (?aynocht) and Kyllevarie'. The last place is evidently Cille Bharra, the principal church of Barra. The other name, which eluded the transcriber and may have been misunderstood by the original writer, is most likely to represent 'Eynort', referring to the church of St Maol-rubha at Clachan Aoineart in the MacLeod territory of Minginish on the west coast of Skye.[24] Also subscribing to the obligation is 'Jone Makpherson vik neill', Iain mac a' Pheursain mhic Néill, son and heir of Dòmhnall and probably the man known in 19th-century Barra tradition as Am Peursan Mór, the Big Parson.

The bond raises the possibility that by the mid-1580s Ruairidh an Tartair, chief of the MacNeils, anticipating opposition from the sons of his legal family to the fulfilment of certain obligations he had made to Màiri MacLeod and her now-deceased father, charged Dòmhnall mac Néill, parson of Cille Bharra, together with the parson's son and heir, Iain, to ensure that these promises were kept. Aligned through his father with the MacLeod faction of the chiefs' sons, and apparently administering church lands in both MacNeil and MacLeod territories, the Peursan Mór, as we shall see shortly, would find himself a target for subsequent MacDonald aggression.

I have suggested that one reason behind the MacNeils' ambitious and costly voyages may have been to reinforce a fragmented clan élite through the companionship fostered by far-flung travel and combat. The corollary was that expeditions were expected to return home laden with plunder and profit. The MacNeils' basic need for spoil, and their tense and unsettled relationships with erstwhile associates, are hinted at in the problems arising from the kindred's association with Gráinne O'Malley, Granuaile the 'pirate queen' of Erris, Co. Mayo. As well as the straightforward piracy for which she remains celebrated today, the latter clearly profited from hiring out her galleys as troop-transports to Ireland for Scottish mercenary redshanks. Such long-standing associations enabled repeated military subventions from the Hebrides in support of the MacWilliam Burke rebellions, of which Granuaile was a major champion, against the governor of Connacht, Sir Richard Bingham, during the late 1580s.[25]

Nevertheless, co-operation between the MacNeils and the O'Malleys soon broke down. It is probable that MacNeils headed the 600 redshanks recorded as being 'of the sept of the Barrones', who disembarked at Erris in September 1589, having been recruited from the Hebrides by Granuaile's son. Dismissed after meeting with violent local opposition, they ravaged the countryside and carried off the hides and tallow of more than 1000 cows.[26] In June 1591 a 700-strong force of Macleans, MacLeods, and MacNeils arrived in Erris to fight for the Burkes, shortly after most of that kindred had sued for peace. Finding no opportunity for combat, the mercenaries devastated north Mayo instead. In the ensuing clash with Granuaile's forces, Ruairidh's son 'Owen' (Gill'-Eóghanan) MacNeil was killed, following which the Highlanders took to their galleys with O'Malley herself in hot pursuit.[27] This setback did not deter the MacNeils from undertaking a further expedition as far afield as Munster two years later, taking in a pilgrimage to Croagh Patrick in Co. Mayo during the voyage home.[28]

Following the lead of their patrons the Macleans of Duart, the MacNeils did not play an active rôle in the Nine Years' War in Ireland in the 1590s. There may have been a rapprochement between themselves and the O'Malleys under the auspices of the Macleans, then co-operating with the English Crown in order to thwart MacDonald-led mercenary support for the Ulster Rising: 'threscore muscataris and hagbuttaris of omailyeis Lands' were reported to be with Lachlann Mór Maclean of Duart in July 1598, 'and from him ar past fardar north in the ylis' – perhaps to Barra?[29] But after the Macleans' catastrophic defeat by the MacDonalds at the Battle of Gruineart in Islay the following month, in which the chief Lachlann Mór was slain, the Mull kindred were no longer a force to be reckoned with, in the Isles or beyond. Although the MacNeils later participated in a revenge attack on MacDonald lands in Islay, Jura, and Colonsay around August 1602, they could no longer depend on the patronage and protection of a powerful and influential overlord.[30] It is probably no coincidence that shortly after the Battle of Gruineart the MacNeils were deprived of their northernmost possessions, the island of Eirisgeigh/Eriskay and the district of Baghasdail/Boisdale in South Uist, by their rivals the MacDonalds of Clan Ranald.[31]

With the accession of James VI to the throne of England in 1603, the political situation in the Hebrides was transformed. The Nine Years' War in Ulster had been brought to a successful conclusion, and the king was at last able to give teeth to the policy of pacifying the western Highlands which had been developed over the previous two decades. Through the agency of various regional magnates, the Campbells of Argyll, the Gordons of Huntly, and the MacKenzies of Seaforth, with the support of Lowland burghs and merchants eager to develop and profit from the rich west-coast fisheries, and wielding the threat of a new 'British Navy', the Crown began vigorously to assert its authority over the region.[32]

In the northern Hebrides one of the Crown's principal objectives was to ensure the success of a second plantation of Lewis by the Fife Adventurers for use as a fishing-station, together with the final dispossession of the island's erstwhile possessors, the MacLeods of Lewis or Sìol Torcail. The first attempt, launched in October 1598, had ended in humiliating failure when the Adventurers were ignominiously routed in a midnight assault by the islanders, probably in February 1602; at least 50 of them were killed and their two principal leaders abducted. A royal proclamation made some four years later not only held the MacNeils of Barra to blame for organising and supporting the raid in concert with the MacLeods of Harris, but also accused Ruairidh an Tartair himself of detaining the kidnapped leaders 'in secret firmance and captivuitie'.[33]

In autumn 1605 a second plantation attempt was launched, accompanied by overwhelming military force. The seriousness with which the Adventurers set about their undertaking convinced the major neighbouring clans, including the MacLeods of Harris, that it would be judicious to acquiesce in despatching levies in support of the Fifers. As the months progressed, however, the Lowland soldiers, unpaid, began to return home, while islanders escalated their relentless harassment of those who remained. After enduring a harrowing three-week siege of their stronghold in Stornoway in autumn 1606, the remaining settlers, by now nearly destitute, abandoned their attempt the following spring. Once again, the MacNeils were identified by the authorities as principal abettors of the MacLeods. This time, however, their allies were named as the MacDonalds of Clan Ranald, their erstwhile adversaries: more specifically, the MacDonalds in South Uist under the leadership of Raghnall mac Ailein of Benbecula, who was effectively ruling the island wing of the territories as his own personal fiefdom independently of the recognised head of the kindred, his brother Dòmhnall.[34]

Although both the MacLeods of Lewis and the MacNeils had recent experience of warfare in Ireland, it would be too hasty to claim that the successful strategies adopted by local resistance to the Fife Adventurers were influenced by the example of Aodh O'Neill in the Nine Years' War. Nevertheless, in their refusal of pitched battle, in their preference for lightning raids followed by swift withdrawal, in their organised harassment of the enemy from afar until he was weakened by disorder, fatigue, scarcity of resources, and loss of morale, the islanders' tactics had much in common with the policies of O'Neill in the previous decade.[35]

The continuing military assistance and refuge given by the two clans to the rebel Sìol Torcail clearly lies behind the Crown's instructions to the reluctant Marquis of Huntly in 1607 to 'extirpate and rute out … McNeill Barra, with his clan' along with the neighbouring MacDonalds.[36] The following year Andrew Knox, Bishop of the Isles, and Andrew Stewart, Lord Ochiltree, having received a royal commission to crush the inhabitants of the Outer Hebrides south of Lewis, launched a major expedition to the islands. Invited to a parley on board, nearly every island chief was kidnapped, taken south, and imprisoned in Lowland fastnesses. Only two chiefs, too astute to accept the invitation, had evaded capture: Sir Ruairidh MacLeod of Harris, and Ruairidh an Tartair of Barra.[37]

The abduction of most island leaders, along with the political implications of the defeat of Cathair Ó Dochartaigh's rising in Ulster the following year, worked to render previous aggressive plantation strategies undesirable and even impractical.[38] At the beginning of June 1609 James VI granted another commission to Andrew Knox, Bishop of the Isles, for a fresh expedition to the Hebrides. In the middle of the month the island chiefs, having agreed terms with the authorities, were at last released from captivity. On 23 August they would reconvene on the island of Iona in order to subscribe their names to a series of statutes intended to impose royal authority on the Hebrides through socio-economic, religious, educational, legal, and military reforms. For a decade the forceful policies of the Crown in the west had placed clan élites throughout the Hebrides under increasing pressure: should they co-operate and seek accommodation, or should they choose to resist? In the case of two major kindreds, Clan Donald South and Sìol Torcail, the MacLeods of Lewis, such disputes exacerbated existing internal dynastic struggles between competing factions and eventually led to wholesale forfeiture and extirpation.[39] Ruairidh an Tartair may have avoided capture the previous year, but it was now imperative for the MacNeils to decide what future strategy to adopt regarding the new Crown ascendancy.

Two major events in 1609 suggest that trouble was already brewing in Barra. Firstly, there is the murder alluded to in a charge laid against Raghnall mac Ailein, the leader of Clan Ranald in South Uist, by Archibald Campbell, Lord Lorne, in 1633:

> Item ye sd Rannald m^callane v^eane alias McDonald in ye monethe of Junii 1609 yeirs Came to ye yll of Bara and y^r maist cruellly wickedlie and unmerciefullie killed & slew to ye deathe umq^ll Johne M^cniell persone & minister of Bara.[40]

The victim must be none other than the cleric known to tradition as Iain Mac a' Pheursain, the Peursan Mór, identified as a supporter of the MacLeod faction in Barra in the bond of obligation in 1585. Nineteenth-century island tradition, as recorded by the folklorist Alexander Carmichael from the parson's descendant John MacPherson at a céilidh in the latter's house in Ceann Tangabhal in 1872, had fashioned the incident into a gripping tale of crime and punishment:

> The Pearsan Mor was chapl[a]in & son to Macneil. He had [a] house at Ciolla & [was] m[arried] to a da[ugh]t[er] of Clanranald. He used to go shooting to Aird Ghrin [*del*: where] There was an oth[er] girl at Cliat upon his wife thought he was fond of her & she was giadach rithe [jealous of her]. She sent for her 12 co[mh][dh]altan [foster brothers] to Uist & they came. He was gone to Aird Ghrin as usual. His wife told them where he was gone & told them to wait him at Ciste nan Cli'eaun where they would hear his dog's coinneal (chain) com[in]g thro[ugh] the ciste. They met & attacked him. He & his dog killed 10 [*supra*: out] of the 12 & the other 2 lived till morn[in]g. He fo[ugh]t them till he fell at Meallach where he was buried & a caibeal [chapel] was built over him.[41]

If the Peursan Mór, Iain MacPherson, was indeed killed in June 1609, the context must unquestionably be linked to the kidnapping of most of the island chiefs the previous year. As we have seen, the 1585 bond of obligation suggests that MacPherson was bound to uphold the interests of MacLeod of Harris in Barra – and thus of the sons of Ruairidh an Tartair by Màiri MacLeod. He would thus undoubtedly incur the enmity of Ruairidh's other sons, the 'legal heirs' from Mòr MacDonald, sister of Raghnall mac Ailein of Benbecula. As we have seen, the MacNeils and the MacDonalds of Clan Ranald together supported the MacLeods of Lewis against the second Fife plantation, suggesting a growing rapprochement between the two kindreds. This new entente may have been thrown into doubt after Ruairidh MacLeod of Harris was left as the only major chief at liberty in the Hebrides. With Ruairidh an Tartair growing old, both factions of sons growing impatient and apprehensive, against the background of chaotic, unpredictable regional political circumstances, Raghnall mac Ailein may have decided to take the initiative on behalf of his own kindred, and dispose of one of the principal allies of his rivals.[42]

The other critical event in the history of Barra during this period probably occurred in late 1609. A merchant ship from Bordeaux under the command of Abel Dynes, 'laden with Spanish wine', anchored off Barra. Some of the islanders boarded the ship and despoiled it, killing or wounding at least five of her crew in the process.[43] So far the MacNeils of Barra had carefully managed to stand apart from the major political upheavals on the western seaboard: Ruairidh an Tartair had been 'the only notable absentee' from the signing of the Statutes of Iona in August, while all other island chiefs had pledged themselves henceforth answerable to the authorities.

The plundering of Dynes's ship in the aftermath of the Statutes offered an opportunity for each faction of the sons of Ruairidh an Tartair to attempt to play the other off against the legal authorities in Edinburgh. The blatant act of piracy also provided an opportunity for the outside clans with an interest in Barra to prove their loyalty by being seen to impose order and bring miscreants to justice in an island hitherto beyond the reach of the Crown. Contemporary sources suggest that the outcome was a ratcheting-up of pressure within the Clan MacNeil until one group effectively broke the other.

In January 1610 Eachann Òg Maclean of Duart, the chief upon whom MacNeil was 'a dependair', was given a commission to apprehend Ruairidh an Tartair on charges of committing 'all kind of barbaritie' on the inhabitants of Barra; James VI expressed his irritation that 'such an unworthie cative [miserable wretch] sould be sufferit without controlment so long to continew rebellious or to braith the air of our cuntrey'.[44] But Maclean's rival Dòmhnall MacDonald of Clan Ranald appears to have forestalled Maclean: later the same month he seized Iain MacNeil, Ruairich's eldest son by Màiri MacLeod, and despatched him to the Tolbooth in Edinburgh. Soon afterwards, according to the official records, Iain MacNeil 'endit this lyffe' in captivity.[45] According to tradition, his detention led his foster-mother to compose the waulking song *Iain Òg mac Mhic Néill*, recorded by Alexander Carmichael from Marion MacNeil on 2 December 1870:

Cha'n e chreach mi –	It is not that which destroyed me, [but]
Mo chui[r]tear donn	My noble courtier
An laimh an Glaschu	In captivity in Glasgow
'S iad a ruitheadh	And them [?binding him]
Chuir a Shasunn	To send him to England
No Dhun-eideann nan ard fasan[46]	Or to Edinburgh of the high fashions.

Iain MacNeil's fate is described in the accompanying narrative:

> *Thainig an toir eir Iain og agus rugadh eir agus e tighinn eir tir a sgoth iasgaich agus*
> *thugadh eir falbh e phriosanach e mach do Ghlascho. Is e bas a thug iad da a chur ann an*
> *togsaid agus biorann iaruin troimh na clair agus an tosgaid a leigeil le beinn an dala [del:*
> *cuid] h-aite an Duneideann no an Sasunn.*[47]

> Iain Òg was pursued, and he was captured disembarking from a fishing boat. He was
> taken away as a prisoner to Glasgow. The way they killed him was to put him in a
> hogshead barrel with iron spikes through the boards, and to roll the hogshead down a
> slope, either in Edinburgh or in England.

Whether true or not, this anecdote serves as a reminder that Highlanders as well as
Lowlanders could entertain prejudices and fears concerning the habitual barbarity
and violence of the inhabitants of the other half of the country.

In retaliation, Eachann Òg Maclean of Duart apprehended and sent south Niall
Uibhisteach, eldest son of Mòr, Clan Ranald's sister, and legitimate heir to the estate,
on a similar charge of piracy. But nothing could be proved, and at the end of July
1610 Niall was permitted to return to the island on bail, with his uncle, the Captain
of Clan Ranald, going surety.[48] Although the case was reconvened at the end of 1611,
Niall Uibhisteach was clearly and understandably reluctant to return to Edinburgh;
it was not until January 1613 that he was exhibited before the Privy Council there.[49]
His eventual appearance was probably calculated to win favour with the authorities,
given recent reported events in Barra.

In October 1612, Niall Òg and Gill'-Eóghanan, the two surviving sons of Ruairidh
an Tartair and Màiri MacLeod, were reported as having carried out a violent, well-
armed attack on the stronghold of Ciosmul: they captured their father, detained him
in irons along with Gill'-Eóghanan Òg, the other surviving son of Mòr MacDonald of
Clan Ranald, and garrisoned Ciosmul for themselves.[50] Although the Privy Council
gave Dòmhnall MacDonald of Clan Ranald a commission to arrest them, no further
action was taken.[51] Perhaps the two brothers enjoyed popular support, and were too
well secured against attack. On the other hand, the account of their attack on Ciosmul
may in fact have been an opportune fiction: this at any rate was Niall Òg's contention
in the late 1620s, with the two supposed captives, conveniently, 'being many yeirs
agoe depairtit yis Lyff'.[52] The Clan Ranald kindred may have been incapable of taking
decisive action, given that the kindred was riven by internal dissension, with the Uist
wing effectively separated under Raghnall mac Ailein, while Dòmhnall made peace
with his erstwhile rival Sir Ruairidh MacLeod of Harris.[53] For the authorities, Barra
was just too remote and unimportant to deal with directly. The status quo prevailed:
Niall Òg was now *de facto* chief, his position strengthened by a timely marriage in
1614 to Màiri, sister of Eachann Òg Maclean of Duart.[54]

Niall Òg MacNeil, the eldest son of Màiri MacLeod, appears to have triumphed.
It is clear, however, that the legitimate heir, Niall Uibhisteach, the son of Mòr
MacDonald of Clan Ranald, remained a force to be reckoned with. From the evidence
of the anonymous description of the island composed *c*.1620, the aged Ruairidh an

Tartair had resumed his chieftaincy before his death.[55] It is unclear, however, whether this peace involved some form of settlement and reparations with the defeated Niall Uibhisteach. A formal arrangement was certainly achieved by 1622, around the time of the death of Ruairidh an Tartair, who appears to have resumed the chieftaincy some time previously, and a year after the exceptionally able and ruthless Ruairidh MacKenzie of Cóigeach had assumed the superiority of Barra.[56]

It is likely that, in hammering out a settlement, MacKenzie was assisted by the capable, ambitious, and well-respected second son of Lachlann Mór Maclean of Duart, Lachlann Òg, known also to contemporaries as Lachlann Barrach, Lachlann the Barraman. In 1617 Lachlann had assumed the titles to the clan lands of the Macleans of Duart – now administered as a free barony by Ruairidh MacKenzie of Cóigeach – in place of his elder and less capable brother the chief Eachann Òg.[57] Lachlann's nickname suggests that he was fostered in Barra, in the household of Ruairidh an Tartair; it is intriguing to note that of Lachlann's three wives, the first was a half-sister of the MacLeod side of the MacNeils, while the third was a first cousin of the MacDonald of Clan Ranald side.[58] These may have been love-matches; but they also look very much like marriage as diplomacy by other means. If Lachlann Barrach was fostered by Ruairidh an Tartair, he is likely to have taken part in expeditions to Ireland along with his foster-father and foster-brothers. He would be bound to both factions of the MacNeils both by ties of affiliation and by ties of marriage – and also by the fact that they had sailed together and fought together.

In return for a payment of 1000 merks and yearly rent of 3s.4d. Scots thereafter, Niall Uibhisteach was effectively allowed his own fiefdom in the north of Barra, that part of the island closest to his foster-kin in South Uist: liferent on a swathe of exceptionally productive farms, with a further tack of these lands to be held by his heirs for 21 years after his death.[59] It is clear that the reconciliation between these half-brothers was not entirely amicable: the unusually firm tenor of the document explicitly binds allegiance to the chiefly house on Niall Uibhisteach and his heirs 'aganis all personis qtsomever (his Majesteis auctoritie onlie exceptit)'. The bond was subsequently renewed three times over the following decade. Niall Uibhisteach readily converted to Catholicism in 1626 while Niall Òg continued to adhere to Protestantism in order to protect his position. He also persisted in threatening the usurper with litigation in later years.[60]

⁂ ⁂ ⁂

The lengthy career of Ruairidh an Tartair demonstrates how political circumstances gradually circumscribed the reach of the MacNeils, from multinational engagements throughout these islands, to a straitened confinement within their own immediate island group. For all their dynamism, versatility, ambition, and occasional ruthlessness, a small, predatory kindred was no match for the might of a predatory state and its allies; the MacNeils of Barra were put firmly in their place. Paradoxically, the kindred's lack of two separate territorial wings, island and mainland, may have exacerbated dissension within it. The example of Clan Ranald shows how, where the clan *dùthchas* was effectively split between two brothers in the early 17th century, widely dispersed clan territories could be subject to fragmentation. At the same time, a looser structure might allow 'spaces for dissent' to which malcontent members of the clan could withdraw. The fractious Clan MacNeil, confined within a small island group, had to live cheek by jowl.

Barra also offers an intriguing example of an island kindred not directly affected by the Statutes of Iona. Its chief Ruairidh an Tartair was not kidnapped and held captive, and did not subscribe his name to the measures in August 1609. Nevertheless, the ratification of the Statutes of Iona appears to have represented a turning-point for the MacNeils. As was the case with a number of other kindreds, the measures appear to have exacerbated existing internal dissension. The prospect of official favour encouraged two competing factions to jockey for influence, both within Barra itself and with the Edinburgh authorities, while other clans were prepared to employ violence and litigation in attempts to demonstrate their authority over a particularly recalcitrant neighbour. The victorious MacNeil faction, the supporters of the 'MacLeod' heir against the 'Clan Ranald' one, relying on the island's remoteness and insignificance, was able to pursue a calculated policy of sitting tight and ignoring Crown authority.

But if this period encouraged fresh discord, events also seem to testify to the ability of clan élites to manage internal conflict without provoking major bloodshed, so as to avoid courting potential outside interference and the fate of the forfeited MacLeods of Lewis and the MacDonalds of Dùn Naomhaig. Despite a brief period of internecine strife, events in Barra at this time demonstrate how kindreds working in tandem could bring a measure of reconciliation, and a sometimes precarious peace to contending factions, through a form of restorative justice. Readers will have noticed the irony that, if indeed Lachlann Barrach played a significant role in mediating between rival factions, the crisis of legitimacy caused by serial marriage customs may have been rectified by a figure who had himself strengthened ties of affiliation with both parties through serial marriage. Again, it hardly needs to be stated that, despite their significance, ties of fosterage tend to be hidden by conventional genealogies.[61]

My aim in this account has been to place Barra at the centre of the story, adopting a perspective complementary to conventional government-focused approaches to Highland history: a vernacular vantage-point facing south-east, we might say, rather than north-west, one in which the usual 'Highland Problem' is balanced by an equivalent 'British Problem', or, perhaps, an 'Edinburgh Problem'. This Barra perspective demonstrates that the MacNeils' strategies were framed and fashioned within the dynamic political and economic contexts of wider archipelagic matrices: the international ('British') North-East Atlantic archipelago; and, on the north-western edge of that larger island group, the 'archipelagic borderland' of the Hebrides.[62]

Barra in Martin Martin's
Description of the Western Islands of Scotland

A key text in any attempt to develop and elaborate indigenous Hebridean perspectives in early modern history is Martin Martin's *Description of the Western Islands of Scotland*, published in London in 1703. The account of Barra it contains demonstrates that at the end of the 17th century Barra was no more remote from the rest of the country than it had been a century previously.[63] Martin describes how islanders were heavily addicted to tobacco, and records how every summer fishing-boats from Orkney took part in the cod and ling fisheries there, a reminder of how inhabitants of different island groups could be brought together by co-operation and commerce, as well as divided by mutual hostility and suspicion.[64]

It is clear, however, from Martin's account that he was met with suspicion during what appears to have been his only visit to Barra – the island was off the main sea-route between his native Skye and the Lowlands on which he travelled on clan business for his chief Sir Donald Macdonald of Sleat. Martin's cold reception at Ciosmul may have resulted from his status as Macdonald's employee: Sir Donald claimed superiority of Barra.[65] As a result, Martin writes, MacNeil owed Sir Donald a hawk and £40 per annum, as well as being obliged 'to furnish him a certain Number of Men upon extraordinary Occasions'.[66] This last requirement may have been a cause of contemporary concern on the island, given the war raging across Europe, and the prospect of additional Highland regiments being raised to fight the French in Flanders.

Martin was perhaps suspect because of his religion: he was not only a Protestant, but had lately studied divinity at the University of Edinburgh, as a result of which he had assisted the Reverend John Campbell, minister of Harris, in a pastoral visitation to St Kilda in 1697.[67] Religion was a particularly charged issue in the Outer Hebrides towards the end of the 17th century. The newly presbyterianised Synod of Argyll was promulgating an ambitious and aggressive reform policy directed against 'popular superstition', involving a series of visitations to the islands.[68] In an effort to gain favour with the synod, Martin's friend the Reverend Alexander Cooper, erstwhile Episcopalian minister of North Uist, highlighted his attempts to uphold Protestant orthodoxy on that island by imposing church discipline and trying to abolish the Michaelmas festivities, the major annual Hebridean holiday that was an occasion just as important to early modern islanders as Christmas is today.[69]

Customs, beliefs, and objects viewed as sacred by local Catholics were particularly significant at this time. Cooper complained in a letter to the Synod of Argyll 'yt some foolish women in a toun called Carinish blames me for offering to robb them of a bell qch is upon ane altar ther qch yy alledge wes consecrated by the Trinity'.[70] For an outsider such as Martin to arrive in Barra and scoff at local belief in St Barr was to throw oil on the fire.[71] Devotion to the local saint was a central part of Barra identity: the annual Michaelmas celebrations were preceded there by similar festivities in honour of St Barr.[72] Martin's request to view the saint's image at Cille Bharra surely encouraged suspicion that the Skyeman's intention was none other than to take it away and dispose of it.

As stated above, it is vital to bear in mind that the Barra mainland was for centuries at the centre of a whole micro-archipelago of smaller islands, many of them inhabited, each with its own history and traditions. There may have been considerable mobility between the various islands in the *dùthchas* of MacNeil. Martin's narrative runs into problems when he describes the Bishop's Isles, which formed the southern end of the MacNeils' estate. Indeed, we cannot be certain that he visited them at all.[73] The islands of Sandray and Vatersay are confused with each other, while Mingulay seems to have been merged in his account with its smaller neighbour, the island of Berneray at the southern tip of the Outer Hebrides. The map of the Hebrides prepared by Hermann Moll for the *Description* exhibits similar lack of clarity.

Martin's apparent confusion of these last two islands is particularly exasperating given the significance of his remarks in this section about what must be, in spite of his disordered narrative, Mingulay, an island every bit as interesting as St Kilda. Both islands exhibited a similar way of life and administration. Like St Kilda, Mingulay's economy was dominated by fowling.[74] The best climber was known in both islands as the 'Gingich'.[75] Both islands were administered by a Steward representing the chief, who was due an *omer* or amar of barley each year when he and his retinue went to live off the islanders in summer: a kind of marine transhumance.[76] A share of the barley was paid to 'an inferior officer', who must be the headman of Mingulay; other members of the MacNeil chief's household, including the *gocaman* or herald, and the porter, also profited from the tax.[77] It is clear that the people of both St Kilda and Mingulay resented these outside impositions, although the St Kildan case was considerably more extreme, involving an introverted religious revival and eventual outright violence against the Steward and his men.[78]

There are also intriguing parallels between Mingulay and the island of North Rona, not only regarding the significance of fowling for both during the early modern period, but also in terms of levies of barley and the apparent right or duty of the 'administrator' (MacNeil of Barra for Mingulay, the Morrisons of Tàbost for Rona) to arrange marriages for widows and widowers in the island.[79] Here, I suspect that Martin was writing solely about the Bishop's Isles when he described this custom, not about Barra as a whole as has sometimes been suggested. Could these three outlying islands, Rona, St Kilda, and Mingulay profitably be studied together? Their administration, taxation, and exploitation during the early modern period, similar in so many ways, may offer us traces of a much older state of affairs dating back to the Viking era.

Finally, another way in which all three islands were similar was in the vulnerability of their isolated populations to famine, ill-health, and disease introduced from outside, a susceptibility exacerbated by the lack of local physicians. Rona was depopulated in Martin's own time; St Kilda was devastated a generation later; and oral tradition connects Mingulay with at least one utterly destructive plague.[80]

Martin Martin's account demonstrates the value of considering Barra within its immediate and wider archipelagic contexts, once more clearly illustrating how its inhabitants were involved in economic and cultural networks stretching well beyond their immediate environment. But reading Martin's account also underlines the importance of employing comparative approaches. His snapshot of the Hebrides at the end of the 17th century suggests that some social organisation and customary practices often read as distinctive to specific islands and estates might best be understood when compared and contrasted to similar aspects elsewhere. Giving a place to both 'island studies' and 'islands studies' might encourage us to reassess and re-orientate both our mental map of the Hebrides, and our perceptions, preconceptions, and prejudices regarding its people.

Acknowledgements

I would like to thank the British Academy for awarding me the mid-career fellowship that enabled research for this paper. For their kind assistance and advice, I would like to acknowledge my grateful thanks to Abigail Burnyeat, Bill Lawson, Aonghas MacCoinnich, Angus Macmillan, Alasdair Roberts, and Anke-Beate Stahl; to staff at the Centre for Research Collections, Edinburgh University Library; the Clan Donald Archive, Armadale, Skye; the Inveraray Castle Archives; the National Library of Scotland; the National Records of Scotland; the School of Scottish Studies Archive; and to all those who offered suggestions when versions of this paper were read at a seminar at Sabhal Mòr Ostaig, University of the Highlands and Islands, and at the Islands Book Trust Galley-Castle Conference in Barra. I am especially obliged to Calum MacNeil for being so generous in sharing his encyclopaedic knowledge of his native Barra. I engaged with some of the material examined here from a folkloristic perspective in my article 'Murder in Barra, 1609?'[81]

Notes

1. J Lorne Campbell, 1954, 'The MacNeils of Barra and the Irish Franciscans', *Innes Review*, 5, pp.35–7; A MacKenzie, 1889, *History of the MacLeods* (Inverness), pp.24–30, 33, 36–8, 40–4; R C MacLeod (ed.), 1938–9, *The Book of Dunvegan*, 2 vols (Aberdeen), pp.90–8, 212–13; I F Grant, 1959, *The MacLeods: The History of a Clan, 1200–1956* (London), pp.116–26; A Campbell, 2002, *A History of Clan Campbell. Vol. 2: From Flodden to the Restoration* (Edinburgh), pp.74–6. A suggestion that the different legal status of the two sets of sons was accepted by themselves is found in a decree (NRS DI1/53, 15 July 1629) on behalf of Ruairidh an Tartair's successor Niall Òg, son of Màiri MacLeod, in which, repeating the phrasing of the complaint to the Privy Council 16 years earlier by his half-brother (*RPC* 10 (1613–16), pp.6–7), he is referred to as 'Neill oige Mcneill sone natural to umqle rorie Mcneill of barra', while his late half-brother Gill'-Eóghanan is 'Gillievene Oig McNeill his son [i.e. of Ruairidh an Tartair] laull procreat betuixt him and Morye nyen Allan his spous & sister to the laitt Capitane of Clanronald'. The two families were of course not necessarily begotten consecutively: see Edinburgh University Library CW MS90/171, ff.66v–67v for an anecdote concerning a MacNeil of Barra consorting with a noblewoman in Dunstaffnage on mainland Argyll. Regarding the MacDonalds of Clan Ranald, the crucial point here is that they too had suffered internal dissension between two sets of half-brothers, a legal heir, son of the daughter of Alasdair Crotach MacLeod of Harris, and six sons of a second liaison with Seònaid, daughter of Eachann Mór Maclean of Duart: A & A MacDonald, 3 vols, 1896–1904, *Clan Donald* (Inverness), vol 2, pp.291–304, vol. 3, pp.230–1.

2. For traditional accounts of raids by the MacNeils on Shetland, see J MacPherson (ed. J Lorne Campbell), 1961, *Tales from Barra told by the Coddy* (Edinburgh), pp.48–52, 212–15; A Jennings, 2013, 'Latter-day Vikings: Gaels in the Northern Isles in the 16th century', *Journal of the North Atlantic* 4, pp.35–42; S Murdoch, 2010, *The Terror of the Seas? Scottish Maritime Warfare, 1513–1713* (Leiden), pp.118–20, 123–4.

3. For an example, see the tradition recorded in Ness, Lewis, in 1866 concerning a 16th-century Morison judge or brieve there who was 'accustomed to go every alternate year

to Ullapool for wood, a commodity which is to this day very scarce in the Long Island' (Edinburgh University Library, CW MS95 f.51).

4. For an intriguing traditional allusion that might point to the kindred's perceived inexperience in shipbuilding, see the poem *Leagail bheag, is togail bhog*, supposedly composed by Sir Dòmhnall Gorm MacDonald of Sleat on a visit to Barra *c*.1600, advising MacNeil's carpenter on how to construct a galley: A MacLeod (ed.), 1933, *Sàr Òrain* (Glasgow), pp.126–9.

5. NRS RD1/27, 21r–v; N Maclean-Bristol, 1999, *Murder under Trust: The Crimes and Death of Sir Lachlan Mor Maclean of Duart, 1558–1598* (East Linton), pp.44, 45n.30.

6. *RPC* 4 (1585–92), p.160; Campbell, *History of Clan Campbell. Vol. 2*, pp.113–14.

7. *CSP Scotland* 11 (1593–5), p.253; 12 (1595–7), p.37.

8. For a brief overview of Highland galleys, 'of great swiftness by Oars, as are hardly to be followed for good servise by hir Majestys Pynasses' (*CSP Ireland* 5 (1592–6), p.412), see Murdoch, *Terror of the Seas?*, pp.2–4. Sources credit MacNeil with 'a fleet of galleys and smaller boats' (G Hayes-McCoy, 1937, *Scots Mercenary Forces in Ireland* (Dublin & London), p.142), although they were not necessarily all from Barra itself.

9. *CSP Scotland* 12 (1595–7), p.206. For details of the relations between the kindreds of MacNeil and O'Malley, see F A Macdonald, 1994, Ireland and Scotland: Historical perspectives on the Gaelic dimension 1560–1760, unpublished PhD thesis, University of Glasgow, pp.40–1, 68–9, 77. For further historical and archaeological background, see C Kelleher, 2013, 'Pirate Ports and Harbours of West Cork in the Early Seventeenth Century', *Journal of Maritime Archaeology* 8, pp.347–66.

10. NLS Adv. MS 34.2.8 f.187v; J Lorne Campbell (ed.), 1998, *The Book of Barra* (2nd edn, Stornoway), pp.46–7; D Ó hÓgáin, 1999, 'The mystical island in Irish folklore' in P Lysaght, S Ó Catháin & D Ó hÓgáin (eds), *Islanders and Water-dwellers* (Dublin), pp.247–60; see also D Rixson, 1998, *The West Highland Galley* (Edinburgh), pp.39–42.

11. N A M Rodger, 2004, *The Safeguard of the Sea: A Naval History of Britain, 660–1649* (London), p.290.

12. *CSP Scotland* 12 (1595–7), pp.35–7, 45, 53, 58, 138, 145, 159, 171, 200, 221–4, 240–42, and probably 392; *CSP Domestic 1595–7*, p.122; also *CSP Scotland* 13 (1597–1603), pp.892, 894, 945, 1024.

13. J C Appleby, 2009, *Under the Bloody Flag: Pirates of the Tudor Age* (Stroud), pp.17–18, 20, 51, 56, 147.

14. For background, see Appleby, *Under the Bloody Flag*, particularly pp.13, 14–15, 19–20, 51, 56, 59–62, 146–7, 151, 154, 179–87.

15. Appleby, *Under the Bloody Flag*, pp.19, 56, 146–7.

16. *Calendar of Material relating to Ireland from the High Court of Admiralty Examinations*, J C Appleby (ed.), 1992 (Dublin), pp.106–7; Aonghas MacCoinnich, 2015, *Plantation and Civility in the North Atlantic World: The Case of the Northern Hebrides, 1570–1639* (Leiden), pp.294–5.

17. Hayes-McCoy, *Scots Mercenary Forces in Ireland*, pp.3, 10, 11, 68, 141, 142, 202, 205–6, 214, 228, 249, 297; Murdoch, *Terror of the Seas?*, pp.111–40, especially 135–40.

18. J Lorne Campbell & F Collinson (eds), 1969–81, *Hebridean Folksong* , 3 vols (Oxford), vol. 2, ll.1111–19; J Lorne Campbell (ed.), 1999, *Songs Remembered in Exile: Traditional Gaelic Songs from Nova Scotia*, 2nd edn (Edinburgh), p.129; J G Campbell (ed. R Black), 2005, *The Gaelic Otherworld* (Edinburgh), p.286.

19. Edinburgh University Library, CW MS 2 ff.40v–41r.

20. See n.12 for references; for the immediate context, see Maclean-Bristol, *Murder under Trust*, pp.167–8.

21. J Fraser (ed. W Mackay), 1905, *Chronicles of the Frasers. The Wardlaw Manuscript* (Edinburgh), p.233; A M Sinclair, 1899, *The Clan Gillean* (Charlottetown, PEI), pp.144, 146, 148, 163, 164, 171, 172, 173, 457–8. An anonymous informant for the English Crown identified Lachlann as the foremost leader of the Macleans of Duart, 'being valorous': *CSP Ireland* 9 (Mar–Oct 1600), p.118.

22. For a useful comparative discussion on this subject, see S P Ashby, 2015, 'What really caused the Viking Age? The social content of raiding and exploration', *Archaeological Dialogues* 22, pp.89–106.

23. NLS Adv. MS 26.3.7, pp.233–4.

24. C Innes (ed.), 1851–5, *Origines Parochiales Scotiæ: The Antiquities Ecclesiastical and Territorial of the Parishes of Scotland* (Edinburgh), 2 vols in 3, vol. 2.1, p.357. The historical importance of Clachan Aoineart may be suggested by the elaborately sculptured font from that church, now in the National Museums of Scotland: A Carmichael, 1870, 'Donation of baptismal font from Chapel of St Maelrube, Lochaoineart, Skye', *PSAS* 8, pp.237–9. The early associations of the MacPherson parsons of Barra with the MacLeods may explain the curious incorporation of the island into the distant parish of Harris in the 17th century: NLS Adv. MS 33.2.7 f.351; Martin Martin, 1703, *A Description of the Western Islands of Scotland* (London), p.95. For other MacPherson parsons who may be related, see MacLeod (ed.), *Book of Dunvegan*, vol.1, p.38 [David: Roghadail, Harris, 1540]; Innes (ed.), *Origines Parochiales Scotiae*, vol.2.1, pp.141, 358, 377 [Malcolm: Durinish and Harris, 1566]; *Fasti* 7, p.189 [John: Harris (and Barra?), 1625–61].

25. See A Chambers, 1998, *Granuaile: The Life and Times of Grace O'Malley, c.1530–1603* (Dublin), pp.52–3, 80–2, 97–9.

26. Chambers, *Granuaile*, p.106; J Cook, 2004, *Pirate Queen: The Life of Grace O'Malley, 1530–1603* (Cork), pp.112–13; Hayes-McCoy, *Scots Mercenary Forces in Ireland*, pp.202–3; Macdonald, 'Ireland and Scotland', p.68.

27. Chambers, *Granuaile*, p.111; Cook, *Pirate Queen*, p.140; Hayes-McCoy, *Scots Mercenary Forces in Ireland*, p.206; Macdonald, 'Ireland and Scotland', pp.68–9.

28. Hayes-McCoy, *Scots Mercenary Forces in Ireland*, p.214; W C Mackenzie, 1903, *History of the Outer Hebrides* (Paisley), p.134; Macdonald, 'Ireland and Scotland', p.69.

29. *CSP Scotland* 13.1 (1597–9), p.244; see also *CSP Ireland* 7 (1597–9), p.289; Macdonald, 'Ireland and Scotland', pp.73, 77. The O'Malleys may have been in the Hebrides as mercenaries themselves, and even as military instructors, in preparation for Lachlann Mór's ill-starred invasion of Islay a few weeks later. There may have been subsequent contact between the MacNeils and the O'Malleys: in February 1602 'Mcneill Barray and utheris wt him' was reported to be to the north-west of Lough Foyle and considering voyaging to the territory of 'O'Maill' in April, possibly with 'mcClaynes brothir' (Lachlann Barrach must be meant here): *CSP Scotland* 13.2 (1600–03), p.945. For MacNeil involvement in the planned expedition against Aodh O'Neill of Tyrone in summer 1602, see *ibid.*, pp.729, 1024.

30. NRS, PA7/2/1. The revenge attack on these islands was clearly carried out to accompany, or even in place of, the intended expedition against Aodh O'Neill in Ulster.

31. [H MacDonald Buchanan], 1819, *Historical and Genealogical Account of the Clan or Family of MacDonald* (Edinburgh), pp.110–11, app. 25; MacDonald & MacDonald, *Clan Donald*, vol. 2, pp.304–05.

32. See A I Macinnes, 1996, *Clans, Commerce and the House of Stuart* (East Linton), pp.56–87; J Goodare, 1998, 'The Statutes of Iona in context', *Scottish Historical Review* 77, pp.31–57; Aonghas MacCoinnich, 2002, '"His spirit was only given to warre": Conflict and identity in the Scottish Gàidhealtachd, *c.*1580–*c.*1630', in S Murdoch & A Mackillop (eds), *Fighting for Identity: Scottish Military Experience, c.1550–1900* (Leiden), pp.133–62; A MacCoinnich, 2006, '"Mar phòr san t-uisge": Ìomhaigh Sìol Torcail an eachdraidh', in M Byrne, T O Clancy & S Kidd (eds), *Litreachas agus Eachdraidh: Rannsachadh na Gàidhlig 2, Glaschu 2002* (Glasgow), pp.214–31; M MacGregor, 2006, 'The Statutes of Iona: Text and context', *Innes Review* 57, pp.111–81; A Cathcart, 2010, 'The Statutes of Iona: The archipelagic context', *Journal of British Studies* 49, pp.4–27.

33. NRS PA7/1/2; MacCoinnich, *Plantation and Civility*, pp.120–3; Mackenzie, *History of the Outer Hebrides*, pp.200–03; N Macdonald (ed.), 1975, *The Morrison Manuscript: Traditions of the Western Isles, by Donald Morrison, Cooper, Stornoway* (Stornoway), pp.56–7.

34. *RPC* 7 (1604–7), p.255; MacCoinnich, *Plantation and Civility*, pp.128–31; Mackenzie, *History of the Outer Hebrides*, pp.217–19, 225; Macdonald (ed.), *Morrison Manuscript*, pp.58–9.

35. MacCoinnich, *Plantation and Civility*, pp.79–80, 146; C Falls, 1950, *Elizabeth's Irish Wars* (London), pp.72–5; J McGurk, 1997, *The Elizabethan Conquest of Ireland: The Burdens of the 1590s Crisis* (Manchester), pp.220–39; D O'Carroll, 2001, 'Change and continuity in weapons and tactics 1594–1691', pp.222–32, and J S Wheeler, 2001, 'The logistics of conquest', p.177, both in P Lenihan (ed.), *Conquest and Resistance: War in Seventeenth-Century Ireland* (Leiden).

36. *RPC* 7 (1604–7), pp.524–5; also J Spottiswoode (ed. M Napier & M Russell), *History of the Church of Scotland* (Edinburgh), 3 vols, 1847–51, vol. 3, p.192; Cathcart, 'Statutes of Iona', pp.11–12.

37. D Gregory, 1881, *The History of the Western Highlands and Islands* (2nd edn, Glasgow), pp.318–26.

38. Goodare, 'Statutes of Iona', pp.33–4; Cathcart, 'Statutes of Iona'.

39. MacDonald, 'Ireland and Scotland', pp.101–31; A MacCoinnich, 2004, Tùs gu Iarlachd: Eachdraidh Chlann Choinnich *c.*1466–1638, unpublished PhD thesis, University of Aberdeen), pp.298–351; MacCoinnich, 'Mar phòr san t-uisge'; MacCoinnich, 2007, 'Sìol Torcail and their lordship in the sixteenth century' in Islands Book Trust (ed.), *Crossing the Minch: Exploring the links between Skye and the Outer Hebrides* (Port of Ness), pp.7–32.

40. NRS, DI1/59 f.427r; J R N Macphail (ed.), 1934, *Highland Papers vol. 4* (Edinburgh), pp.226–7. In 1633 Lord Lorne acquired substantial debts owed by Clan Ranald; the following year these were exploited in order to extend the feudal superiority of the House of Argyll over the clan's mainland territories of Moidart, Arisaig, and Morar. The accusations levelled at Raghnall mac Ailein 'ic Iain, judged by the late-17th-century historian Niall MacMhuirich as *'duine maith do reir na haimsire ina ttarrla se'* ['a good man according to his times'], are evidently an attempt at eliminating a disruptive, unco-operative figure in the island wing of the clan lands: A Cameron (ed.), 1892–4, *Reliquiæ Celticæ,* 2 vols (Inverness), vol. 2, p.172; Macinnes, *Clans, Commerce and the House of Stuart*, p.86 n.46; Macinnes, 2012, *The British Confederate: Archibald Campbell, Marquess of Argyll, c.1607–1661* (Edinburgh), pp.72–87; Domhnall Uilleam Stiùbhart, 1997, An Gàidheal, a' Ghàidhlig, agus a' Ghàidhealtachd anns an t-seachdamh linn deug, unpublished PhD thesis, University of Edinburgh, pp.134–8, 141–6; S Theiss, 2006, The Western Highlands and Isles, 1619–1649: Allegiances during the "Scottish Troubles",

unpublished PhD thesis, University of Edinburgh, pp.156, 158, 165–75; T Brochard, 2010, The "Civilizing" of the far north of Scotland, 1560–1640, unpublished PhD thesis, University of Aberdeen, p.61.

41. Edinburgh University Library, CW MS 90/111 (ff.43v–44r); see also School of Scottish Studies Archives, Maclagan MS 8223. The *Peursan Mór* had been reconstrued in the communal imagination as an archetypal wicked (Protestant) clergyman. As well as being married, the chaplain consorts with a concubine and hunts with a dog on a chain, probably for the cormorants so plentiful on the headland of Àird Ghrinn: see School of Scottish Studies Archives SA1976/190, 191/A1–3 (Roderick MacPherson, Bruairnis). For further elucidation of the narrative and its context, see D U Stiùbhart, 2013, 'Murder in Barra, 1609? The killing of the '*Peursan Mór*', *Béascna* 8, pp.144–78.

42. Note the 'Hector mcNeil, persone of Barra' among the three clansmen named as being 'directit' by Ruairidh an Tartair to pursue hostilities against the Fife Adventurers in 1602 (NRS PA7/1/2). The *Peursan Mór* may be meant here; on the other hand he may be one of 'the two sons of John the son of the Parson', '*dà mhac Iain mhic a' Phearsain*', recorded in the list of MacNeil warriors incorporated into the 17th-century waulking song *Latha dhomh 's mi 'm Beinn a' Cheathaich*: Campbell and Collinson (eds), *Hebridean Folksongs*, vol. 1, l.1319.

43. *RPC* 9 (1609–13), p.318; 10 (1613–16), p.817; Mackenzie, *History of the Outer Hebrides*, pp.287–8.

44. *RPC* 8 (1607–10), pp.174, 396.

45. *RPC* 10 (1613–16), p.817.

46. Edinburgh University Library, CW MS 7/8 (f.14v).

47. Edinburgh University Library, CW MS 7/8 (f.14); A Carmichael *et al.* (eds), 1900–71, *Carmina Gadelica*, 6 vols (Edinburgh), vol. 5, p.22; Macdonald (ed.), *Morrison Manuscript*, pp.99–100.

48. *RPC* 9, p.32; 10, p.817.

49. *RPC* 9, pp.295–6, 318, 533–4.

50. *RPC* 10, pp.6–7.

51. *RPC* 10, p.28; 14 (Addenda, 1545–1625), p.574.

52. NRS DI1/53 (15 July 1629).

53. *RPC* 10, p.776; J A Stewart, 1982, The Clan Ranald: History of a Highland kindred, unpublished PhD thesis, University of Edinburgh), pp.51–2; Stiùbhart, An Gàidheal, a' Ghàidhlig, agus a' Ghàidhealtachd, pp.121–7, 183–5.

54. NRS DI1/53 (5 August 1629). For the Privy Council's continuing attempts to secure taxes from Barra, note Bishop Andrew Knox being granted feu-ferme of the island in 1612, an offer he did not take up (*RPC* 9 (1609–13), p.753), while in 1617 Sir Dugald Campbell of Auchinbreck was charged with paying four years' tack duty for the 'sevin illis of Barra and small islandis belonging thairto' (probably the Bishop's Isles) (*RPC* 11 (1616–19), p.244; NLS MS 2134, p.7).

55. NLS Adv. MS 34.2.8 ff.187, 187v.

56. NRS GD305/1/68/6–9; Campbell (ed.), *Songs Remembered in Exile*, pp.46–7; MacCoinnich, 'Tùs gu Iarlachd', p.323 n.1179; also Macdonald (ed.), *Morrison Manuscript*, pp.64–5.

57. In 1617 Ruairidh MacKenzie had taken over the administration of the lands of Duart, heavily indebted and now deprived by the Crown of the church lands acquired during the Reformation, from the chief Eachann Maclean, who had himself been fostered with

MacKenzie's elder brother Coinnich, Lord Seaforth. These developments may have facilitated MacKenzie's subsequent appropriation of the superiority of Barra and his probable resolution of the succession dispute: *RMS* 7, no. 203; MacCoinnich, 'Tùs gu Iarlachd', pp.64 n.204, 231–2, 323n.1179; Sinclair, *Clan Gillean*, pp.173–6; Stiùbhart, An Gàidheal, a' Ghàidhlig, agus a' Ghàidhealtachd, pp.102–07; D Watt, 2006, '"The laberinth of thir difficulties": The influence of debt on the Highland elite *c.* 1550–1700', *Scottish Historical Review* 85.1, p.31; Brochard, '"Civilizing" of the far north of Scotland', p.57 n.57.

58. Sinclair, *Clan Gillean*, pp.457–8. Iain, second son of Niall Òg MacNeil, would marry Lachlann's daughter Catrìona (*ibid.*, p.458; R L Macneil of Barra, 1923, *The Clan MacNeil: Clann Niall of Scotland* (New York), p.74). Clearly, these women were rather more than mere pawns and marriage counters.

59. NRS RD1/427 ff.484v–485v; Campbell, 'The MacNeils of Barra and the Irish Franciscans', pp.33–4.

60. NRS DI1/53 (15 July 1629); RD2/4, pp.326–9; F J Shaw, 1980, *The Northern and Western Islands of Scotland: Their Economy and Society in the Seventeenth Century* (Edinburgh), pp.49, 52; C Giblin, 1964, *Irish Franciscan Mission to Scotland 1619–1646* (Dublin), p.77; Campbell, 'The MacNeils of Barra and the Irish Franciscans', pp.33–4; Macdonald, 'Ireland and Scotland', pp.315, 336, 351, 438–9, 466–7; F A Macdonald, 2006, *Mission to the Gaels: Reformation and Counter-Reformation in Ulster and the Highlands and Islands of Scotland* (Edinburgh), p.78; Brochard, '"Civilizing" of the far north of Scotland', p.68. The catalogue of the Clan Ranald muniments refers to an undated obligation (NRS GD1/201/99), now unfortunately missing, outlining how 'McNeill of Oligon[ie]' – clearly Niall Uibhisteach, now of Eòlaigearraidh – will no longer pursue a legal process against his chief 'for the murder of John McNeill, lawful son of the deceased Rorie McNeill of Barray'. The identity of 'John McNeill' is unclear – the Iain Òg who was supposedly captured by Dòmhnall MacDonald of Clan Ranald and despatched to his death in the Edinburgh Tolbooth, or an unknown elder brother of Niall Uibhisteach himself? It may indeed be the former, given that the decision was reached in conjunction with Iain Mùideartach, son of Dòmhnall MacDonald, who 'has disbursed the entire charges'. It seems most unlikely, however, that Niall Uibhisteach could describe Iain Òg as the legal heir, and it may be a confused reference to the slaughter of a 'John McMurche VcNeill' and others *c.*1598, with which Donnchadh Campbell of Glenlyon was charged in 1630 (Macneil of Barra, *The Clan MacNeil*, pp.62, 77–8). If Niall Uibhisteach was the progenitor of the later MacNeils of Vatersay, tensions between the families may have lingered into the early 18th century: J Lorne Campbell & C Eastwick, 1966, 'The MacNeils of Barra in the Forty-Five', *Innes Review*,17, pp.82–3.

61. On the subject of fosterage, see especially P Parkes, 2006, 'Celtic fosterage: Adoptive kinship and clientage in northwest Europe', *Comparative Studies in Society and History* 48, pp.359–95.

62. See Cathcart, 'Statutes of Iona'. In constructing and testing new paradigms, perspectives, and conceptual frameworks for the period, productive comparisons might be drawn with recent approaches to the history of North American indigenous peoples: for example, P Hämäläinen, 2008, *The Comanche Empire* (New Haven, CT); M Witgen, 2012, *An Infinity of Nations: How the Native New World Shaped Early North America*, (Philadelphia); B Gratton *et al.*, 2013, 'Book Forum: P Hämäläinen's *The Comanche Empire*', *History and Theory* 52, pp.49–90.

63. Martin Martin, 1703, *A Description of the Western Islands of Scotland* (London), pp.89–100.

64. Martin, *Description*, pp.90–91.

65. NLS MS 1305, f.48; Clan Donald Archives, Armadale, Skye, NRAS 3273/4121/2; Martin, *Description*, p.100; C J Fraser-Mackintosh (ed.), 1897, *Antiquarian Notes, Historical, Genealogical and Social 2nd series): Inverness-Shire* (Inverness), pp.332, 450.

66. Martin, *Description*, p.100.

67. D U Stiùbhart, 'Martin Martin (*c*.1665–1718)', *Oxford Dictionary of National Biography*.

68. See NRS CH2/557/3, 141, 749 [*recte* 149], 153–4, 158, 177; CH2/557/4, 242; CH2/557/14, np.

69. Inveraray Castle Archives, Bundle 1759, Rev. Alexander Cooper's Address to Synod, 6 June 1699; also Bundle 63, Cooper to Synod, 3 August 1697; Bundle 539, Presbytery of Skye to Synod of Argyll on behalf of Master John Morison, 1699. See Martin, *Description*, p.112; also D U Stiùbhart, 2014, 'Leisure and recreation in an Age of Clearance: The case of the Hebridean Michaelmas', in J Borsje, A Dooley, S Mac Mathúna, and G Toner (eds), *Celtic Cosmology: Perspectives from Ireland and Scotland* (Toronto), pp.207–48.

70. Inveraray Castle Archives, Bundle 539, Cooper to Synod, 10 June 1699; also same to same, 8 June 1699.

71. Martin, *Description*, 92–3, 99–100.

72. Martin, *Description*, 99–100.

73. Martin, *Description*, 93–9; B Buxton, 1995, *Mingulay: An Island and its People* (Edinburgh), p.20.

74. Martin, *Description*, pp.94, 96–7; Buxton, *Mingulay*, pp.9–24, 79–83; L Storey, 2007, *Muinntir Mhiughalaigh* (Glasgow), pp.9–17; also A Gannon & G Geddes, 2015, *St Kilda: The Last and Outmost Isle* ((Edinburgh), pp.87–9, 113; M Harman, 1997, *An Isle called Hirte: A History and Culture of St Kilda to 1930* (Waternish), pp.205–25, 290–7; J A Love, 2009, *A Natural History of St Kilda* (Edinburgh), pp.84–163.

75. Martin, *Description*, pp.96–7; K MacAulay, 1764, *The History of St Kilda* (London), pp.188–9. Compare *Dwelly's Gaelic Dictionary*, s.v. *géinneach*, 'stout', 'strong', derived from *géinn*, 'wedge'; apparently also realised as *geangach*, 'thick and short'; also *gingein*, 'cask', 'thick-set person'.

76. Martin, *Description*, pp.98–9, 289–90; Martin, Martin, 1698, *A Late Voyage to St Kilda* (London), p.93.

77. Martin, *Description*, 99; idem, *Late Voyage*, 97–8.

78. Martin, *Description*, 94. For St Kilda, see *ibid.*, pp.289–90; Martin, *Late Voyage*, pp.92–9; Harman, *Isle called Hirte*, pp.94–5; A Fleming, 2005, *St Kilda and the Wider World: Tales of an Iconic Island* (Macclesfield: Windgather Press), 71–9.

79. Martin, *Description*, 98, 99; also 21, 23–4.

80. See, for example, Buxton, *Mingulay*, 49–50; Storey, *Muinntir Mhiughalaigh*, 65; also Martin, *Description*, 24–5; Harman, *Isle called Hirte*, 259–62; Michael Robson, 1991, *Rona: The Distant Island* (Stornoway), 28–31.

81. *Béascna* 8, 144–78.

GALLEY-CASTLES AND THE ISLE OF MAN?

Peter Davey

THE AIM OF THIS PAPER is to consider the function of those Manx defended sites which were in use during the period of the Kingdom of the Isles, *c.*1079–1266, and whether these merit the title of 'galley-castles'. The evidence for each of the sites will be reviewed and assessed in a number of ways: its formal components, physical location, strategic position, role within local and wider networks and its operation seen through contemporary and later medieval documentary evidence. A number of alternative functional explanations will be discussed and some implications for the archaeology of the wider kingdom will be suggested.

The Manx evidence

The Manx evidence consists of three formal types: motte-and-bailey castles, stone castles and promontory forts (Figure 13.1).

Motte-and-bailey castles

The construction of timber forts on the Isle of Man at the beginning of the 12th century is noted in the *Chronica regum mannie & insularum* for 1102, which also underscores the role of galleys in this period and the importance of Man both as a naval base and as a desirable settlement site:

> But they, in great alarm, advised him [Magnus] to quit Norway as soon as possible. He immediately collected a fleet of 160 ships, and sailed to the Orkney islands, which he subdued, and, passing through all the islands, brought them under his dominion, and arrived at Man. Putting in at the island of St Patrick, he went to visit the site of the battle which the Manxmen had fought between themselves a short time before, for many bodies of the slain still lay there unburied. When he had observed the beauty of the island, he was much pleased; and chose it for his abode, erecting forts which to this day bear his name. He compelled the men of Galloway to cut timber and bring it to the shore for the construction of the forts.[1]

Do these forts exist and, if so where are they? Any identification of a Manx context for motte-and-bailey construction is bound to be tentative, given the lack of independent

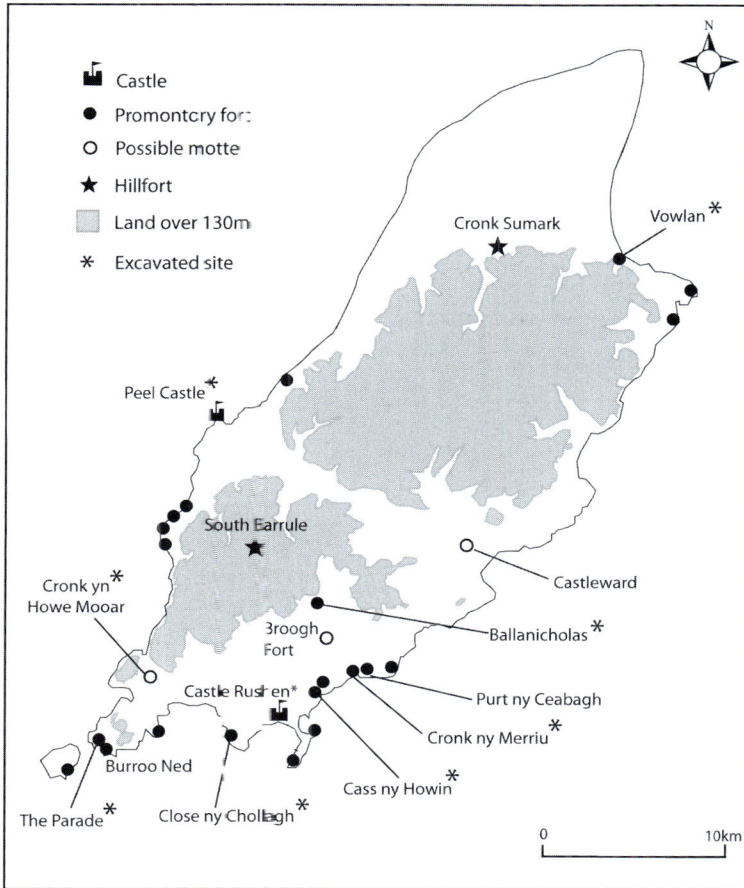

Figure 13.1. *Mottes, castles and promontory forts on the Isle of Man, showing excavated sites. (Peter Davey)*

dating evidence for the building of any of the sites. Four possible candidates will be considered: Cronk yn Howe Mooar, Castletown, Brough Fort and Castleward.

Cronk yn Howe Mooar, Rushen

Spencer Smith has argued convincingly that Cronk yn Howe Mooar (Plate 29) was constructed at the beginning of the 12th century by Magnus Barelegs, king of Norway, after the death of Godred Crovan, and following a second military campaign in Anglesey where he had assisted the Welsh prince Gruffudd ap Cynan in recapturing the Norman motte at Castell Aberlleiniog.[2] The *Brut y Tywysogyon* for 1102 states that:

> In the meantime, Magnus, King of Germany, and with him a fleet, came a second time to Anglesey; and after felling for himself some trees for timber he returned to Man. And there he built himself three castles and a second time filled Man, which he had previously left desolate, with his men.

This proposed context and dating for Cronk yn Howe is to a certain extent confirmed by the nature of the iron arrowhead found by Kermode at the site. At the time of the excavation Montelius in Stockholm commented that 'we have such arrowheads with a tang to be inserted in the wooden shaft; they date from the Viking period'. This identification has recently been confirmed by the Norwegian archaeologists Hofseth and Resi who comment 'only very few types of arrows have split sockets, as your object seems to have. Among the Norwegian spearheads, however, this is the common shape'.[3] Thus Kermode's find would appear to be of a Scandinavian type and of the right period.[4]

Cronk yn Howe Mooar is strategically placed with the movement of galleys in mind. It is 1.5km from Fleshwick Bay which faces the North Channel, the route to the Hebrides and Norway, and about the same distance over a low-lying neck of land from Port St Mary Bay. This would allow a portage which avoids the difficult and often-hazardous Calf Sound in order to reach the fertile south-east of the island and the direct route to England.

Castletown, Malew

Given the important of its south-east-facing harbour, Castletown would be an obvious choice for one of Magnus's 'forts'. In the 1989 excavations of Castle Rushen a wide moat was located apparently surrounding the stone keep, but not concentric with it. It contained 13th-century pottery in its upper fills. As it was not possible to establish the chronological relationship between the keep and the moat, this feature may have survived from an early-12th-century motte-and-bailey timber castle which was replaced in stone between 50 and 100 years later.[5] Only further excavation might clarify this possibility.

The Broogh Fort, Santan

This substantial earthwork consists of a flat-topped mound 25m in diameter and some 5m above the surrounding land-surface. It is surrounded by an 8m-wide flat-bottomed ditch and, on the eastern side, two external concentric banks. To the west and north the site has been severely reduced by ploughing. It has not been excavated and is of unknown date. But it is quite unlike any known form of Manx prehistoric monument, so that some form of motte and bailey is a distinct possibility.

Castleward, Braddan

This is another undated site, situated on a rock outcrop above the River Glass some 2km north-west of Douglas harbour. It has long been considered to be a local version of a Scottish dun, similar to but smaller than the impressive hillfort at Cronk Sumark in the north of the island. Recent examination by members of the hill-fort study group, together with detailed Lidar images which penetrate the dense tree cover, have suggested that a motte and bailey, using an existing outcrop, is at least a possibility.

Stone castles

The two Manx medieval stone castles – Peel on the west coast facing the North Channel and Rushen on the south-east opposite Lancashire and North Wales – are very different in scale, plan, function and occupational history. Both present largely later-medieval towers and curtain-walls, with much less visible from the 12th and 13th centuries. Both command significant harbours.

Peel

Innis Patrick, on which Peel Castle was constructed, is an islet off the west coast of Man some 242m long and 156m wide. It lies 70m off the north end of Peel Hill, and the channel between it and the mainland served as the main route into the harbour until it was closed by a causeway built in the 18th century.

The site has had a complex occupational history, with structures of many periods from the 10th century to the 19th (Plate 30). Investigated on a small scale by Bersu in 1947 and Ralegh Radford in 1962,[6] the major excavations by Freke in the 1980s revealed an intense early Mesolithic occupation, scattered Neolithic and Bronze Age activity and an extensive Iron Age settlement consisting of at least five roundhouses, including a grain-store.[7] Some residual earthworks outside the present circuit of stone walls may represent contemporary defences. At some point between the 5th and 8th centuries AD the islet became home to a monastic community, with a number of chapels and cross-slabs being identified, culminating in the erection of an Irish-style round tower.

The subsequent history of the site sees alternating cycles of military and ecclesiastical use; on occasions the castle appears to have fulfilled both functions at the same time. A Viking interest is represented by a number of elements identified during the Freke excavations: the construction of stone-revetted earth defences at least on the north-east side, a sizeable timber building with sprung wooden floors,[8] a mid-11th-century silver coin-hoard,[9] and a series of 'pagan' burials, that is inhumations with Viking-style grave-goods.[10]

The chronology of these elements is instructive. The coin-hoard was directly associated with the foundations of the timber building for which a thermo-remanent date of AD 1100–1180 was obtained from the uppermost hearth which, itself, was truncated by the transepts of the cathedral probably constructed *c*.1220. The burials lay within a Christian cemetery, many within 'native' lintel-grave coffins. An early-medieval-type chapel was built on the site after the demise of the timber building and before the construction of the cathedral. St German's Cathedral functioned as the headquarters of the medieval diocese of 'the southern isles' (*sodorensis* in contemporary accounts) and then from the late 14th century until the 19th as the seat of the bishops of 'Sodor and Man', actually restricted to Man itself. It saw phases of re-fortification in response to external threats, especially by the Montacutes in the 14th century,[11] the Stanleys in the 15th, 16th and 17th centuries, and the British Government during the Napoleonic wars.

Castle Rushen

Rushen is a much smaller and simpler site than Peel, with no ecclesiastical complex to be sustained. It has a compact plan and is constructed in local limestone which contrasts with the red sandstone and grey Manx-group stone at Peel (Plate 31). Although it lacks a natural sheltered harbour like that at Peel, and the offshore tidal streams are problematic, the tombolo of Langness, which is due east of the castle and connected to the mainland by a sand-bar only 150m wide, creates alternative sheltered anchorages in the south-east in Castletown Bay and in the north-east in Derbyhaven, approachable in almost any sea-conditions. Portage between the two would have been relatively simple. Rushen has the great advantage over Peel in that it faces England and north Wales; access to these coasts became increasingly important as the Manx kings earned significant sums in protection-money from the English.

In its first phase is a keep some 19m square, with later projecting towers, gatehouse and curtain walls. O'Neil in his definitive study suggested a date in the reign of Godred II, soon after 1150, for construction of the original keep; Megaw, followed by McDonald, preferred a date after 1191 in the reign of Reginald I.[12] The castle first appears in the documentary record in 1265 as the place where King Magnus died.[13] The keep has been slighted, probably by Robert the Bruce in 1313, and, on detailed architectural grounds, all the later buildings and defences appear to post-date the transfer of the island to the Montacutes in 1333.[14]

Promontory forts

There are 22 sites where substantial earthworks appear to have been constructed to defend or separate cliff-top promontories from the surrounding lands. All but one is coastal (Figure 13.1). They have traditionally been assigned to the Iron Age, on typological grounds.[15] The seven which have been subject to excavation demonstrate a more complex picture. In 1946 the first to be excavated was the interior of the Vowlam, north of Ramsey,[16] where a series of superimposed, rectilinear timber buildings were identified which, on structural grounds, appeared to be Norse in date. No Iron Age or medieval artefacts were recovered.

Gelling, an Iron Age specialist, investigated four sites between 1950 and 1959. At Ballanicholas he identified a sequence of circular timber buildings within the interior, together with finds indicating a date in the later 1st or earlier 2nd century AD.[17] At Close ny Chollagh he exposed the foundations of three well-built roundhouses together with a cultural assemblage dating from the late 1st century AD. Above these houses a substantial stone rectilinear building, putatively of medieval date, had been constructed; it measured 11m x 7.4m and occupied a majority of the interior.[18] At the other two sites, Cronk ny Merriu and Cass ny Hawin, he found timber buildings of the 11th to 13th century with no Iron Age evidence.[19] In 2000 Darvill excavated a small fort, Hango Brough, at the north end of the Langness peninsular. This also produced a Norse-period radiocarbon date of AD 898–1017 (at 1 sigma).[20] In 2002 a narrow trench through the ramparts and ditches of a trivallate promontory at the

Parade in the south of the island, produced a radiocarbon date of AD 990–1230 (at 2 sigma), implying a Norse-period construction of the fort.[21]

Lidar images of the interior of the unexcavated fort on Barroo Ned appear to show a complex of circular and rectilinear buildings, possibly analogous to those at Close ny Chollagh. A recent gorse fire on Maughold Head exposed a small rectilinear structure at the summit of the fort.

In summary, only one of the seven excavated sites, that of the inland fort of Ballanicholas, produced Iron Age evidence with no later occupation. At Close ny Chollagh Iron Age structures were succeeded by medieval ones and at the other sites only medieval buildings were identified. Thus, while it is not possible to extrapolate with complete confidence to the two-thirds of the forts which have not been excavated, there seems good reason to believe that many of them were first constructed and used in the period of the Kingdom of the Isles. Thus, when trying to find a plausible function for the forts in the medieval period, it must be remembered that few can actually be shown to be contemporary, and that any apparent pattern in their siting may be illusory. Nevertheless their distribution is not even. Apart from the Vowlan there are none in the northern plain; elsewhere they appear to be focused in particular areas. There is a grouping along the southern and eastern coasts, north and south of Castletown, and another on the west, either side of Peel. These two groups make up almost half the 21 sites listed by Gelling.

Function

Galley-castles?

Taking into account the archaeological and documentary evidence there seems no doubt that a major function of the Manx castles was as bases for the fleets of galleys which were essential to the control of an island kingdom and the exploitation of the weakness of its neighbours. A detailed study of the Icelandic sagas, the contemporary Welsh and Irish literature, the English administrative records as well as the *Cronica regum mannie et insularum* makes this only too clear.[22] They may properly be called 'galley-castles'.

Given the growing evidence for the contemporary occupation of a number of the promontory forts, the question arises as to whether the castles and the neighbouring forts constitute a coherent defensive system. Peel Castle is situated on an islet over 20m above sea-level, which projects into the Irish Sea and provides a clear view of over 200°, on a clear day taking in much of the north-west coast of Man to Jurby Head, the North Channel, the Antrim Plateau and the Mountains of Mourne. Only a single, undated, promontory fort can be seen just south of Kirk Michael.

In contrast, Castle Rushen is more-or-less at sea-level and is set within a complicated coastline, with poor visibility to the north, east and south-east. There are eight promontory forts within 10km of the castle. The four excavated forts all produced occupation evidence dating from the 11th to 13th centuries. That at Hango Brooch located a fire-pit and charred gorse which may well represent the site of a beacon.[23] Detailed inspection on the ground has established which of them are inter-visible and/or inter-audible now and which could have been seen directly from Castle Rushen given a structure *c.*2–3m above present-day ground-level (Figure 13.2; Plate 32).[24]

It is clear that these sites could provide forward intelligence of galleys arriving on the south-east coast of the island and give the castle a visual range of some 220° to the north-east, east and south-east, equivalent to, if not better than, Peel Castle gives for the north-west. A signal-station placed on Cronk Mooar might have linked the two forts on the Calf Sound with Close ny Chollagh and Castle Rushen, thus giving warning of any ships passing through the Sound. Both the forts at the Sound have evidence for medieval occupation, whether through typology or by radiocarbon dating. So it does seem that Castle Rushen, the pre-eminent royal focus by the end of the 12th century, was provided with an elaborate early-warning system.

The existence of such a system may be implied by the entry in the Chronicles for 1172:

> … Reginald, son of Echmarcach, and evidently a man of royal stock, came to Man with a large band of men, and in the absence of the king put to flight in the first attack some men who were guarding the coast and killed about twenty of them.[25]

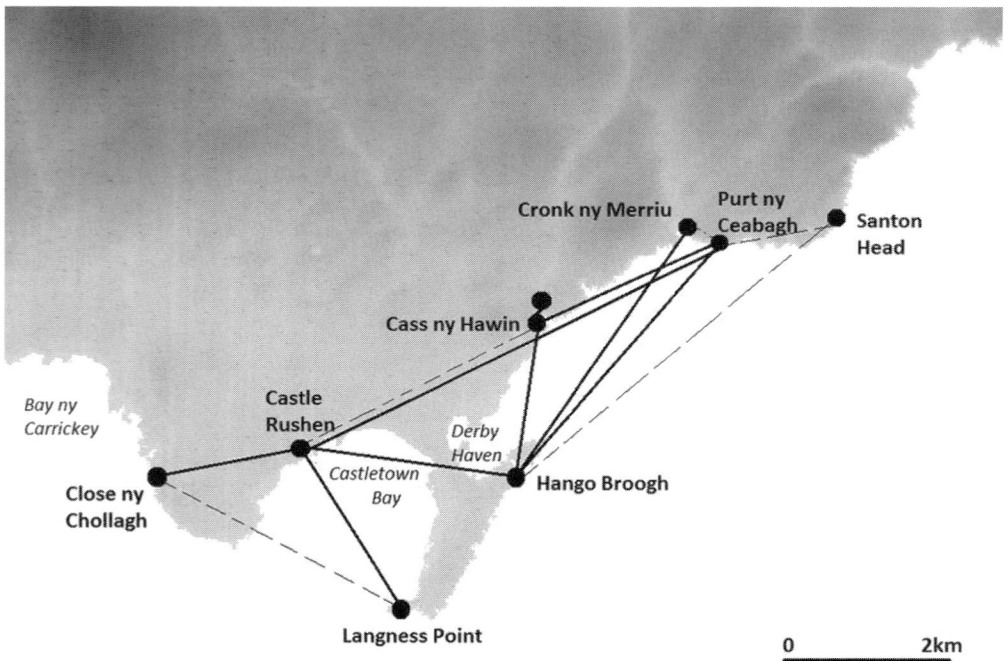

Figure 13.2. The south-east coast of the Isle of Man showing the geographical relationship between Castle Rushen and the coastal promontory forts. The straight lines show modern intervisibility and/or interaudibility between the castle and the local promontory forts. The dashed lines show probable intervisibility given a tower construction of modest height.
(Peter Davey)

and is explicit in the second *Lex scripta* statute for 1417:

> First, that Watch and Ward be kept through your said Land as it ought, upon Pain
> of Life and Lyme; for whosoever fails any Night in his Ward, forfeiteth a Wether to
> the Warden; and to the Warden a second Night a Cowe; and the third Night Life and
> Lyme to the Lord.[26]

It would seem that a system originally devised to protect the capital had, by the
17th century, become island-wide.[27] But is their role as naval bases at the southern
extent of the kingdom of the isles, projecting power into the southern Irish Sea and
beyond, the only or primary function of the two Manx castles? A number of other
possibilities are considered below.

Instruments of conquest

In this period castle-building and town-plantation often accompanied military
conquest and functioned as a key instrument of conquest. Good examples can be
found in the Anglo-Norman adventure in Ulster towards the end of the 12th century
or the Edwardian Welsh campaigns of the 13th. In the case of the Isle of Man this
does not seem to have been so. It is possible that the motte-and-bailey castles may
have fulfilled such a function, but even if the dating of all four possible sites could
be verified, they would only have been able to control the south of the island. The
evidence of the crosses suggests that, in any case, a Norse settlement of the island had
begun early in the 10th century and was very well established by the 11th.[28] By the
time any of the castles was constructed the Norse position within the kingdom was
well secured.

Statements of prestige

The construction of a state-of-the-art stone castle at Rushen in the mid or late 12th
century is one element in a modernising policy pursued initially by Olaf I (1113–53)
and followed by his successors Godred II (1153–87) and Reginald (1187–1228). This
sought to bring the kingdom into the mainstream of European norms. It included
the grant by Olaf of lands to the Savignacs for the foundation of Rushen Abbey in
1134, bringing reformed monasticism to Man and the Isles before it had reached
Ireland, Scotland or Scandinavia. The establishment of the diocese of *sodorensis*,
and of the parochial system later in the century, continued this process. Meanwhile,
during the same period, the Crovan dynasty established more formal economic and
feudal relationships with their neighbours, in particular with the kings of England.[29]
Possession of a 'proper' castle was essential to royal identity both psychologically and
in the eyes of the external world.

Control of external trade

The 12th- and 13th-century ceramic evidence from Peel Castle shows a wide-ranging
network of mainly south-facing commercial relationships, especially with north-west

and south-west England, but also with northern and western France.[30] Although no other site on Man has produced an equivalent and contemporary ceramic assemblage for comparison, it seems most likely that the high proportion of imported wares from Britain and the continent reflects the role of the castles as the entry points for goods traded to the island from overseas. A small, late-medieval assemblage from the mainland settlement at Peel, in which locally-made pottery predominates, seems to confirm this.[31]

In 1406 the Lancashire-based Stanley family became kings of Man.[32] In 1417 the second John Stanley began to record decisions of Tynwald Court in writing, the *Lex scripta*, initially 13 statutes defining his prerogatives as Lord.[33] Further statutes dealing with *corbes* and the role of administrators followed in 1419, and in 1422 the deemsters, the holders of 'breast law', were required to commit to writing the 'Laws of Man'. This they did in a further 99 statutes which form the basis of the modern legal system.[34] The deemsters described the law as 'The Constitution of old Time', and individual statutes are said to follow 'the Use and Custom of long Time'.

It is clear from these earliest statutes that the castles, quite apart from any military function, were central to the control of external trade, the collection of customs,[35] the control of currency[36] and movement of people.[37] The unpublished garrison-roll of 1428 shows how this role was administered and provides a number of interesting examples, such as issues arising over the handling by the garrison, Receiver and Waterbailiff of the cargos of ships carrying salt direct from Brittany.[38]

Internal administration

The first *Lex scripta* statutes between 1417 and 1430 give a clear idea of the roles of the Lord's officers, based at the castles, in the internal administration of the island. They collect agricultural rents[39] from all holdings except those belonging to religious orders, dues to provide an income for the Lord's officers such as the Moars and Coroners,[40] taxes at the sheading courts to support the household when the Lord is present,[41] and also payments in kind such as those on herrings, turf and corn.[42] The chancery courts were held weekly at the castles, where the prisons were also located.[43] Civil weddings continue to be solemnized at Castle Rushen. The 1428 garrison-roll shows many aspects of these functions in actual operation.

Man and the wider kingdom?

The nature and range of the subject-matter of the Galley-Castles Conference made a deep impression on the writer. In particular, it has suggested that more effort should be made by archaeologists working on the 11th to 13th centuries to consider the whole of the kingdom of Man and the Isles as its context, rather than an approach that is based on contemporary political entities.

For example, the galleys which 'dealt death from Man' must have been built somewhere. The Isle of Man lacked deep-water or sheltered harbours and, more significantly, trees. The *Chronica regum mannie & insularum* for 1098 records

Magnus forcing the Gallwegians to cut timber for his Manx castles,[44] and the *Brut y Tywysogyon* for 1102 (above) shows him cutting trees in Anglesey to bring to Man. This lack of timber is reinforced by the pollen evidence, which shows that, by the end of the Iron Age woodland clearance, begun in the early Neolithic in the lowlands, had become total.[45] The island then remained virtually treeless until the early 20th century with very local, very small areas of relict woodland surviving in remote locations.[46]

So where were the Manx galleys built? While suitable timber was certainly available in neighbouring north-east Ireland, Cumbria and Galloway, it seems much more likely that for such a strategically important activity the king would have relied on supplies from another part of the kingdom. Skye would have been most suitable, as well wooded, unlike the Outer Hebrides, and also as an entity that remained within the kingdom despite the ravages of Somerled and his sons. The discovery of a likely shipbuilding facility in the south of Skye, reported on at the conference by Colin Martin (this volume) makes excellent sense as a main shipyard supplying galleys to Man during this period.

Another subject that deserves a more inclusive approach is the study of the medieval ceramic industries throughout the kingdom. The possible connections between these products and the need to consider them together is now recognized, but has not been carried out.[47]

What of the Manx castles themselves in the context of the rest of the kingdom? Was Castle Rushen the sole statement of royal power? Were there contemporary foundations on Islay, Skye or Lewis, for example? Did the king allow castle-building beyond Man, or did any such structures represent the fracturing of central control? Did the Hebridean castles use any kind of formal early-warning system? A key issue here is one of absolute chronology. While the overall political situation and its development is reasonably well dated from documentary sources, the castles are not. Unless the construction of a castle can be closely dated its role in the defence of the kingdom or in its disintegration cannot be determined. The conference included a presentation from Mark Thacker showing how the primary mortar of some Scottish castles could be radiocarbon dated. A wider application of this technique would be of great assistance in determining such questions.

Summary

Peel and Castle Rushen were almost certainly the most important naval bases in the kingdom of Man and the Isles. Castle Rushen, at least, was provided with a sophisticated early-warning system through a 'watch-and-ward' arrangement established on the promontory forts that survived in a more extended form until the early-modern period. In addition, the castles acted as garrisons, as centres of administration, including justice, internal and external trade and for the collection of taxes in cash and in kind. How far the Manx castles and their functions applied to the Hebridean part of the kingdom is a subject still to be studied.

Notes

1. *Cronica Regum Mannie & Insularum,* G Broderick (ed.), 1996 (Douglas), f.35r.
2. S Smith, 2004, 'Castell Aberlleiniog, Anglesey and Cronk Howe Mooar, Isle of Man: related monuments?', *Transactions of the Anglesey Antiquarian Society, pp.*31–45.
3. Smith, 'Castell Aberlleiniog', p.44.
4. The Kermode excavation exposed the stone footings of a rectangular structure on top of the mound; the plan of the later medieval stone defences is compatible with this.
5. D J Freke, 1996, 'Excavations at Castle Rushen, 1989', in P J Davey, D J Freke & D A Higgins, *Excavations in Castletown, Isle of Man 1989–1992* (Liverpool), pp.8, 16.
6. M D Wright, 1982, 'Excavations at Peel Castle, 1947', *Proceedings of the Isle of Man History and Antiquarian Society* 9.1, pp.21–57; Ralegh Radford, 2004, 'St Patrick's Isle, Peel: The Medieval Ecclesiastical Remains and Excavations of 1962', *Proceedings of the Isle of Man Natural History and Antiquarian Society* 11:3, pp.361–93.
7. D J Freke, 2002, *Excavations on St Patrick's Isle Peel, Isle of Man, 1982–88: Prehistoric, Viking, medieval and later* (Liverpool), pp.45–57.
8. Freke, *Excavations on St Patrick's Isle*, pp.132–9.
9. W Seaby, 2002, 'The 1982 coin hoard (82.150/C (262))', in D J Freke, *Excavations on St Patrick's Isle Peel, Isle of Man, 1982–88: Prehistoric, Viking, medieval and later* (Liverpool), pp.320–25.
10. J Graham-Campbell, 2002, 'Tenth-century graves: the Viking age artefacts and their significance', in D J Freke, *Excavations on St Patrick's Isle Peel, Isle of Man, 1982–88: Prehistoric, Viking, medieval and later* (Liverpool), pp. 83–98.
11. W M Ormrod, 2015, 'Man under the Montacutes, 1333–92', in S Duffy & H Mytum (eds), *A new history of the Isle of Man: The medieval period* (Liverpool), pp.151–69.
12. P J Davey, 2013, *After the Vikings: medieval archaeology of the Isle of Man AD 1100–1550* (Douglas), pp.56–64.
13. *Cronica Regum Mannie & Insularum,* f.49v.
14. Ormrod, 'Man under the Montacutes', p.160.
15. P S Gelling, 1978, 'The Iron Age', in P J Davey (ed.), *Man and environment in the Isle of Man* (BAR 54: Oxford), pp.239–41.
16. G Bersu, 1949, 'A promontory fort on the shore of Ramsey Bay, Isle of Man', *Antiquaries Journal* 29, pp.62–7.
17. P S Gelling, 1968, 'Excavation of a promontory fort on Ballanicholas, Kirk Marown, Isle of Man', *Proceedings of the Isle of Man Natural History and Antiquarian Society* 7.2, pp.181–91.
18. P S Gelling, 1958, 'Excavation of a promontory fort at Scarlett, Castletown, Isle of Man', *Proceedings of the Prehistoric Society* 24, pp.85–100.
19. P S Gelling, 1952, 'Excavation of a promontory fort at Port Grenaugh, Santon', *Proceedings of the Isle of Man Natural History and Antiquarian Society* 5.3, pp.307–15; Gelling, 1959, 'Excavation of a promontory fort at Cass ny Hawin, Malew, Isle of Man', *Proceedings of the Isle of Man Natural History and Antiquarian Society* 6.1, pp.28–38.
20. C P Doonan, P Cheetham, B O'Connor, T Eley & K Welham, 2001, 'Investigations at Langness: the 2000 field-season' in T Darvill (ed.), *Billown Neolithic landscape project, Isle of Man Sixth report: 2000* (Bournemouth & Douglas), pp.42–4.
21. P J Davey & D Allwood, 2016, 'Archaeological fieldwork in the Isle of Man in 2015', *Isle of Man Studies* 14, p.146.

22. eg R A McDonald, 2007a, *Manx Kingship in its Irish Sea Setting, 1187–1229: King Rognvaldr and the Crovan dynasty* (Dublin); 2007b, 'Dealing death from Man: Manx sea power in and around the Irish Sea, 1079–1265', in S Duffy (ed.), *The World of the Galloglass* (Dublin), pp.45–76; and this volume.

23. Doonan *et al.* 'Investigations at Langness', p.43; there was no evidence that the fire had been located within a building; the Vowlam also produced an 'open-air hearth which might also have served a similar purpose' (A A C Johnson, 2002, 'Watch and ward on the Isle of Man: the medieval re-occupation of Iron Age promontory forts', in P J Davey & D Finlayson (eds), *Mannin revisited: twelve essays on Manx culture and environment* (Edinburgh), p.73).

24. The sightline between Castle Rushen and Cass ny Hawin is now obscured by spoil from the limestone quarry that lies between them.

25. *Cronica Regum Mannie & Insularum*, f.40r.

26. *The Statutes of the Isle of Man, Vol.1, 1417–1824*, J F Gill (ed.), 1883 (London), p.4.

27. Johnson, 'Watch and ward', pp.75–9.

28. D Wilson, 2008, *The Vikings in the Isle of Man* (Aarhus), pp.58–74.

29. *Monumenta de Insula Manniae*, 2, pp.72–4.

30. P J Davey, 2011, 'Les exportations continentales vers l' île de Man du XVᵉ au XVIIᵉ siècle', in A Bocquet-Liénard & B Fajal (eds), *A propo(t)s de l'usage, de la production et de la circulation des terres cuites dans L'Europe du Nord-Ouest autour des XIVᵉ–XVIᵉ siècles* (Caen), pp.219–31.

31. P J Davey, 2016, 'The ceramic finds from the Peel IRIS excavations', *Isle of Man Studies* 14, pp.71–9.

32. M J Bennett, 2015, 'English rule confirmed: the Isle of Man 1389–1406', in S Duffy & H Mytum (eds), *A new history of the Isle of Man: The medieval period* (Liverpool), p.182.

33. *Statutes of the Isle of Man, Vol.1*, pp.3–6 (1417).

34. *Statutes of the Isle of Man, Vol.1*, pp.6–20 (1422).

35. *Statutes* 1417: 3–4; 1422: 51, 92–3.

36. *Statutes* 1422: 54 and 94.

37. *Statutes* 1417: 4 and 1422: 52.

38. http://isle-of-man.com/manxnotebook/history/peelc/pt7.htm

39. *Statutes* 1417: 5 and 1422: 47–48.

40. *Statute* 1417: 10.

41. *Statute* 1422: 27.

42. *Statutes* 1417: 8–9 and 1422: 99.

43. *Statute* 1422: 53.

44. *Cronica Regum Mannie & Insularum*, f.34v.

45. R Chiverrell, J Innes & J Blackford, 2006, 'Vegetation history of the Isle of Man', in R Chiverrell & G Thomas (eds), *A new history of the Isle of Man 1: the evolution of the natural landscape* (Liverpool), pp.300–326.

46. A Dubbeldam, 2011, *The oak/hazel woodlands of the Isle of Man* (Peel).

47. B Ballin-Smith, 2013, 'Iain Crawford's Udal: the key to ceramic traditions of the western seaboard?', *Medieval Ceramics* 34, p. 43; D Hall, 2013, 'Here be monstrous fabrics: constructing a research agenda for the hand-made wares of the Scottish west coast, highlands and islands', *Medieval Ceramics* 34, p.23.

Galley-Castles in Gaelic Medieval Ireland?

Colin Breen

A decade ago, in a seminal article, Ian R Macneil defined a galley-castle as 'any castle close enough to the sea directly or by portage to have been significantly influenced by the existence of galleys when they were a dominant military factor. Most castles on both the Hebridean islands and Hebridean mainland shores are galley-castles'.[1] He argues that galleys played a central role in the everyday practices of the polities of medieval Hebridean society. His article also recognises the clear correlation between the siting of castles and the sea during this period across mainland Scotland and the islands. Notwithstanding any issues researchers will have about the validity of his argument with regard to Scottish sites, the purpose of this short paper is to question the extent to which the same argument is relevant in an Irish context.

Parts of the island of Ireland and regions within the west of Scotland were bound together both politically and culturally for millennia. In the historic period the Kingdom of Dal Riada, encompassing north-east Antrim, Argyll and the Southern Hebrides, effectively constituted a maritime province, with its peoples sharing a language and a set of cultural traditions in a common political sphere.[2] From the close of the 13th century a series of Argyll and Island families migrated to Ulster and became integrated within the patchwork polities of Gaelic lordship across the island (Figure 14.1). This set of close connections would, by extension, suggest shared architectural traditions and a common relationship to the sea. But to what extent was this true, and did the Gaelic lordships in Ireland negotiate differing relationships with their local and regional maritime worlds? Did galleys, and by extension galley-castles, play a central role in medieval Gaelic society across Ireland's northern and western seaboard?

Scottish migrations and north-coast lordship

This study is particularly concerned with Scottish groups which migrated to Ulster during the High to Late Medieval period. In the 1260s the MacSweens were replaced as Lords of Knapdale by the Stewart Earls of Menteith. John MacSween later failed to recover Castle Sween *c.*1300, and the group moved to consolidate their presence in Ireland. By the close of the 13th century they were established as the leading galloglass force in Ulster, and played a central role in maintaining the strength of the O'Donnells in Donegal. They played a crucial part in the O'Donnell succession conflicts (1333–

80) and were subsequently granted the vassal chieftainship of Fanad.[3] Cadet members were granted the two further territories of Tir Boghaine and Tir Tuatha.

Little archaeological research has been undertaken on the lordship, but the text of a mainly-16th-century document *Leabhar Chlainne Suibhne* (the Book of the MacSweeneys, RIA ms24 f.25) provides important insights into the sept's histories. Folios 66–72, written by Tadhg Mac Fithil between 1532 and 1544, deal primarily with the history of the Fanad branch in north Donegal, but contain important information about the families across all three territories and beyond.[4] The text chronicles the arrival of the clan in Donegal and its subsequent political involvement in this part of north-west Ulster. Their social and cultural interactions in Ireland illustrate how they became more Gaelicised in an Irish sense and lost a number of attributes of their former presence in west Scotland. One key element is the architectural manifestations of lordship that the MacSweeneys adopted. They are associated with five castles or, more properly, tower-houses, across the county.

Figure 14.1. The Gaelic maritime lordships in later medieval Ireland. (Colin Breen)

MacSweeney castles

Tower-houses were the primary residences of Gaelic lords across the island of Ireland. While not overly militaristic in character, they were built to create a visually impressive statement of power and prestige in the landscape. What is of interest here is the relatively late date of these structures in Donegal in comparison with the early castle dates across western Scotland. Of course tower-houses are different architectural entities from castles, but their later construction-dates indicate differing responses to lordship across the Gaelic world.

Of the five structures associated with the MacSweenys two, at Rathmullan, on the western shore of Lough Swilly, and at Killybegs, have been destroyed. Little is known about the latter structure but the Rathmullan site is shown on an early-17th-century map as a typical tower, located adjacent to a sheltered natural bay suitable for the safe anchorage of vessels. We do not have a date for its construction, but it is likely to be early-16th-century on the basis of the establishment of the adjacent Carmelite friary in 1516. Elsewhere in south Donegal Rahan Near, a tower-house with bawn wall on a coastal promontory, first appeared in the historical records in 1524.[5] Moross, a small tower in Mulroy Bay, was reputedly built in 1532, while the primary residence of MacSweeney Doe, Doe Castle, was first mentioned historically in 1544 (Plate 33).

Were these towers galley-castles? While each was deliberately built at a coastal location to take advantage of suitable landing-places, anchorages and access to the sea-lanes, it is unlikely that facilitating galleys was their primary objective. The Mac-Sweeneys' dependence on galleys had lessened since their migrations to Ireland. Indeed, the centralised role galleys played in medieval Scottish island life was not necessarily the case in an Irish context. Yes, maritime trade, traffic and warfare was an intrinsic part of past Gaelic lifeways, but the ownership and operation of galleys was seen as the preserve of a few Irish coastal septs and was not a feature of them all. It could also be argued that, with the ending of the Lordship of the Isles at the close of the 15th century, the power of the galleys and their associated families was greatly weakened as both society and naval technology underwent profound change. The MacSweeneys, in erecting their towers at the opening of the 16th century, were still building in a maritime-specific context, but the period of the galley as the primary instrument of Gaelic power was ending. MacSweeney power lay instead in their role as terrestrial galloglass, and in the relationships they had developed with the O'Donnells and other powerful Gaelic lords.

MacDonnell castles

The southern Clan Donald, or Clan Iain Mhór, acquired the Glens of Antrim following the marriage of Eoin Mhór to Marjorie Bisset c.1390.[6] This effectively marked the first stage of MacDonnell presence in north-east Antrim. It is likely they were associated with Castle Carra, near Cushendun, a late-13th- or 14th-century structure. While the tower has the external appearance of a hall- or chamber-castle it has the dimensions of a tower-house.[7] It was located on the northern shores of a sheltered embayment and would have been ideally suited to facilitate boat traffic and landing from the Isles. Its adjacent bay would effectively have provided the first safe landfall for vessels which had rounded Fair Head with the flooding tide. However, we know little about the castle's medieval history, so little can be said of it in terms of galley use.

A second major period of MacDonnell involvement with Ulster occurred from 1544 when they were invited from their base at Dunyvaig on Islay to fight with the MacQuillans of the Route, a 14th-century lordship in north Antrim, against the O'Cahans, the primary sept located west of the River Bann in Derry. Almost immediately on arrival on the north Irish coast they appear to have built Kinbane Castle, just west of Ballycastle. Possibly in order to create a bridgehead into north Ulster the MacDonnells fortified a projecting chalk promontory at Kinbane with a small two-storey tower and an enclosing wall. Positioned at the base of steep cliffs, it would have been barely accessible from land. Its importance lay in its maritime position, providing a good landfall from Islay for sailing vessels with a knowledge of the prevailing tides and currents. Associated with the castle are two boat-nousts, located 50m to the west of the promontory, above an area of foreshore where boulder clearance is apparent. Limited excavation in the easterly noust produced a sherd of late-medieval Ulster coarse pottery, provisionally linking the boat-shelter features to the castle in date. The castle appears to have been occupied for little more than a decade. In terms of north-east Ulster castles Kinbane was the site most intrinsically linked to the sea. Its original primary purpose was to facilitate landfall and provide a secure provisioning-base for vessels travelling between Ulster and the Isles.

Dunluce Castle, the major fortified centre of lordly power on the north-east Ulster coast, differed from Kinbane in a number of respects (Plate 34). While it was built on the coast, its position on a cliff-edge was not immediately suitable for the accommodation of galley traffic. Originally built *c*.1500 by the MacQuillans, it was taken by the MacDonnells in the 1550s and subsequently refurbished and partially reconstructed.[8] There was no suitable landing-place beneath the castle other than a cave which provided access to the land from the sea. However, this could only have been accessed by small vessels when the sea was exceptionally calm. Such conditions are a rarity on the north coast and the cave must only have been accessible in exceptional circumstances. The closest landfalls were either the sandy beaches near Portrush, 2km west of the castle or Portballintrae, 2km to the east.

When originally built it was intended to be a statement of lordly power and control, more interested in monitoring the coastal waters than accommodating boat traffic. Historical sources indicate that the MacQuillans had only a limited direct engagement with the sea, and their focus was on their terrestrial holdings. The MacDonnells were more engaged with the sea, but by the time they had taken Dunluce and the territory of the Route from the MacQuillans, the purpose of the galley had shifted from being the primary instrument of Gaelic power towards a more utilitarian communication role. Galleys were still important, able to make a swift passage from the islands to Ulster and maintain familial, cultural and political links, but the centrality of and dependence on these vessel-types had shifted.

In choosing Dunluce as their symbolic centre of power the MacDonnells were breaking with medieval Island practice and were instead looking for a castle that would architecturally express their political ambitions and social aspirations. Ultimately, their choice of a cliff-edge castle was to backfire when they attempted to establish a mercantile town at the site in the early 17th century. The absence of a harbour in an age of maritime trade and new larger vessel-types, accommodating bulk trade, rendered the town effectively obsolete, and it went into decline before being abandoned in the middle of the century. Other fortified sites occupied by the MacDonnells followed a similar pattern. Dunineany was built on the edge of a steep cliff, 2km from Ballycastle. While not a castle as such, the site consists of a small promontory fortified by a deep rock-cut ditch. Towards the close of the 16th century the site was refortified with a gate under the authority of the MacDonnells.[9] As with Dunluce this site could not have physically accommodated boats, but instead served as an administrative centre within the lordship.

Across north Ulster different lordships responded and interacted with the sea in different ways. The MacSweeneys maintained their maritime capacity to a degree, but this reduced significantly from the time of their initial arrival. The MacDonnells inhabited a maritime world but their own maritime capacity was somewhat limited. Both the location of their coastal castles and the historical sources indicate that they did not maintain a galley-fleet in Ireland. Similarly, other sept groups in the region had little maritime expertise or capacity. The O'Cahans, for example, whose territory lay on the eastern shores of Lough Foyle, did not have any coastal castles and do not appear to have had vessels of any great size. In terms of Gaelic Irish galley-capacity we need instead to look to the west of Ireland and the lordships of the O'Malleys and the O'Flahertys in particular.

Western seaboard lordship

From the 12th century onwards the O'Malleys controlled the land and seas of the Owles, a territory located along the western seaboard of mid-Connacht, including the islands of Achill, Clare, Inisturk and Inishbofin.[10] They were the pre-eminent seagoing Gaelic family and had a fleet of galleys used for raiding, warfare and general transportation. A galley is shown on a late-medieval armorial funerary plaque on Clare Island, which also bears the family legend 'Strong on land and sea'. By the end of the 15th century they were one of only two Irish Gaelic lordships referred to in an English intelligence report as using 'long galleys'.[11]

A number of castles across the territory are associated with the family. Each was built in a strategic maritime location, at places which could cater for groups of galleys. On Clare Island they built a small tower-house in the mid 16th century on the eastern side of the island, directly above a gently-shelving sandy beach. Overlooking Clew Bay, the site was ideally suited as a galley-base. Interestingly, the small tower-house is not visible on the sea approaches to the island until a boat effectively enters this small bay. Similarly, Rockfleet castle was constructed in the 16th century at the head of a small sheltered inlet near Newport (Plate 35). The tower-house could not have been seen from the main shipping-channels. Both its name and its historical connections suggest that, as with Clare Island, the site served as a galley-base. The fact that both were effectively hidden from the sea further supports the family's reputation for raiding and coastal piracy. A third tower-house on Achill Island was positioned to both monitor and control this important passage, while also serving as an administrative base.

The O'Malleys were intrinsically linked both by geography and by marriage to the O'Flahertys. This sept had migrated west of Lough Corrib following the Anglo-Norman arrival in Connemara at the end of the 13th century.[12] They had a series of castles which had two primary geographical spreads. The first group was centred on lakes, such as Lough Corrib, while a second group consisted of seven castles built on the coast. Ard tower-house on the northern shore of Galway Bay was built by a sheltered inlet. Paul Nassens (pers comm) has recorded a local tradition that the O'Flaherty occupant dammed the stream to an adjacent lake to create a basin for his galleys. As with the O'Malley castles, the site requires specialist knowledge to approach it safely by water, and this is a feature of a number of the O'Flaherty coastal sites.

Bunowen, near Ballyconnelly, is now destroyed and built over by a post-medieval house but it would originally have been in a partly-hidden location within the complex waters and many inlets along this section of Connemara coast. Built above a narrow sheltered beach it would have provided shelter for galleys. Doon castle was built on a rock promontory in the narrow inlet of Streamstown Bay. Renvyle Castle was built further north on the Connemara coast near the entrance to Killary Harbour and overlooks a shallow bay that offered sheltered anchorage as well as beach landing. It was strategically positioned adjacent to the crucial waterway for vessels moving north and south along this section of coast, between the mainland and Inishboffin. Renvyle's occupants were linked by marriage to the O'Malleys, whose territory lay immediately north of the castle.

These Galway and Mayo castles were intrinsically linked to galleys. They were built specifically as focal places for these two maritime lordships, but were also gathering-places for galleys. During periods of conflict these locations would have acted as muster-points for both boats and men, and also have served as provisioning-places. Their sites were suitable for sheltering boats, repairing them and storing them during the winter. It is no coincidence that many of the locations enjoyed limited maritime visibility, in contrast to the overt visible physicality of the north-coast castles, for example. These were locations that often required specialist navigational knowledge to access a safe landing. Both the O'Malleys and O'Flahertys were keen to protect their maritime interests, and this included keeping both their vessels and lordly centres safe from passing vessels and enemy forces. The physical landscape was also conducive to this form of activity, with its complex series of inlets, embayments and dangerous waters.

Lordship in the south-west

It could be argued that the maritime lordships of the south-west had a different emphasis. Here the principal families included the O'Sullivan Mór of the Iveragh Peninsula and the O'Sullivan Beare of Bantry and Beara. Further east both the O'Mahoneys and the O'Driscolls controlled west Cork. Of these groupings the O'Driscolls had close affinities to the O'Malleys and were known as mariners and the controllers of their own fleet.[13] They are also referred to as using 'long galleys' in the 1490 intelligence report.[14] However, while they had this capacity, they played a far less obvious role in raiding and piracy in comparison with the Connemara groups. It may have been that the O'Driscolls occupied territory in a more stable region and were less marginalised than the western groupings, bordering as they did the major port region of Cork. This is not to deny their naval prowess, as they were involved in numerous naval engagements, but their activities were more conventional and seem to have been an accepted part of the everyday political and social conflicts of late-medieval Munster. However, rather than warfare, each of the lordships across this region appears to have been more concerned with the control of maritime resources.

Each had a series of coastal tower-houses dotting this section of the coastline. Unlike their O'Malley counterparts, these were highly-visible structures positioned at recognised places of safe anchorage or harbours, and overlooking key fishing-grounds and important passages. The towers were intrinsically linked to the control of both their marine zones and the associated hinterland. Tower-house location was designed in particular to monitor the local fishery resources. One key aspect of their administration was the imposition of taxes on visiting fishing-fleets. While a number of the lordships may have lacked substantial fleets or large vessels to physically control visiting fleets, they could control anchorage, landfall and the provisioning of these fleets, ensuring a form of landward control over vessels in their waters.

It is important to note the extent of the fisheries during the 16th century in the south-west. Numerous historical sources point to hundreds of vessels coming from the European mainland on an annual basis to fish these waters. Such an annual incursion had major implications for the economy of the south-west as well as for the social and cultural life of its inhabitants. Rather than being perceived as a remote and marginalised area, this coast was instead seen as being an integral part of the broader North Atlantic social world during the Later Medieval period.

A closer examination of the tower-houses of Bantry Bay, the territory of the O'Sullivan Beares, for example, indicates that these were not galley-castles in McNeil's terms. Instead they were key instruments of the social and political control which the lordship exerted over this landscape.[15] They functioned not only as residences of the elite and centres of land administration, but also as physical expressions of that power. Only Dunboy castle, a late-15th-century tower-house, was built directly adjacent to the shoreline beside a natural harbour. This was the principal castle of the lordship and also the centre of the bay's fishery activities. Other tower-houses including Carriganass were built several kilometres from the coast and could not be seen from the sea.

The tower-house on Whiddy Island was placed on one of the highest points of the island and must have been designed to provide good views over the lordship's waters rather than facilitate galleys at the water's edge. Finally, the Taniste's residence at Ardea was built on the edge of a low cliff and overlooks the waters of Kenmare Bay. These were tower-houses built in a landscape of relative stability, where control did not have to depend on galleys. Rather than seeing the structures as facilitating fleets, they were instead built for controlling their associated maritime and terrestrial resources. They served as communication nodes within a broader interconnected maritime landscape, and were an integral part of the socio-political fabric of these places.

Conclusion

Returning to the questions posed at the beginning of this paper we can see that Macneil's definition of galley-castles is problematic in an Irish context. A number of issues immediately present themselves. First, there is the problem of chronology. The Irish coastal tower-houses of the Gaelic lordships tend to be later in date than many of the castles of the Scottish western islands. They therefore post-date the period when galleys were most effective as instruments of power. By the 16th century the power of these vessels had declined and they were gradually being replaced by new vessel-types and by changing socio-economic circumstances. The Irish tower-houses were responding to these evolving times.

Chronological considerations are also important in the context of the emergence of individual lordships. The Ulster MacDonnell lordship on the north coast was only established in the second half of the 16th century, at a time when older medieval norms were being replaced by the advent of modernity. A second consideration is the differing regional responses to maritime lordship in Ireland. Along the north coast lordship was shaped by the complex politics of Ulster and by the region's relationship with Scotland. The mid-western seaboard lordships, while rooted in the structures of Gaelic society, had developed specialisms, and indeed notoriety, as marine fighters who made considerable use of their maritime expertise. By contrast, the south-western lordships were influenced heavily by economic considerations. The castles of each individual lordship reflected the interests of their sept group and the nature of their associated physical landscapes and resources.

There was no single or uniform set of functions associated with these sites. What we can say about them is that they were built by, and belonged to, familial groups bound by their immediate physical and cultural geographies. These tower-houses were built as territorial expressions of power and control, primarily concerned with the protection of their resources as well as their territorial interests. Each sept responded in different ways to the individual needs and requirements of their territory, while their castles reflect regional variations in everyday practice between the groups. The castles also reflect regional hierarchical relationships with the sea, where access to both communications and resources was under the control of the regional elite. Were these galley-castles? The majority were not, although a case can be made that the tower-houses of the O'Malleys functioned as defined by Macneil. Irish coastal tower-houses served many functions, and to label them as galley-castles is overly restrictive and misses the complexities of medieval Gaelic society. Maritime activity was one facet of a range of landscape relationships these castles helped facilitate.

Notes

1. I R Macneil, 2006, 'Kisimul Castle and the origins of Hebridean Galley-Castles: Preliminary Thoughts', in A Kruse & A Ross (eds), *Barra and Skye: Two Hebridean Perspectives* (Edinburgh) pp.21–46.
2. A Lane, E Campbell & J Bayley, 2000, *Dunadd: an early Dalriadic capital* (Oxford).
3. K Simms, 1995, 'Late Medieval Donegal', in W Nolan *et al.* (eds), *Donegal History and Society* (Dublin), pp.183–201.
4. *Leabhar Chlainne Suibhne: an account of the Mac Sweeney families in Ireland with pedigrees*, P Walsh (ed.), 1920 (Dublin).
5. B Lacy, 1983, *Archaeological Survey of County Donegal* (Lifford).
6. S Kingston, 2004, *Ulster and the Isles in the Fifteenth Century: The Lordship of the Clann Domhnaill of Antrim* (Dublin).
7. T E McNeill, 1983, 'The Stone Castles of Northern County Antrim', *Ulster Journal of Archaeology*, pp.101–28.
8. C Breen, 2012, *Dunluce Castle. History and archaeology* (Dublin).
9. T E McNeill, 2002, 'Dunineny castle and the Gaelic view of castle building', *Proceedings of the XX Château Gaillard (Caen, 2000)*, pp.153–61.
10. A Chambers, 1979, *Granuaille—The Life and Times of Grace O'Malley* (Dublin).
11. L Price, 1932, 'Armed Forces of the Irish Chiefs in the Early 16th Century', *Journal of the Royal Society of Antiquaries of Ireland*, 7th ser. 2:2, pp.201–07.
12. P Nassens, 2007, 'Gaelic lords of the sea: the coastal tower houses of south Connemara', in L Doran & J Lyttleton (eds), *Lordship in Medieval Ireland* (Dublin), pp.217–35.
13. C Kelleher, 2013, 'Pirate Ports and Harbours of West Cork in the Early Seventeenth Century', *Journal of Maritime Archaeology* 8.2, pp.347–66.
14. Price, 'Armed Forces'.
15. C Breen, 2005, *The Gaelic Lordship of the O'Sullivan Beare: A Landscape Cultural History* (Dublin).

15

Galley-Castles of the Sound of Mull and Loch Awe: A Gaelic Folklore Perspective

John Macfarlane

This article is very much a personal interpretation. It is intended to give a different but valid perspective and frame of reference when evaluating the papers of the MacNeil conference on galley-castles which are presented here.

The Tobermory where I was born and grew up in the 1940s was a Gaelic place. Beneath the general veneer of a fairly bourgeois respectability, there existed almost a sub-culture in which a genuine oral tradition of song and story still flourished. It sometimes seemed apologetic for its existence, and was almost unsuspected until the advent of the tape-recorder and the gentle probing of folklorists such as Calum Maclean.[1] Old men told tales and young boys like myself exercised their imaginations and dreamed dreams. The blacksmith's shop and convivial gatherings in private houses were bright with tale and song, many of which were ancient in the area.

As far as we were concerned, castles, the sea and boats were workaday objects and sights. It is true to say however, that the tales of strongholds and their leaders, and the folklore of their exploits on land and sea in song and story, were anything but unexceptional. In these media, galleys fought in Bloody Bay and skimmed the short, choppy seas of the tide-race at Bunan nam Biodag between Duart and the Point of Lismore. The songs followed the great exaggerated tone of praise-poetry: golden rudders, fluttering white banners and ropes of silk such as those which, we are told, hanged Colla Ciotach on the decks of his own galley at the anchorage which lies in the shadow of Dunstaffnage Castle.

Galleys were steered by sea-princes (as the Islay song says, '*Mac an Rìgh ga stiùireadh*'). They sailed to and from castles of a fabulous quality: grim and grey outside but candle-lit, awash with light, filled with the gentle pluck of harp-strings and the mirth of wine and strong ales. A Gaelic poetess of the 17th century, Mary MacLeod, known to Highlanders as Màiri Nighean Alasdair Ruaidh, describes one such:

Tigh mòr macnasach meadhrach	That was a high tower blithe and festive, thronged with
Nam macaomh 's nam maighdean,	young men and with maidens, where the clangour of
Far am bu tartarach gleadhraich nan còrn.	the drinking-horns was loud.
Tha do thalla mòr priseil …	thy great and brilliant hall, …
Far am faca mi am fion brìth 'ga òl	where I have seen wine a-drinking.[2]

No one who sailed the zigzag route of the old MacBraynes boat *Lochinvar* from Tobermory to Drimnin, Salen, Lochaline and Craignure and from thence to Oban could miss these castles: Mingary, Aros, Ardtornish, Duart and, out of sight, Loch Buie on Mull. And on the fresh water of Loch Awe, other galley-castles and birlinns.

As we shall see, the history and folklore of these castles and the galleys which sailed from them are inextricably woven with one another in a complex pattern: a tapestry of blood, violence, piracy, cattle-raids, heroic valour, marriage liaisons, necromancy and, sometimes, peaceful social interaction. Each has its stories in local folklore – stories that grow with the telling and display all the hallmarks of genuine orally-transmitted folklore, as it is handed from voice to memory to voice. Exaggeration and decoration occur. Conflation telescopes events and arranges or enhances them in a convenient order to embellish the story. The paranormal intervenes, explaining and clarifying the past, linking it to the present and adding to the dynamic of the tale. Mull was, I regret to say, famous for its its elemental forces, its witches, necromancy, and white witchery. It was an island where, it is alleged, Satan was summoned by the live roasting of cats on a spit and is the origin of the saying '*Ge bu dé a chi thu cum a' tionndadh i*' (whatever you see keep her turning).

The most famous mythical elemental was the *Cailleach Bheithir*, the primeval force who dwelt, among other places, on the rock-girt coast of Gribun, and whose wash-tub was the great maelstrom of Corryvreckan. The most famous Mull witch, a personality to be consulted for good or evil, was *An Doideag Mhuileach*, who features in many a tale of castles, of battles and of other initiatives. She was sometimes accompanied by her frightening counterpart, *Sùil Ghorm*, who had one piercing blue eye in the centre of her forehead. *Sùil Ghorm* was from outwith the area and appears to have been brought in, on a consultancy basis, when extraordinary combined deeds were required. And, of course, there were old men and women who had healing powers or second sight or the power of the evil eye. I myself have seen a woman covering her cow's rear end with her apron while passing a certain house in Tobermory in case an evil eye would affect the buttery property of the milk or the calf-bearing powers of the cow.

In my youth, the men of Tobermory sailed out to the 'Bank', a rich fishing-area found by aligning a scar on the headland above Bloody Bay (Bàgh na Fala) and a church on Morvern. All were aware of Mingary Castle, 13th-century guardian of the Sound of Mull and seat of the MacIains of Ardnamurchan. All knew it had witnessed the heroic sea-battle between the birlinns of John MacDonald, Lord of the Isles and chief of Clan Donald, and his son Angus Òg in the vicinity of Bloody Bay. The precise date of the battle varies in sources, from 1480 to 1483. It is the stuff of great tales: a desperate sea-battle with galley pitted against galley in which the Fairy Flag of the Macleods was unfurled and many lives lost. After the battle, in which Angus Òg Macdonald emerged victorious, he seized power from his father, and held it for a decade. My youth was coloured by the tales of the local cave in Bloody Bay called *Uamh nan Ceann* (Cave of the Heads) where the heads of the vanquished were allegedly thrown after the battle. They may even have been defeated Macleans who came ashore, took refuge in a cave, and were smoked out and killed as they emerged.

My father, Donald Macfarlane, always averred that the 'heads' in question were fish-heads which local lobster fishermen kept in barrels in the cave for baiting their creels – but then he was a cynic! One participant in the battle, Neil Maclean, was called Niall nan Ordag (Neill of the Fingers and Toes) because he was said to show off the bailerfuls of fingers and toes he collected in the enemy galleys! We shall see later that this sort of calculation, where the extent of a victory is measured by the number of body-parts collected, is part of the exaggeration and decoration which enhances the effect of the tale on the listener.

In 1588, matters got worse for Mingary and for the MacIains. It was around this period that a battered Spanish ship escaped the English fleet, came north round Scotland and anchored in Tobermory to repair and take on provisions. She was almost certainly the *San Juan de Sicilia*, a unit of the Squadron of Levant (commanded by Don Martin de Bertendona), a ship of the defeated Spanish Armada. Documents in the possession of the Duke of Argyll identify her as the bearer of coinage to pay Spanish troops. She was said to be of 800 tons, had a complement of 279 soldiers and 63 mariners, and carried 26 guns. Her ordnance stores comprised roundshot, powder, lead and match.[3]

The stories tell that, at this point, MacIain wished to marry the widowed mother of Lachlan Mòr Maclean. She was a daughter of the Earl of Argyll and a woman of considerable dowry. MacIain sailed from Mingary with a strong wedding-party – but not strong enough. The story tells of the marriage at Torloisk in Mull where the happy couple retired to consummate their union. Meanwhile, the heavy drinking continued in the marriage-hall until insults were exchanged, daggers drawn, and the MacIain wedding-party was slaughtered. MacIain himself was in bed with his new wife. Tradition says that he was about to receive the same treatment but the entreaties of his new spouse saved him. Lachlan Mòr Maclean's view of the slaughter has come down in folklore: '*Ma ruitheas am madadh ruadh am broilleach nan gadhar is gun millear e, cò is coireach?*' (If the fox runs up against a pack of hounds and is destroyed who's to blame?).

Fate, however, caught up with the Macleans. In exchange for provisions, they decided to ask for the help of marines from the Spanish ship in order to harry the MacIains yet again. The aim was to ravage the Small Isles and Ardnamurchan and in particular to lay siege to Mingary. The place-name Port nan Spainteach (Port of the Spaniards) near Mingary enshrines this event. They were soundly defeated by MacIain and his Clan Ranald allies and the Spanish galleon with its reputed fabulous hoard of gold blew up in Tobermory Bay where she still lies in the soft silt, wreathed in a plethora of folktale.

Stories tell of the infatuation of Lachlan Mòr's son for the beautiful Spanish princess aboard, who had seen him in a dream as her ideal man. They tell of the fall of a guttering candle which ignited a powder-magazine and blew them to Kingdom Come. Alternatively, they tell of the consultation between Lachlan Mòr and the *Doideag* and *Sùil Ghorm* which resulted in great winds, and in a plague of cats, amphibians and reptiles on her masts and rigging which capsized her. They also relate the tale of the ship's cook who survived the blast to drag himself ashore at Port a' Choit (Port of the Cargo Boat) in Tobermory to father descendants who, even in my own time, were swarthy, hook-nosed, wore bright clothes and were given to owning long-lived parrots!

The Mingary of the 17th century and later is commemorated in folklore as a nest of pirates, the most famous among them being Mac Iain Gheàrr (1628–1684) (Son of Short John). He was famous for sailing out of Ardnamurchan and harrying seafarers in a birlinn which was black on one side and white on the other and which carried double-coloured sails. The Gaelic saying for a two-faced person is: '*Taobh dubh 's taobh bàn air mar a bha bàta Mhic Iain Ghiorr*' (a black side and a fair side on him like Son of Short John's boat). His abilities at theft were given to him by a supernatural being called a *glaistig*, also known as a 'green lady' or *maighdean uaine*, and must have been quite compulsive. Among other stories of cattle-raiding and larceny, he is alleged even to have stolen a pair of carved slabs from Iona and installed them in St Comhgan's Church, Ardnamurchan, to mark his parents' grave. These lie there to this day.

One of the stories tells of his galley drawn up at Ardnacross, in the Sound of Mull, for a reiving expedition against the Macleans. At dead of night he and his men, driving a herd to the beach, saw the glimmer of lights in the ancient chapel of Pennygown,[4] a place where the effigies of a Maclean knight and his wife are alleged to lie outside hallowed ground because of their witchcraft. However, on this occasion, the sorcery was in the opposite direction! Bursting in, Iain and his men found three local *cailleachan* (withered old women) sticking pins into a clay doll or *corp chreadha,* depicting Lachlan Mòr of Duart. At considerable risk to himself, Iain drove the *cailleachan* out at the point of the sword. He immediately took the doll to be broken at Duart where the unfortunate Lachlan recovered from the agonising pains he had been suffering. History – or folklore – does not relate what happened to the stolen Maclean cattle.

Iain Òg MacIain of Ardnamurchan, when on the point of marrying a daughter of the house of Lochiel, about the year 1596, was assassinated by the tutor, his uncle, Mac Mhic Iain. He was his next heir, and wished to obtain possession of the estate. The murderer did not long escape the punishment due to his crime; for, as he was fleeing (strangely enough to Duart under the protection of a band of Macleans), he was soon embattled in a short engagement with the enraged Camerons and MacIains at Leac nan Saighead (or Leac na Saighde – Stone of the Arrows) in Gleann Dubh in Morvern.

In the best traditional fashion, his death has taken a mythical form. He was a gigantic man and was mortally wounded by the arrow from the bow of a legendary Cameron archer whose shaft pinned his hand to his skull as he wiped his brow, even although he was wearing the protection of a (Spanish marine's?) magical helmet which was meant to protect him from all harm. With typical folklore bravado, he is alleged to have said 'it is merely a midge bite', but he did not survive. His body was taken by land and sea to Kiel in Loch Aline . His targe was obtained by the MacLachlainns of Laudale and is still in the possession of a descendant of that family.

Sailing on, we pass the strategic Aros Castle on its rock-face high above the estuary of the River Aros. The only vague reference I can recall is of the abduction of some Highland chiefs. I am presuming this is the incident where Lord Ochiltree, King James VI's lieutenant, in 1608, entertained the principal island chiefs on board his flagship *Moon,* after which he announced to them that they were the king's prisoners and sailed with them to the south where they were imprisoned in the castles of Blackness, Dumbarton and Stirling until they promised to yield to His Majesty's demands.

To the south, well beyond the sea-end of Loch Aline, lies Ardtornish. Tales must abound. From here the funeral procession of John of Islay, Lord of the Isles, sailed through the Sound of Mull to Iona, and it was from here, according to tradition, that his son Donald and his galley-fleet sailed on their way to transport the vassals of the Isles to the bloodstained field of Harlaw. Here treaties with England were made. But I regret that I have no stories about Ardtornish except one unsavoury one which concerns the infamous Patrick Sellar who took over the Ardtornish Estate in the mid-1800s. According to residents of Tobermory who had been cleared from his Ardtornish estate, he had so many curses on him that his eventual death was caused by his body being consumed alive by lice.[5]

I recently heard what I think is an old traditional song which underlines the ancient importance of Duart on the seaways.

Chunna mi do bhàta 's i seòladh o Dhubhairt gu Sléibhte	I saw your boat sailing from Duart to Sleat
's thu fhein air an stiùir oirr'	And you, yourself, steering her
Tha soirbheas an diugh aig an Greumach	The Graham has a fair wind today.[6]

No one who sails in to the eastern end of the Sound of Mull can fail to see the strategic and tactical significance of a castle dominating the seaways of the Sound of Mull, Loch Linnhe and the exit where the Western Sea beckons with all its possibilities.

Despite the vagaries of the Macleans in the fortunes of Mull, the castle and the leaders of its clan loom very large in the folklore. In particular there are many stories about the Battle of the Gruinart Strand in Islay where Sir Lachlan Mòr, 14th chief, perished while trying to wrest control of Islay from his nephew Sir James 9th of Dunyvaig in August 1598. Sir Lachlan consulted the *Doideag Mhuileach*, a 'wise woman', before sailing on his venture. His expedition was, in any case, doomed from the start, because he is alleged to have boldly sailed *tuathal* (anti-clockwise or against the sun) out of the Maclean galley-harbour at Eilean Amalaig (NGR NM 708 229). The witch advised him under no circumstances to sail or land on a Thursday, neither to anchor at Poll-nusaig (the anchoring-pool)[7], nor to plant his standard on Cnoc nan Aighean (Heifer/Deer Hill), nor, indeed, to take off his helmet nor drink out of Tobar Nèill Neònaich (Strange Neil's Well). Inadvertently, he did all these things.

Mull witches were cynical experts at raising storms. Sir Lachlan and his galleys were caught in such a storm and were forced to make landfall in Islay on that day of the week. Being thirsty during battle, Lachlan drank from a spring near the spot, which turned out to be the well in question. He had rejected the offer of help from a *Diùrach* (an islander from the Isle of Jura). As one tale puts it, 'Before battle started, an ugly hunch-backed dwarf called Dubh Sìth (Black Fairy) offered his services to MacLean. His offer was spurned. On offering his services to MacDonald, he was welcomed and armed as one of his men. Dubh Sith hid in a tree above Tobar Nèill Neònaich and killed Sir Lachlan with a crossbow-shot through the eye when the MacLean chief had removed his helmet to drink'.[8] The battle, and Sir Lachlan's death, are recorded in a song which sounds like a piece of *ceòl mòr* (the classical music of the Great Highland Bagpipe), and may be another example of the link between classical pipe music and vocal folk music.[9]

Another, earlier Lachlan Maclean, Lachlan Cattanach, 11th chief, cemented his alliance with the Argylls by marrying Katherine Campbell, daughter of Archibald Campbell 2nd Earl of Argyll. Although politically convenient, the marriage was not a success. Traditional tales tell us she tried to poison him, and he arranged to have her drowned by placing her on a tidal rock in the Sound of Mull which is still known as the Lady Rock.[10] She was rescued by Lismore fishermen just before the high tide overcame her, and was present at Inveraray when Maclean appeared to report her death.[11] Another tale told to me orally said her nephew was with her when she was marooned; that he was brought back to Duart Castle by passing fishermen and was tortured, naked, in a ring of clansmen who stood round a fire in the courtyard and bombarded him with apples, prepared for roasting.[12] A Macgillvray clansman, feeling sorry for him, opened his legs and let him out into the arms of his nurse. Ever thereafter, the boy was known as Iain Gorm (Blue John) from the permanent bruising which resulted.

Many further folktales come from Donald Morrison, a *seanachaidh* or tradition-bearer of the Ross of Mull, who recorded valuable material in old age in the 1970s which connects with the MacLaine galley-castle of Moy at Loch Buie, Isle of Mull (Plate 36). According to Donald, the traditional tales says that lands of Lochbuie had been held in ancient times by MacFadyens who granted the MacLaines a cowhide's worth of land. They cut the hide into bootlace lengths and claimed enough space to build a stronghold. They then drove the MacFadyens out.

Donald's ancestor was the steersman of a sea-going leather-and-wicker *curragh*,[13] which brought 13 soldiers of the Earl of Antrim to restore a MacLaine, Murchadh Geàrr (Short Murdo) who had been dispossessed by the Duarts. Murchadh's father had been imprisoned on Cairn na Burgh Mòr in the Treshnish Isles with the ugliest woman in Argyll to look after him. Inevitably, she became pregnant and was sent to Torloisk, on Mull, to give birth. The Chief of Duart gave instructions to the current doctor of the Beaton medical kindred, that if the child was a son, he was to be strangled. Doctor Beaton, however, let the baby Murchadh Geàrr live and the Duarts got no hold over Lochbuie. As a legitimated adult, Murchadh Geàrr and his warriors went into action and regained possession of Moy Castle through some cunning stratagems, involving a herd of cattle, which add colour to the tale.

I gather that, in reality, the two kindreds of the clan descended from two brothers given land by the Lord of the Isles. Nevertheless, relations between the Duart MacLeans and the MacLaines of Loch Buie who occupied Moy Castle were often strained, but not quite as strained as told in the story of Eòghann a' Chinn Bhig (Hugh of the Small Head). The son of Iain Òg, 5th of Lochbuie, a distinguished soldier, Eòghann was land-hungry and pestered his father for more land. The whole atmosphere became increasingly acrimonious and developed into a feud that would be resolved in 1538 by force of arms. Eòghann died in battle when one of his father's clansmen, standing on a rock, sliced his head off as he joined the thick of the battle. His horse bolted with the headless body still firmly in the saddle, and eventually came to a halt at the Lussa Falls, nearly five miles from the battle-site. Here the body fell and was temporarily buried before being carried to its final resting-place on Iona. From that day forward, whenever a member of the chief's family is about to die, the sound of Eòghann's horse is said to be heard at Lochbuie. In my own lifetime, a local doctor is said to have heard the sound of hoof-beats while ministering to a dying member of the Lochbuie family.

The beaches of Mull have resounded for centuries to the crunch of birlinns coming to shore, and Donald recounts a fine story of an engagement between the MacPhies of Colonsay, who came cattle-reiving to the Ross of Mull.[14] It was the result of a vendetta arising from the murder of a Mull MacGillvray by a mysterious Colonsay man. The man appeared in Mull and enquired where MacGillvray of Glen Caineal was. When told he was hunting in Gleann Mòr, the man asked 'How will I recognise him?', and received the reply that he would be hunting with a hound which had a white ear. The man murdered MacGillvray and left his corpse in the Glen but, on his return to Colonsay, he stopped at Pennyghael and set fire to the house of MacGillvray's brother. On his way to the sea, he met a man who was afoot early and, pointing to the burning house, told him to tell the owner that there was a dead dog in Glenmore which he should bury. The murder enraged Maclean of Duart who sent a message to Colonsay asking that the man be returned so that justice might be done. It is uncertain what happened next. The MacPhies either dumped the body of the messenger on shore in the Ross of Mull with a willow withy through his two eyes, or possibly executed the Colonsay man in this manner and dumped his body without trial on the shores of the Ross.

Whatever happened, the tale recounts that, as a result of this insult, a company of people called 'The Rugged Banner of the Ross of Mull and the Black Men of Brolas' (*Garbh Bhratach an Rois agus Fir Dhubha Bhròlais*) allied themselves to a party of the Macleans of Torloisk who, on receiving news of the incursion, arrived on horseback.[15] Under the able tactical skill of an *eolachan* (a skilled guide who knew the lie of the land) whom Donald Morrison identified as Lachainn Odhar,[16] the Macleans received their orders. He briefed them that there was an ebbing tide and that the Colonsay birlinns would be beached. The shore would be the killing-ground. Under his direction, the Macleans made a tactical withdrawal to the hills, pursued by the *Colbhasaich* (Men of Colonsay). The *eolachan* chose dead ground where a stop-group of Macleans was placed in an ambush, concealed in the heather between the invaders and their galleys. The ambush was to be sprung when the group saw the *eolachan*'s bald head leading the Macleans attacking downhill. On the command of the *eolachan*, the stop-group ambushed the MacPhies. They broke through the ambush, only to find their boats high and dry. A considerable slaughter of the MacPhies took place at what came to be known as Blàr Port Bheathain (NGR NM 405 189) at which nine-times-nine bailerfuls of MacPhie fingers and toes were gathered after the battle: a folklore motif reminiscent of the Battle of Bloody Bay.

On this folklore voyage, we could sail on to the sea-castles of Dunstaffnage (Plate 7) and Dunnollie, but it may be appropriate to conclude this account by drawing attention to the existence of fresh-water galley-castles by citing just one example. When Bruce defeated the MacDougalls at the Battle of the Pass of Brander in 1308 and established his rule in Argyll, local Lorn folklore says that John of Lorn (Iain Bacach or John the Lame) who was recovering from an illness, observed his dispositions from a galley on Loch Awe. When the battle went the wrong way, Iain Bacach fled in his galley to Innischonnel on Loch Awe and eventually died in Kent on a pilgrimage to Canterbury.[17] John Barbour tells it well in his great poem of 1375. The cairns with which the dead were covered lie on the south side of the Pass and are commemorated to this day in local folk memory.

This short account only covers the Sound of Mull and Loch Awe. There must be many other tales connected with the galley-castles of the Western Highlands and Islands, which would merit some research, collection and recording. It is, however, pleasing that our *dualchas* (our hereditary sense of history and culture) and our *dùthchas* (our strong hereditary sense of place and our link to the land) are still alive in Mull and Lorn and well preserved in these myths and stories which link us firmly, if fabulously, to the galley-castles of our past.

Notes

1. https://en.wikipedia.org/wiki/Calum_Maclean.
2. *Gaelic Songs of Mary MacLeod*, https://archive.org/stream/gaelicsongsofmar00macl/ gaelicsongsofmar00macl_djvu.txt.
3. http://canmore.org.uk/site/22320/san-juan-de-sicilia-tobermory-bay-sound-of-mull.
4. http://www.mull-historical-society.co.uk/churches/churches-2/pennygown/.
5. The late Angus Henderson, blacksmith, Tobermory.
6. http://www.tobaranndualchais.co.uk/en/play/85398;jsessionid=9F639994C2EAE3C068 4FAA58E66252FC.
7. This place-name is quoted in n.6 and may be a local Islay(?) equivalent for a noost or nòs-luinge; Poll Nusaig (Poll (pool) + nòs (anchorage) + -aig (diminutive). It could, however, be a corruption of Poll Naoimhaig (Coble Anchorage).
8. http://www.gaelic-rings.com/islay/index.php?top=1mid=4base=2ring=Islay.
9. http://www.tobaranndualchais.co.uk/en/play/7826;jsessionid=165919B6CA69EF2C2B9 27262E657E7BF.
10. Position: 56 27.0 N 005 36.9 W.
11. http://www.clanlivingstone.com/Lady_Rock.htm.
12. Told by Eòghan MacLachlainn, Tobermory, who heard it from the late Ronald Maclean (Raonull Tearlach am 'Fancy'), Tobermory and Edinburgh, a senior member of Clan Maclean.
13. https://en.wikipedia.org/wiki/Currach#Sea-going_currachs.2C_c.17th_century.

14. Eric R Cregeen, 2013, *Recollections of an Argyllshire Drover and other West Highland Chronicles*, Margaret Bennett (ed.), (Crieff, Perthshire), p.174.

15. Cregeen, *Recollections of an Argyllshire Drover*, p.173. Donald Morrison's Gaelic account of the tale, as recorded, is ambiguous at this point. He says: '*Thruis garbh-bhratach a'Rois 's Fir Dhubha Bhròlais 's Cloinn Illeathain Thorrloisgte*. This could be interpreted as 'The Fierce Banner of the Ross gathered both the Black Men of Brolas and the Macleans of Torloisk'. In other words a form of fiery cross or gathering banner was employed.

16. Donald Morrison (Cregeen, *Recollections of an Argyllshire Drover*) identifies the *eolachan* as Lachlan Odhar. There was a Maclean of that name, Lachlan of Ardchraoshinish, nicknamed Odhar (sallow) who was of the Ross and a noted warrior. He fought at the battle of Glenlivet in 1594.

17. John Barbour, *The Brus*, bk. 10 v.95.
    'To Jhone off Lorne it suld displese
    I trow, quhen he his men mycht se
    Oute off his schippis fra the se
    Be slayne and chassyt in the hill'.

16

A Survey of Norse Castles in Orkney

Sarah Jane Gibbon

ORKNEY IS perhaps best known, in the context of castles, for Cubbie Roo's castle (Figure 16.1, 1), thought to be one of the earliest stone-built keeps in Scotland.[1] However, its relationship to other fortified buildings in the earldom, and the role of these buildings in 12th-century Orcadian society, is less well understood. Why was a stone keep built in Orkney in the mid 12th century? From where did the inspiration come? Was it exceptional or did it form part of a wider pattern of 'castle' architecture? To address these questions, Cubbie Roo's castle will be discussed in the context of 12th-century Orkney society and compared with other similar buildings, with particular emphasis on their placement. This study aims to evaluate the evidence in the context of Northern European maritime power and the recent revision of ideas of kingship and feudalism in the wider Scandinavian world.[2]

The Orkney and Caithness earldoms

For most of the saga period (9th–13th centuries) Orkney, Shetland and Caithness, although distinctive cultural and geographical areas, formed the nucleus of the earldoms of Orkney and Caithness. They were ruled by a dynasty of practically-independent earls, whose world was characterised by long-range economic and familial connections.[3] The distinctiveness of Orkney and Caithness as a political unit lies in its 'duality':[4] it was both divided and connected by water, and subject to two overlords; it was two separate entities yet united. The Pentland Firth was not a state border as it was to become after the Treaty of Perth in 1266,[5] but a vital artery connecting these northern maritime earldoms.

According to *Orkneyinga Saga* (*c*.1200) the influence of this polity extended, in the late 10th and early 11th centuries, to include tributary jurisdiction over parts of the Irish Sea region, including the Hebrides and Man. After the 11th century this direct and tributary control decreased, but this did not diminish the earls' position and influence, and there is strong evidence for a wealthy and flourishing society in the North in the 12th century. By the end of the 12th century Shetland had been taken under direct Norwegian control. By the end of the 14th century Caithness was no longer ruled jointly with Orkney, so the maritime connections which had once defined the Norse earldoms had fundamentally changed.[6] Although little mention

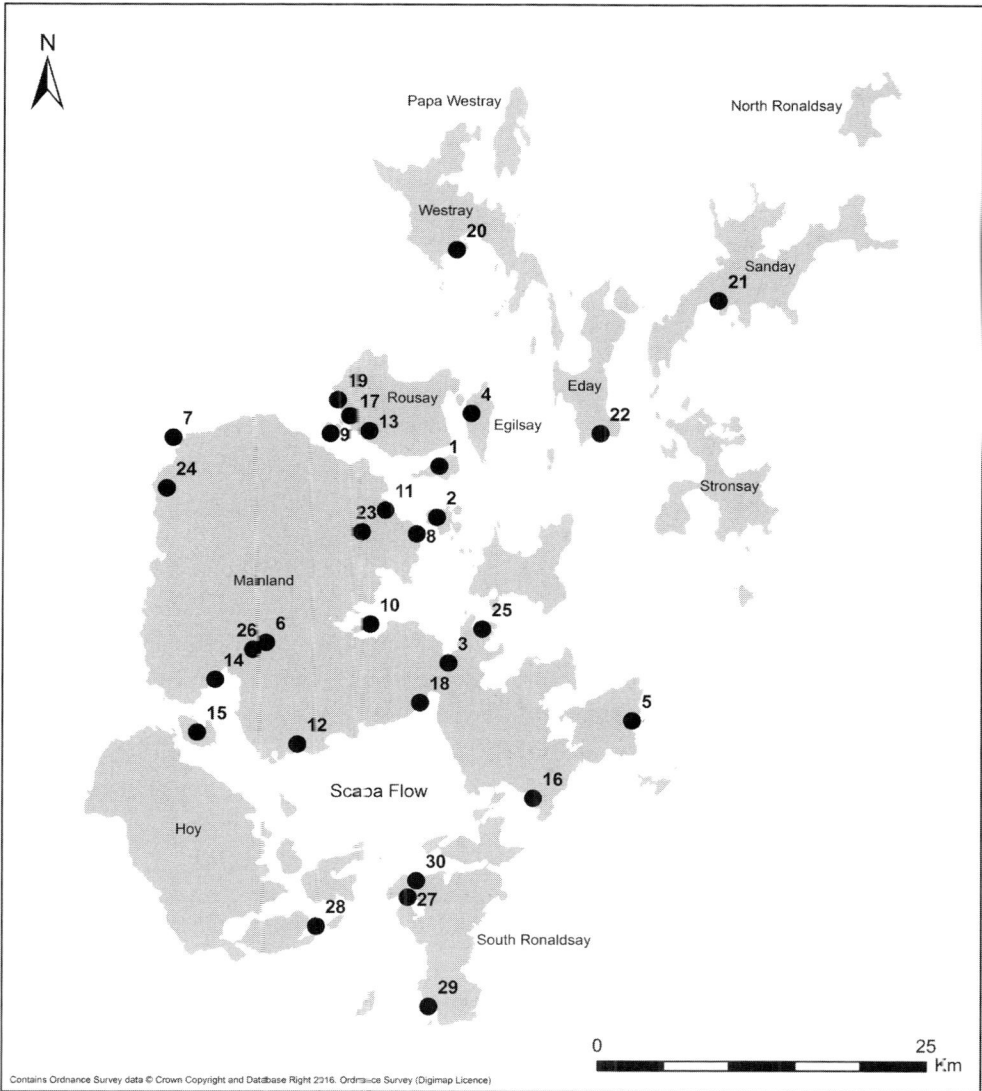

Figure 16.1. *Map of Orkney showing places mentioned in the text.*

1. Cubbie Roo's Castle, Wyre. 2. Gairsay. 3. Kirkwall. 4. St Magnus Church, Egilsay. 5. St Mary's Church, Deerness. 6. Crosskirk, Stenness. 7. St Peter's Church, Brough of Birsay. 8. Tammaskirk, Rendall. 9. Eynhallow Church. 10. Damsay. 11. Tingwall. 12. Bu and Round Kirk. Orphir. 13. Westness. 14. Cairston, Stromness. 15. Graemsay. 16. Castlehowe, Holm. 17. The Wirk. 18. Knarston. 19. Scabra Head. 20. Tuquoy & Crosskirk. 21. Backaskaill. 22. Castle of Stackel Brae. 23. Ellibister, Rendall. 24. Castle, Birsay. 25. Work, St Ola. 26. Gernaness, Stenness. 27. Widewall Bay. 28. South Walls. 29. Burwick. 30. Hoxa.

(James Moore, University of the Highlands and Islands Archaeology Institute)

will be made here of Shetland and Caithness, it is important to appreciate that Orkney was one part of a far-reaching political unit centred in the north of Scotland and controlling the seaways between Norway and the Irish Sea.

In Western Europe the 10th to 13th centuries are typically seen as a time of growth, and Orkney is no exception.[7] *Orkneyinga Saga* portrays a world where heroic earls compete for power in a wider society of prosperous free men. The rich archaeological and environmental evidence confirms this. Place-names indicate a diversity of settlements where farming is developing and habitation expanding, while architectural remains suggest a society with a Scandinavian background and a desire to express power through monumental building emulating the latest in European design, but often incorporating older remains.[8]

The affluence of this society has traditionally been attributed to the geographical position of the earldoms between the Irish Sea, the North Sea and the Atlantic Ocean. But a society cannot prosper on geography alone, and Barrett has argued that the military nature of the economy (which saw Orcadians active as pirates and/or mercenaries in England, Ireland, Norway, Scotland and Wales) up to around the end of the 12th century is fundamental.[9] The earldoms also controlled fertile farmland and fishing-grounds, and it was the combination of piracy and warfare with effective subsistence farming and fishing which created Orkney's thriving society. All this relied on nautical proficiency. This is perhaps most compellingly evident in *Orkneyinga Saga*'s portrayal of Sweyn Asleifsson, and would not be out of place in other contemporary seafaring regions of Britain, such as Moray, Argyll, the Isle of Man and Galloway.[10]

According to *Orkneyinga Saga*, Sweyn was the son of an Orkney chieftain. His estates included Gairsay in Orkney (2) and Duncansby in Caithness. He lived at various times in Caithness, Orkney, the Hebrides and the Isle of Man. He was outlawed, made an earl's steward in Caithness, present at the courts of two kings of Scotland, besieged in his fortress at Lambaborg, entangled in dynastic earldom rivalries and died raiding in Dublin. He divided his time between his farm (being home for springtime and harvest) and raiding in the Irish Sea. His story tells of ties of patronage and clientship, of protection and duty, of how to maintain a retinue by means of farming, fishing and plundering; in short he epitomises the power, prosperity and instability of 12th-century Orkney society.

This society had developed from the late 8th century, reaching its apogee in the 12th century, but came to an end in the 13th century as a result of changes exacerbated by increasingly successful military attention from Scotland and Norway, combined with the loss of the leading men of Orkney in a shipwreck.[11] The height of architectural achievement was also reached in the 12th century, when the restructuring of the earldoms' administrations provided the impetus for the wealthy in society to express power through monumental buildings. Territorially they were often built on or near settlements dating back at least to the Iron Age, and strategically often situated on the coast overlooking waterways and landing-places. This is most clearly expressed in St Magnus Cathedral (3), but is also seen in churches, feasting-halls and 'castles' where towers are a notable feature.[12] The incorporation of earlier buildings can be seen within the context of increased emphasis on defined territories brought about by parochial reform. This is part of a wider European trend where lordships were legitimised by connecting medieval high-status places with buildings and places from the past.[13]

Churches with towers

Of particular note are six churches built in Orkney in the 12th century: St Magnus, Egilsay (4), with a single round tower; St Mary's, Deerness (5), with twin round towers; Crosskirk, Stenness (6), with a single semi-circular tower; St Peter's, Brough of Birsay (7), with a single, probably-never-completed, square tower; Tammaskirk, in Rendall (8), and Eynhallow Church (9), both with single square towers. While square towers are more common throughout Western Europe, the architectural inspiration for the more unusual round-towered churches may have come from Southern Scandinavia or East Anglia.[14] Only one church tower has been suggested as primarily defensive, and that is Tammaskirk.[15] In all instances the towers can be seen as landmarks. All six churches are built either close to the coast or on elevated ground overlooking important sea-routes.

Castles

There are several square or rectangular towers variously described as keep, castle, garderobe-chute or private apartments. These towers were built on large and prosperous estates inhabited by powerful families in 12th-century Orkney, and are all strategically placed with regard to maritime routes and landing-places. Several of them were studied and published by the Orkney antiquarian Joseph Storer Clouston, who found them to be early in date, defensive in nature and similar in construction. He divided the six he had classified as 'castles' into two groups: those of native Norse origin and those of imported design. He saw the 'native castles' drawing influence from a combination of indigenous broch architecture and Norwegian timber fortifications, while the 'imported' castles resulted from European travel by the elite. His analysis was based on architectural attributes and comparison with other areas, but recent archaeological discoveries and theoretical revisions of kingship and power in both Scandinavia and Scotland mean that Clouston's work needs reconsideration.[16] As he coined the term 'Norse Castle', his work will form the basis of this survey, augmented by recent research by the present author and others.

The evidence for medieval castles in Orkney is incomplete, and there is a range of types of source of variable quality.[17] Arguably the most accessible and persuasive source is *Orkneyinga Saga*, but without independent additional evidence this source is limited. In it we find mention of defensive sites variously termed *kastali*, *vigi*, and *borg*.[18] Within it the Broch of Mousa in Shetland (*Morseyjarborg*)[19] is said to have been used as a defensive site not long after Kolbein Hruga had built his stone keep on Wyre, demonstrating the re-use of Iron Age structures.[20] Cubbie Roo's Castle and the Broch of Mousa are at either end of a spectrum of fortifications incorporating

12th-century and prehistoric architecture. This has implications for the identification of medieval fortifications, and Clouston's 'indigenous' and 'imported' classifications need to be reviewed.

In total, there are 29 references to *kastali* in *Orkneyinga Saga*, relating to five castles: three in Orkney, one in Caithness and one in Galicia.[21] The three Orkney *kastali* are three of the six sites designated by Clouston and discussed below. Although one must be cautious when using saga literature as historical evidence, it is reasonable to accept the existence of the castles, as there is no obvious reason to have invented them. Equally, the absence of any mention of a building does not mean it did not exist, merely that it was not relevant to the tales being told.

Damsay

The first Orkney castle reference in *Orkneyinga Saga*, from *c*.1135, concerns a *kastali* on the island of Damsay (10) (Canmore ID 2076), the outermost of two holms at the entrance to the Bay of Firth, with commanding views over the adjacent land and inner north isles. The island is centrally located, allowing the castle to 'guard' the settlements on the fertile coastal strip around the sheltered Bay of Firth, while also monitoring passing ships. The Bay of Firth, between Kirkwall and the assembly-site at Tingwall (11), and south-west of a passage through the islands, is in a central location. The island is hidden by headlands from the route it surveys, and is also conveniently positioned to protect a landing-place suitable for accessing east and west Mainland, and known to have been used to access the earldom estate in Orphir.

The castle had a keeper called Blann Thorsteinsson at the time of the murder of Sweyn Breastrope by Sweyn Asleifsson at the earl's residence in Orphir (12). Sweyn reached the castle by boat from the Bay of Firth, and stayed there until Blann took him by boat to the bishop in Egilsay the next morning. Later in the saga, *c*.1154, Damsay is described as having a large hall (*í skála miklum*) where Earl Erlend (Haraldsson) and his men spend their days drinking, but sleep on board ship for security.[22] This need not mean that there was no castle on the island, as the reference to sleeping aboard appears connected to a plan of immediate escape by sea should the party be ambushed. Later the same year Earl Rognvald spends Yule at Damsay, indicating that this estate was favoured by the earls. Perhaps it was earldom property or belonged to a close kinsman. Local legend tells of a Norse king's castle on Damsay which no house should look out on for fear of being cursed.[23] Several walkover surveys have not identified any conclusive 'castle' features, although what looked like a robbed-out foundation on the highest point of the island was recorded in 1998 as a possible watchtower. This is a slightly raised area measuring 8m x 8m (similar to Cubbie Roo's castle, below) with an outer bank some 25cm high and approximately 1m wide. Magnetometer survey revealed no activity, which makes this less likely as the site of a tower. However, the strategic location and the lack of any other explanation for the feature is hard to ignore.[24]

Clouston's proposed site for the castle was an eroding mound on the north coast. In 1998 this was assessed as a denuded broch, with much of its robbed stone built into a nearby house. Also built into the house were large blocks of red sandstone, not local to the island and reminiscent of those found in St Magnus Cathedral and some medieval parish churches. Clouston made sketches, but the walling he drew could not be located on the ground. This northern shore is where post-medieval settlement was focused, with a two-story house/inn, and the ruins of a 12th-century, lime-mortared, chapel dedicated to St Mary, which is actively eroding into the sea (Canmore ID 2072). The chapel is located on a bank between the shore and a small loch and was once a place of pilgrimage, particularly for women. It has also been interpreted as a nunnery.[25]

On the west of Damsay, a bay affording a safe landing-place was identified in 2009 by the Rising Tides Project. It is close to the landing-place used today and is *c*.240m from the highest point and 190m from the north-shore site.[26] In several places there is evidence of ridge-and-furrow cultivation, including to the north of the east-coast landing-point (Canmore ID 307335). This strategically-situated island, therefore, has evidence for a chapel, drinking-hall, keep and probable farmstead (although we do not know whether some of these elements were combined in a single building). The size and topography of the island is such that it makes little difference, in terms of maritime impact, whether the castle was located on the highest point or on the north shore. It is worth noting, however, that neither possible castle-site is adjacent to the two most likely landing-places on the island.

Cubbie Roo's Castle, Wyre

The second castle mentioned in *Orkneyinga Saga* is found on the island of Wyre.

> Í þann tíma bjó sá maðr í Vigr í Orkneyjum, er Kolbeinn hrúga hét ok var it mesta afarmenni. Hann lét þar gera steinkastala góðan; var þat oruggt vígi. (At that time there lived in Wyre in the Orkneys [a Norwegian] called Kolbein Hruga, and he was the most outstanding of men. He had a fine stone castle built there; it was a safe stronghold).[27]

The passage continues with Kolbein's family connections, telling of his marriage to Herborg, great-grand-daughter of Earl Paul, and naming their five children. Little is known of Kolbein except that he may have been from Sunnfjord and a *lendirman* of Eystein II Haraldsson, as he is listed as a member of the party who accompanied Eystein from Scotland to Trondheim in 1142 to claim his share of the Norwegian crown.[28] Kolbein was clearly a wealthy and powerful man connected to the ruling elites in Orkney and Norway.

A second mention of Kolbein's castle is in *Hakonar's Saga* when in *c*.1231 Earl John's murderers flee to the castle.

> Þeir fóru í Vigr; ok settusk í kastalann, er Kolbeinn hrúga hafði göra látið. Þeir drógu at sér nóg föng ok fjölda nauta, ok varð-veittu í út-kastalanum. En er þetta spurðn vinir jarls í Orkneyjar, sömnuðu þeir miklu liði, ok fórn út í Vigr, ok settusk um kastalann. En þar var óhægt atsókn við at koma.[29] (They went into Wyre, and sat in the castle

which kolbein the burly had let be built. They gathered to them stores enough and a herd of neat, and kept them in the outworks of the castle. But when the friends of the earl in the Orkneys heard that they gathered a great force, and went out into Wyre, and beleaguered the castle. But it was a very unhandy place to attack).[30]

By the 19th century Kolbein Hruga's name had become identified with an infamous bridge-building, rock-throwing giant widely known in Orcadian folklore as Cubbie Roo. This giant has several other landscape features attributed to him across the archipelago, including 'Cubbie Roo's Burden' (Canmore ID 2638), a chambered cairn in south-east Rousay.

The ruinous structure on Wyre has been identified with a building first recorded in the 16th century as the house of a 'tall giant'.[31] In 1688 a more reliable source records the 'Castell of Cubbirow' as a square defensive tower with lime-mortar construction, surrounded by an outer ditch. Wallace mentions a first-floor entrance, a narrow slit window, and 'idle fables' concerning Cubbirow, not fit to be repeated.[32] The structure was surveyed by Marwick in 1927 and preliminarily excavated by Clouston in 1931 before being taken into state care later that year. From 1933 more detailed investigations were undertaken by the Ministry of Works. Ritchie and Ritchie revised the Royal Commission's plan in 1978 and more recently Thacker has analysed lime mortar from the castle.[33]

The tower, described as the 'earliest datable stone castle in Scotland',[34] is located on the small island of Wyre (roughly 2km²), one of the inner north isles of Orkney. The tower, unlike most of the settlement on the island, is located some distance from the shore, c.350m from the nearest landing-place.[35] It is built on top of a considerable rise with commanding views of the surrounding seaways and particularly Wyre Sound, the narrow channel between Egilsay, Wyre, the east side of Rousay and the Mainland. As well as the tower there are outbuildings and outer defences, which enclose an oval area of c.23m x 29m. These comprise a substantial double-ditch and double-bank defence with an internal platform of 14.8m x 16.6m, on which stand the tower and the remains of several phases of outbuildings, which are generally agreed to post-date the tower.[36]

The tower is almost square (three walls are 7.8m long and one 7.9m), expertly built with large cut stones pointed with lime-mortar, and evidence of lime-plaster on the exterior. The walls are c.1.7m thick at the base and 1.66m thick at their maximum surviving height of c.2m. The tower stands to first-floor height with a narrow scarcement visible on the inner face of the north wall. The ground-floor room has no doorway and must have been accessed through a first-floor door. There are two narrow windows, one in the south and one in the west wall, both 0.22m wide on the outside and 0.5m inside with stepped sills and rebated for the insertion of a wooden frame. The floor has a rock-cut tank, roughly rectangular and just off-centre, the only internal feature. The mortar and the quality and style of the stonework is different from the outer defensive walling, but similar to that of the nearby chapel and The Wirk in Rousay (below).[37]

From architectural comparison with similar towers in Scotland, Norway and Europe no firm conclusion was reached by RCAHMS, but a mid-12th-century date was considered 'unsafe'.[38] Others, however, including Clouston in 1931, assign a 12th-century date to the tower.[39] The two saga accounts were written only shortly after the events described and are, therefore, considered reliable. The stonework, lime-mortar and lime-plaster are typical of 12th-century construction in Orkney. The high-quality construction is similar to that of the cathedral in Kirkwall (founded in 1137) and more carefully executed than other known 12th-century structures such as the Round Kirk in Orphir. The outbuildings appear to have been constructed over a considerable time as the site changed from a high-status defensive retreat to a humbler, less-well-defended enclosure with permanent domestic habitation. Evidence for this includes thinner walls, the use of clay rather than lime-mortar, and the removal of the southern ramparts to allow the construction of extra non-defended buildings.

There are several issues to resolve. The relationship between ramparts and tower has not been established; some of the outbuildings' stratigraphy is rather confused; the lack of finds is puzzling; and no physical evidence has been found for an attack on the structure. This may indicate that the construction of the tower was a precautionary defensive measure, or an expression of permanence and authority by the recently arrived Kolbein, asserting his place in a landscape already dominated by important chieftains. But where did the inspiration come from? As Clouston realised, the form of this small stone-built, lime-pointed and -plastered keep suggests influence from northern France or Norman England. There are no contemporary parallels in Norway or mainland Scotland.[40]

Like Damsay, this castle does not stand in isolation but is one of three buildings forming the nucleus of an estate. To the east is a 12th-century chapel dedicated to St Mary, and to the north-west the present-day farm 'Bu of Wyre' stands on an impressive settlement-mound. The 'Bu of' name-form is a later Scots corruption of ON *Bú*, which in medieval Orkney denoted a high-status estate managed as a single unit. There are 22 instances of this name-form in Orkney, and one particularly interesting instance of the form *Buen*.[41] This type of estate can be characterised by central buildings located some distance from the shore, but within 500m of a good landing-place; being central to fertile land; often including a chapel and burial-ground and with evidence of small houses for dependant workers on the estate's periphery.[42] Kolbein's homestead was probably at or near The Bu and not in the tower. This estate was not earldom or bishopric land, but the private (odal) estate of a wealthy and powerful chieftain with Norwegian royal affiliation.

Cubbie Roo's castle is the central element of an estate focused on the north-west side of Wyre (its medieval extent is unknown, but it may well have extended beyond the confines of the island). It commands strategic views of the seaways and, according to saga stories, borders on the south the estates of Sweyn Asleifsson (centred on Gairsay), on the north-east the bishop of Orkney in Egilsay, and on the north-west Sigurd of Westness in Rousay and the monastery of Eynhallow. Considering these neighbours, it is conceivable that the newly-arrived Kolbein decided to mark his presence and his status with an up-to-date keep. There would be a genuine need to keep careful watch over Eynhallow Sound, one of the main sea-routes from Caithness to the inner north isles and onwards to Shetland. *Orkneyinga Saga* includes several accounts where this route is used in stealth, in most instances by Sweyn Asleifsson.[43]

Fortunately this area features more often in the saga than some other parts of Orkney. We learn that ships gathered at Westness (13) on Rousay and were launched from Gairsay, both neighbouring islands to Wyre. In addition the probable assembly-site at Tingwall on the Mainland, not far from Wyre, would no doubt have had a convenient anchorage/landing-point for ships.[44] There is no mention of ships in relation to Wyre in *Orkneyinga Saga* and, unlike the other castles, there is no mention of earls residing there. No doubt there was a suitable landing-place and noust near the castle/farmstead, but no evidence has so far been identified.

This is one of several questions relating to Cubbie Roo's castle. We do not fully understand the relationship between the tower and the outer defences, or have adequate insight into the lack of finds. Clouston and Ritchie considered the outer defences to be of motte design, and yet when viewed in plan and section they convincingly resemble Iron Age defences. This, along with the rock-cut tank in its base, suggest that the tower may have been built on the site of, and adapted the outer defences of, a broch. There is no known broch on Wyre (which is unusual), and the castle's location on fertile land with extensive visibility is a place where a hypothetical broch might have been situated. Without further investigation this can only be conjecture, but it raises some important questions with regard to the 'native' versus 'imported' castle-design model.

The Old Norse words used to describe Kolbein's building are *stein kastala* and *vigi* and it has been inferred that the use of the imported word *kastala* indicates that the structure built by Kolbein was a newly-built tower of imported design as opposed to an existing defensible structure, denoted by *virki, vigi* or *borg*.[45] However, if the keep at Cubbie Roo's castle is built on a former broch then this textual distinction is not convincing. Perhaps the use of both terms could be interpreted as a tower of imported design (*kastala*) built on and making use of a pre-existing fortified site (*vigi*). But it is perhaps more likely to be a literary construct, removing repetition from the saga text. Additional textual analysis from a variety of sources supports a more fluid and complex etymology and use. These terms appear reasonably interchangeable with a range of meanings, and while there is a general association between stone-built architecture and *kastali*, and timber-and-turf structures and *virki/borg*, in an Orkney context this requires further consideration, bearing in mind the ready availability of stone as a building material.[46]

Whatever the precise definitions of words describing fortifications, the possibility that this Anglo-Norman inspired tower's unusual characteristics (outer defences and tank) may be explained through re-use of a broch site is relevant to discussions of castles in the Northern Earldoms, the Western Isles and Europe more widely.[47] This castle stands out in Orkney not only because of its architecture (ramparts particularly), but also its owner's association with Norwegian royal authority, and its key position at the eastern end of Eynhallow Sound – the western entrance to the northern part of Orkney (including Tingwall, the Bay of Firth and Kirkwall).

Cairston, Stromness

The third *kastali* referred to in *Orkneyinga Saga* is Cairston (14).[48] It features in the story of Earl Harald Maddadsson on board ship off Cairston in 1152, who on seeing a warship approach goes ashore into a castle for safety. He and his adversaries battle all day, with many casualties on both sides, and are about to surrender when a settlement takes place.

> Þeir fundu Harald jarl fyrir KjarreksstǫÐum, ok l'a hann 'a skipum. Þat var Míkálsmessumorgin, at þeir Haraldr jarl sá, at langskip fóru at þeim, ok grunuðu, at ófriðr myndi vera. Þeir hljépu af skipunum ok í kastalann, er þar var þá.[49] (They found Earl Harald on board ship off Cairston. It was Michaelmas morning, when Earl Harald and his men saw a warship approaching them, and they feared that it must be a hostile force. They leapt ashore and into the castle that was then there).[50]

Clouston, searching for this castle, thought that 'a certain collection of ruinous walls at the farm of Bu of Cairston … for centuries viewed by uncomprehending eyes (my own among them), might actually be the very '*kastali*' of Cairston mentioned in the *Orkneyinga Saga*'.[51] His survey and partial excavation revealed two building-phases: a 16th-century manor house and an earlier defensive site which he ascribed to the 12th century. There were no datable finds, and the architectural evidence, although not conflicting with a 12th-century date, did not confirm it. There is nothing visible now that suggests a 12th-century castle, but this does not mean there was not one there.

The castle at Cairston, as with Wyre, is associated with a Bu farm name. The Bu is strategically placed between the anchorage of Hamnavoe and the southern access to the Loch of Stenness via the Brig of Waithe opening, and thus an appropriate place to locate a watchtower. Unlike Wyre this 27-pennyland estate was earldom *bordland*, visited regularly by the earl and his retinue as part of peripatetic governance.[52] The site's significance is further demonstrated, not only because it was a wealthy medieval farm (on which a mansion house was built in the 16th century) but because this is where the medieval parish church of Stromness was located. Rescue excavations in 2002 revealed some 120 medieval graves, proving the existence of a sizable cemetery to the south of the manor house.[53] There is an eroding Iron Age site (a probable broch) on the coast alongside the cemetery, and the stonework in the later enclosure wall may well have been robbed from it.

So Cairston is another high-status medieval estate incorporating an Iron Age settlement-site, proprietorial chapel (upgraded to a parish church), large farm and high-status place-name indicator. But was there a castle? The castle mentioned in *Orkneyinga Saga* could have been the probable broch and not a new 12th-century construction, although if this were the case, *borg* would have been the more likely term to have been used (as in the case of Mousa). Without further investigation it is unsafe to ascribe a 12th-century date and castle attribution to the building revealed by Clouston, but this does not mean that a defensive building of some kind did not exist there in the 12th century, and from its situation, a lookout-tower would suggest itself; the existence of a defensive building is likely but its precise location and form remain unknown.

Orkneyinga Saga gives details of some sea-routes within the earldoms, two of which pass within sight of Cairston: one is from Rousay to the Dornoch Firth, via the west of Mainland, going east between Hoy and Graemsay (15), east of the Swelchie and on to the Moray Firth. The second gives less detail but appears to follow a similar route through Scapa Flow[54]. Although not passing Cairston directly, ships taking this route would have been easily observed from Cairston and its slightly out-of-the-way position, to the north of this route, would have ensured some degree of security from what appears to have been a recognised sea-route from mainland Scotland to the islands of the North Atlantic. This is another instance of a castle in a strategic protected position on a recognised sea-route.

Castlehowe, Paplay

Clouston identified a further three sites as Norse Castles. Two are at locations mentioned in *Orkneyinga Saga* as estates, and both have place-names indicative of fortification. The third site, on the available evidence, is unlikely to be a castle.

Castlehowe ('castle mound') at Paplay, in Holm (16), was excavated by Clayton between 1929 and 1931 but not published. It comprises two distinct parts, the upper (built up at the corners by Clayton) is a lime-mortared rectangular structure *c.*8m by 9.8m with walls 2m thick. Clouston considered the stonework to be inferior to that found at Cubbie Roo's Castle and The Wirk (17), noted motte construction on the site, and assigned this building a mid-12th-century date. Underneath the rectangular building is a prehistoric structure, interpreted by RCAHMS as sepulchral, but which has certain similarities with Minehowe, an Iron Age underground structure in the neighbouring parish of St Andrews. It is possible that the later structure incorporated the earlier as a cellar. The site is built on an artificially augmented natural rise, and it is easy to see why Clouston suggested this was a motte. The earthwork has not been dated.

Visibility from the site is excellent, with unrestricted views of the waterways to the south-east of Orkney. This is particularly relevant as *Orkneyinga Saga* states ships were using this eastern sea-route to travel between mainland Scotland and Shetland or Norway. Thorbjorn Clerk is described as sailing 'east into the Firth to Paplay', while other ships mustered at Knarston (18) in Scapa Flow in preparation for conflict, indicating that this was a strategic defensive location and as such an ideal positon for a watchtower.[55] Castlehowe lies on the south-east side of a sheltered bay which would be suitable to beach a boat.

On the north-west side sits the parish church of St Nicholas, which (like Castlehowe) is built on top of a prehistoric site, although in this instance probably a broch. The farm Bu of Skaill (the only Orkney farm-name to combine *Bu* (estate) and *Skali* (hall) elements) lies in the hinterland of this bay, and was once the very large medieval estate (36 pennylands) of Paplay. In *Orkneyinga Saga*, *bú í Papuli* is closely associated with the earls, being the home of Hakon karl Sigurdsson (half-brother of Earl Magnus). It was detached from the earldom by King Magnus Barelegs in 1098 and given as a dowry to Gunnhild on her marriage to Kol Kalisson.[56] The combination of Bu (manor farm), parish church, hall (*skali*), possible keep and saga references indicates a high-status coastal property with strong earldom connections, and although there is little archaeological evidence of a 12th-century settlement here, *bú í Papuli* should be considered alongside the castles described above.

The Wirk, Rousay

In contrast to the freestanding keeps of Wyre, Damsay, Cairston and Castlehowe, the tower at The Wirk in Rousay was never intended to be detached. This site lies less than 40m from the shore in a 2.5km stretch of fertile land with occupation evidence from the Neolithic to the present day. To the south (*c.*900m) lies a Pictish/Viking cemetery at Moaness, a Norse boat-noust (*c.*900m), a late Norse settlement at Westness (*c.*550m), alleged Norse cist burials at the Knowe of Swandro (*c.*530m) and the later ruins of the farm of Skaill (*c.*100m).[57] To the north (*c.*200m) is the house of Brough, the most important house on the island in the 16th century, and yet further north are the remains of Midhowe broch and a Neolithic chambered cairn (*c.*300m). Immediately adjacent to the Wirk is the former parish church of Rousay, dedicated to St Mary, which in its present form dates from the 16th century but is likely to have its origins in the 12th century.[58] Westness (ON *Vestnesi*), according to *Orkneyinga Saga*, was home to Sigurd who was married to Earl Paul's grand-daughter and was one of the leading men in 12th-century Orkney, with a large estate and responsibility for raising arms for the earl in Rousay.[59]

The name Wirk (ON *virki*), is indicative of a fortification of some kind, which is supported by a folk-legend that it was built as a stronghold in which to keep a beautiful woman prisoner.[60] Two such stories of imprisoned damsels feature in *Orkneyinga Saga*, but nevertheless the story of The Wirk being a stronghold is interesting when combined with the place-name and archaeological evidence.

The site was excavated by Clouston and found to comprise a small square tower with a large building appended. The tower is built using similar methods to those at Cubbie Roo's castle, with lime-mortared *c.*2m-thick walls which stand to a height of 2m. The interior space is roughly 8m². Clouston found evidence of a door in the south wall at first-floor height, and in the ground floor a cistern and drain. There were no windows. The adjacent building measured more than 26m x 7m, and in scale is reminiscent of the surviving portions of the 12th-century Bishop's Palace in Kirkwall (see below) begun probably by Bishop William the Old (1102–1168). During excavation a finial carved with human heads was found which, along with a carving of a bishop's coat of arms and the proximity of the site to the parish church, led Clouston to interpret The Wirk as ecclesiastical, as an incomplete 13th-century towered church, and Dietrichson (Norwegian art historian d.1917) to interpret it as a free-standing fortified bell-tower. In 1982 Dunbar suggested The Wirk was a first-floor hall-house with garderobe-tower or strongroom, and most recent scholars agree with this interpretation, including Lowe who surveyed the site in 1984.[61]

The architectural remains, and recently-discovered archive images of the site during investigation, verify that the tower was intended to be an integral part of a larger structure, which contradicts the free-standing bell-tower interpretation.[62] Dunbar's first-floor hall-house suggestion is more plausible than Clouston's unfinished church, although it cannot be completely disregarded, as Clouston was the excavator of the east end of the building. The idea of an undercroft is reinforced by the existence of a stairway and passage in the tower. The presence of a garderobe-chute and drain also suggests that the structure was more than one storey high. If the site were a high-status hall-house then the existence of a defensive tower would not be inconceivable, acting as a status symbol, as well as providing a place of retreat if all other means of escape failed. The thickness of the walls in this tower suggests it was defensive rather than domestic, although the location of the house and lack of outer fortifications does not suggest defence as the main function.

This large building, located close to the shore on the most productive farmland on the island, was part of an estate in a prime location. This is supported by the proximity of two later farms, Skaill and Brough, the late-Norse farmstead of Westness, and the Viking burials at Moaness. The rich Westness graves indicate this was a high-status area in the Viking period, an impression reinforced by the stories of Sigurd in *Orkneyinga Saga*. Sigurd would have required a large hall (*skáli*) to entertain the earl and his retinue and it is not surprising that there is a Skaill farm at Westness. It is possible to interpret The Wirk as a great feasting-hall (a vital and symbolic part of Norse society throughout the North Atlantic)[63] with a tower. There is no indication of date, but because of similarities to Cubbie Roo's castle a 12th-century date is postulated.

At Westness there is evidence for a complex estate, or perhaps multiple estates, with parish church, *skali*, fortified structure, longhouse, boat-noust, cemetery and broch. An unusually rich documentary record for this area indicates a complex tenurial history after the time of Sigurd. Sigurd held an administrative position in the earldom, being responsible for raising a levy in Rousay and providing hospitality for the earl and his retinue.[64] There are five instances in *Orkneyinga Saga* where sea-journeys either begin or end at Westness, including one when a presumed merchant ship is told to report to Westness with its cargo, indicating a trading-post of some kind.[65] As the home of a chieftain, the estate is closely associated with the earls, and the tower at The Wirk is positioned to overlook the western entrance to Eynhallow Sound, a significant routeway, while being hidden from view of those approaching from the west by Scabra Head (19). What we may have here is a medieval chieftain's fortified tower and great hall. The two contenders for chieftain are Sigurd of Westness and the bishop. The existence of a Norse settlement to the south and the proximity of The Wirk to the church, combined with the ecclesiastical architectural fragments, hint at a strong association. Could this be a bishopric hall? The complexity of the later landownership in this area and the sheer quantity of archaeological remains raises interesting questions about the possibility of there being two adjacent contemporary high-status settlements on this fertile coastal strip.

If the Wirk is a towered hall-house located to watch over the local sea-routes then it is not unique. Other strategically-located smaller lime-mortared stone-built halls have been excavated at Tuquoy in Westray (20) and Skaill in Deerness, with several others postulated as a result of eroding remains, including Backaskaill in Sanday (21) and Castle of Stackel Brae in Eday (22). Based on place-name evidence, Ellibster in Rendall (23) (the only site some distance from the shore), Castle in Marwick, Birsay (24) and Work in St Ola (25) have also been identified as possible high-status sites. From the archaeological evidence, a preference for building lime-mortared hall-houses near the shore can be seen across the archipelago in the 12th century. This reflects an essentially Romanesque architectural tradition, which is also seen in several of the remaining medieval churches (Crosskirk, Westray; Round Kirk, Orphir; St Magnus Cathedral).[66] The added value of a watchtower at these high-status estate-centres can be demonstrated in *Orkneyinga Saga*, where time and again internal feuds result in homestead attacks, burnings and kidnaps, usually targeted on the feasting-hall.

Gernaness, Stenness

The last of Clouston's castles is located on the small promontory of Gernaness in the Loch of Stenness (26). Clouston excavated it and believed he had found the remains of a unique castle belonging to his forebear Hakon klό Havardsson. His notes indicate that he uncovered partial remains of a much-disturbed multi-period site of largely prehistoric date. Archive photographs which pre-date Clouston's excavation show how few remains there were.[67] A survey undertaken by the author in 1998 revealed the extent of Clouston's excavation area. Local history records that a mound consisting of black earth was removed from the promontory and spread on the adjacent fields in the late 18th century. In one of the fields four Viking Age rings were subsequently found.[68] Taking all things into consideration it is unlikely that this was a medieval castle. The archaeological remains suggest a prehistoric site and the association with Hakon klό is largely unsubstantiated. There is a muddled tradition of a tall building in the parish of Stenness which Clouston located at this site, but there is more convincing evidence for this building (probably of later date) in another location. This site lacks high-status place-name indicators, or association with a church, and as such the suggestion of a high-status settlement with a Norse castle cannot be supported.

Kirkwall

In addition to the sites referred to above there are two keeps in Kirkwall, only *c.*100m apart, so their wider context is the same. Kirkwall in the early 12th century was a market-town with few houses, yet it was already an ecclesiastical and earldom centre with a church dedicated to St Olaf, and was the preferred location for regular assemblies.[69] Over the course of the 12th century the medieval town developed around the Cathedral of St Magnus and its precinct (founded 1137, in use by *c.*1155) and the merchant quarter extended southward. No towns developed in other Norse colonies, and Kirkwall is comparable to (though smaller than) the medieval towns of Bergen and Trondheim in Norway.[70]

Located at the narrowest point on Mainland, Kirkwall originally had two distinct foci. The mercantile focus was in the north (bounded on the north by Kirkwall Bay, described in *Orkneyinga Saga* as a landing-beach and where the mustering-point for the beacon warning-system may have been) and the ecclesiastical precinct to the south.[71] Both areas faced westward along the shore of a shallow inner bay, much reduced today and named the Peedie Sea. Integral to the town's suitability was its access by sea from north and south and by land from east and west. The southern sea access to Kirkwall was Scapa beach, the northernmost extent of Scapa Flow, some 2km to the south. The earldom estate of Knarston (*knarrarstaðir*) lay on the west side of Scapa Bay and along with Scapa is the place most frequently associated with ships in *Orkneyinga Saga*.[72] For example, the landing-place and the mustering-place for warships for the earldom estate in Orphir, probably in Scapa Bay, was observable from Knarston, demonstrating the strategic importance of this area.[73]

Bishop's Palace

Perhaps the finest and best-preserved 12th-century hall-house in the earldoms was built in the cathedral precinct of Kirkwall. The Bishop's Palace, as it is now known, became the primary residence of the bishops of Orkney after the establishment of St Magnus Cathedral resulted in the administrative centre of the earldom moving from Birsay to Kirkwall.[74] The palace was originally a hall-house, a series of cellars with the major apartment above. Only the lowest portion of the original building survives – a hall *c*.25m by 6m internally with walls 1m thick. The primary masonry corresponds to the earliest Romanesque masonry in St Magnus Cathedral, *c*.1137–1150, while most of the upper parts are a 16th-century rebuild associated with the addition of a round tower by Bishop Reid.[75] The Manse Tower, original to the hall-house and removed in antiquity, was square. Standing to the left of Bishop Reid's 16th-century Moosey Tooer, it may have housed the bishop's private apartments.[76]

Much has changed in this part of Kirkwall, and it is possible that when Earl Patrick built the New Wark, or Earl's Palace, in 1606 he may have demolished the eastern range of the old palace to make way for his own.[77] Although contextually different from the castles described above, the Bishop's Palace is roughly contemporary in date. It is central to the bishopric part of Kirkwall and thus closely associated with the ecclesiastical, administrative, secular and mercantile centre of the earldom. This is the building in which King Hákon of Norway chose to spend the winter after his return to Norway was delayed following the Battle of Largs in 1263, and where he subsequently died. The implication is that this was the most appropriate residence for a king in Orkney at this time. From the top of the Bishop's tower the entire cathedral precinct would have been visible and the wider environs and yet, since St Magnus Cathedral (with a higher tower) was so close, the purpose of the bishop's tower must have been specifically for show rather than as a watchtower.

Kirkwall Castle

This final castle dates to the 14th century, and is included to show the type of towered defensive structure built in Orkney at this time, and also because it may have had a predecessor. It was built by Earl Henry Sinclair between 1379 and 1383, ignoring the no-fortifications condition placed on his rights to the earldom. At his 1434 investiture William Sinclair agreed to surrender the *turris* (tower) to the King of Norway or his heirs.[78] Henry's justification could well have been the need to have a palace as strong as the bishop's, 'which had accommodation for a large garrison'.[79] It was a castle of exceptional strength, according to the earl of Caithness in 1614 who wrote, 'the hous hes neuir bene biggit by the consente of the diuill; for it is one of the strongest houlds in Britane, without fellow'.[80] It was used along with the Bishop's Palace by James V to garrison his army when he came to Orkney in 1540 with a fleet of 12 ships.[81]

Kirkwall Castle had a 'great tower' furnished with turrets, and was enclosed by a curtain-wall with blockhouses which were probably added in the 15th century. It seems to have projected out in the Peedie Sea which served as a defence on three sides, so assailants could only approach from the east. In 1614 the castle comprised a 'great tower' surrounded by 'mantell walls' which included at least one blockhouse. Its total frontage was possibly *c*.30m. Within the keep were probably four or five floors, an overhall, a midhall, a lang hall and a servant hall. We know that one of the halls had a 'king's gallery' and that there were cellars.[82] An order for its demolition was issued in 1614 following a siege, although a reasonable portion of its outer wall remained in a ruinous state until it was removed by the Town Council in 1865, to allow 'Castle Street' to be created.

It has been suggested that there may have been an earlier residence for the Orkney earls somewhere in Kirkwall, but we can only speculate on its location. It could have been near the later Kirkwall Castle, although it is possible that it was further to the north in the mercantile section of town, or again, perhaps Rognvald built a new palace near the cathedral and bishop's palace.[83] An earlier Kirkwall castle, St Magnus Cathedral and the Bishop's tower would have formed a striking skyline visible to all approaching the town. This is particularly relevant as by the mid 12th century Kirkwall was a pilgrimage centre and thus the focus of increased international travel.

We know the 14th-century castle was one of several Sinclair castles in Scotland, built as a blatant expression of the earl's power and authority. Even though it is located in the Norwegian earldom of Orkney, by the time of its construction the ruling elite was Scottish, and it is in a Scottish context that this castle should be viewed, along with Braal and Girnigoe in Caithness.[84] These castles post-date the 12th-century Norse castles discussed above, and deserve detailed study in their own right. They shed light on the motives and purposes of their builders, and are a reminder of the strong connections between the islands and the mainland as the remaining castles in this paper demonstrate.

Thurso, Lambaborg and Old Wick, Caithness

In addition to the three Orkney castles, there are two references in *Orkneyinga Saga* to a castle in Thurso in the earldom of Caithness, where in *c.*1154 Earls Rǫgnvald and Harald met to negotiate the division of the earldoms.

> Kom því svá, at stefnumlagi varð á komit með þeim ok griðum, ok skyldi þeir finnask í kastala einum í Þórsá ok tala tveir einir, en jafnmargir skyldi men hvárs vera hjá kastalanum.[85] (The upshot was that they summoned a meeting and made a truce, and they were to meet in a castle in Thurso and discuss the matter alone; but an equal number of men from each party were to stay outside the castle).[86]

It is thought that this castle stood to the south of Thurso, though it was destroyed in 1198 by William I and no trace remains. Like Cairston it was an earldom stronghold. There is no record of its form, though its existence is not in doubt.[87] However, it is worth considering the position of Thurso in the maritime landscape of the earldoms. There are two Caithness landing-places mentioned in *Orkneyinga Saga* – Thurso, the principal landing-place for various earls, and Duncansby, Sweyn Asleifsson's estate and central to several saga events including those at the fortified site of Lambaborg. This site has not been conclusively identified; Taylor suggests it may have been located at the Broch of Ness near Freswick, whereas Barrett suggests it was the predecessor to nearby Buchollie Castle.[88]

The sailing route from Orkney to Caithness was via Scapa Flow, taking the shortest route across the Pentland Firth, and avoiding the whirlpool known as the Swelchie. Then there were two options. One was eastward past Duncansby, then Lambaborg and then south passing the ruinous Castle of Old Wick, architecturally very similar to Cubbie Roo's Castle and suggested by Crawford to be Earl Harald's castle. The other was westward of Thurso, so ships would pass a fortified site in either direction. These three Caithness sites can be seen in a similar context to the free-standing Orkney keeps – earldom-associated watchtowers located strategically on key sea-routes.

Norse castles in the maritime landscape

Orkney's Norse castles were located to watch over key points on sea-routes around Orkney. The Wirk and Cubbie Roo's Castle are at either end of Eynhallow Sound; Damsay near the entrance to the Bay of Firth; Castlehowe overlooks the eastern coast and access to Scapa Flow; Cairston watches the western entrance to Scapa Flow; and Kirkwall's sites overlook the Flow to the south and Kirkwall Bay to the north. The castles often also protect mustering-, anchoring- and landing-places. In *Orkneyinga Saga* ships are found gathering and landing at certain key places. The landing-place at Westness is between The Wirk and Cubbie Roo's Castle; the mooring and landing-places in the Bay of Firth are protected by Damsay; while the important mooring and landing-places at Knarston and Scapa in Scapa Bay are protected by the watchtowers in Kirkwall, and Cairston and Castlehowe at the entrances to Scapa Flow. Castlehowe also watches over the southern access to the mustering-place east of Deerness. In Caithness, Thurso castle is located at a landing- and assembly-place.[89]

This leaves Widewall (27) in South Ronaldsay and South Walls (28) as two saga mustering-points without apparent castle protection. In the case of South Ronaldsay, three watchmen are stationed at the top of a hill,[90] perhaps negating the need for a watchtower. There are two possible sites in South Ronaldsay, one at Burwick (29) on a headland overlooking the southerly landing-place, and another at Hoxa (30), midway along the northern arm of Widewall bay. The saga tells of fleet gatherings at Walls; in one instance the fleet approached unnoticed by King Olaf, and in the second the fleet assembled there to watch for the enemy arriving from Caithness; both instances imply there was no watchtower. The identified watchtowers and mustering-places cluster around Scapa Flow, the Mainland and the inner north isles. No outer north isles castles or mustering-places are mentioned in the saga; this does not mean they did not exist, although the absence of archaeologically identified sites is notable. Speculatively, the location of Tuquoy fits the model proposed here, it overlooks the Westray firth, with sheltered anchorage and (modern) nousts tucked away in the adjacent bay. It has sufficient evidence for 12th-century monumentality and although no tower was identified by Owen's excavations, its absence may be due to coastal erosion.[91]

This survey has ascribed a 12th-century date to nine probable watchtowers (six in Orkney and three in Caithness), based on a combination of evidence. The remaining two buildings do not fit the same 12th-century context: one dating from the 14th century (perhaps with a 12th-century predecessor) and the other not considered to be a medieval 'castle'. From the written sources, it seems likely that the castles at Cairston and Thurso were no longer standing by the end of the 12th century, and Kolbein's castle, although still defensible in 1231, was soon to be remodelled at the expense of the southern outer defences. None of the Orkney castles (except the two Kirkwall sites) features in surviving 14th-century records, so we can be fairly certain that the life of these castles was reasonably short and their purpose was primarily a 12th-/13th-century one.

Archaeology and textual analysis do not support Clouston's groupings of 'native' versus European castles. Instead there is evidence at most of the towers for re-use of earlier defensive locations, if not the incorporation of Iron Age fabric. The ruling elite of Orkney were building free-standing keeps, fortified halls and towered (possibly fortified) churches in a European style, while at the same time making use of pre-existing fortified structures. They were doing this at a time of change, when Scandinavian lordship was ceasing to be maintained through often-unstable personal relationships based on protection, and instead was being enforced through hierarchical relationships defined by law and tied to landed estates.[92]

Perhaps monumental architecture replaced hoards as evidence of elite investment in 12th-century Orkney. The architectural manifestations of power are associated with large estates managed from central places, often with a tripartite nucleus of farmstead, church and hall, and when located near key seaways they can include a fortified element. It is possible to see these estates as evidence of Orkney moving into a territorially-based society where power is expressed through control or ownership of land. This may explain the impetus behind the choice of architectural expression, which does not stem from state control in Norway or Scotland. The general consensus is that the free-standing stone towers were influenced by contact with European societies further south.[93] In Orkney, we see the choice to build free-standing keeps, but also first-floor halls with towers, in coastally-significant central places, at a time when the volatile warring and feasting maritime society is changing with major reorganisations of secular and ecclesiastical administration. The purposes of the towers are to control the sea-routes, to protect the elite, and to express power in a fashionable continental style, emulating the status symbols of a knightly society on or near earlier monumental structures. In combining defence and control of the seaways with permanence rooted in landed estates these towers epitomise the changing nature of lordship in Norse maritime society.

Notes

1. W D Simpson, 1961, *The Castle of Bergen and the Bishop's Palace at Kirkwall: a study in early Norse architecture* (Edinburgh), p.5; C Tabraham, 1986, *Scottish Castles and Fortifications* (Edinburgh), p.32.

2. B Poulsen & S M Sindbæk, 2011, *Settlement and Lordship in Viking and Early Medieval Scandinavia* (Turnhout); G Steinsland, J V Sigurðsson, J E Rekdal & I Beuermann (eds), 2011, *Ideology and Power in the Viking and Middle Ages* (Leiden).

3. J H Barrett, 2012b, 'Viking Age and Medieval Orkney' in J H Barrett (ed.), *Being an Islander: production and identity at Quoygrew, Orkney, AD 900–1600* (Cambridge).

4. B E Crawford, 2013, *The Northern Earldoms: Orkney and Caithness from AD 870 to 1470* (Edinburgh), ch.1.

5. S Imsen, 2009, 'The Scottish-Norwegian Border in the Middle Ages', in A Woolf (ed.), *Scandinavian Scotland – twenty years after. Proceedings of a Day Conference held on 19 February 2007* (St Andrews), pp.9–30.

6. For the most recent detailed analysis of these earldoms see Crawford, *Northern Earldoms*.

7. Barrett, 'Viking Age and Medieval Orkney', p.12.

8. Barrett, 'Viking Age and Medieval Orkney'; Crawford, *Northern Earldoms*.

9. Barrett, 'Viking Age and Medieval Orkney', p.11; J H Barrett, 2007b, 'The Pirate Fishermen: The Political Economy of a Medieval Maritime Society', in B B Smith, S Taylor & G Williams (eds), *West over Sea: Studies in Scandinavian Sea-Borne Expansion and Settlement Before 1300* (Leiden), pp.299–340.

10. R A McDonald, 2003, *Outlaws of Medieval Scotland: challenges to the Canmore Kings, 1058–1266* (East Linton); S J Grieve, 1999, Norse Castles in Orkney, unpublished MPhil thesis, University of Glasgow, pp.8–9.

11. In *c*.1232 the leading men of Orkney were lost at sea during a return voyage from Norway. See *Icelandic Sagas and other historical documents relating to the settlements and descents of the Northmen on the British Isles*, vol. 2, *Hakonar Saga, and a fragment of Magnus Saga, with appendices*, transl. Sir G Dasent, 1894. (London), ch. 173 and Crawford, *Northern Earldoms*, p.277.

12. Barrett, 'The Pirate Fishermen'; S J Gibbon, 2006, The origins and early development of the parochial system in the Orkney Earldom, unpublished PhD thesis, University of the Highlands and Islands/Open University.

13. M Hansson, 2011, 'Aristocratic expressions in landscape and settlement' in B Poulsen & S M Sindbæk (eds), *Settlement and Lordship in Viking and Early Medieval Scandinavia* (Turnhout), pp.87–93.

14. E Fernie, 1986, 'Early church architecture in Scotland', *PSAS* 116, pp.393–411; E Fernie, 1988, 'The church of St Magnus, Egilsay', in B E Crawford (ed.), *St Magnus Cathedral: Orkney's Twelfth Century Renaissance* (Aberdeen), pp.140–61; R Morris, 1997, *Churches in the Landscape* (London), p.255.

15. J S Clouston, 1932, 'Tammaskirk in Rendall', *Proceedings of the Orkney Antiquarian Society* 10, pp.9–16; R Toolis, 2008, 'Excavation of medieval graves at St Thomas' Kirk, Hall of Rendall, Orkney', *PSAS* 138, pp.239–66.

16. J S Clouston, 1931, *Early Norse Castles* (Kirkwall); J S Clouston, 1929, 'Three Norse Strongholds in Orkney', *Proceedings of the Orkney Antiquarian Society* 7, pp.57–74; R D Oram, 2011, *Domination and Lordship: Scotland 1070–1230* (Edinburgh); R D Oram & G Stell (eds), 2005, *Lordship and Architecture in Medieval and Renaissance Scotland* (Edinburgh); Poulsen & Sindbæk, *Settlement and Lordship*.

17. Grieve, Norse Castles in Orkney.

18. Grieve, Norse Castles in Orkney, Appendix B.

19. *Orkneyinga Saga*, F Guðmundsson (ed.), 1965, *Islenzk Fornrit* 249 (Reykjavík).

20. *Orkneyinga Saga*, A B Taylor (ed.), 1938, (Edinburgh), p.311. This is in contrast to the Western Isles, where a significant period of abandonment of Iron Age fortifications is evidenced, see J Raven & M MacLeod-Rivett, forthcoming, '*Morentur in Domino libere et in Pace*: cultural identity and the remembered past in the mediaeval Outer Isles', in S Stoddart (ed.), *Gardening Time: Reflections on Memory, Monuments and History in Sardinia and Scotland* (Cambridge).

21. *Orkneyinga Saga*, Guðmundsson (ed.), p.34.

22. *Orkneyinga Saga*, Guðmundsson (ed.), p.259, but see also n.3 as the MS versions of OS differ in their terminology here, with *Flateyarbók* using *kastala einum* and *MS325 skála miklum*; *Orkneyinga Saga*, Taylor (ed.), pp.242–4, 319.

23. Grieve, Norse Castles in Orkney, pp.64, 66.

24. Grieve, Norse Castles in Orkney, pp.64–7. The potential of this site as the location of a keep has been supported by Caroline Wickham-Jones who has undertaken several seasons of work in and around the island as part of the Rising Tides Project.

25. R Scarth, recorded in Ordnance Survey site visit 1966, see Canmore ID 2072; J B Craven, 1901, *History of the Church in Orkney from the Introduction of Christianity to 1558* (Kirkwall), p.23; J Firth, 1920, *Reminiscences of an Orkney parish together with old Orkney words, riddles and proverbs* (Stromness); Gibbon, The origins and early development of the parochial system in the Orkney Earldom, pp.508–10; D Griffiths, 2014, 'Firth, Damsay: Landscape, Geophysics, surface and coastal survey, targeted excavation', *Discovery and Excavation in Scotland*, NS14, pp.137–9; B Sandnes, 2010, *From Starafjall to Starling Hill: An investigation of the formation and development of Old Norse place-names in Orkney*, p.185, http://www.spns.org.uk/Starafjall.pdf, and there is an unverified account that the island was associated with St Adomnan, based on the similarity of the island's name with the saint's name.

26. C R Wickham-Jones, S Dawson & R Bates, 2009, *Drowned Stone Age settlement of the Bay of Firth, Orkney, Scotland*, http://www.st-andrews.ac.uk/tzp/NGS%20Reportfinal.pdf; S Dawson & C R Wickham-Jones, 2009, *The Rising Tide: Submerged Landscape of Orkney. Quarterly Report: June 2009*, http://www.abdn.ac.uk/staffpages/uploads/arc007/RT_

interim_June2009.pdf. The project also noted a pier, visible at low tide, on the south-east of the island (*c*.240m from the highest point and 500m from the north-shore site).

27. *Orkneyinga Saga*, Guðmundsson (ed.), p.192; *Orkneyinga Saga*, Taylor (ed.), p.275.

28. Snorri Sturluson: *Heimskringla I (Hákonar saga góða). Íslenzk Fornrit XXVI. Bindi*, Aðalbjarnarson, B (ed.) 2002b, 4th edn (Reykjavík), ch.13.

29. *Icelandic Sagas and other historical documents relating to the settlements and descents of the Northmen on the British Isles. Vol. II. Hakonar Saga, and a fragment of Magnus Saga, with appendices*, G Vigfusson (ed.), 1887 (London), p.150.

30. *Icelandic Sagas and other historical documents relating to the settlements and descents of the Northmen on the British Isles, Vol. IV, The saga of Hacon, and a fragment of the saga of Magnus, with appendices*, transl. Sir G Dasent, 1894 (London), p.171.

31. M Hunter (transl. of a ms in the Advocates' Library, Edinburgh), 1987, A description of the Orchadian Islands by me Jo. Ben who stayed there in the year 1529, unpublished booklet, author's collection, p.9.

32. J Wallace, 1883, *A Description of the Isles of Orkney, reprinted from the Original edition of 1693 … together with the additions made by the author's Son in the Edition of 1700*, J Small (ed.) (Edinburgh), p.31.

33. M Thacker, 2013, The Late Norse 'coral' or mearl-limes of Orkney – an on-site mortar archaeology of Cubbie Roo's castle and chapel, *Proceedings of the 3rd Historic Mortars Conference HMC13*, University of the West of Scotland, Glasgow, 2013. Also, see Thacker's chapter in this volume.

34. Tabraham, *Scottish castles and fortifications*, p.32.

35. A Allen, 1995, *The Maritime cultural landscape of Viking and Late Norse Orkney*, http://etheses.dur.ac.uk/1040/.

36. A Ritchie & G Ritchie, 1978, *The Ancient Monuments of Orkney* (Edinburgh), p.65; RCAHMS, 1946, *Twelfth Report Inventory of the Ancient Monuments of Orkney and Shetland* (Edinburgh). vol. 2, p.237.

37. Clouston, *Early Norse Castles*; Thacker, The Late Norse 'coral' or mearl-limes of Orkney.

38. RCAHMS, *Orkney and Shetland*, vol.2, n.619, p.238.

39. For example, Crawford, *Northern Earldoms*; Grieve, Norse Castles in Orkney; J Graham-Campbell & C E Batey, 1998, *Vikings in Scotland: An Archaeological Survey* (Edinburgh), pp.257–60; C D Morris, 1993a, 'Viking Orkney: A Survey', in C Renfrew (ed.), *The Prehistory of Orkney BC4000–1000AD* (Edinburgh), pp.224–6.

40. Clouston, *Early Norse Castles*; Crawford, *Northern Earldoms*; Grieve, Norse Castles in Orkney.

41. 1st Edition Ordnance Survey Map of Birsay (Sheet LXXXVIII 1882), with thanks to Barbara Crawford (and Brian Smith) for the information.

42. For a more detailed discussion of the Bu place-name in Orkney, see Gibbon, The origins and early development of the parochial system; W P L Thomson, 2008, *Orkney Land and People* (Kirkwall), ch. 1; J S Clouston, 1927, 'The Orkney "Bus"', *Proceedings of the Orkney Antiquarian Society* 5, pp.41–9.

43. *Orkneyinga Saga*, Taylor (ed.), pp.255–6, 321–2, 328.

44. *Orkneyinga Saga*, Taylor (ed.), pp.237–8, 255, 267, 284, 310, 322; S J Gibbon, 2012, 'Orkney's Things' in O Owen (ed.), *Things in the Viking World* (Lerwick), pp.80–93.

45. Clouston, *Early Norse Castles*; Crawford, *Northern Earldoms*.

46. Grieve, Norse Castles in Orkney, ch. 2.

47. Crawford, *Northern Earldoms*, pp.193–7; A Ritchie, 1993, *Viking Scotland* (Edinburgh), p.121; Graham-Campbell & Batey, *Vikings in Scotland*; Raven & MacLeod-

Rivett, 'morentur in Domino libere et in pace'; Hansson, 'Aristocratic expressions in landscape and settlement', pp.87–93.

48. *Orkneyinga Saga*, Taylor (ed.), p.308; *Orkneyinga Saga*, Guðmundsson (ed.), p.245; *Orkneyinga Saga: the history of the earls of Orkney*, H Pálsson & P Edwards (transl.), 1981 (London), p.187.

49. *Orkneyinga Saga*, Guðmundsson (ed.), p.145.

50. *Orkneyinga Saga*, Taylor (ed.), p.308.

51. Clouston, 'Three Norse Strongholds in Orkney', p.57.

52. The 'table' land of the earl, and as such not gifted away, see Thomson, *Orkney Land and People*, pp.71–3.

53. T Stevens, M Melikian & S J Grieve, 2005. 'Excavations at an early medieval cemetery at Stromness, Orkney', *PSAS* 135, pp.371–93; Gibbon, 'The origins and early development of the parochial system', Stromness Inventory.

54. *Orkneyinga Saga*, Taylor (ed.), pp.255–6.

55. *Orkneyinga Saga*, Taylor (ed.), p.317.

56. *Orkneyinga Saga*, Guðmundsson (ed.), pp.101, 103.

57. S H H Kaland, 1993, 'The Settlement of Westness, Rousay', in C E Batey, J Jesch & C D Morris (eds), *The Viking Age in Caithness, Orkney and the North Atlantic* (Edinburgh), pp.308–17; Graham-Campbell & Batey, *Vikings in Scotland*, p.87.

58. C E Lowe, 1984, Archaeological Survey of St Mary's Church and the Wirk, Skaill, Rousay, Orkney, in relation to the collections of architectural fragments at Westside, Trumland and Eynhallow, unpublished report in Orkney SMR, p.1; Gibbon, The origins and early development of the parochial system.

59. *Orkneyinga Saga*, Pálsson & Edwards (transl.), pp.76, 99, 123–4, 137–8.

60. H M Marwick, 1924, 'Antiquarian notes on Rousay', *Proceedings of the Orkney Antiquarian Society* 2, p.17.

61. Grieve, Norse Castles in Orkney, pp.58–63; C D Morris, 1993b, 'Congress Diary, Orkney', in C E Batey, J Jesch & C D Morris (eds), *The Viking Age in Caithness, Orkney and the North Atlantic* (Edinburgh), pp.53–4.

62. Orkney Library and Archive photographic collection: L575–2, 3, 4; L576–1, 2, 3, 4; L577–1.

63. B E Crawford, 1987, *Scandinavian Scotland* (Leicester), p.146.

64. *Orkneyinga Saga*, Taylor (ed.), ch. lxvi, 241.

65. *Orkneyinga Saga*, Taylor (ed.), pp.255–6, 321, 328.

66. O Owen, 2005a, 'History, Archaeology and Orkneyinga Saga: the case of Tuquoy Westray', in O Owen (ed.), *The World of Orkneyinga Saga: 'the Broad-Cloth Viking Trip'* (Kirkwall), pp.192–212; O Owen, 2005b, 'Orkneyinga saga. A brief guide to saga sites to visit in Orkney', *ibid* p.229.

67. Orkney Library and Archive Photographic Collection, TK1230 & TK1231.

68. Grieve, Norse Castles in Orkney, pp.13–16, 49–50, 70–74.

69. *Orkneyinga Saga*, Taylor (ed.), p.221; Gibbon, 'Orkney's Things', pp.80–93.

70. B E Crawford, 2014, 'The Northern Half of the Northern Earldoms' Lordship: A comparison of Orkney and Shetland', in S Imsen (ed.), *Rex Insularum: The King of Norway and His 'Skattlands' as a Political System c.1260-c.1450* (Trondheim), p.157; B E Crawford, 2012, 'St Magnus Cathedral – a proprietory church of the Orkney earls?' in S Imsen (ed.), *'Ecclesia Nidrosiensis' and 'Noregs veldi' the role of the Church in the making of Norwegian domination in the Norse world* (Trondheim), p.181.

71. *Orkneyinga Saga*, Taylor (ed.), pp.183–5, 241.

72. For detailed discussion of Knarston and the role of Scapa Flow in the political geography of the earldom see Crawford, *Northern Earldoms*, p.191 and B E Crawford, 2011, 'Scapa Flow – The nerve centre and Knarr centre of the medieval earldom', *Scapa Flow Landscape Partnership Scheme*, http://www.scapaflow.co/index.php/history_and_archaeology/the_norse/scapa_flow_the_nerve_centre_and_knarr_centre_of_the_medieval_earldom.

73. *Orkneyinga Saga*, Taylor (ed.), pp.242, 259, 261, 307, 317, 331.

74. J Mooney, 1947, *The Cathedral and Royal Burgh of Kirkwall*. 2nd edn (Kirkwall), p.96.

75. Owen, 'Orkneyinga Saga – a brief guide to saga sites', p.227; Simpson, *The Castle of Bergen*, pp.65–76.

76. R Lamb & J Robertson, 2005, 'Kirkwall: Saga, History, Archaeology', in O Owen (ed.), *The World of Orkneyinga Saga: 'The Broad-Cloth Viking Trip'* (Kirkwall), p.170.

77. P D Anderson, 1992, *Black Patie: the life and Times of Patrick Stewart, Earl of Orkney, Lord of Shetland* (Edinburgh), p.43.

78. P Abercromby, 1715, *The martial achievements of the Scots Nation* (Edinburgh), p.402.

79. B H Hossack, 1986, *Kirkwall in the Orkneys* (Kirkwall), p.15.

80. *State papers, and miscellaneous correspondence of Thomas, Earl of Melros*, 1837 (Edinburgh), Vol. 1, p.182, no. CXI, Earl of Caithness to Lord Binning, 7 October 1614.

81. Hossack, *Kirkwall in the Orkneys*, p.15.

82. Anderson, *Black Patie*, pp.163–6.

83. Mooney, *Cathedral and Royal Burgh of Kirkwall*, p.96.

84. B E Crawford, 2005, 'The Sinclairs in the late Middle Ages', in R D Oram & G Stell (eds), *Lordship and Architecture in Medieval and Renaissance Scotland* (Edinburgh), pp.188–203.

85. *Orkneyinga Saga*, Guðmundsson (ed.), p.254.

86. *Orkneyinga Saga*, Taylor (ed.), p.315.

87. Crawford, *Northern Earldoms*, pp.195, 247; Graham-Campbell & Batey, *Vikings in Scotland*, p.260; Grieve, Norse Castles in Orkney, pp.39–40, 51, 95.

88. Taylor in Crawford, *Northern Earldoms*, p.195; J H Barrett, 2005, 'Svein Asleifarson and 12th century Orcadian society', in O Owen (ed.), *The World of Orkneyinga Saga: 'The Broad-Cloth Viking Trip'* (Kirkwall), pp.213–23.

89. *Orkneyinga Saga*, Taylor (ed.), pp.237, 242, 244, 255–6, 259, 261, 310.

90. *Orkneyinga Saga*, Taylor (ed.), ch. 94.

91. O Owen, 1993, 'Tuquoy Westray Orkney: A challenge for the future?' in C E Batey, J Jesch & C D Morris (eds) *The Viking Age in Caithness, Orkney and the North Atlantic, selected papers from the proceedings of the eleventh Viking Congress, Thurso and Kirkwall 22 August–1 September 1989* (Edinburgh), pp. 318–39.

92. Poulsen & Sindbæk, 'Settlement and Lordship', pp.26–8.

93. R D Oram, 2008a, 'Royal and lordly residence in Scotland c1050 to c1250: an historiographical review and critical revision', *The Antiquaries Journal* 88, p.181; Crawford, *Northern Earldoms*; Grieve, Norse Castles in Orkney.

17

WESTERN SEABOARD CASTLES:
HISTORICAL AND ENVIRONMENTAL PERSPECTIVES

Richard Oram

AMONG THE COMPONENT ELEMENTS of traditional visions of medieval lordly might in the maritime West Highlands and Islands, castles are perhaps the most potent. They have long been recognised as unequivocal statements of power, the fortresses of Gaelic warlords set in liminal places which link the terrestrial and marine environments, and the economic, social and cultural spheres on which military and naval might and lordly authority were founded. For the most part, that essentially 19th-century imagining of the castles, which line the Hebrides and west mainland from Sutherland to Galloway, has been little affected by the revisionist trend within wider British and northern European castellology, which has questioned older visions of castles as primarily functional military architecture, and emphasised their symbolic and more practical domestic/administrative functions.[1]

Principally, this apparent detachment of castle-studies in Scotland from research-trends elsewhere reflects the limits of published critical re-evaluation which engages with such work. But it is also a consequence of a deeply-entrenched perception of Scottish castles as the physical manifestation of a culture of feud and social violence that lingered into the mid 18th century.[2] 'Whiggish' visions of a culturally and socially primitive medieval kingdom brought to peace, stability and 'modernity' through union with its more advanced southern neighbour have been debunked by over four decades of historical research; the expressive role of castles, however, remains contested. Whether or not they were practical or representative statements, built as functional fortresses or as symbolic projections of authority, is a debate which has barely begun.[3]

In common with wider European castle-studies, the study of Scotland's western seaboard castles suffers from the legacy of 130 years of 19th-century museological typologising, which projected the physical development of castles as an evolutionary sequence which moved from simple (and by extension 'early') to complex (and by extension 'late') forms just as the morphological development of flint arrowheads was exhibited in museum cases.[4] In 1927 William Mackay Mackenzie cautioned against simply assuming that the physical simplicity of some western seaboard castles signalled their greater antiquity, but his call for circumspection was brushed aside in the 1960s in a new enthusiasm for advancing early dates for their construction, led by Stewart Cruden.[5] His basic arguments, that *prima facie* there was no reason not to posit an early date for structures which exhibited ostensibly early features, and that absence of evidence for early stone castles elsewhere in Scotland was not a sound basis on which to reject the possibility that any western castles were early, appear reasonable.

Cruden was, however, writing in the context of what began in the early 1960s in mainland Europe as an archaeological quest for castle 'origins'. Based largely on the claims advanced for Michel de Boüard's discoveries at the 10th-century castle of Doué-la-Fontaine in Maine-et-Loire, this quest long presented the emergence and spread of the castle idea across Europe in diffusionist terms, with west-central France as cultural epicentre.[6] For the western seaboard castles of Scotland, these origin-seeking and re-dating trends are evident in Cruden's theorising about the sources of inspiration for the region's stone-castle tradition.[7] More recently, the balance has returned to more cautious dating,[8] but until the results of scientific investigation of these castles are published, their chronology will remain a matter of opinion rather than of fact (see Mark Thacker, this volume).

Further potential problems of dating and interpretation lie in the insidious cultural determinism which distorted the mainstream Scottish historical narratives for the Middle Ages, in which Gaelic Highland and Hebridean culture and society was contrasted unfavourably with Anglophone lowland Scotland.[9] A deep-seated prejudice against Gaelic culture coloured much 19th-century historical writing, and a tendency to present the wider Gaidhealtachd as at best culturally conservative consequently became embedded in earlier-20th-century historical narratives. Such views fly in the face of the wide-ranging international connections of the region and its rulers, with the Hebrides forming part of the sea-routes linking the Scandinavian world with Ireland and the Atlantic West of Europe. During the 13th century, when many of the region's castles were possibly first being built, these connections were functioning at their height.

Other contributions in this volume address different dimensions of the difficulties with the historiographical and methodological legacies outlined above. This essay focuses on the historical context for the encastellation of Scotland's Atlantic seaboard, and some environmental factors which potentially contributed to the proliferation of castles throughout the region from the late 13th until the beginning of the 16th century. In a short discussion such as this, however, it is impossible to advance a detailed historical narrative for Hebridean castles, or the environmental history of Scotland's Atlantic seaboard.[10] The focus here, therefore, will be on broad trends.

Apart from spurious tales of a Scottish king ceding the Western Isles to King Magnus Barelegs of Norway in the 1090s, there is no historically-attested evidence for Scottish royal interest in this region before the close of the 11th century.[11] It is in respect of Magnus, however, that the first reference to royal fortification-building occurs in the Isles, when as part of his 1098 expedition he erected *munitiones* in Man. His work perhaps included fortification of St Patrick's Island, Peel, where excavations in the 1980s exposed the remains of a stone-dump rampart, possibly with timber revetting on its outer face, dating from this episode.[12]

What other fortifications throughout the Hebrides were constructed on Magnus's orders is unknown – although possible examples have been suggested – but, if they were similar in form to Peel how these can be differentiated without excavation from enclosures of late-prehistoric or early-medieval date in the Isles is unanswered. Large defensive enclosures on prominent, naturally-strong sites were a feature of contemporary Norwegian fortification, such as that on the Slotsfjellet at Tønsberg constructed in the 12th century. Most such sites, however, did not evolve into permanently-occupied castles of western-European type which combined domestic, administrative, processing and status-enhancing symbolic functions alongside a defensive role. That castle-type appeared first in Sverresborg near Trondheim at the end of the 12th century.[13] In the Isles, while Peel underwent successively more elaborate phases of re-fortification, there is no evidence that fortification trends in general followed the same trajectory as occurred in Norway.

Although Norwegian royal interest in the Hebrides is commonly presented as declining, if not ending, for over 150 years after Magnus's death in 1103, recent scholarship has questioned that perception. As the inclusion from 1152/3 of the diocese of the Isles in the Norwegian archdiocese of Niðarós indicates, through the 12th century the kingdom of Man and the Isles continued to be regarded as a tributary of Norway and part of the so-called Norgesveldet by both Norwegian rulers and the papacy.[14] Across that era the region was part of the zone of Scandinavian cultural dominance which extended from Norway to Man and across the North Atlantic to Greenland.[15]

Although the decline in Norwegian royal power which occurred after Magnus's strong rule worsened during the civil wars that recurred until firm government was restored by King Sverre at the end of the 12th century, Norway's kings maintained their interest in the Hebrides.[16] Other external agents also sought to dominate the Isles during this period of Norwegian weakness. First, Muirchertach ua Briain, king of Munster, and then his nephew and rival Domnall mac Taidc, the latter possibly allied with the kings of Cenél nEógain, intruded their authority. This phase ended *c.*1112 when the English king Henry I established Óláfr, youngest son of the late-11th-century Manx king Guðrøðr Crobán, as king in the Isles.[17] During the second quarter of the 12th century, however, having consolidated his rule in eastern and southern mainland Scotland, the Lowlands-based Scottish king David I (1124–53) looked west at the rulers of the western seaboard and islands. Impelled by the need to confront challenges to his kingship from pretenders who found allies in the Isles, David combined a colonial plantation of 'Anglo-Norman' incomers down the east side of the Firth of Clyde with strategic alliances with local powers – principally King Óláfr – to contain the threat.[18] By the mid 12th century the Western Isles had therefore become subject to conflicting and increasing levels of influence from Norway, Ireland and the principal powers of mainland Britain.

David I's policy of plantation and alliance was maintained by his successors for around a century. Beyond the core zone of their kingdom where their reach was immediate and effective, they projected their authority through proxies whose ambitions complemented theirs. Probably the first arena for such collaboration was the Firth of Clyde, whose waterways linked the mainland zone of Scottish control on their eastern flank to the islands and western-mainland zones occupied by autonomous Norse-Gaelic powers. From David I to Alexander II (1214–49) Scottish kings allied with ambitious west-mainland-based noble families to first dominate and then absorb the Clyde islands and south mainland of Argyll into their kingdom. It was an often violent road to integration, and castle-building formed one significant element in a protracted process of military conquest, colonisation and progressive cultural and political domination.[19]

Chief among the colonial families employed by the Scottish crown were those who became the Stewarts. They had been lords of Renfrew on the inner reaches of the Clyde estuary since late in David I's reign or early in that of his successor, Malcolm IV (1153–65).[20] From Renfrew, Stewart lordship expanded through the acquisition of north Kyle, centred on Dundonald Castle (Plate 37), and across the Clyde into Cowal and Bute, focused on castles at Dunoon, in existence by the later 1220s, and Rothesay (Plate 38), also operative by that period.[21] These castles, in which their administrative agents were based, symbolised the Stewarts' political presence and effective lordship of those districts. Modern perceptions of such castles have seen the Stewarts presented as terrestrial, lowlands-facing and essentially 'Anglo-Norman' interlopers in a water-based, Atlantic-facing and largely Norse/Gaelic world. Yet Renfrew, Dunoon and Rothesay cannot but have operated as static nodes of power in a network that depended on domination of the waterways. From the moment that the Stewarts aspired to dominate the Firth of Clyde they by necessity became a naval power.

With the possible exception of Renfrew, the Stewart castles were probably on sites of older power-centres. Dundonald has possible origins in at least the Early Historic era as a royal stronghold, evidence for imported pottery, elite dyestuffs and the production of high-quality metalwork offering parallels with Dumbarton Rock and Dunadd.[22] In common with other sites, but perhaps less obvious in modern contexts, Dundonald occupies a prominent hill-top close to sheltered beaching-places on the Kyle coast. A more obvious relationship exists between the castle-site and landing-place at Dunoon, but no archaeological investigation has been undertaken here to determine whether the outcrop occupied by the fragmentary medieval ruins was the location of the *dún* from which the later site derived its name.[23] At Rothesay, John Dunbar posited the existence of an earlier earthwork which dominated the adjacent anchorage,[24] but such a low-lying site differs significantly from Dundonald and Dunoon; any precursor to the surviving stone castle might simply have been a preliminary stage in the Stewarts' development of an administrative centre for their newly-acquired lands rather than being re-use of a much older site.[25]

The Stewarts, however, were initially minor players among the west-coast powers. It was the 'native' proxies with whom the Scottish kings allied in their westwards expansion who commanded the greatest naval strength. The most significant down to 1234 were the Lords of Galloway, who enjoyed close blood-links with the English crown, and also had marriage-ties into the Manx royal house. In Scotland they were married into the Morville family, lords of Lauderdale and Cunninghame and constables of the king of Scots, and from 1209 into the royal house itself.[26] They first appear as masters of significant naval resources in 1154, when Fergus of Galloway's ships joined the fleet gathered by the king of Cenél nEógain against Toirrdelbach ua Conchobair, king of Connacht.[27]

Galwegian naval power was greatest in the early 1200s, when Alan of Galloway and his brother campaigned throughout the southern Hebrides and against the Argyll coastlands and Ulster.[28] The Galloways' cousin, Duncan of Carrick, also participated in these operations, allying with John de Courcy, lord of Ulster.[29] Less evidence survives for the active role of the Gaelic lords of the Lennox as a naval power at this time, but annal reference in 1216 to a son of the Earl of Lennox attacking the Cenél Fergusa in modern County Donegal suggests that this kindred, too, participated in the naval warfare of this period.[30]

Although all these kindreds embraced the culture of the Anglo-Norman families with whom they had been intermarrying since the early 1100s, adopting the use of parchment records, seals for authentication of such documents (usually depicting them in the armour of a mounted knight), and employing Anglo-French household organisation and administrative structures, stone castles of Anglo-French form did not form part of the foreign repertoire which they embraced.[31] While their Manx cousin Guðrøðr II Ólafsson, who drew on both Norwegian and English support to consolidate his power in Man, emulated his English patron Henry II's castle-building, or perhaps the great tower built by John de Courcy at Carrickfergus in Ulster, in his donjon at the core of Castle Rushen,[32] the surviving evidence from Galloway, Carrick and the Lennox suggests an adherence to older forms at long-established power-centres. The principal residence of the Galloways from the 1180s onwards, Cruggleton Castle on the Solway coast near Whithorn, occupied a site with late Iron Age and Early Historic origins.[33] When redeveloped after 1185, a castle of motte-and-bailey type was inserted into the innermost sector of the cliff-edge enclosure and it is that structure which is most commonly identified as the stronghold of 'Soumillet of Pelande', father of the eponymous hero of the early-13th-century *Roman de Fergus*, in which it is described as a clay-built tower enclosed by ramparts of earth, clay and wattle.[34]

The structures excavated at Cruggleton, interpreted as a hall with attached tower or solar, were similar in form to those excavated at the contemporary motte-and-bailey at Lismahon in County Down,[35] a similarity that has been used to stress the interconnectedness of Galloway and Ulster at the end of the 12th century. Lismahon, it should be noted, was a re-used Early Historic site associated with John de Courcy's conquest of eastern Ulster after 1177, and should not be seen in a purely Anglo-Norman cultural context. Nothing can be said of the Carricks' coastal stronghold at Turnberry beyond its existence by the 1180s, its heavily-ruined remains being unexcavated. At around the same date the Lennoxes acquired the ancient royal centre of Dumbarton Rock, but there is no firm evidence for their refortification of the citadel that had been the seat of Cumbrian kings down to the third quarter of the 9th century, before the first masonry defences of the royal castle were built *c*.1225.[36]

Reluctance to adopt the Norman-French castle and continued use of Early Historic sites by the nobles of the south-west mainland into the early 1200s is paralleled throughout the Atlantic west. Rushen apart, which has only one contemporary parallel anywhere in the region in the 12th-century castle on Eilean na Comhairle at Finlaggan, which is known only from excavation, there is no documented reference to castles or castle-building by either Guðrøð's sons, between whom the kingdom of Man and the Isles was divided, or his rivals for the kingship, Somerled of Argyll and, after 1164, his sons.[37]

In the absence of firm documentary or archaeological evidence, it is here that discussion of western seaboard castles usually shifts into the realms of speculation concerning the continued use of Early Historic sites or early dates for the origins of the surviving stone structures. Archaeological evidence from coastal dùns at Kildonan Bay and Ugadale Point on the east coast of Kintyre and Dùn Fhinn on its west coast, or at Little Dunagoil on the south-west coast of Bute, indicate that these pre-medieval sites saw re-use as high-status residences into the 13th and in some cases down to the later 15th or 16th centuries.[38] The identity of their occupants can only be conjectured, and little can be said other than that this occupation coincides with possession of Kintyre by Somerled's son Ranald and his heirs.

No castle associated with Dubhgall, the eponymous founder of the senior of the MacSorley lineages, nor the MacRuairi or MacDonald lines descended from his younger brother Ranald, can yet be assigned dates earlier than the 1200s. Excavation has shown that the probable Eilean na Comhairle donjon, underlying the later residence of the MacDonald Lords of the Isles, was erected on top of a dùn which had been constructed no earlier than the 6th century AD, and both it and the wider complex was already functioning as a major lordship centre early in the 12th century.[39] Too little survives of the donjon to be sure of its original form, but its excavator posits King Guðrøð's work at Rushen as a possible exemplar (Plate 39). If correct, that hints at a flow of ideas about the physical expressions of lordship around the Isles between the territories dominated by Guðrøð's sons and those in the hands of the MacSorleys, and greater engagement by them with western European ideals in the second half of the 12th century than has been recognised previously.

Receptiveness to external ideals and symbols of lordship was not restricted to this regnal elite. Indeed, one of the most powerful indicators of the reception of those alien ideals, Castle Sween in Knapdale (Plate 9), was produced for a kindred of second-rank status. The castle's construction is presented as marking a new turn in the physical expression of elite power.[40] While Stewart Cruden argued that through its possession of 'architectural characteristics of the late 11th century in a marked degree' it had a 'reasonable claim to be the earliest existing castle in Scotland', recent discussion more cautiously dates its construction closer to 1200.[41] Even that revision, however, still places it at the beginning of a rapid expansion in the erection of such stone-and-mortar expressions of lordly power throughout southern Argyll, Lorn and the adjacent inner Hebridean group from Mull to Islay. Key examples of such castles are Innis Chonnel on Loch Awe, a building with strong similarities to Castle Sween and where work probably started for the Campbells of Lochawe within the first quarter of the 13th century, and the slightly later Duart on Mull.[42]

The building of Castle Sween pre-dates the resumption of an aggressive assertion of Scottish royal power on the western seaboard which, in parallel with expansionist moves north and west of Inverness, was pursued energetically from the early 1220s.[43] King William had brought a direct royal presence to the Clyde coast with his establishment by 1197 of a royal castle and burgh at Ayr, which was as much about containing the ambitions of the Stewarts as it was about dominating land and sea further west.[44] It was his son Alexander II, however, who asserted Scottish authority in the region, with naval campaigns in 1221 and 1222 securing lordship over the outer Firth of Clyde. This position was consolidated by re-appropriation from the Lennoxes of Dumbarton, where he founded a burgh.[45]

A new castle at Tarbert (Plate 40) became the springboard for the projection of Alexander's power against the MacSorleys and a mechanism for the accelerated integration of southern Argyll into the expanding Scottish realm.[46] By the time that Tarbert was being built, however, the landscape of lordship in Argyll and the islands had changed profoundly from the 12th-century pattern, as the local ruling elite either entered into new relationships of acknowledged subordination to the crown or were displaced in favour of families who recognised Scottish overlordship. Dumbarton, Dunoon (which perhaps fell into royal hands in the 1220s) and Tarbert underscored the immediacy of royal power. The established local regime had either to embrace that fact, and use it to bolster their own legitimacy, or risk marginalisation and potential expulsion as Scottish kings tightened their grip on the region.

Immediacy brought threat but it also brought opportunity and, while the traditional historical record highlights the military and naval campaigns conducted by Alexander II as the principal mechanism of Scottish domination and conquest in the West, other, more subtle, mechanisms were also at work. As Rees Davies explored in the 1990s, economic domination, influence through key appointments within the regional ecclesiastical hierarchy, settlement of colonists and intermarriage between the nobles of the 'dominated' and 'dominating' polities were equally important for acculturation and political integration.[47] Castle-building formed part of the cultural repertoire of the most prominent component of the Scottish nobility of the earlier 13th century, those families of 'Anglo-Norman' descent who had been settled in the kingdom by David I and his heirs. It was, however, embraced progressively by 'native' nobles as they intermarried with and adopted the social, legal and economic norms of the former colonists.[48]

Too much has been made of how different 'native'-built castles were to the types of structure constructed at the same period in eastern Scotland. As with the adoption of castle-building by the Welsh princes in the late 12th and 13th centuries,[49] the lords of western seaboard Scotland adapted a foreign expression of lordship to meet the different cultural and economic conditions of their position, as well as to meet the physical constraints of the local environment and topography. While there is no question of the architectural significance of these buildings, their greatest importance is as indicators of how far the Norse-Gaelic lords of Argyll had been assimilated into the expanding Scottish realm in the early 1200s.

How firm the bonds of the MacSorleys were to the Scottish crown was tested in 1230–31, when King Hákon IV of Norway asserted his authority in the Isles through the proxy of a member of the MacDougall lineage, named in Norwegian sources as Uspak.[50] Accounts of the campaign illuminate conflicts within the wider MacSorley lineage over how to respond to rising Scottish influence in Hebrides; the MacDougall in particular sought to compromise and maintain allegiance to both the Norwegian and Scottish kings for the different portions of their territories.[51] The extension of Scottish power into the Clyde estuary and southern districts of Argyll was, nevertheless, unwelcome to them, and Uspak targeted the chief markers of that spread, the Stewart castles; Rothesay was besieged and stormed. It may have proved ineffectual as a fortress but Rothesay's capture surely underscores the Argyllmen's recognition of such castles as symbols of foreign lordship and as bases from which foreign domination could be extended.

After the temporary reverses of 1230, and intensifying from the 1260s, the crown brought regional powers into direct relationships which reduced the need for its active presence. Instead of the king, regional nobles became the principal castle-building agents as the century progressed. Intermarriage and integration into the Scottish political elite, exemplified by MacDougall-Comyn and MacDonald-Bruce/Stewart bonds, brought greater regional stability after the century of conflict between rival contenders for the kingship of the Isles.[52] The greater familiarity of the leadership of the main Gaelic kindreds with the culture of the heavily English- and French-influenced families with whom they were interacting facilitated the flow of ideas about the form of lordly residence. It was not, however, a question of the western lords aping the traditions of their southern and eastern counterparts, for around the same time as the Lord of Lorn was adding a cylindrical donjon and mural towers to his earlier-13th-century enclosure at Dunstaffnage (Plate 39), Scottish magnates like the earls of Fife and Mar were constructing from-new similar multi-towered castles at Falkland and Kildrummy;[53] the MacDougalls were abreast with architectural fashions.

The description of the Hebrides in the so-called *Gesta Annalia* I, formerly attributed to the late-14th-century chronicler John of Fordun but now posited as his re-working of a late-13th-century text compiled largely by the St Andrews-based cleric Richard Vairement (*fl.*1239–67), offers a glimpse of the nodes of lordly power within the political spheres of the MacDougall, MacDonald and MacRuairi kindreds *c.*1285.[54] While the significance of the inclusion or omission of particular castles can be endlessly and fruitlessly debated, what that list and architectural evidence of 13th-century work in castles as widely dispersed as Brodick and Lochranza on Arran, Achadun on Lismore, and Borve on Benbecula indicate is that castles had been embraced as a symbol of lordly power and their number had proliferated rapidly.[55] In part, this spread was eased by the stability of the extended domains of the MacSorleys and the need of the MacDougalls and the MacRuairis especially for administrative centres from which to defend, control and exploit their far-flung properties. It is in this context that Borve on Benbecula, Dunyvaig on Islay, and Mingary in Ardnamurchan, respectively MacRuairi, MacDonald and possibly MacDougall possessions, should be seen. Along the western fringes of the outer Firth of Clyde, the late-13th-century drum-towered gatehouse at Brodick on Arran and the high-quality mason-work at Skipness underscore the parallel entrenchment of regional domination by the Stewarts and their cadets.[56]

Legislation to institutionalise the post-1266 integration of the western seaboard districts into the kingdom was promulgated in King John Balliol's February 1293 parliament. It planned the creation of sheriffdoms of Skye, Lorn and Kintyre, to be held by the earl of Ross, Alexander MacDougall, lord of Argyll and Lorn, and James the Steward respectively.[57] It is likely that each sheriff would have had his administrative base in either one of their own castles, for example Dunstaffnage in the case of Lorn, or at a mediatised royal castle, such as Tarbert for Kintyre and possibly Eilean Donan for Skye.[58] The 1293 plan, however, was stillborn due to the chaos of the Wars of Independence after 1296. It was only after 1308 that King Robert I actively re-initiated royal intervention in the West following his defeat of the MacDougalls and appropriation of Dunstaffnage.[59] In the 1320s he consolidated his authority over the south-west Highland zone, expanding and refurbishing Tarbert, repairing Dunaverty and resuming royal control of Dumbarton.[60] In the north-west, his nephew Thomas Randolph was ruthlessly imposing the king's peace from Eilean Donan castle,[61] while the Rosses were brought into the fold and served as his agents in Skye and Lewis. At no point, however, did Robert extend a direct royal presence into the Isles proper, instead depending there on the loyal Bishop Bernard of the Isles (former chancellor of Scotland and abbot of Arbroath) and on the less-than-certain support of the MacDonalds and MacRuairis who had expanded into the regional vacuum created by the destruction of MacDougall power.[62] The near-collapse of the Bruce regime following Edward III of England's intervention in 1333 in the renewed Scottish civil war, however, ended the crown's regular involvement in the government of the Isles, and the refurbished royal castles fell into private hands.

For the best part of 165 years after Robert I' death in 1329 the crown reverted to the expediency of government of the West Highlands and Islands through proxies, many of whom operated with *de facto* autonomy. Chief among these were the MacDonalds, who from the 1330s were unquestioned inheritors of the pre-1300 regional leadership of the MacDougalls; Scottish and English royal clerks recognised their status in the style *dominus Insularum* (Lord of the Isles), the Latinised form of the Gaelic *Rí Innse Gall* (King of the Islands of the Strangers) which they had appropriated for themselves. As their power spread beyond Islay, new bases for their authority were needed at more convenient locations than Finlaggan, and castles perhaps associated earlier with the MacDougalls, such as Aros on Mull and Ardtornish in Morvern, became nodes of control in their sea-linked domain.[63] MacDonald cadets, like the MacIains in Ardnamurchan, and Clanranald in Moidart and the Uists, were given possession of older castles like Mingary and Borve, or castles of more recent construction like Tioram,[64] to serve as markers of their social leadership and regional political importance.

In parallel with this process, as MacDonald interests spread into mainland Scotland through their successful claim to the earldom of Ross, a second tier of major lordships emerged in the Isles under an increasingly remote over-arching MacDonald lordship.

A core group in that second tier formed the so-called 'Council of the Isles', which reportedly constituted the Lords of the Isles' advisory council. The council's exact composition is contested, but key members were reported in the 16th century as the heads of the Dunyvaig, Ardnamurchan, Clanranald and Lochaber MacDonalds, the heads of the MacLeans of Duart and Lochbuie, and the MacLeods of Harris and Lewis, and the heads of the MacKinnon, MacQuarrie, MacNeill of Gigha and MacNeil of Barra lines.[65] It is probably a reflection of these men's status that at least seven of the 12 named possessed castles of a recognisably mainstream Scottish form by the mid 15th century, some inherited and expanded 13th-century buildings (like Mingary and Duart) but others of later-14th- to mid-15th-century construction (like Kisimul or Moy).[66] The great towers added in the late 14th century to Duart for the MacLean chief and to Dunvegan for the MacLeod of Harris (Plate 41) are powerful statements of these families' elevated status and ambition, but they also underscore the depth to which the lordly symbolism of lowland Scotland had penetrated the Isles.[67] On the mainland, where families like the Campbells of Argyll and MacDougalls of Lorn were culturally Janus-like in their continued identification with Gaelic culture while being full participants in the political and cultural life of the Anglophone south and east, great towers were widely-represented icons of lordly society.[68] As MacDonald power crumbled after 1475, the proliferation of such structures increased as rising families jockeyed to assert their position in the newly volatile landscape of west-coast lordship.

The political context discussed so far has been the lens through which development of western seaboard castles has most commonly been viewed. More recently, awareness of environmental and economic factors has led to alternative understanding of the context within which the land- and seascape of Hebridean lordship evolved from the 13th to 15th centuries. In this water-connected region, it is now understood that it was the interplay of the two major motors of climate and weather in the North Atlantic – and human cultural responses to them – which influenced the political, cultural and economic idiosyncracies of Isles-based lordship. These motors were the Atlantic Meridional Overturning Circulation of oceanic water, which sees the flow of warmer water north and east across the Atlantic, and the North Atlantic Oscillation (NAO) in the atmospheric-pressure systems (between the permanent Iceland low-pressure and Azores high-pressure cells). Changes in those systems were critical in the establishment of the so-called 'medieval-climate anomaly' which lasted from the later 10th to later 13th centuries, and the 'little ice age' that followed it, through their influence on westerly wind-conditions and eastwards movement of atmospheric moisture. Positive NAO through much of the 10th to mid 13th centuries brought generally more benign weather to the northern and western British Isles, but from the 1250s the NAO weakened, causing greater variation, but principally cooler and wetter summers and intensely cold and stormy winters. The impact of this change was not immediate, but by the end of the 13th century, and more pronouncedly as the 14th and 15th centuries progressed, it became evident that economic regimes which had prevailed since the later 900s were no longer viable.[69]

What did such climate-change mean for the inhabitants of the Hebrides at all social levels? Excavation evidence has shown that 10th- to 13th-century Hebrideans practised intensive arable cultivation, focused in the Uists, Lewis and Harris on the fertile calcareous shell-sand *machair* down the Atlantic-facing seaboard, growing barley, oats, possibly rye and in some areas flax (for linseed).[70] Furthermore, benign sea-conditions facilitated the growth of a commercial fishery, specialising in the processing and export of herring.[71] In short, there was a prosperous economic regime which produced surpluses on which a complex lordship system founded on social display, conspicuous consumption and gift-giving was sustained. Elite craftsmen who produced the high-status items – from jewellery and sculpture to poetry and music – through which this form of lordship was displayed, and the warrior retinues which gave it muscle, were attracted and supported by lords' ability to feed and house them.

The castles of the MacSorleys mark the apogee of that complex exchange-mechanism in the 13th century; confidence, in effect, was reflected in stone. Even as Dunstaffnage, Duart or Borve were being built, however, the economic foundations on which they stood were being exposed to threat. Increasing storminess with attendant episodes of sand-blow rendered that regime increasingly unsustainable, especially in the Outer Isles,[72] with optically stimulated luminescence (OSL) dating from Baleshare in North Uist, for example, suggesting that such incidents increased in frequency from the mid 1200s. Sea-conditions deteriorated also, and changes in bottom-water temperature in sea-lochs which had been rich fishing-grounds, like Mingary-controlled Loch Sunart, possibly brought failures in seasonal herring migration.[73] Palaeo-environmental evidence from excavations throughout the Western Isles has revealed a collapse in the herring-trade in the late 13th and 14th centuries, before a return to boom after *c*.1450.[74]

With the basis of their social positions under threat from environmental stresses on the traditional sources of wealth, western seaboard lords faced a choice of adapting to the changed circumstances and risking a contraction of their power, or finding alternative mechanisms to maintain the status quo. As centres of complex economic networks, castles remained the foci of terrestrial and marine exploitation regimes, but political crisis, warfare, and population contraction from *c*.1300 offered opportunities for lords to secure their positions through off-loading the burdens of maintaining their followings, principally through a return to a predatory culture of raiding, forced quartering of warriors on other men's land, and mercenary service.[75] What had evolved by the later 14th century were militarised kindreds like the MacLeans, MacKinnons and MacAskills, whose martial potential was employed by the Lords of the Isles to extend the reach of their political and economic lordship and, consequently, of the resource-base on which that edifice was sustained. The proliferation of castles across this period reflected the rise of these kindreds and the requirement on their leaders to maintain the culture of elite production and consumption which secured the loyalty of the warriors and craftsmen who serviced that lifestyle. Castles, moreover, became nodal points at which the military and naval resources of these kindreds could be concentrated on the immediate eve of campaigning.

But mercenary service, plunder and forced quartering were not the sole sources of wealth in the late-medieval 'little ice age', for environmental change brought opportunity as well as challenge. Disturbance of the migratory behaviour of herring shoals in the 14th century ended in the 15th century with an apparent return of fish to the Minch, west-coast sea-lochs and Clyde estuary;[76] the MacLeods of Dunvegan and Campbells at Inverary derived a significant component of their wealth and power from exploitation of the fish-trade. In the 1470s and 1480s contracts with east-coast merchants and foreign – often Breton – dealers were commonplace and provided some lords with secure revenue-streams. MacLeod traditions of the Fairy Flag's power being used to bring herring shoals into Loch Dunvegan perhaps preserve a memory of their castle's function as a node in the Hebridean fish-trade network, but further research is needed to establish whether western seaboard castles more generally operated in the manner posited for coastal castles in late-medieval Gaelic Ireland, as control-points at which the profits of that trade were creamed off in the form of tolls rather than as centres of shore-based processing activity.[77]

In conclusion, we can see the origins of the proliferation of castles throughout the western seaboard from the 12th century as a regional response to a general European trend that itself only penetrated south-east mainland Scotland after *c.*1100. There was no one source of inspiration; Isles-based powers were exposed to different manifestations of castle-building culture from Norway, England and Scotland. As Scottish political domination of the region increased from the 1220s onwards, and accelerated through the progressive integration of the MacSorleys into Scotland's social elite, so too did the MacSorleys adopt the cultural baggage of that group, but with adaptations to meet their own socio-cultural needs. Castle-building was part of that acculturation, and reflected acceptance by a widening segment of the region's rulers of the function of castles as expressions of lordship. The increasing remoteness of the MacDonald Lords of the Isles from their ancestral heartlands after *c.*1400 accelerated the rise of a second tier of lords who, like their social superiors, adopted the castle as a projection of their status, and as collection- and control-points for the resources of the land and sea regions which they dominated. In the environmentally volatile conditions of the later Middle Ages, castles came into their own throughout the western seaboard as both arenas for lordly display and relationship-building, and centres for the control and exploitation of the natural resources of their terrestrial and maritime hinterlands.

Notes

1. For trends in the revisionist model, see C Coulson, 1996, 'Cultural realities and reappraisals in English castle study', *Journal of Medieval History* 22:2, pp.171–208; M Johnson, 2002, *Behind the Castle Gate: From Medieval to Renaissance* (Abingdon); C Coulson, 2003, *Castles in Medieval Society: Fortresses in England, France and Ireland in the Central Middle Ages* (Oxford); O H Creighton, 2005, *Castles and Landscapes: Power, Community and Fortification in Medieval England* (London); R Liddiard, 2005, *Castles in Context: Power, Symbolism and Landscape, 1066 to 1500* (Macclesfield).

2. Although focused on the post-1500 period, C A McKean, 2001, *The Scottish Château: the Country House of Renaissance Scotland* (Stroud) and 2006, 'A Scottish problem with castles', *Historical Research* 79: 166–98, constitute the most substantial engagement with these issues. R D Oram, 2008b, 'Castles, concepts and contexts: castle studies in Scotland in retrospect and prospect', *Chateau Gaillard* 23, pp.349–59; and Oram 2010a, 'Medieval Scottish castles: some insights, images and perceptions from archaeological and historical investigation', *Chateau Gaillard* 24, pp.213–22, review the wider difficulties.

3. Important contributions to the debate are made in R D Oram (ed.), 2015, *'A House That Thieves Might Knock At'* (Donington), alongside papers offering comparative European perspectives.

4. The tradition in Scotland begins with D MacGibbon & T Ross, 1887, *The Castellated and Domestic Architecture of Scotland*, vol. 1, pp.61–5 (Edinburgh); Oram, 'Castles, concepts and contexts'.

5. W M Mackenzie, 1927, *The Mediaeval Castle in Scotland* (Edinburgh), p.42; S Cruden, 1981, *The Scottish Castle*, 3rd edn (Edinburgh), pp.15–16.

6. Typified by the Royal Archaeological Institute's 'Origins of the Castle in England' project: A Saunders, 1977, 'Five castle excavations: Reports on the Institute's research project into the origins of the castle in England', *Archaeological Journal* 134, pp.1–156. See O H Creighton, 2012, *Early European Castles: Aristocracy and Authority, AD 800–1200* (London) for a recent review of research and debates on castle 'origins'.

7. Cruden, *Scottish Castle*, pp.18–26.

8. See, for example, discussion of Castle Sween in RCAHMS, 1992, *Argyll: An Inventory of the Monuments, 7, Mid Argyll & Cowal: Medieval and Later Monuments* (Edinburgh), no.119; G Ewart & J Triscott, 1996, 'Archaeological investigations at Castle Sween, Knapdale, Argyll and Bute, 1989–90,' *PSAS* 126, pp.517–58; C J Tabraham, 2005, *Scotland's Castles,* 2nd edn (London), p.28.

9. For discussion of this dichotomy, see R D Oram, 2014a, 'Introduction: A Celtic Dirk at Scotland's Back? The Lordship of the Isles in Mainstream Scottish Historiography since 1828', in R D Oram (ed.), *The Lordship of the Isles* (Leiden), pp.1–39.

10. R D Oram, 2014b, '"The worst disaster suffered by the people of Scotland in recorded history": climate change, dearth and pathogens in the long 14th century', *PSAS* 144, pp.1–22; R D Oram, 2014c, 'From "Golden Age" to Depression: Land Use and Environmental Change in the Medieval Earldom of Orkney,' in H C Gulløv, *Northern Worlds: Landscapes, Interactions and Dynamics* (Copenhagen), pp.203–14; R D Oram, 2010b, 'Innse Gall: Culture and Environment on a Norse Frontier in the Scottish Western Isles', in S Imsen (ed.), *The Norgesveldet in the Middle Ages* (Trondheim), pp.125–48; R D Oram & W P Adderley, 2008, 'Lordship and environmental change in central Highland Scotland *c.*1300 to *c.*1450', *Journal of the North Atlantic* 1, pp.74–84; R D Oram & W P Adderley, 2010, 'Lordship, land and environmental change in West Highland and Hebridean Scotland *c.*1300–*c.*1450', in S Cavaciocchi (ed.), *Economic and Biological Interactions in Pre-Industrial Europe from the 13th to the 18th Centuries* (Florence), pp.257–68.

11. R D Oram, 2012, *Alexander II, King of Scots, 1214–49* (Edinburgh), pp.176–7.

12. *Chronica Regum Manniae et Insularum,* P A Munch (ed.),1860 (Christiania), p.6; D Freke, 2002, *Excavations on St Patrick's Island, Peel, Isle of Man 1982–88: Prehistoric, Viking, Medieval and Later* (Liverpool), pp.3, 132–9.

13. R Meyer, 2010, 'The Zion of the North: the multifunctional role of Sverresborg. A civil-war stone castle near Trondheim', *Château Gaillard* 24, pp.185–94.

14. I Beuermann, 2007, 'Masters of the Narrow Sea: Forgotten Challenges to Norwegian Rule in Man and the Isles, 1079–1266', *Acta Humaniora*, Faculty of Humanities, University of Oslo.

15. Discussed by Andrew McDonald, this volume.

16. For a brief overview, see S Bagge, 2010, *From Viking Stronghold to Christian Kingdom: State Formation in Norway, c.900–1350* (Copenhagen), pp.40–67.

17. R D Oram, 2011, *Domination and Lordship: Scotland 1070–1230* (Edinburgh), p.59.

18. R D Oram, 2004a, *David I: the King Who Made Scotland* (Stroud), ch.7.

19. The mechanisms employed to achieve mastery of the 'Celtic' zones of the British Isles are explored in two volumes by R R Davies, 1990, *Domination and Conquest: The Experience of Ireland, Scotland and Wales 1100–1300* (Cambridge), and 2000, *The First English Empire: Power and Identities in the British Isles 1093–1343* (Oxford).

20. G W S Barrow, 1980, *The Anglo-Norman Era in Scottish History* (Oxford), pp.13–14.

21. G Ewart & D Pringle, 2006, 'Dundonald Castle Excavations 1986–93', *Scottish Archaeological Journal* 26, pp.11–14. For Dunoon, see RCAHMS, *Argyll* 7, no. 127; J G Dunbar, 1981, 'The Medieval Architecture of the Scottish Highlands', in L Maclean (ed.), *The Middle Ages in the Highlands* (Inverness), pp.39–40.

22. S Driscoll & K Forsyth, 2006, 'The Late Iron Age and Early Historic Period', in Ewart & Pringle, 'Dundonald Castle', pp.4–11; E Campbell, 2006, 'Early Historic Imported Pottery', *ibid* pp.90–92.

23. RCAHMS, *Argyll*, 7, pp.273–4.

24. Dunbar, 'Medieval architecture of the Scottish Highlands', p.40.

25. D Pringle, 1995, *Rothesay Castle and St Mary's Church* (Edinburgh), p.4.

26. R D Oram, 2000, *The Lordship of Galloway* (Edinburgh), chs 2–4.

27. *Annals of the Four Masters* http://www.ucc.ie/celt/published/T100005B/index.html - annal M1154.11.

28. Oram, *Lordship of Galloway*, pp.117–120, 122–3, 125–132.

29. Oram, *Domination and Lordship*, pp.155–6.

30. *Annals of Ulster* http://www.ucc.ie/celt/published/T100001B/index.html - annal U1216.4.

31. For discussion, see R Bartlett, 1993, *The Making of Europe: Conquest, Colonization and Cultural Change 950–1350* (London).

32. Dunbar, 'Medieval architecture of the Scottish Highlands', p.44; B H St J O'Neil, 1951, 'Castle Rushen, Isle of Man', *Archaeologia* 94, pp.1–26; C Donnelly, J Ó Néill, T E McNeill & P McCooey, 2005, 'De Courcy's Castle: New insights into the first phase of Anglo-Norman building activity at Carrickfergus Castle, County Antrim', *Medieval Archaeology* 49, pp.311–17.

33. G Ewart, 1985, *Cruggleton Castle. Report of Excavations 1978–1981* (Dumfries), pp.12–18.

34. Ewart, *Cruggleton Castle*, pp.18–22; Tabraham, *Scotland's Castles*, p.15.

35. Ewart, *Cruggleton Castle*, p.22; D M Waterman, 1959, 'Excavations at Lismahon, Co Down', *Medieval Archaeology* 3, pp.139–76; T E McNeill, 1980, *Anglo-Norman Ulster: The History and Archaeology of an Irish Barony 1177–1400* (Edinburgh), pp.85–6.

36. L Alcock & E A Alcock, 1990, 'Reconnaissance excavations on early historic fortifications and other royal sites in Scotland, 1974–84: 4, Excavations at Alt Clut, Clyde Rock, Strathclyde, 1974–75', *PSAS* 120, p.117.

37. D H Caldwell *et al*, Finlaggan Report 7, http://repository.nms.ac.uk/228/1/Finlaggan_report_7_-_eilean_na_comhairle.pdf

38. RCAHMS, 1971, *Argyll*, *1*, *Kintyre* (Edinburgh), nos 204, 220, 228; H Fairhurst, 1939, 'The Galleried Dun at Kildonan Bay, Kintyre', *PSAS* 73, pp.185–228; H Fairhurst, 1956, 'The Stack Fort on Ugadale Point, Kintyre', *PSAS*, 88, pp.15–21; D N Marshall, 1964, 'Report on Excavations at Little Dunagoil', *Transactions of the Buteshire Natural History Society* 16, pp.9, 30–33. For a wider discussion of re-use of prehistoric sites, see A Morrison, 1974, 'Some prehistoric sites in Scotland with medieval occupation', *Scottish Archaeological Forum* 6, pp.66–74.

39. For dating, see D H Caldwell *et al.*, http://repository.nms.ac.uk/214/2/Finlaggan_report_1_-_introduction_and_background.pdf; http://repository.nms.ac.uk/224/1/Finlaggan_report_3-_eilean_mor_excavations_1.pdf; http://repository.nms.ac.uk/228/1/Finlaggan_report_7_-_eilean_na_comhairle.pdf

40. Cruden, *Scottish Castle*, pp.22–5; RCAHMS, *Argyll* 7, no.119; Ewart & Triscott, 'Archaeological investigations at Castle Sween'.

41. Cruden, *Scottish Castle*, p.22; Tabraham, *Scotland's Castles,* p.28.

42. Dunbar, 'Medieval architecture in the Scottish Highlands', pp.44–5; RCAHMS, 1974, *Argyll* 2. *Lorn* (Edinburgh), no.292 [Innis Chonnell]; RCAHMS, 1980, *Argyll* 3, *Mull, Tiree, Coll & Northern Argyll* (Edinburgh), no.339 [Duart].

43. Oram, *Alexander II*, pp.76–81, 175–91.

44. Oram, *Domination and Lordship*, p.157.

45. E P Dennison, 2005, 'Burghs and Burgesses: A Time of Consolidation?' in R D Oram (ed.), *The Reign of Alexander II* (Leiden), pp.274–8.

46. J G Dunbar & A A M Duncan, 1971, 'Tarbert Castle: A Contribution to the History of Argyll', *Scottish Historical Review* 50.1, pp.1–17.

47. Davies, *Domination and Conquest*, especially chs1–3.

48. For native adoption of castle-building, see F Watson, 1998, 'The expression of power in a medieval kingdom: thirteenth-century Scottish castles', in S Foster, A Macinnes & R MacInnes (eds), *Scottish Power Centres from the Early Middle Ages to the Twentieth Century* (Glasgow), pp.59–73; R D Oram, 2003, 'Continuity, adaptation and integration: the earls and earldom of Mar, *c*.1150–*c*.1300', in S Boardman & A Ross (eds), *The Exercise of Power in Medieval Scotland c.1200–1500* (Dublin), pp.57–63; R D Oram, 2008b, 'Castles, concepts and contexts: Castle studies in Scotland in retrospect and prospect', *Château Gaillard* 23, pp.355–6.

49. See for example, Carndochan and Castell y Bere in P R Davis, 2007, *Castles of the Welsh Princes* (Cardiff), pp.39–40, 41–3.

50. See Andrew McDonald, this volume.

51. Oram, *Alexander II*, pp.97–100.

52. A Young, 1997, *Robert the Bruce's Rivals: the Comyns, 1212–1314* (East Linton), p.127.

53. J H Lewis, 1996, 'Dunstaffnage Castle, Argyll and Bute: excavations in the north tower and east range, 1987–94', *PSAS* 126, pp.564, 599–600; RCAHMS, 1933, *Inventory of Ancient Monuments and Historic Constructions in the Counties of Fife, Kinross and Clackmannan* (Edinburgh), pp.135–42; RCAHMS, 2007, *In the Shadow of Bennachie: a Field Archaeology of Donside, Aberdeenshire* (Edinburgh), pp.156–61.

54. *John of Fordun's Chronicle of the Scottish Nation*, ed. W F Skene, trans F J H Skene, 1872, vol. 2 (Edinburgh), pp.39–40; D Broun, 2007, *Scottish Independence and the Idea of Britain: From the Picts to Alexander III* (Edinburgh), pp.49, 236, 252–63.

55. Dunbar, 'Medieval Architecture of the Scottish Highlands', pp.45, 49; RCAHMS, *Argyll* 2, no. 276; D Turner, 1998, 'The Bishops of Argyll and the Castle of Achanduin, Lismore, AD 1180–1343', *PSAS* 128, pp.645–52.

56. RCAHMS, *Argyll* 1, pp.165–78; Dunbar, 'Medieval Architecture of the Scottish Highlands',pp.45, 47.

57. *The Records of the Parliaments of Scotland to 1707*, K M Brown *et al.* (eds), 2007–2015 (St Andrews), 1293/2/16, 1293/2/17, 1293/2/18.

58. For the pre-Wars of Independence castle at Eilean Donan, see R Miket & D L Roberts, 2007, *The Medieval Castles of Skye and Lochalsh*, revised edn (Edinburgh), pp.95–7.

59. For Bruce's capture of Dunstaffnage see John Barbour, 1997, *The Bruce*, ed. A A M Duncan (Edinburgh), pp.366–7.

60. Dunbar & Duncan, 'Tarbert Castle', pp.13–14.

61. For Randolph at Eilean Donan in 1331 see Walter Bower, 1996, *Scotichronicon*, vol 7, eds D E R Watt *et al.* (Aberdeen), p.59.

62. M Penman, 2014, 'The MacDonald Lordship and the Bruce Dynasty, c.1306–c.1371', in Oram (ed.), *The Lordship of the Isles*, pp.72–5.

63. RCAHMS, *Argyll* 3, nos 332, 333.

64. G Stell, 2014, 'Castle Tioram and the MacDonalds of Clanranald: A Western Seaboard Castle in Context', in Oram (ed.), *Lordship of the Isles*, pp.271–96. Stell's dating of Borve (*ibid*, pp.286–7) to the mid 14th century might be revised in light of the re-dating to the later 13th century of the 'Fordun' list in which the castle is named.

65. *Acts of the Lords of the Isles 1336–1493*, eds J Munro & R W Munro, 1986 (Scottish History Society), xlvii–xlviii.

66. RCAHMS, *Argyll* 3, nos 339, 345, 346.

67. Dunbar, 'Medieval Architecture of the Scottish Highlands', pp.53–4; RCAHMS, *Argyll* 3, no. 339.

68. For example, the MacDougalls' 15th-century caput at Dunollie (RCAHMS, *Argyll* 2, no. 286) or the Campbell tower at Carrick (RCAHMS, *Argyll* 7, no. 116).

69. See note 10 above.

70. D Serjeantson, 2013, *Farming and Fishing in the Outer Hebrides AD 600 to 1700: The Udal, North Uist* (Chandlers Ford), pp.73–4, 77–9; N Sharples, 2005a, 'Discussion', in N Sharples *et al.*, 'Resource Exploitation' in N Sharples (ed.), *A Norse Farmstead in the Outer Hebrides: Excavations at Mound 3, Bornais, South Uist* (Oxford), p.169.

71. Serjeantson, *Farming and Fishing*, ch.7; Oram, 'Culture and Environment on a Norse Frontier', pp.133–5, 141–2; Oram & Adderley, 'Lordship, land and environmental change in West Highland and Hebridean Scotland', p.259.

72. S Dawson, A G Dawson & A T Jordan, 2004, 'North Atlantic climate change and Late Holocene windstorm activity in the Outer Hebrides, Scotland', in D Griffiths & P Ashmore (eds), *Aeolian Archaeology: the Archaeology of Sand Landscapes in Scotland*, SAIR 48, http://sair.org.uk/sair48; Serjeantson, *Farming and Fishing in the Outer Hebrides*, p.31; N Sharples, 2005b, 'The End of Settlement on the Machair', in Sharples *et al.*, 'Discussion', in N Sharples (ed.), *A Norse Farmstead in the Outer Hebrides: Excavations at Mound 3, Bornais, South Uist* (Oxford), pp.195–6; D D Gilbertson, J-L Schwenninger, R A Kemp & E Rhodes, 1999, 'Sand-drift and Soil Formation Along an Exposed North Atlantic Coastline: 14,000 Years of Diverse Geomorphological, Climatic and Human Impacts', *Journal of Archaeological Science* 26.4, pp.439–69.

73. A G Cage & W E N Austin, 2010, 'Marine climate variability during the last millennium: the Loch Sunart record, Scotland, UK', *Quaternary Science Reviews* 29, pp.1633–47.

74. M Rorke, 2005, 'The Scottish Herring Trade, 1470–1600', *Scottish Historical Review* 84, pp.150–53, 155; C Ingrem, 2005, 'Fish', in Sharples *et al.*, 'Discussion', in Sharples, *Norse Farmstead*, pp.192–4; Sharples, 'The end of settlement on the machair', in Sharples *et al.*, 'Discussion', *ibid*, pp.195–6.

75. Oram & Adderley, 'Lordship and environmental change in central Highland'; Oram & Adderley, 'Lordship, land and environmental change in West Highland and Hebridean Scotland'.

76. Rorke, 'Scottish Herring Trade', pp.150–55.

77. See for example M W Samuel, 1998, The Tower Houses of west Cork, unpublished PhD thesis, University College London, pp.158–9; C Breen, 2005, *The Gaelic Lordship of the O'Sullivan Beare: a landscape cultural history* (Dublin), p.116.

18

CASTLES OF THE WESTERN SEABOARD: SOME PHYSICAL PERSPECTIVES

Geoffrey Stell

INSTEAD OF spreading observations thinly across a wide range of issues, this essay focuses on two key aspects relating to the contexts and building fabrics of the castles of the western seaboard. It offers, firstly, a summary review of the waterside settings of insular and peninsular castles in the region, both coastal and fresh-water. Secondly, it re-examines briefly the ways in which castle layouts and architectural features have been analysed, classified and dated, matters that have long aroused contention and controversy, and probably always will, given the room for debate that the relative paucity of direct historical evidence permits.

The perspective is largely drawn from an Argyll standpoint, derived from an involvement in RCAHMS's decades-long survey and publication programme.[1] One offshoot of that corpus was a monograph on Argyll castles, published jointly by RCAHMS and Historic Scotland in 1997.[2] Reproducing detailed descriptions of the castles in the care of Historic Scotland, it brought together introductory material on those castles which appeared in five of the seven RCAHMS *Inventory* volumes, together with a composite list and map of all castle-related sites covered in the series, 89 in all.

Physical contexts

Western seaboard castles have come down to us in a wide variety of shapes and sizes, many incapable of tight definition and classification as they merge almost seamlessly with other forms of domestic building. Medieval castles have clearly formed part of a larger socio-architectural kindred which goes back into prehistory and remained wide during the Middle Ages. Old traditions died hard: many ancient or anciently-named sites remained occupied or were re-occupied, while amphibious lifestyles in both salt- and fresh-water contexts were common to a broad range of habitations and places of worship. Intriguingly, many such island dwellings have retained evidence of both a boat-inlet and stone foundations of a causeway or once-timber platform, and a significant number were located in fresh-water lochs or lochans where, as at the limestone-surrounded Loch Finlaggan, Islay, modern-day fishing appears to be better than average.

Overall, the Argyll survey produced evidence of almost 60 sites where waterside castles and churches were associated with identifiable landing-places and anchorages.[3] To the author, one of the most striking examples, clearly visible from the castle parapet, was that which fronted Moy Castle, the mid-15th-century tower residence of the Maclaines of Lochbuie at the head of Loch Buie on the south coast of Mull.[4] The tower's two 18th-century successors, a laird's house of 1752, now part of a steading, and a mansion-house of 1793, stand nearby, while a few metres to the south-east of the tower are the remains of a boathouse, probably also of late-18th- or 19th-century date. Roughly aligned with this structure is a boat-landing which is well defined by two rows of large boulders *c.*4m apart (Plate 42). Although the clarity of its definition probably reflects the latest phases of use, there seems little circumstantial doubt that this landing would have been kept in working order from at least the later Middle Ages. Further out in the bay there is a broad arc of large boulders which appeared partly artificial in origin and which recent aerial photography has defined much more clearly as an anchorage and boat-dock, possibly combined with a fish-trap (Plate 43).[5]

Another memorable, if somewhat unsung, maritime hinterland of archaeological note lay at the opposite, northern, end of Mull on the Mishnish peninsula, where the former MacKinnon stronghold of Dùn Ara remains associated with a landing-beach, an artificially constructed harbour and even traces of a basic form of boat shelter or noust, not as common a surviving feature on the western seaboard as it is in the Northern Isles.[6]

Argyll was once rife with seaborne empires of varying expanse and family cohesion. Physically, still one of the most memorably inter-visible is that of the MacDonalds of Dunivaig on the south-east coast of Islay. From Dunivaig Castle, on clear days, the horizons are bounded by the distant coastlines of Kintyre and Antrim, where the family also exercised lordship during their heyday in the 16th century.[7] An even more remarkable maritime lordship, longer-lasting than the Lordship of the Isles itself, was that of MacDonald of Clanranald, with its mainland station on the tidal Eilean Tioram at the mouth of Loch Moidart (Plate 11). Its history, context and built remains have been explored and set out in detail elsewhere,[8] but it is worth repeating here a couple of 17th-century episodes which illuminate its galley-based character.

As with other West Highland chiefs, compliance with the so-called 'Statutes of Iona' of 1609 and a bond of 1616 placed constraints on Clanranald's customary lifestyle, particularly with regard to the use of only one birlinn of 16 or 18 oars. Castle Tioram was designated as Clanranald's principal residence, but because he did not have a demesne or home farm associated with it he was allowed to nominate and manage another on his estate. His choice of mains at Howbeg and later Ormiclate, South Uist, tells us much about his attitude towards his indivisible, inter-island lordship.[9] Likewise, in the immediate aftermath of the death of Donald, 13th of Clanranald and the last of the line to reside in Castle Tioram, a letter of May 1685 referred to the fact that all the laird's kin and kindred had gone to Uist 'to burry the corps of our maister the Captaine of Clanranald and are not as yet come back', a brief note that conjures up a powerful word-picture of a galley fleet in mourning.[10]

Growing out of the MacRuari lordship of Garmoran in the 14th century, Clanranald came to possess an assemblage of mainland and insular properties which extended from Loch Shiel to Benbecula, and which held together for about four centuries as a water-borne family empire. Among Castle Tioram's secular Hebridean siblings was the 14th-century hall-tower of Borve, Benbecula, which in proportions and general character was probably not dissimilar from the earliest identifiable building at Tioram itself.[11] Its surrounding landscape too was almost certainly less of a topographical contrast with Tioram than now appears to be the case, for early map evidence shows that Borve occupied a promontory site flanking a sea-inlet in a much-indented coastline, quite different from its modern setting on the machair and blown sand. On the other hand, the island setting of Caisteal Bheagram, a South Uist Clanranald property from at least the early 16th century, appears little changed. Standing within sight of the Howmore church complex, also associated with Clanranald, it is a small, two-storeyed island tower, comparable in scale and setting with Castle Sinclair, otherwise known as Dùn Mhic Leoid (Plate 3), which, originally of three storeys, stands on an islet in Loch Tangusdale, Barra.[12]

Borve is a telling illustration of the way in which environmental changes may distort our understanding and appreciation of castle settings. Along the western seaboard few have witnessed more dramatic changes in their surroundings than Rothesay Castle, Bute (Plate 38), although, to date, the relatively extensive literature on this celebrated monument has offered little comment on its somewhat unusual urban context. It occupies a moated site which was redesigned as a landscaped garden in the late 18th century, and is set back from a waterfront which was developed and consolidated from the same period. Originally, however, the castle was once part of an island at the mouth of the Water of Rothesay, a watercourse from Loch Fad which was subsequently canalised for industrial purposes. The island is clearly shown on the map of Bute in the Blaeu Atlas of 1654, and Rothesay's first burgh seal of 1401 displays a galley set immediately in front of the castle. While this may be more symbolic than topographically-precise evidence, all the indications are that in the Middle Ages the castle was directly accessible from Rothesay Bay, which Dean Monro described as a 'gude heavin for schippis to ly on ankers', and was thus more vulnerable to the besieging Norsemen of 1230 than is nowadays apparent.[13]

The original setting of Rothesay Castle reinforces the impression conveyed by many coastal strongholds in neighbouring Argyll where convenience of access by water and close association with sheltered anchorages appears to be a recurrent theme. Among many others, the correlation is readily observable, for example, at Breachacha Castle, Coll (Plate 22), at Castle Sween, Knapdale (Plate 9), and at Tarbert Castle, Kintyre (Plate 40), where the siting of the royal castle was of more than local significance, standing as it did at the eastern end of a mile-wide isthmus and portage across the head of Kintyre, the setting for acts of political theatre in 1098 and 1315.[14] Given these and many other examples, it becomes almost too easy to assume that all waterside medieval sites occupy the very best positions for water-borne communications, and that proximity to the sea automatically bespeaks a logical and convenient spot for a usable boat-landing or anchorage. However, it does not require an expert navigator to detect that this conclusion may be based on a false premiss: on closer investigation many of these sites appear to have conferred limited maritime advantages, and notions of geographical determinism may be misleading.[15]

Take, for example, the much-studied case of Mingary Castle, Ardnamurchan. Compared with Castle Tioram, about which a 17th-century account tells us that 'shipps doeth come to the castle',[16] the nearest fair-weather haven to Mingary is almost two miles to the west in Kilchoan Bay, out of sight of the castle but within view of the rock-built tower outpost, Caisteal Dubh nan Cliar (Black Castle of the Minstrels). The only nearby all-weather anchorage is about three miles in the opposite direction at the mouth of Loch Sunart, again invisible from the castle. While there are tidal landing-points on the foreshore directly beneath the castle, the seaward approach is evidently not an easy one, and, according to modern navigational opinion, these landing-places would be strictly for use in calm weather with small boats. To conclude that Mingary is a site of 'considerable strategic importance in respect of sea-borne communication' is thus to gloss over how its role as an observation-post might have been translated into practical command and control.[17]

Much the same qualifications apply to offshore island castles such as Dùn Chonaill in the Garvellachs and the twin islands which make up Cairn na Burgh Castle in the Treshnish Isles (Plate 8).[18] Although, again like Mingary, 'commanding' sea-routes in the limited sense of being able to overlook them, more often than not these are very difficult islands to embark from or to clamber ashore. At Dùn Chonaill there are landing inlets on either side of the island, but even the principal landing on the leeward, exposed to swells and storms, is still at best a difficult scramble. In the Treshnish group there is no safe anchorage in the vicinity of Cairn na Burgh More and Cairn na Burgh Beg: the two islands are separated by a narrow channel, through which there is a strong tidal flow and from which landings are usually attempted, again full of hazards and probably only by small boats. Curiously, however, for all these limitations, Cairn na Burgh, probably identifiable as Iselborgh, appears to have long been respected as a great strength, and had an active military history down to the middle of the 18th century.

Other coastal settings pose less self-evident hazards and deceptions. The landing-beach in front of Skipness Castle, Kintyre, for example, was described by Angus Graham, who was brought up there, as 'a dangerous lee shore … the Kilbrannan Sound being aimed into the very eye of oncoming Atlantic storms'.[19] It also suffered from marine deposition, and in modern times there has always been a long stretch of sand fronting the shingle foreshore, thus restricting its use to vessels of shallow draught.

The site of the craggy, multi-period MacDonald stronghold of Dunivaig, Islay (Plate 14), prompts other observations about maritime accessibility. It is one of the few castles in Argyll with a sea-gate that opens directly onto a nearby beach (Plate 23), and, twice in the course of a year in 1614–15, MacDonald rebels used this emergency exit. On the first occasion in April 1614 in 'a little boat with six oars which lay at the castle' they managed to negotiate the rocks and the soldiers firing from them.[20] Dunivaig, in fact, faces a comparatively foul, reef-strewn stretch of water with only a narrow channel for small boats, and it does not seem unreasonable to conclude that the expertise and local lore needed to navigate a safe course through treacherous waters such as these may have always been an implicit element in the defence of the castle and its garrison. In these respects, Dunivaig is unlikely to have been an isolated case. The approaches to Castle Stalker, Appin, for example, have long been known to be littered with 'conals' or gravel banks. Although some appear to have been enlarged and regularised as kelp grids in the late 18th and early 19th centuries, a 17th-century description noted that there were 'conals betwixt the toure and the sea that neither ship nor bark can come in anie syde of that tour'.[21]

The assumption that the locations of most if not all coastal castles were to some degree geographically pre-determined, and that, in terms of access and/or protection, they occupied the most favoured sites that the western seaboard had to offer, is again tested when one considers Tobermory Bay, Mull. A first-rate sheltered haven, praised in 1549 and again in 1786 as 'one of the most celebrated, and most frequented bays in the Highlands', this anchorage remained steadfastly castle-less, with no known medieval secular residence for miles in any direction. Its only medieval associations are the fragmentary remains of a chapel and well, from which the late-18th-century planned settlement took its name, the patronage of the chaplainry evidently having passed from the Lords of the Isles to the Crown on their forfeiture in 1493.[22]

Notions of hydro-geological determinism or even consistency are equally difficult to sustain when it comes to assessing whether the supply of fresh water may have influenced the choice of island-castle sites in salt-water surroundings. Famously, Kisimul Castle (Plates 1–2) enjoyed the benefit of two wells, one reportedly in the centre of the courtyard and another in the south-west angle: by the late 19th century the former had been infilled and was no longer visible, but the latter was recorded as being 10ft (3m) deep, covered with large stones, and although partly filled with rubbish, still contained fresh water. In an account partly based on their informant, Donald M'lean of Castlebay, David MacGibbon and Thomas Ross referred to the existence of the spring with characteristic understatement as 'a somewhat remarkable circumstance', a conclusion with which it is hard to disagree.[23] Even more remarkably, it has since been referred to as artesian, that is, self-pumping, although it has proved difficult to pin down a technical authority for this attribute. Given that the castle-island lies within the major Hebridean fault-zone and close to another fault-line, one possible explanation is that the fresh water has issued from fracture-patterns within the prevailing hard and ancient rocks which would otherwise be impervious.[24]

Castle Tioram also possesses a well, for which descriptive details are lacking, but on the western seaboard, as elsewhere around the British coastline, other island sites such as Castle Stalker may have been closer to the norm in making do with water-barrels or with rock-cut or purpose-built cisterns.[25] However, the low-level and unroofed structure which lay to the east of the unrestored ruins of Eilean Donan Castle, and which was interpreted by MacGibbon and Ross as a capacious water-cistern of heptagonal plan, perhaps on the scale of that at Dunnottar Castle, has more recently been tentatively re-interpreted as a storeyed artillery bastion of hexagonal plan.[26]

Building analysis

Our understanding of the castles of the western seaboard is framed within a range of interpretations of the historical background, but it also depends fundamentally on the analysis, classification and dating of the physical evidence that the buildings themselves actually present. It is acknowledged that there have been – and still are – divergent approaches to that evidence and to its interpretation, but, however it is viewed, the built evidence has a right to be examined discretely, on its own terms, avoiding 'force-fits' with such historical evidence as might be available. Long experience has demonstrated that the known or assumed antiquity of a site is not necessarily reflected in the surviving upstanding fabric; on balance, most often it is not. Equally, much that remains visible may not be documented, and that which is documented may no longer be visible.

In recent decades traditional militaristic or quasi-militaristic assumptions about what may have governed the creation, purpose, use and context of castles have come under widespread challenge.[27] However, in regions like the western seaboard where frontier- and authority-zones long remained fluid, both literally and metaphorically, and conflict possibly more endemic, traditional assumptions about the roles of castles have tended to remain strong, while revisionist approaches to castle studies have made less obvious headway. Indeed, the very concept of 'galley-castles' appears to embody a traditional emphasis on command and control, certainly when compared to recent studies of 'equine' or 'pedestrian' castles, centres of lordship where overland communication by horse and foot prevailed.

The historiography of castle studies in the western and northern seaboards has also been rendered even more complex than elsewhere in Scotland as a result of the introduction of other scholarly concepts: firstly, the articulation, mainly on the part of William Mackay Mackenzie and RCAHMS,[28] of a cultural 'time-lag' as applied to the dating of medieval buildings in this region; secondly, the reaction, principally on the part of William Douglas Simpson and Stewart Cruden,[29] to what was viewed as a late-dating syndrome and which led in turn to the creation of an opposite pre-disposition in favour of 'early' dating; and, thirdly, the emphasis that modern historical scholarship has placed on the 13th century as a golden age which hereabouts heralded what has been characterised widely as a Norwegian sunset and Scottish dawn. These second and third strands have now become firmly woven into the fabric of western seaboard castellology, to the extent that the assigning of possible 14th- or 15th-century dates is so often viewed as being at best unnecessarily cautious, or at worst a denial of a castle's claims to a more ancient, and thereby more honourable, interesting or important place in the architectural pantheon.

Given the relative paucity of precise historical sources and criteria, much has rested on assigning castle dates and phases by means of physical features and types. Scientific techniques of various kinds may offer precision with regard to the character and composition of building materials, but dating-brackets may still remain wide. Traditionally, architectural details, including masons' marks, have been much used as dating and/or reference tools, but it has always to be recognised that they may be broad-ranged and ambiguous in the dates that they can suggest. Comparative classifications of layouts are also well-established tools in castle analysis, but, if carried too far into the realms of typology, such techniques may seriously distort, especially if they lead to the creation of fixed period-types and to rigid, qualitative distinctions in place of fine matters of degree. Almost all the well-known western seaboard castle-types – enclosure, courtyard or 'ring-wall' castles, 'hall-houses' and tower-houses – are based on relatively modern taxonomies, but, however far these categories have become enshrined, the extent to which they can be regarded as period-types remains variable and uncertain.

Consider, for example, the celebrated regional family of enclosure- and developed-courtyard castles, which have commanded scholarly attention ever since MacGibbon and Ross first pointed to the distinctiveness and importance of western seaboard castles in the late 19th century.[30] Of the 35 castles which they ascribed to what they designated a 'First Period –1200–1300', almost half – 17 – are in this region, most of them occupying coastal sites and a significant proportion possessing high curtain-walls and irregularly-shaped or rectilinear enclosures. Successively, during the course of the 20th century, this theme has been developed and further elaborated, while hypotheses first put forward tentatively by these great scholar-architects have gradually transformed themselves into certainties and some underlying assumptions have remained unaltered and even untested.

The attribution to the 13th century of most, if not all, of this group is one such assumption. True, some such as Castles Sween, Tarbert, Skipness and Dunstaffnage have firm historical, circumstantial or archaeological evidence to support their 13th-century credentials, but some attributions are not as well-founded as the published literature might suggest. While the existence of what Simpson referred to as a ring- or curtain-wall may have given physical definition to a castle-site, it did not necessarily also define its 13th-century date, as he was wont to assert.

Over his long career Simpson's research and writing came to embrace the medieval architecture of the western seaboard in a significant and enduringly influential manner, spread across about 40 essays.[31] His first major entrance onto this western stage was in 1938 at Dunvegan, Skye (Plate 41), where he tilted at RCAHMS's verdict that the encircling wall was probably an enclosure or barmkin contemporary with the late-14th- or early-15th-century tower (Figure 18.1), another manifestation, in his view, of the late-dating syndrome which had conditioned medieval-building analysis under the Mackenzie regime.[32] Predicating his own view of the physical evidence on the shift from Norwegian to Scottish royal overlordship which would have favoured the creation of a major stronghold and power-base for the emergent MacLeods, Simpson was forceful in his assertion that enclosure or 'ring-wall' was of 13th-century origin and character.

These conflicting interpretations centred on the junction between the tower and curtain-wall and on the nature and character of the walling around the sea-gate which, until the 18th century, was evidently the only designed access to the castle. Harling and later building-works have now made it virtually impossible to assess whether, at the junction of the tower and enclosure-wall, there was structural integration, or whether the two adjacent walls were of distinctly different builds and over a century apart in date. In its existing form, the sea-gate has a dressed masonry surround and altered entrance-passage of 16th-century and later date, so all one can truly say on the basis of the surviving visible evidence is that the wall in which the sea-gate is set is pre-16th-century. However, such a cautious and relatively imprecise verdict has proved no match for bold confidence, and Simpson's assertion of 13th-century origins for Dunvegan has prevailed to this day, serving to underpin the claim that it is the most ancient castle in Scotland which has remained in continuous occupation, a claim which has to be further qualified by the fact that its major medieval feature, the tower, went out of use and became derelict in the course of the 18th century.

Simpson proceeded to apply his theories regarding 'early', that is, 13th-century, ring-walled enclosures, with or without sea-gates, to other castles of the western seaboard most notably to Kisimul, Breachacha, Calvay, Mingary and Tioram.[33] Opportunities for re-assessing Breachacha and Kisimul came up in the 1960s and '70s, and detailed surveys of both confirmed that they adhered to the late-medieval tower-and-barmkin pattern which RCAHMS had first proposed at Dunvegan,[34] a verdict which, in the case of Kisimul, clearly still cuts no ice in Barra. Thankfully, the comparative cords by which Simpson tightly bound together Mingary and Tioram are at last being gradually separated, allowing each to be assessed on its own terms, while his claims on behalf of Castle Calvay as an early enclosure-castle remain to be critically tested.[35]

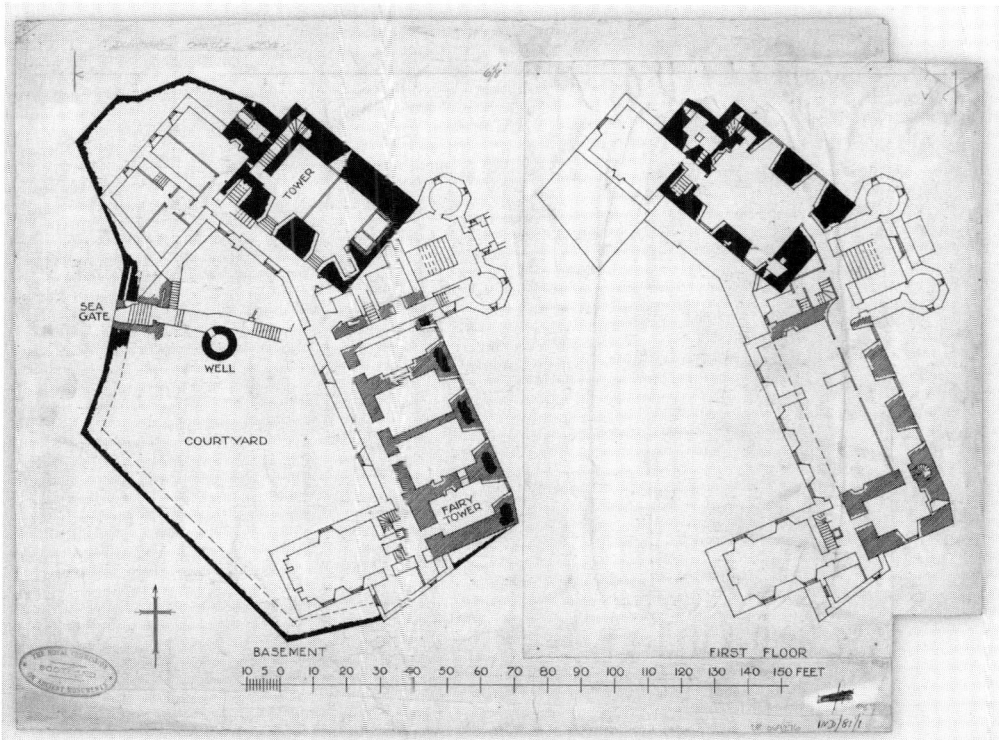

Figure 18.1. Dunvegan Castle, Skye: basement and first-floor plans.
(DP 069276 © Historic Environment Scotland)

In the case of Castle Tioram (Figure 18.2), Simpson's suggestion that the enclosure-wall, simply by reason of its polygonal form and by comparison with others of this type, most notably Mingary, belongs to the 13th century and pre-dates any of the surviving structures within its circuit, is unconvincing. As discussed in detail elsewhere,[36] the alignment of the curtain-wall and the position of the gateway which served as the original main entrance or postern clearly respect the position and extent of the earliest standing building within the enclosure. At the opposite (eastern) end of this same building, formed within an angle of the curtain in a manner which strongly suggests primary work, are the remains of two vaulted mural garderobes which served this block at first- and second-floor levels. The disposition and character of all these features indicate a functional integration between the building and the curtain-wall, a conclusion that is reinforced by the fact that the walls of both are also characterised by closely similar split-boulder masonry techniques. Variously described as a 'keep' or 'tower-house', this relatively modest structure appears originally to have risen to no more than two, possibly three, storeys: it is of a markedly horizontal design and in its elongated oblong proportions is closely akin to the halls and hall-towers found elsewhere in the region.

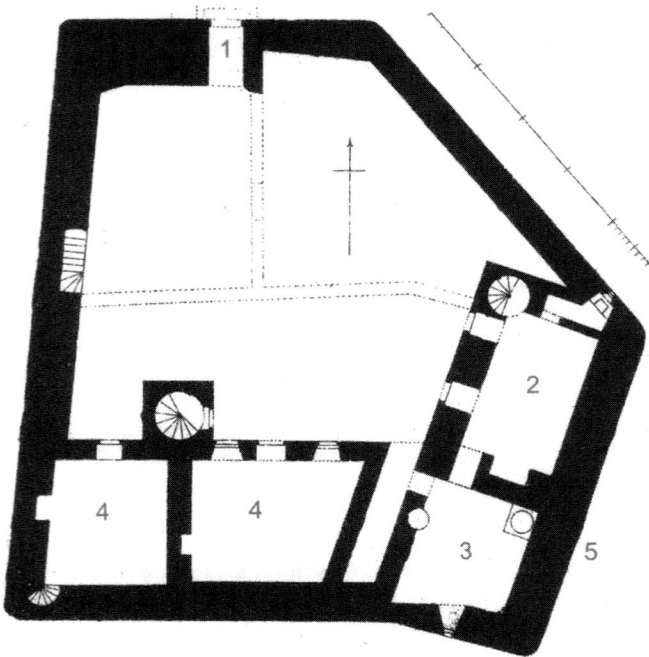

Figure 18.2. Castle Tioram, Moidart: outline plan, showing principal diagnostic features: 1. Entrance-gateway and irregular pentagonal enclosure wall, mid 14th century and later; 2. Eastern range comprising a mid-14th-century hall, later vaulted and heightened into tower; 3. Kitchen, 16th and 17th centuries; 4. Southern tower and hall range, 16th and 17th centuries; 5. Postern gateway, mid 14th century, later blocked. (after MacGibbon & Ross, vol. 3: 56)

For these reasons it is difficult to sustain the argument which draws a clear distinction and century-wide gap between the 'ring-wall' enclosure and the rest of the castle. On balance, the first phases of Castle Tioram as we see it today appear to coincide with the first documented appearance of the castle between 1346 and 1373, and, deriving its layout and design from earlier forms of enclosure and halls, it combines these two elements in a manner previously unrecognised.

Other sites also continue to buck the traditional assumption that polygonal or rectilinear enclosures are necessarily of early date. As one has always to expect, old forms and traditions persisted in the Middle Ages and rarely belonged exclusively to one era. For example, long recognised as one of the group of early polygonal-enclosure castles, Duntrune in its existing form has been shown to have been a product of the 15th century, built by a branch of the Campbell family of Lochawe.[37] As far as rectilinear typology is concerned, Old Castle Lachlan on the shores of Loch Fyne in Cowal incorporates two parallel hall ranges within a rectangular enclosure and is a MacLachlan family residence which is demonstrably of 15th-century date.[38]

Douglas Simpson was also a principal propagator, if not the actual inventor, of modern castle typologies such as 'tower-house' and 'hall-house'. 'Hall-houses' have been defined as establishments in which the principal surviving element is a stone-built hall, although distinguishing them clearly from elongated towers of hall-like proportions is one of many problems to which their creation as a discrete class of castle has given rise.[39] Since Simpson's time buildings classified as 'hall-houses' have been identified all over Scotland, about two dozen altogether, but the genre has been especially conspicuous on the western seaboard where they have been ascribed for the most part to the 13th century. Some, such as Skipness, are demonstrably of this period, but few of the others can be so securely dated.[40]

The problem with 'hall-houses' goes much wider than mere niggling about their dating and definition. As Tadhg O'Keeffe has emphasised in relation to their Irish counterparts, where the current tally is much greater and increasing, one of the most serious aspects of the type-casting of 'hall-houses' is how the process has distorted the ways in which medieval society is viewed and reflected through the medium of surviving buildings.[41] When Scottish 'hall-house' identification was at its height in the third quarter of the 20th century, their erection into a 13th-century period-type of minimally defensive character was equated with peace and domesticity, and it was this interpretation which has since encouraged documentary historians to use them as alleged social barometers in a golden age of peace.[42]

So what, in addition to typology, are the principal architectural or structural dating criteria? At one stage in the course of its survey RCAHMS went so far as to consider timber lintelling of window and door embrasures a 13th-century characteristic,[43] but for the most part dating has traditionally been based on the forms and comparisons of architectural details. Aros Castle, Mull (Plate 19), for example, is judged as a 13th-century MacDougall product, largely on the grounds that it is of 'hall-house' form and was lit by arch-pointed windows, but is it reasonable to assert that a simple two-light, arch-pointed window with chamfer-and-cavetto rebated surround is definitely of pre-1300 date? Could these allegedly classic 13th-century features not equally have been created under the patronage of the MacDonald Lords of the Isles, with whom the castle is known to have been associated in the 14th century?[44]

Across the Sound of Mull at Mingary Castle, Ardnamurchan, the forms of doorways and crenelles add to the evidence of the single and paired lanciform windows to provide a more cumulatively convincing case for a 13th-century date,[45] but can we still be confident of the range of possible dates that these architectural details indicate? Elsewhere, even where the architectural evidence points convincingly to the 13th century, as it does in the case of Dunstaffnage Castle, Lorn (Plate 7), dating brackets may still remain wide or uncertain. At first sight this castle offers an attractive range of potential dating criteria: an enclosure with 'retracted' circular angle-towers, now known to be early additions; arrow-slits of distinctive fish-tailed form; and lanciform hall windows (Figure 18.3), including paired openings, bearing dogtooth ornament comparable to that on the nearby chapel. Despite known revival use of dogtooth ornament, no-one seriously questions the castle's 13th-century credentials, but further precision remains frustratingly elusive. Following earlier commentators, RCAHMS is on record as assigning it to 'about the middle of the 13th century' or 'about the second quarter of the 13th century'.[46]

The even-more-profuse detailing of the nearby chapel at Dunstaffnage is likewise ascribed to 'the second quarter of the 13th century' and, in other words, to 'a date late

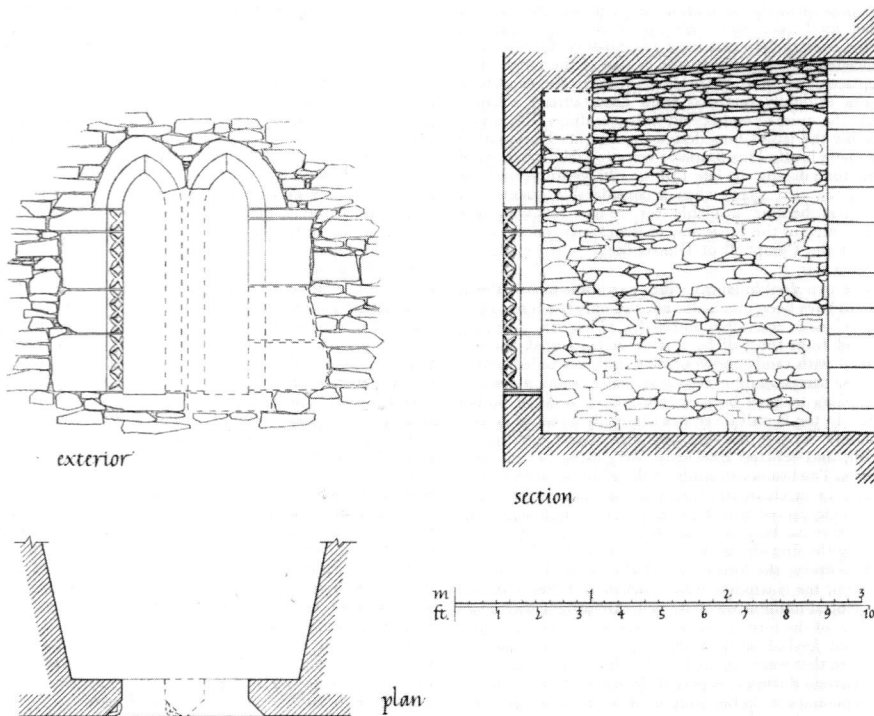

Figure 18.3. Dunstaffnage Castle, Lorn: external elevation, plan and section of southernmost of two pairs of double lancet windows which lit the first-floor hall. (SC 360331 © Historic Environment Scotland)

in the first half of the 13th century'.[47] Richard Fawcett has more recently described the chapel, drawing attention, among other things, to its widely-splayed window embrasures which betray strong Irish influences, but, other than placing his discussion in a chapter which covers the period between 1220 and 1270, he does not venture further to refine its possible dating.[48]

In truth, *pace RCAHMS*, insufficient dating evidence has been adduced to allow us to identify with any degree of certainty which of the successive MacDougall lords of Argyll was mainly responsible for the conception, erection and development of Dunstaffnage Castle and Chapel. To date, the main contenders for that honour have been either Duncan (d.1244–9) or Ewen (d. in or after 1268),[49] but the case for a significant contribution by Alexander MacDougall (d.1310)[50] with Scottish royal backing cannot be ruled out. All that can be stated with complete confidence is that the first documented reference to the castle was in 1308–9, when it was besieged and fell to the forces of Robert Bruce following the Battle of Ben Cruachan.[51]

This issue is more than a few mere quibbles about architectural details. The dating and early phasing of Dunstaffnage Castle are matters of huge regional, even national, historical significance. Yet the creation and the assumed identity of the builder of this castle have for too long been guided, not by hard evidence, but mainly by historical inferences drawn from the changing role and relationships of its MacDougall lords in the middle decades of the 13th century. Events in and after the 1240s have been the subject of abundant recent historical scholarship, but given that we still cannot be sure about the appearance, or even the existence, of this castle in and after Alexander II's expedition in 1249, is it not time to put the spotlight back on such a key strategic centrepiece of the western seaboard and to reassess its architecture and archaeology on their own terms?

Notes

1. RCAHMS, 1971, *Argyll, An Inventory of the Ancient Monuments:* vol. 1, *Kintyre* (Edinburgh); 1974, vol. 2, *Lorn* (Edinburgh); 1980, vol. 3, *Mull, Tiree, Coll & Northern Argyll* (Edinburgh); 1982, vol. 4, *Iona* (Edinburgh); 1984, vol. 5, *Islay, Jura & Colonsay* (Edinburgh); 1988, vol. 6, *Mid Argyll & Cowal, Prehistoric & Early Historic Monuments* (Edinburgh); 1992, vol. 7, *Mid Argyll & Cowal, Medieval & Later Monuments* (Edinburgh).
2. RCAHMS, 1997, *Argyll Castles in the care of Historic Scotland, extracts from RCAHMS Inventories of Argyll, Volumes 1, 2 & 7* (Edinburgh). See also Jane E A Dawson, 1995, 'Argyll: the enduring heartland', *Scottish Historical Review* 74.1, pp.88–94.
3. Geoffrey Stell, 2006, 'Castle Tioram: A Statement of Cultural Significance', http://www. historic-scotland.gov.uk/index/news/indepth/castletioram/castletioram-documents. html), pp.17–19.
4. RCAHMS, *Argyll* 3, no. 346, pl. 76B (http://canmore.org.uk/collection/581241).
5. RCAHMS, aerial photographs, DP 076799–800, taken 1 June 2009: http://canmore. org.uk/collection/1171011–12; R W Munro (ed.), 1961, *Monro's Western Isles of Scotland and Genealogies of the Clans 1549* (Edinburgh) referred to Loch Buie as 'ane fair braid loch with ane gude tak of hering and uther fischings'. The position of the boathouse is shown on plan in RCAHMS *Argyll* 3, fig. 232.

6. RCAHMS, *Argyll* 3, no. 340, fig. 221; J R Hunter, 1996, *Fair Isle: the archaeology of an island community*, pp.156–63 (Edinburgh); Ian Tait, 2012, *Shetland Vernacular Buildings 1600–1900* (Lerwick), pp.469–81.

7. RCAHMS, *Argyll* 5, no. 403; T E McNeill, 2014, 'Organising a Lordship: the castles of the MacDonalds of Dunivaig and the Glens', in Richard D Oram (ed.), *The Lordship of the Isles*, (Leiden), pp.211–26.

8. See above, note 3, and Geoffrey Stell, 2014, 'Castle Tioram and the MacDonalds of Clanranald: a western seaboard castle in context' in Oram, *Lordship of the Isles*, pp.271–96.

9. *RPC*, Henry Paton (ed.), 3rd ser., vol. 10 (1684–5), pp.773–6; Angus & Archibald Macdonald, 1900, *The Clan Donald* (Inverness), vol. 2, pp.306–8, 317–18.

10. John Stewart-Murray, 7th Duke of Atholl, 1908, *Chronicles of Atholl and Tullibardine Families* (Edinburgh), vol. 1, p.235. I am indebted to Athol Murray for this reference.

11. Stell, 'Castle Tioram and the MacDonalds', pp.286–8, and references cited.

12. Stell, 'Castle Tioram and the MacDonalds',pp. 288–9, and references cited. For Dùn Mhic Leoid, see RCAHMS, 1928, *Inventory of Monuments and Constructions in the Outer Hebrides, Skye and the Small Isles* (Edinburgh), no. 440.

13. For the 1654 map of Bute, see NLS, http://maps.nls.uk/atlas/blaeu/page.cfm?id=80, and for a cast impression of the obverse of the burgh seal of 1401, see National Museums Scotland, http://nms.scran.ac.uk/database/record.php?usi=000-180-001-742-C; Munro, *Monro's Western Isles*, p.48.

14. RCAHMS, *Argyll* 3, no. 334; *Argyll* 7, no. 119; and *Argyll* 1, no. 316 respectively. For Tarbert, see also A A M Duncan & A L Brown, 1957, 'Argyll and Isles in the Earlier Middle Ages', *PSAS* 90, pp.192–220, and J G Dunbar & A A M Duncan, 1971, 'Tarbert Castle: a contribution to the history of Argyll', *Scottish Historical Review* 50, pp.1–17.

15. Geoffrey Stell, 1988, 'By Land and Sea in Medieval and Early Modern Scotland', *Review of Scottish Culture* 4, pp.27–8.

16. Sir Arthur Mitchell (ed.), 1908, *Geographical Collections relating to Scotland made by Walter Macfarlane* (Edinburgh), vol. 3, p.167.

17. RCAHMS, *Argyll* 3, no. 345 p.209. A detailed report on the castle by Tom Addyman & Richard Oram in December 2012 at http://www.mingarycastletrust.co.uk/mingarycastletrust/history/analytical-and-historical-assessment/ does not appear to discuss its maritime access and context.

18. RCAHMS, *Argyll* 5, no. 402; and *Argyll* 3, no. 335 respectively.

19. Angus Graham, 1969, *Skipness* (Edinburgh); see also Angus Graham & W G Collingwood, 1923, 'Skipness Castle', *PSAS* 57, pp.285–7.

20. RCAHMS, *Argyll* 5, no. 403; J R N MacPhail (ed.), 1920, *Highland Papers* (Edinburgh), vol. 3, pp.141–2; G G Smith (ed.), 1895, *The Book of Islay: documents illustrating the history of the island* (Edinburgh), pp.156–7.

21. Mitchell (ed.), *Macfarlane Geographical Collections*, vol. 2, p.155.

22. RCAHMS, *Argyll* 3, nos 324 & 361; Munro, *Monro's Western Isles*, p.66; John Knox, 1787, *A Tour through the Highlands of Scotland, and the Hebride Isles, in 1786* (London), p.61.

23. David MacGibbon & Thomas Ross, 1889, *The Castellated and Domestic Architecture of Scotland*, vol. 3 (Edinburgh), pp.54–5.

24. I am grateful to Nigel Ruckley for sharing his preliminary findings. His paper on castle water-supply remains one of the few published explorations of an under-researched theme:

N A Ruckley, 1990, 'Water Supply of Medieval Castles in the United Kingdom', *Fortress* 7, pp.14–26. For the local geological background, see also Noel Fojut, 2006, 'Barra – the physical background' in A Kruse & A Ross (eds), *Barra and Skye: Two Hebridean Perspectives* (Edinburgh), pp.11–20.

25. RCAHMS, *Argyll 2*, no. 285

26. MacGibbon & Ross, *Castellated and Domestic Architecture*, vol. 3, pp.82–5; Roger Miket & David L Roberts, 1990, *The Mediaeval Castles of Skye & Lochalsh* (Portree), pp.89–91

27. Stell, 'Castle Tioram Statement', pp.12–13. See also Richard D Oram, 2008a, 'Royal and Lordly Residence in Scotland c.1050 to c.1250: an historiographical review and critical revision', *Antiquaries Journal* 88, pp.165–89. From a 'traditional' standpoint, castles were products of societies and regions which were to a greater or lesser degree militarised and where defence or, at the very least, security and protection were paramount. The castle's purpose is faithfully reflected in its overall form and features. In other words, its design and detail are regarded as strictly functional and are interpreted in evolutionary terms, undergoing modifications in response to attacking strengths and defensive needs. Throughout, there is a heavy emphasis on design typology and military capability, and military strategy is likewise seen as the key to determining and understanding a castle's location.

   Whilst accepting that defensive considerations may have been critical determinants of castle design and function, 'revisionists' have pointed to the emphasis which medieval societies themselves placed on status, display and symbolism. They have shown, inter alia, that patterns of castle- and tower-building are more closely related to periods of social and economic stability and wealth than to episodes of alleged social and political turbulence. Serious practical investments in time, money and materials apply to the creation of all castles, which are particularly demanding of resources and organisation. This is not to deny that the nature and siting of many castles, especially those which stand in what were medieval frontier-zones like the western seaboard, are likely to have assumed their forms and positions more as a result of considerations of defence and deterrence than of domestic convenience. But there was a balance inherent in any medieval secular building design, and recent studies serve as correctives to assumptions that a castle's many attributes – its commanding or isolated site, its plan-form, its high enclosure-walls or its detailed features at the wall-head or gatehouse – are wholly explicable in military or quasi-military terms and were invariably for real use.

28. RCAHMS, *Outer Hebrides*, and W Mackay Mackenzie, 1927, *The Mediaeval Castle in Scotland* (Edinburgh), passim.

29. Stewart Cruden, 1960 and later editions, *The Scottish Castle* (Edinburgh), passim. For biographical notes on Mackenzie Simpson and Cruden, see Geoffrey Stell, 2010, 'Scottish castellology and castellologists: a brief historical introduction', *Castellologica Bohemica* 12, pp.79–88.

30. MacGibbon & Ross, *Castellated and Domestic Architecture*, vol. 3, pp.41–113.

31. A T Hall, 1991, 'A Bibliography of W Douglas Simpson 1896–1968' in W Douglas Simpson, *Dunollie, Oban, Argyll* (Aberdeen), pp.1–22.

32. W Douglas Simpson in Roderick C MacLeod (ed.), 1938–9, *The Book of Dunvegan* (Aberdeen), vol. I, xv–xlviii, vol. II, xiii–xxxiii; W Douglas Simpson, 1938–68 (16 editions), *Dunvegan Castle, Isle of Skye: official guide* (Aberdeen).

33. W Douglas Simpson, 1941, 'Breachacha Castle in the Isle of Coll', *Transactions of the Glasgow Archaeological Society*, new ser. 10, pp.26–54; W Douglas Simpson, 1954,

'Castle Tioram, Moidart, Inverness-shire; and Mingary Castle, Ardnamurchan, Argyllshire', *Transactions of the Glasgow Archaeological Society*, new ser. 13, pp.70–90; W Douglas Simpson, 1967b, *Portrait of Skye and the Outer Hebrides* (London), pp.150, 154, 162–6.

34. D J Turner & J G Dunbar, 1970, 'Breachacha Castle, Coll: Excavations and Field Survey, 1965–8', *PSAS* 102, pp.155–87; J G Dunbar, 1978, 'Kisimul Castle, Isle of Barra', *Glasgow Archaeological Journal* 5, pp.25–43.

35. RCAHMS, *Outer Hebrides*, no. 369; Noel Fojut, Denys Pringle & Bruce Walker, 1994 (2nd edn 2003), *The Ancient Monuments of the Western Isles* (Edinburgh), p.34.

36. Stell, 'Castle Tioram Statement', pp.46–54; Stell, 'Castle Tioram and the MacDonalds', pp.279–84.

37. RCAHMS, *Argyll* 7, no 128.

38. RCAHMS, *Argyll* 7, no 118.

39. Geoffrey Stell, 1981, 'Late Medieval Defences in Scotland' in D H Caldwell (ed.), *Scottish Weapons and Fortifications 1100–1800* (Edinburgh), pp.23–4.

40. J G Dunbar, 1981, 'The Medieval Architecture of the Scottish Highlands' in Loraine Maclean (ed.), *The Middle Ages in the Highlands* (Inverness), pp.48–9.

41. Tadhg O'Keeffe, 2014, 'Halls, "hall-houses" and tower-houses in medieval Ireland: disentangling the needlessly entangled', *Castle Studies Group Journal* 27, pp.252–62; Tadhg O'Keeffe, 2015, *Medieval Irish Buildings 1100–1600* (Dublin), pp.222–4.

42. Geoffrey Stell, 2015, 'Scottish "hall-houses": the origins and development of a modern castellological concept', *Castle Studies Group Journal* 28, pp.134–9.

43. RCAHMS, *Argyll* 3, p.74. For timber as a possible building material of choice for early castle-builders, see Oram, 'Royal and Lordly Residence in Scotland', pp.182–3.

44. RCAHMS, *Argyll* 3, no. 333; David H Caldwell, 2006, 'Continuity and Change in 12th- and 13th-Century Scotland: an archaeological view', *Review of Scottish Culture* 18, pp.24, 27 n.48.

45. RCAHMS, *Argyll* 3, no. 345; http://www.mingarycastletrust.co.uk/mingarycastletrust/ history/analytical-and-historical-assessment/.

46. RCAHMS, *Argyll* 2, p.27, no.287; J H Lewis, 1996, 'Dunstaffnage Castle, Argyll & Bute: excavations in the north tower and east range, 1987–94', *PSAS* 126, pp.559–603.

47. RCAHMS, *Argyll* 2, p.23, no.243.

48. Richard Fawcett, 2011, *The Architecture of the Scottish Medieval Church* (New Haven & London), p.157.

49. W D H Sellar, 2004a, 'MacDougall, Ewen, lord of Argyll (d. in or after 1268)', *Oxford Dictionary of National Biography* (Oxford), http://www.oxforddnb.com/view/ article/49384.

50. W D H Sellar, 2004b, 'MacDougall, Alexander, lord of Argyll (d.1310)', *Oxford Dictionary of National Biography* (Oxford), http://www.oxforddnb.com/view/article/49385.

51. A A M Duncan (ed.), 1997, *John Barbour, The Bruce* (Edinburgh), pp.362–7; A A M Duncan, 1999a, 'The battles of Ben Cruachan', *West Highland Notes and Queries*, 2nd ser. 20, pp.3–20.

19

Summary and Synthesis

Barbara Crawford

THE PAPERS DELIVERED at the Galley-Castles Conference held on Barra in September 2015 were responding to Ian Macneil's clarion call in a paper presented to the Scottish Society for Northern Studies in 2002. This call was for more openness and comprehensiveness in galley-castle studies, and the need to approach the subject without being hidebound by the shibboleths of castle studies:

♦ That Hebridean and what he called 'Hebridean mainland' buildings lag behind the architectural examples of more southern cultures.

♦ That Hebridean and Hebridean mainland castles are late in the sequence unless proven to be early.

He also regretted the lack of contextual studies and too narrow a focus on individual examples, recommending the need for a broader canvas. Always at the heart of the issue was the dating of Kisimul Castle in Castle Bay and the historical circumstances surrounding the building, adaptation and re-building of this Hebridean castle gem.[1] The Conference, arranged in response to the present chief, Rory Macneil's, wish to further his father's studies into Hebridean galley-castles, was designed to stimulate a comprehensive and comparative approach. The papers presented by him and 19 invited speakers ranged over architectural and historical issues in the relevant geographical and maritime zones of the Hebrides, Ulster, the Isle of Man and northern Scottish locations.

Some of the fundamental issues which have exercised the thoughts and writings of castellologists in recent decades were referred to, in particular the 'revisionist trend' which has questioned the traditional vision of castles as primarily functioning for military purposes, and in particular for the defence of the lord and his family and following. The newer approach which understands such buildings as monuments built for the purpose of enhancing the lord's status was brought into several papers; although it was pointed out that this particular academic debate has not disturbed the more traditional approach to the function of castles north of the Border which is still understood to be primarily defensive (Richard Oram). But was this always the function of castle-building in Scotland? Is the expression of power and status by the owners and builders of these stone fortifications not just as relevant a factor?

The tower-houses of Ireland were described by Colin Breen as 'territorial expressions of power and control' and this mix of military function and political status in the Irish context is a useful combination to bear in mind when considering the significance of castles nearer to home, whether on the western seaboard or in the interior of Scotland. Indeed, the very concept of 'galley-castles' was said, no doubt correctly, 'to embody a traditional emphasis on command and control' (Geoffrey Stell).

A reaction against the traditional typological approach was evident in several of the presentations, and traditional classification according to the structural form and lay-out shown to be misleading and sometimes unhelpful (David Caldwell). The different kinds of enclosure, courtyard or 'ring-wall' castles, along with hall-houses and tower-houses help us to categorise the variables, but, as pointed out by Geoffrey Stell, these are 'relatively modern taxonomies' and cannot be fixed in time. He very helpfully discusses the scholarly history of the different architectural historians, and their theories about the succession of castle-types and dating of the western seaboard examples. Are they primarily 13th-century products, or could they be older in origin? Or maybe even later, the late-dating tendency being a feature of some of the more cautious architectural historians. If historical evidence is supposed to help with giving these famous castles a written pedigree in ascertaining their origin and development, this is sadly very rarely the case, as written evidence from the Hebrides in the medieval period is sparse and unhelpful.

In the absence of historical evidence, and with the many uncertainties about the building histories, it is very important that new evidence in the form of mortar dating is pursued; the current situation regarding the process of carbon-dating masonry fabric was presented by Mark Thacker. The extraction of charcoal from mortar is helping to give some specificity to the dating issues, and the samples taken from Castle Fincharn indicate that the wood for the fuel which was burned in the lime-kiln was felled within the decades 1220–1269 cal. AD (at 95.4% probability). It is likely that the lime mortar was then used fairly quickly after burning. However this scientific analytical process is only just beginning and it will take some time before a full series of carbon dates is produced and analysed for the many undated Hebridean castles. Even then it will have to be a range of estimations taken for the different building elements in these stone structures; for, as was often made clear by speakers, the individual buildings and annexes which go to make up the whole castle complex are from many different periods. The sources of the materials used to build the castles are being studied by Jamie MacPherson and the lime mortar and green stone featuring in Kisimul Castle is in the process of being analysed.

Another factor brought to our attention is that many of these medieval structures were located on sites which had been defensive for a long time – far back into the Iron Age and when hostile tribal societies were in process of establishing their social and military pre-eminence. A wide range of excavated duns, brochs and crannogs on the western seaboard have provided evidence of modification and re-use in the medieval centuries (John Raven). This raises the vitally important issue of geographical circumstances dictating the location of Hebridean castles on sites which had already proved suitable for Iron Age residences; in this respect the importance of maritime connections and locations defensible from seaborne attack is paramount. These circumstances are absolutely fundamental to the 'galley-castle' concept and the understanding of Kisimul's own status and role as a galley-castle. Movement by sea and maritime 'mobility and connectivity' in the western seaways was the theme of the powerful keynote lecture by Andrew MacDonald. He used the saga account of Sveinn Asleifarson's movements along the western seaways from Orkney to the Scilly Isles, and Earl Alan of Galloway's reference to his campaign in the Western Isles, moving from island to island with his army in his galleys; these historical accounts from contemporary sources vividly demonstrate how the seaways were the routeways for the ambitious and powerful. This wide-ranging keynote paper encapsulated many of the thematic requirements of the Conference's focus.

Maritime mobility and connectivity necessitate basic requirements for defensive refuges at the lordly seats – along with sheltered harbourage for their ships. The favoured places with natural harbours might be modified by stone breakwaters or landing places, and secluded locations were desirable (Colin Martin). Fortified islands with associated harbours in the extraordinary loch-strewn landscape of North Uist are a special case, while Kisimul's own favoured situation as a look-out place 'well located to exercise surveillance over the southern part of the Outer Hebrides and its approaches' is noted. These features are easy to recognise but the difficulties of travelling by sea are less well-known for those who do not sail on these island waters regularly. The recent voyages of reconstructions of Viking longships and Hebridean birlinns have brought to the fore the dangers of sea-crossings and of strong currents and tidal flow, as elaborated by Donald McWhannell, who also provides performance-tables for these reconstructed vessels. There was an important balance between rowing performance and sailing performance in order to achieve the maximum flexibility in different requirements for different purposes and in different maritime situations. The evidence that galleys were built and sailed for over 900 years gives us proof that they were very appropriate vessels for the Norse-Gaelic seaways throughout this period.

The mention of Viking longships brings to the fore the Scandinavian element, which has to be considered as part of the cultural and especially maritime cultural background. Alan Macniven explores the Scandinavian heritage in the Hebrides with respect to defensive structures, galley-castle sites and the importance of ships and harbours. Above all he brings in the toponymic evidence which is an ever-present reminder of the blending of the Gaelic and Norse languages. The later-medieval vessel which was dominant in these coastal waters was the 'birlinn', a ship-term derived from the Norse *byrðingr*. which was the term for a merchant ship.

The west Highland galley is a significant cultural icon, appearing in a range of Gaelic poems and on Hebridean grave-slabs and crosses (Donald McWhannell). In the absence of any known wreck-sites which would provide important material remains of these ships we are reliant on the spoken and written word and sculptured surviving images. The castles have of course survived and there are plenty of them in the Hebrides and along the west Scottish coastal waters. Defining them as galley-castles is not always – indeed rarely – easy. The galley requirement is not absolutely mandatory, and most of the papers went beyond that when looking at large numbers of fortified sites and medieval lordly structures. The variety and variability of the many castles discussed – and presented on the screen – provided a wonderful tapestry of these dramatic buildings in the landscape, and of the families which built them and the historical circumstances which brought them into existence. How we view them, and how people in the past viewed them, is part of their fascination and the dramatic nature of the reason for their existence. The orally-transmitted folklore and stories reveal the role that they played in Hebridean society, as in 1598 when Sir Lachlan Mor rashly sailed *tuathal* (anti-clockwise or against the sun) out of the Maclean galley harbour at Eilan Amalaig on his way to Islay for a showdown with his nephew, Sir James of Dunivaig. He also failed to heed the warnings of *Doideag Mhuileach* a 'wise woman' and needless to say Sir Lachlan perished in the attempt (John MacFarlane).

The size of the area needed to provide harbourage for a fleet of galleys can be used to estimate the number of galleys, although sometimes this is known from historical evidence. In the case of Alasdair Crotach, chief of the Macleods, it was stipulated in 1498 that he had to provide the service of one galley of 26 oars and two of 16 oars from his lands in Harris and Skye, and these lands were assessed as supporting 1200 warriors (which actually indicates that he would have had to provide possibly 6 galleys from the Skye lands alone according to David Caldwell). Some castles had a significant role as administrative and supply centres for naval expeditions, such as Claig Castle on Jura where a naval force of 32 galleys, along with other boats preparing to sail to Lough Foyle in Northern Ireland, were recorded by a Bristol merchant in 1569 who saw them as he sailed through the Sound of Jura. He was informed that there were 4000 men mustered there to sail in the galleys. The castle is close to a sheltered beach, but it is hard to imagine today that 4000 men could have embarked from that location.

Claig Castle, along with Kisimul and Innis Chonnel and Fraoch Eilean (both on Loch Awe), are only accessible by boat, and therefore fully worthy of the galley-castle designation. But as David Caldwell points out many of the castles in the west would have had access from the land also, even some on islands, like Achanduin on Lismore. Territorial considerations were important to castle-owners, especially those who had nearby lands to farm and estates to administer. Geography is everything when considering the role and function of medieval castles and maritime geography in particular where galley-castles are concerned. The seaways and sailing routes are basic to our appreciation of the role of galley-castles in the Hebridean and west Highland story; and Kisimul's role is only understood in the context of maritime geography close to hand in Barra, and further afield in the Hebrides, as well as in Hebridean history.

Hebridean history is clan history and the building and location of galley-castles cannot be understood without knowing about the different branches of the clans who lived in them. David Sellar guided the Conference through the complexities of the Dunsleve kindred, the leading families of Cowal, Knapdale and Glassary (the MacSweens, Lamonts and MacLachlans). He discusses the disputed origin of the MacNeils of Barra and the MacNeills of Taynish and Gigha, and provides a useful update on the state of DNA research. Lasting answers on the vexed issues of the Celtic or Norse origins of many of these Hebridean families cannot be given yet, and indeed may never be entirely decided, as the ethnic mix of these two cultural types in this locality is surely a foregone conclusion.

A spotlight is cast on the activities of Clan MacNeil in the Hebridean archipelago – and further afield – by Domhnall Uilleam Stiùbhart in his study of the life and times of the 'charismatic' Ruairidh an Tartair, chief of the MacNeils in the final quarter of the 16th and the first quarter of the 17th centuries. As he explains, the clan operated in three different geographical zones – and archipelagos; the local micro-archipelago of Barra and the surrounding islands, the regional meso-archipelago of the Outer Hebrides and the western seaboard of the Scottish Gaidhealtachd, within the wider macro-archipelago of the north-east Atlantic island group of Scotland, Ireland and England. The evidence shows that the MacNeils of Barra operated within that wider maritime framework, to a greater extent than other Hebridean kindreds. Perhaps constrained by the lack of income (and timber) from mainland territorial estates, the MacNeils looked further afield for possibilities of plunder and commercial opportunities. The clan chiefs were at any rate 'significant players in the politics of the western Gaidhealtachd' at this time.

It is hoped that Ian Macneil would have been satisfied that his call for more openness and comprehensiveness was met by the cultural mix of papers and the extensive nature of topics covered. The geographical range was impressive; to understand the variety of maritime castles and their different roles in Ulster, Man and Orkney can only enhance our understanding of the Hebridean situation and Kisimul's own particular circumstances. The Manx evidence consists of three 'formal types' – promontory forts, which abound in Man; motte-and-bailey castles or timber defences (which we know about from the evidence of Magnus Barelegs' saga which tells that he constructed such forts when seeking to impose his authority on the Isle of Man in the late 11th and early 12th centuries); and the superb stone castles at Peel and Rushen which were certainly important naval bases (Peter Davey). Man's particular maritime circumstances in the middle of the northern part of the Irish Sea with hostile kingdoms to the east, west and north meant that its very defence relied on fleets. Where the wood came from to build the galleys is however uncertain, and this is an issue which must have faced castle-builders throughout the Western Isles (as also the Northern Isles). We have always to remember that Man was the political centre of the Kingdom of the Isles in the early period of castle-building, and social and cultural links between the rulers of Man and the myriad castle lords in the Hebrides should have been close. Man itself was of course open to influences coming in from many other directions.

Such influences would have affected the use of castles for political and administrative purposes and not only naval. As is pointed out by Peter Davey the Manx castles 'acted as garrisons, centres of administration, including justice, internal and external trade and for the collection of taxes in cash and in kind'. Maritime lordships in Ireland, which also functioned as key instruments of control of the local economic resources, may not have functioned quite according to the definition of Hebridean galley-castles (Colin Breen). By the later medieval and early-modern period the importance of fishing brought a marked change and meant that the peripheral western maritime zones were becoming actually part of the broader North Atlantic social world. Commerce was an increasingly important element and some castles (such as Claig at the south end of Jura) would have been well located as a toll-collection point (Tom McNeill). Traditional galley assembly-points such as Claig were well suited to act as tax-collection points and market sites.

Moving further outwith the Hebridean maritime zone takes us into different cultural contexts with varying political needs and requirements. The castles of Orkney – some of which are early examples of stone castles – are very much tied into the Norse social and cultural world of the earls of Orkney (and Caithness), whose ships would be direct descendants of the Viking longships (Sarah Jane Gibbon). There is no doubting that the earls had fleets of longships and they would need secure harbours and anchorages to keep them safe from attack. But the evidence of fortified castles is not obviously linked to the security of fleets of warships, although they do seem to watch over key sea-routes. It may be that the castles in Orkney and Caithness were built more for the internal security of the earl or his family and military following, rather than for defence against external attack.

The Barra Conference was designed to stimulate a comprehensive approach by bringing together those researchers and practitioners whose expertise covered a diverse range of disciplines. These form the source evidence which we need to master for a full understanding of the historical circumstances surrounding the building and purpose of Kisimul Castle and the MacNeil lordship. There can be no doubt that Kisimul was a 'galley-castle' but the message coming out of many of the speakers' presentations was that this was only one aspect of the purpose and significance of the many castles which were discussed, in the Hebrides, in Man and Ireland and in the north of Scotland. The plan and design of the buildings seems less significant than it used to be to an older generation of architectural historians. Nowadays what is considered important is their role as seats of lordship, their significance as places from where the clan chiefs or their followers governed their estates, administered their financial affairs and oversaw the trade-routes and the collection of tribute.

All this would have been understandable to those who dwelt in the castles, and probably considered unexceptional. What was exceptional in their lives dominated by the seas and waterways was the elegant and visually appealing longship or galley. It was as enviable a mark of status as their castle was, and probably considered to be a 'must-have' possession. It gave them 'sea-power' and the ability to traverse swiftly the coastal waters which surrounded their residences and lands. Gaelic poetry expresses some of the brilliance of the maritime world and the high regard for its vessels:

Gold and ivory inlaid swords deck
the prow of the brown-sailed barques;
beside a row of bright-tipped spears
shields against the ships' long flanks …

They'd never neglect one of their ships
full of strength and firm resilience
their golden black-crested masts
which they raise in the harbour's eddies

Many a man with sword or breastplate,
many a fit man surpassing his leap,
against the mane of the mad, fierce ocean,
hitting the smooth-peaked ships' height

Artur Dall MacGurcaigh, *Eoin Mac Suibhne's Voyage to Castle Sween* (c.1310).[2]

Notes

1. I R Macneil, 2006, 'Kisimul Castle and the Origins of Hebridean Galley-Castles: Preliminary Thoughts', in A Kruse and A Ross (eds), *Barra and Skye: Two Hebridean Perspectives* (Edinburgh), pp.21–46.
2. *The Triumph Tree. Scotland's Earliest Poetry AD550–1350*, transl. T O Clancy, 1998, pp.302–04.

Bibliography

Abbreviations

BAR	*British Archaeological Reports*
CANMORE	The online front-end for Historic Environment Scotland's database of site records, see https://canmore.org.uk.
CDI	*Calendar of Documents relating to Ireland*
CDS	*Calendar of Documents relating to Scotland*
CRMI	*Cronica regum Mannie & Insularum: chronicles of the kings of Man and the Isles BL Cotton Julius Avii*, ed. and transl. G Broderick, 1996, 2nd edn. Douglas: Manx National Heritage.
CW	Carmichael Watson collection, Edinburgh University Library
HES	Historic Environment Scotland
HMSO	Her Majesty's Stationery Office
HS	*Icelandic Sagas and other historical documents relating to the settlements and descents of the Northmen on the British Isles*, vol. 4: 'The saga of Hacon and a fragment of the saga of Magnus'.
IED	Cleasby, R, Vigfusson, G & Craigie, WA, 1957, *An Icelandic–English Dictionary* (2nd edn). Oxford: Clarendon Press.
LCS	*Leabhar Chlainne Suibhne*, P Walsh (ed.), 1920. Dublin: Dollard.
Lyon Register	*An Ordinary of Arms contained in the Public Register of all Arms and Bearings in Scotland*, Sir James Balfour Paul (ed.), 1893. Edinburgh: William Green & Sons.
NLS	National Library of Scotland, Edinburgh
NRS	National Records of Scotland, Edinburgh
OS	*Orkneyinga saga: the history of the earls of Orkney*
PSAS	*Proceedings of the Society of Antiquaries of Scotland*
RCAHMS	Royal Commission on the Ancient and Historical Monuments of Scotland
RPC	*Register of the Privy Council of Scotland*
SAIR	*Scottish Archaeological Internet Reports*

Manuscript sources

Clan Donald Archives, Armadale, Skye, NRAS 3273/4121/2.

Edinburgh University Library, Carmichael Watson MS 2, 7, 90 and 95.

Glasgow City Archives (Mitchell Library), MS 591702, Hector Mackenzie's manuscript history of the Mackenzies, 1710.

Inveraray Castle Archives
    Bundle 63, Rev. Alexander Cooper to Synod, 3 August 1697.
    Bundle 539, Presbytery of Skye to Synod of Argyll on behalf of Master John Morison, 1699.
    Bundle 1759, Rev. Alexander Cooper's Address to Synod, 6 June 1699.

Macneil, I R, Spreadsheets of data and associated maps on Galley-Castles. Private Collection. http://www.ed.ac.uk/literatures-languages-cultures/delc/nordic-research/resources.

National Library of Scotland
    MS ADV.26.3.7; 29.4.2; 33/2/7; 34.2.8; 72.1.1 ('MS 1467')
    MS 1305
    MS 2134
National Records of Scotland
    CH2/557 Records of the Synod of Argyll
    D11/53 and 59
    GD1/201/99
    GD305/1/68, Cromartie Muniments
    PA7, Supplementary Warrants and Parliamentary Papers
    RD1/27 and 427, Register of Deeds
    RH4/93/3–4, "Report of Voyage" by Edward Nixon and James Watson 20/06/1732.
School of Scottish Studies, University of Edinburgh
    Maclagan MS 8223
    SA 1976/190 and 191

Printed primary sources

The Acts of Alexander III King of Scots 1249–1286, C J Neville & G G Simpson (eds), 2012, *Regesta Regum Scottorum* IV pt I. Edinburgh: Edinburgh University Press.

Acts of the Lords of the Isles, 1336–1493, J Munro & R W Munro (eds), 1986. Edinburgh: Scottish History Society.

Acts of the Parliaments of Scotland, T Thomson & C Innes (eds), 11 vols, 1814–75. Edinburgh: HMSO.

Adam of Bremen, 2002, *History of the Archbishops of Hamburg-Bremen*, transl. Francis J Tschan, new intro. & selected bibliography by Timothy Reuter. New York: Columbia University Press.

Adamnan, Abbot of Hy, *Life of St. Columba founder of Hy*, W Reeves (ed.), 1874. Edinburgh.

Adomnán's Life of Columba, A O Anderson & M O Anderson (eds and transl.), 1961. Edinburgh: Thomas Nelson.

The Aeneid of Virgil translated into Scottish verse by Gawain Douglas, G Dundas (ed.), 1839. Edinburgh: Bannatyne Club, 64.

Annala Rioghachta Eireann: Annals of the Kingdom of Ireland by the Four Masters from the Earliest Period to the Year 1616, J O'Donovan (ed. and transl.), 7 vols, 1851. Dublin: Hodges & Smith.

Annala Uladh: Annals of Ulster: otherwise, Annala Senait, annals of Senat: a chronicle of Irish affairs, W H Hennessy & B MacCarthy (ed. and transl.), 4 vols, 1887–1901. Dublin: HMSO, http://www.ucc.ie/celt/published/T100001B/index.html.

Annals of Connacht, A. Martin Freeman (ed. and transl.), 1970, http://www.ucc.ie/celt/published/T100011/index.html.

Annals of the Four Masters, s.a.1269, Paul Walsh (ed.), 1920. Dublin, see University College Cork's online corpus of electronic texts: http://www.celt.ucc.ie/index.html.

Annals of Loch Cé: a Chronicle of Irish Affairs from AD 1014 to AD 1590, W M Hennessy (ed. and transl.), 1871, 2 vols. London: Longman.

Annals of Tigernach, W Stokes (ed.), 1897, see University College Cork's online corpus of electronic texts: http://www.ucc.ie/celt/published/T100002A.html.

Annals of Ulster, see University College Cork's online corpus of electronic texts: http://www.ucc.ie/celt/online/T100001A/.

The Asloan Manuscript: a Miscellany in Prose and Verse written by John Asloan in the Reign of James the Fifth, W A Craigie (ed.), 1923, vol. 1. Edinburgh: Scottish Text Society.

Atlas of UK Marine Renewable Energy Resources, 2008, ABPmer, http.//www.renewables atlas. info/@Crown Copyright.

Barbour, John, *The Bruce*, 1997, A A M Duncan (ed. and transl.), repr. with corrections 2007. Edinburgh: Canongate.

Benediktsson, J (ed.), 1986, *Íslendingabók, Landnámabók. Íslenzk Fornrit I. Bindi*. Rejkjavík: Hið Íslenzka Fornritafélag.

Bower, Walter, *Scotichronicon*. D E R Watt *et al.* (eds), 9 vols, 1987–97. Aberdeen: Aberdeen University Press.

Calendar of Documents Relating to Ireland, 1171–1307, H S Sweetman (ed.), 5 vols, 1875–86 London: Longman.

Calendar of Documents Relating to Scotland Preserved in Her Majesty's Public Record Office, London, vols 1–4, J Bain (ed.), 1881–88, London: HMSO; vol. 5, J D Galbraith & G G Simpson (eds), 1896. Edinburgh: Scottish Record Office.

Calendar of Material relating to Ireland from the High Court of Admiralty Examinations, John C Appleby (ed.), 1992. Dublin: Irish Manuscripts Commission.

Calendar of Papal Letters xvii, part 1, 1492–1503, A Fuller (ed.), 1994. Dublin: Irish Manuscripts Commission.

Calendar of State Papers Domestic, reign of Elizabeth, 7 vols, 1856–71, vol. 3 *1595–97,* M A E Green (ed.), 1869. London: Longmans, Green, Reader & Dyer.

Calendar of State Papers Relating to Ireland, reigns of Henry VII to Elizabeth, H C Hamilton, E G Atkinson *et al.* (eds) 11 vols, 1860–1911. London: HMSO.

Calendar of State Papers Relating to Scotland, vol. 11 (1593–95), A I Cameron (ed.), 1936; vol. 12 (1595–97), Montague Spencer Giuseppi (ed.), 1952; vol. 13 parts 1 & 2 (1597–1603), J M Mackie (ed.), 1969. Edinburgh: HM General Register House/HMSO.

Chronica magistri Rogeri de Houedene, T. Arnold (ed.), 4 vols, 1868–71. London: Longman.

Chronica Regum Manniae et Insularam, P A Munch (ed.), 1860. Christiania: Brøgger & Christie.

Corpus Iuris Hibernici, D A Binchy (ed.), 1978. Dublin: Dublin Institute of Advanced Studies.

Cronica Regum Mannie & Insularum: Chronicles of the Kings of Man and the Isles (BL Cotton Julius Avii), G Broderick (ed. and transl.), 1996. 2nd edn, Douglas: Manx National Heritage.

De Gestis Regum Anglorum. History of the English Kings, William of Malmesbury, R A B Mynors, R Thomson & M Winterbottom (ed. and transl.), 1998–99. Oxford: Clarendon Press.

Documents Illustrative of the History of Scotland from the Death of King Alexander the Third to the Accession of Robert Bruce, J Stevenson (ed.), 2 vols, 1870. Edinburgh: HM General Register House.

Duanaire na Sracaire (Songbook of the Pillagers). Anthology of Scotland's Gaelic Verse to 1600, W McLeod & M Bateman (eds), M Bateman (transl.), 2007. Edinburgh: Birlinn.

Dwelly, E, 1911, *The Illustrated Gaelic-English Dictionary* (facsimile edn 2011). Edinburgh: Birlinn.

Early Sources of Scottish History AD 500 to 1286, A O Anderson (ed. and transl.), 1922. 2 vols, Edinburgh: Oliver & Boyd; reprinted 1990, Stamford: Paul Watkins.

Egils Saga Skalla-Grimssonar. Islenzk Fornrit II. Bindi: 363–409, A Nordal (ed.), 1933. Reykjavik.

Egil's Saga, H Palsson & P Edwards (eds), 1976. Harmondsworth: Penguin.

Eric the Red's Saga, Verses from, R Perkins (ed.), 2011. London: Viking Society for Northern Research.

Expugnatio Hibernica. The Conquest of Ireland, A B Scott & F X Martin (ed. and transl.), 1978. Dublin: Royal Irish Academy.

Fasti Ecclesiae Scoticanae Medii Aevi ad Annum 1638, D E R Watt & A L Murray (eds), 2003. Edinburgh: Scottish Record Society.

Foedera, Conventiones, Literae et Cujuscunque Generis Acta Publica, Inter Reges Angliae et Alios Quosvis Imperatores, T Rymer (ed.), 1739–45, 10 vols. Hagae Comitis: Johannem Neulme.

John of Fordun's Chronicle of the Scottish Nation, W F Skene (ed.), F J H Skene (transl.), vol. 2, 1872. Edinburgh.

Giraldus Cambrensis, The Topography of Ireland, T Wright (ed.), T Forester (transl.), 1894. London.

Hákonar saga Hákonarsonar, Þ Hauksson & S Jakobsson (eds), 2013, 2 vols. Reykjavík: Hid Íslenzka Fornritafélag.

Historia Norwegie, I Ekrem & L B Mortensen (eds), P Fisher (transl.), 2003. Copenhagen: Museum Tusculanum Press.

Historie and Life of King James the Sext, T Thomson (ed.), 1825. Edinburgh: Bannatyne Club.

History and Topography of Ireland, Gerald of Wales, J J O'Meara (transl.), 1982, revised edn. London: Penguin.

Hrafns Saga Sveinbjarnarsonar, G Helgadóttir (ed.), 1987. Oxford: Oxford University Press.

Icelandic–English Dictionary, R Cleasby, G Vigfusson & W A Craigie (eds), 2nd edn, 1957. Oxford: Clarendon Press.

Icelandic Sagas and other Historical Documents Relating to the Settlements and Descents of the Northmen on the British Isles, vol. 2, *Hakonar Saga, and a fragment of Magnus Saga, with appendices*, Sir G Dasent (transl.) & G Vigfusson (ed.), 1894. London: Eyre & Spottiswoode.

Icelandic Sagas and Other Historical Documents Relating to the Settlements and Descents of the Northmen of the British Isles, vol. 2, *Hákonar Saga, and a Fragment of Magnus Saga, with Appendices*, G Vigfusson (ed.), 2012. Cambridge: Cambridge University Press.

Icelandic Sagas and Other Historical Documents Relating to the Settlements and Descents of Northmen on the British Isles, vol. 4, *The saga of Hacon, and a fragment of the saga of Magnus, with appendices*, Sir G Dasent (transl.) & G Vigfusson (ed.), 1894. London: Eyre & Spottiswoode; new edition, 2012. Cambridge: Cambridge University Press.

Íslendingabók, Landnámabók. Íslenzk Fornrit I. Bindi, J Benediktsson (ed.), 1986. Rejkjavík: Hið Íslenzka Fornritafélag.

The King's Mirror (Speculum Regale-Konungs Skuggsjá), L M Larsen (transl.), 1917. New York: Twayne.

Leabhar Clainne Suibhne, an account of the Mac Sweeney families in Ireland, with pedigrees, P Walsh (ed.), 1920. Dublin.

Lindsay, Alexander, *A Rutter of the Scottish Seas Circa 1540*, I H Adams & G Fortune (eds), 1980, (abridged from the original ms by A B Taylor). Greenwich: National Maritime Museum.

Lyon Register: An Ordinary of Arms contained in the Public Register of all Arms and Bearings in Scotland, Sir James Balfour Paul (ed.), 1893. Edinburgh: William Green & Sons.

Martin, Martin, *A Description of the Western Islands of Scotland Circa 1695* and *A Voyage to St Kilda*, with *A Description of the Occidental i.e. Western Islands of Scotland* by Donald Monro, W J Withers & R W Munro (eds), 1999. Edinburgh: Birlinn.

Monro, Donald, *A Description of the Occidental i.e. Western Islands of Scotland*, in Martin Martin, *A Description of the Western Islands of Scotland Circa 1695* and *A Voyage to St Kilda*, with *A Description of the Occidental i.e. Western Islands of Scotland* by Donald Monro, W J Withers & R W Munro (eds), 1999. Edinburgh: Birlinn.

Monumenta de Insula Manniae, or a Collection of National Documents Relating to the Isle of Man, 3 vols, J R Oliver (ed. and transl.), 1860–62. Douglas: Manx Society.

[*Old*] *Statistical Account of Scotland*, Sir J Sinclair (ed.), 21 vols, 1791–9. Edinburgh.

Orkneyinga Saga: a New Translation with Introduction and Notes, A B Taylor (transl.), 1938. Edinburgh: Oliver & Boyd.

Orkneyinga Saga, F Guðmundsson (ed.), 1965, *Íslenzk Fornrit* 34. Reykjavík.

Orkneyinga Saga: the History of the Earls of Orkney, H Pálsson & P Edwards (transl.), 1978 and 1981. London: Penguin.

The Records of the Parliaments of Scotland to 1707, K M Brown *et al.* (eds), 2007–15. St Andrews.

Register of the Great Seal of Scotland, 1306–1668, J M Thomson *et al.* (eds), 11 vols 1882–1914. Edinburgh.

Register of the Privy Council of Scotland, 3rd ser., Henry Paton (ed.), vols 4, 7, 8, 9, 10, 11 and 14. Edinburgh.

Registrum Monasterii de Passelet, J Stuart (ed.), 1832. Edinburgh: Maitland Club.

Rotuli Chartarum in Turri Londinensi Asservati vol. I.1, 1699–1716, T D Hardy (ed.), 1837. London: Eyre & Spottiswoode.

Scotichronicon by Walter Bower in Latin and English, D E R Watt *et al.* (eds), 9 vols, 1987–97. Aberdeen: Aberdeen University Press.

Snorri Sturluson: Heimskringla I (Hákonar saga góða). Íslenzk Fornrit XXVI. Bindi, B Aðalbjarnarson (ed.), 2002b, 4th edn. Reykjavík: Hið Íslenzka Fornafélag.

Snorri Sturluson: Heimskringla III (Magnúss saga berfœtts). Íslenzk Fornrit XXVIII. Bindi, B Aðalbjarnarson (ed.), 2002a, 4th edn. Reykjavík: Hið Íslenzka Fornafélag.

Snorri Sturluson: Heimskringla: History of the Kings of Norway, L Hollander (transl.), 1991. Austin TX: University of Texas Press for American Scandinavian Foundation.

State Papers, and Miscellaneous Correspondence of Thomas, Earl of Melros, vol. 1, 1837. Edinburgh: Abbotsford Club.

The Statutes of the Isle of Man, vol. 1, 1417–1824, J F Gill (ed.), 1883. London: Eyre & Spottiswoode.

Sverris saga, G Indrebø (ed.), 1920. Kristiana: Riksarkivet.

Sverrissaga: The Saga of King Sverri of Norway, J Sephton (transl.), 1899. London: D. Nutt. Repr. 1992, Felinfach: Llanerch.

The Triumph Tree: Scotland's Earliest Poetry, 550–1350, T O Clancy (ed. and transl.), 1998. Edinburgh: Canongate.

Vitae Dunkeldensis Ecclesiae Episcoporum a Prima Sedes Fundatione ad Annum MDXV, A Myln (ed.), 1823. Edinburgh: Bannatyne Club.

William of Malmesbury, *De Gestis Regum Anglorum. History of the English Kings*, R Mynors, R Thomson & M Winterbottom (eds and transl.), 1998–99. Oxford: Clarendon Press.

Secondary sources

Abercromby, P, 1715, *The Martial Achievements of the Scots Nation*, 2 vols. Edinburgh: R Freebairn.

Addyman, Tom & Oram, Richard, 2012, http://www.mingarycastletrust.co.uk/mingarycastletrust/ history/analytical-and-historical-assessment/.

Ahronson, K, 2015, *Into the Ocean: Vikings, Irish and Environmental Change in Iceland and the North*. Toronto: University of Toronto Press.

Alcock, L & Alcock, E, 1987, 'Reconnaissance Excavations on Early Historic Fortifications and other Royal Sites in Scotland, 1974–84: 2, Excavations at Dunollie Castle, Oban, Argyll, 1978', *PSAS* 117: 119–48.

Alcock, L & Alcock, E A, 1990, 'Reconnaissance Excavations on Early Historic Fortifications and other Royal Sites in Scotland, 1974–84: 4, Excavations at Alt Clut, Clyde Rock, Strathclyde, 1974–75', *PSAS* 120: 95–150.

Allen, A, 1995, The Maritime Cultural Landscape of Viking and Late Norse Orkney, PhD thesis, University of Durham, http://etheses.dur.ac.uk/1040/.

Anderson, P D, 1992, *Black Patie: the Life and Times of Patrick Stewart, Earl of Orkney, Lord of Shetland*. Edinburgh: John Donald.

Appleby, John C, 2009, *Under the Bloody Flag: Pirates of the Tudor Age*. Stroud: History Press.

Armit, Ian, 1996, *The Archaeology of Skye and the Western Isles*. Edinburgh: Edinburgh University Press.

Ashby, Steven P, 2015, 'What Really Caused the Viking Age? The Social Content of Raiding and Exploration', *Archaeological Dialogues* 22: 89–106.

Bagge, S, 2010, *From Viking Stronghold to Christian Kingdom: State Formation in Norway, c.900–1350*. Copenhagen: Museum Tusculanum Press.

Ballin-Smith, B, 2013, 'Iain Crawford's Udal: the Key to Ceramic Traditions of the Western Seaboard?', *Medieval Ceramics* 34: 39–44.

Bannerman, J W M, 1974, *Studies in the History of Dalriada*. Edinburgh: Scottish Academic Press.

Bannerman, J, 1977, 'The Lordship of the Isles', in J Brown (ed.), *Scottish Society in the Fifteenth Century*: 209–40. London: E Arnold.

Bannerman, J, 1993, 'MacDuff of Fife', in A Grant & K Stringer (eds), *Medieval Scotland*: 20–38. Edinburgh: Edinburgh University Press.

Barrett, J H, 2005, 'Svein Asleifarson and 12th-Century Orcadian Society', in O Owen (ed.), *The World of Orkneyinga Saga: the broad-cloth Viking trip*': 213–23. Kirkwall: The Orcadian.

Barrett J H, 2007a, 'Sea Fishing and Long-Term Socio-Economic Trends in North-Western Europe', in J Graham-Campbell & M Valor (eds), *The Archaeology of Medieval Europe Vol. 1: Eighth to Twelfth Centuries AD*: 201–03. Aarhus: Aarhus University Press.

Barrett, J H, 2007b, 'The Pirate Fishermen: The Political Economy of a Medieval Earldom', in B Ballin-Smith, S Taylor & G Williams (eds), *West Over Sea: Studies in Scandinavian Sea-Borne Expansion and Settlement before 1300*: 299–340. Leiden: Brill.

Barrett, J H (ed.), 2012a, *Being an Islander: Production and Identity at Quoygrew, Orkney, AD 900–1600*. Cambridge: MacDonald Institute for Archaeological Research.

Barrett, J H, 2012b, 'Viking Age and Medieval Orkney', in J H Barrett (ed.), *Being an Islander: Production and Identity at Quoygrew, Orkney, AD 900–1600*. Cambridge: McDonald Institute for Archaeological Research.

Barrett, J, Nicholson, R & Cerón-Carrasco, R, 1999, 'Archaeo-Ichthyological Evidence for Long-Term Socio-Economic Trends in Northern Scotland: 3500 BC to AD 1500', *Journal of Archaeological Science* 26: 353–88.

Barrow, G W S, 1980, *The Anglo Norman Era in Scottish History.* Oxford: Oxford University Press.

Barrow, G W S, 2003, *Kingship and Unity: Scotland AD 1000–1300.* 2nd edn, Edinburgh: Edinburgh University Press.

Barrowman, R C, 2015, 'A Local Response to a Wider Situation: the Archaeology of the Clan Stronghold of Dùn Èistean, Isle of Lewis', *Post-Medieval Archaeology* 49.1: 17–56.

Bartlett, R, 1993, *The Making of Europe: Conquest, Colonization and Cultural Change 950–1350.* London: Penguin.

Bennett, J, 2009, *Sailing into the Past.* Barnsley: Seaforth.

Bennett, M J, 2015, 'English rule confirmed: the Isle of Man 1389–1406', in S Duffy & H Mytum (eds), *A New History of the Isle of Man: The Medieval Period*: 170–84. Liverpool: Liverpool University Press.

Bersu, G, 1949, 'A Promontory Fort on the Shore of Ramsey Bay, Isle of Man', *Antiquaries Journal* 29: 62–79.

Besteman, J C, 1999, 'Viking Silver on Wieringen', in H Sarfatij (ed.), *In Discussion with the Past.* Zwolle: SPA Uitgevers.

Beuermann, I, 2007, 'Masters of the Narrow Sea: Forgotten Challenges to Norwegian Rule in Man and the Isles, 1079–1266', *Acta Humaniora*, Faculty of Humanities, University of Oslo.

Beveridge, E, 1911, *North Uist; its Archaeology and Topography.* Wiltshire: Cromwell Press.

Beveridge, E & Callander, J G, 1931, 'Excavation of an Earth-House at Foshigarry, and a Fort, Dun Thomaidh, in North Uist', *PSAS* 65: 299–357.

Beveridge, E & Callandar, J G, 1932, 'Earth-Houses at Garry Iochdrach and Bac Mhic Connain, in North Uist', *PSAS* 66: 32–66.

Biddle, M & Kjølbye-Biddle, B, 1992, 'Repton and the Vikings', *Antiquity* 66: 36–51.

Biddle, M. & Kjølbye-Biddle, B, 2001, 'Repton and the "Great Heathen Army", 873–4', in J Graham-Campbell *et al.* (eds), *Vikings and the Danelaw: Select Papers from the Proceedings of the Thirteenth Viking Congress, Nottingham and York, 21–30 August 1997.* Oxford: Oxbow.

Blair, J, 1993, 'Hall and Chamber: English Domestic Planning 1000–1250', in G Meirion-Jones & M Jones, *Manorial Domestic Buildings in England and Northern France*: 1–21. London: Society of Antiquaries.

Boardman, S, 2006, *The Campbells 1250–1513.* Edinburgh: John Donald.

Boffetta, G, Celani, A, Dezzani, D & Seminara, A, 2008, 'How Winding is the Coast of Britain? Conformal Invariance of Rocky Shorelines', *Geophys. Res. Lett.* 35.3 (http://www.fisica.unige.it/~seminara/publications/rocky.pdf).

Borradaile, G, 1970, 'The West Limb of the Loch Awe Syncline and the Associated Cleavage Fan', *Geological Magazine* 107.5: 459–67.

Borradaile, G, 1977, 'The Dalradian Rocks of Northern Loch Awe', *Scottish Journal of Geology* 13: 155–64.

Bowen, E G, 1970, 'Britain and the British Seas', in D Moore (ed.), *The Irish Sea Province in Archaeology and History*: 13–29. Cardiff: Cambrian Archaeological Association.

Bowen, E G, 1977, *Saints, Seaways and Settlements in the Celtic lands.* Cardiff: University of Wales Press.

Branigan, K, 2012, *Barra: Episodes from an Island's History.* Stroud: Amberley Publishing.

Branigan, K & Foster, P, 2002, *Barra and the Bishop's Isles.* Stroud: Tempus.

Breen, C, 2001, 'The Maritime Cultural Landscape in Gaelic Ireland', in P J Duffy, D Edwards & E Fitzpatrick (eds), *Gaelic Ireland c.1250– c.1650; Land, Lordship and Settlement*: 418–35. Dublin: Four Courts.

Breen, C, 2005, *The Gaelic Lordship of the O'Sullivan Beare: A Landscape Cultural History*. Dublin: Four Courts.

Breen, C, 2012, *Dunluce Castle: History and Archaeology*. Dublin: Four Courts.

Breen, C, Forsythe, W, Raven, J & Rhodes, D, 2010, 'Survey and Excavation at Dunstaffnage Castle, Argyll', *PSAS* 140: 165–78.

Brink, S, 1996, 'Political and Social Structures in Early Scandinavia: a Settlement-Historical Pre-Study of the Central Place', *TOR Tidsskrift för arkeologi* 28: 235–81.

Brink, S, 1997, 'Political and Social Structures in Early Scandinavia II: Aspects of Space and Territoriality – The Settlement District', *TOR Tidsskrift för arkeologi* 29: 389–437.

Brink, S, 1999, 'Social Order in the Early Scandinavian Landscape', in C Fabech & J Ringtved (eds), *Settlement and Landscape*: 423–39. Århus: Jutland Archaeological Society.

Brochard, Thomas, 2010, The 'Civilizing' of the Far North of Scotland, 1560–1640, unpublished PhD thesis, University of Aberdeen.

Broderick, G, 1996, *Cronica Regum Mannie & Insularum*, Douglas: Manx National Heritage.

Broderick, G, 2013, 'Some Island Names in the Former "Kingdom of the Isles": a Reappraisal', *Journal of Scottish Name Studies* 7: 1–28.

Brøgger, A W & Shetelig, H, 1971, *The Viking Ships: their Ancestry and Evolution*. London: Hurst.

Broodbank, C, 2000, *An Island Archaeology of the Early Cyclades*. Cambridge: Cambridge University Press.

Broun, D, 2007, *Scottish Independence and the Idea of Britain: From the Picts to Alexander III*. Edinburgh: Edinburgh University Press.

Bruce-Mitford, R, 1975, *The Sutton Hoo Ship Burial, Volume 1: Excavations, Background, the Ship, Dating, and Inventory*. London: British Museum.

[Buchanan, Hector MacDonald], 1819, *Historical and Genealogical Account of the Clan or Family of MacDonald*. Edinburgh: D Stevenson.

Buxton, Ben, 1995, *Mingulay: an Island and its People*. Edinburgh: Birlinn.

Byock, J, 2001, *Viking Age Iceland*. London: Penguin.

Cage, A G & Austin, W E N, 2010, 'Marine Climate Variability during the Last Millennium: the Loch Sunart Record, Scotland, UK', *Quaternary Science Reviews* 29: 1633–47.

Caldwell, D H, 1991, 'The Battle of Pinkie', in N Macdougall (ed.), *Scotland and War AD 79–1918*: 61–94. Edinburgh: John Donald.

Caldwell, D H, 2003, 'Finlaggan, Islay – stones and inauguration ceremonies', in R Welander, D J Breeze & T O Clancy (eds), *The Stone of Destiny: Artefact and Icon*: 60–75. Edinburgh: Society of Antiquaries of Scotland Monograph 22.

Caldwell, D H, 2006, 'Continuity and Change in 12th- and 13th-Century Scotland: an Archaeological View', *Review of Scottish Culture* 18: 14–27.

Caldwell, D H, 2007, 'Having the Right Kit: West Highlanders Fighting in Ireland', in S Duffy (ed.), *The World of the Galloglass*: 144–68. Dublin: Four Courts.

Caldwell, D H, 2008a, *Islay: The Land of the Lordship*. Edinburgh: Birlinn.

Caldwell, D H, 2008b, 'The Lossit Cymba', *West Highland Notes and Queries* ser 3.12: 3–11.

Caldwell, D H, 2009, 'The Campbell Takeover of Islay – the Archaeological Evidence', in A Horning & N Brannon (eds), *Ireland and Britain in the Atlantic World*: 89–110. Dublin: Wordwell (Irish Post-Medieval Archaeology Group).

Caldwell, D H, 2011, *Islay, Jura and Colonsay: a Historical Guide*. Edinburgh: Birlinn.

Caldwell, D H, 2013, 'An Intelligence Report on the Hebrides, 1595/6', *West Highland Notes & Queries* ser 3.23: 3–11.

Caldwell, D H, 2014a, 'Breacachadh Castle 1595', *West Highland Notes & Queries* ser. 3.24: 24–8.

Caldwell, D H, 2014b, 'The Kingdom of the Isles', in D H Caldwell & M A Hall (eds), *The Lewis Chessmen: New Perspectives*: 70–93. Edinburgh: National Museums Scotland.

Caldwell, D H, 2015, 'The Sea Power of the Western Isles of Scotland in the Late Medieval Period', in J H Barrett & S J Gibbon (eds), *Maritime Societies of the Viking and Medieval World*: 350–68. Leeds: Maney (Society for Medieval Archaeology Monograph 37).

Caldwell, D H & Ewart, G, 1998, 'Excavations at Eyemouth, Berwickshire, in a Mid-16th-Century *Trace Italienne* Fort', *Post-Medieval Archaeology* 31: 61–119.

Caldwell, D H & Hall, M A (eds), 2014, *The Lewis Chessmen: New Perspectives*. Edinburgh: National Museums Scotland.

Caldwell, D H & Ruckley, N A, 2005 'Domestic Architecture in the Lordship of the Isles', in R Oram & G Stell (eds), *Lordship and Architecture in Medieval and Renaissance Scotland*: 97–121. Edinburgh: RCAHMS & John Donald.

Caldwell, D H & Stell, G P, forthcoming, *Achanduin Castle, Lismore, Argyll: an Account of the Excavations by Dennis Turner, 1970–5*. Edinburgh: Society of Antiquaries of Scotland (SAIR).

Caldwell, D H, Stell, G P & Turner, D J, 2015, 'Excavations at Achanduin Castle, Lismore, Argyll, 1970–5: Findings and Commentary', *PSAS* 145: 349–69.

Caldwell, D H *et al.*, http://repository.nms.ac.uk/214/2/Finlaggan_report_1_-_introduction_ and_background.pdf; http://repository.nms.ac.uk/224/1/Finlaggan_report_3-_eilean_ mor_excavations_1.pdf; http://repository.nms.ac.uk/228/1/Finlaggan_report_7_-_eilean_ na_comhairle.pdf.

Callander, G, 1921, 'Report on the Excavation of Dun Beag. A Broch Near Struan, Skye', *PSAS* 55: 110–31.

Cameron, Alexander (ed.), 1892–94, *Reliquiæ Celticæ*, 2 vols. Inverness: Northern Counties Publishing.

Campbell of Airds, Alastair, 2002, *A History of Clan Campbell, Vol. 2: From Flodden to the Restoration*. Edinburgh: Edinburgh University Press.

Campbell of Airds, A, *West Highland Heraldry*, www.heraldry-scotland.co.uk/westhigh.html.

Campbell, D, 1844, 'The Parish of Glassary', in *New Statistical Account of Scotland*, vol. 7 675–700.

Campbell, E, 2003, 'The Western Isles Pottery Sequence', in B Ballin-Smith & I Banks (eds), *In the Shadow of the Brochs: the Iron Age in Scotland*: 139–44. Stroud: Tempus.

Campbell, E, 2006, 'Early Historic Imported Pottery', in G Ewart & D Pringle, 'Dundonald Castle Excavations 1986–93', *Scottish Archaeological Journal* 26: 90–92.

Campbell, John Gregorson, 2005, *The Gaelic Otherworld*, Ronald Black (ed.). Edinburgh: Birlinn.

Campbell, John Lorne (ed.), 1936, *The Book of Barra*, Edinburgh & London: Routledge.

Campbell, John Lorne, 1954, 'The MacNeils of Barra and the Irish Franciscans', *Innes Review* 5: 33–8.

Campbell, John Lorne (ed.), 1998 *The Book of Barra*. 2nd edn. Stornoway: Acair.

Campbell, John Lorne (ed.), 1999, *Songs Remembered in Exile: Traditional Gaelic Songs from Nova Scotia*. 2nd edn. Edinburgh: Birlinn.

Campbell, John Lorne & Collinson, Francis (eds), 1969–81, *Hebridean Folksongs*. 3 vols, Oxford: Oxford University Press.

Campbell, John Lorne & Eastwick, Constance, 1966, 'The MacNeils of Barra in the Forty-Five', *Innes Review* 17: 82–90.

Campbell, M, 1984, *Mid-Argyll: an Archaeological Guide*. Natural History and Antiquarian Society of Mid-Argyll.

Campbell, M & Sandeman, M, 1962, 'Mid-Argyll: a Field Survey of the Historic and Prehistoric Monuments', *PSAS* 95: 1–125.

Campbell, T, 1987, 'Portolan Charts from the Late Thirteenth Century to 1500', in J B Harley & D Woodward (eds), *The History of Cartography, Vol. 1 – Cartography in Prehistoric, Ancient, and Medieval Europe and the Mediterranean*: 371–463. Chicago: University of Chicago Press.

Carmichael, Alexander, 1870, 'Donation of Baptismal Font from Chapel of St Maelrube, Lochaoineart, Skye', *PSAS* 8: 237–9.

Carmichael, Alexander *et al.* (eds), 1900–71, *Carmina Gadelica*. 6 vols, Edinburgh: Scottish Academic Press.

Cathcart, Alison, 2010, 'The Statutes of Iona: the Archipelagic Context', *Journal of British Studies* 49: 4–27.

Chambers, Anne, 1979, *Granuaille—the Life and Times of Grace O'Malley*. Dublin: Wolfhound.

Chambers, Anne, 1998, *Granuaille—the Life and Times of Grace O'Malley, c.1530–1603*. Dublin: Wolfhound.

Chiverrell, R, Innes, J & Blackford, J, 2006, 'Vegetation History of the Isle of Man', in R Chiverrell & G Thomas (eds), *A New History of the Isle of Man 1: the Evolution of the Natural Landscape*: 300–326. Liverpool: Liverpool University Press.

Christaller, W, 1933, *Die Zentralen Orte in Süddeutschland*. Jena: Gustav Fischer.

Christophersen, A, 1991, 'Ports and Trade in Norway during the Transition to Historical Time', in O Crumlin-Pedersen (ed.), *Aspects of Maritime Scandinavia AD 200–1200. Proceedings of the Nordic Seminar on Maritime Aspects of Archaeology 1989*: 159–70. Roskilde: Vikingskibshallen.

Clancy, M T, 1983, *England and its Rulers 1066–1272*. London: Fontana.

Clancy, T O, 2008, 'The Gall-Ghàidheil and Galloway', *Journal of Scottish Name Studies* 2: 19–50.

Clark, W, 1993, *The Lord of the Isles Voyage*. Naas: Leinster Leader.

Clouston, J S, 1927, 'The Orkney "Bus"', *Proceedings of the Orkney Antiquarian Society* 5: 41–9.

Clouston, J S, 1929, 'Three Norse Strongholds in Orkney', *Proceedings of the Orkney Antiquarian Society* 7: 57–74.

Clouston, J S, 1931, *Early Norse Castles*. Kirkwall: The Orcadian.

Clouston, J S, 1932, 'Tammaskirk in Rendall', *Proceedings of the Orkney Antiquarian Society* 10: 9–16.

Cook, Judith, 2004, *Pirate Queen: the Life of Grace O'Malley, 1530–1603*. Cork: Mercier.

Coull, J R, 1996, 'Shetland: the Land, Sea and Human Environments', in D Waugh (ed.), *Shetland's Northern Links: Language and History*: 66–77. Edinburgh: Scottish Society for Northern Studies.

Coulson, C, 1996, 'Cultural Realities and Reappraisals in English Castle Study', *Journal of Medieval History* 22.2: 171–208.

Coulson, C, 2003, *Castles in Medieval Society: Fortresses in England, France and Ireland in the Central Middle Ages*. Oxford: Oxford University Press.

Coventry, M, 1997, *The Castles of Scotland*. Edinburgh: Goblinshead.

Coventry, M, 2006, *The Castles of Scotland*. 4th edn., Edinburgh: Birlinn.

Cowan, E J, 1990, 'Norwegian Sunset – Scottish Dawn: Hakon IV and Alexander III', in N Reid (ed.), *Scotland in the Reign of Alexander III 1249–86*. Edinburgh: John Donald.

Cowan, I B, 1978, 'The Medieval Church in Argyll and the Isles', *Scottish Church History Society Records* 20.1: 15–29.

Cox, R A V, 1989, 'Questioning the Value and Validity of the Term "Hybrid" in Hebridean Place-Name Study', *Nomina* 12: 1–9.

Craven, J B, 1901, *History of the Church in Orkney from the Introduction of Christianity to 1558*. Kirkwall: W Peace.

Crawford, B E, 1987, *Scandinavian Scotland*. Leicester: Leicester University Press.

Crawford, B E (ed.), 2002, *The Papar in the North Atlantic: Environment and History*. St Andrews: St John's House Papers 10; http://www.paparproject.org.uk.

Crawford, B E, 2005, 'The Sinclairs in the late Middle Ages', in R Oram & G Stell (eds), *Lordship and Architecture in Medieval and Renaissance Scotland*: 188–203. Edinburgh: John Donald.

Crawford, B E, 2011, 'Scapa Flow – the Nerve Centre and Knarr Centre of the Medieval Earldom', *Scapa Flow Landscape Partnership Scheme,* http://www.scapaflow.co/index.php/history_and_archaeology/the_norse/scapa_flow_the_nerve_centre_and_knarr_centre_of_the_medieval_earldom.

Crawford, B E, 2012, 'St Magnus Cathedral – a Proprietorial Church of the Orkney Earls?', in S Imsen (ed.), *'Ecclesia Nidrosiensis' and 'Noregs veldi' the role of the Church in the making of Norwegian domination in the Norse world*. Trondheim: Akademika.

Crawford, B E, 2013, *The Northern Earldoms: Orkney and Caithness from AD 870 to 1470*. Edinburgh: John Donald.

Crawford, B E, 2014, 'The Northern Half of the Northern Earldoms' Lordship: a Comparison of Orkney and Shetland', in S Imsen (ed.), *Rex Insularum: the King of Norway and his 'Skattlands' as a Political System c.1260–c.1450*. Trondheim: Fagbokforlaget.

Crawford, I A, 1981, 'War or Peace – Viking Colonisation in the Northern and Western Isles of Scotland Reviewed', in H Bekker-Nielsen, P Foote & O Olsen (eds), *Proceedings of the Eighth Viking Congress*: 259–69 Odense: Odense University Press.

Crawford, I A, 1996, 'The Udal', *Current Archaeology* 147: 84–94.

Crawford, I A & Switsur, R, 1977, 'Sandscaping and C14: the Udal, North Uist', *Antiquity* 51: 124–36.

Crawford, O G S, 1936, 'The Western Seaways', in D Buxton (ed.), *Custom is King*. London: Hutchinson.

Cregeen, Eric R, 2013, *Recollections of an Argyllshire Drover and other West Highland Chronicles*, Margaret Bennett (ed.). Perthshire: Grace Note Publications.

Creighton, O H, 2005, *Castles and Landscapes: Power, Community and Fortification in Medieval England*. London: Equinox.

Creighton, O H, 2012, *Early European Castles: Aristocracy and Authority, AD 800–1200*. London: Bristol Classical Press.

Crone, A, 1998, 'Wooden Objects': 977–82, in G Ewart & F Baker, 'Carrick Castle: Symbol and Source of Campbell Power in South Argyll from the 14th to the 17th Century', *PSAS* 129: 937–1016.

Cruden, Stewart, 1960 and later editions (3rd edn 1981), *The Scottish Castle*. Edinburgh: Thomas Nelson; 3rd edn 1981. Spurbooks.

Crumlin-Pederson, O, 2010, *Archaeology and the Sea in Scandinavia and Britain*, Roskilde: Viking Ship Museum.

Cunliffe, B, 2001, *Facing the Ocean: the Atlantic and its Peoples 8000 BC–AD 1500*. Oxford: Oxford University Press.

Curle, J, 1932, 'An Inventory of Objects of Roman and Provincial Origin found in Sites in Scotland not Definitely Associated with Roman Constructions', *PSAS* 66: 277–98.

Davey, J, 2015, *In Nelson's Wake: the Navy and the Napoleonic Wars*. New Haven & London: Yale University Press.

Davey, P J, 2011, 'Les Exportations Continentales vers l' île de Man du XVe au XVIIe siècle', in A Bocquet-Liénard & B Fajal (eds), *A propo(t)s de l'usage, de la production et de la circulation des terres cuites dans L'Europe du Nord-Ouest autour des XIVe–XVIe siècles*: 219–31. Caen: Centre de recherches archéologiques et historiques anciennes et médiévales.

Davey, P J, 2013, *After the Vikings: Medieval Archaeology of the Isle of Man AD 1100–1550*. Douglas: Manx National Heritage.

Davey, P J, 2016, 'The Ceramic Finds from the Peel IRIS Excavations', *Isle of Man Studies* 14: 71–9.

Davey, P J & Allwood, D, 2016, 'Archaeological Fieldwork in the Isle of Man in 2015', *Isle of Man Studies* 14: 142–9.

Davies, R R, 1990, *Domination and Conquest: the Experience of Ireland, Scotland and Wales 1100–1300*. Cambridge: Cambridge University Press.

Davies, R R, 2000, *The First English Empire: Power and Identities in the British Isles 1093–1343*. Oxford: Oxford University Press.

Davis, P R, 2007, *Castles of the Welsh Princes*. Cardiff: Y Llolfa.

Dawson, J E A, 1995, 'Argyll: the enduring heartland', *Scottish Historical Review* 74.1: 75–98.

Dawson, S & Wickham-Jones, C R, 2009, *The Rising Tide: Submerged Landscape of Orkney. Quarterly Report: June 2009*, http://www.abdn.ac.uk/staffpages/uploads/arc007/RT_interim_June2009.pdf.

Dawson, S, Dawson, A G & Jordan, A T, 2004, 'North Atlantic Climate Change and Late Holocene Windstorm Activity in the Outer Hebrides, Scotland', in D Griffiths & P Ashmore (eds), *Aeolian Archaeology: the Archaeology of Sand Landscapes in Scotland*, Scottish Archaeological Internet Report 48, http://sair.org.uk/sair48.

Dennison, E P, 2005, 'Burghs and Burgesses: a Time of Consolidation?', in R D Oram (ed.), *The Reign of Alexander II*: 274–8. Leiden: Brill.

Dodgshon, R A, 1998, *From Chiefs to Landlords: Social and Economic Change in the Western Highlands and Islands, c.1493–1820*. Edinburgh: Edinburgh University Press.

Donnelly, C, Ó Néill, J, McNeill, T E & McCooey, P, 2005, 'De Courcy's Castle: New Insights into the First Phase of Anglo-Norman Building Activity at Carrickfergus Castle, County Antrim', *Medieval Archaeology* 49: 311–17.

Doonan, C P, Cheetham, P, O'Connor, B, Eley, T & Welham, K, 2001, 'Investigations at Langness: the 2000 Field-Season' in T Darvill (ed.), *Billown Neolithic Landscape Project, Isle of Man Sixth Report: 2000*: 40–47. Bournemouth & Douglas: Bournemouth University School of Conservation Sciences & Manx National Heritage.

Douglas, G, *The Aeneid of Virgil, The Proloug of the Thyrd Buke*, Bannatyne Club 64.1, Edinburgh.

Dressler, C, 1998, *Eigg: The Story of an Island*. Edinburgh: Polygon.

Driscoll, S T, 1998, 'Formalising the Mechanisms of State Power: Early Scottish Lordship from the Ninth to the Thirteenth Centuries', in S Foster, A Macinnes & R MacInnes (eds), *Scottish Power Centres from the Early Middle Ages to the Twentieth Century*: 32–58. Glasgow: Cruithne Press.

Driscoll, S & Forsyth, K, 2006, 'The Late Iron Age and Early Historic Period', in G Ewart & D Pringle, 'Dundonald Castle Excavations 1986–93', *Scottish Archaeological Journal* 26: 4–11.

Dubbeldam, A, 2011, *The Oak/Hazel Woodlands of the Isle of Man*, Peel: Manx Wildlife Trust.

Duffy, Sean, 2002, 'Emerging from the Mist: Ireland and Man in the Eleventh Century', in P J Davey & D Finlayson (eds), *Mannin Revisited: Twelve Essays on Manx Culture and Environment*: 53–62. Edinburgh: Scottish Society for Northern Studies.

Duffy, Sean, 2007a, 'The Prehistory of the Galloglass', in S Duffy (ed.), *The World of the Galloglass*: 106–23. Dublin: Four Courts.

Duffy, Sean (ed.), 2007b, *The World of the Galloglass: Kings, Warlords and Warriors in Ireland and Scotland*. Dublin: Four Courts.

Duffy, S & Mytum, H (eds), 2015, *New History of the Isle of Man. Volume 3: The Medieval Period 1000–1406*. Liverpool: Liverpool University Press.

Dumville, D N, 2002, 'Ireland and North Britain in the Earlier Middle Ages: Contexts for Miniugud Senchasa Fher nAlban', in C Ó'Baoil & N R McGuire (eds), *Rannsachadh na Gàidhlig 2000*: 185–211. Obar Dheathain: An Clo Gaidhealach.

Dumville, D, 2011, 'Political Organisation in Dál Riata', in F Edmonds & P Russell, *Tome: Studies in Medieval Celtic History and Law*: 41–52. Woodbridge: Boydell Press.

Dunbar, J G, 1978, 'Kisimul Castle, Isle of Barra', *Glasgow Archaeological Journal* 5: 25–43.

Dunbar, J G, 1981, 'The Medieval Architecture of the Scottish Highlands', in L Maclean (ed.), *The Middle Ages in the Highlands*: 38–70. Inverness: Inverness Field Club.

Dunbar, J G & Duncan, A A M, 1971, 'Tarbert Castle: a Contribution to the History of Argyll', *Scottish Historical Review* 50: 1–17.

Duncan, A A M (ed.), 1997, *John Barbour, The Bruce*. Edinburgh: Canongate.

Duncan, A A M, 1999a, 'The Battles of Ben Cruachan', *West Highland Notes and Queries*, 2nd ser. 20: 3–20.

Duncan, A A M, 1999b, 'Roger of Howden and Scotland, 1187–1201', in B Crawford (ed.), *Church, Chronicle and Learning in Medieval and Early Renaissance Scotland*. Edinburgh Mercat Press.

Duncan, A A M & Brown, A L, 1957, 'Argyll and Isles in the Earlier Middle Ages', *PSAS* 90: 192–220.

Everett, Paul, 2016, *Building stone assessment: comparison of stone samples from Kisimul Castle (Barra) and the island of Stulaigh (by South Uist) (British Geological Survey)*, http://nora.nerc.ac.uk/514351/.

Everett, P A, Gillespie, M R & Tracey, A E, 2015, *Provenance of building stones in four 'galley castles' in Argyll (British Geological Survey)*, http://nora.nerc.ac.uk/511801/.

Ewart, G, 1985, *Cruggleton Castle. Report of Excavations 1978–1981*. Dumfries: Dumfries & Galloway Natural History and Antiquarian Society.

Ewart, G & Baker, F, 1998, 'Carrick Castle: symbol and source of Campbell power in south Argyll from the 14th to the 17th century', *PSAS* 129: 937–1016.

Ewart, G & Pringle, D, 2004, 'Dundonald Castle Excavations 1986–93', *Scottish Archaeological Journal* 26.

Ewart, G & Triscott, J, 1996, 'Archaeological excavations at Castle Sween, Knapdale, Argyll & Bute, 1989–90', *PSAS* 126: 517–57.

Fairhurst, H, 1939, 'The Galleried Dun at Kildonan Bay, Kintyre', *PSAS* 73: 185–228.
Fairhurst, H, 1956, 'The Stack Fort on Ugadale Point, Kintyre', *PSAS* 88: 15–21.
Falls, Cyril, 1950, *Elizabeth's Irish Wars*. London: Methuen.
Fawcett, Richard, 2011, *The Architecture of the Scottish Medieval Church*. New Haven & London: Yale University Press.
Fernie, E, 1986, 'Early Church Architecture in Scotland', *PSAS* 116: 393–411.
Fernie, E, 1988, 'The Church of St Magnus, Egilsay', in B E Crawford (ed.), *St Magnus Cathedral: Orkney's Twelfth Century Renaissance*: 140–61. Aberdeen: Aberdeen University Press.
Findlay, A, 2004, *Fagrskinna: a Catalogue of the Kings of Norway*. Leiden: Brill.
Finlaggan Reports, D H Caldwell *et al.*:
  http://repository.nms.ac.uk/214/2/Finlaggan_report_1_-_introduction_and_background.pdf;
  http://repository.nms.ac.uk/224/1/Finlaggan_report_3-_eilean_mor_excavations_1.pdf;
  http://repository.nms.ac.uk/228/1/Finlaggan_report_7_-_eilean_na_comhairle.pdf.
Firth, J, 1920, *Reminiscences of an Orkney Parish together with Old Orkney Words, Riddles and Proverbs*. Stromness: W R Rendall.
Fisher, G, 1956, 'Borg', in J Brøndstedt, J Danstrup & L Jacobsen (eds), *Kulturhistorisk Leksikon for Nordisk Middelalder fra Vikingetid til Reformationstid Bd. II*: 135–8. København: Rosenskilde og Bagger.
Fisher, I, 2005, 'The Heirs of Somerled', in R Oram & G Stell (eds), *Lordship and Architecture in Medieval and Renaissance Scotland*: 85–96. Edinburgh: John Donald.
Fleming, Andrew, 2005, *St Kilda and the Wider World: Tales of an Iconic Island*. Macclesfield: Windgather Press.
Fojut, Noel, 2006, 'Barra – the Physical Background', in A Kruse & A Ross (eds), *Barra and Skye: Two Hebridean Perspectives*: Edinburgh: Scottish Society for Northern Studies.
Fojut, Noel, Pringle, Denys & Walker, Bruce, 1994 and 2003, *The Ancient Monuments of the Western Isles*. Edinburgh: Mercat Press.
Forbes, A R, 1923, *Place-Names of Skye and Adjacent Islands with Lore: Mythical, Traditional and Historical*. Paisley: Alexander Gardner.
Foster, S, 2006, 'Kisimul Castle: Recent Work by Historic Scotland,' in A Kruse & A Ross (eds), *Barra and Skye: Two Hebridean Perspectives*: 47–65. Edinburgh: Scottish Society for Northern Studies.
Fox, C, 1932, *The Personality of Britain*. Cardiff: National Museum of Wales.
Frake, C D, 1985, 'Cognitive Maps of Time and Tide Among Medieval Seafarers', *Man* new ser. 20: 254–70.
Fraser, I, 1999, *The Place-Names of Arran*. Glasgow: The Arran Society of Glasgow.
Fraser, I A, 2004, 'The Place-Names of Argyll', in D Omand (ed.), *The Argyll Book*: 243–54. Edinburgh: Birlinn.
Fraser, James, 1905, *Chronicles of the Frasers. The Wardlaw Manuscript*, W Mackay (ed.), Scottish History Society 47. Edinburgh: Constable.
Fraser, J E, 2009, *From Caledonia to Pictland: Scotland to 795*, New Edinburgh History of Scotland, vol. I. Edinburgh: Edinburgh University Press.
Fraser-Mackintosh, Charles J (ed.), 1897, *Antiquarian Notes, Historical, Genealogical and Social (2nd Series): Inverness-Shire*. Inverness: A. & W. Mackenzie.

Freke, D J, 1996, 'Excavations at Castle Rushen, 1989', in P J Davey, D J Freke & D A Higgins, *Excavations in Castletown, Isle of Man 1989–1992*: 5–40. Liverpool: Liverpool University Press.

Freke, D J, 2002, *Excavations on St Patrick's Isle, Peel, Isle of Man, 1982–88: Prehistoric, Viking, Medieval and Later*. Liverpool: Liverpool University Press.

Gammeltoft, P, 2001, *The Place-Name Element Bólstaðr in the North Atlantic Area*. Copenhagen: Institut for Navneforskning, Det humanistiske Fakultet, Københavns Universitet.

Gammeltoft, P, 2004, 'Scandinavian-Gaelic Contacts. Can Place-Names and Place-Name Elements be used as a Source for Contact-Linguistic Research?', *Nowele* 44: 51–90.

Gammeltoft, P, 2006, 'Scandinavian Influence on Hebridean Island Names', in P Gammeltoft & B Jørgensen (eds). *Names through the Looking-Glass. Festschrift in Honour of Gillian Fellows-Jensen. 5 July 2006*. Copenhagen: C A Reitzels Forlag.

Gammeltoft, P, 2007, 'Scandinavian Naming-Systems in the Hebrides – A way of Understanding how Scandinavians were in Contact with Gaels and Picts?', in B Ballin-Smith *et al.* (eds), *West Over Sea: Studies in Scandinavian Sea-Borne Expansion and Settlement Before 1300*: 479–95. Leiden: Brill.

Gammeltoft, P, Hough, C & Waugh, D (eds), 2005, *Cultural Contacts in the North Atlantic Region: the Evidence of the Names*. Lerwick: Scottish Place-Name Society & Society of Name Studies in Britain and Ireland.

Gannon, Angela & Geddes, George, 2015, *St Kilda: The Last and Outmost Isle*. Edinburgh: Historic Environment Scotland.

Gardiner, M & McNeill, T E, 2016, 'Sea-Borne Trade and the Commercialization of Fifteenth and Sixteenth Century Ulster', *Proceedings of the Royal Irish Academy* 116C: 229–62.

Gelling, P S, 1952, 'Excavation of a Promontory Fort at Port Grenaugh, Santon', *Proceedings of the Isle of Man Natural History and Antiquarian Society* 5.3: 307–15.

Gelling, P S, 1958, 'Excavation of a Promontory Fort at Scarlett, Castletown, Isle of Man', *Proceedings of the Prehistoric Society* 24: 85–100.

Gelling, P S, 1959, 'Excavation of a Promontory Fort at Cass ny Hawin, Malew, Isle of Man', *Proceedings of the Isle of Man Natural History and Antiquarian Society* 6.1: 28–38.

Gelling, P S, 1968, 'Excavation of a Promontory Fort on Ballanicholas, Kirk Marown, Isle of Man', *Proceedings of the Isle of Man Natural History and Antiquarian Society* 7.2: 181–91.

Gelling, P S, 1978, 'The Iron Age', in P J Davey (ed.), *Man and Environment in the Isle of Man*: 233–43. BAR 54, Oxford.

Gibbon, S J, 2006, *The Origins and Early Development of the Parochial System in the Orkney Earldom*, unpublished PhD thesis, University of the Highlands and Islands/Open University.

Gibbon, S J, 2012, 'Orkney's Things', in O Owen (ed.), *Things in the Viking World*: 80–93. Lerwick: Shetland Amenity Trust.

Giblin, Cathaldus (ed.), 1964, *Irish Franciscan Mission to Scotland 1619–1646*. Dublin: Assisi.

Gibson, J S, 1967, *Ships of the '45*. London: Hutchinson.

Gilbertson, D D, Schwenninger, J-L, Kemp, R A & Rhodes, E, 1999, 'Sand-Drift and Soil Formation along an Exposed North Atlantic Coastline: 14,000 Years of Diverse Geomorphological, Climatic and Human Impacts', *Journal of Archaeological Science* 26.4: 439–69.

Gillies, W, 1987, 'Heroes and Ancestors', in B Almqvist, P Ó Héalaí & S Ó Catháin (eds), *The Heroic Process: Form, Function and Fantasy in Folk Epic*: 57–74. Dublin: Glendale Press.

Gillies, W, 1994, 'The Invention of Tradition, Highland-Style', in A MacDonald, M Lynch & I Cowan (eds), *The Renaissance in Scotland*: 144–56. Leiden: Brill.

Goodare, Julian, 1998, 'The Statutes of Iona in Context', *Scottish Historical Review* 77: 31–57.

Gordon, R, 1813, *A Genealogical History of the Earldom of Sutherland*. Edinburgh: Constable.

Gower, P, 1977, 'The Dalradian Rocks of the West Coast of the Tayvallich Peninsula', *Scottish Journal of Geology* 13: 125–33.

Graham, Angus, 1969, *Skipness*. Edinburgh: privately printed.

Graham, Angus & Collingwood, W G, 1923, 'Skipness Castle', *PSAS* 57: 266–87.

Graham-Campbell, J, 2001, *The Viking World*. 3rd edn, London: Frances Lincoln.

Graham-Campbell, J, 2002, 'Tenth-Century Graves: the Viking Age Artefacts and their Significance', in: D J Freke, *Excavations on St Patrick's Isle, Peel, Isle of Man, 1982–88: Prehistoric, Viking, Medieval and Later*: 83–98. Liverpool: Liverpool University Press.

Graham-Campbell, J, 2004, '"Danes … in this Country": Discovering the Vikings in Scotland', *PSAS* 134: 201–39.

Graham-Campbell, J & Batey, C E, 1998, *Vikings in Scotland: an Archaeological Survey*. Edinburgh: Edinburgh University Press.

Grant, A, 1988, 'Scotland's "Celtic Fringe" in the Late Middle Ages: the Macdonald Lords of the Isles and the Kingdom of Scotland', in R R Davies (ed.), *The British Isles, 1100–1500: Comparisons, Contrasts and Connections*: 118–41. Edinburgh: John Donald.

Grant, A, 1993, 'Thanes and Thanages', in A Grant & K Stringer (eds) *Medieval Scotland*: 39–81. Edinburgh: Edinburgh University Press.

Grant, I F, 1959, *The MacLeods: the History of a Clan, 1200–1956*. London: Faber & Faber.

Gratton, Brian *et al.*, 2013, 'Book Forum: Pekka Hämäläinen's *The Comanche Empire*', *History and Theory* 52.1: 49–90.

Gregory, Donald, 1881, *The History of the Western Highlands and Islands*. 2nd edn, Glasgow: T D Morison.

Grieve, S J, 1999, Norse Castles in Orkney, unpublished MPhil thesis, University of Glasgow.

Griffiths, D, 2014, 'Firth, Damsay, Landscape, Geophysics, Surface and Coastal Survey, Targeted Excavation', *Discovery and Excavation in Scotland*, new ser. 14: 137–9.

Groome, F H, 1895, *Ordnance Gazetteer of Scotland: a Survey of Scottish Topography*. 6 vols, London: W Mackenzie. http://www.gazetteerofscotland.org.uk.

Haines, R M, 2003, *King Edward II: His Life, his Reign, and its Aftermath, 1284–1330*. Montreal & Kingston: McGill-Queens University Press.

Hall, A T, 1991, 'A Bibliography of W Douglas Simpson 1896–1968', in W Douglas Simpson, *Dunollie, Oban, Argyll*: 1–22. Aberdeen: Centre for Scottish Studies, University of Aberdeen.

Hall, D, 2013, 'Here be Monstrous Fabrics…: Constructing a Research Agenda for the Hand-Made Wares of the Scottish West Coast, Highlands and Islands', *Medieval Ceramics* 34: 19–25.

Hall, D, forthcoming, 'The Pottery', in C Ellis (ed.), *Excavations at Baliscate, Mull*. SAIR.

Hall, Richard, 2010, *Viking Age Archaeology*. Princes Risborough: Shire Publications.

Hallan, N, 1982, 'Skei og Trollskeia' *Trøndelag -82: Årbok for Trøndelag* 16: 91–6.

Hämäläinen, Pekka, 2008, *The Comanche Empire: History and Theory*. New Haven CT: Yale University Press.

Hansson, M, 2011, 'Aristocratic Expressions in Landscape and Settlement', in B Poulsen & S M Sindbæk (eds), *Settlement and Lordship in Viking and Early Medieval Scandinavia*: 87–93. Turhout: Brepols.

Hardisty, J, 1990, *The British Seas: An Introduction to the Oceanography and Resources of the North-West European Continental Shelf*. London & New York: Routledge.

Harman, Mary, 1997, *An Isle called Hirte: a History and Culture of St Kilda to 1930*. Waternish: Maclean Press.

Haswell-Smith, H, 1996, *The Scottish Islands*, Edinburgh: Canongate.

Hayes-McCoy, Gerard A, 1937, *Scots Mercenary Forces in Ireland, 1565–1603*. Dublin & London: Burns, Oates & Washbourne.

Hayes-McCoy, G A, 1964, *Ulster and other Irish Maps*. Dublin: Stationery Office, Irish Manuscripts Commission.

Henderson, J C, 2007, *The Atlantic Iron Age*, London: Routledge.

Herteig, A E, 1989, 'The Coastal Courtyard-Sites in Norway from the 1st Millennium AD', in H Galiniè (ed.), *Les Mondes Normands (VIIIe–XIIe s.)*. Caen: Société d'Archéclogie Médiévale.

Holland, P, 1996, 'The Anglo-Normans and their Castles in County Galway', in G Moran & R Gillespie, *Galway: History and Society*: 1–25. Dublin: Geography Publications.

Holliday, J, 2014, *An Island in 180 Names: The Norse Place-Names of Tiree*. Scarinish: An Iodhlan.

Horden, P & Purcell, N, 2000, *The Corrupting Sea: a Study of Mediterranean History*. Malden MA & Oxford: Blackwell.

Hornell, J, 1946, *Water Transport*. Cambridge: Cambridge University Press.

Hossack, B H, 1986, *Kirkwall in the Orkneys*. Kirkwall: Kirkwall Press.

Hudson, B T, 1999, 'The Changing Economy of the Irish Sea Province', in B Smith (ed.), *Britain and Ireland 900–1300: Insular Responses to Medieval European Change*: 39–66. Cambridge: Cambridge University Press.

Hudson, B T, 2012, 'Prologue: the Medieval Atlantic Ocean', in B T Hudson (ed.), *Studies in the Medieval Atlantic*. New York & London: Palgrave MacMillan.

Hunter, M, 1987, A Description of the Orchadian Islands by me Jo. Ben who stayed there in the year 1529 (transl. of a ms in the Advocates' Library, Edinburgh), unpublished booklet.

Hunter, J R, 1996, *Fair Isle: the Archaeology of an Island Community*. Edinburgh: HMSO.

Hutchinson, G, 1994, *Medieval Ships and Shipping*, London: Leicester University Press.

Imsen, S, 2009, 'The Scottish-Norwegian Border in the Middle Ages', in A Woolf (ed.), *Scandinavian Scotland – Twenty Years After. Proceedings of a Day Conference held on 19 February 2007*. St Andrews: Committee for Dark Age Studies, University of St Andrews.

Ingrem, C, 2005, 'Fish', in Sharples *et al.*, 'Discussion', in N Sharples (ed.), *A Norse Farmstead in the Outer Hebrides: Excavations at Mound 3, Bornais, South Uist*: 192–4. Oxford: Oxbow.

Innes, Cosmo (ed.), 1851, 1854, 1855, *Origines Parochiales Scotiae: The Antiquities Ecclesiastical and Territorial of the Parishes of Scotland*. Bannatyne Club 97, 2 vols in 3. Edinburgh: W H Lizars.

James, Heather, 2009, Medieval Rural Settlement: a Study of Mid-Argyll, Scotland, unpublished PhD thesis, University of Glasgow.

Jennings, Andrew, 2013, 'Latter-Day Vikings: Gaels in the Northern Isles in the 16th Century', *Journal of the North Atlantic* 4: 35–42.

Jennings, A & Kruse, A, 2005, 'An Ethnic Enigma – Norse, Pict and Gael', in A Mortensen & S V Arge (eds), *Viking and Norse North Atlantic, Selected Papers from the Proceedings of the Fourteenth Viking Congress, 19–30 July 2001, Tórshavn, Faroe Islands*: 251–63. Tórshavn: Føroya Fróðskaparfelag.

Jennings, A & Kruse, A, 2009, 'From Dál Riata to the Gall-Ghàidheil', *Viking and Medieval Scandinavia* 5: 123–49.

Johnson, A A C, 2002, 'Watch and Ward on the Isle of Man: the Medieval Re-occupation of Iron Age Promontory Forts', in P J Davey & D Finlayson (eds), *Mannin Revisited: Twelve Essays on Manx Culture and Environment*: 63–80. Edinburgh: Scottish Society for Northern Studies.

Johnson, M, 2002, *Behind the Castle Gate: From Medieval to Renaissance*. Abingdon: Routledge.

Johnston, J B, 1903, *Place-Names of Scotland*. Edinburgh: David Douglas.

Kaland, S H H, 1993, 'The Settlement of Westness, Rousay', in C E Batey, J Jesch & C D Morris (eds), *The Viking Age in Caithness, Orkney and the North Atlantic*: 308–17. Edinburgh: Edinburgh University Press.

Kelleher, C, 2007, 'The Gaelic O'Driscoll Lords of Baltimore, Co. Cork', in L Doran & J Littleton (eds), *Lordship in Medieval Ireland*: 130–59. Dublin: Four Courts.

Kelleher, C, 2013, 'Pirate Ports and Harbours of West Cork in the Early Seventeenth Century', *Journal of Maritime Archaeology* 8.2: 347–66.

Kingston, S, 2004, *Ulster and the Isles in the Fifteenth Century: the Lordship of the Clann Domhnaill of Antrim*. Maynooth Historical Studies, Dublin: Four Courts.

Knox, John, 1787, *A Tour through the Highlands of Scotland, and the Hebride Isles, in 1786*. London: J Walter.

Kruse, A, 2015, 'Laithlinn', *Namn og Nemne* 32.3: 49–86.

Kruse, A & Ross, A (eds), 2006, *Barra and Skye: Two Hebridean Perspectives*. Edinburgh: Scottish Society for Northern Studies.

Lacy, B, 1983, *Archaeological Survey of County Donegal*. Lifford: Donegal County Council.

Lamb, R & Robertson, J, 2005, 'Kirkwall: Saga, History, Archaeology', in O Owen (ed.), *The World of Orkneyinga Saga: the broad-cloth Viking trip*. Kirkwall: The Orcadian.

Lane, A, Campbell, E & Bayley, J, 2000, *Dunadd: an Early Dalriadic Capital*. Oxford: Oxbow.

Leirfall, J, 1979, *West Over Sea: Reminders of Norse Ascendency from Shetland to Dublin*, transl. K Young. Belfast: Appletree Press.

Lennon, C, 1981, *Richard Stanihurst the Dubliner, 1547–1618*. Dublin: Irish Academic Press.

Lew, A, Hall, C & Dallen, T, 2008, *World Geography of Travel and Tourism: a Regional Approach*. Oxford: Elsevier.

Lewis, A R, 1958, *The Northern Seas: Shipping and Commerce in Northern Europe AD 300–1100*. Princeton: Princeton University Press.

Lewis, J H, 1996, 'Dunstaffnage Castle, Argyll & Bute: Excavations in the North Tower and East Range, 1987–94', *PSAS* 126: 559–603.

Liddiard, R, 2005, *Castles in Context: Power, Symbolism and Landscape, 1066 to 1500*. Macclesfield: Windgather Press.

Lobay, Meredith, 2009, *Contextual Landscape Study of the Early Christian Churches of Argyll. The Persistence of Memory*. BAR 488, Oxford: Archaeopress.

Loeber, R, 2001, 'An Architectural History of Gaelic Castles and Settlements, 1370–1600', in P Duffy, D Edwards & E Fitzpatrick (eds), *Gaelic Ireland: Land, Lordship and Settlement, c.1250–c.1650*: 271–314. Dublin: Four Courts.

Love, John A, 2009, *A Natural History of St Kilda*. Edinburgh: Birlinn.

Lowe, C E, 1984, Archaeological Survey of St Mary's Church and the Wirk, Skaill, Rousay, Orkney, in Relation to the Collections of Architectural Fragments at Westside, Trumland and Eynhallow, unpublished report in Orkney SMR.

MacAulay, J, 1996, *Birlínn: Long-hips of the Hebrides*. Cambridge: White Horse Press.

MacAulay, Rev. Kenneth, 1764, *The History of St Kilda*. London: T Becket & P A de Hondt.

MacBain, A, 1922, *Place-Names, Highlands and Islands of Scotland*. Stirling: Eneas MacKay.

MacCárthaigh, C (ed,), 2008, *Traditional Boats of Ireland*, Cork: Collins.

McCaughan, M & Appleby, J (eds), 1989, *The Irish Sea: Aspects of Maritime History*. Belfast: Institute of Irish Studies & Ulster Folk and Transport Museum.

MacCoinnich, Aonghas, 2002, '"His spirit was given only to warre": Conflict and Identity in the Scottish Gàidhealtachd, *c.*1580–*c.*1630', in S Murdoch & A Mackillop (eds), *Fighting for Identity: Scottish Military Experience, c.1550–1900*: 133–62. Leiden: Brill.

MacCoinnich, Aonghas, 2004, Tus gu iarlachd: Eachdraidh Chlann Choinnich *c.*1466–1638, unpublished PhD thesis, Aberdeen University.

MacCoinnich, Aonghas, 2006. '"Mar phòr san t-uisge": Ìomhaigh Sìol Torcail an eachdraidh', in M Byrne, T O Clancy & S Kidd (eds), *Litreachas agus Eachdraidh: Rannsachadh na Gàidhlig 2, Glaschu 2002*: 214–31. Glasgow: Celtic & Gaelic, University of Glasgow.

MacCoinnich, Aonghas, 2007, 'Sìol Torcail and their Lordship in the Sixteenth Century', in Islands Book Trust (ed.), *Crossing the Minch: Exploring the Links between Skye and the Outer Hebrides*: 7–32. Port of Ness: Islands Book Trust.

MacCoinnich, Aonghas, 2015, *Plantation and Civility in the North Atlantic World: the Case of the Northern Hebrides, 1570–1639*. Leiden: Brill.

McCullough, D A, 2000, Investigating Portages in the Norse Maritime Landscape of Scotland and the Isles, unpublished PhD thesis, University of Glasgow (available from ethos.bl uk).

Macdonald, Angus & Macdonald, Archibald, 1896, 1900, 1904, *The Clan Donald*, 3 vols. Inverness: Northern Counties Publishing.

Macdonald, Fiona A, 1994, Ireland and Scotland: Historical Perspectives on the Gaelic Dimension 1560–1760, unpublished PhD thesis, University of Glasgow.

Macdonald, Fiona A, 2006, *Mission to the Gaels: Reformation and Counter-Reformation in Ulster and the Highlands and Islands of Scotland 1560–1760*. Edinburgh: John Donald.

McDonald, F & Keogh, E, 2010, 'Fortress Uncovered: Co Louth Viking Site of International Importance', *The Irish Times, 17 September 2010*: http://www.irishtimes.com/news/fortress-uncovered-co-louth-viking-site-of-international-importance-1.651715.

Macdonald, Norman (ed.), 1975, *The Morrison Manuscript: Traditions of the Western Isles, by Donald Morrison, Cooper, Stornoway*. Stornoway: Stornoway Public Library.

McDonald, R A, 1997, *The Kingdom of the Isles: Scotland's Western Seaboard c.1100–c.1336*. East Linton: Tuckwell Press.

McDonald, R A, 2003, *Outlaws of Medieval Scotland: Challenges to the Canmore Kings, 1058–1266*. East Linton: Tuckwell.

McDonald, R A, 2007a, *Manx Kingship in its Irish Sea Setting, 1187–1229: King Rognvaldr and the Crovan Dynasty*. Dublin: Four Courts.

McDonald, R A, 2007b, 'Dealing Death from Man: Manx Sea Power in and around the Irish Sea, 1079–1265', in S Duffy (ed.), *The World of the Galloglass: Kings, Warlords and Warriors in Ireland and Scotland*: 45–76. Dublin: Four Courts.

MacGibbon, David & Ross, Thomas, 1887, 1887, 1889, 1892, 1892, *The Castellated and Domestic Architecture of Scotland*. 5 vols, Edinburgh: David Douglas.

McGrail, 2014, *Early Ships and Seafaring: Water Transport in Europe*. Barnsley: Pen & Sword.

MacGregor, A A, 1929, *Summer Days among the Western Isles*. Edinburgh & London: Nelson.

MacGregor, A A, 1930, *Over the Sea to Skye*. London: Chambers.

MacGregor, A A, 1966, *The Enchanted Isles*. London: Michael Joseph.

MacGregor, Martin, 2006, 'The Statutes of Iona: Text and Context', *Innes Review* 57: 111–81.

MacGregor, M, 2014, 'Warfare in Gaelic Scotland in the Later Middle Ages', in E M Spiers, J A Crang & M Strickland (eds), *A Military History of Scotland*: 209–31. Edinburgh: Edinburgh University Press.

McGurk, John, 1997, *The Elizabethan Conquest of Ireland: the Burdens of the 1590s Crisis*. Manchester: Manchester University Press.

Macinnes, Allan I, 1996, *Clans, Commerce and the House of Stuart, 1603–1788*. East Linton: Tuckwell.

Macinnes, Allan I, 2012, *The British Confederate: Archibald Campbell, Marquess of Argyll, c.1607–1661*. Edinburgh: John Donald.

MacInnes, J, 1974, 'West Highland Sea Power in the Middle Ages', *Transactions of the Gaelic Society of Inverness* 48: 518–56.

McKean, C A, 2001, *The Scottish Château: the Country House of Renaissance Scotland*. Stroud: Alan Sutton.

McKean, C A, 2006, 'A Scottish Problem with Castles', *Historical Research* 79: 166–98.

McKechnie, Hector, 1938, *The Lamont Clan 1235–1935*. Edinburgh: Clan Lamont Society.

McKee, E, 1983, *Working Boats of Britain*. London: Conway Maritime.

MacKenzie, Alexander, 1889, *History of the MacLeods*. Inverness: A & W MacKenzie.

Mackenzie, W C, 1903, *History of the Outer Hebrides*. Paisley: Alexander Gardner.

Mackenzie, W Mackay, 1927, *The Mediaeval Castle in Scotland*. Edinburgh: Methuen.

MacKie, E, 1969, 'Dun Lagaidh', *Current Archaeology* 12: 8–13.

MacKie, E, 1974, *Dun Mor Vaul: an Iron Age Broch on Tiree*. Glasgow: Glasgow University Press.

MacKie, E, 2000, 'The Scottish Atlantic Iron Age: Indigenous and Isolated or Part of a Wider European World?', in J C Henderson (ed.), *The Prehistory and Early History of Atlantic Europe. Papers from a Session held at the European Association of Archaeologists 4th Annual Meeting in Göteborg 1998*: 99–100. BAR S861, Oxford: Archaeopress.

MacKie, E, 2007, *The Roundhouses, Brochs and Wheelhouses of Atlantic Scotland, c.700 BC–AD 500: Architecture and Material Culture*. BAR 444, Oxford.

Maclean, Charles, 1997, *The Isle of Mull: place-names, meanings and stories*. Dumfries: Maclean Publications.

Maclean-Bristol, Nicholas, 1995, *Warriors and Priests: the History of Clan Maclean, 1300–1570*. East Linton: Tuckwell.

Maclean-Bristol, N, 1999, *Murder Under Trust: the Crimes and Death of Sir Lachlan Mor Maclean of Duart 1558–1598*. East Linton: Tuckwell.

MacLellan, Angus, 1962, *The Furrow Behind Me*, transl. J Lorne Campbell. London: Routledge & Kegan Paul.

MacLeod, Angus, 1933, *Sàr Orain: Three Gaelic Poems*. Glasgow: An Comunn Gàidhealach.

Macleod, G, (Seòras Chaluím Sheòrais), 2005, *Muir is Tir (Sea and Shore)*. Stornoway: Acair.

MacLeod, Roderick C (ed.), 1938–9 *The Book of Dunvegan*. 2 vols, Aberdeen: Third Spalding Club 9.

McNamee, C, 1997, *The Wars of the Bruces: Scotland, England and Ireland, 1306–1328*. East Linton: Tuckwell.

Macneil, Ian R, 2006, 'Kisimul Castle and the Origins of Hebridean Galley-Castles: Preliminary Thoughts', in A Kruse & A Ross (eds), *Barra and Skye: Two Hebridean Perspectives*: 21–46. Edinburgh: Scottish Society for Northern Studies.

Macneil, Robert Lister, 1923, *The Clan Macneil: Clann Niall of Scotland*. New York: Caledonian Publishing.

Macneil, Robert Lister, 1964, *The Castle in the Sea*. London & Glasgow: Scotpress.

McNeill, T E, 1980, *Anglo-Norman Ulster: the History and Archaeology of an Irish Barony 1177–1400*. Edinburgh: John Donald.

McNeill, T E, 1983, 'The Stone Castles of Northern County Antrim', *Ulster Journal of Archaeology* 3rd ser. 46: 101–28.

McNeill, T E, 2002, 'Dunineny Castle and the Gaelic View of Castle Building', *Proceedings of the XX Château Gaillard (Caen, 2000)*: 153–61.

McNeill, T E, 2004, 'Excavations at Dunineny Castle, Co. Antrim', *Medieval Archaeology* 48: 167–200.

McNeill, T E, 2014, 'Organising a Lordship: the Castles of the MacDonalds of Dunivaig and the Glens', in R D Oram (ed.), *The Lordship of the Isles*: 211–26. Leiden: Brill.

Macniven, A, 2014, 'Navigating the Nomenclature: the Validity of Gaelic *Tairbeart as Evidence for Pre-Norse Survival in Lewis and the West of Scotland', in D H Caldwell & M A Hall (eds), *The Lewis Chessmen: New Perspectives*: 121–50. Edinburgh: National Museums Scotland.

Macniven, A, 2015, *The Vikings in Islay: the Place of Names in Hebridean Settlement History* Edinburgh: John Donald.

MacPhail, James R N (ed.), 1914–34, *Highland Papers*. 4 vols, Edinburgh: Scottish History Society.

MacPherson, John, 1961, *Tales from Barra told by the Coddy*, J Lorne Campbell (ed.), 2nd edn. Edinburgh: Johnston & Bacon.

MacPherson, John, 1992, *Tales from Barra Told by the Coddy*, J Lorne Campbell (ed.). Edinburgh: Birlinn.

MacPherson, N, 1879, 'Notes on Antiquities from the Island of Eigg', *PSAS* 12: 577–97.

MacQueen, Rev. Edward, 1998, 'Barra in 1794', in John Lorne Campbell, *The Book of Barra*: 54–67. Stornoway: Acair.

McWhannell, D C, 2000, 'Ship Service and Indigenous Sea Power in the West of Scotland', *West Highland Notes & Queries*, ser 3.1: 5.

McWhannell, D C, 2002, 'The Galleys of Argyll', *Mariner's Mirror* 88.1: 14–32.

McWhannell, D C, 2003, 'Campbell of Breadalbane and Campbell of Argyll Boatbuilding Accounts 1600 to 1700', *Mariner's Mirror* 89.4: 405–24.

McWhannell, D C, 2014a, 'Difficulties with the Ua Néill Pedigrees, Anrothan and the Ancestry of Donnsléibhe, Father of Suibhne', *West Highland Notes and Queries* ser. 3.24: 3–14.

McWhannell, D C, 2014b, 'The family of Donnsléibhe, the father of Suibhne', *West Highland Notes and Queries* ser. 3.25: 3–11.

Mandelbrot, B B, 1967, 'How Long is the Coast of Britain? Statistical Self-Similarity and Fractional Dimension', *Science* 156: 636–8, (http://users.math.yale.edu/~bbm3/web_pdfs/howLongIsTheCoastOfBritain.pdf)

Manwaring, G E & Perrin, W G, 1922, *The Life and Works of Sir Henry Mainwaring*. 2 vols, Navy Records Society 54.

Marcus, G J, 1980, *The Conquest of the North Atlantic*. Woodbridge, Suffolk: Boydell.

Márkus, G, 2012, *The Place-Names of Bute*. Donnington: Sean Tyas.

Marsden, John, 2003, *Galloglas: Hebridean and West Highland Mercenary Warrior Kindreds in Medieval Ireland*. East Linton: Tuckwell.

Marshall, D N, 1964, 'Report on Excavations at Little Dunagoil', *Transactions of the Buteshire Natural History Society* 16: 3–69.

Marshall, D, 1983, 'Excavations at Macewen's Castle, Argyll, in 1968–69', *Glasgow Archaeological Journal* 10: 131–42.

Martin, C J M, 2009, 'Maritime Transport on the Western Seaboard from Prehistory to the Nineteenth Century', in K Veitch (ed.), *Transport and Communications*: 137–67. Edinburgh: John Donald.

Martin, C J M, 2014a, 'The Sea World of the Chessmen', in D H Caldwell & M A Hall (eds), *The Lewis Chessmen: New Perspectives*: 185–99. Edinburgh: National Museums Scotland.

Martin, C J M, 2014b, 'A Maritime Dominion – Sea Power and the Lordship', in R D Oram (ed.), *The Lordship of the Isles*: 176–99. Leiden: Brill.

Martin, Martin, 1698, *A Late Voyage to St Kilda*. London: D Brown & T Goodwin.

Martin, Martin, 1703, *A Description of the Western Islands of Scotland*. London: Andrew Bell.

Martin, Martin, 1999, *A Description of the Western Islands of Scotland circa 1695*. Edinburgh: Birlinn.

Marwick, H M, 1924, 'Antiquarian Notes on Rousay', *Proceedings of the Orkney Antiquarian Society* 2: 17.

Matheson, W, 1950, 'Traditions of the MacKenzies', *Transactions of the Gaelic Society of Inverness* 40: 193–228.

Mattingly, H (transl.), 1948, *Tacitus on Britain and Germany*. Harmondsworth: Penguin.

Meek, D E, 1997, '"Norsemen and Noble Stewards": the MacSween Poem in the Book of the Dean of Lismore', *Cambrian Medieval Celtic Studies* 34: 1–49.

Megaw, B R S, 1941, 'A Thousand Years of Watch and Ward: from Viking Beacon to Home Guard', *Journal of the Manx Museum* 5.64: 8–13.

Meulengracht-Sørensen, P, 2000, 'The Prosimetrum Form 1: Verses as the Voice of the Past', in R E Poole (ed.), *Skaldsagas: Text, Vocation, and Desire in the Icelandic Sagas of Poets*: 172–90. Berlin: De Gruyter.

Meyer, R, 2010, 'The Zion of the North: the Multifunctional Role of Sverresborg. A Civil-War Stone Castle near Trondheim', *Château Gaillard* 24: 185–94.

Miket, R & Roberts, D L, 1990, *The Mediaeval Castles of Skye & Lochalsh*. Portree: Maclean Press.

Miket, R & Roberts, D L, 2007, *The Mediaeval Castles of Skye & Lochalsh*, revised edn. Edinburgh: Birlinn.

Millar, H & Kirkhope, J, 1964, 'Fincharn Castle', *Discovery & Excavation in Scotland*.

Millea, N, 2007, *The Gough Map: the Earliest Road Map of Great Britain?* Oxford: Bodleian Library.

Mitchell, Sir Arthur (ed.), 1906–8, *Geographical Collections relating to Scotland made by Walter Macfarlane*, vols 2 & 3. Edinburgh: Scottish History Society.

Moffat, A & Wilson, J, 2011, *The Scots: a Genetic Journey*. Edinburgh: Birlinn.

Mollat, M, 1993, *Europe and the Sea*, transl. T L Fagan. Oxford: Blackwell.

Mooney, J, 1947, *The Cathedral and Royal Burgh of Kirkwall*. 2nd edn. Kirkwall: W R Mackintosh.

Moore, D W, 2005, *The Other British Isles: a History of Shetland, Orkney, the Hebrides, Isle of Man, Anglesey, Scilly, Isle of Wight and the Channel Islands*. Jefferson NC & London: McFarland & Co.

Morken, R, 1968, 'Norse Nautical Units and Distance Measurement', *Mariner's Mirror* 54.4: 393–401.

Morris, C D, 1993a, 'Viking Orkney: a Survey', in C Renfrew (ed.), *The Prehistory of Orkney BC4000 – 1000AD*: 210–42. Edinburgh: Edinburgh University Press.

Morris, C D, 1993b, 'Congress Diary, Orkney', in C E Batey, J Jesch & C D Morris (eds) *The Viking Age in Caithness, Orkney and the North Atlantic*: 53–4. Edinburgh: Edinburgh University Press.

Morris, R, 1997, *Churches in the Landscape*. London: Phoenix.

Morrison, A, 1974, 'Some Prehistoric Sites in Scotland with Medieval Occupation', *Scottish Archaeological Forum* 6: 66–74.

Munro, R W (ed.), 1961, *Monro's Western Isles of Scotland and Genealogies of the Clans 1549* Edinburgh: Oliver & Boyd.

Murdoch, Steve, 2010, *The Terror of the Seas? Scottish Maritime Warfare 1513–1713*. Leiden Brill.

Murray, N, 2002, 'A House Divided Against Itself: a Brief Synopsis of the History of Clann Alexandair and the Early Career of "Good John of Islay" c.1290–1370', in C Ó Baoill & N R McGuire (eds), *Rannsachadh Na Gàidhlig 2000*: 221–30. Obar Dheathain: An Clo Gaidhealach

Murray, W H, 1973, *The Islands of Western Scotland*. London: Methuen.

Myhre, B, 1998, 'The Archaeology of the Early Viking Age in Norway', in H B Clarke M Ní Mhaonaigh *et al.* (eds), *Ireland and Scandinavia in the Early Viking Age*: 3–35. Dublin Four Courts.

Nassens, P, 2007, 'Gaelic Lords of the Sea: the Coastal Tower Houses of South Connemara' in L Doran & J Lyttleton (eds), *Lordship in Medieval Ireland*: 217–35. Dublin: Four Courts

Nicholls, Kenneth, 2007, 'Scottish Mercenary Kindreds in Ireland, 1250–1600', in S Duffy (ed.), *The World of the Galloglass Kings, Warlords and Warriors in Ireland and Scotland*: 86–105. Dublin: Four Courts.

Nicolaisen, W F H, 1969, 'Norse Settlement in the Northern and Western Isles', *Scottish Historical Review* 48: 6–17.

Nicolson, A, 1994 (3rd edn, ed. Cailean Maclean), *History of Skye*. South Lochs, Lewis Islands Book Trust.

Nieke, M R, 2004, 'Secular Society from the Iron Age to Dálriata and the Kingdoms of the Scots', in D Omand (ed.), *The Argyll Book*: 60–70. Edinburgh: Birlinn.

Noble, G & Stevens, F, 2008, 'An Island of Fluctuating Perceptions: the Landscape and Archaeology of Bute', in G Noble, T Poller, J Raven & L Verrill (eds), *Scottish Odysseys: the Archaeology of Islands*: 37–60. Stroud: History Press.

Noble, G, Poller, T, Raven, J & Verrill, L (eds), 2008, *Scottish Odysseys: The Archaeology of Islands*. Stroud: History Press.

Noort, R van de, 2011, *North Sea Archaeologies: a Maritime Biography, 10,000 BC to AD 1500* Oxford: Oxford University Press.

Nyman, E, 2006, 'Words for 'Portage' in the Scandinavian Languages, and Place-Names indicating Old Portages', in C Westerdahl (ed.), *The Significance of Portages: Proceedings of the 1st International Conference on the Significance of Portages, 29 Sept–2 Oct 2004, Lydal Vest-Agder, Norway*. 169–72. BAR S1499, Oxford: Archaeopress.

O'Brien, E & Breathnach, E, 2011, 'Irish Boundary *Ferta*: their Physical Manifestation and Historical Context', in F Edmonds & P Russell, *Tome: Studies in Medieval Celtic History and Law*, pp.53–64. Woodbridge: Boydell Press.

O'Carroll, Donal, 2001, 'Change and Continuity in Weapons and Tactics 1594–1691', in Pádraig Lenihan (ed.), *Conquest and Resistance: War in Seventeenth-Century Ireland*: 210–55. Leiden: Brill.

Ó Corráin, D, 1980, 'Book Review: Studies in the History of Dál Riada, John Bannerman', *Celtica* 13: 168–82.

Oftedal, M, 1954, 'The Village Names of Lewis in the Outer Hebrides', *Norsk tidsskrift for sprogvidenskap* 17.

Ó hÓgáin, Dáithí, 1999, 'The Mystical Island in Irish Folklore', in P Lysaght, S Ó Catháin & D Ó hÓgain, *Islanders and Water-Dwellers*: 247–60. Dublin: Four Courts.

O'Keeffe, Tadhg, 2014, 'Halls, "Hall-Houses" and Tower-Houses in Medieval Ireland: Disentangling the Needlessly Entangled', *Castle Studies Group Journal* 27: 252–62.

O'Keeffe, Tadhg, 2015, *Medieval Irish Buildings 1100–1600*. Dublin: Four Courts.

O'Neil, B H St J, 1951, 'Castle Rushen, Isle of Man', *Archaeologia* 94: 1–26.

O'Neill, P, 2014, 'Control of the Means of Production in Early Irish Law', *Studia Celtica Fennica* 10: 87, http://ojs.tsv.fi/index.php/scf/article/view/8228/14657.

O'Neill, T, 1987, *Merchants and Mariners in Medieval Ireland*. Dublin: Irish Academic Press.

Oppenheim, M (ed.), 1902, *The Naval Tracts of Sir William Monson, v*ol. 3, Navy Records Society 43.

Oram, R D, 2000, *The Lordship of Galloway*. Edinburgh: John Donald.

Oram, R D, 2003, 'Continuity, Adaptation and Integration: the Earls and Earldom of Mar, *c*.1150–*c*.1300', in S Boardman & A Ross (eds), *The Exercise of Power in Medieval Scotland c.1200–1500*: 46–66. Dublin: Four Courts.

Oram, R D, 2004a, *David I: the King Who Made Scotland*. Stroud: Tempus.

Oram, R D, 2004b, 'The Lordship of the Isles: 1336–1493', in D Omand (ed.), *The Argyll Book*: 123–39. Edinburgh: Birlinn.

Oram, R D, 2008a, 'Royal and Lordly Residence in Scotland *c*.1050 to *c*.1250: an Historiographical Review and Critical Revision', *Antiquaries Journal* 88: 165–89.

Oram, R D, 2008b, 'Castles, Concepts and Contexts: Castle Studies in Scotland in Retrospect and Prospect', *Chateau Gaillard* 23: 349–59.

Oram, R D, 2010a, 'Medieval Scottish Castles: some Insights, Images and Perceptions from Archaeological and Historical Investigation', *Chateau Gaillard* 24: 213–22.

Oram, R D, 2010b, 'Innse Gall: Culture and Environment on a Norse Frontier in the Scottish Western Isles', in S Imsen (ed.), *The Norgesveldet in the Middle Ages*: 125–48. Trondheim: Tapir Press.

Oram, R D, 2011, *Domination and Lordship: Scotland 1070–1230*. Edinburgh: Edinburgh University Press.

Oram, R D, 2012, *Alexander II, King of Scots, 1214–49*. Edinburgh: Birlinn.

Oram, R D, 2014a, 'Introduction: a Celtic Dirk at Scotland's Back? The Lordship of the Isles in Mainstream Scottish Historiography since 1828', in R D Oram (ed.), *The Lordship of the Isles*: 1–39. Leiden: Brill.

Oram, R D, 2014b, '"The Worst Disaster Suffered by the People of Scotland in Recorded History": Climate Change, Dearth and Pathogens in the Long 14th Century', *PSAS* 144: 1–22.

Oram, R D, 2014c, 'From "Golden Age" to Depression: Land Use and Environmental Change in the Medieval Earldom of Orkney,' in H C Gulløv, *Northern Worlds: Landscapes, Interactions and Dynamics*. Copenhagen: National Museum of Denmark.

Oram, R D, 2014d, *The Lordship of the Isles*. Leiden: Brill.

Oram, R D (ed.), 2015, *'A House That Thieves Might Knock At'*. Donington: Sean Tyas.

Oram, R D (nd) *Mingary Castle, the MacIans and the Lordship of Ardnamurchan*. http://www.mingarycastletrust.co.uk/mingarycastletrust/history/analytical-and-historical-assessment/.

Oram, R D & Adderley, W P, 2008, 'Lordship and Environmental Change in Central Highland Scotland *c.*1300 to *c.*1450', *Journal of the North Atlantic* 1: 74–84.

Oram, R D & Adderley, W P, 2010, 'Lordship, Land and Environmental Change in West Highland and Hebridean Scotland *c.*1300–*c.*1450', in S Cavaciocchi (ed.), *Economic and Biological Interactions in Pre-Industrial Europe from the 13th to the 18th Centuries*: 257–68. Florence: Florence University Press.

Oram, R D & Stell, G (eds), 2005, *Lordship and Architecture in Medieval and Renaissance Scotland*. Edinburgh: John Donald.

Ormrod, W M, 2015, 'Man under the Montacutes, 1333–92', in S Duffy & H Mytum (eds), *A New History of the Isle of Man: the Medieval Period*: 151–69. Liverpool: Liverpool University Press.

O'Sullivan, A, McCormick, F, Kerr, T & Harney, L, 2013, *Early Medieval Ireland, AD 400–1100: the Evidence from Archaeological Excavations*. Dublin: Royal Irish Academy.

Owen, O, 1993, 'Tuquoy, Westray, Orkney: A challenge for the future?', in C E Batey, J Jesch & C D Morris (eds), *The Viking Age in Caithness, Orkney and the North Atlantic, selected papers from the proceedings of the eleventh Viking Congress, Thurso and Kirkwall, 22 August–1 September 1989*: 318–39. Edinburgh.

Owen, O, 1999, *The Sea Road: a Viking Voyage through Scotland*. Edinburgh: Historic Scotland.

Owen, O, 2005a, 'History, Archaeology and Orkneyinga Saga: the case of Tuquoy Westray', in O Owen (ed.), *The World of Orkneyinga Saga: 'the Broad-Cloth Viking Trip'*: 192–212. Kirkwall: The Orcadian.

Owen, O, 2005b, 'Orkneyinga Saga – a Brief Guide to Saga Sites to Visit in Orkney', in O Owen (ed.), *The World of Orkneyinga Saga: 'The Broad-Cloth Viking Trip'*: 224–31. Kirkwall: The Orcadian.

Palit, D K, 1953, *The Essentials of Military Knowledge*. Aldershot: Gale & Polden.

Parker, A J, 2001, 'Maritime Landscapes', *Landscapes* 2.1: 22–41.

Parker-Pearson, M & Sharples, N, 1999, *Between Land and Sea: Excavations at Dun Vulan, South Uist*. Sheffield: Sheffield Academic Press.

Parker-Pearson, M, Sharples, N & Symonds, J, 2004, *South Uist: Archaeology and History of a Hebridean Island*. Stroud: Tempus.

Parkes, Peter, 2006, 'Celtic Fosterage: Adoptive Kinship and Clientage in Northwest Europe', *Comparative Studies in Society and History* 48: 359–95.

Penman, M, 2014, 'The MacDonald Lordship and the Bruce Dynasty, *c.*1306–*c.*1371', in R D Oram (ed.), *The Lordship of the Isles*: 62–87. Leiden: Brill.

Pennant, T, 1998, *A Tour in Scotland and Voyage to the Hebrides 1772*. Edinburgh: Birlinn.

Perkins, R (ed.), 2011, *Verses in Eric the Red's Saga*. London: Viking Society for Northern Research.

Petersen, H C, 1986, *Skinboats of Greenland*. Roskilde: Arkrisk Institute.

Petre, J S, 1992, 'Mingary in Ardnamurchan: a Review of Who Could Have Built the Castle', *PSAS* 144: 256–76.

Phillips, C, 2006, 'Portages in Early Medieval Scotland: The Great Glen Route and the Forth-Clyde Isthmus', in C Westerdahl (ed.), *The Significance of Portages: Proceedings of the 1st International Conference on the Significance of Portages, 29 Sept –2 Oct 2004, Lydal, Vest-Agder, Norway*: 191–8. BAR S1499, Oxford: Archaeopress.

Pocock, J G A, 2005, 'The Atlantic Archipelago and the War of the Three Kingdoms', in J Pocock, *The Discovery of Islands*. Cambridge: Cambridge University Press (essay originally published 1996).

Poulsen, B & Sindbæk, S M, 2011, *Settlement and Lordship in Viking and Early Medieval Scandinavia*. Turnhout: Brepols.

Price, L, 1932, 'Armed Forces of the Irish Chiefs in the Early 16th Century', *Journal of the Royal Society of Antiquaries of Ireland*, 7th ser. 2.2: 201–07.

Pringle, D, 1995, *Rothesay Castle and St Mary's Church*. Edinburgh: HMSO.

Pye, M, 2015, *The Edge of the World: How the North Sea made us who we are*. London: Penguin.

Radford, R C A, 2004, 'St Patrick's Isle, Peel: the Medieval Ecclesiastical Remains and Excavations of 1962', *Proceedings of the Isle of Man Natural History and Antiquarian Society* 113: 361–93.

Raven, J, 2005, Medieval Landscapes and Lordship in South Uist, unpublished PhD thesis, University of Glasgow.

Raven, J & MacLeod-Rivett, M, forthcoming, '*Morentur in Domino libere et in Pace*: Cultural Identity and the Remembered Past in the Mediaeval Outer Hebrides', in S Stoddart (ed.), *Gardening Time: Reflections on Memory, Monuments and History in Sardinia and Scotland*. Cambridge: Cambridge University Press.

Ravn, M, 2016, *Viking-Age War Fleets: shipbuilding, resource management and maritime warfare in 11th-century Denmark*. Roskilde, Denmark: Viking Ship Museum.

Regan, R, 2012, *Dun Mhuirich, North Knapdale*, http://www.kilmartin.org/docs/dunMhurichExcavation2012DSR.pdf.

Regan, R, 2013, *Dun Mhuirich, North Knapdale*, http://www.kilmartin.org/docs/dunMhurichExcavation2013DSR.pdf.

Reid, W S, 1960, 'Sea-Power in the Anglo-Scottish War, 1296–1328', *Mariner's Mirror* 46: 7–23.

Rennell, R, 2010, 'Islands, Islets, Experience and Identity in the Outer Hebridean Iron Age', *Shima: The International Journal of Research into Island Cultures* 4.1: 47–64, http://www.shimajournal.org/issues/v4n1/g.%20Rennell%20Shima%20v4n1%2047–64.pdf.

Riach, A, 2015, *The Birlinn of Clanranald*. Newtyle, Angus: Kettillonia.

Ridel, E, 2007, 'From Scotland to Normandy: the Celtic Sea Route of the Vikings', in B Ballin-Smith, S Taylor & G Williams (eds), *West Over Sea: Studies in Scandinavian Sea-Borne Expansion and Settlement before 1300*. Leiden: Brill.

Ritchie, A, 1993, *Viking Scotland*. Edinburgh: Batsford.

Ritchie, A, 1996, *Orkney*. Edinburgh: HMSO.

Ritchie, A & Ritchie, G, 1978, *The Ancient Monuments of Orkney*. Edinburgh: HMSO.

Rixson, D, 1998, *The West Highland Galley*. Edinburgh: Birlinn.

Robson, Michael, 1991, *Rona: The Distant Island*. Stornoway: Acair.

Rodger, N A M, 2004, *The Safeguard of the Sea: a Naval History of Britain, 660–1649*. London: Penguin.

Roesdahl, E, 2001, 'Trelleborg Fortresses', in P Crabtree (ed.), *Medieval Archaeology An Encyclopedia*: 344–7. New York: Garland Publishing.

Roesdahl, E, Sindbaek, S M, Pedersen, A & Wilson, D M (eds), 2014, *Aggersborg. The Viking Age settlement and fortress*. Højbjerg: Jutland Archaeological Society, Moesgard Museum.

Rorke, M, 2005, 'The Scottish Herring Trade, 1470–1600', *Scottish Historical Review* 84: 149–65.

Royal Commission on the Ancient and Historical Monuments of Scotland, 1928, *Inventory of Monuments and Constructions in the Outer Hebrides, Skye and the Small Isles*. Edinburgh: HMSO.

Royal Commission on the Ancient and Historical Monuments of Scotland, 1933, *Inventory of Ancient Monuments and Historic Constructions in the Counties of Fife, Kinross and Clackmannan*. Edinburgh: HMSO.

Royal Commission on the Ancient and Historical Monuments of Scotland, 1946, *Inventory of the Ancient Monuments of Orkney and Shetland*, 3 vols. Edinburgh: HMSO.

Royal Commission on the Ancient and Historical Monuments of Scotland, 1951, *The City of Edinburgh*. Edinburgh: HMSO.

Royal Commission on the Ancient and Historical Monuments of Scotland, 1971, *Argyll, An Inventory of the Ancient Monuments* vol. 1, *Kintyre*. Edinburgh: HMSO.

Royal Commission on the Ancient and Historical Monuments of Scotland, 1974, *Argyll, An Inventory of the Ancient Monuments* vol. 2, *Lorn*. Edinburgh: HMSO.

Royal Commission on the Ancient and Historical Monuments of Scotland, 1980, *Argyll, An Inventory of the Ancient Monuments* vol. 3, *Mull, Tiree, Coll & Northern Argyll (excluding the Early Medieval and Later Monuments of Iona)*. Edinburgh: HMSO.

Royal Commission on the Ancient and Historical Monuments of Scotland, 1982, *Argyll, An Inventory of the Ancient Monuments* vol. 4, *Iona*. Edinburgh: HMSO.

Royal Commission on the Ancient and Historical Monuments of Scotland, 1984, *Argyll, An Inventory of the Ancient Monuments* vol. 5, *Islay, Jura & Colonsay*. Edinburgh: HMSO.

Royal Commission on the Ancient and Historical Monuments of Scotland, 1988, *Argyll, An Inventory of the Ancient Monuments* vol. 6, *Mid Argyll & Cowal, Prehistoric & Early Historic Monuments*. Edinburgh: HMSO.

Royal Commission on the Ancient and Historical Monuments of Scotland, 1992, *Argyll, An Inventory of the Ancient Monuments* vol. 7, *Mid Argyll & Cowal, Medieval & Later Monuments*. Edinburgh: HMSO.

Royal Commission on the Ancient and Historical Monuments of Scotland, 1997, *Argyll Castles in the care of Historic Scotland, extracts from RCAHMS Inventories of Argyll, Volume 1, 2 and 7*. Edinburgh HMSO.

Royal Commission on the Ancient and Historical Monuments of Scotland, 2007, *In the Shadow of Bennachie: a Field Archaeology of Donside, Aberdeenshire*. Edinburgh: HMSO.

Ruckley, N A, 1990, 'Water Supply of Medieval Castles in the United Kingdom', *Fortress* 7: 14–26.

Samuel, M W, 1998, *The Tower Houses of West Cork*, unpublished PhD thesis, University College London.

Sandnes, B, 2010, *From Starafjall to Starling Hill: an Investigation of the Formation and Development of Old Norse Place-Names in Orkney*, http://www.spns.org.uk/Starafjall.pdf.

Sandnes, J & Stemshaug, O (eds), 1990, *Norsk Stadnamnleksikon 3. Utgåva*. Oslo: Det Norske Samlaget.

Sanmark, A & Semple, S J, 2010, 'The Topography of Outdoor Assembly Sites in Europe with Reference to Recent Field Results from Sweden', in H Lewis & S J Semple (eds), *Perspectives in Landscape Archaeology*: 107–119. BAR S2103, Oxford.

Sansum, P, 2004, Historical Resource-Use and Ecological Change in Semi-Natural Woodland: Western Oakwoods in Argyll, Scotland, unpublished PhD thesis, University of Stirling.

Sansum, P, 2005, 'Argyll Oakwoods: Use and Ecological Change 1000 to 2000 AD – a Palynological-Historical Investigation', *Botanical Journal of Scotland* 57.1–2: 83–97.

Saunders, A, 1977, 'Five Castle Excavations: Reports on the Institute's Research Project into the Origins of the Castle in England', *Archaeological Journal* 134: 1–156.

Sayers, 2006, 'What's in a Nonce?', *Scandinavian Studies* 78: 111–28.

Seaby, W, 2002, 'The 1982 Coin Hoard (82.150/C (262)', in: D J Freke, *Excavations on St Patrick's Isle, Peel, Isle of Man, 1982–88: Prehistoric, Viking, Medieval and Later*: 320–25. Liverpool: Liverpool University Press.

Sellar, W D H, 1966, 'The Origins and Ancestry of Somerled', *Scottish Historical Review* 45: 124–42.

Sellar, W D H, 1971,'Family Origins in Cowal and Knapdale', *Scottish Studies* 15: 21–37.

Sellar, W D H, 1981, 'Highland Family Origins – Pedigree Making and Pedigree Faking', in L Maclean (ed.), *The Middle Ages in the Highlands*: 105–08. Inverness: Inverness Field Club.

Sellar, W D H, 2004a, 'MacDougall, Ewen, Lord of Argyll (d. in or after 1268)', *Oxford Dictionary of National Biography*. Oxford: Oxford University Press, http://www.oxforddnb.com/view/article/49384.

Sellar, W D H, 2004b, 'MacDougall, Alexander, Lord of Argyll (d. 1310)', *Oxford Dictionary of National Biography*. Oxford: Oxford University Press, http://www.oxforddnb.com/view/article/49385.

Sellar, W D H, Maclean, A & Nicholson, C B H, 1999, *The Highland Clan MacNeacail (MacNicol): a History of the Nicolsons of Scorrybreac*. Waternish, Skye: Maclean Press.

Serjeantson, D, 2013, *Farming and Fishing in the Outer Hebrides AD 600 to 1700: The Udal, North Uist*. Chandlers Ford: Highfield Press.

Severin, T, 1978, *The Brendan Voyage*, New York: Arrow.

Sharples, N, 2005a, 'Discussion', in N Sharples *et al.*, 'Resource Exploitation', in N Sharples (ed.), *A Norse Farmstead in the Outer Hebrides: Excavations at Mound 3, Bornais, South Uist*. Oxford: Oxbow.

Sharples, N, 2005b, 'The End of Settlement on the Machair', in Sharples *et al.*, 'Discussion', in N Sharples (ed.), *A Norse Farmstead in the Outer Hebrides: Excavations at Mound 3, Bornais, South Uist*: 195–6. Oxford: Oxbow.

Sharples, N, 2005c, *A Norse Farmstead in the Outer Hebrides: Excavations at Mound 3, Bornais, South Uist*. Oxford: Oxbow.

Sharples, N & Parker-Pearson, M, 1999a, 'Norse Settlement in the Outer Hebrides', *Norwegian Archaeological Review* 32: 41–62.

Sharples, N & Parker-Pearson, M, 1999b, *Between Land and Sea: Excavations at Dun Vulan, South Uist*. Sheffield: Sheffield Academic Press.

Sharples, N & Smith, R, 2009, 'Norse Settlement in the Western Isles', in A Woolf (ed.), *Scandinavian Scotland – Twenty Years After. The Proceedings of a Day Conference held on 19 February 2007*. St Andrews: Committee for Dark Age Studies, University of St Andrews.

Shaw, Frances J, 1980, *The Northern and Western Islands of Scotland: Their Economy and Society in the Seventeenth Century*. Edinburgh: John Donald.

Shaw, J, 2008, '"Gaelic/Norse Folklore Contacts" and Oral Traditions from the West of Scotland', in T A Gunnell (ed.), *Legends and Landscape: Articles based on Plenary Lectures Presented at the 5th Celtic-Nordic-Baltic Folklore Symposium, Reykjavík, 2005*. Reyjavík: University of Iceland Press.

Shaw, Robert L, 1985, *Fighter Combat: Tactics and Maneuvering*. Wellingborough: Patrick Stephens.

Sigurðson, J V & Bolton, T, 2014, *Celtic-Norse Relationships in the Irish Sea in the Middle Ages*. Leiden: Brill.

Simmons, A (ed.), 1998, *A Tour in Scotland and Voyage to the Hebrides 1772 by Thomas Pennant*. Edinburgh: Birlinn.

Simms, Katharine, 1995, 'Late Medieval Donegal', in W Nolan *et al.* (eds), *Donegal History and Society*: 183–201. Dublin: Geography Publications.

Simms, Katharine, 2007, 'Images of the Galloglass in Poems to the MacSweeneys', in S Duffy (ed.), *The World of the Galloglass*: 106–23. Dublin: Four Courts.

Simpson, W Douglas, 1938–68 (18 editions), *Dunvegan Castle, Isle of Skye: Official Guide*. Aberdeen: Aberdeen University Press.

Simpson, W Douglas, 1941, 'Breachacha Castle in the Isle of Coll', *Transactions of the Glasgow Archaeological Society* new ser. 10: 26–54.

Simpson, W Douglas, 1953, 'Crookston Castle', *Transactions of the Glasgow Archaeological Society* 12: 1–14.

Simpson, W Douglas, 1954, 'Castle Tioram, Moidart, Inverness-shire; and Mingary Castle, Ardnamurchan, Argyllshire', *Transactions of the Glasgow Archaeological Society* new ser. 13: 70–90.

Simpson, W Douglas, 1961, *The Castle of Bergen and the Bishop's Palace at Kirkwall: a study in early Norse architecture*. Edinburgh: Oliver & Boyd.

Simpson, W Douglas, 1967a, 'Castle Sween', *Transactions of the Glasgow Archaeological Society* 15: 3–14.

Simpson, W Douglas, 1967b, *Portrait of Skye and the Outer Hebrides*. London: Hale.

Sinclair, Alexander Maclean, 1899, *The Clan Gillean*. Charlottetown, PEI: Haszard & Moore.

Sindbæk, S M, 2009, 'Open Access, Nodal Points and Central Places: Maritime Communication and Locational Principles for Coastal Sites in South Scandinavia, c.AD 400–1200', *Estonian Journal of Archaeology* 13.2: 96–109.

Skene, W F, 1880, *Celtic Scotland: a History of Ancient Alban*. 3 vols, Edinburgh: David Douglas.

Smith, G G (ed.), 1895, *The Book of Islay: Documents Illustrating the History of the Island*. Edinburgh: privately printed.

Smith, S, 2004, 'Castell Aberlleiniog, Anglesey and Cronk Howe Mooar, Isle of Man: Related Monuments?', *Transactions of the Anglesey Antiquarian Society and Field Club*: 31–45.

Solberg, B, 2003, *Jernalderen i Norge: c.500 f.Kr–1030 e.Kr.* Oslo: Cappelen Akademisk Forlag.

Spottiswoode, John, 1847–51, *History of the Church of Scotland*, M Napier & M Russell (eds). 3 vols, Edinburgh: Spottiswoode Society.

Stahl, Anke-Beate, 1999, Place-Names of Barra in the Outer Hebrides, unpublished PhD thesis, University of Edinburgh.

Stahl, Anke-Beate, 2006, 'On the Verge of Loss: Lesser Known Place-names of Barra and Vatersay', in A Kruse & A Ross (eds), *Barra and Skye: Two Hebridean Perspectives*: 94–115. Edinburgh: Scottish Society for Northern Studies.

Stanton, C D, 2015, *Medieval Maritime Warfare*. Barnsley: Pen & Sword.

Steer, K A & Bannerman, J W M, 1977, *Late Medieval Monumental Sculpture in the West Highlands*. Edinburgh: RCAHMS.

Steinsland, G, Sigurðsson, J V, Rekdal, J E & Beuermann, I (eds), 2011, *Ideology and Power in the Viking and Middle Ages*. Leiden: Brill.

Stell, Geoffrey, 1981, 'Late Medieval Defences in Scotland', in D H Caldwell (ed.), *Scottish Weapons and Fortifications 1100–1800*: 21–54. Edinburgh: John Donald.

Stell, G, 1985, 'The Scottish Medieval Castle: Form, Function and 'Evolution', in K Stringer (ed.), *Essays on the Nobility of Medieval Scotland*: 195–209. Edinburgh: John Donald.

Stell, Geoffrey, 1988, 'By Land and Sea in Medieval and Early Modern Scotland', *Review of Scottish Culture* 4: 25–43.

Stell, Geoffrey, 2006, 'Castle Tioram: a Statement of Cultural Significance', http://www.historic-scotland.gov.uk/index/news/indepth/castletioram/castletioram-documents.html). http://www.historic-scotland.gov.uk/tioram-stell-fullversion-part1and2.pdf.

Stell, Geoffrey, 2010, 'Scottish Castellology and Castellologists: a Brief Historical Introduction', *Castellologica Bohemica* 12: 79–88.

Stell, Geoffrey, 2014, 'Castle Tioram and the MacDonalds of Clanranald: a Western Seaboard Castle in Context', in R D Oram (ed.), *The Lordship of the Isles*: 271–96. Leiden: Brill.

Stell, Geoffrey, 2015, 'Scottish "Hall-Houses": the Origins and Development of a Modern Castellological Concept', *Castle Studies Group Journal* 28: 134–9.

Stevens, T, Melikian, M & Grieve, S J, 2005, 'Excavations at an Early Medieval Cemetery at Stromness, Orkney', *PSAS* 135: 371–93.

Stewart, James A jun., 1982, The Clan Ranald: History of a Highland Kindred, unpublished PhD thesis, University of Edinburgh.

Stewart, T W, 2004, 'Lexical Imposition: Old Norse vocabulary in Scottish Gaelic', *Diachronica* 21.2: 393–420.

Stewart-Murray, John, 1908, *Chronicles of Atholl and Tullibardine Families* vol. 1. Edinburgh: privately printed.

Stiùbhart, Domhnall Uilleam, 1997, An Gàidheal, a' Ghàidhlig, agus a' Ghàidhealtachd, unpublished PhD thesis, University of Edinburgh.

Stiùbhart, Domhnall Uilleam, 2013, 'Murder in Barra, 1609? The Killing of the "Peursan Mór"', *Béascna* 8: 144–78.

Stiùbhart, Domhnall Uilleam, 2014, 'Leisure and Recreation in an Age of Clearance: The Case of the Hebridean Michaelmas', in J Borsje, A Dooley, S Mac Mathúna, and G Toner (eds), *Celtic Cosmology: Perspectives from Ireland and Scotland*: 207–48. Toronto: Pontifical Institute of Medieval Studies.

Stiùbhart, Domhnall Uilleam, nd, 'Martin Martin (*c*.1665–1718)', *Oxford Dictionary of National Biography*.

Storey, Lisa, 2007, *Muinntir Mhiughalaigh*. Glasgow: Clàr.

Stout, G, nd, *Eight Acres and a Boat*. Dundee: Dundee City Council.

Stringer, K J, 1993, 'Periphery and Core in 13th-Century Scotland: Alan Son of Roland, Lord of Galloway and Constable of Scotland', in A Grant & K J Stringer (eds), *Medieval Scotland: Crown, Lordship and Community*: 82–113. Edinburgh: Edinburgh University Press.

Stylegar, F-A & Grimm, O, 2003, 'Place-Names as Evidence for Ancient Maritime Culture in Norway', *Norsk Sjøfartsmuseum Årbok* 2002: 79–115.

Stylegar, F-A & Grimm, O, 2004, 'Court Sites in SW Norway – Reflections of a Roman Period Political Organisation?', *Norwegian Archaeological Review* 37.2: 111–33.

Sutherland, D G, 1997, 'The Environment of Argyll', in G Ritchie (ed.), *The Archaeology of Argyll*: 10–24. Edinburgh: Edinburgh University Press.

Sweetman, P, 1998, 'The Hall-House in Ireland', *Archaeology Ireland* 12.3: 13–16.

Swift, C, 2004, 'Royal Fleets in Viking Ireland, The Evidence of Lebor na Cert, AD 1050–1150', in J Hines, A Lane & M Redknap (eds), *Land, Sea and Home: Settlement in the Viking Period*: 189–208. Society for Medieval Archaeology Monograph.

Sykes, B, 2004a, *The Seven Daughters of Eve*. London: Corgi.

Sykes, B, 2004b, *Adam's Curse: a Future Without Men*. London: Corgi.

Sykes, B, 2007, *The Blood of the Isles*. London: Corgi.

Tabraham, C J, 1986, *Scottish Castles and Fortifications*. Edinburgh: HMSO.

Tabraham, C J, 1988, 'The Scottish Medieval Towerhouse as Lordly Residence in the Light of Recent Excavation', *PSAS* 118: 267–76.

Tabraham, C J, 1997, *Scotland's Castles*. London: Batsford.

Tabraham, C J, 2005, *Scotland's Castles,* 2nd edn. London: Batsford.

Tait, Ian, 2012, *Shetland Vernacular Buildings 1600–1900*. Lerwick: Shetland Times.

Thacker, M, 2011, An Archaeology of the Lime and Shell-Lime Mortars of the Western Isles, unpublished MA dissertation, University of York.

Thacker, M, 2013, 'The Late Norse "Coral" or Mearl-Limes of Orkney – an on-site Mortar Archaeology of Cubbie Roo's Castle and Chapel', *Proceedings of the 3rd Historic Mortars Conference HMC13, University of the West of Scotland, Glasgow, 2013*, https://invenio.itam.cas.cz/record/2223?ln=en.

Thacker, M, 2016, Constructing Lordship in North Atlantic Europe: the Archaeology of Masonry Mortars in the Medieval and Later Buildings of the Scottish North Atlantic, unpublished PhD thesis, University of Edinburgh.

Theiss, Sherrilynn, 2006, The Western Highlands and Isles, 1619–1649: Allegiances during the 'Scottish Troubles', unpublished PhD thesis, University of Edinburgh.

Thomas, F W L, 1876, 'Did the Norsemen Extirpate the Inhabitants of the Hebrides in the Ninth Century?', *PSAS* 11: 472–507.

Thomas, S E, 2014, 'From Cathedral of the Isles to Obscurity – the Archaeology and History of Skeabost Island, Snizort', *PSAS* 144: 245–64.

Thomson, W P L, 2008, *Orkney Land and People*. Kirkwall: The Orcadian.

Toolis, R, 2008, 'Excavation of Medieval Graves at St Thomas' Kirk, Hall of Rendall, Orkney', *PSAS* 138: 239–66.

Toop, N, 2009, Eilean Donan Castle, Ross-shire, Archaeological Evaluation Report. Unpublished Report. Field Archaeology Specialists.

Turner, D, 1998 'The Bishops of Argyll and the Castle of Achanduin, Lismore, AD 1180–1343', *PSAS* 128: 645–52.

Turner, D J & Dunbar, J G, 1970, 'Breachacha Castle, Coll: Excavations and Field Survey, 1965–8', *PSAS* 102: 155–87.

Wallace, J, 1883, *A Description of the Isles of Orkney, reprinted from the Original edition of 1693 … together with the Additions made by the Author's Son in the Edition of 1700*, J Small (ed.). Edinburgh: William Brown.

Waterman, D M, 1959, 'Excavations at Lismahon, Co Down', *Medieval Archaeology* 3: 139–76.

Watson, F, 1997, 'Rights and Responsibilities: Woodland Management as seen through Baron Court Records', in T C Smout (ed.), *Scottish Woodland History*: 100–114. Dalkeith: Scottish Cultural Press.

Watson, F, 1998, 'The Expression of Power in a Medieval Kingdom: Thirteenth-Century Scottish Castles', in S Foster, A Macinnes & R MacInnes (eds), *Scottish Power Centres from the Early Middle Ages to the Twentieth Century*: 59–78. Glasgow: Cruithne Press.

Watson, W J, 2004, *The History of the Celtic Place-names of Scotland*, with introduction by Simon Taylor. Edinburgh: Birlinn.

Watt, Douglas, 2006, '"The Labrinth of thir Difficulties": The Influence of Debt on the Highland Elite *c*. 1550–1700', *Scottish Historical Review* 85.1: 28–51.

Waugh, D, 2005, 'What is an Aith? Place-Name Evidence for Portages in Shetland', *The New Shetlander* 232: 33–8.

Waugh, D, 2006, 'Place-Name Evidence for Portages in Orkney and Shetland', in C Wester-dahl (ed.), *The Significance of Portages: Proceedings of the First International Conference on the Significance of Portages, 29 Sept – 2 Oct 2004, in Lyngdal, Vest-Agder, Norway, arranged by the County Municipality of Vest-Agder, Kristiansand*: 239–49. BAR S1499, Oxford: Archaeopress.

Waugh, D, 2010, 'On *Eið*-Names in Orkney and other North Atlantic Islands', in J Sheehan & D Ó Corráin (eds), *The Viking Age in Ireland and the West:* 545–54. Dublin: Four Courts.

Westerdahl, C, 1989, *Norrlandsleden I.* Örnköldsvik.

Westerdahl, C, 2002, 'The Cognitive Landscape of Naval Warfare and Defence. Toponymic and Archaeological Aspects', in A N Jørgensen, J Pind, L Jørgensen & B Clausen (eds), *Maritime Warfare in Northern Europe. Technology, Organisation Logistics and Administration 500 BC–1500 AD*: 169–90. Copenhagen: National Museum of Denmark.

Whaley, D, 2005, 'The Semantics of *Stöng/Stang*', in P Gammeltoft, C Hough & D Waugh (eds), *Cultural Contacts in the North Atlantic Region: the Evidence of the Names*: 244–70. Lerwick: NORNA, Scottish Place-Name Society & Society for Name Studies in Britain and Ireland.

Wheeler, James Scott, 2001, 'The Logistics of Conquest', in P Lenihan (ed.), *Conquest and Resistance: War in Seventeenth-Century Ireland*: 177–205. Leiden: Brill.

Whitfield, Alan, 1995, *Island Pilot.* Lerwick: Shetland Times.

Wickham-Jones, C R, 1986, 'The Procurement and Use of Stone for Flaked Tools in Prehistoric Scotland', *PSAS* 116: 1–10.

Wickham-Jones, C R, 1990, *Rhum: Mesolithic and Later Sites at Kinloch, Excavations 1984–86.* Edinburgh: Society of Antiquaries of Scotland.

Wickham-Jones, C R, Dawson, S & Bates, R, 2009, *Drowned Stone Age Settlement of the Bay of Firth, Orkney, Scotland*, http://www.st-andrews.ac.uk/tzp/NGS%20Reportfinal.pdf.

Williams, D G E, 1997, 'The Dating of the Norwegian Leiðangr System: a Philological Approach', *Nowele* 30: 21–3.

Wilson, D, 2008, *The Vikings in the Isle of Man.* Aarhus: Aarhus University Press.

Witgen, Michael, 2012, *An Infinity of Nations: How the Native New World Shaped Early North America.* Philadelphia: University of Pennsylvania Press.

Woodham-Smith, C, 1962, *The Great Hunger: Ireland 1845–9.* London: Hamish Hamilton.

Wooding, J M, 1996, *Communication and Commerce along the Western Sealanes AD 400–800.* BAR S654, Oxford: Tempus Reparatum.

Woolf, A, 2004, 'The Age of Sea-Kings: 900–1300', in D Omand (ed.), *The Argyll Book*: 94–109. Edinburgh: Birlinn.

Woolf, A, 2007, *From Pictland to Alba 789–1070.* Edinburgh: Edinburgh University Press.

Wright, J, 2008, 'Islandscapes and Standing Stones: Changing Perceptions', in G Noble, T Poller, J Raven & L Verrill (eds), *Scottish Odysseys*: 61–72. Stroud: History Press.

Wright, M D, 1982, 'Excavations at Peel Castle, 1947', *Proceedings of the Isle of Man Natural History and Antiquarian Society* 91: 21–57.

Young, A, 1956, 'Excavations at Dun Cuier, Isle of Barra, Outer Hebrides', *PSAS* 89: 290–328.

Young, A, 1997, *Robert the Bruce's Rivals: the Comyns, 1212–1314.* East Linton: Tuckwell.